About the Authors

Roger Matuz develops print and electronic information resources and writes on American history and popular culture. He wrote the five-volume *Complete American Presidents Sourcebook* (2001), edited works on literature, baseball, film, wine, and his other hobbies, and managed the development of a database of hundreds of historical American magazines and journals that date back to the 1740s.

Gina Misiroglu is a fourteen-year veteran of the West Coast publishing industry, specializing in the development and editing of popular culture, biography, and history titles. Misiroglu is the author of *The Handy Politics Answer Book* (2002). Recent edited works by Misiroglu include *The Superhero Book: The Ultimate Encyclopedia of Comic-Book Icons and Hollywood Heroes* (2004); *Girls Like Us: 40 Extraordinary Women Celebrate Girlhood in Story, Poetry, and Song* (1999), winner of the New York Public Library's "Best Book for Teens" award; and *Imagine: The Spirit of Twentieth-Century American Heroes* (1999).

Larry Baker brings a near-lifetime of interest in presidential history and 23 years of publishing experience to *The Handy Presidents Answer Book*. His editorial talents have been seen in such titles as *Complete American Presidents Sourcebook, The Handy Politics Answer Book, American Civil War Reference Library,* and *Bowling, Beatniks, and Bell-Bottoms: Pop Culture of 20th-Century America.* His presidential history geekiness is demonstrated by his memberships in the William McKinley Presidential Library and Museum and Rutherford B. Hayes Presidential Center, his attendance at the Calvin Coolidge Symposium, and his collection of books about the presidents.

The Handy Answer Book® Series

Please visit us at visibleink.com.

THE
HANDY
PRESIDENTS
ANSWER
BOOK

THE HANDY PRESIDENTS ANSWER BOOK

Roger Matuz

with Gina Misiroglu and Lawrence W. Baker

Detroit

THE HANDY PRESIDENTS ANSWER BOOK

Visible Ink Press®
43311 Joy Rd. #414
Canton, MI 48187–2075

Visible Ink Press is a registered trademark of Visible Ink Press LLC.

Most Visible Ink Press books are available at special quantity discounts when purchased in bulk by corporations, organizations, or groups. Customized printings, special imprints, messages, and excerpts can be produced to meet your needs. For more information, contact Special Markets Director, Visible Ink Press, at www.visibleink.com or (734) 667-3211.

Art Director: Mary Claire Krzewinski
Typesetting: The Graphix Group

ISBN 1-57859-167-8

Cataloging-in-Publication Data is on file with the Library of Congress.

Front cover images of John F. Kennedy inauguration, Theodore Roosevelt, and the presidential seal courtesy AP/Wide World; Dwight D. Eisenhower button courtesy the Granger Collection, New York.

Back cover images of Jimmy Carter button courtesy Getty Images; button collection courtesy comstock.com; and Bill Clinton whistle stop, Harry S. Truman playing piano, and Ronald Reagan with Mikhail Gorbachev courtesy AP/Wide World.

For Mary Claire & Michael, la dolce vita.
(Roger Matuz)

For Luke and Oliver.
(Gina Misiroglu)

Much love to Beth—my first lady; and to Charlie, Dane, Sam, and Tess—my cabinet.
Thanks for putting up with all those nights of me sitting at the kitchen table!
(Larry Baker)

"A popular government, without popular information, or the means of acquiring it, is but a prologue to a farce or a tragedy.... A people who mean to be their own governors must arm themselves with the power which knowledge gives."

—James Madison, "Father of the Constitution" and fourth President of the United States

Contents

Introduction

The opening phrase of the U.S. Constitution, "We the People of the United States, in Order to form a more perfect Union," indicated that the form of government the document outlined was meant to be dynamic and evolving. Power ultimately rests with the people and their votes, and means are available to improve on imperfections of the government and its laws. This holds true for the presidency as well, an office that has significantly recalibrated and expanded (and, occasionally, contracted), often from president to president, with and without the people's consent. Now the most powerful position in the world, the American presidency is still historically adolescent, and it is certain to endure significant change as the new century unfolds. But, as *The Handy Presidents Answer Book* demonstrates, history often has a remarkable way of repeating, or at least resonating, with current events.

The evolution of the American presidency is an intriguing, adventuresome tale, filled with historic moments upon which the Republic twisted and turned. For instance, in 1841 William Henry Harrison became the first president to die in office, less than a month after being sworn in. There was no precedent as to what should happen next. The Constitution was vague, and many believed Vice President John Tyler would act as interim president until Congress decided on a successor. Tyler cut short the debate by having himself sworn in and assuming the office. After some additional discussion, Congress agreed. His opponents derisively referred to him as "His Accidency" or "Vice President Acting President Tyler." But his decisive action was an important development for the country, eventually formalized in the Presidential Succession Act of 1947 and the Twenty-fifth Amendment, adopted in 1967.

With the United States created in part as a reaction to imperial English rule, the role, or mere existence, of the chief executive was debated passionately at the Constitutional Convention of 1787. The delegates practiced what they preached. The notion of a chief executive was first met with an "embarrassed pause" by the assembled, according to James Madison, who made lengthy notes on the proceedings. Edmund Randolph (a delegate from Virginia) broke the silence that followed James Wilson's (Pennsylvania) suggestion by reminding the delegates that they wanted "no semblance of a monarch," and the Convention moved on to other matters. But the delegates later returned to the idea of a chief executive, debated various approaches to such a position, forged a system of checks and balances, and eventually enumerated powers that continue to guide the presidency midway through three centuries of federal leadership.

To better understand the shaping and influencing of the presidency, the challenges confronted by each president, and the development of the political system as we know it today, *The Handy Presidents Answer Book* addresses more than 800 broad, fundamental questions about the office itself as well as specific issues about each president and their campaigns, elections, and achievements, or lack thereof. It also covers the notable losers who might have led the country down a different path, such as progressive William Jennings Bryan. Bryan, who ran as a Democrat in 1896, 1900, and 1908, eventually became secretary of state under Woodrow Wilson in 1913 before resigning in 1915 in protest over the handling of the sinking of the British cargo and passenger ship, *Lusitania,* torpedoed by a German submarine in the midst of World War I.

Handy Presidents's question-and-answer format provides information in an easy-to-read, straightforward manner. Programs, policies, and philosophies are balanced with attention to the human factor—personalities, experiences, families—that play no small role in the life of leaders. Life in the White House is also inspected, from staff to chores to pets to romance. *Handy Presidents* notes, for example, that two presidents have married while in office (John Tyler and Grover Cleveland). But only Cleveland held his wedding at the White House, an event that would send today's media into frenzy for months.

The Handy Presidents Answer Book employs a unique arrangement that follows the development of the presidency—from its origins at the Constitutional Convention of 1787 to legacies of the presidents. Each of the book's fourteen chapters is divided into sections that focus on a specific element of the chapter's main topic. The chapter "The President Leads: Foreign Policy," for example, has the sections "Programs and Statements," "Treaties and Trade," and "Crisis and Diplomacy" to help readers more easily locate and follow questions and answers pertaining to those topics.

In addition, each section generally progresses along a chronological sequence, helping the reader to follow history as it developed and to compare and contrast the actions of presidents. On occasion, the chronological approach is abandoned when several questions on a topic are better clustered together than artificially spread apart by a strict chronology. For example, the section "Social Programs and Civil Rights" in the chapter "The President in Action: Domestic Issues" begins with a question on the suspension of rights that occurred with the Alien and Sedition Acts of 1798. Since similarities exist between government suspension of rights in 1798, the Sedition Act of 1918, and the USA PATRIOT Act of 2001, the information is better served by grouping the questions and answers together than by a chronological structure that would have placed events from three different centuries at the beginning, middle, and end of the section, respectively.

The first three chapters of the book set the stage. After addressing the origins and development of the responsibilities and duties of the president, *Handy Presidents* turns its attention to the electoral process with a chapter on presidential campaigns. It follows the campaign trail wherever it may lead. For instance, popular demand led political parties to woo the likes of military heroes Zachary Taylor and Dwight D. Eisenhower, neither of whom had ever held elected office. Other candidates emerged more conventionally, from such methods as the modern state primary system to the more traditional "smoke-filled rooms" at party and state conventions and caucuses. The development of campaign financing is traced. The practice of financing public elections dates back to George Washington, who, while running for a seat in the Virginia House of Burgesses, appealed to voters in his district with rum and hard cider. Expenditures remained rather understated until 1828, when professional campaign management emerged and the practice of buying votes became considerably more expensive.

A chapter on presidential elections follows, topics ranging from the act of voting to the counting of the votes (apparently still a challenge) and the development and real-life misadventures of the electoral college, which the founding fathers advocated as a method to lessen election corruption and manipulation. Let's hope they had a sense of humor. *Handy Presidents* supplies the scoop on remarkable elections—landslides, surprises, upsets, and controversies. Harry S. Truman's upset of Thomas Dewey remains the standard by which we judge modern cliffhangers, though the election of 2000 is obviously another high point on the low road of presidential contests. There it is joined by the election of 1824, when war hero Andrew Jackson won the most popular *and* electoral votes but still managed to lose the election. Splitting the vote with John Quincy Adams, Henry Clay, and William Crawford (respectively, the secretary of state, speaker of the house, and secretary of the treasury), he failed to receive the necessary electoral majority. In accordance with the Twelfth Amendment, the election was thrown into the House of Representatives, which, led by its speaker, voted by a narrow margin for Adams. Four years later, Jackson had his revenge with a sweeping victory against the incumbent Adams. Not surprisingly, Jackson became the first major American politician to advocate abolishing the electoral college, a debate still going on today.

Winners of presidential elections and those who assumed the office are profiled in two chapters. "The President Takes Office" covers presidential inaugurations, ducks behind the curtain to look at life in the White House, examines the personalities, styles, and families of the presidents, and measures the initial benchmark for evaluating a president—the first one hundred days in office. "Presidential Administrations" concentrates on presidents interacting with their teams, including the development of the vice presidency, cabinet, and other advisory positions, with attention devoted to those officials who exerted the most influence on presidential policies and the character of the administration. Here we answer questions such as, "Has a woman ever served as vice president?" Only men have held the office, though in 1984 Democrat Geraldine Ferraro became the first woman to run on a major party ticket, joining Walter Mondale.

To capture the complexities and dynamics of serving as president, seven chapters address the president in action, including his role as commander in chief. The expansion of executive power is followed, as well as presidential leadership in domestic affairs (including social reform, civil disturbances, slavery, and civil rights), economic policy, and foreign policy, including war, peace, crisis, and diplomacy. *The Handy Presidents Answer Book* then confronts the sudden challenges and interruptions that often happen during a presidency—illness, death, assassination, and scandal. *Handy Presidents* examines the mortal coil, including those presidents who hid illnesses during their tenure in office, the strange death of President Harding, and the continuing medical problems of Presidents Eisenhower and Kennedy. Among other fascinating, often tragic events worthy of an American Shakespeare, you'll learn how simple twists of fates doomed or spared presidents, including the story behind the eyeglass case that saved Theodore Roosevelt's life during an assassination attempt.

Interaction between the president and two other branches of the federal government is covered in two chapters. "Presidents and Congress" highlights effective and contentious relationships with the legislative branch ranging from issues of war, economic hardship, and civil rights, to confrontations over federal spending, legislation, use of executive power, and partisan positions. Impeachments, McCarthyism, Watergate, and other crimes and misdemeanors all have their day in the sun. "Presidents and the Judiciary" includes attempts by presidents to influence the federal courts—from Thomas Jefferson's attempts to scale back the federal court system, to Franklin D. Roosevelt's plan to "pack" the Supreme Court, to the "litmus test" of conservative philosophy employed in the judicial appointments of Ronald Reagan, George Bush, and George W. Bush. The influence of the judiciary on the presidency is also addressed, from *Marbury v. Madison* (1803), in which the Supreme Court defined its power of judicial review, to more contemporary rulings on such issues as affirmative action and "enemy combatants." The focus on the presidency concludes with "Legacies of the Presidents," which includes historical and contemporary assessments and rankings.

"I desire you would remember the ladies," wrote future first lady Abigail Adams to her husband, John Adams, while he was in Philadelphia in 1776 attending the Continental Congress that would approve the Declaration of Independence. "Be more generous to them than your ancestors," she advised. We remember Adams and other first ladies in the concluding chapter. Among other intriguing factoids on presidential spouses, you'll discover that in the mid-nineteenth century, Sarah Polk was an activist first lady resembling Hillary Clinton in her role as political confidante to the president.

In all, *Handy Presidents* offers a wide array of factual, anecdotal, historical, and contemporary perspectives on the presidency and the challenges facing those who have held the office. An enormous number of print and Web resources were consulted to collect and organize the information, from plentiful government resources to exhaustive and detailed biographies, articles, and overviews of presidents, historical eras, and political ideologies. An appendix of resources provides more information on most of these sources.

Sprinkled throughout are helpful charts—on the closest presidential elections, the number of vetoes by each president, the most inventive campaign slogans, and more—plus illustrations and key passages from significant documents and speeches. Finally, for those wanting lighter fare, additional trivia on the presidents, landmarks associated with the presidents, and a list of all the presidents and vice presidents appear as appendices. The Constitution of the United States, including amendments, is printed at the end of the book.

Encompassing complex matters to entertaining trivia, *The Handy Presidents Answer Book* accommodates a variety of reader needs ranging from specific information quests to more leisurely overviews. Whatever your information aspirations, we invite you to immerse yourself in a non-partisan, wide-ranging resource that, like a candidate, pledges to have something for everyone. We hope to have played our part in an informative and enjoyable manner, with an arrangement that brings the information into clear context.

Acknowledgments

An enormous number of print and Web resources were consulted to collect and organize the information contained in this book, from plentiful government sources, including the U.S. National Archives and Records Administration (NARA; www.nara.gov) and the Library of Congress (www.loc.gov), to exhaustive and detailed biographies, articles, and overviews of presidents, historical eras, and political ideologies.

The authors thank Visible Ink Press for the swift and collaborative process of developing this project, including Marty Connors and Christa Gainor for their editorial vision, and Roger Jänecke and Mary Beth Perrot for marketing savvy; Sue Salter and Brad Morgan for editorial assistance; Diane Sawinski and Chris Scanlon for assisting with illustrations, and Marcia Schiff at AP/Wide World Photos and Anthony Sullivan at Getty Images; Robert J. Huffman, imager and adventurer; Mary Claire Krzewinski for ever-resourceful and creative book design; and Marco Di Vita of Graphix Group, typesetter.

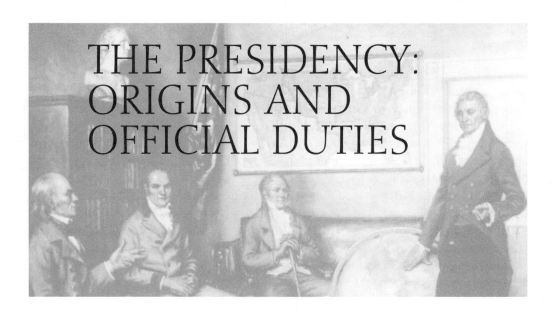

THE PRESIDENCY: ORIGINS AND OFFICIAL DUTIES

THE CONSTITUTIONAL CONVENTION: THE ORIGINS OF THE U.S. PRESIDENCY

What was the **Constitutional Convention and when did it convene**?

Beginning on May 25, and running until September 17, 1787, the Constitutional Convention consisted of an assembly of delegates representing twelve of the thirteen original states (Rhode Island did not send delegates) who convened in Philadelphia, Pennsylvania, at Independence Hall (then called the Pennsylvania State House). They initially met to discuss revisions to the Articles of Confederation, the guidelines under which the colonial government operated since 1781, but soon abandoned the revision in order to create a new constitution that would allow for a strong federal government.

Who **called for the Constitutional Convention**?

The delegates of the Annapolis Convention, held in September 1786 under the leadership of Alexander Hamilton, issued a call for a convention that would have full authority to amend the Articles of Confederation. At the urging of James Madison, the delegates in Annapolis who supported the concept of a national government asked the legislatures of all the states to appoint commissioners to meet "to devise such further provisions as shall appear to them necessary to render the Constitution of the Federal Government adequate to the exigencies of the Union." When the Constitutional Convention convened, it did so under the name Federal Convention.

What **issues surrounded the call to convene the Constitutional Convention**?

Under the Articles of Confederation, the United States of America was operating under an inadequate framework of government, known as the Confederation Congress. A limited national government was entirely dependent upon the states for power and funds, and had no authority to regulate trade between the states, negotiate with other nations, borrow money, or levy taxes. Most importantly, the Articles of Confederation failed to provide for a national chief executive. By 1787, many of the nation's leaders were especially concerned that the tyrannical majorities in state legislatures threatened fundamental freedoms, including freedom of religion and the rights of property holders. Internal problems—such as the huge debt caused by the American Revolution, multiple state currencies, different state taxation policies, intrastate treaties, and the recent Shays' Rebellion of Massachusetts farmers over foreclosures on their properties—convinced many of the nation's leaders that America's postwar plight was the result of an unchecked democracy. As the embodiment of "mob rule," Shays' Rebellion helped accelerate the movement away from the Articles of Confederation toward a stronger central government.

Who **attended the Constitutional Convention**?

Every state except Rhode Island sent delegates, although the delegates were in attendance at varying times. In all, seventy-four men were appointed as delegates, fifty-five attended at one time or another, and approximately forty were responsible for the hands-on work of developing a constitution. The delegates were the elite of the American republic: lawyers, merchants, physicians, planters, and at least nineteen slave owners. Twenty-six were college-educated, thirty-four were lawyers or had studied law, three were physicians, approximately forty had served in the Confederation Congress between 1783 and 1787, thirteen had held state offices, twenty-five had served in the Continental Congress, and as many as fifteen had helped write state constitutions. In addition, eight of the fifty-six signers of the Declaration of Independence attended the Constitutional Convention.

Delegates who attended have become well known to history books and have gained the title of America's Founding Fathers. They include George Washington, James Madison, Edmund Randolph, and George Mason of Virginia; Benjamin Franklin, James Wilson, and Gouverneur Morris of Pennsylvania; Alexander Hamilton of New York; John Dickinson of Delaware; Oliver Ellsworth and Roger Sherman of Connecticut; William Paterson of New Jersey; John Rutledge and brothers Charles Pinckney and Charles Cotesworth Pinckney of South Carolina; Elbridge Gerry of Massachusetts; and Luther Martin of Maryland. Yet many of the prominent businessmen and thinkers of the era did not attend, including John Adams, Samuel Adams, John Hancock, Patrick Henry, Thomas Jefferson, and Richard Henry Lee. When the Constitution was signed, thirty-nine out of fifty-five delegates put their pen to the document.

Who **led the Constitutional Convention**?

The delegates unanimously elected George Washington, who was respected in the political community for his fairness, patience, and diplomacy, to preside over the con-

George Washington, presiding over the Constitutional Convention in Philadelphia, Pennsylvania, in 1787. *Getty Images.*

vention. As the presiding officer, Washington did not engage in any of the constitutional debates. Rather, Washington's presence gave the gathering an air of importance and legitimacy. Initially, Washington doubted that the convention would reach any significant resolutions, or that many prominent leaders would attend. In fact, many accounts of the event note that Washington was torn between the liabilities of lending his name to a potentially ineffective gathering and the fear that his reluctance to attend would hurt his reputation. During the convention's recesses, he went fishing near Valley Forge. Nevertheless, Washington—a delegate to the First and Second Continental Congresses and commander in chief of the Continental Army during the American Revolution—believed in creating a strong central government. After the ratification of the new Constitution, Washington was unanimously elected the first president of the United States.

Why is **James Madison** known as the **"Father of the Constitution"**?

James Madison of Virginia earned the title "Father of the Constitution" for his contributions to the Constitutional Convention. As a political theorist and practical politician, Madison was one of the most vocal leaders who lobbied for a strong national government. In the month before the Convention opened, Madison pored over historical texts and drew on his legislative experience in Congress to analyze the pitfalls of the U.S. government under the Articles of Confederation. In Madison's view, the state constitutions, which existed to protect the people from their rulers, actually contributed to

James Madison, known as the "Father of the Constitution," was a leader of the Constitutional Convention and the nation's fourth president. *Library of Congress.*

a breakdown of social order, because those in power used majority rule to pass laws to protect their private interests. To end this self-interest, Madison advocated the establishment of a large national republic whose legislators would act in the best interests of all the people, thus instigating the formation of the new government as established by the Constitution. Madison took extensive notes of every issue that was discussed at the Convention, and his notes remain the primary source for Convention happenings. On September 17, 1787, after sixteen weeks of deliberation, the finished Constitution was signed by thirty-nine of the forty-two delegates present, including Madison himself.

What was the **significance of the Constitutional Convention** of 1787 on the **presidency**?

The Constitutional Convention was the first time that the development of a strong national government, led by a chief executive who represented the will of the people, was seriously discussed. The Convention created the definition of the chief executive that is found in the Constitution of the United States.

What were the **key debates surrounding the presidency**?

When the delegates began to debate how the executive branch should be structured, there was varying opinion. Three issues dominated the framers' discussion of the role the executive would play in the new government. First, the delegates discussed whether the executive should be a single individual or whether multiple persons, such as a committee of three men, should share the office. Those in favor of the committee approach argued that if each of the three men was selected from a different region of the country, then each region would have equal consideration in all major decisions; others felt that one man could adequately represent all the nation's varied interests while maintaining a national perspective. Second, they debated at length the amount of power the executive should hold, including whether the chief executive should have the power to veto legislation and whether or not he should command the armed forces. Third, delegates debated the length of the executive's term (three-, six-, and seven-year terms were all considered) and discussed whether he should be eligible for reelection. In addition, they debated the best means by which to elect the executive, including whether he should be elected by the state legislatures, by both houses of Congress, by the Senate alone, by the governors of the states, or by citizens.

How did the **topic of the presidency arise,** and what was the response?

When Pennsylvania delegate James Wilson suggested that the executive should consist of one person, a lengthy silence followed. The delegates each had their own conceptions of executive power, and they were leery of granting too much control to a powerful executive who could usurp legislative authority and engage in tyrannical actions. The framers eventually decided upon a single executive, primarily because they felt conflicts would be more easily avoided if there were only one person in the nation's highest office. Also, they believed that Congress could more carefully watch and check a single executive.

What was the result of the **debates regarding the presidency?**

Not until September 8, 1787, did the framers finally settle on the scope and definition of the executive office. A single leader, elected to a four-year term and eligible for reelection, with authority to veto bills enacted by Congress, would rule the nation. The president was also given command of the military and the power to appoint federal officials, subject to confirmation by the Senate. To ensure a balance of power, the legislative and judicial branches were given the ability to check presidential actions. The framers hoped this system of checks and balances would prevent the reign of a tyrannical executive. In addition to finalizing the executive's powers, the framers finalized the methods of selecting the president. Concerned about the people's ability to elect the president directly and cautious of existing legislative bodies to select the president, they designed the electoral college, a group of presidential electors for each state who meet after the popular election to cast their ballots for the president and vice president.

Why did the framers of the Constitution choose a **three-branch government model?**

Although the framers of the Constitution intended to create a stronger central government for the fledgling United States, they also wanted to limit the powers of the government. A three-branch model—the executive branch (the president), the legislative branch (Congress), and the judicial branch (the courts)—distributes the power of the national government among these three authorities, ensuring that not all power is consolidated in one place.

What does the term **"separation of powers"** mean?

Separation of powers means that the power of the federal government is literally "separated" or distributed among its three branches: the executive, legislative, and judi-

Doubts about the Presidency

"A squint toward monarchy" is how Patrick Henry described the presidency. Henry, who had served in the Continental Congress and as Virginia's governor and had uttered the memorable phrase "Give me liberty or give me death" in a speech on the eve of the American Revolution, voted against ratification of the Constitution. He was in favor of the strongest possible state governments and a weak federal government.

cial. Officials of each branch are selected differently, have different responsibilities, and serve different terms. By distributing the essential business of government among three separate but interdependent branches, the framers of the Constitution ensured that the government's powers were not concentrated in any one branch. The principle of separation of powers allows for a system of checks and balances, whereby each branch serves as a check on potential excesses of the others.

What is the concept of **checks and balances**?

Although each branch of the federal government has its own authority, each branch is not completely separate from, or independent of, the others. Instead, the branches are threaded together by a system of "checks and balances" that subjects each branch to a number of constitutional checks, or restraints, by the other branches. For example, the president can veto bills approved by Congress and the president can nominate individuals to serve in the federal judiciary; the Supreme Court can declare a law enacted by Congress or an action by the president unconstitutional; and Congress can impeach the president and federal court justices and judges.

What role did the **Federalists and the Anti-Federalists** play in adopting the new Constitution?

Proponents of the Constitution adopted the name "Federalists." Federalist leaders included men like James Madison, Alexander Hamilton, and John Jay, who together wrote a series of eighty-five newspaper essays collected in a book called *The Federalist* (1788), as well as George Washington and Benjamin Franklin. As nationally known figures, they used their prestige and political finesse to organize support for the Constitution after it was written, with the hopes of having it ratified. According to the language of the Constitution, nine of the thirteen states would have to ratify, or accept, the terms of the document in order for the Constitution to become the ruling law of the land.

On the other hand, most of those against the Constitution were not prominent national leaders and many were small farmers. They vehemently opposed the Constitution for various reasons. Some objected to Congress's taxation power, others to the president's sweeping authority, and others to the omission of a Bill of Rights to protect individual liberties. In general, they feared that the Constitution created a national government that would be dominated by aristocrats whose nearly limitless power would deprive ordinary people of their independence. Prominent opponents of the Constitution included Patrick Henry, Richard Henry Lee, George Mason, and Samuel Adams.

DUTIES AND POWERS

What are the **duties of the president** of the United States?

The president's chief duty is to protect the U.S. Constitution and enforce the laws made by the Congress. However, he also has a host of other responsibilities tied to his job as the nation's leader. These include recommending legislation to Congress; calling special sessions of Congress; delivering messages to Congress; signing or vetoing legislation; appointing federal judges; appointing heads of federal departments and agencies and other principal federal officials; appointing representatives to foreign countries; carrying on official business with foreign nations; acting as commander in chief of the armed forces; and granting pardons for offenses against the United States.

What are the **executive and enumerated, or expressed, constitutional powers of the president**?

Article II of the U.S. Constitution vests the "executive power" in the president. The president is commander in chief of the U.S. armed forces and, when called into action, the National Guard. The president may require the written opinion of military executive officers, and is empowered to grant reprieves and pardons, except in the case of impeachment. The president receives ambassadors and other public ministers, ensures that the laws are faithfully executed, and commissions all officers of the United States. The president has power, by and with the advice and consent of the U.S. Senate, to make treaties, provided that two-thirds of the senators present concur. The president also nominates and appoints ambassadors, other public ministers and consuls, justices of the Supreme Court, federal judges, and other federal officers, by and with the advice and consent of the Senate. The president has the power to temporarily fill all vacancies that occur during the recess of the Senate. In addition, the president may, under extraordinary circumstances, convene "emergency" sessions of Congress. Further, if the two houses disagree as to the time of adjournment, the president may adjourn the bodies. In addition to these powers, the president also has enumerated powers that allow him to directly influence legislation. The Constitution directs the president to periodically inform Congress on the State of the Union, and to recommend legislation that is considered necessary and expedient. Also, Article I, Section 7, of the Constitution grants the president the authority to veto acts of Congress.

Constitutional Duties of the President

The president's duties, as outlined by Article II, Section 2, of the U.S. Constitution:

> The President shall be Commander in Chief of the Army and Navy of the United States, and of the Militia of the several States, when called into the actual Service of the United States; he may require the Opinion, in writing, of the principal Officer in each of the executive Departments, upon any Subject relating to the Duties of their respective Offices, and he shall have Power to grant Reprieves and Pardons for Offences against the United States, except in Cases of Impeachment.

> He shall have Power, by and with the Advice and Consent of the Senate, to make Treaties, provided two thirds of the Senators present concur; and he shall nominate, and by and with the Advice and Consent of the Senate, shall appoint Ambassadors, other public Ministers and Consuls, Judges of the supreme Court, and all other Officers of the United States, whose Appointments are not herein otherwise provided for, and which shall be established by Law: but the Congress may by Law vest the Appointment of such inferior Officers, as they think proper, in the President alone, in the Courts of Law, or in the Heads of Departments.

> The President shall have Power to fill up all Vacancies that may happen during the Recess of the Senate, by granting Commissions which shall expire at the End of their next Session.

What are the **implied constitutional powers of the president**?

The president possesses certain powers that are not enumerated in the U.S. Constitution. For example, although the Constitution does not grant the president the expressed power to remove administrators from their offices, as the chief executive the president holds power over executive branch officers, unless such removal power is limited by public law. Note, however, that he does not have such implied authority over officers in independent establishments. For instance, when Franklin D. Roosevelt removed a member of the Federal Trade Commission, an independent regulatory agency, the Supreme Court in 1935 ruled the act invalid. Another implied constitutional power is derived from the president's authority as commander in chief. Although Congress has the explicit power to declare war, the president holds the responsibility to protect the nation from sudden attack and has the ability to initiate military activities overseas without a formal declaration of war. Through the War Powers Resolution of 1973, Congress sought to define more clearly the conditions under which presidents unilaterally can authorize military action abroad.

Are there any **constitutional amendments that clarify the president's powers**?

During the debates on the adoption of the Constitution, opponents repeatedly charged that the Constitution as drafted would invite tyranny by the central government. The Anti-Federalists demanded a "bill of rights" that would spell out the rights of individual citizens, and that would place limitations on the Congress, the executive branch, and the courts. After the Constitution was ratified in June 1788, and George Washington was inaugurated president of the United States in April 1789, the Congress proposed a Bill of Rights.

These first ten amendments to the Constitution, known as the Bill of Rights, were ratified by two-thirds of the states in December 1791, thus becoming law. The purpose of the ten amendments was to give each of the three branches definite, restricted boundaries. The Second, Third, and Fourth Amendments clearly place limitations on the executive branch: the executive branch is not to infringe on the right of the people to bear arms (II), may not arbitrarily take houses for a militia (III), and shall not engage in the search or seizure of evidence without a court warrant (IV). In addition, both the Ninth and Tenth Amendments place limits on the national government as a whole, stating that all rights not enumerated in the Constitution are reserved to the states or the people.

What are the **president's various roles**?

Although the U.S. Constitution clearly assigns to the president only the roles of chief executive and commander of the country's armed forces, today the president of the United States assumes six basic roles: (1) chief executive; (2) chief of state/foreign relations; (3) commander in chief; (4) chief legislator; (5) chief of party; and (6) chief citizen, or popular leader.

What is the president's role as **chief executive**?

When wearing the hat of chief executive, sometimes called chief administrator, the president has four main duties: (1) enforcing federal laws and court rulings; (2) developing various federal policies; (3) appointing federal officials; and (4) preparing the national budget. Within the executive branch, the president has broad powers to manage national affairs and the workings of the federal government. The president can issue rules, regulations, and instructions called executive orders, which have the binding force of law upon federal agencies but do not require congressional approval. The president may also negotiate with foreign countries "executive agreements" that are not subject to Senate confirmation. The president nominates—and the Senate confirms—the heads of all executive departments and agencies, together with hundreds of other high-ranking federal officials. In addition, the president solely appoints other important public officials, including aides, advisors, and hundreds of other positions. Presidential nomination of federal judges, including members of the Supreme Court, is subject to confirmation by the Senate. Another significant executive power involves granting a full or conditional pardon to anyone convicted of breaking a federal law—except in a case of impeachment. In addition, as the nation's chief executive, the president prepares the national budget.

What types of **executive orders** does a president generally make?

From the founding of America, U.S. presidents have developed and used various types of presidential or executive directives. The best-known directives are executive orders and presidential proclamations—written instructions or declarations issued by the president that carry the full force of the law. These vary from formalities, such as the presidential proclamation of Earth Day or a National Day of Prayer, to orders that effect major policy changes, such as President Bill Clinton's executive orders calling for preferential treatment in federal contracting based on race or ethnicity.

It is not uncommon for executive orders to proliferate in times of crisis, and in reaction to the nation's social or economic circumstances. Harry S. Truman integrated the armed forces under executive order, and Dwight D. Eisenhower desegregated schools with one. Presidents John F. Kennedy and Lyndon B. Johnson both used them to bar racial discrimination in federal housing, hiring, and contracting. President Ronald Reagan used an executive order to bar the use of federal funds for advocating abortion, a decision President Bill Clinton reversed upon coming into office. According to the Federal Register, George W. Bush issued 85 executive orders in 2001–2002, some of which were a direct response to the September 11, 2001, terrorist attacks; these included the executive order that established the Office of Homeland Security and the Homeland Security Council.

What is the president's role as **chief of state**?

As the chief of state, the president is the ceremonial head of the United States. Under the Constitution, the president is the federal official primarily responsible for the relations of the United States with foreign nations. As chief of state, the president appoints ambassadors, ministers, and consuls, subject to confirmation by the Senate, and receives foreign ambassadors and other public officials. With the secretary of state, the president manages all official contacts with foreign governments. On occasion, the president may personally participate in summit conferences where chiefs of state meet for direct consultation. For example, President Woodrow Wilson headed the American delegation to the Paris conference at the end of World War I; President Franklin D. Roosevelt met with Allied leaders during World War II; and every president since Roosevelt has convened with world leaders to discuss economic and political issues and to reach foreign policy agreements.

Through the Department of State, the president is responsible for the protection of Americans abroad and of foreign nationals in the United States. The president decides whether to recognize new nations and new governments, and negotiates treaties with other nations, which become binding on the United States when approved by two-thirds of the Senate.

What is the president's role as **commander in chief**?

Article II, Section 2, of the U.S. Constitution states that the president is the commander in chief of the U.S. Army, Navy, and, when it is called into federal service, state militias (now called the National Guard). Historically, presidents have used this authority to commit U.S. troops without a formal declaration of war. However, Article I, Section 8, of the Constitution reserves to Congress the power to raise and support the armed forces as well as the sole authority to declare war. These competing powers have been the source of controversy between the legislative and executive branches over war making, so much so that in 1973 Congress enacted the War Powers Resolution, which limits the president's authority to use the armed forces without specific congressional authorization, in an attempt to increase and clarify Congress's control over the use of the military. In addition, the armed forces operate under the doctrine of civilian control, which means that only the president or statutory deputies—such as the secretary and deputy secretary of defense—can order the use of force. The chain of command is structured to ensure that the military cannot undertake actions without civilian approval or knowledge.

How is the president the **chief legislator**?

Despite the constitutional provision that "all legislative powers" shall be vested in the Congress, the president, as the chief formulator of public policy, plays a major legislative role. The president can veto any bill passed by Congress and, unless two-thirds of the members of each house vote to override the veto, the bill does not become law. Much of the legislation dealt with by Congress is drafted at the initiative of the executive branch. In his annual and special messages to Congress, the president may propose legislation he believes is necessary. If Congress should adjourn without acting on those proposals, the president has the power to call it into special session. But beyond this official role, the president, as head of a political party and as principal executive officer of the U.S. government, is in a position to influence public opinion and thereby the course of legislation in Congress.

To improve their working relationships with Congress in recent years, presidents have set up a Congressional Liaison Office in the White House. Presidential aides keep abreast of all-important legislative activities and try to persuade senators and representatives of both parties to support administration policies.

What is the **president's "veto power"**?

There are two types of vetoes available to the president. The regular veto, called a "qualified negative veto," is limited by the ability of Congress to gather the necessary two-thirds vote of each house for constitutional override. The other type of veto is not explicitly outlined in the U.S. Constitution, but is traditionally called a "pocket veto." As an "absolute veto" that cannot be overridden, it becomes effective when the president fails to sign a bill after Congress has adjourned and is unable to override the veto. The president's veto authority is a significant tool in legislative dealings with Congress. It is not only effective in directly preventing the passage of legislation undesirable to the president, but serves as a threat, thereby bringing about changes in the content of legislation long before the bill is ever presented to the president.

What is a **line-item veto**?

The Line Item Veto Act of 1996 gave the president the authority to cancel certain new spending and entitlement projects, as well as the authority to cancel certain types of limited, targeted tax breaks. The president could make these cancellations within five days of the enactment of a bill providing such funds. These line-item vetoes could then be subject to a two-thirds veto override by the House and Senate. For example, President Bill Clinton used the line-item veto to make eighty-two cancellations, and Congress overrode thirty-eight of the cancellations, all within a single military construction bill. In 1998, the U.S. Supreme Court ruled the line-item veto unconstitutional, in violation of the Presentment Clause in Article I, Section 7, of the Constitution, which requires that every bill that passes the House and Senate must be presented to the president for either approval or disapproval.

When can a president call a **special session with Congress**?

Article II, Section 3, of the U.S. Constitution gives the president power to convene Congress, or either house, "on extraordinary [or special] occasions." It is usual for the president when calling an extra session to indicate the exact matter that needs the attention of Congress. However, once convened, Congress cannot be limited in the subject matter that it will consider. The president is also empowered by the Constitution to adjourn Congress "at such time as he may think proper" when the House and Senate disagree with respect to the time for adjournment; however, to date no president has exercised this power. Many constitutional experts believe the provision applies only in the case of extraordinary sessions.

Have any **presidents ever called special sessions with Congress**?

In total, on twenty-seven occasions presidents have called both houses of Congress into session to deal with urgent matters of war and economic crisis. Two early presidents— George Washington and John Adams—were known for utilizing the Senate as a kind of executive council in addition to its constitutional role as the upper house of the Congress. In 1794, Washington called the Senate into special session to consider Jay's Treaty, for example, and in 1797, Adams called the Senate alone into session in order to discuss relations with France. In 1861, Abraham Lincoln called a special session of Congress to explain his actions at the outbreak of the Civil War. The last president to convene Congress was Harry S. Truman in 1948, who did so to urge enactment of his domestic legislative agenda that expanded the New Deal programs of his predecessor, Franklin D. Roosevelt. Although it is constitutionally permissible for the president to do so, no president has ever called the House of Representatives into a special session by itself.

How is the president the **chief of party**?

As chief of party, or party leader, the president is the acknowledged leader of the political party that controls the executive branch. He helps form the party's position on policy issues, and strives to elect party members to Congress so that his party dominates in both the House and the Senate. While most presidencies are divided governments—that is, one party controlling the executive office and another party controlling the Congress—a unified party in both the executive and legislative departments makes it much easier for the president to propel his legislative agenda.

One of the roles of the president is to serve as the country's chief citizen, welcoming dignitaries and people of achievement. President Herbert Hoover is pictured with aviatrix Amelia Earhart in June 1932 before presenting her with the National Geographic Society gold medal in recognition of her solo flight across the Atlantic Ocean. *AP/Wide World Photos.*

In what ways is the president the **chief citizen**?

President Franklin D. Roosevelt probably summed up the duties of this role best when he called the presidency "preeminently a place of moral leadership." As a representative of the nation's people, the president automatically assumes the role of its chief citizen, or popular leader. The nature of this role mandates a certain trust between the president and the people, since it is the president's duty to work for the public interest amidst competing private interests, and to place the nation's best interests above the interests of any one group or citizen. In turn, the president relies on public support to help pass his legislative agenda through Congress—gaining the trust of the public with regard to these issues through exposure, straightforwardness, and strong leadership.

What is the **president's power to pardon**?

Article II, Section 2, of the U.S. Constitution states that "the president shall have the power to grant reprieves and pardons for offenses against the United States, except in cases of impeachment." The pardon power is exclusive to the executive branch, with no requirement for consent from any other branch of government. Of all of the president's responsibilities, the pardon power is perhaps the most delicate and political, in that it is meant to be an instrument that rights the wrongs of those who have violated federal laws, and is purely subjective on the part of the president. Presidents may exercise this power on behalf of a particular person or a group of people.

What are some **notable historical pardons**?

Presidents have used the pardon power as both an act of mercy and as a strategic decision to restore stability and peace among the American people. For example, in 1795 George Washington achieved this result when he granted amnesty for two participants in the previous year's Whiskey Rebellion, a series of riots made in protest against an excise tax placed on alcohol. During and after the Civil War (1861–1865), Presidents Abraham Lincoln and Andrew Johnson used the power to provide amnesty to thousands of Confederate soldiers, including a controversial one to Jefferson Davis, the president of the Confederacy, in efforts to bring a war-torn nation together. Both Gerald Ford and Jimmy Carter pardoned Vietnam War draft evaders, and—in one of the most controversial and talked-about pardons in history—Ford pardoned former president Richard Nixon in 1974 from prosecution for his involvement in the Watergate scandal, which had divided the nation. In another controversial move, President George Bush pardoned former secretary of defense Casper Weinberger and five other participants in the Iran-Contra affair. In total, President Bill Clinton issued 395 pardons between 1993 and January 20, 2001. The vast majority were issued in the last three years of his presidency, and 140 were issued on his last day in office, the most notable of which was to fugitive commodities trader Marc Rich. The pardon prompted hearings by the Senate Judiciary Committee to investigate whether or not it was related to financial contributions made by Rich and his ex-wife to Clinton's presidential campaign.

REQUIREMENTS

What are the **qualifications for becoming president**?

According to Article II, Section 1, of the U.S. Constitution, any person seeking the presidency must be a natural-born citizen, at least thirty-five years old, and a resident of the United States for at least fourteen years. Constitutional scholars have debated whether a child born abroad of an American parent constitutes "a natural-born citizen." While most maintain that such a person should qualify as a natural-born citizen, no definitive consensus has been reached.

Are there any **unwritten requirements for becoming president**?

In addition to the requirements outlined in the Constitution, Americans typically elect a president who meets a set of informal criteria, such as strong leadership skills—particularly leadership within the political arena or in one of the two major political parties—moral uprightness, extensive experience in running for and gaining political office, and an adeptness at communicating with the media and the citizenry. Although millions of Americans are legally eligible to run for president, those who have a decided advantage are those who have held political office, especially as governors and members of the U.S. Congress. In America's history, sixteen former governors and twnety-four former members of one or both houses of Congress have served as president. The two leading presidential candidates in 2000, George W. Bush and Al Gore, both held political posts: Bush served as the governor of

Cartoon depicting the transition of power from one president to another. Theodore Roosevelt hands off a baby, symbolizing his policies, to his successor, William Howard Taft, who had served as Roosevelt's secretary of war. *Library of Congress.*

Texas from 1994 to 2000, and Gore served in both houses of Congress from 1976 to January 2, 1993, before serving as vice president from 1993 to 2001. John Kerry, who ran against Bush in 2004, was elected to the U.S. Senate in 1984 and served three terms.

How many **terms** can a president serve?

Article II, Section 1, of the U.S. Constitution mandates that the president serve a four-year term. This time period was chosen because the framers agreed that four years was enough time for a president to have learned the ropes, demonstrated his leadership abilities, and established sound policies. The Constitution placed no limit on the number of terms that a president might serve until 1951, with the adoption of the Twenty-second Amendment, which states that "no person shall be elected to the office of the President more than twice, and no person who has held the office of President, or acted as President, for more than two years of a term to which some other person was elected President shall be elected to the office of the President more than once." As a result, a person may be elected president twice to serve a maximum of eight years in office; however, a president who has succeeded to the office beyond the midpoint in a term to which another person was originally elected could potentially serve for more than eight years. In these exceptional cases, the president would finish out his predecessor's term and then seek two full terms on his own. Under these conditions, the maximum amount of time that he could serve would be ten years.

How and when was the **concept of the term limit challenged**?

While early presidents, beginning with George Washington, refused to seek more than two terms of office and established the unwritten rule of not pursuing a third term, Franklin D. Roosevelt broke tradition by winning a third term in 1940 and a fourth term in 1944. He was the only president to ever serve more than two terms, since shortly thereafter the Twenty-second Amendment was passed, placing term limits on the executive office. The Twenty-second Amendment, proposed in 1947 and ratified in 1951, restores the tradition established by George Washington by legally restricting a president to two terms in office.

Have **other term limits** been suggested?

Since the Twenty-second Amendment was passed in 1951, several presidents—including Harry S. Truman, Dwight D. Eisenhower, and Ronald Reagan—have called for its appeal. Their main argument has centered on the fact that the amendment places an arbitrary time limit on the office, and that the ultimate will of the people should be regarded when electing their chief officer, despite the amount of time that he has already served. Critics of the amendment concur, saying the time limit undercuts the authority of a two-term president, especially in the latter half of his second term. Still other presidents, most recently Jimmy Carter, have lobbied for a single, nonrenewable six-year term, arguing that this time period would allow the president to more feasibly focus on implementing long-term policies that would benefit the nation and release him from the pressure of campaigning for a second term—a cumbersome task that ultimately distracts him from the day-to-day responsibilities of the office.

Which **presidents pledged to serve only one term**?

In an era when presidents consistently seek a second term in office, few people can believe that several presidents *chose* to serve only one term in office. James K. Polk (served 1845–1849), Rutherford B. Hayes (served 1877–1881), and James Buchanan

Lyndon B. Johnson is sworn in as president of the United States on *Air Force One* after the assassination of President John F. Kennedy on November 22, 1963. To his right stands his wife, Lady Bird Johnson, and to his left is the grief-stricken Jacqueline Kennedy. Federal judge Sarah T. Hughes is administering the oath. *Getty Images.*

(served 1857–1861) make the list of those presidents who pledged to serve one term and fulfilled their promise.

When does the president actually **begin his term**?

When the Constitution was ratified, Congress was given power to determine the date for beginning the operations of the new presidential administration, and it set the date of March 4, 1789. Although George Washington did not take the oath of office until April 30 of that year, his term officially began on March 4. Later, the Twentieth (or so-called "lame duck") Amendment, which was ratified in 1933, established January 20 as the date on which presidents would be inaugurated. In 1937, Franklin D. Roosevelt became the first president to take the oath on January 20.

The change of date eliminated the often-awkward "lame duck" period of four months, during which an outgoing president's power was realistically diminished. The need for a longer timeframe between election and inauguration earlier in history was due to the more modest means of travel and communication of the times.

What is the **presidential oath**?

The oath of the office for the president is outlined in Article II, Section 1, of the U.S. Constitution, and reads as follows: "I do solemnly swear (or affirm) that I will faithfully execute the office of President of the United States, and will, to the best of my ability,

17

preserve, protect, and defend the Constitution of the United States." Usually, the chief justice of the Supreme Court administers the oath, although there is no provision made for this within the Constitution. In fact, throughout American history other judges have administered the oath at times of unexpected presidential succession.

Which **president in history did not swear to the oath**?

Franklin Pierce, the fourteenth president of the United States, was the only president in history to affirm rather than swear the oath of office. Pierce's objection to "swear" was a religious one. In addition, he did not kiss the Bible.

What are the president's **salary and benefits**?

As of the term that began on January 20, 2001, the president' salary is $400,000 per year. Congress sets the president's salary, which cannot be increased or decreased during a presidential term. In addition, the president is allocated a $50,000-per-year taxable expense allowance to be spent however he chooses. During his term in office, the president also enjoys many perks, including living in the White House, orchestrating office suites and a large staff, sailing on the presidential yacht, flying in his private jet (*Air Force One*), holding meetings at the Camp David resort in Maryland, and enjoying abundant travel and entertainment funds, among other benefits. In addition, since 1959, each former president has received a lifetime pension.

Can a president be **removed from office**?

Yes. Presidential power is not absolute, but rather limited and kept in check by both constitutional and political constraints. The ultimate limit on presidential power is removal from office by Congress through "Impeachment for, and Conviction of, Treason, Bribery, or other high Crimes and Misdemeanors," as outlined in Article II, Section 4, of the U.S. Constitution.

What is **impeachment**?

Impeachment is the process by which the president, vice president, federal judges and justices, and all civil officials of the United States may be removed from office. Officials may be impeached for treason, bribery, and other high crimes and misdemeanors. The

House of Representatives has sole authority to bring charges of impeachment, by a simple majority vote, and the Senate has sole authority to try impeachment charges. An official may be removed from office only upon conviction, which requires a two-thirds vote of the Senate. The Constitution provides that the chief justice shall preside when the president is tried for impeachment.

How many **presidents have been impeached**?

Throughout America's history, only two presidents have been impeached: Andrew Johnson and Bill Clinton. In 1868, impeachment proceedings were initiated against Johnson by the House of Representatives, who charged Johnson with usurpation of the law, corrupt use of veto power, interference at elections, and various misdemeanors. However, the fifty-four-member Senate proceedings acquitted Johnson by one vote. In December 1998, the House of Representatives brought two articles of impeachment against President Clinton: perjury under oath before a federal grand jury about the precise nature of his sexual relations with White House intern Monica Lewinsky, and obstruction of justice by withholding evidence about, and influencing others to conceal, his affair with Lewinsky. Ultimately, the U.S. Senate rejected both charges, and Clinton remained in office.

How many presidents have **resigned from office**?

Just one: Richard Nixon. While many people cite Nixon in the list of impeached presidents, it is a misnomer. During the Watergate scandal, the House Committee on the Judiciary approved in July 1974 three articles of impeachment against President Nixon, including the obstruction of justice and the abuse of presidential power. However, on August 9, 1974, Nixon resigned before being formally impeached.

In cases of **impeachment or resignation, who succeeds the president**?

According to the Twenty-fifth Amendment, adopted in 1967, the vice president succeeds to the office if the president dies, resigns, or is removed from office by impeachment.

How many **vice presidents have succeeded to the presidency because of a vacancy** in that office?

Nine: John Tyler, Millard Fillmore, Andrew Johnson, Chester Alan Arthur, Theodore Roosevelt, Calvin Coolidge, Harry S. Truman, Lyndon B. Johnson, and Gerald Ford.

Who would **succeed to the presidency if the office becomes vacant and there is no vice president?**

According to Article II, Section 1, of the Constitution, Congress fixes the order of succession following the vice president. According to the effective law on succession, the

The original wording of the Constitution was vague on who should succeed a president unable to complete his term. When it happened for the first time—in 1841, William Henry Harrison died after less than a month in office—many believed Congress would choose a successor. Vice President John Tyler, however, had himself sworn into office and began performing the duties of president. Congress agreed, after debate, but when Tyler made unpopular decisions he was quickly referred to as "His Accidency" and "Vice President Acting President Tyler."

Presidential Succession Act of 1947, should both the president and vice president vacate their offices, the Speaker of the House of Representatives would assume the presidency. Next in line is the president pro tempore of the Senate (a senator elected by that body to preside in the absence of the vice president), and then cabinet officers in designated order: secretary of state; secretary of the treasury; secretary of defense; attorney general; secretary of the interior; secretary of agriculture; secretary of commerce; secretary of labor; secretary of health and human services; secretary of housing and urban development; secretary of transportation; secretary of energy; secretary of education; and secretary of veterans affairs. (See also Illness and Death, Assassination and Scandal: Assassination Attempts.)

THE WHITE HOUSE

Where does the **president reside**?

The president of the United States lives and works in the White House in Washington, D.C., located at 1600 Pennsylvania Avenue. The White House is three stories high, with offices, public rooms, guest rooms, and the family's living space taking up most of the 55,000 square feet of the building. All told, there are 132 rooms (including 16 family guest rooms, 1 main kitchen, 1 diet kitchen, 1 family kitchen, and 31 bathrooms) in the residence. There are 412 doors, 147 windows, 28 fireplaces, 8 staircases, and 3 elevators. In addition, the property houses a tennis court, a jogging track, a swimming pool, a gym, a movie theater, and a bowling lane. It is surrounded by approximately 18 acres of lawns and gardens.

Who was the **first president to reside in the White House**?

In December 1790, President George Washington signed the Residence Act, declaring that the federal government would reside in a district "not exceeding ten miles square … on the river Potomac." Although President Washington was in office when construction began on the White House, he never lived in it. It was not until November 1800, when the White House was nearly completed (but still undergoing internal renovation), that its first residents, President John Adams and his wife Abigail, moved in. The couple had previously resided in Philadelphia, Pennsylvania, which was the temporary capital of the United States while the White House was undergoing construction. Thomas Jefferson (served 1801–1809) was the first to spend his entire presidency in the White House.

Where did **President Washington live**?

As president, George Washington lived at 190 High Street in Philadelphia, Pennsylvania, in a four-story house that served as the executive mansion from 1790 to 1800, during the city's tenure as the nation's capital. Before the White House in Washington, D.C., was constructed, he lived in the house on High Street for more than six years, until his second term ended in 1797. (John Adams also lived there for almost four years before moving to the White House for the final few months of his administration.) In these living quarters, Washington performed all the duties and social obligations of president. The Market Street house was built in the late 1760s and, before the Washingtons, was home to several men of note, including Richard Penn, grandson of Pennsylvania's founder William Penn; British general Sir William Howe, who was headquartered there during the American Revolution; Benedict Arnold; and Robert Morris.

Before moving to Philadelphia, Washington resided at 3 Cherry Street in New York City, and then later in a second executive mansion on lower Broadway, near the city's Federal Hall, where the fledgling national government met.

What was the **White House like originally**?

The original White House was designed by Irish American architect James Hoban, and built between 1792 and 1800. When workers first built the presidential home out of gray stone, it was called the "Executive Mansion." The building was first made white with lime-based whitewash in 1798, when its walls were finished, primarily as a means of protecting the porous stone from freezing. The Adamses moved into a house that was still unfinished; in fact, many of the plaster walls were still wet and about half of the thirty-six rooms had not been plastered at all. The largest room in the house, the East Room, was also unfinished. Because Abigail Adams thought that the president's laundry should not be hung to dry outside on the lawn for the public to see, she set up drying lines in the East Room.

Is it true that **slaves built the White House**?

Yes. On October 13, 1792, workers laid the cornerstone of the President's House, as it was then commonly called. The decision to place the capital in Washington, D.C., on

Citizens celebrate the end of World War I in front of the White House in 1918. *Getty Images.*

land assigned to two slave states, Virginia and Maryland, led to the use of slave labor to meet construction needs. Although the D.C. commissioners originally planned to import Europeans to build the residence of America's chief executive, a low turnout persuaded them to recruit both free and enslaved African Americans to perform the labor for this as well as other early government buildings, including the U.S. Capitol.

When was it **officially called the White House**?

Although the term "White House" was used to describe the building as early as 1809, President Theodore Roosevelt officially adopted the moniker in 1901, when he engraved it on his stationery. Before then, the building was referred to as the Executive Mansion, the Presidential Palace, or the Presidential Mansion. First Lady Dolley Madison called it the President's Castle.

When did the **White House burn down**?

In 1814, during the War of 1812, the British completely burned down the White House. President James Madison immediately ordered the rebuilding of the destroyed mansion, insisting that it be restored to its original condition. To ensure authenticity, Madison enlisted the help of the White House's original architect, James Hoban. Workers used the stone slabs that had survived the fire to rebuild the White House, and afterward gave it a fresh coat of white paint. The rebuilding took a total of three years, and was reopened by President James Monroe for a New Year's party in 1818.

Today, approximately three hundred gallons of white paint are used to cover the exterior of just the center section of the White House, excluding the East and West Wings. Only one other fire tinged the building in its history: In 1929, the West Wing caught on fire during Herbert Hoover's administration.

During which administrations did the White House receive significant updates and remodeling?

Before major restoration began in the late 1940s, the White House had already undergone many changes. In the 1820s, workers added extra pavilions and porticos (ornamental, deck-like structures with columns supporting a roof), after the design of architect Benjamin Latrobe, who also designed the U.S. Capitol. In 1833, water pipes were added; in the 1850s, a stove was added; in 1881, an elevator was added. The first telephone was wired into the White House during Rutherford B. Hayes's administration (1877–1881); during Benjamin Harrison's administration, in 1891, the White House was wired for electricity. The one-story West Wing offices were constructed during the term of Theodore Roosevelt, in 1901–1902, because the president needed the second-floor office area for living space for his large family. A new east entrance was also built to allow groups of carriages to enter the property. And in 1909, President William Howard Taft remodeled the president's office, creating the Oval Office in the center of the West Wing. In 1927, President Calvin Coolidge and his wife relocated to nearby Dupont Circle while the White House roof was raised and replaced, and a third floor was added to allow for guest bedrooms and additional storage. In 1933, engineers installed air conditioning in the White House's private quarters.

When was the White House renovated?

During President Harry S. Truman's administration, the White House was found to be structurally unsound. Under Truman's recommendation, the residence underwent major renovation. From 1948 to 1952, construction workers tore down the entire interior, retaining only the third floor and the original outer walls that architect James Hoban built. Using steel instead of wood, workers reinforced the building, adding several rooms, and restoring the existing rooms to their original appearance.

Where did President Truman live while the White House was being restored?

Throughout much of Truman's presidency, the interior of the White House was completely gutted and renovated while the Trumans lived at Blair House, right across Pennsylvania Avenue.

Who pays for the purchase of new furniture, artwork, and renovations to the White House?

The U.S. federal government pays for the operation and maintenance of the White House. For major refurbishings of the public rooms, the White House Endowment   23

Fund provides the funds; for major acquisitions of artwork and furnishings, the White House Acquisition Trust provides the funds. Both of these sources are administered by the White House Historical Association from an endowment raised from public contributions. The Historical Association also receives objects as gifts from private donors.

What are some of the **White House's famous rooms**?

One of the most famous rooms in the White House is the Lincoln Room, named for President Abraham Lincoln. In Lincoln's administration, it was his cabinet room and the room in which he signed the 1863 Emancipation Proclamation. Under President Harry S. Truman's orders, furniture of Lincoln's that had been scattered about the White House was put in this room. The furniture includes Lincoln's bed, which Theodore Roosevelt and Calvin Coolidge slept in. Today, the president's guests often sleep in the Lincoln Room and the Rose Room.

The East Wing (which houses offices for executive branch workers) and the West Wing (where the president and the president's staff work) are on either side of the main building. The Oval Office, located in the West Wing, is familiar to most Americans because this is the location from which president's speeches are often broadcast. The East Room, the largest public room, is where the president often hosts receptions, dances, and concerts. Also used for receptions are the Blue Room (which received its name in 1837), the Green Room (which received its original name, the "Green Drawing Room," from John Quincy Adams sometime between 1825 and 1829), and the Red Room (which received its name in 1840), all three of which are named for the color of their decorations. The State Dining Room accommodates more than one hundred guests. The China Room, originally donned the "Presidential Collection Room," was designated by first lady Edith Wilson in 1917 to display the growing collection of White House china. Although more than one million visitors tour the White House every year, the public is not allowed on the second or third floors; the second floor is where the president and his family reside.

What **changes** have been made to the White House **post–September 11**?

For two years following the terrorist attacks of September 11, 2001, the White House had limited access to the public in order to strengthen security and redecorate several areas. In January 2002, President George W. Bush unveiled a redecorated Oval Office, featuring bronze silk damask draperies, an oval custom-made rug featuring the presidential seal, cream-colored sofas, and Texas landscape paintings. Upstairs in the president's private quarters, longtime Bush family decorator Ken Blasingame remade several of the president's rooms. White House curator William Allman said, "To the naked eye, nothing much has changed," though several rooms have been redecorated, including the East Room, which has had a $200,000 update. Some historic paintings in the Red, Green, and Blue Rooms have been reframed, and gardeners planted a new row of crab apple trees in the Rose Garden.

PRESIDENTIAL CANDIDATES AND CAMPAIGNS

PARTIES AND PLATFORMS

How did **early candidates enter the presidential race**?

During the fledgling years of the nation, the government was still small, loosely organized, and remote from the people. The legislative leaders met together, planned their political strategy, and decided upon candidates, a process known as the congressional caucus. Leaders discussed relevant matters, tried to gain the support of like-minded men, and then attempted to affect the next election by taking their ideas back to the electorate, which at this point in history was reserved to white, property-owning males. During the presidential elections of 1796 and 1800, members of the national Congress met unofficially in caucus in order to solidify support for the nation's presidential candidates. In 1804, the Democratic-Republican congressmen openly met in caucus in order to nominate Thomas Jefferson for his second term. This practice assumed the title "King Caucus," and subsequently was used to nominate both James Madison and James Monroe. Though the caucus system of nomination gained acceptance as a mechanism of election management, it was criticized for its tendency toward secrecy and elitism. By the presidential elections of 1824 and 1828, candidates were nominated through a mix of methods: state legislatures, state conventions, and congressional caucuses.

Is it true that **George Washington was elected without** the help of a **political party**?

Yes. Believing that political parties were complicated, if not outright detrimental to society, America's Founding Fathers were set on developing a system for electing presidents without the aid of political parties and national campaigns. When George Washington was elected president in early 1789, he was the first and last president to do so without the support of a political party. When the Constitution of the United States was ratified, the electoral college unanimously elected Washington president, an act they repeated in 1792. Although this method worked fine for Washington, its weaknesses were revealed with the development of political parties, and ultimately the original design of the electoral college system lasted only through four presidential elections.

What did **George Washington** have to say about **political parties**?

The U.S. Constitution does not mention political parties, and indeed many of the nation's founders, including George Washington, detested the concept of parties, or factions, because they did not want any political group in the nation to become too powerful. In his Farewell Address to the nation, first published in Philadelphia's *American Daily Advertiser* on September 19, 1796, rather than delivered orally, Washington waned against the party system in America. Cautioning the public "in the most solemn manner" against the "baneful effects of the spirit of Party," Washington said the party system "serves to distract the Public Councils, and enfeeble the Public Administration … agitates the Community with ill founded Jealousies and false alarms; kindles the animosity of one … against another … opens the door to foreign influence and corruption.… Thus the policy and the will of one country, are subjected to the policy and will of another." Washington was referring to divisions that had already arisen in his cabinet and leaders whom had each begun to sew the seeds of the party system.

How did the **first two political parties evolve**?

The first two parties, the Federalists and the Democratic-Republicans, were shaped during the administration of the country's first president, George Washington. The Federalist Party was a creation of Alexander Hamilton, secretary of the treasury under Washington. Hamilton believed that the success of the new government would depend on its economic stability, and as such favored full funding of the entire federal debt and the assumption of the states' debts by the federal government. The issues of funding and assumption, coupled with other major economic issues such as the charter of the Bank of the United States and an imposition of an excise tax, began to divide the government. The opposition party, the Jeffersonian (or Democratic) Republicans, was organized by congressman James Madison and Thomas Jefferson, who served as secretary of state during Washington's first term. The Democratic-Republicans formed around opposition to many of Washington's economic policies, denouncing many of Hamilton's decisions, such as the ratification of Jay's Treaty with Great Britain. Although Washington did not call himself a Federalist per se, his policies reflected those of the Federalists, and Washington was considered a candidate of the Federalist Party for his second-term election in 1792.

What were the key **differences between the Federalists and the Democratic-Republicans**?

The Federalists were a powerful and wealthy party, made up mostly of lawyers, big businessmen, bankers, merchants, and professionals, and were influential in New

George Washington Warns Americans
of the Dangers of Political Parties

George Washington "delivered" his farewell address to the American people by way of Philadelphia's *American Daily Advertiser* on September 19, 1796. In it, he expressed his concerns about political parties:

> The alternate domination of one faction over another, sharpened by the spirit of revenge natural to party dissension, which in different ages & countries has perpetrated the most horrid enormities, is itself a frightful despotism. But this leads at length to a more formal and permanent despotism. The disorders & miseries, which result, gradually incline the minds of men to seek security & repose in the absolute power of an Individual: and sooner or later the chief of some prevailing faction more able or more fortunate than his competitors, turns this disposition to the purposes of his own elevation, on the ruins of Public Liberty.

> Without looking forward to an extremity of this kind (which nevertheless ought not to be entirely out of sight) the common & continual mischiefs of the spirit of Party are sufficient to make it the interest and the duty of a wise People to discourage and restrain it.

> It serves always to distract the Public Councils and enfeeble the Public Administration. It agitates the Community with ill founded Jealousies and false alarms, kindles the animosity of one part against another, foments occasionally riot & insurrection. It opens the door to foreign influence & corruption, which find a facilitated access to the government itself through the channels of party passions. Thus the policy and the will of one country, are subjected to the policy and will of another.

England and the northern part of the United States where big business thrived. In terms of political thought, the Federalists believed in strong government leadership and a loose constructionist interpretation of the Constitution, meaning that key philosophies were implied by or simply understood by the wording of the Constitution, and thus could be adapted to the day-to-day running of the government. They also supported improved relations with England over France. In contrast, the Democratic-Republicans, known as the "party of the common man," were made up of farmers, small businessmen, and laborers, and influenced the southern and western parts of the United States, where agriculture was strong. The Democratic-Republicans adopted a strict constructionist interpretation of the Constitution, meaning that if an issue wasn't written or referred to directly in the Constitution then the federal government had no authority to regulate or manage those affairs. Both parties were relatively short-lived: besides Washington, an ipso facto Federalist, John Adams was the only Federalist president (served 1797–1801); four presidents were Democratic-Republicans: Thomas Jefferson (served 1801–1809); James Madison (served 1809–1817); James Monroe (served 1817–1825); and John Quincy Adams (served 1825–1829).

What role did **political parties** play in the **elections of 1796 and 1800**?

The development of political parties accidentally resulted in the election outcomes of 1796 and 1800. Under the framers' method of electing a president (described in Article II, Section 1, of the Constitution), each elector cast two votes without indicating which vote was for the president and which vote was for the vice president. As a result, a number of mishaps could occur. For example, in the election of 1796, this system produced a president from one party, Federalist John Adams, and a vice president from another party, Thomas Jefferson of the Democratic-Republicans. In the presidential election of 1800, the electors of the Democratic-Republican Party gave Thomas Jefferson and Aaron Burr, who were both of that same party, an equal number (seventy-three) of electoral votes. Because the votes were tied, the election was thrown to the House of Representatives, where each state voted as a unit to decide the outcome of the election. Since the Federalist-dominated House consistently divided its votes between the two men, the deadlock wasn't broken until the thirty-sixth ballot, when Jefferson gained the majority of necessary votes to claim presidential victory. The final results were ten states in favor of Jefferson, and four in favor of Burr. To prevent tie votes in the electoral college that were made probable by the rise of political parties, in 1804 Congress and the states adopted the Twelfth Amendment to the Constitution, which provides that electors "name in their ballots the person voted for as president, and in distinct ballots the person voted for as vice president."

What became of the **Federalists**?

The Federalists' tenure in the White House was short-lived, and with the exiting of John Adams from the White House in 1800, the Federalists began to fade from view. During Adams's presidency, Alexander Hamilton wrote a scathing criticism of Adams's performance as president in an effort to throw Federalist support to presidential hopeful Charles Cotesworth Pinckney; instead this act split the Federalists and helped give the presidential victory to Thomas Jefferson, the leader of the Democratic-Republicans. Although the Federalists continued to be a major political party in New England and the Northeast, they never regained control of the presidency or the Congress. With the retirement of Adams and the death of Hamilton in a famous duel with Aaron Burr in 1804, Federalists lacked a strong leader, and grew steadily weaker as a political force. After their defeat in the presidential election of 1816, the Federalists did not run a presidential candidate against the Democratic-Republicans in 1820.

What happened to the **Democratic-Republicans**?

With the demise of the Federalists, the Democratic-Republicans dominated the political landscape for twenty-four years, without any serious opposition during the administrations of Thomas Jefferson (served 1801–1809), James Madison (served 1809–1817), and James Monroe (served 1817–1825). When Monroe ran virtually unopposed in the election of 1820, the "the era of good feelings"—a term that describes the national mood of the United States from about 1815 to 1825— had reached its peak. Shortly afterward, the Democratic-Republicans split into two parties: the Democratic Party, led by Andrew Jackson, and the Whig Party, which was formed in opposition to Jackson's principles.

What were the **major contributions** of this **first party system**?

The first party system ushered in the concept of modern political parties. During the late 1700s, American parties became an important, integrated part of the national government. Distinctly different from any other entity that existed before, parties allowed leaders to legitimately oppose government policies without opposing the concept of government itself. The leaders of the Democratic-Republicans, especially, learned how to become sensitive to the will of the people and how to respond to changing social conditions, something that the Federalists never fully grasped and which quickly brought about their demise. With a distinct national ideology, the Democratic-Republicans became an enduring organization through several administrations, learning how to rally support for their causes from like-minded leaders. Parties used the congressional caucus as a means of nominating candidates, and they recruited candidates for all offices, developing a party structure that would continue to be shaped into the nineteenth century.

What **other parties were in existence until 1832**?

Though the first American party system is generally framed within a discussion of the Federalists and the Democratic-Republicans, there were other political parties that existed in the 1820s and early 1830s. The development of political parties was closely linked to the extension of voting rights, as property-owning qualifications for voting were lifted during the early 1800s. With a vastly expanded electorate, politicians needed a means to mobilize masses of voters, and political parties became institutionalized to accomplish this essential task. Amidst the reign of the Democratic-Republicans, two parties enjoyed brief popularity, the National Republicans and the Anti-Masonics.

Who were the **National Republicans**?

The National Republicans were the administration party during John Quincy Adams's presidency (served 1825–1829). Adams's supporters adopted the name National

Republicans because they favored strong economic nationalism, much like the defunct Federalist Party. The National Republicans stood in opposition to Andrew Jackson's Democratic-Republican Party, which favored a limited national government and opposed economic aristocracy. As the National Republicans dissolved in the mid-1830s, the Whigs emerged.

Who were the **Anti-Masonics**?

Formed in New York in 1828, the Anti-Masonic Party was the first third party to appear in American national politics. It was formed primarily in response to America's suspicion of secret societies like the Masons and in reaction to the Masonic threat to public institutions that was perceived to be occurring at that time in American history. The Anti-Masonic Party was the first party to hold a nominating convention and the first to announce a platform—nominating William Wirt of Maryland for president and Amos Ellmaker of Pennsylvania as his running mate in September 1831. However, the political effect of the first-time entrance of a third party into a U.S. presidential election drew support from presidential contender Henry Clay and helped then-president Andrew Jackson, who was a Mason, win reelection by a wide margin. Although the Anti-Masonics enjoyed some results (Vermont elected an Anti-Masonic governor, William A. Palmer), after the elections of 1836 the Anti-Masonic party declined and was eventually absorbed into the Whig Party.

Is it true that **today's Democratic Party roots** can be traced back to the **1820s**?

Yes. After the Democratic-Republicans splintered following the 1824 election, a group of supporters rallied around Andrew Jackson and became the Democratic Party. Through the work of Jackson and Martin Van Buren of New York, the first modern political party was created by joining together local party organizations and newspapers. Jackson's early, aggressive campaigning—which reached an expanded electorate wherein almost the entire male population could vote—allowed him to win the elections of 1828 and 1832. With the states' lifting of property qualifications for voting and holding office, the United States evolved from a republic of property holders into more of a mass democracy. The Jacksonian Democrats spent most of Jackson's presidency crafting the chief executive's image and building support for the president. Although the Democrats had originally consisted of southern agrarians and egalitarian New York residents, by this time party followers lived across the nation, which allowed the party to sidestep discussion of the slavery issue that was dividing the country in favor of less heated domestic issues. In addition, this party single-handedly created the national convention process—a means of nominating presidential candidates by delegates from each state—when it held its first national convention in 1832. They created the party platform, and built party spirit by unifying the party on the issue of states' rights.

Who were the **Whigs**?

The Whig Party emerged during the second quarter of the nineteenth century, formed to oppose President Andrew Jackson and the Democratic Party. The term "Whig" came into popular parlance in 1834 and continued until the party disbanded after the presidential election of 1856. The anti-Jackson group drew upon the political history of two revolutions, the American Revolution and seventeenth-century English, for their name, during which the opposition to the king had called themselves Whigs. The party's leading figures, Henry Clay of Kentucky and Daniel Webster of Massachusetts, supported a nationalistic economic policy called the "American System," which entailed a program of tariff protection, federally sponsored communication projects (internal improvements), continuation of the national bank, and a conservative public land sales policy, the essence of which harkened back to Alexander Hamilton's Federalist economic policy of 1791. Although they enjoyed some successes, Whigs were hindered by the rising power of the Jacksonians, who were thereafter called Democrats. During the time of the Whigs and the Democrats, America's true two-party system developed.

Why did the **Whigs** run **regional candidates** in 1836?

In 1836, the Whig Party organized its first presidential campaign, running three regional candidates against Democratic candidate Martin Van Buren. Military leader and former U.S. senator and representative William Henry Harrison of Indiana hoped to gain support in the West; lawyer, orator, and U.S. senator Daniel Webster of Massachusetts hoped to appeal to New England voters; and lawyer and U.S. senator Hugh Lawson White of Tennessee hoped to win votes in the South. The Whigs wanted to ensure that no candidate received a majority of electoral votes, thus throwing the election into the House of Representatives, where the Whigs held the majority and could then unite behind a single candidate. Despite their attempts, Van Buren polled well in all sections of the country and won the presidency with 170 electoral votes, compared with Harrison's 73, White's 26, and Webster's 14. After Van Buren's tenure, Harrison was elected president in 1840. He became the first Whig to win the presidency and the first president to die in office.

Why did the **Whig Party disappear**?

When Vice President John Tyler, a defender of slavery, succeeded to the presidency in 1841 after the death of president William Henry Harrison, he rejected the Whig's political platform. Tyler's attempt to annex Texas made the slavery-extension controversy a heated political issue, and soon the Whigs abandoned Tyler and expelled him from the party. When Whig Millard Fillmore succeeded his fellow Whig, President Zachary Taylor, following the latter's death in 1850, the Whigs were already showing deep signs of fracture. Key members had joined alternative parties, such as the Free-Soil Party, which opposed the extension of slavery in the western territories. In the election of 1852, the Whigs supported the antislavery presidential candidate, General

Winfield Scott, instead of states' rights candidate Fillmore. Scott lost the presidential race, winning only forty-two electoral votes, and the antislavery faction, mostly comprised of northern Whigs, joined the newly formed Republican Party in 1854. The election of 1856 was the last time a Whig ran for president.

What other **political parties** dominated the political scene **between 1844 and 1856**?

During the mid-1800s, several political parties rose up, mainly in response to the slavery issue that had divided the nation. Three parties garnered headlines at this point in America's history: the Liberty Party; the Free-Soil Party; and the American Party, colloquially referred to as the Know-Nothings.

What was the **Liberty Party**?

The Liberty Party was a short-lived mid-nineteenth-century political party that supported abolitionism. Formed by members who broke away from William Lloyd Garrison's American Anti-Slavery Society (1833–1870), the Liberty Party nominated James G. Birney for president in 1840 and 1844. The party never quite got off the ground, and in 1848 members joined with other like-minded leaders to form the Free-Soil Party.

Who were the **Free-Soilers**?

Another short-lived political party, the Free-Soil Party was in existence for only about four years, from 1848 to 1852. Formed to oppose the extension of slavery into the territories, the Free-Soil Party was a melding of abolitionists from the Democratic Party, the Whig Party, the Liberty Party, and a group known as the Barnburners, a radical antislavery arm of the New York Democrats. The party held its first convention in 1848. Free-Soilers nominated a ticket of former U.S. president Martin Van Buren and former Massachusetts state senator Charles Francis Adams (son of former U.S. president John Quincy Adams). Although Van Buren did not win any electoral votes, he received some popular support: his support in New York took enough votes from Democrat Lewis Cass to help Whig Zachary Taylor carry the state. The Free-Soilers had some representation in Congress (two senators, fourteen representatives), but ultimately it was unable to compete with the stronger, pro-abolition Republican Party. Its members eventually joined the Republicans.

Who were the **Know-Nothings**?

More formally known as the American Party, the Know-Nothing Party was founded in New York City in 1849. It was organized to oppose the large influx of immigrants who entered the United States after 1846. Because Know-Nothings believed that these primarily Irish and Roman Catholic immigrants threatened to destroy America, the party strove to use government power to uphold its vision of an Anglo-Saxon Protestant society. Their platform outlined a limited immigration policy, proposed that only native-born Americans could hold public office, and advocated a twenty-one-year mandatory waiting period for immigrants before they were granted citizenship and voting rights. Despite their strength that came with the election of 1856, in which they supported former president Millard Fillmore, the Know-Nothings declined as a national party when many members defected to the Republican Party. Although their numbers remained strong in several northern states in the late 1850s, the party had eroded as a national presence before the presidential election of 1860.

What is the **origin of the Republican Party**?

The Republican Party was born in the early 1850s by antislavery activists and individuals who believed that government should grant western lands to settlers free of charge. The first official Republican meeting took place on July 6, 1854, in Jackson,

Martin Van Buren became increasingly involved in the antislavery movement after his presidency. Van Buren joined the movement that led to the Free-Soil Party and became its candidate for president in 1848. His support in New York took enough votes from Democrat Lewis Cass to help Whig Zachary Taylor carry the state. *Getty Images*.

Michigan, during which the name "Republican" was chosen because it alluded to equality and reminded individuals of Thomas Jefferson's Democratic-Republican Party. At the Jackson convention, the new party adopted a platform and nominated candidates for office in Michigan. In 1856, the Republicans became a national party when former U.S. senator John C. Frémont of California was nominated for president. Even though the Republican party was considered a "third party" because the Democrats and Whigs constituted the two-party system at the time, it wasn't long before Republicans passed the Whigs. In the 1860 election, Abraham Lincoln became the first Republican to win the White House.

What were the **oddities associated with Abraham Lincoln's election of 1860**?

In May 1860, the Republicans gathered in Chicago for their second national convention and nominated Lincoln as their candidate on a platform that denounced the expansion of slavery. The Democrats, divided over the expansion of slavery, nominated two candidates: U.S. senator Stephen A. Douglas of Illinois (a Northern Democrat) and Vice President John C. Breckinridge (a Southern Democrat). A third party, the Constitutional Union Party, composed mostly of former Whigs and Know-Nothings, nominated former U.S. senator John Bell of Tennessee. The contest was actually two elections, one in the North and one in the South. In the North, Lincoln and Douglas vied for victory; in the South, Breckinridge and Bell campaigned against one another. Lincoln did not even appear on the ballot in most southern states, and Breckinridge gained support in only a few northern states. Lincoln won the election by carrying 17 free states and 180 electoral votes, while Breckinridge won in 11 slave states with 72 electoral votes. Lincoln's Republican Party controlled the White House after 1860, leading the nation through the Civil War and into Reconstruction; the Democratic Party won only 4 of the next 17 elections (twice by Grover Cleveland and twice by Woodrow Wilson) and never fully regained its political strength until 1932, with the election of Franklin D. Roosevelt.

Why is **Lincoln's election of 1864 noteworthy**?

The election of 1864 took place amid the much-criticized Civil War, and at a time when no sitting president had been reelected in over three decades—since Andrew Jackson won his second term in 1832. The Republicans met in Baltimore, Maryland, for their national convention under the name National Union Party, with the intention of gaining the support of Democrats opposed to the Confederacy. The party chose Democrat Andrew Johnson, the Union military governor of Tennessee, as Lincoln's running mate. Lincoln won the election with 212 electoral votes. After Lincoln was assassinated in 1865, Johnson became president, eventually denouncing the plans of the Republicans and creating his own agenda.

What were some of the **political parties** that dominated the landscape during the **1880s and 1890s**?

Two parties were popular during this time frame: the Greenbacks, who were active between 1874 and 1884, and the Populists, who nominated a presidential candidate in 1892. The Greenbacks took their name from the paper money called "greenbacks" that was issued during the Civil War (1861–1865). Made up of farmers who had been financially devastated by the Panic of 1873, the Greenbacks believed the government should issue larger amounts of money in an effort to help people, especially farmers, by raising prices and making their debts easier to pay. In the presidential election of 1876, the Greenbacks nominated inventor Peter Cooper; in 1880, they nominated former U.S. representative James B. Weaver of Iowa, who advocated a pro-agriculture agenda and the prohibition of alcohol.

Who were the **Populists**?

Also known as the People's Party, the Populist Party was formed by a group of small farmers and sharecroppers to oppose large-scale commercial agriculture that they feared would put them out of work. The national party was officially founded in 1892 through a merger of the Farmers' Alliance and the Knights of Labor. That year, the Populist presidential candidate, James B. Weaver, won over one million votes. The populists also elected ten representatives, five senators, three governors, and approximately fifteen hundred members of state legislatures. Between 1892 and 1896, however, the party was intimidated by southern Democrats, and after 1896 the party began to decline.

Populists advocated federally regulated communication, transportation, and banking systems to offset the economic depression and prevent poverty among working-class families. Progressive Republican Theodore Roosevelt resurrected many Populist ideas and recast them in new forms as he expanded the federal regulation of business corporations, and addressed many People's Party concerns in his Progressive policies. Other Populist ideas—particularly those calling for aid to farmers and employment on public works projects in times of economic depression—became reality during the 1930s with the New Deal programs of Democratic president Franklin D. Roosevelt.

Why were the **Populists popular among the African American population** in the 1890s?

In the 1890s, both black and white farmers—threatened by common poverty, the loss of their farms, and escalating national business interests—attempted to build an interracial political alliance and challenge mainstream politics, which they felt was unresponsive to their needs. The Populist Party recruited blacks, many of whom continued to vote in large numbers in the South, to help move forward their campaign of political equality. As white populist leaders spoke out against the poll tax, literacy tests, and residence requirements that disenfranchised blacks, African Americans saw the Populists as potential allies against the country's existing racism. As a result, many blacks campaigned for Populist candidates at the state level; in 1892 and 1894, Populists were successful in legislative, congressional, and local elections.

What is significant about **political parties between 1840 and 1890**?

Historians call the period from 1840 to 1890 the Golden Age of Parties. During this time, the major political parties—first the Democrats and Whigs until the mid-1850s, then the Democrats and Republicans—were the strongest they have been in American history. Party leaders used patronage and campaign practices to ignite enthusiasm for their causes and gain a wide, loyal membership. Voter turnout during this period was the highest in American history: between 70 and 80 percent of qualified voters turned out for presidential elections, and sometimes higher figures emerged in state and local contests.

What election "firsts" did the **Progressives** establish?

During the 1890s, the Progressive movement—a broad-based reform movement of mainly middle-class, urban Americans seeking to alleviate many of the social ills

Theodore Roosevelt was a passionate speaker and vigorous leader. He brought excitement and power to the presidency, as he led Congress and the American public toward progressive reforms and a strong foreign policy. *AP/Wide World Photos.*

plaguing American society—picked up momentum. While the movement was not cohesive or organized, the Progressives began to make inroads at the state level to reform government, with a larger goal of undermining the power of party bosses and restoring sovereignty to the people. They advocated a wide range of political reforms, including adoption of the secret ballot, direct primaries, the initiative, the referendum, and direct election of senators. The direct primary is a mechanism that enables voters, rather than party heads, to choose party candidates; by 1916, all but three states had adopted the direct primary. Less widely adopted was the recall, which allows voters to remove from office any public servant who has betrayed their trust. The adoption of the concepts of referendum (the practice of referring a measure proposed or passed by a legislature to the vote of the electorate for approval or rejection), initiative (the procedure whereby voters, by petition, may propose a law or constitutional amendment and have it submitted to the voters), and recall were created to make office holders more directly responsible to the voting public.

The three Progressive-minded presidents were Theodore Roosevelt (served 1901–1909), William Howard Taft (served 1909–1913), and Woodrow Wilson (served 1913–1921).

What was Teddy Roosevelt's **Progressive "Bull Moose" Party**?

Also known as the Bull Moose Party, the Progressive Party was formed in 1912 by former Republican president Theodore Roosevelt (served 1901–1909). Progressives supported women's suffrage, environmental conservation, tariff reform, stricter regulation of industrial combinations, and prohibition of child labor. Unhappy with the conservative policies of William Howard Taft and dominant Republicans, Roosevelt and many liberal Republicans transferred their allegiance to the Progressives. They nominated Roosevelt for president and California governor Hiram W. Johnson for vice president in the campaign of 1912. Roosevelt bested his former close Republican colleague, incumbent president Taft, in the popular vote, and by a margin of 88 to 8 in the electoral vote, but the split in the Republican vote resulted in a victory for the Democratic candidate, New Jersey governor Woodrow Wilson. Progressive candidates for state and local offices did poorly, and the party disappeared in 1916 when Roosevelt returned to the Republican Party. Two other presidential candidates—U.S. senator Robert La Follette of Wisconsin and former vice president Henry Wallace—briefly resurrected their own versions of the Progressive Party, and the party officially disbanded after the 1952 presidential election.

Who were the **Dixiecrats**?

The Dixiecrats were a small group of southern Democrats in the election of 1948 who opposed President Harry S. Truman's civil rights program and revolted against the civil rights plank adopted at the Democratic National Convention. A group of states' rights leaders met in Birmingham, Alabama, and nominated South Carolina governor Strom Thurmond for president, hoping to force the election into the House of Representatives by preventing either Truman or his Republican opponent, New York governor Thomas E. Dewey, from obtaining a majority of the electoral votes. However, their plan failed with Truman's election. Thurmond garnered 39 electoral votes and 1.1 million popular votes. Many Dixiecrats switched their allegiance to the Republican Party or remained a Democratic voting bloc that supported conservative policies.

What are the **two dominant political parties** in the United States today?

In the United States today, two parties dominate the political landscape: the Democrats and the Republicans. "In America the same political labels—Democratic and Republican—cover virtually all public officeholders, and therefore most voters are everywhere mobilized in the name of these two parties," notes political scientist Nelson W. Polsby in *New Federalist Papers: Essays in Defense of the Constitution* (1997). The Democratic Party tends to draw its base of support from the poor and lower-middle-class, ethnic and religious minorities, women, and union members. Generally, their platform deals with such issues as support for government programs; support for the public sector; and support for affirmative action, reproductive rights, gay rights, and gun control. Conversely, the Republican Party tends to draw its support from the upper-middle-class and elite, business owners, and Protestant Anglo-Saxon men. The party tends to support a strong private sector, business and military interests, gun rights, and tax cuts. As a rule, Republicans are hesitant to embrace rights-based policies like affirmative action, and have a history of opposing welfare and government-based programs.

How does the **Democratic Party today differ from its original incarnation**?

From 1828, when Andrew Jackson was elected president, to 1860, when James Buchanan exited the White House, the Democratic Party was the dominant force in national politics. From these early roots, the party opposed national banks, supported states' rights and slavery, and favored farms and rural independence. In 1860, the issue of slavery split the Democrats, and although they enjoyed some successes at the national level, the party didn't fully regain its strength until the election of Franklin D. Roosevelt in 1932. Beginning in the late 1800s with Grover Cleveland, the party became more urban and socially progressive, and began to take on a strong Progressive stance with presidents Woodrow Wilson (served 1913–1921), Franklin D. Roosevelt (served 1933–1945), and Harry S. Truman (served 1945–1953). For nearly four decades after 1932, the Democratic Party remained America's majority party, controlling both Congress and the White House, while consistently aligning itself with the rights and interests of immigrants, blue-collar workers, women, seniors, and minorities. By the 1960s, the Democrats supported extensive government involvement in social issues like education and urban renewal. By the 1980s, the Democrats had broadened their base among women and African Americans, and in the 1990s and 2000s have sought to further strengthen this base of support, as well as widen it to include Hispanics. The party has grown more liberal over the years, supporting issues such as stronger environmental protection laws, affirmative action, gay rights, gun control, increased Medicare funding, reproductive rights, and workers' rights.

How does the **Republican Party today differ from its original incarnation**?

When the Republican Party formed in 1854, it opposed the extension of slavery in the free territories. By the election of 1860, Republican platforms appealed to commercial interests, with Republicans favoring homesteading, internal improvements, the building of a transcontinental railroad, protective tariffs, and the containment of slavery. The Republican Party became more business-oriented and socially conservative beginning in 1880s, a trend that has continued to this day. Platform planks during the late nineteenth century stressed the protection of U.S. businesses through tariffs, a strong currency, low taxes, and increased international trade.

Presidents during most of the late nineteenth century and the early part of the twentieth century were Republicans. While the Democrats and Franklin D. Roosevelt tended to dominate American politics in the 1930s and 1940s, for twenty-eight of the forty years from 1952 through 1992 the White House was in Republican hands. With the election of Richard Nixon in 1968, Republicans introduced their platform of "New Federalism," which advocated a reduction of federal power and a return of that power to the states. The party took another distinctive turn in 1980 with the election of Ronald Reagan, as conservative Christians, Southern whites, affluent ethnic suburbanites (often called "Reagan Democrats"), and young conservatives formed a "New Right" that supported Reagan and his platform of strict laws against crime, drugs, and pornography; opposition to abortion; tax cuts; and increase in defense spending. Generally, the party supports business interests, a large defense budget, faith-based initiatives, the privatization of Social Security, and abortion restrictions. Beginning in the 1980s, the party saw the rise of the Religious Right, who were attracted to the party because of its opposition to abortion and support for school prayer.

Which presidents are known for **switching parties**?

Most presidents remained associated with a certain political party from early in their careers until the ends of their lives, though a few changed their affiliations. Before he was elected to the vice presidency in 1840, John Tyler switched his political allegiance from the Jackson Democrats to the newly formed Whig Party. Once Tyler succeeded to the presidency after President William Henry Harrison died in office, he abandoned many Whig principles, lost the support of his Whig cabinet, and was ejected by the party. In the 1930s and 1940s, Ronald Reagan was a Democrat; however, he gradually adopted a more conservative political ideology and officially changed his political affiliation to Republican in 1962. Reagan served as Republican governor of California from 1967 to 1975 and as the Republican president for two terms, from 1981 to 1989.

Three presidents changed their party affiliation after their presidency: Martin Van Buren, a Democrat, became a candidate for the Free Soil Party; Millard Fillmore, a Whig, became a candidate for the American, or Know-Nothing, Party; and Theodore Roosevelt, a Republican, founded the Progressive, or Bull Moose, Party.

What are some **third parties that are active today**?

Any political party that is not Republican or Democratic, receives a base of support, and plays a role in influencing the outcome of an election is considered a minor party or "third party." There are many third parties in today's political playground, including the American Independent Party, the American Reform Party, the Communist Party USA, the Green Party, the Independence Party, the Libertarian Party, the Natural Law Party, the Peace and Freedom Party, the Reform Party, and the Socialist Party USA. Third parties often voice a protest vote against one or both of the major parties, and often enter a political race to deflect votes from one of the major candidates.

Which **third-party presidential bids have been noteworthy** in the post–World War II era?

No third-party candidate has ever come close to winning the presidency, and only eight minor parties have managed to win a single state's electoral votes. However, historians agree that there have been four noteworthy third-party presidential bids since World War II, when third-party or independent candidates have garnered more than 7 percent of the popular vote. In 1948, two independent candidates for president challenged the Republican candidate, Thomas E. Dewey, and the Democratic contender, then-President Harry S. Truman. On the right, Strom Thurmond—then a Democratic governor from South Carolina—ran as the nominee of the Dixiecrats or States' Rights Party, a group of dissident Democrats in favor of racial segregation. On the left, Henry Wallace, a former vice president under Franklin D. Roosevelt, ran as the nominee of the Progressive Party. Thurmond won 22 percent of the vote in the South, the only area of the country in which he campaigned; Wallace garnered slightly more than 2 percent of the vote.

In 1968, George Wallace, the pro-segregation governor of Alabama, ran as the presidential nominee of the American Independent Party. Wallace, who won 13.8 percent of the vote, was thought to have taken votes away from both major-party candidates, Democrat Hubert Humphrey and Republican Richard Nixon. In 1980, U.S. representative John Anderson of Illinois ran as the presidential nominee of the National Unity Movement. It was assumed that Anderson, a moderate, would take votes away from both the Democratic nominee, President Jimmy Carter, and the Republican nominee, Ronald Reagan. In the end, Anderson won 7 percent of the vote, which hardly dampened Reagan's landslide victory. Recent examples of significant third-party candidates include H. Ross Perot, who in 1992 ran as the presidential nominee of United We Stand America, the precursor of the Reform Party. Political commentators argue that Perot's strong garnering of 19 percent of the vote probably hurt the Republican candidate, President George Bush, while helping elect Democratic nominee Bill Clinton. And some could argue that Ralph Nader's presence in the 2000 presidential race—small that it was, with only a little under 3 percent of the popular vote—siphoned key votes from Democratic candidate Al Gore, who despite gaining the majority of popular votes lost the electoral vote to George W. Bush.

Who is **Shirley Chisholm**?

Democrat Shirley Chisholm of New York became the first African American woman elected to the U.S. House of Representative in 1968. In 1972, she ran for president on the Democratic ticket. The 1972 Democratic National Convention marked the first major party convention in which a woman was considered for the presidential nomination. Her campaign brochure utilized her familiar slogan, "Unbossed and Unbought," and emphasized her support of the urban poor. Although she did not win the party nomination, she received 151 of the delegates' votes. As the first African American woman to campaign for the presidency, Chisholm blazed a trail for other candidates like herself who, as she noted in her autobiography *The Good Fight* (1973), "will feel themselves as capable of running for high political office as any wealthy, good-looking white male." Chisholm continued to serve in the House of Representatives until 1982. Since that time, she has remained active in politics, supporting Jesse Jackson's campaigns for presidency and acting as chairperson of the National Political Congress of Black Women.

Who is **John Anderson**?

John B. Anderson, a ten-term Republican representative from Illinois, ran for president as a moderate independent on the National Unity Party ticket in 1980. As a major third-party contender, Anderson appealed to the public's dissatisfaction with the incumbent president, Democrat Jimmy Carter, and Republican challenger Ronald Reagan. In the Republican primaries, Anderson campaigned heavily against Reagan's conservative policies. With a likely Reagan primary victory in sight, Anderson dropped out to start his own independent campaign. In the presidential election, Anderson received six million popular votes and no electoral votes. Besides being a credible third-party candidate

Major Third Parties in Presidential Campaigns

Third party	Year	% Popular vote	Electoral votes	Fate in next election
Anti-Masonic	1832	7.8	7	Endorsed Whig candidate
Free Soil	1848	10.1	0	Received 5 percent of vote; provided base of Republican supporters
Whig-American	1856	21.5	8	Party dissolved
Southern Democrat	1860	18.1	72	Party dissolved
Constitutional Union	1860	12.6	39	Party dissolved
Populist	1892	8.5	22	Endorsed Democratic candidate
Progressive (T. Roosevelt)	1912	27.5	88	Returned to Republican Party
Socalist	1912	6.0	0	Received 3.2% of vote
Progressive (LaFollette)	1924	16.6	13	Returned to Republican Party
States' Rights Democrat	1948	2.4	39	Party dissolved
Progressive (H. Wallace)	1948	2.4	0	Received 1.4 percent of vote
American Independent (G. Wallace)	1968	13.5	46	Received 1.4 percent of vote
John B. Anderson	1980	7.1	0	Did not run in 1984
H. Ross Perot	1992	18.9	0	Formed the Reform Party and ran again in 1996
Reform Party (H. Ross Perot)	1996	8.4	0	Perot engaged in struggle for control of Reform Party

"Third Parties in Presidential Elections," U.S. Department of State. http://usinfo.state.gov/products/pubs/archive/elect00/table.htm (accessed on July 5, 2004).

in the late twentieth century, Anderson was the first third-party candidate to participate in televised presidential debates. Since that time, only one other third-party candidate, H. Ross Perot in 1992, has been included in presidential debates.

Who is **H. Ross Perot**?

Billionaire Texan H. Ross Perot is the founder of the Reform Party, the most successful third party in late-twentieth-century American politics. Perot enjoyed a fair measure of success in the presidential elections of 1992, when he ran for president as a nominee of United We Stand America, and again in 1996 under his newly formed Reform Party. In the 1992 elections, Perot ran against Republican president George Bush and the Democratic contender, Bill Clinton. In that race, Perot garnered 19 percent of the popular vote, the highest percentage of the popular vote as a third-party candidate since former president Theodore Roosevelt won 27 percent in 1912 on his Progressive ticket. Perot won 9 percent of the popular vote in 1996, making him the only third-party presidential candidate in history to receive more than 5 percent of the popular vote in two consecutive elections.

Who is **Ralph Nader**?

An environmental and consumer rights advocate, Ralph Nader ran for the presidency on the Green Party ticket in 1996 and 2000. In the 2000 race, Nader ran under the campaign slogan "Not for Sale," calling for corporate responsibility, campaign finance reform, environmental justice, and universal health care. Nader won less than 3 percent of the popular vote. According to the exit polls conducted by Democratic pollster Stanley Greenberg, 25 percent of Nader's votes came from Republicans, 38 percent from Democrats, and the remainder from people who would not have voted. Nader received criticism from the Democratic Party for garnering votes in Florida that might have gone to Democratic nominee Al Gore, who narrowly lost the state and the overall 2000 election to Republican George W. Bush, following a ruling by the U.S. Supreme Court. In February 2004, Nader announced his decision to run as an independent (not affiliated with any political party) in the 2004 race to "challenge the two-party duopoly" that he believes is damaging to American democracy. Because of his Independent status, Nader had to undergo the time-consuming and expensive process of getting ballot access in all fifty states.

CAMPAIGNS AND NOMINATIONS

How are **political parties and political campaigns related**?

While political parties perform a variety of functions, they are mainly involved in nominating candidates for office and organizing their elections. Their major responsibilities include recruiting candidates for local, state, and national office; nominating candidates through caucuses, conventions, and the primary election; "getting out the vote" for their candidates and providing voters with information about candidates and their parties; and facilitating mass electoral choice—that is, helping voters recognize their options and encouraging electoral competition. In addition, they influence the institutions of national government and the policy-making process. For example, Congress is organized around the two-party system, and the Speaker of the House position is a party office. Parties determine the makeup of congressional committees, including those who chair the committees, whose positions are no longer based solely on seniority.

What is a **primary**?

A primary is a state-run election for the purpose of nominating party candidates to run in the general election. Presidential primaries perform this function indirectly, because voters elect delegates to a national convention rather than directly seeking presidential candidates. Most states restrict voting in a primary to party members; such states are called closed primary states. Open primary states allow the voter to choose either party's ballot in the voting booth on primary day, and none of the open primary states require voter registration by party. Today, more than three-fourths of the states use presidential primaries; in the 2000 presidential election, approximately 84 percent of the Democratic delegates and 89 percent of the Republican delegates were chosen in the primaries.

When was the **primary introduced**?

The primary was introduced in 1904, when Florida became the first state to adopt the primary as a way of choosing delegates to nominating conventions. By 1912, fifteen states provided some type of primary election, and that year was also the first in which a candidate sought to use primaries as a way to obtain the presidential nomination (former president Theodore Roosevelt challenged incumbent William Howard Taft; Roosevelt won nine primaries to Taft's one, but lost the nomination). By 1916, twenty state Democratic and Republican parties selected their delegates in primaries. The introduction of the primary is significant to election history because it expanded democratization of the nominating process by enabling party members to choose delegates. However, in its infancy stage, the primary failed to attract many voters, and some states even abandoned it. It didn't fully recapture the electorate's attention until 1969, when the Democratic National Committee formed the McGovern-Fraser Commission to reform and revive the delegate selection process.

What are **caucuses and state conventions**?

A caucus is a meeting of party members or leaders to select nominees for public office and to conduct other party business. In the presidential nominating process, it is often used in combination with a state convention to elect delegates to the national nominating convention. Approximately twelve states use a caucus or convention system (or both) for choosing delegates, and each state's parties and legislature regulate the methods used. The caucus or convention is the oldest method of choosing delegates, and it differs from the primary system because its focus is on party organization.

Why are the **Iowa caucus** and the **New Hampshire primary** important?

Since the last few decades of the twentieth century, two states—Iowa and New Hampshire—have risen to the forefront of the presidential primary season. Because of custom and party rule, these two states hold the nation's first caucus and primary, respectively, of the campaign season. The voting in Iowa and New Hampshire has become critical to presidential candidates because candidates who do well in these states garner early media attention and are instantly dubbed their parties' front-runners. Although victories in these states often set the tone for the presidential race, success isn't automatic, as evidenced by two late-twentieth-century examples: In 1980, George Bush beat Ronald Reagan in the Republican Iowa caucuses, but Reagan won the party's nomination for president; in 1996, journalist Patrick Buchanan won the New Hampshire primary in a victory over former U.S. senator Bob Dole of Kansas, but Dole received the Republican nomination. In an effort to gain more control over the nomination process, a number of states have moved their primaries ahead on the campaign calendar.

What is **Super Tuesday**?

"Super Tuesday" is the term used to describe a Tuesday in early March of a presidential year when the most states simultaneously hold their primary elections, and the single day when the largest number of nominating delegates can be won. This day is key for presidential candidates, who must do well if they hope to secure their party's nomination. The phrase "Super Tuesday" was first used during the slate of primary elections that took place in Alabama, Georgia, Kentucky, Texas, Florida, Tennessee, Oklahoma, Louisiana, and Mississippi on March 8, 1988. Since then, the particular states holding primaries on Super Tuesday has varied from year to year. The 2004 "Super Tuesday" was held on March 2, during which California, Connecticut, Georgia, Maryland, Massachusetts, New York, Ohio, Rhode Island, and Vermont held Democratic primaries, while a caucus was conducted in Minnesota.

What happens at the **national party convention**?

The delegates elected in primaries, caucuses, or state conventions meet at their national party convention in the summer before the November election to choose the party's presidential and vice presidential candidates, ratify the party platform, elect officers, and adopt rules. Up until the mid-twentieth century, delegates arrived at national nominating conventions with differing levels of commitments to presidential candidates, and thus the convention was an event of excitement and fervor. However, today the nominee is usually known well in advance of the convention, based on the accumulation of a majority of delegate votes. As a result, the convention characteristically serves to ratify a choice already arrived at by party primaries, caucuses, and state conventions. Sometimes the nominee reveals his choice for running mate during the convention. In almost every national convention since 1956, one candidate has gone to each party's convention with a clear, strong lead in delegate totals.

When did **national party conventions** arise?

The election of 1824 brought an end to the congressional caucus as a nominating device, after which state legislative caucuses, conventions, and other methods were used to nominate presidential candidates. However, 1831 marked the first year that the national convention was used: The Anti-Masonic Party met in Baltimore in September of that year to choose William Wirt as its presidential candidate; in 1832, both the Democrats and National Republicans followed suit. Because the national convention was made up of delegates chosen by party holders, activists, and office-holders in each state, it was a natural extension on the national level of the way party conventions worked at the state level.

What is the concept of **political bosses and smoked-filled rooms**?

In their early incarnation, national conventions were often unruly, strongly contested meetings, and often many ballots and extensive political maneuvering were required before a presidential candidate could be nominated. A political party's nominee for president was often selected by influential party members and leaders (called "party bosses") at the party's national convention, after a lot of negotiation in "smoked-filled rooms"—where the air was filled with intrigue, not to mention cigar and cigarette smoke. The term came into use at the 1920 Republican National Convention in Chicago, when Republicans met to select a front-runner for the presidential nomination. After the first day of balloting, the convention adjourned without a nominee from among the eleven candidates, forcing party leaders and U.S. senators to meet in a smoke-filled room at the Fairbanks Hotel to choose a candidate. The result was U.S. senator Warren G. Harding of Ohio, a candidate acceptable to both the conservative and progressive wings of the party. Realizing that this was not a democratic method of choosing a major-party presidential candidate, the Democratic and Republican parties began opening up the process to voters through the primary and caucus system.

What is a **"dark horse" candidate**?

The early convention atmosphere and a fear of deadlock among the most popular candidates (based on the Democratic Party rule that a presidential candidate needed to win two-thirds of the convention delegates to capture his party's nomination), led to the occasional selection of a "dark horse" candidate. The term is used to describe a minor candidate or party figure who was not originally considered but who steps in as a compromise choice. A dark horse, in betting parlance, is not among the betting favorites. The first dark horse candidate to win nomination was Tennessee politician James K. Polk, who emerged from the Democratic Convention of 1844 and went on to win the presidency. The opposition Whig Party had used the slogan, "Who is James K. Polk?"

Other dark horse candidates in history include New Hampshire politician Franklin Pierce, New York politician Horatio Seymour, Ohio governor Rutherford B. Hayes, U.S. representative James A. Garfield of Ohio, U.S. senator Warren G. Harding of Ohio, and former U.S. representative John W. Davis of West Virginia. Of these, Pierce, Hayes, Garfield, and Harding were elected president.

What are some **notable early presidential conventions**?

Several early conventions are known for their "deadlock" stances, where delegates' were unable to reach a consensus on candidate choice or platform issues. These include the 1844 Democratic Convention, which resulted in the selection of "dark horse" candidate James K. Polk, who was chosen on the ninth ballot; the 1852 Democratic Convention, which chose Franklin Pierce after 48 ballots; the 1860 Democratic Convention, which selected U.S. senator Stephen Douglas of Illinois only after 59 ballots and two conventions; the 1880 Republican Convention, where delegates rallied together on behalf of James A. Garfield on the 36th ballot; and the Democratic Convention of 1924, where Democrats cast 103 ballots before nominating John W. Davis. Since World War II, only one presidential nominating convention, the Democratic National Convention of 1952, went beyond a first ballot.

During at least two conventions, heated factional debates were the order of the day. At the 1860 Democratic National Convention in Charlston, South Carolina, the Democrats were sharply divided over the issue of slavery. When the delegates adopted Stephen Douglas's plank to support nonintervention in the territories, fifty Southern Democrats walked out of the convention, protesting because their plank calling for the passage of a more radical federal slave code was dismissed. Because a 1832 convention rule required a two-thirds vote for a nomination, the convention was dismissed. Reconvening in Baltimore, Maryland, several weeks later, 110 Southern delegates stormed out of the convention and nominated their own candidate, Vice President John Breckinridge. Though Douglas won the nomination, he lost the election to Republican Abraham Lincoln. In 1912, Theodore Roosevelt challenged the renomination of his one-time protégé, William Howard Taft. After a bitter debate over the seating of contested delegates, Roosevelt's supporters withdrew and formed the Progressive Party.

What was so special about the **convention of 1896**?

On July 9, 1896, William Jennings Bryan delivered his famous "Cross of Gold" speech at the Democratic National Convention in Chicago, causing delegates to rush the stage and give him a standing ovation that lasted for more than one hour. The issue being discussed on the convention floor was whether to endorse the free coinage of silver money, a measure popular among the debt-ridden farmers of the day. In his speech, Bryan criticized the gold standard and advocated inflating the currency through the free coinage of silver, delivering one of history's most oft-quoted lines, "You shall not press down upon the brow of labor this crown of thorns, you shall not crucify mankind upon a cross of gold." Although Bryan was a little-known former congressman from Nebraska before he gave the speech, he succeeded in winning the presidential nomination that year. Bryan was nominated by the Democratic Party again in 1900 and 1908, but never was elected to the White House.

Which **twentieth-century conventions are notable**?

Although presidential conventions have come a long way since the days of haggling over nominees in smoked-filled rooms, there are several twentieth-century conventions that enjoyed their fair share of controversy and notoriety. Chief among these is the 1932 Democratic Convention, during which Franklin D. Roosevelt's supporters worked with convention organizers to rearrange the seating so that delegates who opposed Roosevelt were engulfed by a sea of supporters. Convention-floor microphones were strategically positioned so that the roar of the crowd always favored Roosevelt. At this convention, Roosevelt became the first presidential candidate to give an acceptance speech during the convention. Before this time, candidates accepted their nominations in a ceremony weeks later. Other talked-about conventions include the 1968 Democratic National Convention in Chicago, during which ten thousand anti-Vietnam war protestors clashed with local police and the National Guard, draining attention from the main Democratic contenders, U.S. senator Eugene McCarthy of Minnesota and Vice President Hubert Humphrey; the 1972 Democratic National Convention, which saw its nominee, U.S. senator George McGovern of South Dakota, give his acceptance speech in the early-morning hours rather than at the regularly scheduled prime-time appointment, causing most of the news media to doze off; and the 1992 Republican National Convention, during which Patrick Buchanan and other speakers alienated many mainstream viewers because of their extreme right-wing discussions of religious and cultural issues.

What role does **convention location** play, if any?

Chicago holds the record as the city to host the most presidential nominating conventions, with twenty-five major-party conventions to its credit. A convention provides the perfect opportunity for a city to profile itself and its history to tourists but, more importantly, the location of a convention has political connotations. Swing states (which could either vote Democrat or Republican in an election) are often the site of conventions: swing-state Pennsylvania hosted the 2000 Republican National Convention, and electoral vote–rich California hosted the 2000 Democratic National Convention. Similarly, pro-labor city Detroit was the site of the 1980 Republican convention, as Republicans courted the labor vote in Michigan that year. However, there is no tried-and-true formula for picking up electoral votes in states that host party conventions: Democrat Al Gore won Pennsylvania in 2000, home of the Republican convention that year, and in 1996 Democratic Bill Clinton won California, where Bob Dole accepted the Republican Party nomination earlier that year. In 2004, the Republicans held their convention in New York City, the site of the September 11 terrorist attacks just three years prior, providing incumbent president George W. Bush with a strong patriotic backdrop for his campaign; and the Democrats chose Boston, marking the

47

first time a major political party has held its convention in that city. Other cities that have hosted conventions since 1960 include San Francisco, Miami Beach, Kansas City, Dallas, New Orleans, Houston, San Diego, Atlanta, and Atlantic City.

What are some **convention firsts**?

At the Democratic Convention of 1920, Laura Clay became the first woman to receive votes for either president or vice president when she received one vote for the presidential nomination. At the Democratic Convention of 1936, the two-thirds rule, in which a candidate must receive two-thirds of the convention vote to gain a nomination for the presidency, was abolished. At the 1968 Democratic National Convention in Chicago, Rev. Channing Phillips became the first African American nominated for the presidency at a major party's convention. And several years go down in history as media firsts: 1924 was the first year of radio coverage of the conventions, 1948 saw the first live television broadcast of the entire convention, and 1996 marked the first year during which the public could view the conventions live on the Internet.

How are **running mates chosen**?

According to current practice followed by both parties, the presidential candidate chooses his vice presidential running mate. Elements involved in nominations include political ideology (a conservative presidential nominee will often choose a more liberal running mate, and vice versa), political history (particularly Senate and House voting record if the candidate is a congressperson or previous member of Congress), geography, and age. Franklin D. Roosevelt (particularly in 1940 and 1944) is cited as the first president to impose his vice presidential choice upon delegates. In 1948, the Republican nominee, New York governor Thomas Dewey, followed in Roosevelt's footsteps when he chose California governor Earl Warren as his running mate. Before these precedents were set, party leaders usually selected the vice presidential nominee, who was either an unsuccessful presidential candidate with wide support, or one who was perceived as adding geographical balance to the ticket.

What are some **notable selections of running mates**?

In 1956, Democratic nominee Adlai Stevenson broke selection tradition when he encouraged open nominations for vice president from the convention floor. Although U.S. senator Estes Kefauver of Tennessee won the nomination on the third ballot after a spirited debate, other names that were considered included U.S. senator Albert Gore Sr. of Tennessee, U.S. senator Hubert Humphrey of Minnesota, U.S. senator John F. Kennedy of Massachusetts, and New York mayor Robert Wagner. And while incumbent presidents generally select their current vice presidents as running mates, in 1956 some Republican leaders unsuccessfully tried to persuade President Dwight D. Eisenhower to replace Vice President Richard Nixon. In 1976, then–Vice President Nelson Rockefeller announced he would not seek the nomination, presumably to open the slot to a more conservative candidate and to increase President Gerald Ford's chances at reelection. Ford picked conservative U.S. senator Robert Dole of Kansas but the pair lost the election to former Georgia governor Jimmy Carter and U.S. senator Walter Mondale of Minnesota. The most recent example of a president who broke selection tradition can be found with Bill Clinton, an Arkansas governor who chose a running mate (U.S. senator Albert Gore Jr. of Tennessee) who was also from the same geographical location (the South), was roughly the same age, and shared many of the same policy views.

What different **campaign styles** have made history?

Throughout the nineteenth and early twentieth centuries, presidential campaigns were conducted at the grassroots level, often by party leaders and officeholders, but seldom by the candidate himself. One notable exception is William Jennings Bryan's 1896 tour of the country by rail in order to deliver his Democratic message to the American people. Other nominees held "front porch" campaigns, during which candidates didn't leave the privacy of their own homes. Introduced by Benjamin Harrison, the front-porch campaign became notable in 1896 when 750,000 voters flocked to William McKinley's Canton, Ohio, home to hear the candidate speak. A modern example of the front-porch campaign is the "Rose Garden" campaign, whereby sitting presidents seeking reelection minimize their travel schedule and instead deliver announcements from the White House, in an effort to simultaneously campaign and maintain their demanding executive agenda. The term "front-porch" campaign has come to denote any campaign conducted close to home without extensive travel or one-on-one interaction with the populace.

Active campaigning became more prominent with Franklin D. Roosevelt, who in 1932 conducted the first modern "whistle stop" campaign, traveling thirteen thousand miles by train and visiting thirty-six states in an effort to reach voters. The "whistle stop" campaign—during which candidates toured the country by train and delivered speeches from the rear platform—became a tried and true campaigning method. Historians generally cite Harry S. Truman as the candidate who holds the record for the most stops, covering thirty-two thousand miles and delivering an average of ten speeches per day in his successful 1948 election campaign. Roosevelt is also known for another groundbreaking act—in 1932, he flew from New York to Chicago to accept the Democratic nomination—ushering in an era of campaign travel by air. A thoroughly modern campaigning device, air travel allows candidates to touch base in media markets across the country and gain media exposure. According to media reports, George W. Bush paid about $3 million to charter his own private plane during his twenty-month bid for the presidency in 2000.

Do modern candidates go back to **campaign methods of previous eras**?

Interestingly so, yes. Although air travel is by far the most expedient way of reaching the voting populace, several recent candidates tried a more grassroots approach. In both 1992 and 1996, for example, Democrat Bill Clinton and his running mate, Al Gore Jr., launched their campaign with an extensive bus tour across several states. The public seemed refreshed by this method of campaigning, as supporters cheered them on at bus stops and along the highways. In 1992, Republican nominee George Bush reenacted the "whistle stop" campaign era, as he traveled by train to several cities, delivering his message from the rear platform of the train.

How have **candidates used the media to their advantage** during the campaigning process?

Today, the media covers early campaign strategy, presidential primaries, party conventions, presidential debates, and dozens of other campaign happenings up until the November election. Presidential candidates use the media to showcase their platform issues and personalities, playing to a host of radio, television, and Internet opportunities. In the early days of campaigning, this precedent was set by Theodore Roosevelt, who encouraged media coverage of his family, and greatly expanded upon by Warren G. Harding and his wife, Florence, during his 1920 campaign. In the 1930s and 1940s, radio and then film emerged as a major campaign communications tool, and candidates took advantage of radio and newsreels in an effort to reach a mass audience at unprecedented levels. Notwithstanding the large circulation rates of the daily newspapers, from 1920 to 1950, radio continued to be the major political information source for most Americans. Television surpassed radio's dominance during the presidential election of 1952, when an estimated 53 percent of the population watched television programs on the Dwight Eisenhower–Adlai Stevenson race.

Since 1952, when full-scale television coverage of the national conventions began, the media took on a new dimension for the presidential candidate. That year Dwight D. Eisenhower spent almost $2 million on television advertising. Since that time, television has been used to project the candidate's image and stance on various issues. Paid advertising, news coverage, and presidential debates have thrived on television. In fact, *New York Times* columnist Russell Baker wrote that after the high-profile 1960 televised debates between Richard Nixon and John F. Kennedy, "television replaced newspapers as the most important communications medium in American politics." In 1992, television reached new heights in the campaigning process, as billionaire H. Ross Perot bought air time to produce infomercials and made the rounds on the morning and late-night talk-show circuits. The 1990s also saw the dramatic rise of the candidates' use of e-mail, fax, direct-mail videos, and other alternate media formats. Blogs, website forums for communication among supporters of a candidate, became popular in the 2004 presidential campaign. Pioneered by Democratic dark horse candidate Howard Dean, blogs were quickly created for nominees George W. Bush and John Kerry.

What were some of the **first historically notable debates**?

Historians cite the 1858 Illinois senatorial debate between Republican Abraham Lincoln and incumbent Democratic senator Stephen Douglas as the most significant early debate. Douglas agreed to the joint appearances only after Lincoln followed him around the state and questioned him from the audience. Finally, seven separate debates were held, one in each of the state's congressional districts. Without the aid of a moderator or a press panel, Lincoln and Douglas debated the hot issue of the day, slavery. Then relatively unknown, Lincoln received nationwide attention for his now-famous "House Divided" speech, during which he maintained that the "government cannot endure, permanently half slave and half free." The Lincoln-Douglas debates were controversial because they occurred in front of the voting public, even though state legislatures elected U.S. senators at that time in history. The debates were followed by newspaper and telegraph synopses, but did not ignite a trend in candidate debates. Lincoln lost the Senate race, but beat Douglas in the 1860 race for the U.S. presidency, during which there were no debates.

Before 1960, neither political candidates nor the voting public had a deep interest in public presidential debates. There were no general election debates during this time, only primary debates that occurred in the years 1948, 1952, and 1956. In 1948, Republicans Harold Stassen and Thomas Dewey held a radio debate several days before the Oregon primary. In May 1952, the first nationally televised debate took place between Republican and Democratic contenders and their representatives as they answered just a few questions at the annual convention of the League of Women Voters. In May 1956, Democrats Estes Kefauver and Adlai Stevenson exchanged words in the first nationally televised intraparty primary debate, just days before the Florida primary.

The 1960 presidential debate was the first general election debate held in U.S. history, and it ushered in a new era of debating in the twentieth century. As part of a larger movement to reform presidential campaigns, Congress suspended the equal time provision of the Communications Act of 1934 to permit a two-man televised debate. Before an audience of seventy million, in four debates over the course of September and October, the Republican contender, Vice President Richard Nixon, and the Democratic hopeful, U.S. senator John F. Kennedy of Massachusetts, debated both domestic issues—including health care, education, and taxes—and foreign affairs. Television provided the first real opportunity for millions of voters to see their candidates in competition, and political commentators often cite Kennedy's good looks and honed oratory skills as key to his winning favor with the voting public.

What are some **notable debates of the late twentieth century**?

For a variety of reasons, including candidates' reluctance and the equal-time provision of the Communications Act, no presidential debates took place between 1960 and 1976. By 1976, both the law and candidates' attitudes had changed, and the 1976 debates between incumbent Gerald Ford and challenger Jimmy Carter were significant: it was the first time a sitting president participated in televised presidential debates, and the first time that vice presidents were included in debates.

After the high-profile 1960 televised debates between Richard Nixon and John F. Kennedy, television became the most important mode of communication in American politics. *AP/Wide World Photos.*

The 1980s and 1990s marked an era where presidential debates became the most talked-about aspect of a candidate's campaign. The September 1980 Ronald Reagan–John Anderson debate marked the first time only one major party candidate (Reagan) participated in a general election debate (Democrat Jimmy Carter did not want to debate independent Anderson and refused to participate). In 1992, presidential debates were at an unprecedented high; ninety-seven million viewers tuned in for the presidential debate between incumbent president George Bush, Democratic contender Bill Clinton, and independent H. Ross Perot. This debate marked the first time a third-party candidate participated in general-election debates with both major-party candidates. Later in 1992, in Richmond, Virginia, the three candidates debated the issues in front of some two hundred average Americans who questioned them for approximately ninety minutes. The debate's "town meeting" format garnered unprecedented attention because it featured the candidates meeting face-to-face with the populace.

How are **town hall debates** significant to a presidential campaign?

In 1860, Abraham Lincoln conducted his entire election campaign from his "front porch"—without ever leaving his hometown of Springfield, Illinois, and without delivering one single speech. Today, candidates visit all fifty states, deliver hundreds of speeches, and travel thousands of miles in an effort to reach voters. Some presidential candidates have used this person-to-person forum, known as the town meeting, more effectively than others, and recently it has been the format of several debates. Of the

In 1992, ninety-seven million viewers tuned in for the presidential debate between President George Bush (left), independent H. Ross Perot, and Democratic contender Bill Clinton. This debate marked the first time a third-party candidate participated in general-election debates with both major-party candidates. *AP/Wide World Photos.*

four debates held in 1992, the Richmond, Virginia, town hall debate was the most heavily viewed. During that debate, moderator Carole Simpson of ABC News took unscripted questions from an audience of voters. Commenting on the success of the debate, Simpson observed that voters are eager to see other voters talking with the candidates and asking them "real" questions. "They want that connectedness," she confirmed.

Is it true that the **League of Women Voters** is involved in the presidential debates?

Yes. Few people realize the League of Women Voters (LWV), a nonpartisan political organization, is a primary source of information during the debates. The organization's involvement in the debating process dates to 1952, when a joint televised appearance before the LWV national convention—the precursor to the modern televised debate—included several presidential candidates or their representatives discussing the issues. In 1976, the League of Women Voters sponsored four Democratic primary debates that were nationally broadcast. They also sponsored three ninety-minute presidential debates between nominees Jimmy Carter and Gerald Ford and one vice presidential debate. Their 1976 format included follow-up questions, rebuttals, and closing statements in front of a live audience. Because candidate debates are a key component of a political campaign, the LWV often sponsors or cosponsors presidential debates, as it did in 1976 and in 1992, with cosponsor CNN.

53

How was **image** used in some of the **early presidential campaigns**?

One of the earliest campaigns to make use of image occurred in 1828 between incumbent John Quincy Adams and Democratic contender Andrew Jackson. It was the first campaign to extensively use election paraphernalia such as campaign buttons, slogans, posters, tokens, flasks, match boxes, and mugs. To publicize Jackson's image, his supporters capitalized on his nickname, "Old Hickory," by distributing hickory sticks, hickory toothpicks and canes, and firing up hickory chip barbeques.

Another notable example of early image-making in politics was the "Log Cabin and Hard Cider" campaign of 1840. Although Whig nominee William Henry Harrison came from an aristocratic Virginia family, the Whigs focused on his long life on the frontier and depicted him as a simple man of the people. When a Democratic newspaper editor suggested sarcastically that Harrison would be satisfied to retire to a log cabin with a barrel of hard cider, the Whigs introduced log cabins and cider barrels as their party symbols. Harrison's opponent, incumbent president Martin Van Buren, was depicted as a wine-drinking urban sophisticate. In fact, that year the Whigs didn't even construct a party platform and avoided all discussion of political issues during their campaign. Instead, their campaign featured political songs, rallies, carnivals, and the now-famous slogan, "Tippecanoe and Tyler Too." With a definite goal to "keep [William] Harrison vague and [John] Tyler quiet" the Whigs were successful in securing the presidency in 1840.

How did **twentieth-century campaigns** capitalize on a candidate's **image**?

The growth of radio, television, and the Internet, coupled with the late-twentieth-century predominance of political consultants and image-makers, has transformed the modern political campaign into one based on candidate image. A key turning point in the importance of a candidate's image took place during the 1960 presidential debates. Many listening to the debates on radio declared Richard Nixon the winner, while those watching the debates on television were certain that John F. Kennedy would claim the presidency. Kennedy, a tanned, good-looking and well-rested orator, appeared relaxed and assured, and stood in stark contrast to an ill, gaunt, and sweating Nixon. More than thirty years later, Democrat Bill Clinton pioneered the "talk-show campaign" when he appeared in 1992 on the late-night *Arsenio Hall Show* playing his saxophone. As the "candidate for a new generation," Clinton aimed to reach a younger audience and perpetuate his image of a maverick who could change a stale Republican government. In 2000, both candidates Al Gore and George W. Bush were interviewed on the *Oprah Winfrey Show* in an effort to attract women voters. Most recently, image played a role in 2004's Democratic presidential candidate, John Kerry, who announced his candidacy in front of an aircraft carrier to underscore his military credentials as a decorated Vietnam veteran.

What were some **historic issues** during the **campaigns**?

Political commentators have often said that current events define the issues of a campaign. Indeed, slavery, war, foreign relations, the American economy, and the candidate's character and lifestyle have all been backdrops for key elections. When Abraham Lincoln ran for the presidency in 1860, slavery divided the nation. Prohibition was a dominant issue in the presidential campaign of 1928, which juxtaposed "wet" New York governor Alfred E. Smith against "dry" Herbert Hoover. The Great Depression drove the campaign of 1932, and Franklin D. Roosevelt's vision of "Three R's—relief, recovery and reform" won him the presidency. Presidential contenders Theodore Roosevelt, Franklin D. Roosevelt (in 1944), Dwight D. Eisenhower (in 1952), and Richard Nixon (in 1968) framed their successful campaigns around discussions of war.

Later elections have clearly pitted foreign relations against domestic matters. Jimmy Carter was plagued with the Iranian hostage crisis during his campaign for reelection in 1980; Republican challenger Ronald Reagan took advantage of this issue, as well as economic hardships at home, to ask Americans, "Are you better off than you were four years ago?" In 1992, Democratic contender Bill Clinton emphasized the state of the economy throughout his entire campaign, discussing at length the failures of the George Bush administration in handling America's stagnant economy. In 1996, amidst economic security and an optimistic populace, the issue at stake was not the economy, but rather Bill Clinton's character. And in the 2004 presidential campaign, the perceived failure of the Bush administration to adequately combat the war on terrorism gave Democratic contender John Kerry an opportunity to emphasize returning America's energies to domestic issues such as the economy, job renewal, and health care.

What is considered the **dirtiest presidential campaign** on record?

In his book *Presidential Campaigns,* author Paul F. Boller Jr. noted, "Presidential campaigns are a lot nicer today than they used to be. What respectable person today would think of calling one of the candidates for the highest office in the land a carbuncled-faced old drunkard? Or a howling atheist? Or a pickpocket, thief, traitor, lecher, syphilitic, gorilla, crook, anarchist, murderer? Yet such charges were regular features of American presidential contests in the nineteenth century." Although many early campaigns contained their share of derogatory remarks, historians agree that the 1828 presidential campaign between Andrew Jackson and incumbent president John Quincy Adams was probably history's dirtiest. Having its roots in the controversial 1824 election between the same two candidates, in which Jackson had won the popular vote but neither candidate won the necessary number of electoral votes, mudslinging ranged from accusations of adultery against Andrew and Rachel Jackson to suggestions that President Adams had spent thousands of federal dollars to stock the White House with gambling equipment. Attacks against Jackson included criticism of his leadership abilities, name-calling involving his mother and wife, and allegations that he was involved in dueling and brawling. Words used to describe him included "slave trader," "gambler," and "promoter of cock fights and horse races." Despite this unprecedented attack on the candidates' personalities, the campaign resulted in Jackson's landslide victory, the revival of a two-party system, and the creation of a new national party, the Democratic Party of the United States.

What other presidential campaigns had their fair share of **mudslinging**?

The period between the election of Andrew Jackson in 1828 and the election of Abraham Lincoln in 1860 has many examples of mudslingling, lies, name-calling, deceit, and trickery. In the election of 1840, sitting president Martin Van Buren was ridiculed for the lavishness of the White House and the money he spent on furnishings and dinners. In the election of 1844, Democrats who supported James K. Polk insisted that opponent Henry Clay had broken every one of the Ten Commandments, stating that the "history of Mr. Clay's debaucheries ... is too shocking, too disgusting to appear in public print." During the campaign of 1848, General Zachary Taylor called the attacks that were made on his military record and character "the vilest sladers of the most unprincipled demagogues this or any other nation was ever cursed with." Franklin Pierce was called the "Fainting General" in 1852, after he collapsed in battle during the Mexican War. And as Abraham Lincoln hit the campaign trail in 1860, Lincoln's physical appearance was called into question, being described as a "horrid looking wretch ... of the umcomeliest visage, and of the dirtiest complexion.

What were some notable **campaign slogans**?

Many memorable presidential campaigns slogans can be found in political history. Slogans often express something of the character or platform of the candidate, or they may just be catchy phrases crafted to attract voters. In 1840, presidential hopeful William Henry Harrison and his running mate John Tyler ran for election under one of the catchiest campaign slogans in history, "Tippecanoe and Tyler Too!" In 1844, James K. Polk ran under the slogan "54°40' or Fight!" The slogan referred to the latitude parallel of 54 degrees, 40 minutes—the area of the Oregon Territory subject to dispute with Great Britain. Those that adopted this slogan stood by Polk's desire to have the United States own this territory, or go to war for it. In 1856, western explorer and national hero John Frémont won the first Republican presidential nomination with the slogan, "Free Soil, Free Men, Frémont," which referred to the antislavery platform of Frémont and the Republicans. Although he did not win the general election, he won eleven states in a three-man contest.

During his reelection campaign of 1864, when the country was divided by war and party, Lincoln encouraged voters, "Don't swap horses in the middle of the stream." In 1869, during the era of Reconstruction, Ulysses S. Grant ran on the slogan "Let Us Have Peace." In 1896, "Patriotism, Protection, and Prosperity" were the key words for William McKinley. In 1924, Calvin Coolidge and his supporters touted "Keep Cool with Coolidge," a slogan that reflected the public's sense of optimism over the economy. In 1928, Herbert Hoover promised "A Chicken in Every Pot, and a Car in Every Garage." Harry S. Truman ran under the slogan "Give 'em Hell, Harry!" for his 1948 campaign, with which he was forever associated. In 1952, voters liked the catchy "I Like Ike" slogan that Dwight D. Eisenhower adopted.

Late-twentieth-century slogans have tended to discuss the concept of a new America. In 1980, Ronald Reagan invited voters, "Let's Make America Great Again." In 1988, George Bush promised "A Kinder, Gentler Nation." In 1996, Bill Clinton promised he was, "Building a Bridge to the 21st Century." George W. Bush's campaign slogan of "Compassionate Conservatism" also became a catchphrase for his first administration.

Dwight Eisenhower's catchy "I Like Ike" slogan showed up on campaign posters and buttons all over the country in the months leading up to the 1952 presidential election. *Getty Images.*

What **nicknames** have been used to describe candidates during their campaigns?

As candidates rise in popularity or come under intense ridicule, they often acquire nicknames. Other times, they are an invention of the candidates themselves (Bill Clinton called himself "The Comeback Kid" in 1992 after first dipping, then rising, in the polls.) Nicknames can be a reflection of administration policies or actions (such as the "New Dealer" for Franklin D. Roosevelt or "Tricky Dick" for Richard Nixon), or attached to a president after the fact, as perspective is given to the president's legacy (perhaps the best-known example of this is George Washington, who is called "Father of His Country").

One of the most interesting nickname stories centers on Martin Van Buren, who was dubbed "Old Kinderhook" after his birthplace of Kinderhook, New York. Echoing a popular acronym of the day (O.K. for "Oll Korrect"), O.K. became the battle cry of the Old Kinderhook Club, a political organization supporting Van Buren during the 1840 campaign. The popular and positive nickname didn't benefit Van Buren, who was defeated in his bid for reelection, but the expression "O.K." lives on in American vernacular.

Other nicknames for presidents include: the "Sage of Monticello," for Thomas Jefferson; "Old Hickory" for Andrew Jackson; "Old Tip" and "Tippecanoe" for William Henry Harrison, who earned his nickname as the commanding general of the American forces during the Battle of Tippecanoe in the Ohio River Valley in 1811. Zachary Taylor is called "Old Rough and Ready," a nickname he earned in the Battle of Buena Vista in 1847 during the Mexican War; the never-married James Buchanan is called the "Bachelor"; and historians consistently identify Abraham Lincoln, who is immortalized as the president who freed the slaves, as the "Great Emancipator." Ulysses S. Grant earned the nickname "Unconditional Surrender Grant" in 1862, when he led the Union Army to victory in the Battle of Fort Donelson. Teddy Roosevelt has been called the "Rough Rider"; William Howard Taft, "Big Bill"; Woodrow Wilson, the

Presidential Campaign Slogans

Campaign	Candidate	Slogan
1840	William Henry Harrison	"Tippecanoe and Tyler Too!"
1844	James K. Polk	"54°40' or fight"
1844	Henry Clay	"Who is James K. Polk?"
1856	John C. Frémont	"Free soil, free labor, free speech, free men, and Frémont"
1860	Abraham Lincoln	"Vote yourself a farm"
1864	Abraham Lincoln	"Don't swap horses in the middle of the stream"
1884	Grover Cleveland	"Blaine, Blaine, James G. Blaine, the continental liar from the state of Maine"
1884	James Blaine	"Ma, Ma, where's my Pa, gone to the White House, ha, ha, ha"
1888	Benjamin Harrison	"Rejuvenated republicanism"
1896	William McKinley	"Patriotism, protection, and prosperity"
1900	William McKinley	"A full dinner pail"
1916	Woodrow Wilson	"He kept us out of war"
1920	Warren G. Harding	"Return to normalcy"
1924	Calvin Coolidge	"Keep cool with Coolidge"
1928	Herbert Hoover	"A chicken in every pot and a car in every garage"
1952	Dwight D. Eisenhower	"I like Ike"
1956	Dwight D. Eisenhower	"Peace and prosperity"
1976	Jimmy Carter	"Not just peanuts"
1988	George Bush	"A kinder, gentler nation"
1992	Bill Clinton	"Don't stop thinking about tomorrow"
1992	H. Ross Perot	"Ross for boss"
2000	George W. Bush	"Compassionate conservatism"

"Schoolmaster"; and Calvin Coolidge, "Silent Cal," for his low-key style. Harry S. Truman was called the "Haberdasher" after his previous occupation—he owned a haberdashery shop after serving in World War I. Ronald Reagan acquired the nickname "the Gipper" based on his 1940 film role as George "the Gipper" Gipp in the film *Knute Rockne, All American.*

Which presidents participated in **antiwar activities**?

Before he was president of the United States, Abraham Lincoln protested the Mexican-American War of 1846–1848 because he felt it was an unnecessary and unconstitutional war of conquest, designed to add more slave states to the union. More than one hundred years later, during Bill Clinton's 1992 presidential campaign, American citizens learned that the presidential contender participated in antiwar activities and sidestepped the draft while a student at Oxford University in England. Grover Cleveland avoided the Civil War draft by taking advantage of a section of the Enrollment Act of 1863, which allowed draftees to pay $300 to a substitute to serve for them. Cleveland paid a thirty-two-year-old Polish immigrant to serve in his place as a private in the Seventy-sixth New York Infantry.

In whose campaigns was **religion** was an issue?

In early political campaigns, no issue was beyond scrutiny, including a candidate's religion. In 1856, the American Party expressed its hostility to the Irish Catholics that were immigrating to the United States. In that year's presidential election, the American Party charged that Republican candidate John C. Frémont was a Catholic, a claim that Frémont refused to publicly deny because he maintained it was not a legitimate issue. In 1928, the Democratic candidate for president, New York governor Alfred E. Smith, was criticized for being a Catholic. Also a proponent of the repeal of Prohibition, Smith was the butt of slurs and jokes by opponents of a Catholic voice in American politics. The periodical *Fellowship Forum* stated, "The real issue in this campaign is Protestant Americanism versus rum and Romanism." Smith lost the election by a wide margin to his Protestant opponent, Republican Herbert Hoover.

In 1960, Democratic candidate John F. Kennedy encountered anti-Catholic bias emanating from a suspicion that a Catholic president would submit his presidential decision-making authority to the pope in Rome. Kennedy responded with a televised speech, in which he refuted claims that Catholicism was incompatible with the secular office of president and proclaimed his allegiance to the separation of church and state. The speech was edited into a commercial broadcast frequently throughout the campaign, and Kennedy won by a thin margin of the popular and electoral votes.

As a sign of a more religiously tolerant populace, 2000 vice presidential candidate Joseph Lieberman experienced wide support among Democrats of all religions for his candidacy. Political analysts agree that Lieberman's Orthodox Judaism—which holds strictly to traditional Jewish beliefs and practices—only helped the image of presidential running mate Al Gore.

How much **money is spent on presidential campaigns**?

The amount of money spent on presidential campaigns has skyrocketed since the mid-twentieth century. In 1952, presidential candidates spent a combined $16 million on their campaigns. By 1972, this amount rose to $90 million. And in 1996, the amount had totaled $120 million. These figures represent an increase of 750 percent from 1952 to 1996.

What was **campaign financing** like in the early presidential races?

The practice of financing public elections dates back to George Washington, who, while running for a seat in the Virginia House of Burgesses, appealed to voters in his district with rum and hard cider. For the first half century after Washington's inauguration, campaign costs were relatively low. If candidates campaigned at all, they did so via no- or low-cost public meetings and rallies, the distribution of handbills, and newspaper advertisements. Thus, the candidates themselves, or their friends and associates, covered the costs of the campaign, and fundraising was unnecessary. As the population grew, and property and religious stipulations were lifted from voting requirements, this situation began to change.

William McKinley's presidential campaign is touted as the first modern political advertising campaign, featuring the distribution of regular press releases, millions of posters, buttons, and billboards, and 300 million campaign fliers printed in nine different languages. *Library of Congress.*

In 1828, professional campaign managers emerged, as did the practice of buying votes, which further increased the costs of campaigning. By the 1840s and 1850s, a mutual dependence between candidates and financial interests began to arise, as candidates needed more money in order to campaign, and America's businesses leaders increasingly sought favors from the government. In 1864, President Abraham Lincoln called these developments "a crisis approaching."

What was so special about the **election of 1896 and campaign financing**?

The presidential election of 1896 was a landmark event because it set a record for campaign expenditures that was unsurpassed for the next quarter century. According to George Thayer, author of *Who Shakes the Money Tree? American Campaign Practices from 1789 to the Present* (1974), Republican victor William McKinley raised and spent between $6 million and $7 million, while his opponent, William Jennings Bryan, was able to raise and spend only $650,000. In addition, the 1896 election marked the beginnings of systematic fundraising techniques. Marc Hanna, the chairman of the Republican National Committee and the mastermind behind McKinley's campaign, introduced the practice of regularly assessing businesses for campaign contributions to the Republican Party. Besides being heralded for its campaign-finance achievements, McKinley's campaign, which was run by Hanna, is touted as the first modern political advertising campaign, featuring the distribution of regular press releases, millions of posters, buttons, and billboards, and 300 million campaign fliers printed in nine different languages.

What is **campaign financing** like today?

Since 1975, when the post-Watergate campaign reforms went into effect, presidential candidates have relied on a combination of public subsidies and voluntary contributions by individuals, groups, and political parties to fund their campaigns. In the 1980s and 1990s, significant amounts of money given to presidential campaigns came in the form of "soft money"—unlimited financial contributions made by corporations, labor unions, and wealthy individuals. During the 1996 elections, the Democratic and Republican parties raised $172.5 million in soft-money contributions, Philip Morris being the largest single contributor, with donations totaling $1.7 million. In the 2000 primary, private donors provided 74 percent of George W. Bush's funding and 65 percent of Al Gore's. In addition, businesses and labor groups spend large sums on what are termed "independent expenditures," such as media campaigns to endorse or oppose specific candidates, and the political parties themselves can also make campaign expenditures, as long as they are independent of their own candidates. In addition, candidates spend unlimited amounts of their own personal funds on their campaigns. In the 2000 election cycle, the Bush campaign reported more than $191 million raised, including federal funds; and contender Al Gore reported raising just over $133 million.

The Bipartisan Campaign Reform Act, signed into law by President George W. Bush in 2002, prohibits national political parties from raising or spending soft money, and bans states and local parties from spending soft money on federal elections, with the exception of voter registration and turnout efforts.

PUBLIC OPINION POLLS

How is **public-opinion polling** linked to presidential campaigns?

Campaign strategists poll voters and monitor polls conducted by news organizations to know what voters are thinking, to gauge how their campaigns are faring, and to adjust their campaign strategy. John F. Kennedy's team was the first political campaign organization to use sophisticated polling. Although the value of public-opinion polls drew increasing favor from political analysts in the 1970s and 1980s, the expense of polling reserved the method primarily for national campaigns. In the late 1980s and 1990s, innovations in polling techniques and computer technology made polling less costly, and national and statewide polls are now a staple of every election.

Polls, however, have been criticized because pollsters often know the results of an election well in advance of the actual voting. For example, President Bill Clinton's lead over opponent Bob Dole in 1996 was so large, and his lead in some states was so wide, that political analysts claimed his reelection was assured well before election day. Critics of the polls also claim that polls often deflate voter turnout and have the ability to alter the results of an election.

What are **exit polls**?

Exit polls are a survey of selected voters taken soon after they leave their voting place. Pollsters use this sample information, which is collected from a small percentage of voters, to track and project how all voters or specific segments of the voters sided on a particular campaign race or ballot measure.

What is a **representative sample**?

Assessments of citizen attitudes about political candidates are based on polling a "representative sample," or pool, of the total population. Therefore, if 1,000 persons are polled, and of them 750 select "Candidate A" as their presidential choice, then, according to pollsters, that statistic should linearly scale up to the entire population: If there are 1 million votes to be cast, then 750 x 1000, or 750,000—give or take a 5 percent or less margin of error—should select the same candidate. However, because some segments of the voting population are not included in the "representative" sample, critics maintain that there is a larger margin of error than pollsters are willing to account for.

How is **polling done on election night** to forecast the winner?

As a routine part of election campaigns, polls are used to forecast the results of a particular race. On election night, communications companies conduct "exit polls," which, unlike electoral surveys, are not concerned with the intended vote, but are based on the answers given by voters selected at random after they have voted. These are not results that have already been counted and verified after the closing of the polls, but rather what the person says he or she has voted, therefore they are relatively reliable.

What caused the **2000 election night forecast on all the major network outlets to be so in error**?

On election night, the networks largely base their projections on exit polling data supplied to them by the Voter News Service (VNS), a consortium funded by the networks and the Associated Press, which had produced figures predicted Al Gore defeating George W. Bush in Florida. Although VNS supplies the raw polling data, it is the networks' on-staff political experts who make the networks' final calls. Around 8:00 P.M. Eastern Standard Time, the major networks—including ABC, CBS, NBC, CNN and

Election Night Embarrassment

"We don't just have egg on our face. We have omelet all over our suits." So said NBC anchorman Tom Brokaw about news agencies that began projecting Al Gore as the likely winner of the 2000 election shortly after 8:00 P.M. Eastern Standard Time, based on exit polls. Around 10:00 P.M., the agencies retracted their projection and declared the race "too close to call." At 2:15 A.M., news agencies began projecting George W. Bush as the winner.

The candidates did not fare much better. Gore called Bush at 2:30 A.M. to congratulate him and concede the race. After Gore received word of voting irregularities in Florida, he called Bush again at 3:45 A.M. to retract his concession. The two had a tense exchange. "As you may have noticed," said Gore, "things have changed." Over a month later, the election results were finalized by a Supreme Court ruling.

Fox—called the state of Florida for Democratic contender Al Gore. The Associated Press and PBS followed suit a bit later. A few hours later, however, the networks began reversing themselves, as the actual counted votes did not match the projections, and the historical night of predicting which candidate would win Florida's twenty-five electoral votes began. According to the networks, the decision to call Florida for Gore was based on two factors: exit polls indicating a narrow Gore lead, and initial returns that may have been incorrectly entered into the networks' databases, causing their computer models to anticipate a larger Gore vote than was ultimately recorded.

Are there **other examples in history where the polls were incorrect**?

Yes. The most notorious failure of polling was the *Literary Digest* survey of 1936 that incorrectly predicted a landslide victory for the Republican Kansas governor Alfred Landon over incumbent Democrat Franklin D. Roosevelt. Although the magazine had correctly predicted the winner of every presidential election since 1916, it incorrectly made its prediction for Landon (who they said would garner 56 percent of the vote to Roosevelt's 44 percent) because their questionnaire of 2.4 million failed to include many working-class and poor Americans, an ignored portion of the population who largely voted for Roosevelt. In fact, Roosevelt ended up sweeping 62 percent of the popular vote, compared to Landon's 38 percent.

What was the **Dewey-Truman miscall** all about?

In 1948, three major polls (including the Gallup Poll) incorrectly predicted that Republican New York governor Thomas Dewey would defeat incumbent Harry S. Truman, largely based on their improper use of quota sampling, which did not accurately reflect the voting population and hence was not totally representative. Although Gallup predicted that Dewey would win 50 percent and Truman 44 percent of the popular vote, the results were almost exactly reversed, with Truman garnering 50 percent of the popular vote, and Dewey 45 percent. From this campaign, most remember the *Chicago Daily Tribune*'s famous headline, "Dewey Defeats Truman." The 2000 presidential election aside, since that time polls have correctly predicted the presidency, with the percentage of error typically less than 4 percent.

PRESIDENTIAL ELECTIONS

Chicago Daily
DEWEY DEFEATS
G.O.P. Sweep Indicated in State;

WHO VOTES?

How has the **body of voters changed** through the years?

Although the electorate today is all-encompassing, that wasn't always the case. Five years after he penned the Declaration of Independence, Thomas Jefferson estimated that more than half of the white men in Virginia who paid taxes and served in the militia were not allowed to vote. From America's founding to the Civil War (1861–1865), the decision of who could vote fell to the individual states. Generally speaking, only property-owning, white males aged twenty-one years or older and some black males in certain nonslave states were eligible to vote. Since this time, through a series of constitutional amendments and legislative enactments, Congress and the states have progressively extended the right to vote to other groups—until it became universal for almost anyone over the age of eighteen.

The Fifteenth Amendment (ratified in 1870) guarantees the right to vote regardless of "race, color, or previous condition of servitude"; the Seventeenth Amendment (1913) provides for direct popular election to the Senate; the Nineteenth Amendment (1920) extended the vote to women; the Twenty-third Amendment (1961) established the right to vote in presidential elections for citizens of the District of Columbia; the Twenty-fourth Amendment (1964) prohibits the payment of any tax as a prerequisite for voting in federal elections; and the Twenty-sixth Amendment (1971) extended the vote to citizens eighteen years or older.

Were any political parties involved in the **early efforts to expand voting rights**?

Yes. Organized political parties were instrumental in expanding the right to vote, as politicians made an increased effort to appeal to masses of voters. Specifically, the Democratic Party, led by the followers of Andrew Jackson, mobilized urban voters, and

The Constitutional Amendments on the Right to Vote

"The right of citizens of the United States to vote shall not be denied or abridged by the United States or by any state on account of race, color, or previous condition of servitude." —Fifteenth Amendment to the U.S. Constitution (1870)

"The right of citizens of the United States to vote shall not be denied or abridged by the United States or by any state on account of sex." —Nineteenth Amendment (1920)

"The right of citizens of the United States to vote in any primary or other election ... shall not be denied or abridged ... by reason of failure to pay any poll tax or other tax." —Twenty-fourth Amendment (1964)

"The right of citizens of the United States, who are eighteen years of age or older, to vote, shall not be denied or abridged by the United States or by any state on account of age." —Twenty-sixth Amendment (1971)

led the fight to expand the franchise and lift property requirements. In the 1820s, states began to rewrite their constitutions and extend the voting franchise to all free white males. By Jackson's election in 1828, far more people voted than in the four years prior, and the states were beginning to open more convenient polling places and let the people select presidential electors. Although Jackson was a wealthy landowner by the time he assumed the presidency, he had humble origins and was a war hero, and was thus able to draw support from every social class, but especially the "common man" of the Western states and the South. With an increased voter turnout, Jackson defeated incumbent president John Quincy Adams with 56 percent of the popular vote.

When did **African Americans get the right to vote**?

After the Fourteenth Amendment (1868) granted former slaves the rights of citizenship, male African Americans received the right to vote with ratification of the Fifteenth Amendment in 1870. However, states still prevented African Americans from voting through the loophole "grandfather clause," which stated that one could not vote unless his grandfather had voted, an impossibility among most blacks. Although the Supreme Court struck down the grandfather clause in 1915, states used a variety of other methods—namely, the poll tax, literacy tests, fraud, and intimidation—to keep African Americans away from the polls.

What was the **poll tax**?

The poll tax—a capital tax levied equally on every voting adult—was enacted in southern states between 1889 and 1910. The poll tax disenfranchised many Africans Americans and poor whites because payment of the tax was a prerequisite to voting. Of the ten southern states, the five that passed restrictive legislation before 1892 (Arkansas, Florida, Georgia, Mississippi, and South Carolina) all had low voter turnout levels—below 60 percent during the 1890s. The five states that had not initiated poll taxes, literacy tests, and other restrictive legislation experienced a seventy percent voter turnout. By the 1940s, certain states had abolished these taxes, and in 1964 the Twenty-fourth Amendment outlawed their use. By 1966, this prohibition was extended to all elections in the United States by the Supreme Court, which ruled that the tax violated the equal protection clause of the Fourteenth Amendment.

When did **African Americans begin to realize full rights as voters**?

It wasn't until the 1960s—with the passage of the Civil Rights Acts of 1957, 1960, and 1964 and the Voting Rights Act of 1965, which suspended all tests and similar devices that had been used to discriminate against minority groups, particularly blacks—that African Americans began to experience fewer instances of discrimination at the polls and truly gained the opportunity to exercise their voting rights. Recognizing the power behind releasing African Americans into the voting populace, the August 16, 1965, issue of *U.S. News and World Report* headlined "A Million New Negro Voters?" Before 1965, only 23 percent of voting-age blacks were registered to vote; by 1969, 61 percent were registered. In 1975, Congress again extended the Voting Rights Act, enacting a permanent nationwide ban on the use of tests and devices, expanding the act to provide coverage for minority groups not literate in English, and requiring affected states and jurisdictions to offer certain types of bilingual assistance to voters. Although voter rights for African Americans and other minorities have come a long way, as recently as the 2000 presidential election the National Association for the Advancement of Colored People (NAACP) maintained that voting irregularities plagued African American voters in Florida, charging that voters were unlawfully turned away from polls by sheriff's deputies and improperly stricken from voter rolls.

When did **Native Americans get the right to vote**?

Technically, Native Americans received the right to vote in 1870 when the Fifteenth Amendment was passed, opening voting up to citizens regardless of "race, color, or previous condition of servitude." However, it wasn't until 1924, with the passage of the Indian Citizenship Act—in which Congress granted citizenship to all Native Americans born in the United States—that Native Americans began exercising their right to vote. Even so, Native Americans participated at the polls on a very limited basis, since state law governed suffrage, and many states prohibited them from voting. In 1948, the Arizona Supreme Court struck down a provision of its state constitution that prohibited Indians from voting. Other states followed suit, and in 1962 New Mexico became the last state to fully enfranchise Native Americans. Like African Americans, Native Americans became the brunt of unfair voting mechanisms, such as poll taxes

Property and the Right to Vote

In early America, the best known prerequisite for voting was property owner-ship. Most men in the late eighteenth century believed that voting was a privi-lege to be exercised by those who had enough money or land to be politically responsible. Of the original thirteen states, ten restricted voting to those who owned property, while the remaining three—Georgia, New Hampshire, and Pennsylvania—limited voting to taxpayers. Founding father Benjamin Franklin mocked the property requirements when he said:

> Today a man owns a jackass worth fifty dollars and he is entitled to vote; but before the next election, the jackass dies. The man in the meantime has become more experienced, his knowledge of the prin-ciples of government, and his acquaintance with mankind, are more extensive, and he is therefore better qualified to make a proper selec-tion of rulers—but the jackass is dead and the man cannot vote. Now gentlemen, pray inform me, in whom is the right of suffrage? In the man or the jackass? —From *The Casket, or Flowers of Literature, Wit and Sentiment* (1828)

Property qualifications for voting in either state or national elections did not extend beyond the original thirteen states. When Vermont was admitted into the union as the fourteenth state in 1791, it was the first to separate property owner-ship from the right to vote. In 1792, Kentucky entered the Union with a liberal constitution, and New Hampshire eliminated a taxpaying requirement for the right to vote, indicating that the movement toward universal suffrage extended beyond one localized region. By the late 1820s, most states had dropped the property and taxpaying qualifications for voting in state and national elections. One state—North Carolina—held out until 1859 before abandoning property qualifications.

and literacy tests. With the passage of the Voting Rights Act in 1965, Native American voting rights were strengthened.

When did **women get the right to vote**?

Women received the right to vote with the ratification of the Nineteenth Amendment in 1920. However, it took many years of organized struggle for women to gain the right to vote. The women's rights convention held in Seneca Falls, New York, on July 19 and 20, 1848, was considered a historical step in the long process for gaining women the right to vote, and between that time and the ratification of the Nineteenth Amendment certain states granted women the right to vote. After years of vigorous lobbying by suffragettes such as Elizabeth Cady Stanton, Susan B. Anthony, Lucretia Mott, and Lucy Stone, in 1890 Wyoming became the first state to recognize women's right to vote and provide for it in a state constitution. In 1893, women got the vote in Colorado, followed by Utah (1896), Idaho (1896), Washington (1910), California (1911), Arizona (1912), Kansas (1912), Oregon (1912), Illinois (1913), Nevada (1914), and Montana (1914).

What is the significance of **Seneca Falls**?

"We hold these truths to be self-evident, that all men and women are created equal...." These words, written in 1848 at the first Women's Rights Convention held in Seneca Falls, New York, announced the opening of a new American revolution in which the goal was to overthrow masculine "tyranny" and to establish political, social, and economic equality between the sexes.

A circa 1920s poster urging women to exercise their right to vote. *Getty Images.*

Although the campaign for the vote created the greatest public outcry, it was one facet of the larger struggle of women to enter the professions, to own property, and to enjoy the same legal rights as men. It would be seventy-two years from the Seneca Falls convention before the Nineteenth Amendment to the Constitution universally gave women the right to vote, which they first exercised in the 1920 presidential election.

What events triggered the **lowering of the voting age**?

Until the 1970s, most states defined voting-age "adults" as those over the age of twenty-one. Arguments about the validity of the voting age began to surface as those under twenty-one served in the armed forces in World War II, and people questioned why men old enough to risk their lives for their country were not old enough to vote. Beginning in 1942, Congress entertained a number of amendments to lower the voting age, and slowly states began to lower their voting-age requirements, beginning with Georgia in 1943. In the 1950s and 1960s, Presidents Dwight D. Eisenhower, Lyndon B. Johnson, and Richard Nixon pressured Congress to adopt an amendment that would allow those under the age of twenty-one to vote. Congress finally reacted to Vietnam War protesters—who argued that they didn't have a voice in the election of those who were sending them to fight in Southeast Asia—by passing the Voting Rights Act in 1970. However, the U.S. Supreme Court ruled that the act only applied to federal elections. In order to make the age applicable to state and local elections, the Twenty-sixth Amendment was passed and ratified by the states in June 1971. The amendment was passed in record time, just two months after it was proposed, immediately enfranchising eleven million young people. Despite the larger electorate, voting turnout for the 1972 presidential election was not substantial. According to the U.S. Bureau of the Census, 58 percent of young adults ages eighteen to twenty registered to vote, and 48 percent actually voted.

Who **votes today**?

Statistics reveal that only about half of the U.S. citizens in America vote. In the 1996 presidential elections, voter turnout was 58 percent. Although more than 105 million Americans cast their vote during the 2000 Bush-Gore presidential race, the 2000 elections only represented a 2 percent increase in voters, bringing that year's turnout rate for citizens to 60 percent. Beyond this general statistic, studies on voter demographics reveal the following specifics: Whites are more likely to vote than minorities, although there is not much difference in voter turnout between whites and African Americans; college graduates are much more likely to vote than people with less than eight years of education; senior citizens are much more likely to vote than people in the 18-to-24 age category; and higher income groups are more likely to vote. The U.S. Census Bureau adds the following observation: "The characteristics of people who are most likely to go to the polls are a reflection of both the racial/ethnic composition of the citizen population and the attributes of people with the biggest stakes in society: older individuals, home-owners, married couples, and people with more schooling, higher incomes, and good jobs."

According to the U.S. Census Bureau, in the 2000 presidential election, 57 percent of African American citizens voted; 43 percent of Asian American and Pacific Islander citizens voted; and 45 percent of Hispanic citizens voted. Also, although men historically have voted at higher rates than women, women were more likely than men to vote in the 2000 election, at 61 percent compared to 58 percent.

How many voters are **Democrats** and how many are **Republicans**?

During Franklin D. Roosevelt's administration, 49 percent of voters said they were Democrats. For most of the period between the 1930s and the beginning of the twenty-first century, most Americans were affiliated with the Democratic Party. In Pew Research Center polls conducted during 1997 and 1998, 33 percent of adults said they thought of themselves as Democrats, and 28 percent called themselves Republicans. These general figures persisted through the presidential campaign period of 2000 and the post-election period in 2001. The September 11, 2001, terrorist attacks, and President George W. Bush's response to the attacks, marked a major turning point in party identification in the United States. Republican party identification rose to 30 percent, while the Democrats fell to 31 percent, placing the parties in a more equitable stance.

Will this **change in party identification** affect the 2004 presidential election?

Historically, most voters cast their ballots for the candidates of their party. However, party affiliation is only one factor in voting trends. Ultimately, elections are won and lost because individual voters decide one candidate most closely matches their beliefs. However, political analysts note that because Republicans traditionally turn out to vote in higher numbers than do Democrats, the current division in party affiliation among the public could provide the Republican Party with a slight electoral advantage, all other things being equal. Republicans have made notable gains in a number of key "swing" states—states that could vote either way in a presidential election. Michigan, Minnesota, and Iowa—three Midwestern states Democratic nominee Al Gore won in 2000 by very slight margins—have all experienced shifts in party identification toward the Republicans. And though the Republicans have gained ground in several other swing states, notably Florida, the Democratic Party still has a stronghold on the Northeast.

When was **Election Day** set?

Election Day takes place every two years, in even numbered years, on the first Tuesday after the first Monday in November. The presidential election occurs every four years, in years divisible by four (for example, 2000, 2004, and 2008). In accordance with Congressional legislation passed earlier that year, on November 4, 1845, Americans participated in the first uniform Election Day in history. (Congress chose November because it was the most convenient month for farmers and citizens living in rural areas to get to the polls; since reaching polling places required an overnight horse-and-buggy ride, holding the elections on Tuesday allowed people plenty of time to get there.) The law, which ensured the simultaneous selection of presidential electors in each state, increased the power of political parties and strengthened the democracy of elections. As late as 1816, the citizens of nine states were not able to vote in presidential elections. Instead, previously elected state legislators chose the presidential electors who then determined the outcome of the election.

THE ELECTORAL COLLEGE

Is the presidential candidate who gets the **highest number of popular votes** the winner?

No. The president and vice president of the United States are not elected directly by the popular vote, but rather are elected by electors, individuals who are chosen in the November general election in presidential election years. Known collectively as the electoral college, it is this entity that votes directly for the president and vice president.

What is the **electoral college**?

When Americans vote for a president and vice president, they are actually voting for presidential electors, known collectively as the electoral college. It is these electors, chosen by the people, who elect the chief executive. The Constitution assigns each state a number of electors equal to the combined total of the state's Senate (always two) and House of Representatives delegation (which may change each decade according to the size of each state's population as determined in the U.S. Census); at the time of the 2004 presidential election, the number of electors per state ranged from 3 to 55, for a total of 538.

In each presidential election year, a group (called a ticket or slate) of candidates for elector is nominated by political parties and other groupings in each state, usually at a state party convention, or by the party state committee. In most states, voters cast a single vote for the slate of electors pledged to the party presidential and vice presidential candidates of their choice. The slate winning the most popular votes is elected; this is known as the winner-take-all, or general ticket, system. Maine and Nebraska use the district system, under which two electors are chosen on a statewide, at-large basis, and one is elected in each congressional district. Electors assemble in their respective states on the Monday after the second Wednesday in December. They are pledged and expected, but not required, to vote for the candidates they represent. Separate ballots are cast for president and vice president, after which the electoral college ceases to exist for another four years.

How are the **electoral votes tabulated**?

The electoral vote results are counted and certified by a joint session of Congress, held on January 6 of the year succeeding the election. A majority of electoral votes is required to win. In the 2004 presidential election, this number is 270 of the 538 electors. If no candidate receives a majority, then the president is elected by the House of Representatives, and the vice president is elected by the Senate, a process known as a contingent election.

How are **electors chosen**?

The U.S. Constitution left the method of selecting electors up the states, so methods vary. Generally, the political parties nominate electors at their state party conventions (in thirty-six states) or by a vote of the party's central committee in each state (in ten states). Aside from members of Congress and employees of the federal government, who are prohibited from serving as an elector in order to maintain the balance between the legislative and executive branches of the federal government, anyone may serve as an elector. Since electors are often selected in recognition of their service and dedication to their political party, they are often state-elected officials, party leaders, or persons who have a personal or political affiliation with the presidential candidate. Today, all states choose their electors by direct statewide election, except for Maine and Nebraska.

Were the **electors always chosen by popular election**?

No. While today all presidential electors are chosen by eligible voters, in the early republic more than half the states chose electors in their legislatures, thus eliminating any direct involvement of the voting public in the election. After 1800, this practice changed, as voting rights expanded to include a larger section of the population. By 1836, all the states except South Carolina selected their electors by a statewide popular vote. South Carolina continued to choose its electors through the state legislature until 1868.

What is **electoral reapportionment**?

Each state's electoral votes are equal to the combined numerical total of its House of Representatives delegation (currently ranging from one to fifty-three, depending on population) and Senate membership (two for each state). The number of electoral votes per state, based on the 2000 census, ranges from three to fifty-five. These totals are adjusted following each census, taken every ten years, in a process called reapportionment. This process reallocated the number of members of the House of Representatives to reflect changing rates of population growth or decline among the states. Thus, a state may gain or lose electors following census reapportionment. The 2000 census allocations will be in effect for the presidential elections of 2004 and 2008. The next time electoral votes will be reallocated is following the 2010 census, which will be in effect for the first time for the 2012 presidential election.

Is **Washington, D.C.**, allocated any **electoral votes**?

Yes. The Twenty-third Amendment grants the District of Columbia the number of electors it would be entitled to if it were a state, but not more than that of the least populous state. In 2000, the District of Columbia received three electors. Wyoming, the least populous state, has three electors.

How does the **electoral college relate to the popular vote**?

Civil rights leader Martin Luther King Jr. once said, "The most important step that a person can take is a short walk to the ballot box." Within his or her state, a person's vote is significant. Under the electoral college system, the people do not elect the president and vice president through a direct nationwide vote, but a person's vote helps decide which candidate receives that state's electoral votes. It is possible that an elector could ignore the results of the popular vote, but that occurs very rarely.

The Founding Fathers devised the electoral college system as part of their plan to share power between the states and the national government. Under the federal system adopted in the U.S. Constitution, the nationwide popular vote has no legal significance. As a result, it is possible that the electoral votes awarded on the basis of state elections could produce a different result than the nationwide popular vote. The electoral vote totals determine the winner, not the statistical plurality or majority a candidate may have in the nationwide vote totals. Forty-eight out of the fifty states award electoral votes on a "winner-takes-all" basis (as does the District of Columbia), whereby the candidate who receives the most popular votes in a state wins all that state's electoral votes.

What is a "faithless elector"?

A faithless elector is the term used to describe an elector in the electoral college who does not follow the will expressed by the presidential popular vote. Instead, he or she casts an electoral vote for another candidate. For example, in the presidential election of 1976, Republicans carried the state of Washington; however, one Republican elector from that state refused to vote for Republican presidential nominee Gerald Ford. The most recent example occurred in 1988, when a Democratic elector for West Virginia voted for Lloyd Bentsen for president and Michael Dukakis for vice president—instead of the other way around. However, the vote of a faithless elector has never influenced the results of a presidential election. Although most states legally require electors to vote for the candidates to whom they are pledged, the U.S. Constitution allows electors discretion in the voting process.

Why was the electoral college created?

The Founding Fathers established the electoral college as a compromise between election of the president by Congress and election by popular vote. They were attempting to create a blueprint that would allow for the election of the president without political parties, without national campaigns, and without disturbing the carefully designed balance between the presidency and the Congress, and between the states and the federal government. It sought to meet a number of democratic needs: to provide a degree of popular participation in the election process, give the less populous states some additional leverage in the election process, and generally insulate the election process from political manipulation.

Were other presidential election ideas considered?

Yes. At the Constitutional Convention of 1787, America's Founding Fathers considered several methods of electing the president, including selection by Congress; selection by the states' governors; selection by the state legislatures; selection by a special group of

The Lone Elector

The years that followed the end of the War of 1812 are defined as the Era of Good Feelings, primarily because the American people were politically united and a strong spirit of nationalism dominated the country. Incumbent president James Monroe, who was elected in 1816, faced no opposition in his bid for reelection in 1820.

With only his name on the ballot, Monroe would be expected to garner a unanimous win in the electoral college. He would have, except that a strong-willed elector, William Plumer of New Hampshire, cast his vote for John Quincy Adams, Monroe's secretary of state, rather than for Monroe, to whom he was pledged. The final vote count was 231–1. Plumer's act denied Monroe the possibility of duplicating George Washington's record as the only president to have won every electoral vote in his elections of 1789 and 1792.

Historians have debated Plumer's motivation as a "faithless elector." He reportedly said he felt that only Washington deserved a unanimous election, but historians often contest this claim. They note that Plumer voted for Adams as an act of protest against the Monroe administration, which he viewed as incompetent. While Plumer is noted in the political record as a member of the New Hampshire constitutional convention, a U.S. senator, and a governor of New Hampshire, he will be remembered in history books as the lone elector to cast his vote in opposition to the reelection of James Monroe.

Congressional members; and election by direct, popular vote. Congressional selection was soon rejected because some delegates felt that this method would ultimately be too divisive, giving way to political bargaining and corruption. Similarly, state-legislature selection was denounced out of concern that a president beholden to the state legislatures might allow the states to erode federal authority, thus undermining the concept of federalism, which calls for a separation of state and federal power. Heated debate centered on the concept of the direct, popular vote. While Founding Father James Madison favored popular election of the president, other delegates, such as George Mason of Virginia and Elbridge Gerry of Massachusetts, dreaded "the ignorance of the people." The Framers feared that without sufficient information about candidates from outside their home state, people would naturally vote for their "favorite son" from their own state. Eventually, all ideas gave way to the concept of an electoral college. After widespread approval by the delegates, this plan for electing the president was written into the U.S. Constitution.

What were some **early flaws in the electoral college**?

Though the electoral college system worked in theory, it was flawed in practice. It did not take into account the fact that political parties and their distinct ideologies would enter into politics at the national level. Under the original system, each elector cast two votes for president (for different candidates) and no vote for vice president. The candidate who received the most votes was elected president, provided it was a majority of the number of electors, and the runner-up automatically became vice president. While this early voting method worked for the elections of 1789 and 1792, problems arose with the election of 1800.

What happened in the **election of 1800**?

By 1800, the fledgling Federalist and Democratic-Republican parties had begun to take shape. The Democratic-Republican Party ran incumbent vice president Thomas Jefferson as its presidential candidate and Aaron Burr as its vice presidential candidate. The Federalist Party ran incumbent president John Adams and diplomat Charles C. Pinckney. However, an equal number of electors voted for both Jefferson and Burr (Adams received sixty-five votes and Pinckney got sixty-four votes). While their intention was to elect Jefferson as president and Burr as vice president, the vote showed that both men were tied for the presidency with seventy-three electoral votes each. Burr seized the opportunity to become president, and the Federalist Party seized the opportunity to help defeat Jefferson and claim the presidency. Amid bitter infighting, the election was thus thrown into the House of Representatives—where each of the states then in existence had one vote—to decide the fate of the election. Before Jefferson finally received a majority of the votes, the House voted thirty-six times, casting ballots over a period of six days. In the end, ten states voted for Jefferson and four states voted for Burr. As the runner-up, Burr became vice president.

The election of 1800 exposed the flaws of the early electoral college system and led to the adoption of the Twelfth Amendment, which was ratified by the states in September 1804. According to this amendment, electors cast separate ballots for president and vice president. The amendment also says that if no candidate receives an absolute majority of electoral votes, then the House of Representatives selects the president among the top three contenders—with each state casting only one vote and an absolute majority needed to claim the presidency.

How did the **electors finally choose Jefferson**?

When the election of 1800 was thrown into the House of Representatives, a number of Federalists schemed to elect Aaron Burr as president. In order to do this, they had to defeat Democratic-Republican Thomas Jefferson with a majority of votes. To beat Jefferson, a number of Federalists planned to vote for Burr, even though he was a Democratic-Republican. In the end, one man was responsible for Jefferson's victory: his old political rival, Federalist Alexander Hamilton. Because Hamilton thought that Burr would make a poor ruler and thus could not support his party's choice due to principle, he persuaded enough Federalists to cast their votes for Jefferson. Never one to forgive an offense, in 1804 Vice President Burr shot and killed his rival Hamilton in a duel. Scholars cite the election of 1800 as one of the most colorful in American history—especially given its ultimate conclusion.

What happened in the **1824 election**, and why was it called a **"corrupt bargain"**?

In 1824, four strong contenders vied for the presidency: Andrew Jackson, John Quincy Adams, William Crawford, and Henry Clay. All the candidates were Democratic-Republicans, though each held sectional interests and very different views of the presidency. The electoral vote totals were divided, and no candidate received the necessary majority to become president. Jackson finished with 99 electoral votes, Adams with 84 votes, William Crawford with 41, and Henry Clay with 37.

An 1824 celebration commemorating the ninth anniversary of the Battle of New Orleans included such guests as Andrew Jackson (left) and John Quincy Adams (far right), both of whom vied for the presidency that year. *Getty Images.*

(Vice presidential contender John C. Calhoun received 182 votes, enough to become vice president, so his victory was never in question.) In accordance with the Twelfth Amendment, the election was thrown into the House of Representatives, whose members voted by a narrow margin to select Adams as president—despite the fact that Jackson had obtained the greater number of electoral and popular votes. Given his numbers, Jackson expected to win; however, Clay used his influence as Speaker of the House to persuade the legislative body to vote for Adams, with whom he shared a similar political ideology. After being elected by the House on the first ballot, Adams became the sixth president of the United States. Adams clearly returned the favor, appointing Clay with the well-regarded position of secretary of state—leading Jackson and many of his supporters to call the election a "corrupt bargain."

As for Jackson, he ran for president against incumbent Adams four years later, in 1828, and won in a sweeping victory. Interestingly, Jackson became the first major American politician to call for an elimination of the electoral college.

Why is the **1824 election considered a "first"**?

The 1824 election was the first one in which the candidate who obtained the greatest number of popular votes, Andrew Jackson, failed to be elected president. Because Jackson did not receive a majority of electoral-college votes, the election was thrown to the House of Representatives. When John Quincy Adams was selected as president, Jackson's supporters claimed that the will of the people had been dismissed. However, this claim does not reflect certain voting realities of the time. While technically true, in 1824 the popular vote was not an accurate indicator of the will of the people. Very few states had all four candidates that were running for election on the ballot. And six of the twenty-four states did not have a public vote, but chose their electors in the state legislature. This election is, however, the only one in which a president was elected by the House of Representatives.

Is the election of 1824 the only election where a **candidate won the popular vote, but lost the presidency**?

No. Since electoral vote totals—and not the statistical majority of popular vote totals a candidate receives—determine the winning candidate, it is quite possible that a candidate who collects the most votes on a nationwide basis will not win the electoral vote. Although this is less likely to occur in a two-candidate race, two nineteenth-century elections fit this scenario: the Rutherford B. Hayes and Samuel Tilden election of 1876 and the Benjamin Harrison and Grover Cleveland election of 1888. Though the circumstances of the elections were very different, both popular-vote winners (Tilden and Cleveland, respectively) did not garner the majority of electoral votes necessary to win the election. This scenario was repeated in the 2000 presidential election, during which Vice President Al Gore won the nationwide popular vote but lost the election to Texas governor George W. Bush, who received a majority of electoral votes (271 to Gore's 267).

What happened in the **election of 1876**?

Against a backdrop of the tumultuous era of Reconstruction, a deep economic depression, and scandal surrounding the incumbent administration of Republican Ulysses S. Grant, the Democratic Party nominated popular New York governor and reformer Samuel Tilden and Indiana politician Thomas Hendricks for its presidential ticket in the 1876 election. The Republicans nominated war veteran and three-term Ohio gov-

Controversial Hayes Victory

The controversy over the election of 1876 led Congress to create a special electoral commission. The commission was intended to be politically balanced: it consisted of five senators (three Republicans and two Democrats), five representatives (two Republicans and three Democrats), and five associate justices of the Supreme Court (two Republicans, two Democrats, and one independent). However, the one independent member refused to serve and was replaced by another Republican. The committee's final votes on the winners in the disputed states went strictly along party lines, eight Republicans voted Hayes the winner, and seven Democrats voted Samuel Tilden the winner. By taking the electoral votes of the four remaining states, Hayes was officially declared winner of the 1876 presidential election on March 2, 1877, two days before he was to take the oath of office. Those who believed Tilden had won the election referred to President Hayes as "Old 8 to 7."

ernor Rutherford B. Hayes as their presidential candidate and U.S. representative William Wheeler of New York as Hayes's running mate. When the election was over, Tilden had won the popular vote by a thin margin, and gained 184 undisputed electoral votes (just one vote short of a majority) to Hayes's 166. However, late on election night, electoral-vote ballots totaling 19 electoral votes were contested in three southern states—Louisiana, South Carolina, and Florida—all of which were strongly divided between whites and recently enfranchised blacks. In addition, 1 electoral vote from Oregon was in question. In a true historical anomaly, electors from each of the southern states submitted two sets of electoral ballots: one for Hayes and one for Tilden. Democratic-controlled local administrators had Tilden as the winner, while Republican federal officials in the states had Hayes as the winner.

After extended partisan debate and discussion, during which both parties were accused of using forms of fraud, intimidation, and violence to gain the popular-vote edge, a special fifteen-member congressional electoral commission was set up to determine which set of electoral votes from the contested Southern states would be counted and accepted. The commission decided—by one vote in each case—to honor Hayes's electoral votes from all three states. In addition, the Commission also awarded Hayes the disputed Oregon vote. Hayes claimed the presidency with a total of 185 electoral votes to Tilden's 184, even though Tilden won the popular vote by 3 percent (4.3 million to Hayes's 4 million). Historians generally agree that two of the three disputed states were really won by Tilden, but that the Republican-heavy electoral commission awarded Hayes all the disputed states.

Once president, Hayes pacified the outraged Democrats by ending military occupation in the South and the Reconstruction Era. In addition, he appointed one Southern Democrat to his cabinet. Nevertheless, the election was called "the great fraud of 1876–1877" by the Democratic Party. Others called the electoral commission's vote the Compromise of 1877, believing Hayes's victory came with the provision that he would end federal occupation in the South.

What **legislation resulted from the election of 1876?**

The results of the 1876 election prompted Congress to write a reform law to handle similar disputed presidential elections in the future. In the Electoral Count Act of 1887, Congress gave each state the final authority over the legality of its electoral votes. The legislation also required a concurrent majority of both houses of Congress to reject any electoral vote. The next time the Electoral Count Act's language would be seriously discussed was in the wake of the controversial presidential election of 2000.

Why was the **election of 1888 significant?**

During the election of 1888, Democratic incumbent Grover Cleveland won the popular vote (by 1 percent) but lost in the electoral college by sixty-five votes to Republican Benjamin Harrison, marking the first clear-cut instance that the electoral college vote went contrary to the popular vote. Cleveland won the popular vote because he racked up huge majorities in several of the eighteen states that supported him, especially in the Democrat-heavy South, while Harrison won only by a slim popular-vote majority in some of the larger, electoral-heavy states that supported him (including Cleveland's home state of New York, which carried thirty-four electoral votes). Historians also cite Pennsylvania's electoral votes, which went to Harrison: Republican senator Matthew Quay of Pennsylvania used power and money to buy votes in that state, which may have provided the Harrison victory there. Although the 1888 election made Harrison the winner, he lost to Cleveland in a rematch four years later, making Cleveland the only president to serve non-consecutive terms.

Why was the **2000 election notable?**

The 2000 presidential election is a twenty-first century example of the nationwide popular-vote winner, Democrat Al Gore, losing the election to an opponent who secured the electoral-college majority, Republican George W. Bush. The 2000 election hinged on the key state of Florida, which held 25 electoral votes. Charges of voter irregularities in several Florida counties prompted Gore to call for a recount. Several hundreds of thousands of votes in that state were under scrutiny, as faulty voting equipment, confusing ballots, voter error, and problems at polling places surfaced. Although recounts began in several contested Democratic counties in Florida, in December 2000 the Supreme Court ruled that the recount process could not continue on constitutional grounds because Florida's lack of uniform standards for the recounting process violated the Fourteenth Amendment's equal protection guarantees. Thus, the original, certified popular-vote count in Florida stood, representing a 537-vote-margin win for Bush. Bush's popular-vote victory in that state gained him the necessary electoral votes he needed for presidential victory: 271 to Gore's 266. (For more on the 2000 election, see Presidents and the Judiciary—The Judiciary Influences the Presidency.)

What are the **criticisms of the electoral college**?

Detractors of the electoral college tend to be proponents of the popular vote, and often mention the fact that the electoral college can result in a president being elected, as in the election of 1824, with fewer popular and electoral votes than his opponent. Opponents also point to the risk of faithless electors, although there has never been an instance of a faithless elector changing the outcome of a presidential election. Depressed voter turnout is another result critics cite when mentioning the institution of the electoral college; they maintain, for example, that because each

During the 2000 presidential election, faulty voting equipment, confusing ballots, voter error, and problems at polling places resulted in a manual recount of hundreds of thousands of votes in Florida. *Getty Images.*

state is entitled to the same number of electoral votes regardless of voter turnout, there is no incentive for states to encourage their citizens to go to the polls at election time. Another argument is that the results of the electoral-college election can fail to accurately reflect the national popular will. This can happen because of the "winner-takes-all" system, whereby the presidential candidate with the most popular votes in the states wins all of that state's electoral votes (this is true for forty-eight of the fifty states, as well as for Washington, D.C.). Even if a third-party candidate were to win as many as 25 percent of the voters nationwide, he or she could still not potentially end up with any electoral college votes. According to the National Archives and Records Administration, the American Bar Association has criticized the electoral college, calling it "archaic" and "ambiguous," and its polling showed sixty-nine percent of lawyers favored abolishing it in 1987.

What are the **arguments in favor of the electoral college**?

Mandated by the U.S. Constitution and modified by the Twelfth and Twenty-third Amendments, the "College of Electors," as the Founders called it, has served as the nation's method for selecting its highest official for over 200 years. Besides its durability and longevity as an election method, proponents argue the electoral college contributes to the cohesiveness of the United States because it requires that candidates receive a distribution of popular support in order to be elected president. In the 2000s, no one region of the country contains the absolute majority (270) of electoral votes required to elect a president. Therefore, there is an incentive for presidential candidates to pull together coalitions of states. Proponents also mention that the electoral college contributes to democracy by encouraging a healthy, two-party system. It is extremely difficult for third-party candidates to secure enough popular votes in enough states to win a presidential election. In addition to protecting the executive office from fleeting third parties, the electoral college system forces third-party movements to converge into either the Republican or Democratic Party. The result is two large political parties that tend to fall within the center of public opinion, rather than multiple third parties with divergent fringe views. Surveys of political scientists have supported continuation of the electoral college.

Why does the **United States still have the electoral college**?

Because the electoral college process is part of the original design of the U.S. Constitution, a constitutional amendment would need to be passed in order to change this system. While critics have suggested many different proposals to alter the presidential election process (some seven hundred over the years, according to the National Archives and Records Administration), none has been passed by Congress and sent to the states for ratification. However, the Twelfth Amendment, which deals with the expansion of voting rights and the use of the popular vote in the states as the vehicle for selecting electors, substantially changed the electoral college process and made it more tangible to American voters.

DISPUTES, ANOMALIES, AND CLOSE-CALLS

Which are the **most disputed elections in American history**?

Historians generally rank the elections of 1824, 1876, and 2000 as the most controversial elections in American history. In the 1824 election, Andrew Jackson won the popular vote in a four-way race, but lost the presidency to John Quincy Adams after the election was thrown into the House of Representatives. Jackson supporters maintained there was a "corrupt bargain" between Adams and the fourth-place finisher, Speaker of the House Henry Clay. There were claims that Adams's appointment of Clay to the post of secretary of state—a position then viewed as a stepping-stone to the presidency—was part of a deal struck in return for Clay persuading his House supporters to select Adams over Jackson. The 1876 election, conducted in the tense decade following the Civil War (1861–1865), also failed to determine a winner in the electoral college. Democrat Samuel Tilden won the popular vote but ultimately lost to Republican Rutherford B. Hayes in a vote of a Republican-majority election commission. Like the 2000 election, Florida also played a key role in the election of 1876, as one of the hotly contested states. The election of 2000 between Al Gore and George W. Bush has unquestionably been the most disputed election of modern times—raising issues of balloting problems, including high rates of spoiled, unmarked, or uncounted ballots in Florida and in other states; the vote-counting and certification process; the legal validity of absentee ballots; and the legal parameters of vote counts, an issue that reached the U.S. Supreme Court. In fact, some have drawn parallels to the election of 1876, claiming that Bush "stole" Florida, much like Hayes "stole" the southern states more than 120 years ago.

Which presidents were elected to the office with a **national popular vote of less than 50 percent**?

Fourteen presidential candidates became president with a popular vote of less than 50 percent of the total ballots cast nationwide. They are: John Quincy Adams (32 percent in 1824); Zachary Taylor (47 percent in 1848); James Buchanan (45 percent in 1856); Abraham Lincoln (40 percent in 1860); Rutherford B. Hayes (48 percent in 1876); James A. Garfield (48.3 percent in 1880); Grover Cleveland (49 percent in 1884 and 46 percent in 1892); Benjamin Harrison (48 percent in 1888); Woodrow Wilson (42 percent in 1912 and 49 percent in 1916); Harry S. Truman (49 percent in 1948); John F. Kennedy (49.7 percent in 1960); Richard Nixon (43.4 percent in 1968); Bill Clinton (43 percent in 1992 and 49 percent in 1996), and George W. Bush (48 percent in 2000). In fact, only three successful presidential candidates since 1960—Lyndon B. Johnson in 1964, Richard Nixon in 1972, and Ronald Reagan in 1984—have captured more than 55 percent of the popular vote.

Which are the **closest elections**?

The two closest elections, if measured by popular-vote totals, were in 1796 and 1800. In both cases, John Adams and Thomas Jefferson won the election with a few hundred popular votes. However, at that time in America's history, the electorate was composed solely of property-owning white males. With only one electoral vote separating the two candidates, the election of 1876 was the closest electoral-vote election in all of history. The following election, of 1880, was also close, as Republican James A. Garfield received just ten thousand more popular votes than Democrat Winfield Hancock. The election of 1884 was another close election, as Democrat Grover Cleveland broke his party's almost-thirty-year hiatus when he won the election by twenty-nine thousand popular votes. In 1888, Cleveland won the popular vote by a narrow 1 percent, but his opponent, Benjamin Harrison, picked up more electoral votes and

Cartoon depicting President James A. Garfield riding an eagle over the White House in triumph after becoming the twentieth president of the United States. *Getty Images.*

eventually claimed the election. Cleveland returned victorious in 1892, becoming the only president to win two non-consecutive terms.

Which elections make up the **twentieth century's close-call list**?

In the twentieth century, five elections stand out as true close-calls: 1916, 1948, 1960, 1976, and 2000. In 1916, Democratic incumbent Woodrow Wilson beat his Republican challenger, former governor of New York Charles Evans Hughes, by more than a half a million popular votes. However, Wilson nearly lost the presidency because of the close race in California, where early returns indicated Hughes had won the state. Wilson eventually took California by approximately 3,000 votes—bringing his electoral vote victory to 277 to Hughes's 254.

In 1948, all eyes were focused on Republican Thomas Dewey of New York beating incumbent Democrat Harry S. Truman, whose election was threatened by the insurgent candidacies of Dixiecrat Strom Thurmond of South Carolina and Progressive Henry Wallace of Iowa. After embarking on a thirty-thousand-mile "whistle-stop" campaign—in which he delivered some three hundred speeches to six million voters—Truman defeated Dewey by some two million votes—despite pollsters and newspaper headlines incorrectly calling Dewey the victor on election night.

In the 1960 presidential election, some 119,000 votes ended up separating incumbent Republican vice president Richard Nixon and Democrat John F. Kennedy, making it one of the closest elections of the twentieth century. When it became clear that

A jubilant Harry S. Truman holding up the front page of the *Chicago Daily Tribune,* which erroneously reported that Thomas Dewey had won the 1948 election. *Getty Images.*

Kennedy, a U.S. senator from Massachusetts, had won the state of Illinois by approximately 8,000 popular votes, thus picking up that state's electoral votes, Nixon conceded the election. The 1976 election between sitting Republican president Gerald Ford and Democratic challenger Jimmy Carter was close in the electoral college, but Carter won by almost 2 million votes in the national popular-vote totals. Despite these close races, no election in history has come down to such a margin as the 537-popular-vote difference in Florida that ultimately decided the 2000 presidential contest between Democrat Al Gore and Republican George W. Bush.

What were the circumstances surrounding the **closeness of the 1960 election**?

After a campaign in which the major issues of the national economy and the communist challenge were batted back and forth, in October 1960 pollster George Gallup predicted a close race, which he refused to forecast in exact numbers. In fact, Democrat John F. Kennedy ended up winning the presidency by a plurality of 119,450 votes—the closest popular-vote contest since the Harrison-Cleveland race of 1888. Although Republican Richard Nixon won more individual states than Kennedy, Kennedy eventually prevailed by winning key states with many electoral votes, such as Illinois, New York, Pennsylvania, and Texas—despite former president Dwight D. Eisenhower's lobbying on Nixon's behalf in those closely contested states. The key state was Illinois, worth 27 electoral votes, which Kennedy won amidst serious allegations of fraud in that state and Texas. Although the news media launched a series of investigative arti-

Close Presidential Elections

Year	Presidential candidate (Party)	Popular votes	Electoral votes
1824	John Quincy Adams (Democratic-Republican)	108,740 (29.5%)	84
	Andrew Jackson (Democratic-Republican)	153,544 (41.6%)	99
	William H. Crawford (Democratic-Republican)	47,136 (12.8%)	41
	Henry Clay (Democratic-Republican)	46,618 (12.6%)	37
1844	James K. Polk (Democratic)	1,337,243 (49.5%)	170
	Henry Clay (Whig)	1,299,062 (48.1%)	105
1848	Zachary Taylor (Whig)	1,360,099 (47.3%)	163
	Lewis Cass (Democratic)	1,220,544 (42.5%)	127
	Martin Van Buren (Free Soil)	291,263 (10.1%)	0
1876	Rutherford B. Hayes (Republican)	4,036,298 (47.8%)	185
	Samuel J. Tilden (Democratic)	4,300,590 (51.0%)	184
1880	James A. Garfield (Republican)	4,454,416 (48.3%)	214
	Winfield Scott Hancock (Democratic)	4,444,952 (48.2%)	155
1888	Benjamin Harrison (Republican)	5,444,337 (47.8%)	233
	Grover Cleveland (Democratic)	5,540,309 (48.6%)	168
1892	Grover Cleveland (Democratic)	5,556,918 (46.0%)	277
	Benjamin Harrison (Republican)	5,176,108 (42.9%)	145
	James B. Weaver (Populist)	1,041,028 (8.7%)	22
1896	William McKinley (Republican)	7,104,779 (51.3%)	271
	William Jennings Bryan (Democratic)	6,509,052 (47.0%)	176
1916	Woodrow Wilson (Democratic)	9,129,606 (49.3%)	277
	Charles Evans Hughes (Republican)	8,538,221 (46.1%)	254
1948	Harry S. Truman (Democratic)	24,105,695 (49.5%)	303
	Thomas E. Dewey (Republican)	21,969,170 (45.1%)	189
	J. Strom Thurmond (States' Rights Democratic)	1,169,021 (2.4%)	39
	Henry Wallace (Progressive)	1,156,103 (2.4%)	0
1960	John F. Kennedy (Democratic)	34,227,096 (49.7%)	303
	Richard M. Nixon (Republican)	34,107,647 (49.5%)	219
1968	Richard M. Nixon (Republican)	31,710,470 (43.4%)	301
	Hubert H. Humphrey (Democratic)	31,209,677 (42.7%)	191
	George C. Wallace (American Independent)	9,893,952 (13.5%)	46
1976	Jimmy Carter (Democratic)	40,977,147 (50.0%)	297
	Gerald R. Ford (Republican)	39,422,671 (48.1%)	240
2000	George W. Bush (Republican)	50,456,167 (47.88%)	271
	Al Gore (Democratic)	50,996,064 (48.39%)	266

James T. Havel. *U.S. Presidential Candidates and the Elections.* New York: Macmillan Library Reference USA, 1996; "Report: Gore Won Popular Vote by 539,897." *Washington Post* (December 21, 2000).

cles on voting fraud at the hands of the Democrats, Nixon did not pursue a vote recount and quietly conceded the election. Like other notable losers of presidential elections before him, Nixon ran again. In 1968, he defeated Democratic contender Hubert Humphrey by a clear majority of electoral votes.

Given the closeness of the 2000 race, what did **political analysts say about the 2004 race**?

Many political commentators noted that incumbent president George W. Bush and his Democratic contender, U.S. senator John Kerry of Massachusetts, had diverging views on the economy, taxes, national security, and abortion rights. Most analysts, however, focused instead on the contentiousness of the two candidates, noting that in recent history the close presidential races have tended to pit a moderate Democrat against a moderate Republican, such as in the close presidential races of 1960 (Kennedy/Nixon), 1968 (Humphrey/Nixon), 1976 (Carter/Ford), and 2000 (Gore/Bush). During the spring of 2004, the presidential contenders endured large swings in various polls. Americans tend to give sitting presidents a second term, so history would tend to favor Bush in this regard. However, that was not the case with his father twelve years earlier.

Which **eighteenth- and nineteenth-century elections were landslides**?

America's very first election, in 1789, was America's first landslide election, where all 69 electors of the electoral college voted unanimously for George Washington. In 1792, Washington again won the vote of every elector, making him the only president in history to be elected unanimously. During 1820's "Era of Good Feelings," incumbent president James Monroe stood unopposed for reelection. His victory was *near*-unanimous: one of the 231 electors voted instead for Secretary of State John Quincy Adams, a noncandidate—supposedly to preserve Washington's record as the only unanimously elected president in history. Andrew Jackson's 1828 victory was another landslide election; "Old Hickory" claimed the electoral vote victory by 178 to incumbent president John Quincy Adams's 83 votes. In addition, a greatly expanded electorate gave Jackson some 648,000 votes to Adams's 507,000. Further, most historians rank the election of Abraham Lincoln to a second term in 1864 as one of the nineteenth-century's most interesting landslide elections.

Was the **election of 1864 considered a landslide**?

Historians mention the election of 1864 as unparalleled in American history. It was a landslide victory for sitting president Abraham Lincoln, who remained in office while America was in the midst of its only civil war. Lincoln won the election, despite criticisms over his handling of the war and the odds of history against him: no president had won a second term since Andrew Jackson more than thirty years prior. While

87

some people voted to replace Lincoln, the Union Army successes (including General William Sherman's capture of Atlanta), Lincoln's release of Union soldiers to go home on furlough (and vote), and Lincoln's campaign slogan, "Don't swap horses in the middle of the stream" won out over Democratic challenger George B. McClellan. Lincoln received 212 electoral votes to McClellan's 21. Lincoln's most vocal critics were in Southern states that seceded from the Union.

Which twentieth-century elections were landslides?

The 1920 presidential election was the first landslide victory in the twentieth century. The Republican contender, U.S. senator Warren Harding of Ohio, beat his Democratic opponent, Ohio governor James Cox, by a whopping 26 percent of the popular vote. Also notable is the election of 1924, during which Republican incumbent Calvin Coolidge beat Democratic opponent John W. Davis of West Virginia. Coolidge campaigned little because of his teenage son's sudden death during the summer, but the country was prosperous, the nation was at peace, and his catchy Republican campaign slogan, "Keep Cool with Coolidge," attracted voters. Franklin D. Roosevelt was one of America's most popular presidents, and is often cited in historian polls as the best of the twentieth-century presidents. Roosevelt won his second-term election in 1936, garnering 61 percent of the popular vote to the 37 percent received by his Republican contender, Kansas governor Alf M. Landon. In the election of 1948, when most of the nation had prophesied a Harry S. Truman defeat, the incumbent Democrat beat his Republican contender, New York governor Thomas E. Dewey, in a landslide election. Truman won more than 24 million popular votes, 49 percent of the national total, to Dewey's 22 million, and won 303 electoral votes.

The only late-twentieth-century president to win with a landslide was Republican Ronald Reagan, who beat incumbent Democratic president Jimmy Carter in 1980. The former California governor's platform of steep tax cuts, a balanced budget, decontrol of oil and gas prices, and a greater reliance on nuclear power resonated with a nation riddled with rising unemployment, runaway inflation, a severe gasoline shortage, and the lingering American hostage crisis in Iran. Amidst America's growing discontent with Carter, Reagan's sense of humor and personal appeal scored high with the one hundred million viewers who watched the presidential debates and—despite periodic language slip-ups throughout his campaign—Reagan conveyed confidence and strength. He won the presidency with forty-three million votes to Carter's thirty-five million. Reagan also gained the electoral votes of forty-four states—making Carter's defeat the most significant of any sitting president since Herbert Hoover's loss to Franklin D. Roosevelt in 1932.

What were some notable election oddities?

Two early elections claim the title of odd elections, but historians sometimes discuss them as controversial elections, too. The election of 1836 is the only election in which a

Like Father, Like Son?

Americans tend to give sitting presidents a second term, so history would tend to favor George W. Bush over John Kerry in 2004. But that's not always the case. The presidential father-and-son tandem of John Adams and John Quincy Adams each lost as incumbents, and the elder George Bush lost as an incumbent.

vice presidential candidate did not receive a majority of electoral votes, but is mainly remembered for the Whig Party's strategy of running multiple candidates in an effort to throw the election into the House of Representatives. The election of 1872 involved the first time a candidate died (Democrat Horace Greeley) after the general election, but before the electoral college met to cast their votes, forcing electors to split their votes among other, minor candidates. These elections present oddities more than perhaps any others in the nineteenth century. And one little-known fact is hidden in between these elections: the election of 1852 has its own military-history oddity (see below).

What happened during the **election of 1836**?

In the 1836 presidential election, Martin Van Buren was enthusiastically received as the man of choice for the Democratic Party that he helped found. Van Buren was the hand-picked successor of popular president Andrew Jackson. The Whig Party attempted to derail Van Buren's campaign by running several different regional candidates, including future president William Henry Harrison, with the hopes of denying Van Buren a majority and throwing the election to the House of Representatives. Ultimately, the Whigs were unsuccessful: Van Buren won the election with nearly 60 percent of the electoral votes and 51 percent of the popular vote.

However, Van Buren's vice presidential running mate, U.S. representative Richard M. Johnson of Kentucky, fell under a storm of controversy. Upon hearing that Johnson had children with an African American woman, the twenty-three Democratic electors of Virginia refused to give him their votes. Without these twenty-three votes, Johnson did not receive the majority he needed within the electoral college to claim the vice presidency. Under the terms of the Twelfth Amendment, the decision was deferred to the Senate—a historical first (and last)—where Johnson was finally elected by a majority vote. The Democratic Party declined to nominate Johnson in 1840.

What was **unusual about the election of 1852**?

In the election of 1852, Whig candidate and military war hero Winfield Scott ran against Democratic nominee Franklin Pierce. Although Scott's military record brought him a healthy popular vote total of almost 1.4 million, the results in the electoral college were a landslide for Pierce, who won the presidency with 254 electoral votes to Scott's 42. Several prominent men had served under Scott, who was appointed general in chief of the U.S. Army in 1841. He commanded the U.S. forces during the Mexican War of 1846–1848, where Brigadier General Franklin Pierce served under him. Although Pierce was injured when he fell from his horse on the front lines in the Battle of Churubusco in August 1847, he stayed with his troops until they captured Mexico City. Another man of note who served under Scott in 1847 was Ulysses S. Grant, an inspirational leader who would become commander of the Union armies during the Civil War and president of the United States in 1868.

Why is the **election of 1872 unusual**?

During the 1872 presidential election, when his administration was riddled with corruption, sitting Republican president Ulysses S. Grant faced opposition from Horace Greeley of New York, a liberal Republican who was also endorsed by the Democrats. Though few at first took seriously Greeley's campaign, which called for a "more honest government" and the end of radical Reconstruction policies, the prominent journalist and founder of the *New York Tribune* quickly gained support. Though he lost to Grant, Greeley claimed 44 percent of the popular vote—or 2.8 million votes—on Election Day. Greeley would have received 66 electoral votes had he not died on November 29, after the general election but before the electoral college met to cast their votes. With no precedent to guide them, Greeley's electors split his 66 votes among four minor candidates: Thomas A. Hendricks of Indiana (42); Benjamin Gratz Brown of Missouri (18); Charles J. Jenkins of Georgia (2); and David Davis of Illinois (1). Three votes were not counted. Grant had already won an absolute majority of the electoral votes so the results of the election were not affected by the vote-splitting. Grant is credited with the sweeping victory of 286 electoral votes to Greeley's 0. Greeley, remembered for having popularized the phrase "Go west, young man," had a rough 1872: he was smeared and ridiculed in the presidential campaign, endured the death of his wife, lost the presidential election, and lost control of his newspaper, the *New York Tribune*. Greeley died a broken man within a month after the 1872 election.

What **election oddities** surfaced in the **twentieth century**?

In the election of 1912, Democrat Woodrow Wilson defeated *two* presidents in one election: incumbent Republican president William Howard Taft, and former Republican president Theodore Roosevelt, who ran on the Progressive Party ticket. In one of the more colorful anecdotes of twentieth-century elections, Eugene Debs, the Socialist candidate of the 1920 presidential election, spent his entire campaign in the Atlanta penitentiary on charges that he violated the Espionage Act during World War I. Nevertheless, he received 915,000 popular votes. Another oddity of the 1920 election is that three of the presidential candidates were active journalists: the winner, U.S. senator Warren Harding of Ohio, was editor and publisher of the *Marion Star*. Another, Socialist candidate, Norman Thomas, ran six times for the presidency—in 1928, 1932, 1936, 1940, 1944, and 1948—and lost all six elections. In 1932, New Deal promises won Franklin D. Roosevelt almost 23 million popular votes to incumbent president Herbert Hoover's 16 million, the first of four election wins for Roosevelt, the only American president to ever hold office for more than two terms. Two twentieth-century presidents, Hoover and Dwight D. Eisenhower, never ran for public office prior to their presidential nominations. They join three presidents before them, Zachary Taylor and Ulysses S. Grant, who also never held public office prior to the presidency.

What was the influence of **multiple candidates in notable nineteenth-century elections**?

The presidential election of 1836 saw the Whigs rally behind not one, but four, candidates in an effort to rob Democrat Martin Van Buren of a majority of electoral votes. The leading Whig vote-getter,

Political poster advocating the candidacy of Horace Greeley and Benjamin Gratz Brown. Though few at first took seriously Greeley's campaign, which called for a "more honest government," Greeley quickly gained support. *Getty Images.*

William Henry Harrison, still came in a distant second (with 73 electoral votes) to Van Buren (with 170 electoral votes). The presidential election of 1844 featured James K. Polk, the first "dark horse" compromise candidate for a major political party (the Democrats). Polk won the election against Whig opponent Henry Clay of Kentucky thanks to abolitionist James G. Birney of Michigan, whom the Liberty Party nominated for the presidency. Although Birney could not even muster up enough votes to carry one state, he cost Clay enough northern Whig votes to tip the election to Polk. If Clay had won the electoral vote–rich state of New York, where Birney did well, he would have won the presidency. However, Polk picked up the state of New York, ringing in a total of 170 electoral votes to Clay's 105. Four years later, in the election of 1848, the Whigs were successful in claiming the presidency with Zachary Taylor.

In the election of 1860, the Republicans rallied around candidate Abraham Lincoln, providing a united front against slavery. But the Democrats were regionally divided, with northern Democrats favoring popular sovereignty and Democratic nominee Stephen Douglas of Illinois, and pro-slavery Southern Democrats (who called themselves National Democrats) favoring nominee John Breckinridge of Kentucky. Though Douglas won 1.3 million popular votes, he only picked up the electoral votes of one state (Missouri), while Lincoln won the majority in 18 states, clinching his presidency.

What **influence did multiple candidates have in the election of 1912**?

One of the most notable third-party candidates to make a strong showing was Theodore Roosevelt in the presidential election of 1912. Running on the Progressive, or Bull Moose, ticket, Roosevelt called for the New Nationalism of an interventionist government and comprehensive social welfare legislation. He stood in contrast to Democrat Woodrow Wilson, who campaigned on a New Freedom platform that stood for antimonopoly policies and a return to small businesses. After the campaign was interrupted by an assassination attempt on Roosevelt, the former president finished second to Wilson in electoral votes (taking 88 of the 266 electoral votes needed to win). Because the Republicans were divided between incumbent president William Howard Taft and Roosevelt from the start of the campaign, Wilson was almost assured of a victory, which he claimed with a total of 435 electoral votes. In fact, historians note that Wilson owed his presidential victory not so much to popularity (the popular vote was divided among the three primary candidates that year), but rather to division within the Republican Party: Wilson won the presidency with fewer popular votes than three-time loser William Jennings Bryan in his defeats of 1896, 1900, and 1908.

What **role did third-party candidates play in the elections of 1948 and 1968**?

During President Harry S. Truman's reelection campaign in 1948, the third-party States' Rights Democrats (called Dixiecrats) chose South Carolinian Strom Thurmond as their presidential candidate. Though the pro-segregation Dixiecrats didn't expect Thurmond to win the election (he only carried four southern states), they were hoping to divert enough electoral college votes from the pro–civil rights Truman to throw his contest with Republican Thomas Dewey into the House of Representatives. Once there, the Dixiecrats hoped Truman would need to negotiate his civil rights agenda in order to garner favor from the powerful southern House committee chairman. Although Truman won the presidency with a majority of electoral votes in twenty-eight states, several states were lost to Dewey, including electoral-rich New York and Pennsylvania. Thurmond picked up electoral votes in Alabama, Louisiana, Mississippi, and South Carolina.

Civil rights issues and the Vietnam War contributed to a tumultuous presidential election of 1968. George Wallace of Alabama ran on the American Independent ticket on a pro-segregation platform. Though the party did not expect to win the election, they hoped to divert enough votes from the major-party candidates, Republican Richard Nixon and Democrat Hubert Humphrey, to prevent either major party from winning a preliminary majority in the electoral college. In what was a very close election, Nixon and Humphrey were separated by only 1 percent of the popular vote. Ultimately, Nixon won the presidency with 301 electoral votes to Humprhey's 191.

Historians note that candidates with strong regional appeal—such as Thurmond and Wallace—may win blocks of electoral votes in one region, such as the South, and affect the election's outcome somewhat, though never enough to substantially challenge the major-party winner. In 2000, Green Party presidential candidate Ralph Nader challenged that statement. His strong showing of nearly one hundred thousand votes in Florida may have siphoned votes from Democratic contender Al Gore, who lost the popular-vote total in that state, and the election, to George W. Bush.

Why was the **1992 election unique**?

Independent candidate and Texas billionaire H. Ross Perot won 19 percent of the popular vote in the 1992 presidential election, although he received no electoral votes because he was not particularly strong in any one state. Perot received the most popular votes of any third-party candidate since Theodore Roosevelt in 1912. While history has shown that any candidate who wins a majority or plurality of the popular vote stands a good chance of winning in the electoral college, one only has to consider the results of the elections of 1824, 1876, 1888, and 2000 to know there are no guarantees. Sheer tenacity, millions of dollars with which to finance his own campaign, and a unique campaign appeal made Perot successful. In addition, Perot propelled his campaign by debating the two major-party candidates, Republican George Bush and Democrat Bill Clinton, and presented his platform through infomercials, a new form of political media advertising he single-handedly pioneered. Although Perot ran again under his newly formed Reform Party in 1996—even claiming 9 percent of the popular vote—his second campaign was not equal to his first.

Who are some **notable losers** of presidential elections?

"For every winner, there is a loser, and everyone who makes it to the top leaves someone at the bottom," Ernest Fitzgerald said in *How to Be a Successful Failure* (1978). Consider these unfortunate candidates: George Clinton, who ran as a Democratic Republican in 1789, 1792, and 1796, and as an Independent-Republican in 1808; Henry Clay, who ran as a National Republican in 1832, without a party in 1836, and as a Whig in 1844; William Jennings Bryan, who ran as a Democrat in 1896, 1900, and 1908; Eugene Debs, who ran on the Socialist Party ticket five times, in 1900, 1904, 1908, 1912, and 1920; Norman Thomas, who ran on the Socialist Party ticket in every election from 1928 to 1944 (only once, in 1932, did he receive more than 2 percent of the popular vote); and—last but not least—Gus Hall, who ran on the Communist Party ticket in 1972, 1976, 1980, and 1984. However, the candidate who holds the record for the most attempts to become president is Republican Harold Stassen, who sought the executive office nine times between the years 1944 and 1992—and never won his party's nomination.

How many **incumbent presidents were defeated in their bid for another term?**

Ten incumbent presidents were defeated in their bids for reelection: John Adams (1800), John Quincy Adams (1828), Martin Van Buren (1840), Grover Cleveland (1888), Benjamin Harrison (1892), William Howard Taft (1912), Herbert Hoover (1932), Gerald Ford (1976), Jimmy Carter (1980), and George Bush (1992). Five sitting presidents, John Tyler (1844), Millard Fillmore (1852), Franklin Pierce (1856), Andrew Johnson (1868), and Chester Alan Arthur (1884), wanted to run but did not win their party's nomination.

What are some **notable twentieth-century "coattail" elections?**

The "coattail" effect of elections refers to a presidential candidate who carries into office "on his coattails" a substantial number of congressional candidates of the same party. The coattail effect is the result of voters casting their ballots for the president of a particular party and then voting for the remainder of the party's ticket. When President Harry S. Truman won reelection in 1948, for example, the Democrats gained seventy-six House seats and nine Senate seats. Such was also the case for Dwight D. Eisenhower in 1952, when the Republicans gained twenty-four House seats and two Senate seats. However, the late-twentieth century witnessed a decline in the coattail effect as party identification weakened. In each of the presidential elections from 1956 through 1996, "split-ticket" voting was the norm, and at least 23 percent of America's congressional districts voted for a presidential candidate of one party and a House candidate of the other. Except for Ronald Reagan's 1980 presidential victory, when the Republicans gained a substantial thirty-three House and twelve Senate seats, gains have been minimal for the party of the presidential victor. Even in landslide presidential years such as Richard Nixon's victory in 1972 and Ronald Reagan's sweep in 1984, there was not a notable coattail effect. In fact, when George Bush won the presidency in 1988, the Republicans *lost* three House seats and one Senate seat.

Which **vice presidents were later elected president?**

As the first person in the presidential line of succession, nine vice presidents have assumed the presidency upon the death or resignation of the president. They are: John Tyler, Millard Fillmore, Andrew Johnson, Chester Alan Arthur, Theodore Roosevelt, Calvin Coolidge, Harry S. Truman, Lyndon B. Johnson, and Gerald Ford. However, fewer vice presidents have gained the presidency by election. The first two vice presidents, John Adams and Thomas Jefferson, were elected to the presidency after formally running for office. After Jefferson, only two incumbent vice presidents were immediately elected to the presidency—Martin Van Buren in 1836 and George Bush in 1988—and more than 150 years separated those successes. Richard Nixon also won the presidency by election, but only during his second campaign in 1968, which was eight years after, as the sitting vice president, he lost to John F. Kennedy.

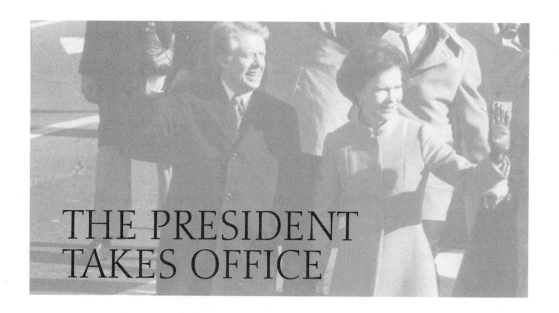

THE PRESIDENT TAKES OFFICE

INAUGURATIONS AND THE FIRST ONE HUNDRED DAYS

What is **Inauguration Day**?

Inauguration Day marks the beginning of a president's new term. The Oath of Office is the main focus of the day, and the only activity required by law. As mandated by Article II, Section 1, of the U.S. Constitution, the president-elect recites the oath, "I do solemnly swear (or affirm) that I will faithfully execute the office of President of the United States, and will to the best of my ability, preserve, protect, and defend the Constitution of the United States." George Washington added the words, "so help me God," and most presidents have followed suit. President Washington also set the precedent of kissing the Bible after taking the oath, although not all presidents have followed this custom (most notably Franklin Pierce, who preferred simply to place his left hand on it, and Theodore Roosevelt, who didn't use a Bible at all but an upraised hand). Washington also followed his swearing-in with the nation's first inaugural address, a tradition most presidents have adopted. Since the early days of Washington, each president has added his own stamp on the day's events, so Inauguration Day reflects the personality and tastes of the incoming chief executive.

Is **Inauguration Day always held on the same day**?

Yes. Inauguration Day originally took place on March 4, giving electors from each state nearly four months after Election Day to cast their ballots for president. In 1933, the Constitution's Twentieth Amendment officially changed the date to January 20, in an effort to expedite the change in presidential administrations. Franklin D. Roosevelt's second inauguration in 1937 was the first to take place on the new date.

95

Jimmy Carter, seen here with his wife Rosalynn, was the first president to walk from the Capitol to the White House after his inauguration ceremony. *Getty Images*.

What are some **Inauguration Day firsts** and **little-known facts**?

George Washington delivered the shortest inaugural address in history—just 135 words—during his second inauguration in 1793. John Adams began the tradition of having the oath of office administered by the chief justice of the Supreme Court. During his first inauguration in 1801, Thomas Jefferson became the first, and probably only, president to walk to and from his inaugural. In 1828, Andrew Jackson became the first president to take the oath of office on the East Portico of the Capitol in Washington, D.C., a tradition many presidents have since followed. While most presidents have read their inaugural addresses from written notes, Franklin Pierce broke tradition in 1853 when he recited his address. In 1945, Franklin D. Roosevelt took the presidential oath on the White House South Portico to spare himself an exhausting day, as America was engaged in World War II. In 1977, Jimmy Carter was the first president to walk from the Capitol to the White House with his family after the ceremony. In 1981, Ronald Reagan became the first president to take the presidential oath on the West Front of the U.S. Capitol (facing West in honor of his tenure as California's governor), where every president after him has followed suit. In 1985, Reagan participated in two inaugural addresses—a private ceremony on January 20 and a public ceremony the next day—so as not to conflict with the festivities of Super Bowl Sunday.

Among all the **inaugural addresses,** which ones are **most memorable**?

In inspiring Americans as their new leader, inaugural addresses have been carefully composed and edited by presidents and their trusted advisors. Abraham Lincoln's first

Lincoln the Orator

Abraham Lincoln's second Inaugural Address (1865) is considered among his greatest speeches. With the Civil War drawing to a close, Lincoln sought to set the terms for reunifying the nation:

> With malice toward none, with charity for all, with firmness in the right as God gives us to see the right, let us strive on to finish the work we are in, to bind up the nation's wounds, to care for him who shall have borne the battle and for his widow and his orphan, to do all which may achieve and cherish a just and lasting peace among ourselves and with all nations.

inaugural address made no mention of the Republican Party platform, which clearly condemned slavery. Against a backdrop of succession and strife, Lincoln instead admonished listeners, "In *your* hands, my dissatisfied fellow-countrymen, and not in *mine,* is the momentous issue of civil war." Until the final draft, Lincoln's address had ended with a question for the South: "Shall it be peace or sword?" However, the famous concluding paragraph ended instead on the less contentious note: "We are not enemies, but friends. Lincoln' Second Inaugural Address, in which he pled for peace and reconciliation, is considered among his best speeches. President Lincoln called on Americans to "finish the work we are in, to bind up the nation's wounds."

John F. Kennedy's 1961 inaugural address challenged Americans to live up to the nation's ideals and outlined his ideas on foreign policy. Kennedy's conclusion, "Ask not what your country can do for you—ask what you can do for your country," is among the most famous lines from an inaugural address. The inauguration also featured Robert Frost, who read his poem "The Gift Outright" in front of an audience of thousands. Nearly thirty years later, Bill Clinton paid homage to Kennedy when he asked Arkansas native and poet Maya Angelou to read her poem "The Rock Cries Out to Us Today" at his 1993 inauguration.

The words of inaugural addresses not only usher in a new leader and set the country on its course, they encourage and calm Americans during uncertain times. In 1933, Franklin D. Roosevelt assured those discouraged by the Great Depression by promising, "This great nation will endure as it has endured, will revive and will prosper." He added, "The only thing we have to fear is fear itself."

What is notable about **William Henry Harrison's inaugural address**?

President William Henry Harrison holds several records: he delivered the longest inaugural speech of any of the presidents; he was the first president to die in office; and he served the shortest term. And some say he is one of the first presidents to exercise poor judgment. On March 4, 1841, Harrison delivered his two-hour-long inaugural address in freezing-cold weather. In the middle of a snowstorm, as the crowds shivered, "Old Tip" Harrison (of "Tippecanoe and Tyler Too" fame) stood without a hat, coat, or gloves to deliver his eighty-six-hundred-word speech, which was carefully penned by Harrison but heavily edited by wordsmith Daniel Webster, his secretary of state. Harrison broke precedent by beginning his address, taking the presidential oath, and then resuming his address. Shortly afterward, he caught a cold, and he died of pneumonia one month later.

Although George Washington's inauguration was held outdoors, it was Andrew Jackson's inauguration in 1829 that set the precedent for outdoor ceremonies to celebrate a president of the people. Except in cases of extreme weather, the day's activities are held outdoors. One recent example of an indoor ceremony was in 1985, when Ronald Reagan was sworn-in indoors because of bitter cold temperatures.

What is noteworthy about **Abraham Lincoln's first Inauguration Day**?

The celebratory happenings of most Inauguration Days contrast sharply with those of President Abraham Lincoln, who arrived in Washington, D.C., in March 1861 amidst the dampened national mood of the secession of seven Southern states from the Union. Fearing violence, Lincoln arrived at his inauguration via a secret route, carefully guarded by General Winfield Scott's soldiers. Lincoln arrived safely with outgoing president James Buchanan at the Capitol, where he took the oath of office on the East Portico. In his inaugural address, Lincoln appealed for the preservation of the Union, vowing not to use force to maintain the Union or interfere with slavery in the states in which it existed. Despite his appeal, a little more than a month later, the Confederates launched the first attack of the Civil War.

What happened on **Inauguration Day 1877**?

In 1877, the Democrats boycotted Republican Rutherford B. Hayes's inauguration in order to protest his controversial electoral victory. In the election of 1876, the Republican governor of Ohio lost the popular vote to Democrat Samuel J. Tilden, but won the election in a disputed contest finally settled days before the inauguration. During his inaugural address, Hayes made a nonpartisan commitment to run his government, saying, "He who serves his country best serves his party best." Nevertheless, much ill feeling surrounded the day, and Hayes's supporters even feared assassination. The March 4, 1877, edition of the *New York Sun* headlined, "His Fraudulency Surrounded by a Horde of Schemers." During this heated emotional climate, a reader wrote a letter to the *Sun* editor, pleading, "Please request the people throughout the country to continue with half-masted flags, tolling bells, minute guns on the day of inauguration."

What was unique about **Calvin Coolidge's "inauguration"**?

Historians call Calvin Coolidge's swearing-in "the lamplit inaugural." At 2:47 A.M. on August 3, 1923, Vice President Calvin Coolidge was sworn into office by his father,

John C. Coolidge, a Vermont notary public, in his father's Vermont farmhouse, where the vice president had been vacationing with his wife. President Warren G. Harding had died just hours before in a San Francisco hotel, but it took four hours for a telegram announcing the news to reach the East Coast. The Plymouth Notch home had no electricity, so by the light of a kerosene lamp, Coolidge became the thirtieth president of the United States. Coolidge was the only president to be sworn in by his father and in his family's home.

In his autobiography, written in 1929, Coolidge recalled the event: "Where succession to the highest office in the land is by inheritance or appointment, no doubt there have been kings who have participated in the induction of their sons into their office, but in republics where the succession comes by an election I do not know of any other case in history where a father has administered to his son the qualifying oath of office which made him the chief magistrate of a nation. It seemed a simple and natural thing to do at the time, but I can now realize something of the dramatic force of the event."

What were the circumstances surrounding **Gerald Ford's speech upon becoming president**?

On August 9, 1974, Gerald Ford was sworn in as president of the United States after Richard Nixon resigned amidst the Watergate scandal. After taking the oath, Ford delivered a straightforward speech that beseeched the confidence of the American people. Acknowledging that "our long national nightmare is over," Ford admitted, "The oath that I have taken is the same oath that was taken by George Washington and by every President under the Constitution. But I assume the presidency under extraordinary circumstances never before experienced by Americans. This is an hour of history that troubles our minds and hurts our hearts." Ford had been nominated and then approved as vice president in late 1973 after his predecessor, Spiro Agnew, had resigned due to his own personal scandal. Former New York governor Nelson Rockefeller succeeded Ford as a non-elected vice president in December 1974. Ford and Rockefeller were the first and only, thus far, to reach office under the provisions of the Twenty-fifth Amendment.

Why is President **George W. Bush's inaugural address notable**?

President George W. Bush delivered his inaugural address among a sea of supporters and detractors, some of whom protested the November 2000 election outcome with signs that read, "Not My President." The ceremony took place at the Capitol's West Front in Washington, D.C., where Bush delivered a speech laden with acknowledgment of the days behind and promises of the days ahead: "While many of our citizens prosper, others doubt the promise—even the justice—of our own country," Bush said. "The ambitions of some Americans are limited by failing schools, and hidden preju-

99

dice, and the circumstances of their birth. And sometimes our differences run so deep, it seems we share a continent, but not a country. We do not accept this, and will not allow it…. Everyone belongs, everyone deserves a chance." Despite an optimistic and timely message, shouts of protesters intermittently drowned out the marching bands and cheers, reflecting Americans' divisiveness over the election results and their hesitancy toward the new president.

Which **presidents did not deliver an inaugural address**?

Five presidents assumed the presidency after taking the constitutional oath without participating in an inauguration ceremony (and without later winning a presidential election on their own): Vice President John Tyler, who became president in April 1841 upon William Henry Harrison's death one month after his inauguration; Vice President Millard Fillmore, who assumed the presidency in July 1850 after President Zachary Taylor died; Vice President Andrew Johnson, who took the executive oath in April 1865, after the assassinated Abraham Lincoln died in a house across the street from Ford's Theatre in Washington, D.C., where he had been shot; Vice President Chester Alan Arthur, who became president in September 1881, upon the death of President James A. Garfield; and Vice President Gerald Ford, who took the oath in August 1974 after President Richard Nixon resigned from office. (Ford made some brief comments, acknowledging the drama of the moment.)

When did the **Inaugural Day Parade** come into custom?

After his second inauguration in March 1805, Thomas Jefferson rode on horseback from the Capitol to the President's House while being surrounded by military band music from the nearby naval yard. This impromptu procession eventually grew into the modern Inaugural Parade so many people recognize today. Like the inaugural speech and other events of the day, the parade reflects the personality of the incoming president. For example, in 1837, Martin Van Buren became the first president to use floats during his inauguration—complementing the many balloons, fireworks, and flag-draped grandstands that have been a staple of presidential inaugural events. President Abraham Lincoln's 1865 inaugural parade saw African Americans participate officially for the first time in history.

In 1905, thirty-five thousand participants enjoyed Theodore Roosevelt's parade, which was led by cowboys, miners, and his former Spanish American War cavalry regiment. Woodrow Wilson's inaugural parade, in 1913, included an unprecedented forty thousand enthusiasts. Jimmy Carter's parade unfolded a giant peanut-shaped balloon in honor of his career as a peanut farmer. George W. Bush's 2001 inaugural parade featured six U.S. military bands and thirty-eight marching bands.

A gathering in front of the White House during Andrew Jackson's first inaugural reception in 1829. The peaceful gathering turned rowdy, and destructive partiers in the White House were finally lured out by tubs of punch placed on the lawn. *Library of Congress.*

When was the **first inaugural ball** held?

Although George Washington hosted an informal ball after his inauguration in 1789, the first official inaugural ball was held in honor of James Madison who, along with his wife Dolley, danced the night away at Long's Hotel in Washington, D.C. As time went on, the balls became more elaborate: Martin Van Buren's inauguration featured two inaugural gala balls, and President William Henry Harrison held three to meet his supporters' demand for tickets. Later inaugurations have featured specially built pavilions for dancing, multiple ball sites throughout the capital, and even inaugural parties in other cities. Nine inaugural balls were held in honor of President George W. Bush in 2001.

Which **inaugural parties go down in history**?

Andrew Jackson's first inauguration in 1829 is famous for its public reception. For the first time in history, Jackson invited the public to attend an inaugural party—an invitation that attracted thousands of newly enfranchised supporters, including old soldiers, backwoodsmen, and immigrants, to the White House. Their enthusiasm over the day's events and downright rowdiness caused thousands of dollars of property damage and forced the new president to narrowly escape out a window. A fourteen-hundred-pound wheel of cheese was consumed in two hours. Meanwhile, White House staff members placed tubs of punch on the lawn in an effort to draw the crowd out of the White House, and then carefully locked the doors behind them. Though one eyewitness compared the event to the "inundation of the northern barbarians into Rome," Amos Kendall, an editor from Kentucky, heralded, "It was a proud day for the people. General Jackson is *their own* president." Four years later, Jackson delivered his second inaugural address to a more subdued crowd in the Capitol's Hall of Representatives.

Jackson's bash laid the groundwork for most twentieth-century presidents, who have enjoyed glitz and glamor consistently since Warner Bros. Studios sent a trainload of Hollywood stars to Franklin D. Roosevelt's inauguration in 1932. In 1961, John F. Kennedy turned inaugural events into a nationwide happening when he televised his gala, which was hosted by Frank Sinatra and attended by the movie stars of the day. Bill Clinton was determined to outdo those presidents before him, reportedly spending as much on the inauguration events of 1993 as he did on his campaign for president a year earlier. The central event of his inaugural celebration was a Call for Reunion concert at the Lincoln Memorial in Washington, where artists such as Aretha Franklin, Michael Bolton, Tony Bennett, Bob Dylan, Diana Ross, and LL Cool J performed. At a televised party, the rock group Fleetwood Mac reunited to sing "Don't Stop Thinking About Tomorrow," Clinton's campaign theme song.

Why are the **first one hundred days a significant benchmark** for the president?

Since the election of Franklin D. Roosevelt in 1932, historians and political commentators have used a president's first one hundred days in office as a first benchmark for judging his performance. When Roosevelt delivered his first inaugural address, America was in the depths of the Great Depression, with an unemployment rate of 25 percent, a severe banking crisis, and a populace that was fearful of its future. President Roosevelt took immediate action with Congress on his New Deal program. By the end of his first one hundred days, Congress had passed fifteen bills, and Roosevelt was well on his way to enacting his program of social recovery. Although the first one hundred days is a contrived timeline, observers use this time frame not only to discuss how a president has performed out of the starting gate, but also as a gauge of how he will do for the rest of his administration.

Which people stepped into the presidency under **particularly challenging circumstances**?

In his 1981 inaugural address, Ronald Reagan said the following about Inauguration Day: "The orderly transfer of authority as called for in the Constitution routinely takes place, as it has for almost two centuries, and few of us stop to think how unique we really are. In the eyes of many in the world, this every-four-year ceremony we accept as normal is nothing less than a miracle." Although presidential transitions are generally smooth, that hasn't always been the case.

"Hail to the Chief"

The song "Hail to the Chief," though long associated with the president of the United States, has origins in the theater. It was created for a stage adaptation of Sir Walter Scott's romantic poem "The Lady of the Lake," with music by English composer James Sanderson. The song was first associated with a president in 1815, when it was played (under the title "Wreaths for the Chieftain") both in honor of the late George Washington's birthday and the end of the War of 1812. According to the Library of Congress, the first recorded instance of a president being present when the tune was played was at an 1828 ground-breaking ceremony for the Chesapeake and Ohio Canal attended by President John Quincy Adams. However, Andrew Jackson was the first living president to be personally honored by "Hail to the Chief" in 1829. The tune was among several played for Martin Van Buren's inauguration ceremony in 1837, and was often summoned for social occasions during his administration.

Julia Tyler, the second wife of President John Tyler, was responsible for requesting the song be played to announce the president's arrival on official occasions. However, it was first lady Sarah Polk, who had a personal affinity for the song and ritualized its use. Although it was played at her husband James K. Polk's inauguration in 1845, it had deeper meaning for this particular president. According to historian William Seale, because of Polk's height (five-foot-eight), "Some announcement was necessary to avoid the embarrassment of his entering a crowded room unnoticed." It was played at almost every formal event in the White House during his administration.

President Chester Alan Arthur was not fond of the tune and asked American composer John Philip Sousa to compose a new tribute. Sousa, then director of the U.S. Marine Band, responded with "Presidential Polonaise," but the song never endured. President Harry S. Truman, an amateur musicologist who liked to play the piano, traced the origins of "Hail to the Chief" and in 1954 the U.S. Department of Defense established it as the official musical tribute to the U.S. president. Since that time, only one president—Gerald Ford—has preferred to omit the performance of the song upon his arrival. Ford preferred the college fight song from his alma mater, the University of Michigan.

Abraham Lincoln assumed the presidency in 1861 just after several states had seceded from the Union, and he continued as president through the nation's only civil war (1861–1865). Franklin D. Roosevelt took office in 1933, in the midst of the country's Great Depression, and held the helm through America's involvement in World War II (1941–1945). When Dwight D. Eisenhower became president in 1953, the government was deeply divided; the Republicans dominated the White House and the two

Annual Message / State of the Union Milestones

1790   George Washington delivered the first Annual Message to Congress on January 8 in New York, then the nation's capital.

1823   In his written message, James Monroe set forth the Monroe Doctrine, opposing European intervention in the Americas: "... as a principle in which the rights and interests of the United States are involved, that the American continents, by the free and independent condition which they have assumed and maintain, are henceforth not to be considered as subjects for future colonization by any European powers."

1862   As the Civil War raged on, Abraham Lincoln penned his famous message, justifying the war: "Fellow citizens, we cannot escape history ... the fiery trial through which we pass will light us down in honor or dishonor to the latest generation. In giving freedom to the slave we assure freedom to the free—honorable alike in what we give and what we preserve."

1913   Woodrow Wilson revived the practice of delivering the annual message in person, giving a dramatic speech calling for tariff reform. Realizing that the oral delivery of the State of the Union and the British tradition were interwoven, Wilson felt the need to separate the delivered address from its monarchical past. He expressed that he did not expect a formal response from Congress: "I am very glad indeed to have this opportunity to address the two Houses directly and to verify for myself the impression that the President of the United States is a person, not a mere department of the Government hailing Congress from some isolated island of jealous power, sending messages, not speaking naturally and

houses of Congress, but lost them during Eisenhower's tenure. And four men—Andrew Johnson, Chester Alan Arthur, Theodore Roosevelt, and Lyndon B. Johnson—assumed the presidency after the presidents under whom they served had been assassinated. Gerald Ford assumed the presidency in 1974, after Richard Nixon resigned from office under the threat of impeachment and amidst unprecedented public distrust of the executive office. George W. Bush assumed the presidency after a contentious election and at a time when the Senate was evenly divided between Republicans and Democrats.

What is the president's **State of the Union address**?

As outlined by Article II, Section 3, of the U.S. Constitution, the president's State of the Union address is an annual message from the president of the United States to Congress and the nation. During the address, the chief executive reports on conditions in

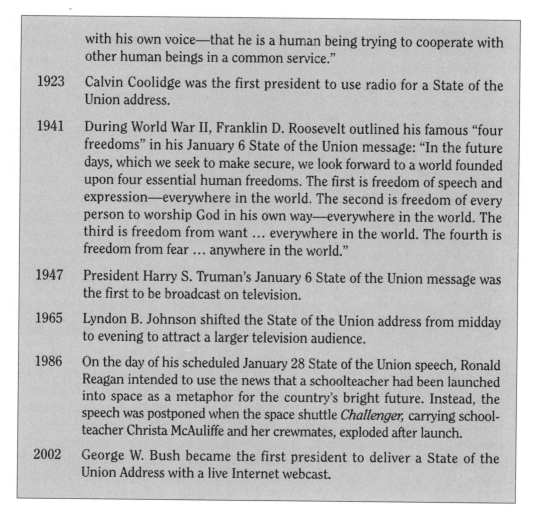

with his own voice—that he is a human being trying to cooperate with other human beings in a common service."

1923   Calvin Coolidge was the first president to use radio for a State of the Union address.

1941   During World War II, Franklin D. Roosevelt outlined his famous "four freedoms" in his January 6 State of the Union message: "In the future days, which we seek to make secure, we look forward to a world founded upon four essential human freedoms. The first is freedom of speech and expression—everywhere in the world. The second is freedom of every person to worship God in his own way—everywhere in the world. The third is freedom from want … everywhere in the world. The fourth is freedom from fear … anywhere in the world."

1947   President Harry S. Truman's January 6 State of the Union message was the first to be broadcast on television.

1965   Lyndon B. Johnson shifted the State of the Union address from midday to evening to attract a larger television audience.

1986   On the day of his scheduled January 28 State of the Union speech, Ronald Reagan intended to use the news that a schoolteacher had been launched into space as a metaphor for the country's bright future. Instead, the speech was postponed when the space shuttle *Challenger*, carrying schoolteacher Christa McAuliffe and her crewmates, exploded after launch.

2002   George W. Bush became the first president to deliver a State of the Union Address with a live Internet webcast.

the United States and abroad; recommends a legislative program for the coming session of Congress; and frequently presents his views of, and vision for, the present and future. The message was generally known as "the President's Annual Message to Congress" until well into the twentieth century. Although some historians suggest that the phrase "State of the Union" emerged after World War II, Franklin D. Roosevelt actually coined the phrase: His 1934 message is identified in his papers as his "Annual Message to Congress on the State of the Union."

Who delivered the **first State of the Union address**?

On January 8, 1790, President George Washington delivered the first message before a joint session of Congress in New York. During Washington's administration and that of John Adams, it was custom for the president to appear before a joint session of Congress and deliver the address personally. Each House subsequently debated and approved official replies to the president's message, which were then delivered personally to the president by delegations of senators and representatives. America's third president, Thomas Jefferson, began the precedent of sending written reports, which continued until Woodrow Wilson convened Congress in 1913 to hear his message delivered verbally.

Is there a **State of the Union address every year**?

Since World War II, there have occasionally been times when a president has not delivered an annual address. Several recent presidents—Ronald Reagan in 1981, George Bush in 1989, and Bill Clinton in 1993—have chosen not to give an official State of the Union address the year they were first inaugurated as president. Other presidents, such as Reagan and Bush, have chosen

President Harry S. Truman, seen here with movie star Lauren Bacall, was an amateur musicologist who liked to play the piano. *AP/Wide World Photos.*

not to deliver a message immediately prior to their departure from office (although President Reagan delivered a televised farewell address from the Oval Office on January 8, 1989). And both incoming and outgoing presidents have occasionally given State of the Union messages within weeks of each other. President Dwight D. Eisenhower's first message, delivered to Congress on February 7, 1953, followed on the heels of President Harry S. Truman's final message, delivered to Congress just a month earlier.

What are some of the most **notable speeches and documents** made by presidents?

In carrying out his roles of popular leader and chief executive, the president often makes compelling speeches in order to rally the American people around a national goal or during a time of crisis. While each president has made a memorable speech or proffered key words of wisdom that can be attributed to him, some of the more time-less and poignant deliveries include George Washington's farewell address (1796); James Monroe's State of the Union address proclaiming the Monroe Doctrine (1823); Abraham Lincoln's Gettysburg Address (1863) and his Second Inaugural Address (1865); Woodrow Wilson's war message, advising Congress to declare war on Germany (1917); Franklin D. Roosevelt's first inaugural address and first fireside chat (1933) and his war message (1941); John F. Kennedy's inaugural address (1961); Lyndon B. Johnson's State of the Union address proposing his "Great Society" program (1965); Richard Nixon's resignation speech (1974); and Ronald Reagan speaking in Germany near the Berlin Wall, imploring Soviet premier Mikhail Gorbachev to "tear down this wall" (1987).

PERSONALITIES AND LEADERSHIP STYLES

What are some **personality quirks of presidents**?

A variety of personalities and character traits have embodied America's forty-three presidents. Despite a public persona of seriousness, some presidents, such as Abraham Lincoln, were known for their wit and sense of humor. Other presidents, such as John Adams, were called vain and cantankerous. Some, such as Thomas Jefferson, go down in history as inventors and intellectuals. And others, such as "Silent Cal" Coolidge, were labeled for their reserved and contemplative manner. Harry S. Truman was known as a no-nonsense type, but one who liked to tell a joke, play the piano, or get in a round of poker. John F. Kennedy was so attached to his role as president that many likened him to a royal king living in a royal palace, and even called the White House under his tenure "Camelot." President Jimmy Carter was considered one of the most unassuming presidents of the modern times, often wearing cardigan sweaters instead of suits, insisting on carrying his own luggage, and asking the Marine band to refrain from playing "Hail to the Chief" upon his arrival to official events.

To identify personality traits one only has to review presidential nicknames, such as "Old Hickory" Andrew Jackson, "Old Rough and Ready" Zachary Taylor, "Honest Abe" Lincoln, "The Plodder" James K. Polk, "White House Iceberg" Benjamin Harrison, "His Obstinacy" Grover Cleveland, and "Mr. Nice Guy" Gerald Ford. These nicknames often carried over into a president's accomplishments as chief executive: George Washington is the best-known example as "Father of His Country," Lincoln is called "The Great Emancipator" for his pursuit of ending slavery, and Ronald Reagan was called "The Great Communicator" for his oratory skill and polished public appearances.

Caricature depicting the wildly different personalities of U.S. presidents throughout the years. Eisenhower reaches for a golf ball, Taft sits in his specially-built bathtub, and John Quincy Adams gazes through a telescope; Coolidge, dressed for a photo op in a cowboy outfit, rejects an offer of jelly beans from Reagan; Lincoln reads a joke book, T. Roosevelt, dressed in his Rough Riders uniform, holds a teddy bear, and Washington examines Lyndon B. Johnson's gall bladder scar; Nixon is secretly taping the event, while Jefferson plays the violin and Truman the piano. *Library of Congress.*

What are some **leadership styles** of the presidents?

The role of the president has changed over history, as office holders have shaped the presidency and interpreted their powers in a variety of ways. George Washington, America's first president, was unanimously elected to office because all members of the electoral college considered him the embodiment of the American president. His commitment and leadership to the country brought legitimacy to the new national government. Two of Washington's cabinet members, Secretary of Treasury Alexander Hamilton and Secretary of State Thomas Jefferson, differed in their views of the role government should play, and their distinct political philosophies have characterized leadership styles adopted by subsequent presidents.

Hamilton believed in an active government and strong leadership. Presidents who have exhibited this type of leadership style include Abraham Lincoln, Theodore Roosevelt, Woodrow Wilson, Franklin D. Roosevelt, Harry S. Truman, and Lyndon B. Johnson. Most historians cite Franklin D. Roosevelt as the embodiment of the Hamiltonian personality because his strong leadership skills enabled him to greatly expand the role of the federal government, which ultimately brought the country through the Great Depression. Jefferson, on the other hand, believed in a less active government. Andrew Jackson, William Howard Taft, Warren G. Harding, Calvin Coolidge, Herbert Hoover,

Traits of an Effective Leader

In his book *The American Presidency* (1976), presidential scholar Ernest Griffith describes the traits of an effective national leader, however idealized:

[The president] will, by example, image, and appeal, try as best he can to lead in the ideals and traditions of the past, and be sensitive to the national missions that lie ahead. He will try to unify the people around these national missions so as to realize the dreams of a way of life for the United States.... He will be President of *all* the people.

He should be steeped in our national history and traditions. He will thereby recognize the elements of greatness in our greatest Presidents—Washington, Jefferson, Lincoln, the two Roosevelts, Wilson, and Truman.

He should also recognize the conflicting, confusing, and dangerous elements in our contemporary society and the world at large—and the elements of promise. With deep understanding of all these, with a combination of determination and humility as God gives him to see the right, he will be the biggest man he can be, adding to his own strength the strength of others who like him would recapture a sense of mission for our people.

and Ronald Reagan all demonstrated a more hands-off Jeffersonian leadership style, even being called passive by some of their detractors. President Hoover, for example, initially refused to offer federal aid during the Great Depression because he believed government intervention in private matters should be limited. Likewise, President Reagan's administration was characterized by reduced federal regulations of business and industry and a return of power to the states. Yet Jefferson, in fact, was an active president—from authorizing an undeclared war against pirates, to making the Louisiana Purchase (1803), to ordering a shipping embargo (1807) against England and France.

How did the **early presidents expand the role of the presidency**?

Although they are known for different achievements, each of the first three presidents contributed significantly to the president's role as chief executive. As the nation's first president, George Washington (served 1789–1797) had the formidable task of both creating and running the new national government. Washington was a strong believer in the authority of the federal government, and insisted that people respect both the office of the presidency and the president as a person. He fostered an administration of inclusion and began the practice of regular meetings with his advisers, which evolved

Nine Steps to Achieving a Successful Presidency

In his book *Presidential Power: The Politics of Leadership* (1960), presidential scholar and White House adviser Richard Neustadt outlines the following nine steps to achieving a successful presidency, all of which center around Neustadt's classic concept of the power to persuade:

1. A president must have a will for power.

2. He must be the person who sets the agenda for the national government, and his ability to ingratiate others is key to persuading other government institutions to act.

3. A president must be receptive to the thoughts, ideas, and agendas of others in order to reach effective compromises to national issues.

4. He must have an ability to work with Congress and convince members that his agenda is in their best interest.

5. Any effective president must be able to weather the storm of crisis and conflict.

6. As a strong, national leader, the president must own his role as chief politician, and not delegate that role to anyone. He must own his own actions.

7. A president must assume the role of the expert, even if he is not an expert in the issue at hand, since the public's trust in him depends upon his knowledge of key issues.

8. Popularity and prestige are musts for a successful president. Public disapproval discourages others in the Washington community from working with the president and adapting his programs.

9. A smart president is mindful of the power of persuasion, negotiation, and the art of the deal, and avoids confrontational mandates that alienate people.

into today's cabinet system. And, finally, Washington took a lead in foreign affairs, negotiating treaties under the scrutinizing eye of Congress. Washington mandated that the Senate's role was to approve treaties once they were negotiated, not initiate discussions of negotiation. Washington can be called the "President of Precedents." When John Adams (served 1797–1801) assumed the presidency, his poor leadership skills stood in stark contrast to Washington, and his administration is known for fostering the development of political parties. After Adams, Thomas Jefferson (served 1801–1809) used the fledgling party system to his advantage to establish a strong relationship with Congress and expand the role of the chief executive in the legislative process. Jefferson used his inherent powers as president to double the size of the United States through the Louisiana Purchase (1803), making the still-young country one of the largest nations in the world.

What was **John Quincy Adams** like as a president?

John Quincy Adams, the first son of a president to become president himself, was already an accomplished politician and diplomat when he assumed the executive office. As secretary of state under James Monroe, he was the main proponent for the Monroe Doctrine, one of the most significant and enduring statements of U.S. foreign policy. However, Adams's strength as a leader was overshadowed by his aloof personality, which Adams himself called "reserved, cold, austere, and forbidding." Many suggest that he inherited these traits from his father and the nation's second president, John Adams, whom Alexander Hamilton, the nation's first secretary of the treasury, called "petty, mean, erratic, egoistic, eccentric, jealous." As a distant ruler, the younger Adams never enjoyed a familiar popularity with the people.

Adams captured the presidency after the contentious election of 1824. Tension characterized his relationship with Congress, whose members refused to support many of Adams's ideas, including a national system of roads and canals and a national university. His answers to dealing with the stresses of the executive office lay in keeping a strict schedule. As a man enveloped by routine, Adams exercised self-discipline in all areas of his life: He regularly rose at 6:00 A.M. to swim in the Potomac River, and his deep religious convictions led him to read the Bible several times each day, often in three different languages. Although Adams once said, "I never was and never shall be what is commonly termed a popular man," he became more highly regarded after the presidency. Adams served for seventeen years in the U.S. House of Representatives (1831–1848), gaining a reputation as a persuasive speaker—so much so that his nickname was "Old Man Eloquent." Adams was the only man to hold office in the House after his presidential term ended.

Why was **Andrew Jackson** called **"King Andrew"**?

Andrew Jackson, who assumed the presidency as party politics were becoming more polarized, found himself labeled as nothing short of a dictator by his Democratic Party's opposition, the Whigs. Unlike previous presidents, Jackson used his popularity and power as president to fill his cabinet with loyal Democratic followers. Jackson did not consult Congress in policymaking and used his power of the veto to assume control of the national government. As a result, many of Jackson's detractors and the political cartoonists of the day labeled Jackson "King Andrew." Whig leaders, such as Henry Clay and Daniel Webster, claimed that Jackson was more of an authoritarian and bully than a balanced president, often citing his relentless use of veto power. In

1832, Jackson vetoed the bill to recharter the controversial Second Bank of the United States, claiming, "The bank is trying to kill me, but I will kill it!" Jackson vetoed bills for political reasons, or simply because he disliked them, thus rejecting the tradition originated by George Washington that vetoes were rarely to be exercised by presidents in a republic. During his two terms in office, Washington used the veto power just twice; Jackson used it twelve times, more than all of his predecessors combined.

Is it true that **Zachary Taylor never voted**?

Yes. By all accounts, Zachary Taylor was at heart a very simple man, who was raised and home-schooled in Kentucky before joining the army in 1808. He was assigned to the Seventh Infantry Regiment that year by his second cousin, Secretary of State James Madison, and would continue to serve as a career military officer until his nomination to the presidency in 1848. In the army, Taylor acquired his nickname "Old Rough and Ready," for his rugged demeanor and simple, unkept dress. Of the presidency, he once said, "The idea that I should become President seems to me too visionary to require a serious answer. It has never entered my head, nor is it likely to enter the head of any sane person." Nevertheless, Whig politicians recruited Taylor, despite his never voting in a national election, primarily on the strength of his victories during the Mexican War (1846–1848) and his subsequent popularity among the people. Riding on the wave of his war-hero reputation, Taylor was well liked as president. His short-lived administration was consumed with deciding whether the national government should allow the spread of slavery into several Western states. Taylor died unexpectedly of inflammation of the stomach sixteen months into his presidency, and was succeeded by Vice President Millard Fillmore.

Despite his many successes, why was **Abraham Lincoln criticized**?

Because Lincoln dealt with the unprecedented crisis of America's civil war, he assumed unprecedented powers. Faced with a national emergency while Congress was not in session, Lincoln expanded the size of the army above congressionally approved ceilings, spent war funds prior to congressional appropriation, and ordered a blockade of Southern ports, which in effect initiated war without the approval of Congress. Scholars maintain that Lincoln limited civil rights when he suspended the writ of habeas corpus, thus allowing for the indefinite detainment of those suspected of sympathizing with the Southern cause. (Habeas corpus, which is guaranteed by the U.S. Constitution, dictates that someone accused of a crime will be brought before court to decide the legality of the charges.) Lincoln justified his actions according to the inherent powers of the presidency, maintaining that it was necessary to circumvent the Constitution in order preserve the nation. Lincoln's broad interpretation of executive power was only approached by two wartime presidents, Woodrow Wilson (World War I) and Franklin D. Roosevelt (World War II).

What is the **"bully pulpit"**?

Persuading the public of the validity of a presidential agenda is a key part of a president's job. Theodore Roosevelt (served 1901–1909) referred to the presidency as a "bully pulpit," which he used to gain support for his progressive programs, including social legislation and government regulation of industry. When he entered the presidency, Roosevelt had a distinct vision to see America as a great world power. His strong leadership style—which was built around the bully pulpit and an effective use of rhetoric, stories, and symbols—transformed America's domestic program and turned the nation's foreign-policy approach of isolationism to true internationalism. Roosevelt was able to institute wide-sweeping social reform and see the country through some difficult challenges, including regulation of the food and drug industry and the dismantling of corporate trusts. In 1906, Roosevelt became the first American to win the Nobel Peace Prize, and he is generally ranked as one of the top presidents in U.S. history.

How have other **twentieth-century presidents rallied support from the public**?

In the wake of World War I, Woodrow Wilson tried to garner public support for his idea of a League of Nations by embarking on a "whistle-stop" train tour around the country. Although Wilson's attempts were unsuccessful and the United States never participated in the League of Nations, historians view Wilson as one of America's most visionary presidents. Franklin D. Roosevelt was the personification of a "personal president." His fireside chats, press conferences, and ability to befriend the public helped him to gain tremendous support for his programs. John F. Kennedy used the format of the press conference to his ultimate advantage. In an effort to gain support from reporters, Kennedy always answered them in a respectful tone, engaging them with flattery and charm, and consistently thanked them for the facts they chose *not* to publish. The elite of print and television journalism considered themselves Kennedy's friends, and often mentioned their shared burden of helping Kennedy shape the country and its future. Ronald Reagan was perhaps the best communicator of all the late-twentieth-century presidents. As a former actor, he played to the medium of television and was successful in getting public support for his tax-cut program. Reagan attempted to use the bully pulpit to win support for public school prayer and for anti-abortion legislation.

Which president **first used the press conference** to his advantage?

Although he distrusted the media, Woodrow Wilson made many attempts to interface with it. He was the first president to hold a presidential news conference and pioneered the concept as a way of molding public opinion and rallying support for the administration. Wilson's personal appeal to the media also translated to Congress: In 1913, he broke Thomas Jefferson's precedent of submitting the then-named Annual Message to Congress in writing by delivering the address to Congress in person, thus setting a precedent for today's State of the Union Address.

Despite the effectiveness of the press conference as a tool for communicating their ideas, presidents vary in their use of it. Ronald Reagan held only seven press conferences during his first year in office. His successor, George Bush, held more press conferences during his first eighteen months than Reagan held during his entire two terms.

Which three presidents required the press to submit their questions in writing in advance?

Not wanting to be taken by surprise, three presidents in succession—Warren G. Harding (served 1921–1923), Calvin Coolidge (served 1923–1929), and Herbert Hoover served (1929–1933)—required the press to submit their questions in writing to them or their secretaries in advance. This allowed time to prepare a politically advantageous response and more carefully control the information that was disseminated to both the press and the public. Interestingly, Harding initiated the practice of holding biweekly press conferences, an act that Coolidge continued. Because of his openness and availability to the press (having held some five hundred such meetings during his six years in the White House), Coolidge enjoyed great popularity among the Washington press corps.

Why is Franklin D. Roosevelt considered one of the twentieth-century's best communicators?

Probably one of the most successful communicators was Franklin D. Roosevelt, who used the popular medium of the radio, by that time in over half of America's households, to his political advantage. From the room now known as the Diplomatic Reception Room of the White House, Roosevelt addressed the nation with more than thirty so-called "fireside chats"—heart-to-heart conversations he held directly with Americans about the problems they were facing during the Great Depression of the 1930s and World War II in the 1940s. The chats were immensely popular, primarily because Roosevelt's calming voice and everyday language assured Americans that despite the country's current crises, the United States had the resiliency to survive as a nation. Their effect ultimately instilled Americans' faith in Roosevelt as president, convincing them he was working hard to correct their problems. Radio was also a means for the president to bypass the partisan newspapers that were generally critical of New Deal reforms, instead giving his administration direct access to citizens, which ultimately boosted his popularity as a leader and allowed him to move forward with his presidential agenda. Roosevelt's chats were so successful that presidents Jimmy Carter and Bill Clinton tried to replicate the technique.

How else did Franklin Roosevelt reach the populace?

President Roosevelt made effective use of the media to reach the public. He held 998 news conferences during his 12-year presidency. He began the trend on March 8, 1933, as soon as he was sworn into office, and continued holding press conferences steadily throughout his tenure. Unlike his predecessor, Herbert Hoover, who asked the press to prepare their questions and submit them to him prior to any press dealings, Roosevelt's off-the-cuff, frank nature established a fresh relationship with the press. And this translated to the American public, and ultimately to the success of his presidency.

Roosevelt also holds the title of the first president to appear on television, which occurred when he spoke at the opening ceremonies of the New York World's Fair on April 30, 1939. NBC telecast the event from the Federal Building on the Exposition Grounds. Three-and-a-half years later, Roosevelt took another "first" as the first president to broadcast in a foreign language. On November 7, 1942, Roosevelt addressed the French in their own language from Washington, D.C., in coordination with the U.S. Army's invasion of the French territorial possessions in Africa.

Which president used the saying "The buck stops here" to define his presidency?

A plain-spoken man, Harry S. Truman often drew on sayings such as "The buck stops here" (which he had made into a desk plaque) and "If you can't stand the heat, get out of the kitchen" during his presidency. Scholars describe Truman as a strong leader. He assumed the presidency in 1945 after the death of a very popular president, Franklin D. Roosevelt. During his presidency Truman made some tough foreign-policy decisions that fed his reputation as a determined leader. He created the Truman Doctrine, which provided economic aid to Greece and Turkey to help those countries resist Soviet influence. His administration soon outlined a strategy of "containment" aimed at "containing" communism and blocking its expansion, which shaped the outcome of the Cold War. Truman oversaw the implementation of the Marshall Plan, a reconstruction plan for war-torn Europe that took place in the aftermath of World War II, and the creation of the North Atlantic Treaty Organization (NATO), a military alliance of countries united against potential Soviet threat. Under his administration, presidential power expanded as Truman made unprecedented moves, such as sending U.S. troops to Korea without Congress's approval.

Although Truman was a media "first"—he was the first president to appear on television from the White House when he spoke about the world food crisis on October 5, 1947—he had trouble relating to the press. Critical of journalists and shy of the press, Truman frequently got himself in trouble by coming unprepared to press conferences and offering impromptu answers. Truman frequently relied on his press secretary, Charles Ross, to brief him on trial questions and issue clarifications to any of his off-the-cuff answers, such as when he implied at a 1950 conference that he might use nuclear weapons in Korea.

What was Dwight D. Eisenhower's personality like?

Peter Lyon's biography of the president, *Eisenhower: Portrait of a Hero* (1974), describes the president as an easygoing, gentle man. Lyon said, "Eisenhower wanted to like people, he wanted people to like him; he was distressed when it failed to happen so." Indeed, Eisenhower was enormously popular with the public from his time as a commander of the Allied forces in Europe during World War II through his death in 1969. However, many political analysts have mixed opinions of Eisenhower, and many have ranked him as a weak leader. Criticisms include his weak speaking ability, especially to the press, his intermittent bursts of anger, and his passivity in dealing with troublesome personalities, such as U.S. senator Joseph McCarthy of Wisconsin, whose anti-communist crusading dominated the news for some time.

After the Eisenhower administration's records came into the public domain over the years, many scholars changed their view of Eisenhower's legacy. Princeton professor Fred Greenstein called Eisenhower "a skilled political operator with an interesting and complex personality who engaged in the kinds of politicking that many believed he left to subordinates." His indirect approach to political matters preserved his popularity and left his administration to carry out controversial policies, including Central Intelligence Agency covert operations in Iran and Guatemala. Ultimately, Eisenhower commanded the respect necessary to reconcile foreign-relations issues, helping to bring an end to the Korean War and improve relations with the Soviet Union. An interesting personality quirk is that Eisenhower was a bit superstitious: He always carried three lucky coins in his trouser pockets.

Will **Richard Nixon's failures overshadow his accomplishments**?

While historians recognize Nixon's accomplishments, primarily in the area of foreign relations, many scholars believe they will forever be overshadowed by his weaknesses as president. Nixon veered from post World War II American policy by reaching out to communist China in an effort to transform U.S.-China relations. He was the first U.S. president to visit China, and the first to visit a nation with a communist government that had no prior diplomatic relations with the United States. He signed the 1972 SALT (Strategic Arms Limitation Talks) Agreement with Soviet leader Leonid Brezhnev in an effort to limit nuclear-weapon production. Nevertheless, these milestones are overshadowed by the Watergate scandal that began in 1972, which resulted in President Nixon being charged with authorizing the break-in into Democratic National Headquarters. The investigation that followed the break-in uncovered a long list of wrongdoings at the hand of the president, which eventually caused him to resign the office under the threat of impeachment in August 1974.

Even before the Watergate scandal, the press's relationship with the president was adversarial. Nixon was often uncomfortable around reporters, always disclosing as little information as possible. Because of his failures as president, the Nixon personality has been subject to extended discussion by historians and psychoanalysts alike. Dr. David Abrahamsen, in his book *Nixon vs. Nixon* (1977), described him as being severely conflicted, driven by loneliness, hypersensitivity, narcissism, and secretiveness. Others have described Nixon as a compulsive liar driven by a deep fear of failure. In the aftermath of Nixon's resignation, Americans cited great disillusionment with the national government, and with the president in particular. Many have charged Nixon with creating a breach of trust between the citizenry and its leaders that in some ways has never been restored.

What was **Jimmy Carter's weakness** when it came to **dealing with the press**?

Political commentators often cite Jimmy Carter's inability to communicate effectively with the press and public as his greatest weakness. Often viewed as the harbinger of bad news, Carter's non-television-friendly persona and elevated speaking style contributed to his image of an ineffectual leader who was overwhelmed by his administration's crises, including uncontrollable inflation rates at home, the hostage crisis in Iran, and the Soviet Union's invasion of Afghanistan. Carter was also apathetic toward the press, which fostered a new aggressiveness toward the executive office in the aftermath of the Watergate scandal. Carter's crumbling relationship with the press mirrored his low approval ratings, which had dropped to 31 percent—lower than Richard Nixon's before his resignation—by the election of 1980.

How did **Ronald Reagan's former career as an actor** influence his role as president?

Some analysts acknowledge that Ronald Reagan's celebrity image of a Hollywood "good guy" was successful at the polls and helped him identify with the public as president. Others argue that his former career as an actor ultimately hurt him. Indeed, the press frequently used Reagan's Hollywood background to discredit his presidency, linking his weakness as a leader with lack of qualifications. Many asserted that as president, Reagan was simply playing a role or participating in a public performance. His detractors emphasized the fact that certain administration priorities were drawn from the scripts of his most popular movies, calling attention, for example, to his proposed 1983 Strategic Defense Initiative as a copycat of the Hollywood-devised technology "the Inertia Projector" of his 1940 film *Murder in the Air.*

Reagan himself did much to perpetuate his image as an actor, frequently making analogies to Hollywood when discussing his presidential responsibilities. When addressing students in Moscow during his 1988 summit meeting with Soviet leader Mikhail Gorbachev, Reagan presented his view of the presidency and role as president by comparing himself to the director of a film. He asserted that a good director makes sure that the star actors and all the bit players know their parts and comprehend the director's vision of what the film is all about. Nevertheless, Reagan's nickname as "The Great Communicator" reflects the consensus that he communicated well with both the media and the public, a trait that was undoubtedly honed during Reagan's years as a successful actor.

How have historians described **Bill Clinton's personality**?

Ambitious, self-confident, and full of charisma and charm, Bill Clinton captured the allegiance of many during his two terms as president (served 1993–2001). Historians and scholars describe Clinton as personal and outgoing. Despite these admirable traits, his presidency was beset by rumors of scandal, beginning with Whitewater, during which members of the Republican Party accused Clinton and his wife, Hillary, of covering up financial misdealings of Arkansas investments made prior to Clinton's presidency. Weaknesses in Clinton's ethics and personality came to the fore in his relationship with Washington intern Monica Lewinsky, with whom he was accused of sexual misconduct. The investigation of the Lewinsky scandal eventually led to Clinton's 1998 impeachment by the House of Representatives on charges of lying and obstructing justice. The press reminded the public of Clinton's nickname, "Slick Willie," as a moniker for evading the truth. Unlike President Richard Nixon before him, Clinton chose not to resign from office, but to fight back against his accusers.

In the wake of the scandal, many Americans questioned Clinton's decision-making abilities and said that Clinton's trademark of playing "fast and loose" with the truth had eroded the president's image as the moral figurehead of the nation. Even so, a majority of Americans opposed Clinton's impeachment, and after sitting on the sidelines for nearly four years after the end of his presidency, Clinton reemerged with the publication of his enormously best-selling memoirs. He drew large crowds at book signings and strong ratings in television and radio appearances.

What are **George W. Bush's personality quirks**?

During Bush's campaign and early presidency, some media commentators made light of his occasionally confusing word choices, inability to accurately answer questions about history and foreign policy, and vague ideas about his presidential agenda. Bush's personal traits include his down-home Texas attitude, joke-cracking persona, and habit of personally nicknaming members of his staff. In the aftermath of the September 11, 2001, tragedy, Bush's job approval rating averaged 89 percent, and many politicians, Republicans and Democrats alike, rose to compliment the president as a leader. Although some political commentators criticized President Bush's handling of the subsequent war with Iraq, specifically his tendency to act unilaterally, most Americans still viewed Bush as a strong national leader.

LIFE IN THE WHITE HOUSE

Do presidents maintain a **large personal staff for their living quarters**?

Yes. There isn't one first family who has lived in the White House without staff. The people who help make the president and his family's lives easier include those who

Presents Talking About the Job

John Adams: "Let me have my farm, family and goose quill, and all the honors and offices this world has to bestow may go to those who deserve them better and desire them more. I court them not."

Andrew Jackson (1821): "I know what I am fit for. I can command a body of men in a rough way; but I am not fit to be President."

James Polk (1847): "The passion for office and the number of unworthy persons who seek to live on the public is increasing beyond former example, and I now predict that no President of the United States of either party will ever again be reelected. The reason is that the patronage of the government will destroy the popularity of any President, however well he may administer the government."

James Buchanan, to successor Abraham Lincoln (1861): "If you are as happy, my dear sir, on entering this house as I am in leaving it and returning home, you are the happiest man in the country."

Abraham Lincoln: "Being President is like the man who was tarred and feathered and ridden out of town on a rail…. A man in the crowd asked how he liked it, and his reply was that if it wasn't for the honor of the thing, he would much rather walk."

Chester Arthur: "I may be President of the United States, but my private life is nobody's damned business."

Grover Cleveland (1892): "Why should I have any desire or purpose to return to the Presidency? I do not want the office. It involves a responsibility beyond human strength to a man who brings conscience to the discharge of his duties."

William Howard Taft (1913): "I'll be glad to be going—this is the loneliest place in the world."

Warren G. Harding (1923): "My God, this is a hell of a job! I have no trouble with my enemies…. But my damn friends, they're the ones that keep me walking the floor nights."

Franklin D. Roosevelt (1932): "The Presidency is not merely an administrative office. That's the least of it. It is more than an engineering job, efficient or inefficient. It is pre-eminently a place of moral leadership."

Harry S. Truman: "Within the first few months, I discovered that being a President is like riding a tiger. A man has to keep on riding or be swallowed."

Richard Nixon (1964): "Character is the most important qualification the President of the United States can have."

cook, serve, clean, sew, wash, chauffeur, feed and walk their pets, place their telephone calls, and do odd jobs around the house. A rotating staff of housekeepers and chief ushers answer directly to the president and the first lady. In *My Turn* (1989), former first lady Nancy Reagan described a brief glimpse of this service: "Every evening, while I took a bath, one of the maids would come by and remove my clothes for laundering or dry cleaning. The bed would always be turned down. Five minutes after Ronnie came home and hung up his suit, it would disappear from the closet to be pressed, cleaned or brushed. No wonder Ron used to call the White House an eight-star hotel."

Before the administration of William Howard Taft, the presidents paid their staffs' wages. Afterward, they were placed on the federal payroll. Nevertheless, the government only pays for state dinners and receptions, and the first family is responsible for paying for its own groceries, as well as incidentals such as dry cleaning and toiletries.

Did any of the **presidents like to do chores** themselves?

Although it is a temporary residence, many presidents quickly adapt to the White House as if were their own home. Upon arriving at the newly built White House, John Adams ordered a garden to be prepared. The third president of the United States, Thomas Jefferson, enjoyed the garden, claiming later that "no occupation is so delightful to me as the culture of the earth, and no culture comparable to that of the garden." Although he grew the majority of his vegetables at his Virginia estate Monticello, Jefferson was known to get his hands dirty in White House soil. John Quincy Adams continued this tradition in the 1820s, when he established a formal gardening program, although he, too, personally planted many of the herbs and vegetables.

President Millard Fillmore tinkered in the kitchen, being the first president to install a modern heating system and new stove in the White House. Noticing that his cooks were working over open fireplaces, Fillmore ordered a large stove, personally installed it, and then guided the kitchen staff through a demonstration of the new appliance. Presidents who liked to cook include Dwight D. Eisenhower, who read cookbooks and called soups and stews his specialty; Gerald Ford, who toasted his own English muffins; and Bill Clinton, who prepared enchiladas. And although William Howard Taft isn't noted in the historical record as a cook, he did insist on fresh milk, and as such kept a cow on the White House lawn to provide his daily supply. He was the last president to do so. It is not a matter of record that presidents and their wives consistently engaged in chores, although Grover Cleveland was known to answer the White House phone personally, Bess Truman cooked and cleaned on the maids' days off, and Jackie Kennedy often moved her own furniture while decorating and rearranging rooms.

What **hobbies** did the presidents engage in?

Rest and recreation break the stress of the president's fast-paced lifestyle. The hobbies of presidents have changed over time, reflecting the evolution of leisure activities for

Americans. George Washington's favorite sports were fox hunting and fishing. John Quincy Adams enjoyed swimming nude in the Potomac River. Andrew Jackson loved to watch a good cockfight. Abraham Lincoln's favorite sport was wrestling. Rutherford B. Hayes was a dedicated hunter and fisherman who loved to play chess. Warren G. Harding played poker at least twice a week, and once gambled away an entire set of expensive White House china. Calvin Coolidge got a kick out of riding mechanical horses—and had one installed in the White House so he could ride at his whim. Richard Nixon liked to bowl. Fortunately for Nixon and many other presidents, they could indulge in pastime pursuits right at the White House—which has been renovated over time to include its own swimming pool, bowling alley, golf area, tennis courts, and movie theater.

In 1933, a heated indoor swimming pool was built in the West Wing for Franklin D. Roosevelt's polio therapy. John F. Kennedy swam daily in the pool, heated to ninety degrees, to alleviate his back pain. After the indoor pool eventually gave way to the construction of a White House pressroom, the Ford administration installed an outdoor pool in 1975. Gerald Ford swam laps in the pool almost daily, and even once hosted a press conference from the pool. In order to satiate his love of golf, Dwight D. Eisenhower had a putting green and bunker installed outside the Oval Office, and discussed the benefits of golf at a 1958 news conference. He joins other avid White House golfers: William Howard Taft, the first president to golf while in office; John F. Kennedy, one of the best of the presidential golfers; and Gerald Ford, George Bush, Bill Clinton, and George W. Bush. Although bowling lanes were first constructed in 1947 in the basement of the West Wing, in 1969 Nixon had a one-lane alley built in an underground workspace below the driveway leading to the North Portico. George Bush invited tennis champions to play with him on the ground's courts, which were first built in 1902 behind the West Wing, and then moved to the south lawn in 1909 to make way for the expansion of executive office space. And because Bill Clinton loved to jog, a jogging track was constructed around the driveway of the south grounds during the president's first term. Other White House amenities include a small movie theater, converted from a long cloakroom, which was installed in the East Wing in 1942, and a game room, complete with billiard and ping-pong tables, which was built in 1970.

Who established a **White House library**?

Although Millard Fillmore (served 1850–1853), the thirteenth president of the United States, is often credited with establishing the White House library, first lady Abigail Fillmore was the brainchild behind its development. Before Fillmore's tenure, there was no permanent collection of books in the White House. Although Fillmore refused an honorary degree from Oxford University on the grounds that he had "neither literary nor scientific attainment," the president felt it was his duty to establish a reading room. Abigail, an avid reader who took immense pleasure in teaching others, urged her husband to obtain the congressional funds necessary to acquire the books. With a

121

special appropriation from Congress, the first lady spent hours selecting books for the upstairs room. More than just a depository for reading materials, the new library hosted small gatherings and prompted lively discussions about the politics of the day. In the 2000s, the refurbished White House library is located on the ground floor.

Do presidents have a **safe place to get away** from it all?

Camp David is the private presidential retreat where presidents can unwind and relax in a private setting with their family and guests. Tucked away in Maryland's Catoctin Mountains, the vast, wooded retreat was envisioned during the administration of Franklin D. Roosevelt as a presidential getaway and originally called Hi-Catoctin. The lands were cleared in 1939 and the Civilian Conservation Corps and the Works Progress Administration—both New Deal programs under Roosevelt—built the retreat, which now includes ten cabins, a lodge, a conference room that seats fifty, a presidential office, a skeet range, and basketball courts. After he assumed office in 1953, Dwight D. Eisenhower renamed the mountain-top establishment Camp David after his grandson.

In addition to being a private getaway for rest and relaxation, Camp David has been the site of historical events. President Eisenhower held his first cabinet meeting at this location, rather than in the White House. Visiting heads of state, such as British prime minister Winston Churchill, Soviet premier Nikita Khrushchev, and Soviet president Leonid Brezhnev, have been entertained there, and the Jimmy Carter–hosted 1978 Middle East peace talks between Israeli prime minister Menachem Begin and Egyptian president Anwar Sadat concluded with the Camp David Accords. President Ronald Reagan spent more time at Camp David than any other president. Besides enjoying horseback riding and woodworking, he and wife Nancy entertained British prime minister Margaret Thatcher. In 2000, Bill Clinton hosted a summit meeting with Palestine Liberation Organization chairman Yasser Arafat and Israeli prime minister Ehud Barak, in an to attempt to resolve the Israeli-Palestinian conflict.

In addition to getting away at Camp David, presidents also enjoy flying in a private jet, *Air Force One,* and sailing on the presidential yacht.

Why did few Americans know about **Franklin D. Roosevelt's paralysis**?

When Franklin D. Roosevelt died on April 12, 1945, few Americans knew how disabled he was and the pains he took to conceal his physical disability, polio. During his earlier political career, Roosevelt denied his disability in order to not compromise public perception of him as a viable candidate, and he continued to hide his condition throughout his presidency, fearing political ramifications. Sitting mostly at his desk or at a lectern, Roosevelt was rarely seen by the public in the wheelchair he used daily for two decades. Reporters and photographers followed an unwritten rule to keep the disability secret, and media appearances were orchestrated with the president seated

Warren G. Harding being photographed in front of the White House with his pet dog Laddie Boy. *Library of Congress.*

or able to reach a podium with minimal movement. Of the more than thirty-five thousand pictures taken of Roosevelt, only two show him in a wheelchair, while political cartoonists did much to dispel the illness myth by drawing him running, jumping, or leaping. The media acquiesced to FDR's public persona primarily because they were continuing an earlier trend of emphasizing the public performance and personality of the president while avoiding his private life.

Who are some of the more famous **White House pets**?

Setting a precedent that would be followed by virtually every president to occupy the White House, George Washington loved animals and kept pets. He never thought twice about dispensing orders to have his staff brush the teeth of his six white horses. Washington didn't live in the White House on Pennsylvania Avenue, but subsequent chief executives either brought their pets with them or acquired new ones.

Thomas Jefferson had a mockingbird that flew freely around the White House unless Jefferson was entertaining guests. The bird, named Dick, rode proudly on Jefferson's shoulder as the president scurried about the White House on official business, even taking bits of food from Jefferson's mouth. Bears brought back from Lewis and Clark's expedition were displayed in cages on the White House lawn, earning the front yard the nickname the "president's bear garden." Indeed, the president's lawn has sometimes resembled a pasture, having been home to Zachary Taylor's horse, Old

123

Whitey, who served the former general in the Mexican War and roamed the grounds freely, and a flock of sheep under Woodrow Wilson's watch, including the president's personal favorite, the tobacco-chewing "Old Ike."

Andrew Jackson was the White House's most serious equestrian. The president owned five horses, including Truxton, a champion racehorse. Jackson was also the proud owner of Poll, a talking parrot who had to be removed from Jackson's funeral ceremony because its word choices were less than appropriate. Martin Van Buren owned two tiger cubs as pets. William Henry Harrison, though he spent only a month in the White House, had a pet goat named His Whiskers, who carted grandson Benjamin "Baby" McKee over the White House grounds. Goats were used by Abraham Lincoln's son to pull his wagon. William McKinley kept a parrot that could whistle "Yankee Doodle." Warren G. Harding enjoyed the company of a pet canary named Bob and a dog named Laddie Boy.

Calvin Coolidge owned numerous dogs and cats, insisting that "any man who does not like dogs and want them about, does not deserve to be in the White House." Coolidge also owned a donkey named Ebenezer, a goose that had starred in a Broadway play, and a raccoon called Rebecca, who occasionally rode on the president's or the first lady's shoulder. Herbert Hoover's son Allan kept a pair of pet alligators in the upstairs bathtub. Franklin D. Roosevelt had a dog named Fala who accompanied the president almost everywhere, including, it is rumored, to the Yalta Conference during World War II. He also had a German shepherd named Major that was famous for biting politicians. Later presidents seem to follow in Roosevelt's footsteps with the conventional dog or cat: Lyndon B. Johnson's famous beagles, Him and Her, provided many Kodak moments for the Washington press corps, including a controversial occasion when the president pulled his dogs up by the ears; Jimmy Carter had a dog named Grits and a Siamese cat called Misty Malarky Ying Yang; George Bush and his wife Barbara loved their dog Millie so much that the first lady "helped" Millie "write" her own book; Bill Clinton owned a cat named Socks and a Labrador retriever named Buddy who were infamous for not getting along; and George W. Bush had two dogs upon entering the White House, a Scottish terrier named Barney and an English springer spaniel named Spot. First lady Laura Bush enjoyed the company of her cat, India.

Why were a **flock of sheep grazing on the White House lawn**?

During Woodrow Wilson's term, a flock of sheep were raised on the White House lawn, where they were free to roam and graze. The flock of eighteen helped with White House expenses during World War I (1914–1918) by trimming the grass. The sheep were fleeced of almost one hundred pounds of raw wool, which was auctioned off for more than $50,000 for the Red Cross. During the war, the White House sheep were only one reminder of the first family's support for the troops and the war effort. The Wilsons discontinued entertaining at the White House and first lady Edith Wilson instituted meatless days, heatless days, and gasless days as America underwent wartime rationing. Mrs. Wilson sang to raise money for the troops, organized celebri-

President Calvin Coolidge with his wife Grace, their two sons, John and Calvin Jr., and their pet white collie named Rob Roy. *Getty Images.*

ty-filled war bond rallies, and spent hours at her sewing machine making pajamas for wounded soldiers in hospital wards.

Which president is called the **"bachelor president?"**

As the only president who never married, James Buchanan (served 1857–1861) is nicknamed the "bachelor president." During the summer of 1819, Buchanan, then a lawyer in Lancaster, Pennsylvania, was engaged to Ann Coleman, the daughter of a wealthy iron manufacturer and one of America's first millionaires. While Coleman's parents questioned Buchanan's reputation (he was dismissed from Dickinson College for poor performance and lack of discipline), they reluctantly endorsed the engagement. During the financial panic of 1819, Buchanan focused more on his law practice than his finances, and rumors circulated about his sincerity. Although the specifics of their tensions are unknown, Coleman quickly called off the engagement, presumably because she felt Buchanan was marrying her for her family's fortunes. When she died a few days later at her sister's home in Philadelphia, rumors circulated that a distraught Coleman had committed suicide. Although Buchanan was denied permission to attend Coleman's funeral, he wrote to her family, "I may sustain the shock of her death, but I feel happiness has fled from me forever." In later years, Buchanan said that he possessed documents and materials that would explain the breakup, although on his deathbed the sealed materials were found with a note that requested they be destroyed. Because Buchanan was a bachelor, his niece, Harriet Lane, served as the official White House hostess during his administration.

125

Gossip about Grover

Grover Cleveland was the only president to enter the White House as a bachelor and leave as a married man. Gossip mongers began swirling news of a presidential romance when Cleveland entertained Emma Folson, a widow, and her daughter Frances, at the White House. The Folsoms went on a European vacation, and Cleveland is alleged to have said about the gossip, "I don't see why the papers keep marrying me to old ladies." When the Folsoms returned to New York, their ship was anxiously awaited by reporters, but the ship was met by a boat chartered by Cleveland's secretary and the Folsoms were sped away to a safe harbor. The next morning, however, news reports featuring stories about Emma Folsom caused the president to issue a statement. The forty-nine-year-old president was indeed engaged, but he was marrying twenty-one-year-old Frances Folsom, not her mother, Emma.

Which presidents have been **married in the White House**?

While John Tyler was the first president to marry while in office (it was his second marriage; his first wife, Letitia, died in September 1842, nearly two years before his marriage to Julia), one man holds the record for the only president to be married in the White House itself. Grover Cleveland, who was both the twenty-second (served 1885–1889) and twenty-fourth (served 1893–1897) president, is the only president to hold his wedding at the White House. In June 1886, the forty-nine-year-old Cleveland, the second bachelor to become president, married twenty-one-year-old Frances Folsom, the daughter of his former law partner, in a private ceremony. While the press speculated whom the "confirmed bachelor" would marry for weeks leading up to the big event, Cleveland kept the public wondering about his bride-to-be. After the wedding, Cleveland sent off two wedding guests in the presidential carriage as a decoy, allowing he and his wife to escape the event.

During the early years of their marriage, the press continued to cover the first lady, especially after she had given birth to their daughter Ruth. Mrs. Cleveland often played with the baby on the White House lawn, which soon became the day's headlines. Ruth became so popular that a candy bar was named after her: Baby Ruth. Despite their age difference, the president and first lady remained married until Cleveland's death in 1908.

Which presidents had **family members as advisers**?

From time to time, presidents have hired family members as their most trusted advisers or appointed them to government posts. George Washington originally appointed John Quincy Adams as minister to the Netherlands and then, later, to Portugal; however, when John Adams became president, he changed his son's appointment to minis-

Campaign as Family Affair

Historian Betty Boyd Caroli notes that "Americans have come to accept the fact that the candidate's wife and children will be packaged as part of the campaign, and a president's family, especially those members who reside in the White House, will be scrutinized, tutored, and implicated in any evaluation of an administration. The presidency now seems to extend to the entire family. How else can we explain the public attention given to Amy Carter's school choice, Nancy Reagan's wardrobe, and Chelsea Clinton's cat?"

ter to Prussia. Adams served as minister to Prussia during his father's entire administration, from 1797 to 1801, during which he finalized the Prussian-American Treaty of 1799. In the nineteenth century, it was accepted practice for the president and other dignitaries to use their close relatives as private secretaries. The president was given no public money beyond his salary, so having a family member serve this key role undoubtedly cut down on expenses. John Quincy Adams hired his son, John II, as his secretary in 1825, although the younger Adams frequently bickered with the Washington press. Likewise, Martin Van Buren's oldest son, Abraham, served as his father's private secretary during the president's term from 1837 to 1841, as did James Hayes, Rutherford B. Hayes's son, for his father. James Buchanan hired his nephew, James Buchanan Henry, as his private secretary.

In the twentieth century, President Dwight D. Eisenhower often consulted his brother, Milton Eisenhower, president of Johns Hopkins University, who was an unofficial adviser to the president. However, most people recall John F. Kennedy when it comes to the subject of nepotism: Kennedy was the only president to appoint a family member to a cabinet post. Robert F. Kennedy served as attorney general from 1961 to 1964, under both JFK and his successor, Lyndon B. Johnson.

Which presidents' **children grew up in the White House**?

Generally speaking, when a president wins the election, his entire family takes office. While the first lady has typically assumed the most celebrated role, first families have received their share of both praise and criticism. For those presidents who had younger families at the time of their electoral victory, the family typically moved into the White House with them.

Thomas (Tad) Lincoln, the youngest son of Abraham Lincoln, was known for his practical jokes. He once discovered how to make all of the White House bells ring at the same time, much to the chagrin of the White House staff. He often played dress-up in a Union Army uniform, bombarding the house with a toy cannon. He once accused and convicted a doll for insubordination, upon which President Lincoln wrote a note

Tad Lincoln, the youngest son of Abraham Lincoln, standing next to his father in 1864. *Library of Congress.*

pardoning the doll. Irvin and Abram Garfield were ages eleven and nine when their father, James A. Garfield, assumed the presidency. Although the Garfields lived only a few months in the White House before the president's assassination in 1881, the boys still had time to throw pillow fights in the East Room and race their "big-wheels" (called velocipedes) on the slick wood floors. Theodore Roosevelt's raucous family turned the White House upside down, and anecdotes of the Roosevelt children's antics abound. The younger children roller-skated through hallways and shot spitballs at presidential portraits. When one of Roosevelt's sons, Archie, got the measles and was bedridden, his brother Quentin smuggled the family pony onto an elevator and into Archie's upstairs bedroom.

Despite glimpses into the lives of these and other first children, it was John F. Kennedy's two young children, Caroline and John Jr., who were consistently courted by the press. Human-interest stories of the children's visits to their father's Oval Office (including the infamous photo of John Jr. hiding under the president's desk, which the boy called "my house"), the president's doting upon his children, and the children's pets—including Caroline's pony named Macaroni—made headlines and catapulted the children into the spotlight. Since Kennedy's tenure, other celebrated White House children include President Richard Nixon's children, Tricia and Julie, who along with Julie's husband, David Eisenhower (the grandson of President Dwight D. Eisenhower), enjoyed family many dinners in the White House, and stood by Nixon during the darker days of the Watergate scandal; Amy, President Jimmy Carter's daughter, who moved into the White House at the age of nine, and whose treehouse summer slumber parties were closely guarded by the Secret Service; and Bill Clinton's daughter Chelsea, who traveled with her parents and was buffered from constant attention. George W. Bush's twin daughters, Barbara and Jenna, were away at college for most of their father's 2001–2005 term. They joined him on the campaign trail in 2004.

Which presidents had **children who grew up to be successful in politics**?

Two presidents' sons became presidents themselves: John Quincy Adams in 1825 and George W. Bush in 2001. William Henry Harrison's grandson, Benjamin Harrison,

President John F. Kennedy's children's visits to their father's Oval Office made headlines and catapulted the children into the media spotlight. *AP/Wide World Photos.*

claimed the presidency in 1888, making the pair the only grandfather and grandson to have reached the nation's highest public office. Other presidents' children have also tried their hand at politics, including John Quincy Adams' youngest son, Charles, who served in the U.S. House of Representatives from 1859 to 1861; Abraham Lincoln's oldest son, Robert, who became secretary of war under James A. Garfield and Chester Alan Arthur and minister to Great Britain under Benjamin Harrison; both of Garfield's sons, Harry and James, whose careers included posts in the U.S. Food Administration during World War I and the U.S. Department of Commerce and Labor, respectively; and William Howard Taft's son, Robert, who served as U.S. senator from Ohio from 1939 to 1953. Franklin D. Roosevelt's oldest son, James, participated in politics, serving several terms in the U.S. House of Representatives in the 1950s and 1960s. George Bush's son Jeb was elected governor of Florida in 1999 and reelected in 2002.

Of the twenty-six living children of U.S. presidents, several have made a mark for themselves, though not necessarily in politics. One of the most established is Michael Reagan, the adopted son of President Ronald Reagan and his first wife, actress Jane Wyman. Reagan hosts a nationally syndicated radio talk show and enjoyed success in his first career as a champion power-boat racer. Caroline Kennedy Schlossberg, daughter of John F. Kennedy, is an author and president of the Kennedy Library Foundation. Schlossberg's brother, John, founded and ran a political magazine, *George,* before he died in a plane crash in 1999. Amy Carter is a board member at the Carter Center, the human rights and diplomacy organization established by her father, President Jimmy Carter. After graduating from Stanford University in 2001, President Bill Clinton's daughter, Chelsea, earned a master's degree in international relations from Oxford University. In 2003, she joined the New York consulting firm McKinsey and Company, earning a reported six-figure salary.

PRESIDENTIAL ADMINISTRATIONS

EARLY ADMINISTRATIONS

What is a **president's administration**?

A president's administration primarily refers to the tenure of the president; that is, the happenings of the president and his staff during the president's term of office. A detailed discussion of a president's administration rests on an understanding of the structure of the executive branch. Almost three million Americans work in the executive branch, which includes fifteen cabinet-level departments and more than fifty independent agencies and commissions comprised of two thousand bureaus, divisions, branches, and other government subunits. Executive departments—like the Department of Defense or the Department of Justice—tend to be the largest federal organizations with the broadest directives. Independent agencies and commissions, such as the U.S. Postal Service, the Central Intelligence Agency, and the National Aeronautics and Space Administration (NASA), tend to be smaller and have more narrowed responsibilities. While the executive departments are directly beholden to the president, the independent agencies and regulatory commissions are more independent and do not come under the direct, immediate authority of the president.

What was the **first administration** like?

As America's first president, George Washington was responsible for creating and developing a strong central government that could accommodate the diverse needs of the new country. Congress quickly created the Department of State and the Department of Treasury. Washington appointed Thomas Jefferson as secretary of state and Alexander Hamilton as secretary of the treasury. Congress established the federal judiciary—setting up a Supreme Court with one Chief Justice (John Jay) and five associate

President George Washington (left) and his cabinet members (from left): Henry Knox, secretary of war; Alexander Hamilton, secretary of the treasury; Thomas Jefferson, secretary of state; and Edmund Randolph, attorney general. *AP/Wide World Photos.*

justices—as well as three circuit courts and thirteen district courts. Congress also established a Post Office Department.

In the first administration, Washington appointed both a secretary of war (Henry Knox) and an attorney general (Edmund Randolph). Because Washington generally preferred to make decisions only after consulting key men, he embraced three leaders whom he could trust—Jefferson, Hamilton, and Knox—as his personal "cabinet" of advisers. Thus, the American cabinet was born, consisting of the heads of any executive departments that Congress might approve. Especially in his first term as president from 1789 to 1793, Washington's nationwide popularity and stature as a leader greater enhanced the legitimacy of the executive office and the national government as a whole.

How have **presidential administrations changed**?

In his book *The Federalists* (1956), scholar Leonard White described the beginnings of the federal government of 1790 as a "foreign office with John Jay and a couple of clerks to deal with correspondence from [Vice President] John Adams and [Secretary of State] Thomas Jefferson in London." Since that time, administrations have grown more bureaucratic and complex. As early as Thomas Jefferson's term, presidents have been promising to downsize government, although it became virtually impossible in the early years as Jefferson's Louisiana Purchase (1803) doubled the size of the United States. The Louisiana Purchase was a key event that introduced corruption into the federal government, through the General Land Office's clerks who set aside the best pieces of land for themselves. The corruption eventually climaxed into the public awareness and anger that moved Democrat Andrew Jackson into office in 1828. Jackson's administration was responsible for cleaning house and introducing the "spoils system" into government, which maintained that party loyalists should be rewarded to key federal posts. Jackson defended his decision to replace hundreds of officials on the grounds that it furthered democracy to replace government leaders with "new blood" every few years. Jackson insisted that a newly elected president needs officials whom he can trust to carry out executive decisions, an argument that has pervaded to this day. No matter what President Jackson's intentions, the spoils system ignited a wave of future administration bribery and poor job performance that continued through much of the nineteenth century.

In 1881, President James A. Garfield attempted to return prestige to the executive office by fighting corruption. Garfield's successor, Chester Alan Arthur, pressured Congress to pass the Pendleton Act, which set up a merit system for evaluating and hiring federal employees. Though presidents of the twentieth century have generally chosen their administration officials and advisers on merit, the shaping of an administration is a highly personalized creation. The president makes high-level political appointments based on a variety of qualifications, including past accomplishments, diplomatic skill, partisanship, talent, and personality. At the same time, presidents use the appointment process to establish links to powerful political and economic constituencies. Increasingly, the White House staff, composed mainly of analysts and advisers, has played a critical role in the management of the administration. Like other parts of the federal government, its size and role have grown.

What role does the **White House staff** play?

The White House office houses the White House staff—key personnel and political staff whose offices are located in the East and West wings of the White House. The White House staff exists to help the president carry out his role of chief executive. The chief of staff directs the president's more than four hundred staff members. The staff includes the president's most trusted aides, the counsel to the president, a number of senior advisers, and top officials who work with the president in the areas of foreign policy, the economy, national health care, the media, and defense. It also includes the president's press secretary, the president's physician, and the staff of the first lady. Of these, the most important positions are the chief of staff, the special counsel, the national security adviser, the press secretary, the domestic policy adviser, and the personnel office director.

ROLE OF THE VICE PRESIDENT

What is the **role of the vice president**?

The limited role of the vice president is introduced in Article II, Section 1, of the U.S. Constitution, which provides that the president "shall hold his Office during the Term of four Years … together with the Vice President.…" In addition to his role as president of the U.S. Senate, the vice president is empowered to succeed to the presidency, according to Article II and the Twentieth and Twenty-fifth Amendments to the Constitution. His right of succession has often been mentioned as his most coveted privilege. The executive functions of the vice president include participation in cabinet meetings and, by statute, membership on the National Security Council and the Board of Regents of the Smithsonian Institution.

Although the Constitution spends little time assigning any roles to the office of vice president and traditionally the office has not been highly regarded, more recent presidents have assigned larger roles to their vice presidents. These include advising the president in domestic and foreign policy matters and carrying out a host of political and diplomatic duties in the name of the executive office. However, one of the reasons that the vice presidency has not increased in scope beyond its present-day definition is because, unlike other members of the president's staff, the vice president is not subject to removal from office at the hand of the president. Under no circumstances may the president formally remove his vice president.

What are the **qualifications for vice president**?

The qualifications for vice president are the same as the president. According to the constitutional requirements for the president outlined in Article II, Section 1, of the U.S. Constitution, the vice president must be a natural-born citizen, at least thirty-five years old, and have been a resident of the United States for at least fourteen years.

What were the **first vice presidents** like?

The nation's first two vice presidents, John Adams and Thomas Jefferson, acquired the office as runners-up in presidential contests, with the support of party members who believed they were qualified to hold the executive office. However, in assuming the new and largely undefined position of vice president, each man had to carve out his own niche—particularly because the Constitution assigns few responsibilities to the vice president other than breaking a tie vote in the U.S. Senate. Adams summed up the role when he said, "I am Vice President, in this I am nothing, but may be everything."

During his two vice presidential terms under President George Washington (served 1789–1797), Adams maintained a cordial, but distant, relationship with the president, who asked his advice only occasionally. In the Senate, Adams played a more active role, persuading senators to vote against legislation he opposed, and he frequently lectured the body on procedural and policy matters. Unlike Adams, who shared the political ideology of his president, Thomas Jefferson and his president (John Adams, in fact) belonged to different political parties. Instead of aligning himself with President Adams, Jefferson spent his four-year term (served 1797–1801) strengthening the organization of the Democratic-Republican Party and preparing himself for a presidential victory in the election of 1800. As the Senate's presiding officer, Jefferson drafted a guidebook on legislative procedures, *A Manual of Parliamentary Practice,* which members of Congress still consult today.

Who were some **notable nineteenth-century vice presidents**?

During the nineteenth century, the vice presidency was essentially a legislative position. Those who held it rarely attended cabinet meetings or became involved in executive branch business. Their benefit to the president—in terms of attracting voters from key regions of the country—generally ended with the election. The vice presidency seldom led to the White House, primarily because vice presidents of the era were seldom men of presidential stature. Of the twenty-one men who held that office from 1805 to 1899, only Martin Van Buren was elected president (served 1837–1841). Despite these realities, several men deserve mention for their actions or precedents as vice presidents.

The committee members chosen to draft the Declaration of Independence in 1776: from left to right, Benjamin Franklin, Thomas Jefferson, John Adams, Philip Livingston, and Roger Sherman. Adams and Jefferson later served as president and vice president despite being from two different political parties. They would not speak to each other for more than a decade after Jefferson defeated the incumbent Adams in the 1800 presidential election. *AP/Wide World Photos.*

John C. Calhoun, vice president (served 1825–1832) under both John Quincy Adams and Andrew Jackson, is best known for his theory of nullification, which proposed that a state could nullify, or disregard, a federal law it believed was harmful to its interests. This theory helped link the ideas of slavery, states rights, and secession together in the antebellum South. Calhoun resigned from the vice presidency near the

135

end of Jackson's first term after he was elected to the U.S. Senate from South Carolina, where he became one of the leading voices during the second quarter of the nineteenth century until his death in 1850.

Richard Mentor Johnson, Martin Van Buren's vice president (served 1837–1841), was the only vice president to assume office via a vote of the Senate because he did not receive the necessary number of electoral votes to win. Johnson was a controversial figure who had openly acknowledged his slave mistress and mulatto daughters and spent more time attending to the customers of his tavern than his Senate duties.

Johnson's successor as vice president, John Tyler, was the first to succeed to the presidency following the death of a president. (William Henry Harrison died after only a month as president.) Tyler rejected the concept that he was an "acting president," and established himself as president in his own right by holding to his political convictions. His boldness in claiming the full duties and benefits of a president set an important precedent. Almost a decade later, when Vice President Millard Fillmore succeeded to the presidency after Zachary Taylor's death in 1850, no serious question was raised about his role as president.

Several vice presidents took their job of residing over the Senate very seriously. Individuals such as George Dallas (served 1845–1849 under James K. Polk), Levi Morton (served 1889–1893 under Benjamin Harrison), and Garret Hobart (served 1897–1899 under William McKinley) studied the Senate's rules and precedents and were effective presiding officers. Others, such as Henry Wilson (served 1873–1875 as Ulysses S. Grant's second vice president), turned their attentions elsewhere. For example, Wilson authored a three-volume history of slavery before dying in office in 1875.

How has the **role of the vice president evolved in the twentieth century**?

The role of the vice president has evolved over time, reflecting the personality, priorities, and the management style of various presidents. The office has become more visible since the mid-twentieth century, beginning with Richard Nixon's vice presidency. Nixon folded into President Dwight D. Eisenhower's desire to remain above the political fray and to create a much more active vice president. In the years since, presidents have relied to a greater or lesser extent on their vice presidents. Of the late-twentieth-century presidents, President Jimmy Carter was the first to give his vice president, Walter Mondale, more than ceremonial duties, and Mondale became a close adviser to the president. Vice presidents have become major players in the administration, influencing policy. For example, Ronald Reagan entrusted Vice President George Bush, a former director of the Central Intelligence Agency, with heading the National Security Crisis Management team. When he succeeded to the presidency, Bush appointed Vice President Dan Quayle as chair of the National Space Council. Vice President Al Gore played an important role as a general adviser to President Bill Clinton, and headed Clinton's initiative of reinventing government. Vice President Dick Cheney broke new ground in 2001 by heading the presidential transition team and helping staff the new

> ## "I Will Indeed Be Your Moses!"
>
> **D**uring the difficult campaign for Abraham Lincoln's reelection in 1864, vice presidential hopeful Andrew Johnson did much to endear voters. At the urging of the renowned Republican orator Robert Ingersoll, who insisted "the people want to see and hear you," Johnson reached out to large numbers of voters. Historian Mark O. Hatfield, in a book he penned with the Senate Historical Office, *Vice Presidents of the United States, 1789–1993* (1997), put it this way:
>
> > Late in October 1864 [Johnson] addressed a large rally of African Americans in Nashville. Johnson noted that, since Lincoln's emancipation proclamation had not covered territories like Tennessee that were already under Union control, he had issued his own proclamation freeing the slaves in Tennessee. He also asserted that society would be improved if the great plantations were divided into many small farms and sold to honest farmers. Looking out over the crowd and commenting on the storm of persecution through which his listeners had passed, he wished that a Moses might arise to "lead them safely to their promised land of freedom and happiness." "You are our Moses," shouted people in the crowd. "We want no Moses but you!" "Well, then," replied Johnson, "humble and unworthy as I am, if no other better shall be found, I will indeed be your Moses, and lead you through the Red Sea of war and bondage, to a fairer future of liberty and peace."

Bush administration. In the aftermath of the September 11, 2001, terrorist attacks, President George W. Bush relied heavily on his vice president, drawing on Cheney's experience as secretary of defense during the 1991 Gulf War (during Bush's father's administration) and chief of staff (during Gerald Ford's administration) to help deal with the tragedy. Indications are that the importance of the vice presidential role will continue in 2005 and beyond with either Cheney or John Kerry's running mate, U.S. senator John Edwards of North Carolina.

Has there ever been a **president / vice president team from different parties**?

Only two times in American history has a president and his running mate been from different political parties. John Adams, the second president of the United States, was a Federalist, and his vice president, Thomas Jefferson, was a Democratic-Republican. In the election of 1796, Jefferson ran against Adams for president. Because Jefferson received the second highest number of electoral votes, he automatically became vice president under the electoral system rules that existed at the time. The second president to have a vice president from another party was Republican Abraham Lincoln, whose reelection campaign of 1864 saw Andrew Johnson, the tough-minded war governor of Tennessee who had remained loyal to the Union, as Lincoln's running mate. Johnson was a War Democrat who ran on a fusion ticket with President Lincoln.

Has there ever been a **woman vice president**?

In the history of the United States, only men have held the office of vice president. However, women have been considered as vice presidential running mates as early as 1924. In 1984, Democrat Walter Mondale ran with U.S. representative Geraldine Ferraro of New York, marking the first time a woman had been nominated as a running mate on a major-party ticket. In 2000, attention focused on both Republican George W. Bush and Democrat Al Gore, both of whom considered women as vice-president running mates, although they ultimately decided to run with men. According to *USA Today,* "Vice presidential nominees are typically considered from two groups—people who have run for president themselves and governors. And despite women's advancement through the ranks of politics, very few women fall into either group."

Is the **vice president automatically next in line for the presidency**?

Yes. The vice president serves concurrently with the president and holds the right of succession. According to the Twenty-fifth Amendment, adopted in 1967, the vice president succeeds to the office if the president dies, resigns, or is removed from office by impeachment. The amendment details the specific conditions under which the vice president is empowered to take over the office of president if the president should become incapacitated. It also provides for resumption of the office by the president in the event of his recovery. In addition, the amendment enables the president to name a vice president, with congressional approval, when the second office is vacated.

Under what circumstances have **vice presidents assumed the presidency**?

Out of the forty-six men who have served as vice president, fourteen have reached the presidency. In fact, the majority of those vice presidents have assumed the presidency after the natural death, assassination, or resignation of a sitting president. Two vice presidents, Hannibal Hamlin and Henry Wallace, were dropped from the ticket after their first term, only to see their successors become president months after taking office, when the assassination of Abraham Lincoln made Andrew Johnson president in 1865 and the death of Franklin D. Roosevelt elevated Harry S. Truman to the presidency in 1945. Before Theodore Roosevelt, none of the four vice presidents who replaced a sitting president went on to win election to a full term in his own right. Roosevelt was vice president to President William McKinley from March to September 1901, when McKinley was assassinated, leading to Roosevelt's ascension to the presidency. The enormously popular Roosevelt easily won the Republican Party's nomination and

presidential election in 1904. After Roosevelt, three other vice presidents who replaced

Twenty-fifth Amendment

In 1967, the Twenty-Fifth Amendment was adopted, addressing presidential disability and succession.

1. In case of the removal of the President from office or of his death or resignation, the Vice President shall become President.

2. Whenever there is a vacancy in the office of the Vice President, the President shall nominate a Vice President who shall take office upon confirmation by a majority vote of both Houses of Congress.

3. Whenever the President transmits to the President pro tempore of the Senate and the Speaker of the House of Representatives his written declaration that he is unable to discharge the powers and duties of his office, and until he transmits to them a written declaration to the contrary, such powers and duties shall be discharged by the Vice President as Acting President.

4. Whenever the Vice President and a majority of either the principal officers of the executive departments or of such other body as Congress may by law provide, transmit to the President pro tempore of the Senate and the Speaker of the House of Representatives their written declaration that the President is unable to discharge the powers and duties of his office, the Vice President shall immediately assume the powers and duties of the office as Acting President.

Thereafter, when the President transmits to the President pro tempore of the Senate and the Speaker of the House of Representatives his written declaration that no inability exists, he shall resume the powers and duties of his office unless the Vice President and a majority of either the principal officers of the executive department or of such other body as Congress may by law provide, transmit within four days to the President pro tempore of the Senate and the Speaker of the House of Representatives their written declaration that the President is unable to discharge the powers and duties of his office. Thereupon Congress shall decide the issue, assembling within forty eight hours for that purpose if not in session. If the Congress, within twenty one days after receipt of the latter written declaration, or, if Congress is not in session, within twenty one days after Congress is required to assemble, determines by two thirds vote of both Houses that the President is unable to discharge the powers and duties of his office, the Vice President shall continue to discharge the same as Acting President; otherwise, the President shall resume the powers and duties of his office.

presidents who died in office won subsequent elections to a full four-year term: Calvin Coolidge, Harry S. Truman, and Lyndon B. Johnson.

How many **vice presidents have been elected to the presidency directly after completion of their vice presidential term**?

Only four men. In the eighteenth century, the only two vice presidents advanced to the presidency by election directly after completing their vice presidential term: John Adams in 1796 and Thomas Jefferson in 1800. In the nineteenth century, only Martin Van Buren in 1836 claimed this accomplishment. And the same is true for the twentieth century: Only George Bush, in 1988, was elected to the presidency directly after completing his vice presidential term.

Which **vice presidents were temporarily in charge of the presidency**?

When President Dwight D. Eisenhower was out of town, Vice President Richard Nixon presided over cabinet meetings. He also presided over White House meetings when President Eisenhower was recuperating from a heart attack in 1955. At this time, there was no constitutional language for the transfer of power from a disabled president to the vice president, which only came with the ratification of the Twenty-fifth Amendment in 1967. While Eisenhower was hospitalized in Denver, Colorado, his adviser Sherman Adams spent most weekdays with him, then flew to Washington for the Friday cabinet meetings held by Nixon. Similarly, after an assassination attempt on President Ronald Reagan in March 1981, Vice President George Bush worked closely with the recuperating president to keep the government running smoothly. He routinely presided over cabinet meetings and met with staff members, members of Congress, and others for about two weeks until President Reagan returned. On July 13, 1985, presidential powers were transferred to Bush for an eight-hour period, during which President Reagan underwent intestinal-cancer surgery.

Has a **vice president ever resigned**?

Yes, two vice presidents have resigned. John C. Calhoun resigned on December 28, 1832, three months before his term expired, to become senator from South Carolina. Spiro T. Agnew resigned on October 10, 1973, after pleading no contest to a charge of federal income tax evasion. Following Agnew's resignation, President Richard Nixon nominated Gerald Ford, the minority leader of the House, to fill the vice presidential vacancy. In accordance with the provisions of the Twenty-fifth Amendment under which Ford was nominated, the Senate and House approved the nomination and Ford was sworn into office on December 6, 1973. On August 9, 1974, less than a year later, Ford became president following Nixon's resignation. Shortly thereafter, Ford nominated Nelson A. Rockefeller to be vice president, who was confirmed and sworn into office on December 19, 1974. Thus, in about one year, two situations arose for using the provisions of the Twenty-fifth Amendment to fill a vacancy in the vice presidency.

President Gerald Ford (right) and Vice President Nelson Rockefeller ran the U.S. government from 1974 to 1977 without being elected to their posts as president and vice president. Both reached office under the provisions of the Twenty-fifth Amendment. *AP/Wide World Photos.*

When was the **first—and only—time that a president/vice president team was not elected by the people**?

The Gerald Ford/Nelson Rockefeller team ran the U.S. federal government from 1974 to 1977 without being elected to their posts as president and vice president. Both reached office under the provisions of the Twenty-fifth Amendment.

Under the Richard Nixon presidency, Vice President Spiro Agnew resigned on October 10, 1973, leaving the position vacant. In accordance with the Twenty-fifth Amendment, President Nixon nominated Gerald Ford, House Republican leader from Michigan, as his vice president. Upon Senate confirmation, Ford assumed that role until President Nixon resigned the presidency, and Ford assumed the nation's highest executive office. Ford was then left to nominate a vice president, choosing Nelson Rockefeller on August 20, 1974. After protracted hearings, Rockefeller was sworn in on December 19, 1974, as the new vice president of the United States.

How is **Richard Nixon a vice presidential and presidential first**?

Richard Nixon is the only person to serve two terms as vice president and be elected to two terms as president. He served as vice president for Dwight D. Eisenhower from 1953 to 1961 and served as president from 1969 to 1974, when he resigned from office under the threat of impeachment. Nixon is the only vice president to win election to

Vacancies in the Vice Presidency

James Madison was twice left without a vice president. His first-term vice president, George Clinton, died in 1812, leaving the vice presidency vacant until 1813. Madison's second-term vice president, Elbridge Gerry, died in 1814, leaving the vice presidency vacant until 1817.

Andrew Jackson's first-term vice president, John C. Calhoun, resigned from office in December 1832 after being elected as a U.S. senator from South Carolina. The position was not filled for the remainder of Jackson' term.

John Tyler was William Henry Harrison's vice president in 1841. When Tyler assumed the presidency after Harrison's death, the position of vice president was not filled.

Millard Fillmore was Zachary Taylor's vice president from 1849 to 1850. The position was not filled when Fillmore assumed the presidency.

Franklin Pierce won the presidency in the election of 1852. At the time, his vice presidential running mate, William Rufus DeVane King, was terminally ill with tuberculosis. Although King was sworn in as vice president (in Cuba, where he was seeking medical treatment), he died before assuming his duties as vice president and was not replaced.

Andrew Johnson was Abraham Lincoln's vice president from March to April 1865. When Johnson succeeded to the presidency upon Lincoln's assassination, the position of vice president was not filled.

Ulysses S. Grant's second-term vice president, Henry Wilson, died in office in 1875 and was not replaced, leaving Grant without a vice president for more than a year.

Chester Alan Arthur was James A. Garfield's vice president, and the position was not filled when Arthur assumed the presidency.

Grover Cleveland's first-term vice president, Thomas Hendricks, was not replaced after dying in 1885, just nine months into his term.

William McKinley's first vice president, Garret Hobart, died in office in 1899, and was not replaced until March 1901, when Theodore Roosevelt became vice president.

Theodore Roosevelt served as William McKinley's second-term vice president from March 1901 until September 1901. When Roosevelt assumed the presidency after McKinley's assassination, the position of vice president was not filled until Roosevelt was elected for his own term as president in 1904.

William Howard Taft's vice president, James Sherman, died in 1912, shortly before the end of Taft's term, and was not replaced.

Calvin Coolidge served as Warren G. Harding's vice president from 1921 to 1923. When Coolidge assumed the presidency after Harding's sudden death, the position of vice president was not filled until Coolidge was elected for his own term as president in 1924.

Harry S. Truman served as Franklin D. Roosevelt's last vice president, from January to April 1945. When Truman assumed the presidency after FDR's death, the vice presidential position was not filled until Truman ran for the presidency in 1948.

Lyndon B. Johnson was John F. Kennedy's vice president. When Johnson assumed the presidency upon JFK's death in 1963, the vice president's position was not filled until Johnson was elected for his own term as president in 1964.

Richard Nixon's first vice president, Spiro Agnew, resigned in December 1973, nearly nine months into his second term in office due to a tax scandal. Gerald Ford was approved as Agnew's successor almost two months later.

Gerald Ford was Nixon's vice president from December 6, 1973, to August 9, 1974, when he became president following Nixon's resignation as president. Nelson Rockefeller was approved as Ford's vice president about four months later.

the presidency after losing a previous election for the presidency. He was defeated in 1960 by Democrat John F. Kennedy.

THE PRESIDENT'S CABINET AND ADVISERS

What is the **president's cabinet**?

The president's cabinet is comprised of the chief administrators, or secretaries, of the major departments of the federal government. The president's cabinet has been commonly regarded as an institution whose existence has relied more upon custom than law. Article II, Section 2 of the U.S. Constitution indirectly provides for the cabinet, by stating that the president "may require the Opinion, in writing, of the principal Officer in each of the executive Departments, upon any subject relating to the Duties of their respective Offices." The historical origins of the cabinet can be traced to the first president, George Washington. After the first Congress created the state, treasury, and war departments and established the office of the attorney general, Washington made

143

appropriate appointments and, subsequently, found it useful to meet with the heads of the executive departments. These executive department secretaries, who came to be known collectively as the "cabinet" by about 1793, were envisioned by Washington to be the president's primary advisory group. In practice, however, presidents have used their cabinets, along with other advisers and ad-hoc arrangements, as they deemed necessary. The cabinet often meets as a group, but does not make decisions as a collective body. Because cabinet terms are not fixed, any secretary may be replaced at any time by the president.

Who makes up the cabinet?

Traditionally, the membership of the cabinet has consisted of the heads of the executive departments. All executive departments are headed by a secretary, except the Department of Justice, which is headed by the attorney general. Cabinet secretaries are appointed by the president with the consent of the Senate. A department secretary cannot be a member of Congress or hold any other elected office. In President George W. Bush's administration, there are fifteen departments: the Departments of Agriculture, Commerce, Defense, Education, Energy, Health and Human Services, Homeland Security, Housing and Urban Development, the Interior, Justice, Labor, State, Transportation, the Treasury, and Veterans Affairs. From the earliest days, presidents have also included others in cabinet meetings; in recent years, the vice president, the president's chief of staff, the director of Central Intelligence, and the director of the Office of Management and Budget, among others, have been accorded cabinet-level rank. In addition, under Bush, cabinet-level rank has been accorded to the administrator of the Environmental Protection Agency, the director of the Office of Management and Budget, the director of the National Drug Control Policy, and the U.S. trade representative.

Which were the first and last executive departments to be created?

The first four departments were created during the administration of George Washington: the Department of State, the Department of the Treasury, the Department of War (now called the Department of Defense), and the Department of Justice were all created in 1789. With the signing of his Homeland Security Act of 2002 by President George W. Bush, the Department of Homeland Security was created. The new department combines all or parts of 22 existing federal agencies and employs approximately 170,000 workers. It also represents the largest reorganization of the U.S. government since President Harry S. Truman reorganized the Department of War into the Department of Defense in 1947.

What is a "kitchen cabinet"?

The term "kitchen cabinet" refers to a president's group of informal advisers. Sometimes, members of a kitchen cabinet are also members of the official cabinet. The term dates to the administration of Andrew Jackson, who regularly consulted his kitchen cabinet during the early years of his first administration, from 1829 to 1831. Jackson felt it necessary to turn to a key group of men he could trust because his official cabinet was rife with factionalism, primarily due to the rivalry between Vice President John C. Calhoun and Secretary of State Martin Van Buren. Jackson's kitchen cabinet consisted of two members of his official cabinet, Van Buren and Secretary of War John H. Eaton, and influential men from the business community, including Amos Kendall, a journalist and later postmaster general, *Washington Globe* editor Francis P. Blair, and Andrew Jackson Donelson, the president's nephew and secretary. It wasn't long before Jackson abandoned regular cabinet meetings altogether, and instead turned to his kitchen cabinet to formulate policy. The group reportedly held its meetings in the White House kitchen, thus the origin of the term.

What were the **early presidential cabinets like**?

George Washington's cabinet consisted of four members: Thomas Jefferson, secretary of state; Alexander Hamilton, secretary of the treasury; Henry Knox, secretary of war; and Edmund Randolph, attorney general. These four men were truly Washington's advisers, though two of them, Jefferson and Hamilton, were notable for their ideologies and ways of doing business. Jefferson believed in a strict interpretation of the Constitution to limit the powers of the central government and conserve states' rights; Hamilton believed in a broad interpretation of the Constitution to strengthen the central government. When George Washington's vice president, John Adams, was elected to the presidency in 1796, he retained Washington's cabinet, truly a rarity in presidential administrations. Jefferson had resigned as secretary of state and was elected Adams's vice president. Hamilton emerged as the leader of the cabinet and advocated more aggressive federal policies than Adams. By 1798–1799, Adams's cabinet was clearly working against his policies, although Adams did create a Department of the Navy and managed to avoid war with France with his Treaty of 1800. The treaty negotiations split the Federalist Party, leading to the dismissal of key cabinet members, and resulted in a Democratic-Republican Party victory with the election of Thomas Jefferson in 1800.

How has the **cabinet system evolved in the twentieth century**?

Twentieth-century presidents have varied in their reliance upon cabinet members. Some presidents, such as Harry S. Truman and Dwight D. Eisenhower, met often with their cabinets, especially at the beginning of their terms. Eisenhower in particular made great use of his cabinet, preparing detailed agendas for cabinet meetings and appointing a cabinet secretary. While Eisenhower was known for delegating responsibilities and being spared administrative detail, Truman was willing to steer clear of departmental matters but insisted on having the final say when it came to policy decisions. Other presidents did not rely on cabinet members' advice or hold regular cabinet meetings. John F. Kennedy, Lyndon B. Johnson, and Richard Nixon all preferred small conferences with key advisers and individuals involved with a particular issue and rarely held cabinet meetings. Some presidents were selective: Woodrow Wilson took little interest in domestic administrative matters after his initial programs were enacted and World War I erupted in his second year in office. Instead, Wilson preferred to appoint trustworthy secretaries to carry out the day's duties. When it came to foreign affairs, Wilson was intricately involved with the work of the state department, much to the dismay of Wilson's secretary of state, William Jennings Bryan, who remained in the post only two years.

Both Jimmy Carter and Ronald Reagan tried to revive the concept of the cabinet as a presidential advisory team, and as such met frequently with their cabinets during their first two years in office. Nevertheless, several of Carter's cabinet members resigned in 1979, suggesting his administration lacked focus. President George W. Bush showed a preference for calling together small groups of cabinet members as needed. Some presidents have relied on an "inner cabinet," the National Security Council (NSC). The NSC was established by law in 1947 and is made up of the president; the vice president; the secretaries of state, defense, and the Treasury; the attorney general; and other key officials. Indeed, the head of the NSC has gained cabinet-level rank in most of the late-twentieth-century administrations.

How many **women and minorities** have served in the **president's cabinet** to date?

Through George W. Bush's present administration, only a few dozen people of color have held cabinet posts. While Bill Clinton chose more women, more African Americans, and more Hispanics than any of his predecessors, Bush's administration has followed suit with a broad mix of women and people of color. In fact, seventeen of the twenty-nine women who have been in the cabinet or in cabinet-level positions were appointed by either President Clinton or President Bush.

Bush's cabinet included three women (Secretary of Agriculture Ann M. Veneman, Secretary of Interior Gale Norton, and Secretary of Labor Elaine Chao), three African Americans (Secretary of State Colin Powell, Secretary of Housing and Urban Development Alphonso Jackson, and Secretary of Education Rod Paige), and two Asian Americans (Secretary of Labor Chao and Secretary of Transportation Norman Mineta). With her appointment, Chao became the first Asian American woman to serve in a cabinet post. Mineta was the first Asian Pacific American to serve in a president's cabinet when he began his stint as secretary of commerce under President Clinton. Another African American, Condoleezza Rice, serves in a high-ranking role as the president's national security adviser.

Which **women were cabinet firsts**?

A total of twenty-nine women have held cabinet or cabinet-level positions in the history of American government. Frances Perkins became the first woman appointed to a presidential cabinet when she was selected in 1933 by Franklin D. Roosevelt. As FDR's secretary of labor, Perkins served for Roosevelt's entire twelve-year administration (one of only two people in the cabinet to do so), and was responsible for drafting much of the New Deal legislation relating to labor. Patricia Roberts Harris was the first African American woman to serve in the cabinet, and the first woman to hold two different cabinet posts. She was secretary of housing and urban development (served 1977–1979) and secretary of health and human services (served 1979–1981) in Jimmy Carter's administration. Elizabeth Dole served as a White House aide in the Lyndon B. Johnson administration before becoming Ronald Reagan's secretary of transportation in

Frances Perkins became the first woman appointed to a presidential cabinet when she was selected in 1933 by Franklin D. Roosevelt as his secretary of labor. *AP/Wide World Photos.*

1983. After serving in Reagan's cabinet, she was appointed secretary of labor in the administration of George Bush and later ran for president in 2000.

Bill Clinton's administration is heralded as a breakthrough in cabinet posts for women: thirteen cabinet or cabinet-level positions were filled by women. The most notable of these is Madeleine K. Albright, who served as United Nations ambassador during Clinton's first term, and then secretary of state during his second, becoming the first woman to serve as secretary of state and the highest-ranking woman in American government. In 1997, Aida Alvarez became the first Hispanic woman to hold a cabinet-level position when she became the administrator of the Small Business Administration. Janet Reno was Clinton's attorney general for both of Clinton's terms, becoming the first woman in history to head the Justice Department.

Who was **Henry Knox**?

Henry Knox, the first secretary of war, was a natural selection for this post, having served as chief of artillery and close adviser to General George Washington during the American Revolution (1775–1781) and as secretary of war for the First Continental Congress(1785–1789). As secretary of the War Department from 1789 to 1794, Knox advocated both a strong navy and a strong central government. Although Knox's 1790 plan for a national militia failed to win congressional approval, he oversaw the development of a regular navy, laying the groundwork for the formation of the Department of Navy after Washington's second term. During his tenure, Knox dealt with the growing resistance by Native Americans against settlers streaming into the Ohio valley and

Great Lakes regions and was responsible for negotiating treaties that are still in force today. He oversaw the inclusion of the Springfield Armory as one of two national facilities. When Knox resigned, President Washington appointed Thomas Pickering as his new secretary of war.

Has a **secretary of state ever been fired**?

Yes. Thomas Pickering, a holdover from the Washington administration, served as John Adams's secretary of state from 1797 to 1800. When the president discovered that he had been conspiring with Alexander Hamilton against administration policy, Adams asked him to resign. When Pickering refused, Adams dismissed him, and Pickering became the first—and only—secretary of state to be fired.

Did **James Madison serve in a cabinet** before becoming president?

Yes. James Madison was Thomas Jefferson's secretary of state for both of President Jefferson's administrations. In his day-to-day role as secretary of the busy office, Madison exceeded at the foreign-policy demands placed upon a secretary of state. Madison oversaw the Patent Office, issued all federal commissions, ensured that new public laws were printed, and served as liaison between President Jefferson and the governors of states and territories. Madison also co-signed treaties between the U.S. government and Native American tribes and nations.

As an early master of U.S. foreign policy, Madison played a key role in the Jefferson administration. He supported the Louisiana Purchase from France in 1803, one of the most significant land acquisitions in U.S. history. By supporting President Jefferson and overseeing the purchase, Madison ensured that the French could no longer restrict American ships from using the Mississippi River and dominate trade routes, and extended boundaries that provided protection from French aggression. Madison pressed for the passage of the Embargo Act of 1807, which restricted trading with England and France during the Napoleonic Wars, and as such laid the groundwork for the use of economic sanctions in preference to war.

What was **James Monroe's role in the administration of James Madison**?

After dismissing his first secretary of state, Robert Smith, for ineffectiveness and for badmouthing his administration, James Madison appointed James Monroe as his secretary of state in 1811, a post he held until the end of Madison's administration in 1817. Monroe had acquired sharp negotiating skills, having studied law with and served in the administration of his friend Thomas Jefferson. Monroe tried to avert the impending War of 1812 with Great Britain, but soon felt that the war was unavoidable. When the British landed on the Maryland coast, he personally led a force of scouts and discovered that the British were headed for Washington, D.C. Monroe ordered all State Department records and valuable documents, including the Declaration of Independence, removed from Washington. Widely respected for his practical sense and ability to unify conflicting interests, Monroe established a good working relationship with Congress and won Republican support for President Madison's policies as the United States became involved in the War of 1812. Madison appointed Monroe his secretary of war, a post he held simultaneously with his secretary of state position from 1814 to 1815.

Monroe's acclaimed performance in both positions led to his victory as the next president in the election of 1816. Once president, Monroe made strong cabinet choices himself, naming southerner John C. Calhoun as his secretary of war, and northerner John Quincy Adams as his secretary of state.

Why was **Henry Clay** important?

Despite accusations that Henry Clay was awarded his secretary of state post for supporting John Quincy Adams during the presidential runoff election in Congress in 1824, Clay managed to hang on in Adams's administration until the end of the president's term. As secretary of state, he negotiated a number of commercial treaties and sought unsuccessfully to have the United States participate in the inter-American Congress at Panama in 1826. Though Clay's position of secretary of state, widely viewed as a stepping stone to the presidency, has always been discussed in relation to the contentious election, Clay was a successful statesman in his own right. His legacy includes three-time presidential candidate (1824, 1832, 1844), intermittent member of the House of Representatives (served 1811–1825), and member of the U.S. Senate (served 1831–1842; 1849–1852). Clay led the Senate for the only time in its history to vote to censure a president—Andrew Jackson, for behavior considered dictatorial and unconstitutional. A unifier, Clay was known as the Great Compromiser for having negotiated several agreements on politically divisive issues.

What role did **Martin Van Buren** play in the **Jackson administration**?

After helping found the Democratic Party following the election controversy of 1824, Martin Van Buren was Andrew Jackson's influential secretary of state from 1829 to 1831. He solidified his relationship with Jackson by encouraging the president's use of the "spoils system" of rewarding his political supporters with office appointments. Van Buren was a key member of Jackson's close inner circle, known as the kitchen cabinet, although he resigned as part of a general cabinet shakeup in 1831. Immediately afterward, the Senate rejected Van Buren's nomination as ambassador to Great Britain. Never dismayed, Jackson chose Van Buren as his vice presidential running mate in 1832, specifically so that Van Buren would be well positioned to succeed him when Jackson's term came to a close. Jackson so believed in Van Buren's ability to lead the Democratic Party onward that he seriously considered resigning from office so that Van Buren could assume the presidency without having to risk an election campaign.

Van Buren convinced Jackson that an unprecedented move of that caliber would doom his presidency from the starting gate, and so Jackson abandoned the idea. As vice president from 1833 to 1837, Van Buren publicly supported Jackson on administration policies, including his more controversial decisions, such as his withdrawal of federal funds from the Bank of the United States, and continued as the president's trusted confidante. Van Buren was elected to the presidency in 1836 by a wide margin.

Did a **cabinet ever walk out on its president**?

Yes. Called "His Accidency" by his opponents, John Tyler was the first vice president to assume the office of president upon the death of his predecessor. When President William Henry Harrison died suddenly in 1841, Tyler stepped up as the nation's chief executive and set precedent by insisting upon assuming the full powers of a duly elected president. Tyler vetoed Senator Henry Clay's bill to establish a national bank with branches in several states, and on states' rights grounds vetoed a second bank bill that was passed by Congress. In retaliation, the Whigs threw Tyler out of the Whig Party, and every member of Tyler's cabinet resigned, except for Secretary of State Daniel Webster, who continued to serve until 1843. By the end of his term, Tyler had replaced the original Whig cabinet with southern conservatives, including John C. Calhoun as secretary of state in 1844.

How was **William H. Seward** a lone voice in the Lincoln administration?

When Abraham Lincoln was elected president in 1860, he offered abolitionist William H. Seward the position of secretary of state. During the Fort Sumter crisis that triggered the Civil War (1861–1865), Seward was the lone voice in the Lincoln administration that urged President Lincoln *not* to take action because he felt that an outbreak of war would drive the border states of Kentucky, Maryland, and Missouri "into the arms of the secessionists" and that there was still hope that the Union could be peacefully restored. (Border states were slave states that did not secede from the Union.) Seward's personality drove him to mistakenly assume that in his role of secretary of state he would come to dominate both the president and his administration.

Once the Civil War began, Seward became an unwavering supporter of the war effort and was called by historian John M. Taylor "Lincoln's right-hand man." Seward became head of the government's program to arrest disloyal people living in the North, and soon developed a reputation for using strict methods to deal with Confederate sympathizers. As one of Lincoln's closest advisers, the diplomatic Seward deterred European entry in the Civil War and opposed French intervention in Mexico. He successfully convinced Lincoln to wait to announce the Emancipation Proclamation, the document issued in 1863 that freed the slaves, until a major Union victory had been won. Following Lincoln's assassination in April 1865, Seward continued on as Andrew Johnson's secretary of state until the end of Johnson's term in 1869.

Was President Warren G. **Harding's administration the most corrupt**?

Among corrupt administrations, such as those of President Ulysses S. Grant and President Richard Nixon, scholars consider President Warren G. Harding's one of the most corrupt. The president's self-serving friends made up his cabinet, and they quickly found opportunity for corruption, including the sale of alien properties after World War I and exploitation of oil-rich lands that had been held in reserve during World War I. The latter opportunity evolved into the Teapot Dome Scandal, which fully erupted after Harding's sudden death in 1923. As a result of the scandal, Secretary of the Navy Edwin Denby resigned amidst Congressional pressure, and Secretary of the Interior Albert Fall was sentenced to jail time (see more on the Teapot Dome scandal in Presidents and the Judiciary—The Judiciary Influences the Presidency). Deaths related to the various scandals include Jess Smith, personal aide to Attorney General Harry M. Daugherty, who committed suicide, and Charles Cramer, another suicide victim and aide to Charles Forbes, the corrupt director of the Veterans Bureau who was eventually convicted of fraud and conspiracy.

Did any **cabinet members emerge unscathed from the Harding administration**?

Yes. Although President Harding's administration was rife with scandal and his cabinet filled with unscrupulous men, several men escaped controversy and continued on as successful leaders. At a time when the Teapot Dome business, which involved Secretary of the Interior Albert Fall's secret leasing of naval oil-reserve lands to private companies, was brewing, the upright Andrew W. Mellon served with distinction as secretary of the treasury. During his two years (1921–1923) under Harding, Mellon reduced the national debt by one-third and implemented lower income taxes. Though other Harding cabinet members were convicted of fraud, conspiracy, and bribery, Mellon joins Secretary of State Charles Evan Hughes (who later became chief justice of the U.S. Supreme Court) and Secretary of Commerce Herbert Hoover (who later became U.S. president) as those few capable and exemplary leaders whom Harding recruited to his cabinet.

Mellon continued on in Calvin Coolidge's administration, during which he advocated his pro-business policy and presided over a period of such unprecedented financial prosperity that he was called the greatest Treasury secretary since Alexander Hamilton. Coolidge's "hands-off" method of running the executive office left much room for Mellon and other cabinet members to do their jobs. Although Mellon continued on into the Hoover administration, he was plagued by the stock market crash of 1929 and growing criticism of his close business ties, and eventually resigned in 1932.

What was **FDR's "black cabinet"**?

President Franklin D. Roosevelt's "black cabinet" was not an official cabinet, but rather an informal advisory group that focused on jobs, education, and equal rights for

African Americans. The black cabinet included such notables as Howard University law school dean William Henry Hastie; author Walter White, secretary of the National Association for the Advancement of Colored People; social worker Lawrence A. Oxley; educator and economist Robert C. Weaver, who would later become secretary of housing and urban development in the Lyndon B. Johnson administration, and as such the first African American to serve in a presidential cabinet; and Mary McLeod Bethune, founder of Bethune-Cookman College and the National Counsel of Negro Women and personal friend of first lady Eleanor Roosevelt. From 1936 to 1944, Bethune was President Roosevelt's special adviser on minority affairs, while simultaneously serving as director of the Division of Negro Affairs of the National Youth Administration. When she assumed this office, she became the first black woman ever to head a federal agency. By the mid-1930s, President Roosevelt had appointment forty-five African Americans to serve in his New Deal agencies.

Who were the **powerful secretaries of state** during the **mid-twentieth century**?

When historians mention mid- to late-twentieth-century men of achievement, several secretaries of state names emerge: George Marshall, Franklin D. Roosevelt's army chief of staff (served 1939–1945) and secretary of state (served 1947–1949) under Harry S. Truman; John Foster Dulles, a World War I army veteran and U.S. senator who served as secretary of state (served 1953–1959) in Dwight D. Eisenhower's administration; and Henry Kissinger, national security adviser and later secretary of state (served 1973–1974) under President Richard Nixon, and secretary of state (served 1974–1977) under President Gerald Ford.

All three men had significant knowledge of foreign affairs before they were appointed to their positions as secretary of state, and all men achieved great acts in office. Marshall is best known for devising the European Recovery Plan, or Marshall Plan, in the wake of World War II. Under Marshall's leadership, between 1948 and 1951 the United States contributed more than $13 billion in economic, agricultural, and technical aid to perpetuate the recovery of postwar Europe. Dulles spent his tenure building up the North Atlantic Treaty Organization (NATO) as part of his strategy of controlling Soviet expansion during the Cold War. Dulles was also instrumental in forming the Southeast Treaty Organization (SEATO) in 1954. As secretary of state, Kissinger helped negotiate a truce to the 1973 Yom Kippur War in the Middle East. President Nixon and Kissinger together pursued a policy of "Vietnamization," preparing South Vietnamese soldiers to better defend their nation, and they opened secret peace negotiations with the North Vietnamese. Under President Ford, Kissinger helped bring about the 1975 Sinai Peace Accord between Egypt and Israel.

Although they were all peacemakers as secretary of state, their biographies often describe the influence they had on presidents and other leaders after they finished serving their posts. After the outbreak of the Korean War, Marshall served as secretary of defense for President Harry S. Truman during 1950–1951, and won the Nobel Peace

Prize in 1953. Dulles formulated the "Domino Theory"—in which he spoke of the domino effect Southeast Asia would have on other countries if it became communist—which dominated America's foreign-policy thinking throughout the 1960s and 1970s. For years after he left office, Kissinger was considered America's elder statesman regarding foreign policy and advised numerous presidents in this arena. In 1973, Kissinger shared the Nobel Peace Prize for his efforts in the agreement that ended the U.S. role in the Vietnam War. Kissinger reemerged in the spotlight a year after the September 11, 2001, terrorist attacks, when he was asked by President George W. Bush to lead an independent panel to investigate U.S. intelligence failures before the attacks. But Kissinger stepped down only a month later, due to potential conflicts of interest with his consulting firm.

What was **President Richard Nixon's management style with his cabinet?**

President Richard Nixon promised "a reorganized and strengthened cabinet," rather than a "government of yes-men" in his 1968 campaign for the presidency, and was the first president to have his cabinet sworn in on national television. However, these events hardly characterize how his administration is remembered. According to Richard P. Nathan's *The Plot That Failed: Nixon and the Administrative Presidency* (1975), President Nixon allowed his cabinet members to make subcabinet appointments, a decision he quickly regretted and a power he quickly reassumed. Although Nixon's cabinet was filled with loyalists partial to his policies, he soon came to distrust several members. Even friends and longtime associates such as Robert Finch, secretary of the Department of Health, Education, and Welfare, left their departments over conflicts with Nixon. Others, such as Secretary of the Interior Walter J. Hickel, were alienated until an opportune time for their dismissal.

Early in his presidency, Nixon created a domestic counterpart to the National Security Council, called the Domestic Security Council. This new department included all cabinet members except the secretaries of state and defense, but this newly organized group was not effective. Nixon asked Congress to approve a reorganized cabinet, but Congress refused. After his successful reelection campaign in 1972, Nixon in essence achieved the same result by reorganizing the White House, even amongst murmurs that he sidestepped Congress. When cabinet members Attorney General Elliot Richardson and Deputy Attorney General William D. Ruckelshaus resigned after refusing to follow Nixon's orders to discharge Special Prosecutor Archibald Cox, the official in charge of investigating Watergate, their critical statements upon exiting the White House furthered demand for the impeachment or resignation of the president.

What was President **Jimmy Carter's 1979 cabinet reorganization?**

Upon his election to the presidency in 1976, Jimmy Carter promised to give his cabinet members carte blanche in policy formation, saying, "I believe in Cabinet adminis-   153 tration.... There will never be an instance while I am President where members of the White House staff dominate or act in a superior position to the members of our Cabinet." But it wasn't long before Carter sensed disorganization within his administration and, with the help of a team of advisers, identified dissension as the primary culprit. He thus asked for the resignations of his entire cabinet, five of which he accepted, in the great cabinet purge of 1979. Those who resigned were Brock Adams, secretary of transportation; Griffin Bell, attorney general; Michael Blumenthal, secretary of the treasury; Joseph A. Califano, secretary of health, education, and welfare; and James Schlesinger, secretary of energy. Interestingly, Patricia Roberts Harris, secretary of housing and urban development, one of President Carter's most vocal critics, survived the reorganization.

What were some **problems George W. Bush encountered when putting together his cabinet**?

In assembling his cabinet, President George W. Bush borrowed heavily from the administrations of past Republican presidents, including his father, George Bush. Nevertheless, he did have some trouble getting his cabinet off the ground. Bush's first choice to head the Department of Labor, Linda Chavez, withdrew her nomination after it was revealed that she housed and possibly employed an undocumented immigrant, an illegal alien. The press likened Chavez's withdrawal to the nomination of Zoe Baird, President Bill Clinton's first choice for attorney general. Baird withdrew after it was revealed that she had employed undocumented immigrants and had failed to pay Social Security taxes for them. After Chavez withdrew, Bush named Elaine Chao as his labor secretary and the Senate quickly confirmed her. John Ashcroft, a former U.S. senator from Missouri, was Bush's choice for attorney general. He faced a difficult confirmation process, as some criticized him for being too conservative on individual rights and Democrats questioned whether he would enforce laws with which he did not agree. They also criticized his record of attempting to outlaw abortion and of denouncing gun control proposals. In the end, Ashcroft won confirmation to his post by a 58–42 vote. Despite some concerns from environmentalists, former Colorado attorney general Gale Norton was named secretary of the interior.

Who is **Condoleezza Rice?**

President George W. Bush's high-profile national security adviser, Condoleezza Rice, was the first woman and second African American in history (Colin Powell was the first) to occupy this key post. Her impressive academic credentials, including having been the youngest, the first female, and the first non-white provost of Stanford University, her gender, and background make her one of the most distinctive women to hold a high-ranking government position. She served in the senior Bush administration as senior director of Soviet and East European Affairs in the National Security

Council, and as special assistant to the president for national security affairs. In this function, Rice received accolades for co-formulating the strategy of President Bush and Secretary of State James A. Baker in favor of German reunification in the wake of the Soviet Union's collapse.

Rice immediately made her mark on George W. Bush's administration by leading the negotiation with Russia over missile defense. Although Rice has been one of the most outspoken supporters of the 2003 war in Iraq, she became a controversial figure when she refused to testify under oath before the National Commission on Terrorists Attacks Upon the United States, commonly called the 9/11 Commission. With her role in counterterrorism policy under question, President Bush agreed to allow her to publicly testify before the commission, and when she did so in April 2004 she became the first sitting national security adviser to testify on matters of policy.

National security advisers' profiles and power over policy have varied, depending upon the administration in which they served. Rice's mentor, Brent Scowcroft, was a low-profile coordinator of foreign policy in his role as national security adviser to the senior George Bush. Others, such as Henry Kissinger of the Nixon administration and Sandy Berger of the Clinton administration, were more visible leaders.

Condoleezza Rice makes remarks after President-elect George W. Bush named her to serve as his national security adviser in 2000. *AP/Wide World Photos.*

THE PRESIDENT LEADS: DOMESTIC ISSUES

INTERNAL IMPROVEMENTS AND CONSERVATION

How does the Constitution define the **President's role concerning internal improvements**?

The Constitution does not specifically address the President's role in this area. Infrastructure improvement programs fall under the powers noted in Article II, Section III, which outlines the President's relationship with Congress: "He shall … recommend to their Consideration such Measures as he shall judge necessary and expedient."

When did **internal improvements first become a major issue**?

What became known as "internal improvements" first became a major concern during the administration of Thomas Jefferson, when construction of canals would have greatly improved transportation and commerce. Jefferson believed in a limited federal government and was against the idea of raising and collecting taxes to fund federal projects. The waning Congressional power of the opposition party, the Federalists, who supported a more powerful central government, ensured that national planning of a transportation network would be subordinated and left to individual states.

The first national project was the Cumberland Road, running from Cumberland, Maryland (at the head of navigation on the Potomac River) to the Ohio River (at present-day Wheeling, West Virginia). Because a portion of government revenue from the sale of public land was available for internal improvements, Congress approved the interstate road and Jefferson signed the measure in 1806.

Jefferson's secretary of the treasury, Albert Gallatin, prepared a report and a plan in 1808 detailing a comprehensive system of canals and roads for federal construction.

When "Road Under Repair" Signs Were Rare

Despite recognizing the need for a comprehensive national system of roads and canals, Presidents Jefferson, Madison, and Monroe, who served from 1801 to 1825, stuck to their constructionist principles and refused to endorse federal appropriations for much-needed construction of transportation systems. The three presidents believed a constitutional amendment was necessary to authorize federal spending on internal improvements.

No action was then taken either by Jefferson or by his successor, James Madison, who shared Jefferson's limited federal government approach.

Why did **President Madison veto a major internal improvements bill**?

Following the official end of War of 1812 in 1815, the United States was flush with pride and nationalism. Speaking before Congress in 1816, President James Madison called for "a comprehensive system of roads and canals, such as will have the effect of drawing more closely together every part of the country." U.S. representative John C. Calhoun of South Carolina led Congress to pass the Bonus Bill, which provided $1.5 million to be used for internal improvements.

But Madison insisted that a constitutional amendment was needed to authorize Congress to use public funds for internal improvements. When Congress approved the Bonus Bill, Madison vetoed it.

What was the outcome of **President Monroe's program for internal improvements**?

When James Monroe followed Madison to the presidency he championed internal improvements, yet, like Madison, believed a Constitutional amendment was necessary to empower the federal government to act. Monroe tried a new strategy: he tied internal improvements with national defense. Monroe had been secretary of state under Madison during the War of 1812 and improved the U.S. war effort—helping stop a series of U.S. military losses and making Britain less inclined to prolong the war. Recalling his wartime experience, where Britain had relatively easy access to American ports on the Atlantic and Great Lakes, Monroe ordered the State Department to repair important roads and ports, claiming they were vital to national security. Construction of a network of coastal fortifications to guard against future invasions was begun, but the program was reduced after the Panic of 1819, when government revenues fell sharply.

Monroe was challenged in Congress by Henry Clay, Speaker of the House. Clay was a great supporter of internal improvement programs, but he opposed Monroe's

> ## Star-Gazing President
>
> John Quincy Adams had many enemies during his presidency. Critics pounced on his proposal to include an astronomical observatory among national construction programs. But nearly two decades later, in 1843, Adams was invited to attend the opening of the first American observatory, which was built on a hill named Mount Adams, near Cincinnati, Ohio.

use of a presidential order as a means to initiate internal improvements. Instead, Clay championed legislation he called "the American System," but it stalled when Monroe announced he would veto any improvement bills until a Constitutional amendment authorized Congress to pursue such action.

Clay continued maneuvering and cited popular support for internal improvements. He was able to pass through Congress and pressure Monroe to sign measures providing for a subsidy to the Chesapeake and Delaware Canal, an appropriation for the extension of the Cumberland Road, and modest amounts for surveys and additional roads.

Which president pursued the **American System**?

Henry Clay's proposal for taxes and tariffs to fund internal improvements, called the American System, was adopted and expanded by John Quincy Adams, who followed Monroe as president and named Clay his secretary of state. The American System was an ambitious, far-reaching federal program. Internal improvement elements included construction of an interstate network of roads and canals and establishment of the Department of the Interior to regulate use of natural resources. Also proposed were expeditions to map U.S. territories beyond the twenty-four states that comprised the Union at that time. Adams was especially enthusiastic for a naval academy, a national university, and construction of astronomical observatories.

Why was the **American System controversial**?

The disputed election of 1824 split the nation between supporters of President John Quincy Adams, who wanted to expand the powers and influence of the federal government, and those of Andrew Jackson, who emphasized a limited federal government. Jacksonians had enough support in Congress to debate and delay all of Adams's major proposals. Some smaller subsidies and federal land donations were passed for canals in the Ohio Valley and Great Lakes regions.

Ironically, Jacksonians portrayed themselves as champions of the people against the large-landowning and New England base of Adams, but the American System

159

would have greatly benefited common people, particularly through land development and a public education system.

Why was there **little federal action on internal improvements until the 1850s?**

Like Thomas Jefferson, James Madison, James Monroe and those congressmen who frustrated John Quincy Adams's attempts for internal improvement programs, Andrew Jackson was a staunch supporter of a limited federal government. He was elected president in 1828, and his influence was so great that the years 1829 (when he took office) to 1848 are often called the Age of Jackson by historians. His limited federal government approach was followed by his successors, Martin Van Buren (served 1837–1841), the major political force behind Jackson, and James K. Polk (served 1845–1849). Even John Tyler (served 1841–1845), who became president following William Henry Harrison's death after only one month in office, held similar views on limiting the role of the federal government despite his intense dislike of Jackson.

Though Jackson wanted to limit federal influence, he was one of the more powerful presidents, and sometimes used his authority to supersede the powers of states. Internal improvement programs, however, were not one of those areas. His 1830 veto of the Maysville Road bill, which would have provided federal funds for much-needed construction of roads within Kentucky, set the tone for his policy on internal improvements. But demand persisted and more modest expenditures for canals, roads, and harbors passed annually during Jackson's administration.

When were **significant internal improvement programs first enacted** by the federal government?

During the 1840s, the United States acquired the territory spanning from Texas (which became a state in 1845) to California (which became a state in 1850) as well as sole possession of Oregon Country (present-day states of Washington, Oregon, and Idaho). The need for railroad construction overwhelmed the long-standing concern of constructionist presidents (those who believe a president can act only in ways specifically addressed in the Constitution). Westward expansion, in effect, turned internal improvements from a constitutional to a budgetary matter.

In 1850, President Millard Fillmore threw his support behind U.S. senator Stephen Douglas of Illinois and his plans to secure federal funds for providing grants for railroad construction. Congress granted 3.75 million acres of land to aid in constructing a line of railroad from Illinois to the Gulf of Mexico at Mobile, Alabama. By 1871, over 130 million acres of land were granted as subsidies to railroads, and the government made large loans to the Union and Central Pacific railroads. Since the

1850s, presidents and Congress have pursued and debated internal improvement programs without concern for a constitutional amendment.

What were some **notable internal improvement programs of the twentieth century**?

Since the 1920s, the federal government has consistently authorized programs for road construction. Typically, more money is spent on roads in any given year than was spent by state and federal governments on internal improvements in the entire pre–Civil War period. Federal expenditure on harbors, waterways, and airports has also been consistently high since the 1920s.

The Tennessee Valley Authority (TVA), instituted as part of Franklin D. Roosevelt's New Deal program in 1933, was a public corporation that built multipurpose dams to control floods and generate cheap hydroelectric power. The TVA also manufactured fertilizer and promoted soil conservation.

With the increasing use of automobiles for long-distance travel in the 1930s, the Pennsylvania Turnpike was built across the state from the Delaware River to the Ohio border. The turnpike was begun in 1938 with the aid of a loan from the Public Works Administration, an agency that was part of Roosevelt's New Deal program.

Federal grants replaced loans for the building of roads beginning in 1944. In 1956, during the Eisenhower administration, Congress enacted the Highway Revenue Act, which provided matching grants (at a 9-to-1 ratio) to states for construction of toll-free interstates.

Lyndon B. Johnson's Great Society program in the 1960s included ambitious plans to improve public housing and urban areas. In contrast, beginning in the 1970s and especially with the presidency of Ronald Reagan during the 1980s, federal funds for internal improvements were scaled back. Reagan's approach was a return to the principle of most pre-1850 U.S. presidents: a limited federal government and a president against raising taxes to fund federal projects.

When an electric power outage left much of the northeast without power in August 2003 from one to three days, President George W. Bush called for updating the electrical power grid. Like Reagan, Bush emphasized improvement through private interests with limited government oversight.

When did **conservation of natural resources** become a presidential concern?

The American System, proposed by John Quincy Adams and his secretary of state, Henry Clay, during the mid-1820s, included the first serious proposal for conservation and called for creation of the cabinet-level Department of the Interior to oversee exploitation of natural resources. The plan was never approved by Congress.

The great 1840s expansion of American territory in the west made land management a formidable challenge. President James K. Polk created a federal agency for land management.

In 1871, geologist Ferdinand Hayden led an expedition that included artist Thomas Moran and photographer William H. Jackson. They brought back images to help convince Congress that the area known as Yellowstone needed to be protected and preserved. In 1872, President Ulysses S. Grant signed a law declaring that Yellowstone would forever be "dedicated and set apart as a public park or pleasuring ground for the benefit and enjoyment of the people." During the 1890s, Sequoia, Yosemite, and Mount Rainier were set aside as national parks.

President Theodore Roosevelt with conservationist John Muir at Glacier Point, Yosemite National Park in 1903. *Library of Congress.*

Which **president championed conservation**?

Theodore Roosevelt was the first president to actively promote conservation and wise use of natural resources. He supported conservationists who advocated planned and orderly use of resources, guided by science and regulated by government. Always taking advantage of opportunities for publicity, Roosevelt went on a western camping trip with conservationist John Muir in 1903 to promote the benefits of the great outdoors. Conservation gained steadily in popularity.

During Theodore Roosevelt's administration, government standards were set for power and irrigation sites, mining, logging, and grazing. The Newlands Act of 1902 provided for construction of dams and aqueducts in the arid west. Roosevelt mandated the first Federal Bird Reservation—at Pelican Island, Florida—in 1903. He created 50

> ## "Is there any law that will prevent me from declaring Pelican Island a Federal Bird Reservation?"
>
> President Theodore Roosevelt asked an aide that question, and he replied that there was not. "Very well, then I so declare it."

more bird sanctuaries during his presidency. In 1905, Roosevelt greatly expanded the National Forestry Service. The nation's largest single natural resource agency, the Forestry Service, began with an act of Congress in 1876. Preserving federal forest land was not common until Roosevelt was president. During Roosevelt's administration alone, 230 million acres were set aside as preserves, park, and refuges.

How did **conservation and infrastructure improvement assist the New Deal of Franklin D. Roosevelt**?

The Civilian Conservation Corps (CCC), the first New Deal agency specifically charged with providing relief for unemployed young people, placed nearly three million single men from age seventeen to twenty-five on a variety of conservation-related jobs between 1933 and 1942.

A quarter million veterans of World War I and ninety thousand Native Americans were among the workers. Reforestation was their major contribution: more than half of all the public and private tree-planting ever done in the United States was performed by the CCC. Erosion control, fire prevention, land reclamation, and pest eradication were among other activities performed by these workers.

Other New Deal environmental initiatives included the Soil Conservation Service, which was founded in 1935 to reduce the erosion of agricultural land, and the 1937 Pittman-Robertson Act, which established a fund from proceeds of federal taxes on hunting and fishing equipment to help replenish state fish and wildlife programs.

Which **presidents were progressive on environmental quality** following World War II?

In 1946, President Harry S. Truman merged the General Land Office, one of the oldest federal bureaus, with the Grazing Service, one of the newest, to create the Bureau of Land Management. The Bureau developed a land inventory, classification, and planning system that assisted in identifying areas in the environment in need of attention.

As the modern environmental movement gained momentum during the early 1960s, President John F. Kennedy began advocating environmental improvement in his speeches. President Lyndon B. Johnson, in his 1964 and 1965 State of the

Union addresses to Congress, emphasized the importance of safeguarding wilderness and repairing damaged environments. Stewart L. Udall, secretary of the interior for Kennedy and Johnson, greatly increased government planning and land use controls.

Kennedy signed the Federal Clean Air Act of 1963. Johnson signed the Wilderness Act of 1964, the Land and Water Conservation Fund Act of 1965, the National Historic Preservation Act of 1966, and the Wild and Scenic Rivers Act of 1968, and another bill in 1968 strengthened the Federal Water Pollution Control Act of 1956.

Which president supported the **formation of the Environmental Protection Agency**?

The National Environmental Policy Act of 1969, which included the formation of the Environmental Protection Agency (EPA), culminated a decade of environmental improvement measures. President Richard Nixon signed it into law. In 1969 and 1970, Nixon approved and directed sweeping environmental protections. He presented Congress with a thirty-seven-point message on the environment, requesting four billion dollars for the improvement of water treatment facilities, improvement of national air quality standards, and research to reduce automobile pollution. Nixon also ordered a clean-up of polluting federal facilities, supported legislation to end the dumping of wastes into the Great Lakes, proposed a tax on lead additives in gasoline, and approved the National Contingency Plan for the treatment of oil spills.

What are some of the **notable conservation and environmental improvement initiatives** championed by presidents since the establishment of the EPA?

The Safe Water Drinking Act was passed in 1974 and signed into law by President Gerald Ford. President Jimmy Carter called for the reorganization of national energy policy, stressing reduction in consumption of fossil fuels and development of alternative energy technologies. Carter called the energy shortage that hit the United States during the 1970s "the moral equivalent of war." He proposed the creation of the Department of Energy, and Congress passed legislation to create the new Cabinet department. Mandatory automobile mileage requirements, the fifty-five-mile-per-hour speed limit, and incentives for weatherization of public and private buildings were other regulations in the legislation. Carter signed the bill into law on August 4, 1977, establishing a comprehensive U.S. energy policy. He also supported a law preserving vast wilderness areas of Alaska.

Significant amendments to the Clean Air Act of 1970 were passed with the support of President George Bush in 1990 to tighten pollution control requirements in major cities. Bill Clinton used executive orders to protect coastal reefs and wilderness areas and to expand several national parks.

EXPANSION

What were some of the **early presidents' concerns about expanding the United States beyond the original thirteen states**?

Several of the early presidents—George Washington, Thomas Jefferson, James Monroe, and John Quincy Adams—were concerned about encroachment on Native American lands in American territory outside of the states. Washington, for example, wanted to avoid duplicating in North America the forceful dispossession of land that had occurred in South America and Mexico by Spanish colonists. In addition, Spain, France (until 1803), and Great Britain all held possessions in North America. Expansion would involve conflict over those territories or acquisition of them.

The spread of slavery was another concern, and it became a reality in 1819 when Missouri territory applied for statehood. Slavery had existed in the territory when it was occupied by Spanish and French settlers before the Louisiana Purchase of 1803 and the subsequent arrival of American settlers.

Why did **George Washington encourage armed conflict in the Ohio Valley**?

Native American tribes that occupied the region from the Great Lakes to the Ohio River fought western expansion, but settlers from the east continued to flow in. The growing number of settlers was welcomed by President Washington as a way to help keep in check the British military presence around the southern portion of the Great Lakes.

When U.S. forces sent to protect settlers were routed in 1790 and 1791, the American government authorized the raising and equipping of a four thousand–man army. Washington wanted to use the army as a show of strength during negotiations with Native American tribes, but skirmishes continued. General Anthony Wayne defeated a combined force of two thousand Native Americans in the Battle of Fallen Timbers (near present-day Toledo, Ohio) in 1794. When British forces failed to aid Native Americans, their ability to resist settlers was broken and in 1795 they signed the Treaty of Greenville, which opened much of the Northwest Territory and a small part of Indiana to white settlement. American settlers moved into the region so rapidly that Ohio qualified for statehood and entered the Union in 1803.

Why was **Thomas Jefferson hesitant to authorize the Louisiana Purchase**?

Jefferson was a "strict constructionist," interpreting the Constitution as strictly as possible to give the federal government the minimal authority necessary for its operation. He believed a constitutional amendment was necessary to give him the authority to make the Louisiana Purchase. He abandoned that principle because the opportunity to make the deal with France was brief. French emperor Napoleon Bonaparte was motivated to make the transaction to help finance his expansionist aims in Europe. American negotiators were convinced he might retract the offer to sell Louisiana at any time.

165

Was the Louisiana Purchase legal?

The Louisiana Purchase was transacted despite questions about the legality of the deal. When Spain ceded Louisiana territory to France in 1801, Napoleon agreed not to resell it to another country. Meanwhile, Thomas Jefferson doubted the Constitution authorized him to make such a purchase. In essence, then, Jefferson made a purchase for which his authority was questionable from a country that did not have the authority to sell.

By treating the purchase as a treaty with France, Jefferson was acting in accord with the Constitution under the president's authority to make treaties. Nevertheless, Jefferson went against his principle of modest government spending by making a huge federal expenditure. The Louisiana Purchase—the largest-ever real estate deal—was a bargain: $15 million for 512 million acres (less than three cents per acre). However, the purchase increased the U.S. public debt by 20 percent.

What was the **impact of the Louisiana Purchase**?

The acquisition of Louisiana virtually doubled the territory of the United States, bringing a new sense of national pride and making later expansion to the Pacific Ocean possible. Jefferson set a presidential precedent for acquiring foreign territory through treaty.

Why did **Thomas Jefferson commission the Lewis and Clark expedition**?

In addition to having the expedition explore and report on the new Louisiana territory, Jefferson wanted scientific information on flora and fauna, a report on lands stretching to the Pacific Ocean, and contact with Native American nations. Meriwether Lewis and William Clark, accompanied by forty-one other explorers, set out west from St. Louis in 1804 and had numerous gifts and tokens to pay tribute to Native American tribes they would encounter. The expedition reached the Pacific Ocean in November 1805 and returned to St. Louis a year later.

Why was **statehood for Missouri so controversial** during James Monroe's presidency?

Nine states entered the Union without controversy between 1791 and 1819. Statehood for Missouri would have tipped the majority to slave states over free states (there were eleven of each at the time). Missouri's application touched off a fierce sectional dispute between North and South, free states and slave states.

After much debate in Congress, the Missouri Compromise combined the admission of Missouri as a slave state with that of Maine as a free state and prohibited the introduction of slavery into the remaining portions of the Louisiana Purchase north of latitude 36°30' north (the southern border of Missouri).

Slavery had existed in Missouri since before the Louisiana Purchase. When Missouri applied for statehood, there were about ten thousand slaves counted among the sixty thousand people required for a territory as part of its application statehood. Present-day Maine had been part of Massachusetts since colonial times. The idea of separation from Massachusetts began surfacing as early as 1785, but popular pressure rose with the War of 1812. Maine was primarily rural and sided with Democratic-Republicans (Presidents Jefferson, Madison, and Monroe), while Boston was a base for Federalists.

How long did the **Missouri Compromise** last?

The Missouri Compromise worked as intended until the 1840s. When the United States added huge new territories in the southwest and the Pacific coast in the mid-1840s, the power of Congress to exclude slavery from new territories was questioned, as it had been prior to the Missouri Compromise. In 1848, Congress passed the Oregon Territory bill prohibiting slavery in that region. President James K. Polk signed the bill because the territory was north of the Missouri Compromise line.

The Kansas-Nebraska bill of 1854 prepared those territories north of the Missouri Compromise line to petition for statehood and allowed them to decide by popular sovereignty whether or not to be free or slave states. With the passage of the Kansas-Nebraska bill, the Missouri Compromise was repealed in 1854.

What were presidents' views on the **annexation of Texas**?

While Mexican dictator Antonio López de Santa Anna marched an army of six thousand men north into the Mexican state of Texas in 1836, delegates from across Texas met in a convention and declared themselves an independent republic. After the Texans were defeated at the Alamo, the rebel army led by Sam Houston, a former Tennessee congressman and governor, defeated the Mexican force in a battle on the San Jacinto River near present-day Houston. Houston's forces captured Santa Anna and forced him to sign a treaty granting Texas independence.

Houston was elected president of the Republic and petitioned for annexation to the United States as a slave state. President Andrew Jackson delayed a decision, not wanting to provoke war with Mexico or address the volatile issue of expanding slavery. On his final day in office, Jackson formally recognized the Republic of Texas, but he and his successor, Martin Van Buren, did not act on the request for annexation.

William Henry Harrison succeeded Van Buren, but he died just a month into his term. His successor, John Tyler, began attempts to annex Texas, leading his secretary of state Daniel Webster, to resign because Texas would add another slave state to the Union. Tyler replaced Webster with John C. Calhoun, a longtime South Carolina con-

Do the "Constitutional Sidestep"

During the final year of John Tyler's presidency (June 1844 to March 1845), the White House was alive with the sound of music. The fifty-four-year-old Tyler had married twenty-four-year-old Julia Gardiner, a debutante who liked holding formal dinners followed by dancing to a lively orchestra. Tyler, normally serious in manner and strictly constructionist in political matters, learned to enjoy dancing around the White House and the Constitution. Stymied by the U.S. Senate in his attempts to have them approve the Texas Annexation Treaty (which required two-thirds majority approval), Tyler sidestepped the normal constitutional procedure and introduced the annexation of Texas as a resolution to Congress. A resolution requires only a simple majority approval in both houses of Congress. The resolution passed, and annexation of Texas became Tyler's last dance as president—he signed the annexation into law three days before leaving office.

gressman and former vice president (during Jackson's first term). Calhoun (pro-slavery) and Webster (anti-slavery) had engaged in debate over slavery in Congress in 1833. Calhoun negotiated a treaty of annexation with Sam Houston, president of the independent Republic of Texas. The treaty was signed by both men in April 1844.

How did **President Tyler sidestep the Constitution** to win approval for the annexation of Texas?

In 1844, the treaty for annexation of Texas was presented by President Tyler to the Senate, where two-thirds majority vote was needed for approval. The Senate, led by members of the Whig Party, who were against the expansion of slavery, narrowly rejected the treaty.

Later that year, James K. Polk ran for president and distinguished himself from his opponent, Henry Clay, by supporting the annexation of Texas. When Polk won the election, the lame duck President Tyler tried a new scheme to annex Texas in which he compromised his firm constructionist principles. Knowing he was unlikely to get two-thirds of the Senate to approve the treaty, Tyler introduced the annexation of Texas as a resolution. A treaty requires two-thirds majority of the Senate for approval, while a resolution requires only a simple majority in the House and the Senate. The resolution easily passed the House and squeaked by in the Senate by two votes. Three days before leaving office, Tyler signed the resolution to annex Texas.

When did the term **"Manifest Destiny"** first become popular?

James K. Polk became known as the Expansionist President during the 1840s, when the United Sates took possession of California and Oregon Country. With the annexation of Texas in 1845 and enthusiasm in the United States for taking sole sovereignty of Oregon Country, instead of continuing to share it with Great Britain, a strong spirit for westward expansion permeated the nation. To emphasize the "moral obligation" of the United States to spread democracy, the phrase "Manifest Destiny" was used by John O'Sullivan, editor of the *United States and Democratic Review,* in an editorial in the July 1845 issue. He used it again later in the year (December 27, 1845) in an editorial in the *New York Morning News* that argued the United States had the "true title" to Oregon Country.

What issues surrounded the **acquisition of Oregon Country**?

Oregon Country—spanning west from the Rocky Mountains to the Pacific Ocean and from the northern California border to the southern Alaska border—was claimed by both England and the United States during the early nineteenth century. The nations agreed to joint occupation in 1827. In July 1843, an Oregon convention was held in Cincinnati, Ohio, where a resolution was adopted that demanded 54°40' latitude as the American boundary (the southernmost point of present-day Alaska). In 1844, U.S. senator William Allen of Ohio used the phrase "54°40' or Fight!" to describe America's willingness to go to war over the area.

"54°40' or Fight!" became a campaign slogan for the expansionist-minded Democratic Party and its nominee, James K. Polk. Elected president in 1844, Polk insisted in his inaugural address that the United States was entitled to the whole of Oregon Country. Britain insisted on sovereignty over present-day British Columbia and south to the Columbia River in present-day Washington (south of 49° latitude) to the Pacific Ocean. Polk offered to use the 49° line, which already served as the boundary between the United States and Canada east of the Rockies, to continue from the Rockies west to the Pacific.

When the British minister to the United States rejected the proposal, Polk stated in his first annual message to Congress that the United States was ready to support its claim to all of Oregon. Invoking the Monroe Doctrine, which warns European nations from interfering in the affairs of the Americas, Polk insisted that he was opposing the establishment of a European "colony or dominion" on the North American continent. His warning is known as the "Polk corollary" to the Monroe Doctrine.

Congress passed a resolution empowering Polk to terminate the Oregon joint occupation arrangement after one year. When the year elapsed, the United States and Great Britain faced conflict. But the British government of the time was preoccupied with a political power struggle and a domestic dispute. They agreed on a treaty with the boundary set at 49° and a guarantee of free navigation of the Columbia River. Polk received this proposal officially on June 6, 1846. On June 10, he sent the treaty without change to the Senate. The Senate approved it two days later. Instead of war, the United States won a great diplomatic success with the Oregon settlement.

Why did the **drive for statehood for Kansas lead to violence**?

Dispute over the expansion of slavery in the western federal territories stirred up in 1854 when U.S. senator Stephen A. Douglas of Illinois, chairman of the Committee on Territories, presented a bill to organize the country west of Iowa and Missouri as the territory of Nebraska. The territory was to be divided into two parts, Kansas and Nebraska. The bill permitted the people of the territories, acting through their representatives, to decide whether the territory should be slave or free.

President Franklin Pierce pressured Northern Democrats to support the bill. The growing abolitionist movement was outraged, and passage of the Kansas-Nebraska Act reopened sectional conflicts. Wanting to ensure that Kansas would be a slave state, proslavery people from Missouri flooded into the territory, obtained the right to vote, and organized a proslavery legislature in Lecompton, Kansas. At the same time, abolitionists moved into Kansas, organized their own legislature in Topeka, and fought for free-state status. Meanwhile, the situation between residents and transients, pro-slavery and abolitionists, erupted into a civil war, called "Bloody Kansas," in 1856.

How did Presidents Pierce and Buchanan react to **"Bloody Kansas"**?

Both Franklin Pierce and James Buchanan were presidents from the north who believed in the rights of states to determine whether or not to permit slavery. They contended that the violence in Kansas was provoked by abolitionists. When both the Lecompton legislature (proslavery) and the Topeka legislature (antislavery) petitioned for statehood, Pierce only recognized the LeCompton petition as legitimate.

Buchanan tried to ease matters by supporting legislation that would admit Kansas as a slave state, but with a reduced federal land grant. Congress passed the bill, but by the time Kansas actually became a state in 1861, the antislavery majority was victorious, and Kansas entered as a free state.

Did the United States add any **new states during the Civil War**?

Yes. West Virginia entered the union in 1863 and Nevada in 1864.

In what way did President Lincoln encourage **westward movement**?

Abraham Lincoln helped champion the Homestead Act (1862), which provided an opportunity for people to claim a frontier lot of 160 acres for a small fee. They would become owner of the lot by remaining there for five years.

Why was the **Alaska Purchase** controversial?

Most Americans were caught by surprise when the proposed treaty to purchase what was commonly called Russian America was revealed in 1867. Talks between Russia and the United States about the United States purchasing Alaska occurred in 1854 and

Presiding over a divided nation, President James Buchanan's struggles to avoid war between the states angered many and alienated those from his own party. Buchanan, fourth from left, is pictured with his cabinet on January 1, 1860. *Getty Images.*

1860, under Presidents Franklin Pierce and James Buchanan, respectively. Talks were renewed in March 1867, led by President Andrew Johnson's secretary of state, William Seward. An agreement was quickly made: the United States would purchase Russian America for $7,200,000.

A few hours after the signing, President Johnson forwarded the treaty to the Senate for its consent. Because Congress and President Johnson were engaged in a bitter struggle over Reconstruction policies, approval of the treaty was not secured until it was championed by U.S. senator Charles Sumner of Massachusetts, who was otherwise a staunch anti-Johnson Republican. On April 9, 1867, he made a three-hour speech that summarized arguments for the purchase. Later that day, the Senate gave its approval by a 37-to-2 vote.

There was some hostility toward the treaty in the press. Some newspapers called the purchase "Johnson's Polar Bear Garden," "Seward's Icebox," "Seward's Folly," and "Walrussia," believing that what was then called Russian America was a vast, icy wasteland.

Why was the **annexation of Hawaii so controversial** that it spanned three presidential administrations?

In 1892, the monarchy that ruled Hawaii was overthrown by a group encouraged by American businessmen. A constitutional government was quickly formed and they negotiated a treaty of annexation with the United States. President Benjamin Harrison signed the treaty and sent it to the Senate for approval. Harrison was defeated in the election of 1892, however, and the treaty was not voted on by the time he left office.

In 1893, newly elected president Grover Cleveland rescinded the treaty to annex Hawaii. Cleveland was concerned about American imperialism—action by a stronger nation to dominate a weaker one. Cleveland wanted to investigate whether the action by Americans in helping overthrow the monarchy of Hawaii was legal. He believed evidence showed that the revolt against the Hawaiian monarchy was carefully planned by Americans.

Nevertheless, the revolutionaries in Hawaii held a constitutional convention and established an independent republic in 1894. Cleveland did not recognize the republic. William McKinley, Cleveland's successor, recognized the Republic of Hawaii following his election in 1896. McKinley encouraged Congress to vote on annexation of Hawaii as a joint resolution (which requires a simple majority in both houses of Congress). Congress approved the resolution and McKinley signed it on July 8, 1898. Transfer of sovereignty to the United States took place a month later.

What **other lands outside the continental United States were targeted for annexation** by U.S. presidents during the nineteenth century?

Cuba was targeted for annexation during the 1850s during the administrations of Franklin Pierce and James Buchanan. They were backed by proslavery forces concerned that Spain would free its slaves in Cuba or the island would be overrun by a slave revolt. The necessary support in Congress never materialized.

Santo Domingo (now Haiti and the Dominican Republic) was eyed by President Ulysses S. Grant. Santo Domingo had switched several times between French and Spanish rule before becoming independent. In 1870, a faction within Santo Domingo wanted to return to Spanish rule. Grant, with the support of Congress, promised to help keep Santo Domingo independent. Grant wanted to go further and annex Santo Domingo, but there was little support for annexation in Congress (and even in Grant's own cabinet). Nevertheless, Grant persisted in his failed effort through the end of his presidency in 1877.

SOCIAL PROGRAMS AND CIVIL RIGHTS

Which presidents supported **acts that compromised the Bill of Rights**?

John Adams signed the Alien and Sedition Acts, passed by the Federalist-dominated Congress of 1798. He was preparing for war with France and wanted to expose pro-French sympathizers while also putting an end to criticism of the government by the opposing political party, the Democratic-Republicans, thus compromising freedom of speech. While Adams sided with Great Britain in a dispute with France, Democratic-Republicans favored France. The Alien and Sedition Acts were allowed to expire in 1801.

The Sedition Act of 1918, supported by President Woodrow Wilson, made it a felony to interfere with the U.S. effort in World War I, but went further to make it illegal to insult the government, the Constitution, or the armed forces. The Sedition Act of 1918 was used by Attorney General A. Mitchell Palmer to make mass arrests of political and labor agitators before it was repealed in 1921.

How does the **2001 USA PATRIOT Act reduce rights**?

Under the USA PATRIOT Act, which stands for Uniting and Strengthening America by Providing Appropriate Tools Required to Intercept and Obstruct Terrorism, the government can arrest those it suspects may have ties to terrorism. The government can resist requests for information regarding detainees, deny detainees access to legal representatives, and conduct hearings in secret. The Federal Bureau of Investigation received expanded powers for search and surveillance and was given the ability to detain citizens and non-citizens indefinitely, without formal charges.

The PATRIOT Act follows precedents established by previous presidents in their duty as commander in chief during wartime. President George W. Bush described himself as a "war president" following the terrorist attacks on the United States on September 11, 2001. Like the Alien and Sedition Acts of 1798 and the Sedition Act of 1918, as well as presidential actions during the Civil War and World War II, the PATRIOT Act is viewed by Congress and the president as a series of emergency interim regulations during a time of crisis or war.

How have presidents reacted to **emergency regulations** once the **state of emergency has ended**?

Usually, emergency regulations cease once the emergency (war or the threat of war) has ended. Presidents have generally attempted to make amends for losses of freedom and property that occurred when rights were suspended during times of national emergency. For example, the Alien and Sedition Acts passed in 1798 were set to expire in 1801. President Thomas Jefferson took office that year and allowed the Acts to expire, then subsequently pardoned all people convicted under the act. Congress eventually voted to repay all fines levied against the convicted. Calvin Coolidge (served 1923–1929) acted similarly in regard to the Sedition Act of 1918.

In some cases, freedom or apologies came much later. Within weeks after the December 7, 1941, bombing of Pearl Harbor, the U.S. government forced over 120,000 people of Japanese ancestry—seventy percent of whom were American-born citizens—to leave their homes and move to internment camps. Nearly fifty years later, in

1988, President Ronald Reagan signed an act that provided an apology and $20,000 to each surviving internee. By then, almost half of the internees had died.

What were the views of early presidents on **Native American relations**?

By the time the U.S. government began operating, Native Americans had little land left from Virginia northward, and in the 1820s they were losing land as well in the Carolinas and Georgia. Despite attempts by early presidents to form a positive approach, Native Americans continued to be pushed westward.

George Washington had hoped that the United States would not repeat in North America the conquest and domination exhibited by Spain in the new world. When Americans began spilling over into the Ohio Valley and settling there, however, Washington supported raising an army to protect them. The army crushed Native American resistance and imposed a treaty where the tribes relinquished their claim to the Ohio Valley.

Thomas Jefferson supported a policy that emphasized education and private ownership of land for Native Americans. James Monroe wanted legislation that set aside certain areas as Native American for "as long as the grass shall grow and rivers run." John Quincy Adams attempted to introduce national protections for Native Americans and their lands. Adams faced derision during his 1828 reelection campaign as an "Indian supporter."

Early presidents generally negotiated removal treaties. The first major removal treaty was signed by the Delaware tribe and the Monroe administration in 1818. After having had progressively moved westward, the Delaware in 1818 were vacating Indiana. The following year the Kickapoo tribe of Illinois agreed to resettle on lands in Missouri. In the southeast, treaties aimed at migration were signed by the Choctaw tribe in 1820 and the Creek tribe in 1821.

In his final message to Congress in January 1825, President Monroe called removal the only means of solving "the Indian problem" of continual encroachment and skirmishes. Monroe urged Congress to provide "a well-digested plan" for governing Native Americans that would not only "shield them from impending ruin, but promote their welfare and happiness." Congress, however, did not act.

What presidents **forced migration of Native Americans**?

In 1827, the Cherokee Nation adopted a written constitution that asserted complete jurisdiction over its own territory in Georgia. The government of Georgia countered the Cherokee tribe move by extending state authority and law over the Cherokee lands.

When Andrew Jackson became president in 1829, he refused to support the Cherokees and suggested in his Annual Address to Congress that the Cherokees move across the Mississippi River or submit to the laws of Georgia. Jackson influenced Congress to authorize the president to negotiate for the removal of Native Americans. In 1830, Congress passed the Indian Removal Act and appropriated $500,000 to force Native American migration to the West. Jackson's administration negotiated ninety-four removal treaties, and almost all Native Americans in the East and South were removed by 1840.

In 1831, the Choctaw tribe moved west with a promise of assistance that never materialized. Thirty-five hundred Creeks lost their lives during migration in 1836. President Jackson and his successor, Martin Van Buren, used federal troops to remove the Cherokees: four thousand Cherokees died on the march to their new home in what is commonly called "The Trail of Tears." The Seminoles of Florida resisted by force and were removed after several years of war.

Which presidents participated in **military campaigns against Native Americans**?

George Washington fought in the French and Indian Wars (1754–1763) as a colonist under the British. The war was fought between the French and their Native American allies on one side, and the British and their Native American allies on the other.

As commander of the Southern District of the U.S. Army in 1817, Andrew Jackson led punitive expeditions against the Seminole Indians of Florida (then under Spanish control) after Seminole warriors had conducted a raid in southern Georgia.

William Henry Harrison fought in the Battle of Fallen Timbers in 1794 that resulted in Native Americans surrendering the Ohio Valley. He was governor of Indiana Territory when the Shawnee warrior Tecumseh began an Indian confederacy to war against American settlers. Harrison defeated a group led by Tecumseh's brother, Tenskwatawa (also known as The Prophet) in the Battle of Tippecanoe in 1811. Harrison would later become known as "Old Tippecanoe" when he ran for president in 1836 and 1840.

Zachary Taylor fought against Tecumseh's forces (who had allied with the British) during the War of 1812. Later, in 1832, he was a colonel during the Black Hawk War and secured the surrender of Chief Black Hawk. In the late 1830s, he commanded a unit in Florida that broke the resistance of Seminole Indians and forced them to leave their homeland.

Abraham Lincoln volunteered to serve in a military unit during the Black Hawk War, but he never saw action.

How did the **president's role in Native American relations change after the Civil War**?

On March 3, 1871, Congress passed the Indian Appropriations Act, which terminated treaty-making between the tribes and the federal government. With the Act, Native American affairs were conducted through legislation approved in Congress, rather than through treaties negotiated by the executive branch and approved by the Senate.

Settlers pouring into the western frontier had reached Oregon by the 1840s. Presidents after the Civil War faced the same pressure from voters as their predecessors to protect settlers and encourage expansion. For example, after petitioning from Chief Joseph of the Nez Perce, President Ulysses S. Grant issued an Executive Order in 1873 recognizing the Wallowa Valley (in Oregon) as Nez Perce territory. Two years later, however, he rescinded the order after pressure by the Bureau of Indian Affairs to permit the building of a wagon road that would bring more settlers into the region.

The Dawes Act became law on February 8, 1887. Hailed by Grover Cleveland's administration as the "Indian Emancipation Act," it authorized the President to allot reservation lands to individual Native Americans instead of being held in common by the tribe. Between 1887 and 1933, however, over half of the tribal land base was lost to land thieves, tax sales, and governmental sales of "surplus lands."

What are **differences in approaches to Native American relations** by twentieth-century presidents?

Early presidents who were sympathetic to Native American rights sponsored programs for assimilation (Thomas Jefferson) or legal protection (John Quincy Adams). By 1890, however, the last major battles over land were completed, and the cause of "Manifest Destiny" (American democracy and occupation spreading from the Atlantic to the Pacific Oceans) had been accomplished.

Presidents in the twentieth century have supported the federal government's increased recognition of tribal self-determination, rather than assimilation. With the backing of President Calvin Coolidge, Congress granted citizenship to all Native Americans in 1924.

The Indian Reorganization Act (IRA) of 1934 was sponsored by the Franklin D. Roosevelt administration. The IRA encouraged tribes to develop their own constitutions, and tribal governments were recognized as the means through which to implement federal policies pertaining to Native Americans. For the first time in over fifty years, the right of Native Americans to sustain distinct tribal entities was upheld.

However, the U.S. government attempted to force constitutions on some tribes. During the Truman and Eisenhower administrations, over one hundred Native American groups lost their status as federally recognized tribes. Thousands of acres of Native American lands protected by treaty were condemned and taken over by the federal government.

During the Lyndon B. Johnson administration, special provisions for Native Americans were part of the Voting Rights Act, the Fair Housing Act, and the Equal Employment Opportunity Act. Many tribal governments participated in Johnson's

Great Society programs, including Headstart, the Comprehensive Older Americans Act, and the Elementary and Secondary Education Act.

During the Jimmy Carter administration, the Indian Child Welfare Act reestablished tribal authority over the adoption of Native American children. In 1979, the American Indian Freedom of Religion Act sought to honor and nurture traditional Native American religious rituals and practices.

What were the **early presidents' views on slavery**?

As president, John Adams made few public pronouncements on slavery. Presidents George Washington, Thomas Jefferson, and James Madison were ambiguous in their views on slavery. All wanted to see the institution abolished, yet all three owned slaves. As president, each refused to interfere with the course of slavery, viewing it as an issue for states, not the federal government. During Jefferson's administration, the slave trade was ended in 1808. Almost all slaves afterward would be born on American soil.

Presidents Jefferson, Madison and James Monroe advocated colonization as a feasible method of ending slavery. After leaving office in 1817, Madison proposed a gradual emancipation that would resettle freed slaves in western territories. Monroe served as president of the American Colonization Society, an organization that proposed gradual emancipation of slaves and resettling them in Africa with compensation for their former owners. In 1822, the society named its first settlement on the west coast of Africa (in present-day Liberia) Monrovia, in his honor.

Which **early president was the most fervent against slavery**?

John Quincy Adams attempted initiatives to stem slavery, but he had no effective power as president to enact change—Congress was generally hostile toward his policies and he faced a solid block of opposition to all of his programs.

Adams proved most effective against slavery after he left the presidency. He was elected to the House of Representatives, where he earned the nickname "Old Man Eloquent" for his frequent, impassioned speeches against slavery and for repeal of a gag order that endured from 1831 to 1844 and limited debate over issues related to slavery . He called the powerful faction of Congress made up of large Southern landowners a "slavocracy."

At the end of the 1830s, Adams argued the defense in the *Amistad* case before the Supreme Court. The *Amistad* defendants were captives on a Spanish slave ship bound for the Caribbean. They mutinied, but were tricked into sailing to New York, where the ship was seized by American forces. President Martin Van Buren wanted the slaves returned to Spanish authorities, but Adams was successful in arguing their defense and having them returned to their native Africa.

177

Despite the fact that President Zachary Taylor owned a farm and slaves, he was against the Compromise of 1850 and the spread of slavery to new territories. *Library of Congress.*

Was there any support for the **growing abolitionist movement** by presidents during the **Age of Jackson** (1829–1849)?

President Andrew Jackson condemned the abolitionist movement as an infringement on states' rights. Jackson and his congressional supporters implemented a gag rule on discussion and debate in Congress and outlawed abolitionist mailings. Martin Van Buren pledged not to interfere with slavery. After his defeat in the 1840 presidential election, however, Van Buren began to work for forces opposed to the expansion of slavery. In 1848, he headed the presidential ticket for the Free-Soil party, which aimed at banning slavery from western lands.

William Henry Harrison, who died less than a month after his inauguration as president, did not give an indication that he would take a leadership role on slavery. However, antislavery advocate Daniel Webster was prominent in his administration. John Tyler, who succeeded Harrison, supported states' rights on slavery. His call for annexation of Texas and having it enter the Union as a slave state led to Webster's resignation. James K. Polk, like his predecessors, wished to keep the subject of slavery out of national politics. After the annexation of Texas in 1845, Polk pressed and then initiated war with Mexico to secure the acquisition of California and New Mexico. When the territory was taken in the Mexican War, the expansion of slavery became a more volatile issue of national political debate.

What was the **Compromise of 1850,** and why was President **Zachary Taylor against it**?

The Compromise of 1850 was intended to settle divisive debates about the spread of slavery. As part of the compromise, California was admitted to the Union as a free state; the territories of New Mexico and Utah (encompassing present-day Utah and Nevada) would determine for themselves whether or not to permit slavery; and the Fugitive Slave Law permitted slave owners to enter non-slave states to pursue, capture, and return fugitive slaves.

President Zachary Taylor owned a farm and slaves but he was against the spread of slavery to new territories. Taylor believed the institution of slavery was an economic need in the South that did not apply to the western frontier. Even as Congress planned to pass the measures known as the Compromise of 1850, Taylor was adamant that he would veto any legislation that allowed the expansion of slavery.

Which **presidents supported the Compromise of 1850**?

Taylor's vice president, Millard Fillmore, a Northerner, believed the Compromise of 1850 offered a "final statement" on the issue of slavery. He informed President Taylor that if called upon in his duty as vice president to cast the tie-breaking vote in the Senate, he would vote for the measure.

Fillmore became president when Taylor died while in office in 1850. The Compromise of 1850 passed Congress and Fillmore signed it into law. Subsequent presidents Franklin Pierce and James Buchanan, also northerners, like Fillmore, shared his view that the Compromise of 1850 was the final statement on slavery.

Why wasn't the **Compromise of 1850 the final statement on slavery**?

The Compromise of 1850 only fueled abolitionist sentiments. The Fugitive Slave law was especially abhorrent to many Northerners and led them to take a more active stand against slavery. The publication of Harriet Beecher Stowe's *Uncle Tom's Cabin*— first as a serialized story in a periodical before becoming a best-selling novel in 1852— further impassioned abolitionists with its depiction of the human cost of slavery. The growing anti-slavery sentiment led to the downfall of the Whig Party during the 1850s, as anti-slavery proponents sought a more forceful and dedicated party to counter Democrats, the states-rights defenders of slavery. The Republican Party was formed from this sentiment in 1854.

Far from being the final statement on slavery, the Compromise of 1850, especially the Fugitive Slave Law, contributed to greater national divisiveness over slavery.

What effect did President Lincoln's **Emancipation Proclamation** have on ending slavery?

The Emancipation Proclamation of 1862 helped fuel momentum for the end of slavery and was a strong symbolic gesture. After January 1, 1863, every Union victory became an act of liberation since the Emancipation Proclamation applied to states that had seceded from the Union. As territory was taken, slaves were freed.

Abraham Lincoln delayed announcing the proclamation until after the beleaguered Union army made a strong showing. That came at the Battle of Antietam in mid-September 1862, which was essentially a standoff, but the strongest Union army showing to date. The Emancipation Proclamation allowed African Americans to be recruited into the federal army. By the end of the Civil War in 1865, over 10 percent of the Union army was African American.

Lincoln Careful to Emphasize His Constitutional Powers

The following excerpt from the Emancipation Proclamation shows how Abraham Lincoln was careful to emphasize that his action was in accordance with the Constitution. The excerpt includes the third, fourth and fifth paragraphs of the nine-paragraph document.

> Now, therefore I, Abraham Lincoln, President of the United States, by virtue of the power in me vested as Commander-in-Chief, of the Army and Navy of the United States in time of actual armed rebellion against the authority and government of the United States, and as a fit and necessary war measure for suppressing said rebellion, do, on this first day of January, in the year of our Lord one thousand eight hundred and sixty-three, and in accordance with my purpose so to do publicly proclaimed for the full period of one hundred days, from the day first above mentioned, order and designate as the States and parts of States wherein the people thereof respectively, are this day in rebellion against the United States, the following, to wit:
>
> Arkansas, Texas, Louisiana (except the Parishes of St. Bernard, Plaquemines, Jefferson, St. John, St. Charles, St. James Ascension, Assumption, Terrebonne, Lafourche, St. Mary, St. Martin, and Orleans, including the City of New Orleans), Mississippi, Alabama, Florida, Georgia, South Carolina, North Carolina, and Virginia, (except the forty-eight counties designated as West Virginia, and also the counties of Berkley, Accomac, Northampton, Elizabeth City, York, Princess Ann, and Norfolk, including the cities of Norfolk and Portsmouth[)], and which excepted parts, are for the present, left precisely as if this proclamation were not issued.
>
> And by virtue of the power, and for the purpose aforesaid, I do order and declare that all persons held as slaves within said designated States, and parts of States, are, and henceforward shall be free; and that the Executive government of the United States, including the military and naval authorities thereof, will recognize and maintain the freedom of said persons.

What were **presidents' views on civil rights issues pertaining to African Americans following the Civil War to the end of World War I**?

Andrew Johnson wanted no major change in the relationship between the national government and the states. But, Republican majorities in Congress, fearing that freedmen's basic rights of citizenship would not be recognized, passed laws to protect the rights of the ex-slaves in 1866. Johnson vetoed the measures as unconstitutional.

Ulysses S. Grant, Johnson's successor, was upset by the lack of progress in race relations. Grant issued a proclamation celebrating the Fifteenth Amendment (which affirms that voting rights shall not be abridged by the federal government or any state "on account of race, color, or previous condition of servitude"). Grant supported the Enforcement Act of 1870 that authorized the use of federal troops to protect voting rights of African Americans. The Ku Klux Klan Act of 1871, which Grant supported, was intended to rid racial violence in the south. In his 1874 Annual Address to Congress, Grant countered concerns about federal interference in the affairs of Southern states: "Treat the negro as a citizen and a voter, as he is and must remain, then we shall have no complaint of sectional interference."

The Civil Rights Act of 1875 prohibited segregation in public housing and transportation, but the Supreme Court ruled it unconstitutional in 1883. U.S. Supreme Court opinions invalidated most of the civil rights legislation passed by the Congress during this period, concluding that Congress had acted unconstitutionally in trying to protect the newly freed slaves from racial segregation and discrimination over states' authority.

Rutherford B. Hayes proclaimed the end of Reconstruction (the government program for readmitting Confederate states into the Union) in an 1877 speech in Atlanta, Georgia, offering his respect for "Republicans, Democrats, colored people, white people, Confederate soldiers, and Union soldiers." Despite his efforts as president to improve race relations, Hayes later admitted that he failed: "My task was to wipe out the color line, to abolish sectionalism.... I am forced to admit the experience was a failure."

Theodore Roosevelt made symbolic gestures: he became the first president to host a White House dinner for an African American, inviting noted educator Booker T. Washington. Roosevelt urged federal and state leaders to appoint more African Americans to government positions.

What were the actions of presidents on civil rights issues pertaining to African Americans after World War I?

Warren G. Harding was the first of three presidents during the 1920s who favored limited actions by the federal government. Harding made speeches calling for political, economic, and educational equality among the races, but took no specific actions.

During the 1930s, Franklin D. Roosevelt delayed action on civil rights, fearing that he might alienate Southern congressmen and lose key support for his New Deal legislation. In 1941, however, Roosevelt issued Executive Order 8802 to establish the Fair Employment Practices Committee to prevent racial discrimination in the booming defense industry. Roosevelt was motivated, in part, by concern that a planned civil rights march on Washington, to protest severe unemployment rates among African Americans, might turn violent. Executive Order 8802 is considered an early form of affirmative action.

President Lyndon B. Johnson meeting in his White House office in January 1964 with civil rights leaders (left to right) Roy Wilkins, James Farmer, Martin Luther King Jr., and Whitney Young. *AP/Wide World Photos.*

Harry S. Truman issued an Executive Order for desegregation of the military. The Executive Order, his establishment of the President's Committee on Equality of Treatment and Opportunity in the Armed Forces, and his support for civil rights legislation in 1946 (fair employment and an end to "Jim Crow" laws that maintained segregation in the South) failed to interest Congress and worked against Truman. Many Southern Democrats rallied around presidential candidate Strom Thurmond, the governor of South Carolina, as "Dixiecrats," and they mounted an unsuccessful challenge to Truman's reelection campaign in 1948.

Dwight D. Eisenhower was president during the birth of the modern Civil Rights movement and the momentous *Brown v. Board of Education* decision in 1954 that ruled separate schools for white and African American children were inherently unequal. When a mob obstructed integration of a high school in Little Rock, Arkansas, in 1957, Eisenhower tried to convince state authorities to enforce a federal court order. When they refused, he dispatched military units to Little Rock. However, momentum on civil rights stalled when Republican senators joined with Southern Democrats to allow filibusters against civil rights legislation. Protection of voting rights in acts passed in 1957 and 1960 were largely insignificant.

John F. Kennedy was only beginning to make progress in domestic leadership when he was assassinated in 1963. Earlier that year in a nationally televised address, he stated that frustration by African Americans over discrimination and lack of opportunities amounted to a "moral crisis" in the United States. Kennedy sent a message to Congress calling for extensive civil rights legislation. Congress delayed action.

Kennedy's successor, Lyndon B. Johnson, implored Congress to pass the sweeping and significant Civil Rights Act of 1964. With a nation still shocked and grieving over Kennedy's assassination, Johnson stated, "No memorial or eulogy could more eloquently honor President Kennedy's memory than the earliest passage of the civil rights bill for which he fought so long." The Act outlawed discrimination on the basis of race, religion, and ethnic origins, with provisions for action in such areas as employment, education, housing, and public accommodations.

How have presidents reacted to **affirmative action**?

Unemployment rates for African Americans were extremely high following World War II. A mandatory affirmative action employment policy was considered during the Dwight D. Eisenhower administration but not acted upon. Two months after John F. Kennedy took office, he issued Executive Order 10925, which established a President's Committee on Equal Employment Opportunity. This action strengthened equal opportunity employment efforts and required government contractors to agree not to "discriminate against any employee or applicant for employment because of race, creed, color or national origin." The Order actually used the term "affirmative action": government contractors were to "take affirmative action to ensure that applicants are employed, and that employees are treated during employment, without regard to their race, creed, color, or national origin."

President Lyndon B. Johnson also used Executive Orders in his effort on a national employment policy. Executive Order 11246 required firms that conduct business with the federal government and suppliers to those firms to take affirmative action. Executive Order 11375 required government contractors in "good faith" to set goals and timetables for employing previously "underutilized" minority group members available and qualified for hire.

During the 1970s, affirmative action programs in education and employment lost some support, especially from presidents who favored limited action by the federal government. During the 1980s, Presidents Ronald Reagan and George Bush campaigned and governed against government-imposed quotas on employers and institutions of higher education. While Bill Clinton was a supporter of affirmative-action policies, George W. Bush, who succeeded Clinton, cited concern about government-imposed quotas as an infringement on employers and educational institutions. His administration actively supported a court case that challenged the legality of an affirmative-action program by the University of Michigan Law School that set admission percentage goals for minority students.

What roles did presidents play in **civil rights issues pertaining to Asian Americans**?

Both Rutherford B. Hayes and Chester Alan Arthur vetoed legislation intended to restrict Chinese immigration during the late 1870s and early 1880s, respectively.

Hayes vetoed a Chinese exclusion bill enacted by Congress because, in his view, it violated treaty obligations. His administration then reached an agreement with the Chinese government permitting the United States to regulate immigration of Chinese laborers. Arthur vetoed a Chinese exclusion bill barring Chinese nationals from admission as immigrants to the United States. His veto was overridden.

In 1907, Theodore Roosevelt forced the San Francisco school board to rescind an order for school segregation of Japanese American children. In return, the Japanese government placed restrictions on the immigration of laborers to the United States. This arrangement was dubbed "the Gentlemen's Agreement."

Following the surprise Japanese attack on Pearl Harbor in December 1941, Franklin D. Roosevelt issued Executive Order 9066 that established 10 internment camps to house all Japanese American citizen and non-citizens residing on the west coast of the United States. None of the over 120,000 Japanese American inmates had committed criminal acts or were tried in court. After petitioning by young Japanese American men, Roosevelt issued another Executive Order, this time establishing a special army combat team consisting of Japanese American volunteers. Upon issuing the Order, Roosevelt stated, "Americanism is a matter of the mind and the heart; Americanism is not, and never was, a matter of race or ancestry."

Why was there **little social reform leadership** by presidents in the nineteenth century?

Presidents prior to the Civil War largely favored limiting the influence of the federal government. Following the Civil War, from 1865 to 1884, Congress exerted more power over national policies than the president. Grover Cleveland, elected to non-consecutive terms in 1884 and 1892, was a powerful president, but he did not support instituting new federal programs.

William McKinley, who succeeded Cleveland following his second term, was preoccupied with economic, trade, and foreign affairs issues, including the Spanish American War (1898), during his first term. There was evidence he would address social concerns after being reelected in 1900, but McKinley was assassinated during the first year of his second term.

What **reform programs** were championed by the **Theodore Roosevelt administration**?

In addition to business reforms, President Roosevelt took the lead in social reform. Many social problems as well as solid evidence of political and business corruption were brought to public attention through exposé journalism, which began flourishing in the mid-1890s. Unsanitary conditions in meat-packing plants was the focus of *The Jungle,* a 1901 novel by Upton Sinclair, and articles in several magazines exposed the exploitation of child labor, slum conditions, racial discrimination, and extravagant claims about medicines. Roosevelt championed and signed into law in 1906 the Pure Food and Drug Act, enacted "for preventing the manufacture, sale, or transportation of adulterated or misbranded or poisonous or deleterious foods, drugs, medicines, and liquors, and for regulating traffic therein, and for other purposes."

Why did Theodore Roosevelt chastise **exposé journalists as "muckrakers"**?

In a speech at the Gridiron Club in Washington, D.C., on April 15, 1906, Roosevelt condemned journalists and reformers who exaggerated seamy social conditions to further their personal, financial, or political cause. Drawing on *The Pilgrim's Progress,* a moral allegory by Englishman John Bunyan published in 1678, Roosevelt lumped sensationalist journalists with a character Bunyan called "the Man with Muck rake," someone who sees only the vile parts of life.

Ironically, reputable exposé journalists like Ida Tarbell, Lincoln Steffens, and Roy Stannard Baker adopted Roosevelt's term as their identity. "Muckraker" persists as a term to describe an exposé journalist. Literary historians recognize the muckraking movement in American literature, usually dating its heyday from 1900 to 1912.

What were presidents' views on the **constitutional amendment prohibiting sale and consumption of alcohol**?

As momentum for Prohibition grew during World War I, presidential candidates Woodrow Wilson and Charles Evans Hughes in 1916 found it politically valuable to support the proposed constitutional amendment. Twenty-one states had outlawed saloons by that time, and in the Congressional elections that year, "dry" candidates (supporters of Prohibitions) beat "wet" ones by a 2-to-1 ratio. The Eighteenth Amendment, ratified in 1919, stated: "The manufacture, sale, or transportation of intoxicating liquors within, the importation thereof into, or the exportation thereof from the United States and all territory subject to the jurisdiction thereof for beverage purposes is hereby prohibited." In 1933, the Twenty-first Amendment repealed the Eighteenth Amendment, and consumption of alcohol was once again a local issue.

Prohibition grew out of the Temperance Movement of the nineteenth century, which began from concern about alcohol abuse in the United States. In 1851, Maine outlawed the manufacture and sale of intoxicating liquors, and thirteen states adopted such laws by 1855.

At the federal level, several first ladies belonged to the temperance movement. Consumption of alcoholic beverages was frowned upon by first lady Lucy Hayes, for example, earning her the nickname "Lemonade Lucy." On the other hand, President Warren G. Harding was known to have enjoyed alcohol while in the White House, despite the fact that Prohibition was in effect. His wife, Florence Harding, was a good mixer—she served booze to Harding and his friends.

Herbert Hoover tightened law enforcement of Prohibition following his election in 1928. It was during Hoover's presidency that Eliot Ness of the Justice Department served with a special unit designed to catch Al Capone, a notorious Chicago gangster known for bootlegging and tax evasion. Hoover ordered the Capone investigation, which was headed by Ness and involved nine other agents. The adventures and success of Ness in seizing breweries run by Capone, and Capone's efforts to thwart the government, inspired several films and television programs. Franklin D. Roosevelt supported the repeal of Prohibition.

What **cultural and social programs** were part of Franklin Roosevelt's **New Deal**?

The Works Projects Administration sponsored programs that supported artists, writers, and musicians. In addition, the Social Security Administration was formed, providing pensions for Americans upon retirement. (For a full description of New Deal programs, see The President Leads: The Economy—Policies and Programs, Booms and Busts.)

What was the **Great Society program** of Lyndon B. Johnson?

Lyndon B. Johnson described his vision for the Great Society in the spring of 1964. In an address on the campus of the University of Michigan, Johnson told the crowd, "In your time we have the opportunity to move not only toward the rich society and the powerful society, but upward to the Great Society. The Great Society rests on abundance and liberty for all. It demands an end to poverty, and racial injustice, to which we are totally committed in our time."

Through an amazing amount of legislation that rivaled Franklin D. Roosevelt's New Deal, the Great Society of Lyndon Johnson offered sweeping reforms and introduced new government programs spanning economic, social, and cultural areas.

How have presidents viewed **social programs since the New Deal and the Great Society**?

The role of government in addressing social issues has been a topic of debate since the founding of the United States. Enacted to battle the effects of the worst depression in American history, the New Deal represented the largest involvement of federal government programs in American history.

Harry S. Truman's Fair Deal and Lyndon B. Johnson's Great Society agendas included federal programs intended to improve social inequalities. The costs of these programs and their mixed results are cited by presidents who favor a limited government approach.

During the 1980s, Ronald Reagan stopped the momentum of large-scale government social programs that began with the New Deal. During his first term, the presi-

The Great Society Programs of the Johnson Administration

President Lyndon B. Johnson's Great Society plan covered six major areas:

Education
- The Elementary and Secondary Education Act provided funds to strengthen public urban and rural schools and special education programs.
- The Higher Education Act launched scholarship, work-study, and student loan programs.

Health
- Medicare provided health care coverage for the nation's elderly.
- Medicaid provided health care coverage for low-income Americans.

Civil Rights
- The Fair Housing Act barred landlords, sellers, or real estate agents from refusing to rent or sell because of the buyer's racial, religious, or ethnic origin.
- The Immigration Reform Act erased a quota system for immigration to the United States that had been largely favorable to European immigration.

Internal Improvements
- The Model Cities Act provided federal funds for job training, community centers, medical clinics, and other social services.
- The Department of Housing and Urban Development was created as a cabinet-level department to better address problems of urban decay.

Labor
- The Fair Labor Standards Act raised the minimum wage.

Culture
- The National Foundation for the Arts and Humanities was created and founded the National Endowment for the Arts and the American Ballet Theater.
- The Corporation for Public Broadcasting was formed.

dent sought to shift dozens of federal programs to the state and local levels under his system of "new federalism." Reagan decreased social programs and increased appropriations for defense.

Bill Clinton introduced government-sponsored social programs at a reduced scale. His popularity increased with the growing strength of the economy during his presidency, but he also won support by fighting cutbacks in services for the poor, anti-immigrant legislative proposals, and attempts to rescind affirmative-action programs. A college-loan payback plan, the Family and Medical Leave Act, appropriations for crime fighting, and a welfare reform bill that ended federal guarantees were signed into law by Clinton.

George W. Bush worked to cut many programs or shift them to state levels. He proposed faith-based programs that would provide limited government assistance to religious organizations that would be responsible for administering the programs.

What presidents proposed **national health care programs**?

Presidents Harry S. Truman, Jimmy Carter, and Bill Clinton proposed national health care programs, but none of the programs received much serious congressional attention. Truman faced congressional majorities opposed to his plans. Carter faced limitations from a poor economy. The Clinton health care program was generally viewed as complicated and requiring a large amount of government oversight.

Lyndon B. Johnson was the most successful president with government health care initiatives. He pushed for Medicare, a program that provided insurance coverage benefits for the nation's elderly population, and Medicaid, which provided access to health care for low-income Americans. President George W. Bush supported and signed into law the Medicare Prescription Drug, Improvement, and Modernization Act of 2003, intending to foster competition in the private sector and provide Medicare recipients more choices.

DISTURBANCE, SECURITY, AND ENFORCEMENT

When was the first time a **president acted against a domestic uprising**?

When rioting occurred in western Pennsylvania in 1794, President George Washington directed fifteen thousand troops—the militias of New Jersey, Virginia, and Maryland—to restore order. Called the Whiskey Rebellion, the uprising was a protest against the Excise Tax of 1791, which was instituted to pay off interest on the national debt (an excise tax is a tax on the production or sale of a particular item). A tax on whiskey was especially hard on small farmers. Because of high costs of shipping corn to market, many small farmers distilled some of their corn crop into whiskey, which they could store easily and sell locally.

Which presidents responded to **sectional disputes prior to the Civil War**?

South Carolina attempted to nullify federal tariffs in 1828 and 1832, which many in the South believed were especially hard on their region. John C. Calhoun, who served as vice president during Andrew Jackson's first term and had been a powerful congressman from South Carolina, announced his Theory of Nullification in 1828, claiming states had the right to disobey federal mandates they deemed harmful to their interests. Following his election to the Senate in 1832, Calhoun resigned as vice president shortly before the end of Jackson's first term.

When another tariff passed in 1832, Calhoun announced that South Carolina would nullify the law and would consider seceding from the Union. Jackson responded with a Nullification Proclamation and a call for a congressional bill to authorize military suppression of any state defiance of federal law. A lower tariff, called the Compromise Tariff of 1833, prevented a showdown.

Later, during the fierce debate over the expansion of slavery in 1850, there was fear of civil war over the possibility that the Texas militiamen would attempt to drive the U.S. Army out of Santa Fe in New Mexico territory. President Zachary Taylor made it clear that he would not hesitate to employ the full authority of his office to quell rebellion in any form.

Weeks after Abraham Lincoln's election to the presidency in 1860, South Carolina seceded from the Union. James Buchanan, the lame duck president, hoped to stop further states from seceding. He urged Lincoln to join him in a call for a constitutional convention. When Lincoln rejected this proposal, Southern members of Buchanan's cabinet resigned, and six more southern states seceded. They formed the Confederacy on February 4, 1861. Buchanan was advised to send troops to Southern ports to protect federal property. He refused, believing the action would provoke violence. When forces of the Confederacy fired upon the federal Fort Sumter shortly after Lincoln took office, the Civil War effectively began.

Buchanan's inaction has proven to be his legacy. Upon his death in 1868, an obituary in the *New York Times* stated that "he met the crisis of secession in a timid and vacillating spirit, temporizing with both parties, and studiously avoiding the adoption of a decided policy."

Which president put out a bounty for the **capture of abolitionist John Brown**?

James Buchanan announced a $250 bounty for the capture of John Brown. Brown responded by issuing a $2.50 bounty for the capture of James Buchanan.

Following the Compromise of 1850, Brown began advocating violence as a means to end slavery. His five sons traveled from the northeast to Kansas to settle during the period when pro- and anti-slavery advocates journeyed to Kansas to influence whether Kansas would enter the union as a free state or a slave state. When Brown's sons informed their father that violence was imminent between pro- and anti-slavery factions, Brown traveled west to Kansas with an arsenal. The Browns engaged in a battle in which five pro-slavery people were killed. President Buchanan ordered federal involvement in capturing Brown.

Brown returned to the northeast with the intention of gaining support for arming slaves for revolt. With a squad of twenty-one fighters (sixteen white and five black), Brown led an assault on the federal arsenal at Harper's Ferry, Virginia (in present-day West Virginia). Local militia fought with Brown's squad until the arrival of federal forces led by future Confederate general Robert E. Lee. Brown was caught, tried, found guilty of treason, and hanged.

How did **President Lincoln define the Civil War** in order to carry out his constitutional duties as commander in chief?

When forces representing the Confederate States of America fired on Fort Sumter, a federal fort in South Carolina, in 1861, Lincoln declared that the attack opposed federal laws in a manner "too powerful to be suppressed by ordinary judicial proceedings." Using his authority under the Militia Act of 1792, Lincoln called for seventy-six thousand militia volunteers. Four states—Virginia, North Carolina, Tennessee, and Arkansas—responded by joining the Confederacy.

Throughout the war, Lincoln was careful to make it clear his main purpose as president was to preserve the union. His actions were taken to suppress a rebellion and to protect free national elections.

What **powers did Lincoln employ beyond those listed or implied in the Constitution**?

Congress was not in session when Fort Sumter was attacked. Moving swiftly to mobilize the Union by executive order, Lincoln suspended the writ of habeas corpus so that known secessionists and persons suspected of disloyalty in the north could be held without trial. Before asking for congressional authorization, and in violation of the Constitution, Lincoln ordered an increase in the size of the army and navy, and he also entrusted public funds to private agents in New York to purchase arms and supplies. By the time Congress assembled in a special session on July 4, 1861, the president, acting in his capacity as commander in chief, had put himself at the head of the whole Union war effort. Lincoln took on more powers than those claimed by any previous president.

What are some **modern examples of presidents using force to quell civil disturbance**?

In 1932, a group of World War I veterans rode trains across the country to march on Washington, D.C. They were demanding an early pay-off on adjusted compensation ("bonus") certificates that had been awarded to them in 1925 for their military service. Congress passed a bill in 1931 that would allow certificates to be redeemed from $250 to $400 per veteran, but President Herbert Hoover vetoed the bill.

Genesis of the Office of Homeland Security

The U.S. Commission on National Security/21st Century was formed in 1998 and completed their work in February 2001, having been charged by Congress to investigate new threats to national security that developed since the 1980s and how to combat them. The Commission concluded that the United States is vulnerable to a catastrophic terrorist attack, and the government is unequipped to handle it. They recommended that Congress should create a new Cabinet-level homeland security department and the National Guard should be retrained to serve as U.S.-based anti-terrorism troops. After the terrorist attacks of September 11, 2001, the idea for a Department of Homeland Security was renewed and was finally created in the summer of 2002.

Images of down-and-out veterans cooking meals over open fires while waiting for a few hundred dollars of relief became one of the starkest reflections of the Great Depression. Most veterans left after participating in the Bonus March, but some two thousand remained. After they resisted police efforts to remove them, Hoover ordered a military squad led by General Douglas MacArthur to evict the veterans with restrained force. When tear gas was fired at the veterans, an unruly mob set upon them and set fire to their cardboard huts.

In May 1954, the Supreme Court declared segregation in public schools unconstitutional. It set no time schedule for compliance, and President Dwight D. Eisenhower took no immediate action to enforce the ruling. In 1957, however, a mob obstructed the integration of a high school in Little Rock, Arkansas. Eisenhower tried to get state authorities to enforce the federal court order. When they refused, the president dispatched military units to Little Rock.

Racial tensions boiled over into rioting during the 1960s, most notably in the Watts district of Los Angeles, California (where thirty-five people died), and in Detroit, Michigan, in 1967 (where forty-one people died). Johnson ordered the National Guard to help restore order in Detroit.

How did the **Department of Homeland Security** develop?

The Department of Homeland Security was established in the wake of the terrorist attacks on the United States on September 11, 2001. The National Strategy for Homeland Security and the Homeland Security Act of 2002 was passed to mobilize and organize the nation for security from terrorist attacks. The Department of Homeland Security was intended to coordinate a national network of organizations and institutions involved in security efforts and employs over 180,000 men and women.

The idea for a cabinet-level home security department was put forth in late 2000 by the Congress-appointed U.S. Commission on National Security/21st Century. The Commission was convened in 1998 to investigate threats to national security and how they can be addressed. The idea was endorsed by William Cohen, Bill Clinton's secretary of defense, but at the time the Clinton presidency was in its final months.

President George W. Bush, Clinton's successor, was originally opposed to establishing an Office of Homeland Security, but he submitted an expanded plan Congress in summer 2002 just before legislators were scheduled to debate the issue. The Department of Homeland Security under Bush brought together groups and agencies that had previously been spread among various government agencies and cabinet departments. The Department is comprised of five major divisions, or directorates: Border & Transportation Security; Emergency Preparedness & Response; Science & Technology; Information Analysis & Infrastructure Protection; and Management.

REFORMING GOVERNMENT

What was the **spoils system** and when did it begin?

The practice by presidents of assigning federal positions to reward loyalty and friendship, sometimes over more skilled and qualified people, occurs in every administration. It first became a notable concern during the administration of Andrew Jackson, the seventh president. The first five presidents had served with one another in some political or military capacity, and the sixth president, John Quincy Adams, was the son of the second president, John Adams. Many federal workers remained in their positions when presidential administrations changed.

Having campaigned against what he called the old "aristocratic corruption" that he believed symbolized as the administration of John Quincy Adams, Andrew Jackson portrayed himself as a champion of the common people and promised "reform" and "rotation in office." His wholesale changes brought in a new wave of federal workers, many of whom were rewarded for loyalty to Jackson and certainly all of whom agreed with Jackson's policies. Experience and qualifications gave way to loyalty and friendship to varying degrees in subsequent administrations.

Who was the **first president to take effective action against the spoils system**?

The spoils system was especially prominent following the Civil War, when northern politicians dominated the federal government and the New York political machine dominated the Republican Party, which held the presidency from 1868 to 1884. Numerous scandals of the Ulysses S. Grant administration, perpetrated by Grant appointees who had benefited from the spoils system, inspired public demand for reform. President Rutherford B. Hayes, who succeeded Grant, introduced the first serious reforms in 1877. Hayes issued an executive order early in his administration to forbid federal civil servants to take an active part in politics. Hayes lost some political clout by butting heads against the New York political machine, but he was successful in removing two strategic cogs in that machine—both of whom were fellow Republicans. One of them, Chester Alan Arthur, collected taxes at the New York Customhouse.

Arthur would survive his dismissal. He benefited when the New York political machine was appeased at the Republican convention of 1880 for having been passed over with their preferred presidential candidate. To help keep their support, Arthur was named vice presidential candidate.

President Chester Alan Arthur, nicknamed "Elegant Arthur," was associated with the New York political machine called the "Stalwarts." As president, however, he surprisingly pushed for reforms that would curtail the power of political machines. *Library of Congress.*

What **reform championed by James A. Garfield** led an assassin to kill the president?

Garfield continued the momentum in civil service reform begun by Hayes, his predecessor. He was assassinated by a deranged man who was angry that he lost his civil service job because of new employment qualifications imposed by Garfield.

Why was **President Arthur a surprise government reformer**?

Chester Alan Arthur was an important player in and benefactor of the New York political machine called the "Stalwarts" that rewarded loyal Republicans with political appointments to civil service positions. Arthur became a nominee for vice president when the Stalwarts' favored candidate for the 1880 Republican presidential nomination, Ulysses S. Grant, could not muster enough support. A rival political machine, the "Half-Breeds," arranged a compromise at the convention that provided enough delegates for James A. Garfield to become the party's nominee. To appease the rival Stalwarts and to ensure the Republican Party would carry the state of New York in the election, Arthur was named vice presidential nominee, though he had never held an elected position.

Upon becoming president, Garfield initiated reforms that began to curtail the power of political machines. After Garfield was assassinated in the summer of 1881, his first year in office, Arthur succeeded to the presidency and was expected to ignore reform. Instead, Arthur pushed for change in the civil service in 1882, but Congress ignored him. To pressure Congress, Arthur turned to the public, which had demanded reforms, and aligned himself with a grassroots agency called the National Civil Service Reform League. Arthur drafted legislation that was sponsored by U.S. senator George Pendleton of Ohio. The momentous Pendleton Civil Service Reform Act was passed by Congress and signed into law by Arthur in 1883. The Act established the Civil Service Commission to oversee federal appointments, administer competency tests, and ensure that civil service employees do not actively participate in partisan efforts.

What **other presidents instituted government reform**?

Even after the Pendleton Civil Service Reform Act, presidents were pressured to appoint friends and party loyalists. Grover Cleveland in 1884 was the first Democrat elected president since 1856, and Democrats expected to fill government positions long denied to them. Instead, Cleveland selected a variety of qualified individuals from both parties, and he was the first president since the Civil War to include Southern Democrats in his cabinet. Cleveland held true to his credo, "A public office is a public trust."

Among other government reforms, Cleveland changed the system through which Civil War veterans requested pensions for disabilities. Some veterans had taken advantage of the system through which they made a pension claim to their local congressman, who would then appropriate money through a "pension bill." Cleveland carefully reviewed each pension claim and ended up rejecting over two hundred of them.

William Howard Taft attacked a wasteful appropriations process by creating the Commission on Economy and Efficiency, the forerunner to the modern Office of Management and Budget. More wasteful processes were streamlined by the businesslike administrations of Warren G. Harding, Calvin Coolidge, and Herbert Hoover, spanning from 1921 to 1933.

What are some **major government reforms led by modern presidents**?

After news stories surfaced about illegal activities conducted internationally by the Central Intelligence Agency (CIA) and domestically by the Federal Bureau of Investigation (FBI), President Gerald Ford presented an intelligence reorganization plan in February 1976. The program improved supervision and tightened rules to better enforce the activities of those agencies. Most of the president's recommendations were put into effect by executive order.

More evidence of illegal activities was revealed when the Senate's Select Committee to Study Governmental Operations published its report in April 1976 after lengthy hearings. The report detailed assassination attempts against foreign leaders during the Eisenhower and Kennedy administrations as well as extensive wiretapping by the FBI of presumed radicals during the 1960s that included civil rights leaders. Most of these occurred without consent by the president in charge at the time. The establishment of a permanent Senate Committee on Intelligence, with legislative and budgetary authority over the CIA and other federal intelligence activities, complemented Ford's reorganization of intelligence agencies.

Jimmy Carter introduced governmental reforms that made it easier to remove officials deemed incompetent. He created new departments of education and energy. The Bill Clinton administration streamlined federal processes, significantly trimming the number of federal employees.

THE PRESIDENT LEADS: THE ECONOMY

THE TREASURY, BANKS, AND MONEY

Why was the establishment of the **federal treasury and federal banks controversial**?

Upon taking office as the first president, George Washington turned to Alexander Hamilton, whom he named secretary of the treasury, to establish a financial system for the United States. Combined with legislation passed by the first Congress, the Federalist program of Washington and Hamilton provided for the payment of debts incurred during the American Revolution and created a sound, uniform currency. Congress passed and Washington signed into law the Tariff Act (1789), the Tonnage Act (1789), and the Excise Act (1791), all of which levied taxes and brought in enough revenue for the government to function.

All of these measures were challenged by those who believed in limiting the powers of the federal government. Led by Thomas Jefferson in Washington's administration and by James Madison in Congress, the group that became known as anti-Federalists denounced Hamilton's plans and began debates over taxes, government spending, and federal power. Nevertheless, almost all elements of Hamilton's financial plan passed through Congress and were signed into law by Washington.

Plans for a national bank, which Hamilton introduced in December 1790, were also hotly debated. Jefferson argued that Congress was not authorized to charter a national bank. Hamilton countered by noting that Congress was granted by the Constitution the right to levy taxes, coin money, and pay the nation's debts, all of which are functions of a national bank. Washington considered both sides of the debate before approving Hamilton's plan. Congress chartered the First Bank of the United States, and President Washington signed it into law in February 1791. The Bank Act set up a nationwide banking structure, owned mainly by private citizens, authorized

The Flexibility of the Constitution

The establishment of the Federal Bank immediately brought attention to one of the most fundamental questions of the American political system—the flexibility of the Constitution. Those who argue that if the Constitution is to be meaningful it must be interpreted literally are called constructionists. Others contend the Constitution is intended as a framework and a guide: its principles are to be upheld and followed, but the Constitution is open to interpretation.

to issue currency that could be used for tax payments as long as it was redeemed in coin on demand. The Coinage Act (1792) directed the government to mint both gold and silver coins.

Disagreements among different factions concerning the Constitution, taxes, federal authority, and the bank became so contentious that the unity of the young nation was threatened. Washington had planned to retire following his term as president, but was persuaded to run again in 1792. Meanwhile, the differences led to the formation of political parties—the Federalists of Washington, Hamilton, and John Adams (Washington's vice president); and what became the Democratic-Republicans (also called the Anti-Federalists), led by Jefferson and Madison.

Why wasn't the **charter for the First Bank of the United States** renewed in 1811?

The First Bank of the United States was chartered in 1791 for twenty years. Leading the opposition to its formation were two men who would later become president, Thomas Jefferson and James Madison. Though the First Bank performed well for two decades, Democratic-Republicans like Jefferson and Madison continued to claim it was unconstitutional. They also believed it favored money interests of northern states and that it violated states' rights and responsibilities. As president and head of the dominant Democratic-Republican party in 1811, Madison led the party against renewing the bank's charter, and the First Bank was allowed to expire.

Economic disorder resulted, compounded by financial needs for fighting the War of 1812, which lasted through 1815. State banks did not have gold and silver (specie) reserves to back the currency they issued, and the federal government no longer had a safe depository for its funds.

When the War of 1812 ended, a new spirit of nationalism prevailed. Democratic-Republicans were more receptive to the bank, and Madison agreed that some measure of expanding federal authority was needed. Congress granted the First Bank a second twenty-year charter in 1816.

Why did **Andrew Jackson's actions against the national bank lead to the "bank war"**?

Like Jefferson and Madison, Andrew Jackson questioned the authority of the federal government to maintain a national bank. Additionally, by bitterly denouncing the bank as favoring northeastern money interests, Jackson won popular support outside the northeast. Jackson planned to lead the charge against renewing the First Bank of the United States when its charter was set to expire in 1836. However, Congress moved to renew the charter ahead of schedule—in 1832, an election year. Henry Clay, a U.S. senator from Kentucky at the time, was the leading presidential candidate against Jackson and a leading supporter of the National Bank.

The bill to renew the national bank was passed by Congress in July 1832. Jackson vetoed the measure and sent a message explaining his veto to Congress: "I can perceive none of [the] modifications of the bank charter which are necessary, in my opinion, to make it compatible with justice, with sound policy, or with the Constitution of our country." Jackson viewed the bank as a monopoly, "subversive to the rights of the States, and dangerous to the liberties of the people...."

U.S. senator Daniel Webster of Massachusetts accused the president of overstepping his authority. Nevertheless, Jackson won: his veto was sustained, and he soundly defeated Clay in the 1832 presidential election.

What were President Jackson's **"pet banks"**?

Following his victories with the bank veto and with the electorate in 1832, Jackson ordered federal deposits to be moved from vaults of the First Bank and distributed to a select group of state banks he called "pet banks."

The U.S. Senate adopted a formal resolution censuring Jackson for arbitrary and unconstitutional action (the Senate would later vote to remove the censure from the Senate Record). Jackson's actions contributed to the formation of the Whig Party, which was represented as a combined force of all anti-Jacksonians.

What was the **result of the bank war**?

Moving funds from federal to "pet" (state) banks contributed to a severe financial crisis (called the Panic of 1837) that began in 1836, took hold in 1837, and lasted until the early 1840s. Many people who borrowed money from pet banks were unable to repay the loans, and thousands of citizens lost their savings. Meanwhile, the lack of a central banking authority contributed to wild expansion of money, risky land speculation, and inflation. President Jackson attempted to halt inflation by requiring federal obligations to be paid in gold or silver (The Specie Circular Act of 1836), but the measure was not effective.

Martin Van Buren, Jackson's second-term vice president and hand-picked successor, won the presidential election of 1836 and was plagued throughout his presidency

President Andrew Jackson vetoed an attempt to renew the charter of the Bank of the United States on the grounds that it was a tool of the rich. He ordered federal deposits to be distributed to a select group of state banks he called "pet banks." This cartoon, called "The Downfall of Mother Bank," shows Jackson brandishing his veto message as pandemonium ensues. Journalist Seba Smith, who wrote under the pseudonym Major Jack Downing, cheers Jackson on. *Getty Images.*

by a weak economy. He succeeded in pushing an Independent Treasury bill through Congress in 1840 as a temporary measure for controlling federal funds.

Another bank war erupted during the 1840s. Congress passed two bills to create a new Bank of the United States, but President John Tyler vetoed both as unconstitutional. Tyler had been the first vice president to become president following the death of the president. For his daring vetoes, which outraged Congress and his own Whig Party, Tyler was nicknamed "His Accidency," advised that he should resign, and was kicked out of the Whig Party.

Tyler's successor, James K. Polk, was receptive to reestablishing the Independent Treasury system. The Independent Treasury was renewed in 1846 and would remain the nation's banking system until 1913, when the Federal Reserve System was instituted.

What were **greenbacks**?

"Greenbacks" were notes issued during the Civil War as legal tender but were not backed by gold reserves. They served as the standard of value in ordinary commercial transactions. Some $450 million in greenbacks was authorized, but was later reduced to under $350 million. Greenbacks spurred inflation, depreciated during the Civil War, and contributed to financial problems following the war.

Brother-in-law Blues

Jim Fisk and Jay Gould wanted to involve President Grant in their scheme to corner the gold market. They bribed Abel Rathbone Corbin, who was married to Grant's sister and claimed to have access to the president. Corbin had a low-level job in the administration. Grant turned away Fisk and Gould, then quickly and effectively acted against their caper, but the Grant administration's relationship with the financiers became the subject of a congressional investigation and public embarrassment for Grant.

The Ulysses S. Grant administration delayed in acting on greenbacks until Congress passed the Resumption Act of 1875. The delay contributed to poor economic conditions during the 1870s. The Act redeemed greenbacks and they were completely out of circulation by 1879.

How did an **1869 conspiracy to corner the gold market** affect the U.S. economy?

Two wealthy men, Jay Gould and Jim Fisk, bought large amounts of gold in 1869, making the precious metal more valuable. The value of greenbacks plummeted, ruining many individuals and banking institutions that held them.

Meanwhile, the gold purchase created a financial crisis in the stock market, causing the market to close on September 24, 1869—a day called "Black Friday." President Ulysses S. Grant authorized the U.S. government to sell some of its gold reserves to help reduce the value of the precious metal. Investors who had purchased gold at higher prices lost money.

Some low-level government officials had been bribed as part of the conspiracy to corner the gold market. Historians generally credit Grant for acting quickly to sell government gold and to fire government officials who participated in the scheme to corner the market.

What other presidents addressed **crises related to gold reserves**?

U.S. gold reserves were depleted during the 1880s and early 1890s. When an economic depression hit the country in 1893, much of the privately held gold was moved to Europe. President Grover Cleveland called on banker J. P. Morgan to form a syndicate of American and European bankers to lend gold to the U.S. government to prop up reserves and stem the flow of gold from the country.

In 1933, President Franklin D. Roosevelt declared a four-day nationwide bank moratorium shortly after taking office to combat a steadily worsening economic crisis.

201

President Franklin D. Roosevelt, speaking to the nation on radio from the White House in 1933, explains the measures he planned to take to solidify the nation's shaky banking system. *AP/Wide World Photos.*

Banks were forbidden to pay out gold or to export it. In April 1933, he ordered all gold coins and gold certificates in hoards over $100 turned in for other money. The government took in $300 million of gold coin and $470 million of gold certificates by mid-May. Later that month, he imposed a permanent embargo on gold exports, claiming there was not enough gold to pay all the holders of currency and of public and private debts. Earlier, in 1931, the gold standards of Austria, Germany, and Great Britain successively collapsed, and they joined several other nations in leaving the gold standard.

Following the establishment of the International Monetary Fund (IMF) in 1944, U.S. gold reserves fell drastically. Each IMF member nation was assigned a quota of gold to pay to the IMF as a means for creating international monetary stability. With gold reserves low in the 1960s, President John F. Kennedy introduced regulations on gold in the United States. In August 1971, President Richard Nixon announced that the U.S. Treasury would no longer redeem dollars in gold for any foreign treasury or central bank. This action took the U.S. off the gold standard. The value of the United States dollar suffered for over a decade.

How did the popular movements for **bimetallism and "free silver"** affect the presidency?

Bimetallism is a monetary system in which two metals (usually gold and silver) form the standard in which the unit of value is expressed. From 1792 until the Civil War, the United States, with a few brief exceptions, was on a bimetallic standard. Early in the Civil War, the country turned to a paper money standard called "greenbacks." The value of greenbacks fell consistently following the war.

In 1873, the United States went exclusively on the gold standard. The currency laws of the federal government were revised and codified. The standard silver dollar was dropped from the list of coins authorized by law for minting.

When the American economy fluctuated from the mid-1870s to the early 1890s, farmers, laborers, and others with modest incomes were the hardest hit. They became a large voting bloc seeking economic relief, and they blamed economic hard times on a low money supply and the switch from bimetallism to the gold standard. Politicians

The Ironies of Bimetallism

During the 1890s, political parties and presidents flipped their political coins on bimetallism and the coinage of silver.

- Republican president Benjamin Harrison struck a blow for bimetallism by supporting the Sherman Silver Purchase Act (1890), which increased the amount of silver that could be coined.

- Democratic president Grover Cleveland, who preceded and followed Harrison, pushed Congress to repeal the Sherman Purchase Act in 1893 to help slow inflation and stave off an economic depression.

- The 1896 Republican presidential candidate, William McKinley, who had supported bimetallism as a U.S. congressman for over twenty years, abruptly dropped his support for bimetallism early in the campaign and became the favored candidate of business leaders.

- Democratic presidential candidate William Jennings Bryan led the free silver and bimetallism causes in the elections of 1896 and 1900. Bryan lost both elections to McKinley, and bimetallism lost when the Gold Standard Act became law in 1900.

took up the cause of bimetallism and free silver. "Free silver" was a slogan representing the desire for unlimited coinage of silver by the U.S. government for anyone bringing the metal into the U.S. Mint.

The grassroots support for bimetallism and free silver grew into the Populist movement and peaked during the 1890s. The Populist Party (also called the People's Party) nominated former U.S. representative James B. Weaver of Iowa as its presidential candidate in 1892. Weaver collected over a million votes in the 1892 election (of about twelve million cast) and won twenty-two electoral votes. However, Democrat Grover Cleveland was elected (he had previously been president from 1885 to 1889) and refused to veer from the gold standard.

When a depression hit the United States in 1893, the Populist movement grew stronger. William Jennings Bryan, the 1896 Democratic Party candidate, embraced the unlimited coinage of silver in his famous "Cross of Gold" speech. Speaking to those who supported currency backed only by gold, primarily Republicans, Bryan proclaimed, "You shall not press down upon the brow of labor this crown of thorns, you shall not crucify mankind upon a cross of gold." Populists embraced Bryan, but he lost a close election to William McKinley in 1896 and lost again to McKinley in 1900.

Bimetallism faded as an issue with the Gold Standard Act of 1900, which declared the gold dollar "shall be the standard unit of value, and all forms of money issued or coined by the United States shall be maintained at a parity of value with this standard and it shall be the duty of the Secretary of the Treasury to maintain such parity."

When was the **Federal Reserve established**?

President Woodrow Wilson, working with U.S. representative Carter Glass of Virginia, wrote the Federal Reserve bill to establish twelve Federal Reserve banks to perform central banking functions for the United States. A Federal Reserve Board of presidential appointees was to coordinate the system. A new currency, Federal Reserve notes, issued by Federal Reserve banks against gold and commercial credits, was created. The House approved the bill in September 1913, but Wilson had to fight hard in the Senate against supporters of private banking interests. The Senate finally passed the Federal Reserve Act in mid-December 1913. Still in effect in the twenty-first century, the Federal Reserve is easily the longest running central banking system in U.S. history.

What **influence does the president have over the Federal Reserve**?

The Federal Reserve Board is composed of seven members appointed by the president and confirmed by the Senate. Each member serves a term of fourteen years, and the seven terms are staggered so that one ends every two year years.

The Federal Reserve acts independent of the president. For example, Arthur Burns had served as an advisor to President Dwight D. Eisenhower and to 1960 Republican presidential candidate Richard Nixon. Burns then served in the Kennedy administration after John F. Kennedy defeated Nixon in the election of 1960. Burns continued to serve in the administrations of Lyndon B. Johnson and Richard Nixon before being named by Nixon as chairman of the Federal Reserve in 1969.

Similarly, Alan Greenspan, who became chairman of the Federal Reserve in 1987, has been respected by presidents of both major political parties. Reports on the economy by Greenspan, in his role as chairman of the Federal Reserve, are anxiously awaited by the president. Greenspan is credited with having helped thwart inflation in the early 1990s by raising interest rates, then consistently reducing them as the economy improved and helping to sustain the longest period of economic growth in the nation's history.

Greenspan has been described as the second most powerful man in the world, behind the president, but the approval ratings of presidents can rise and fall with the actions and reports of the Federal Reserve chairman. Greenspan has been reappointed chairman three times to extend his tenure, which was originally set to end in 2001. In 2004, Greenspan was nominated by President George W. Bush for a final term.

TAXES

What were some of the **early arguments for and against taxes**?

The first attempt at American government, under the Articles of Confederation, failed in part because the government was not empowered to enact and collect national taxes. The Constitution addressed the issue by authorizing Congress to levy taxes. When George Washington became the first president of the United States in 1789, he wanted to avoid repeating the failure of the Articles of Confederation. He encouraged and then endorsed the financial plans of Alexander Hamilton, his secretary of the treasury, for levying taxes to provide the government with revenue. Despite opposition from Thomas Jefferson, Washington's secretary of state, and James Madison, a congressional leader, Hamilton's plan was approved by Congress and the president.

Jefferson became president in 1801. By the following year, he ended the system of excise duties and direct taxes established by Washington and continued by John Adams, Washington's successor. For revenue, Jefferson relied on customs receipts, land sales, and a small tax on postal services.

Why did **James Madison abandon his anti-tax position** when he became president?

The Madison presidency began in 1809 in difficult economic times. With the added burden of the War of 1812, Congress was forced to find additional sources for funding. Taxes on houses, land, and slaves were enacted in 1813, 1815, and 1816, with additional duties on liquor licenses, auction sales, carriages, and refined sugar, among other items. Following the war, the economy of the United States improved considerably. President James Monroe, Madison's successor, toured the states at the beginning of his first term in 1817 and ushered in what was called the "Era of Good Feelings." The duties and taxes levied during the war were repealed late in 1817.

What were presidents' **tax policies from the Era of Good Feelings to the Civil War**?

From 1817 until the outbreak of the Civil War, the national government made no use of excise, stamp, income, inheritance, or direct property taxes. Government expenses were met principally from customs duties, supplemented by the income from the sale of public lands. Whenever there were revenue shortfalls the Treasury secured temporary loans and avoided imposing new taxes, even during the Mexican War (1846–1848).

What **new taxes were imposed during the Civil War**?

The administration of Abraham Lincoln (served 1861–1865) attempted to avoid introducing new taxes to finance the war effort by relying on the sale of government bonds and increases in tariff rates, along with proceeds from the sale of public lands. The sale of bonds, principally through the efforts of Salmon P. Chase, secretary of the treasury, largely financed the Union war effort, but the administration was also battling a massive deficit that began with an economic downturn in 1857 and was compounded by the loss of revenue from states that seceded from the Union. Congress passed a series of tax bills between 1861 and 1865 to generate revenue, including the first national income tax, an inheritance tax, excise taxes on liquor, tobacco, and carriages, and many other levies.

What were the **tax policies of presidents after the Civil War to the end of the century**?

After the war, government expenditures decreased and taxes were reduced. After 1883, liquor and tobacco were the only commodities taxed. The income tax was reduced in 1867 and 1870 and then allowed to expire in 1872. Proposals for restoring the income tax were promoted by southern and western congressmen representing agrarian interests during this period, when industrialism was taking dominance and the number of small farms was decreasing. However, Republicans held the presidency from 1868 to 1884 and primarily represented the interests of industry from New York and New England to Illinois. The income tax was not renewed because it would have been especially taxing on voters in those regions.

A severe economic crisis called the Panic of 1893 brought a renewal of the income tax—2 percent on annual incomes (including gifts and inheritances) that exceeded $4,000—during the administration of Grover Cleveland. In 1898, President William McKinley supported Congressional action to double tobacco and beer taxes, to adopt special stamp and occupation taxes, and to impose a tax on legacies to help support the costs of the Spanish-American War.

When was a **corporate income tax** levied?

In 1909, President William Howard Taft supported a bill in Congress that instituted the first federal corporation tax since the Civil War.

When did the **federal income tax become permanent**?

The Sixteenth Amendment to the Constitution, adopted in 1913, granted power to Congress to levy income taxes without apportionment among the states. Previously, states paid a portion of national taxes based on population. The maximum income tax in 1913 was 7 percent on personal net income over $500,000. However, increasing defense expenditures after the United States entered World War I led to a series of new tax laws designed to meet about one-third of the total war costs. Congress passed and President Woodrow Wilson approved four major revenue acts between 1914 and 1919 that increased the rates of personal income taxes. Among other taxes introduced during wartime were a special tax on munitions manufacturers, an estate tax, an excess profits tax, a war profits tax, transportation taxes, and a wide variety of new excise taxes on goods and services.

When did **taxes first become a major political issue** during the twentieth century?

The presidential election of 1920 occurred the year after the end of World War I. While Democrats focused on sustaining the international focus and legacy of incumbent president Woodrow Wilson, Republicans campaigned on a "return to normalcy" theme that emphasized tax cuts, reductions in government spending, and fewer regulations on business and industry. An economic downturn following the war helped the Republican cause: U.S. senator Warren G. Harding of Ohio was elected president in a landslide.

Harding's economic program helped usher in a period of general economic prosperity—the "Roarin' '20s." For the most part, from 1920 to 1933, the presidents—Harding, Calvin Coolidge, and Herbert Hoover—ran "business administrations." They checked expenditures, maintained low tax rates, and believed that government should intervene only to curb unfair business practices and unhealthy working conditions. The government maintained an active role in regulating only a few developing industries and technologies, most notably radio and aviation.

How did the **Great Depression affect tax policies**?

After the stock market crash of 1929 and the immediate economic downturn, President Herbert Hoover maintained confidence that the economy would recover. A federal budget deficit soon began growing and Hoover eventually agreed that government spending was needed for social welfare and economic stimulus. Congress and the president raised corporate and personal income tax rates, doubled estate tax rates, imposed numerous manufacturer excise taxes, and introduced new sales taxes on gasoline and a host of luxury items, banking transactions, and uses of communications.

Franklin D. Roosevelt won the 1932 election in a landslide over Hoover in large part based on his pledge for more aggressive government action against the poor economic conditions. His New Deal policies for relief, recovery, and reform required massive government spending to finance unemployment relief and public works. Tax laws were passed to prevent an unjust concentration of wealth and economic power and to induce businesses to adopt certain recovery policies. In 1933, Congress enacted a corporation excess profits tax, a capital stock tax, and an increase in the gasoline tax.

In 1935, the corporate income tax and the excess profits tax were increased. The Social Security Act established retirement insurance for qualified workers through payroll taxes on both employers and employees. In 1936, a graduated corporate income tax was levied in order to induce corporations to distribute their earnings to their stockholders. This highly controversial measure was modified in 1938 and repealed in 1939. Partly as compensation for this repeal, the corporate income tax was increased in 1938 and 1939.

How did **World War II affect tax policies**?

The most significant and lasting tax policy introduced during World War II was the employee withholding tax (1942). For the first time, a large percentage of the American population was subject to the income tax. The federal government needed to raise an unprecedented amount of money to spend on the war effort.

Since the new income tax was creating a much larger percentage of new taxpayers, there was concern in the U.S. government that people hadn't prepared to save money to pay the taxes, and the Treasury Department was worried about confronting massive tax evasion. A group of financial advisers to President Roosevelt, led by Beardsley Ruml (treasurer of R. H. Macy & Company, the department store giant) recommended tax amnesty for all Americans in 1942. Payments on the new income tax would then be spread over an entire year, beginning in 1943, as opposed to being paid all at once. The outcome was a plan that forced employers to regularly collect taxes from their employees' salaries and send the money directly to the federal government.

How did **tax policy change in the decade after World War II**?

The employee withholding tax remained. Shortly before World War II ended in September 1945, Congress began easing the tax capital–reconversion burdens of American businesses through the 1945 Tax Adjustment Act. Corporate and personal income tax rates were moderately reduced, and tax exemptions were given to members of the armed forces below the rank of commissioned officer on service pay received during the war. With the support of President Harry S. Truman, Congress postponed reduction of many of the wartime excise taxes that were due to expire.

In 1948, Congress instituted reductions in the personal income, estate, and gift taxes over Truman's veto. The trend to lower taxes was halted by the outbreak of the Korean War in June 1950. Three revenue bills enacted in 1950 and 1951 raised personal and corporation income taxes. An excess profits tax was revived, and excise taxes were increased.

In 1954, one year after the Korean War ended, Congress repealed the excess profits tax and, with the blessing of the Dwight D. Eisenhower administration, reduced the income tax to stimulate business and remove inequalities in the treatment of taxpayers. However, between 1950 and 1958, Social Security taxes and the accompanying benefits were raised on five different occasions. A few changes in the excise taxes were also made, the biggest of which were increases affecting motorists to finance massive highway building projects.

Guns and Butter

Tax cuts in 1964 and 1965 helped stimulate the economy. As the economy grew robustly, enough tax revenue returned to the government to help finance Lyndon B. Johnson's Great Society of government support for social and economic programs. Johnson believed the economy could also support the United States' growing involvement in the Vietnam War, but, in the popular terminology of the time, the government found they could not pay for both "guns and butter."

What presidents have proposed **tax cuts to stimulate the economy**?

Previous to the 1960s, tax cuts were generally introduced as relief or rollbacks following a period of tax hikes enacted to meet wartime needs. During the early 1920s and late 1950s, tax cuts had an additional intention of helping stimulate an economy in recession.

Leading officials in the administration of John F. Kennedy were influenced by the economic theories of John Maynard Keynes, who argued that at times a national government must spend more than it collects in order to stimulate economic growth. Tax cuts were part of the Kennedy administration's plans to increase consumer spending and stimulate jobs to produce consumer goods. Kennedy counteracted the recession of 1961 with a $6.2 billion increase in government spending and an investment tax credit for businessmen.

A larger tax cut stalled in Congress in 1963. Following Kennedy's assassination, Lyndon B. Johnson focused on passing the tax cut and a sweeping civil rights act that Kennedy had been championing. Johnson pushed through Congress in 1964 a bill providing $11.5 billion in income tax reductions for 1964 and 1965. The resulting improved economy led to increased tax revenues that helped finance Johnson's Great Society programs.

Ronald Reagan introduced sweeping tax cuts during his first term, both for economic stimulus and tax relief. Reagan argued that tax relief increased consumer spending and stimulated jobs to produce consumer goods. Because the Reagan plan, dubbed "Reaganomics," also involved massive cuts in social programs and large increases in defense spending, critics charged that Reaganomics primarily benefited wealthy individuals, promoting a "trickle down" effect—massive tax relief for the wealthiest who would spend and invest their tax returns.

Reagan's domestic program during his second term focused on tax reform. Late in 1986, Congress passed a major tax bill that reduced the number of tax rates, removed millions of low-income persons from the tax rolls, and eliminated most deductions.

Why did the phrase **"Read my lips: no new taxes"** haunt George Bush?

During the 1988 presidential campaign, George Bush wanted to draw on the conservative support of outgoing president Ronald Reagan while appealing to more moderate voters by acknowledging the need for government action and spending in such areas as education and the environment. To ensure he would not abandon Reaganomics (which he had called "voodoo economics" when running against Reagan for the 1980 Republican presidential nomination), Bush insisted that he would not raise taxes to support his new spending plans. To counter continued skepticism, especially among conservatives, Bush uttered the memorable phrase, "Read my lips: no new taxes."

After winning the election, however, Bush faced an economy dogged by a large and ever-increasing budget deficit. By 1990, Bush was forced to admit that new or increased taxes were necessary. Many Republican conservatives were critical of this shift. Congressional Republicans helped defeat a deficit-reduction plan because it included new and increased taxes. The government was almost forced to shut down for lack of money while a new budget proposal was drafted.

By the end of 1990, the president and Congress reached a compromise on a budget package that increased the marginal tax rate and phased out exemptions for high-income taxpayers. Bush hoped to maintain support among conservatives by demanding a reduction in the capital gains tax, but had to give in on this issue as well. Bush's popularity among Republicans never fully recovered, and the compromise plan he had negotiated with Congress had only a slight effect on reducing the deficit.

What **tax cuts** occurred during the administration of **Bill Clinton**?

In 1997, Congress enacted a major tax cut, the first since 1981, while Clinton negotiated a deficit-reduction package that projected a balanced federal budget in 2002. Unlike the tax cuts of 1981 and 2001, the 1987 tax cut did not contribute to the national debt. In fact, the United States had a budget surplus the following year.

Though the relationship between Clinton and the Republican-dominated Congress was acrimonious, both sides achieved goals—targeted spending plans and reduction of taxes and the national debt.

What was the effect of **tax cuts championed by George W. Bush**?

With the backing of Republican majorities in both houses of Congress, Bush signed into law a broad federal tax cut—the largest in the nation's history—in 2001, with provisions for making the tax cuts permanent. Bush argued that the tax cuts would stimulate an economy that had stagnated. The first signs of economic growth began to show in 2004, but it was offset by continued sluggishness in other areas of the economy. In addition, the national debt had quickly accumulated.

How did Republican **George W. Bush** and Democrat **John Kerry represent different strategies towards taxes** in the 2004 election campaign?

Bush argued that tax relief provides Americans with spending power that stimulates economic growth. Kerry argued that broad tax relief saps economic growth by making the government vulnerable to debt. In addition, critics of the Bush plan link it with the so-called "trickle down" element of Ronald Reagan's tax cuts in the 1980s, where wealthier Americans benefit from large tax refunds that they are expected to spend or invest as a means for stimulating the economy. Kerry would reduce the tax cuts for Americans with incomes over $200,000 annually.

Like the debates that occurred over taxes at the very beginnings of American government, those in favor of reducing taxes argue that the strategy helps place limits on government spending and therefore limits the federal government's authority and ability to impose policies and programs on states and individuals. Meanwhile, those who favor maintaining or increasing tax rates want to fund government programs for internal and social improvements.

TARIFFS

Have **tariffs** ever been a **major issue confronting presidents**?

Yes. In fact, tariffs were a major issue in virtually every presidency until the Great Depression (1929–1941). Tariffs protect American industry, but they also create higher consumer prices for goods. Tariffs have provided the government with surplus revenue and have been blamed for economic recessions. The first tax in U.S. history was a tariff, passed by the first Congress (on July 4, 1789) to protect American manufacturers and bring revenue to the federal government. From 1789 to 1861, the federal government derived its main revenue from customs duties on goods imported into the United States. The nation nearly faced a secession crisis over tariffs thirty years prior to South Carolina's secession from the union in 1860. Tariff issues have contributed to winning and losing presidential campaigns as well as the impeachment proceedings against John Tyler. The only time a president ever focused his entire Annual Address (called the State of the Union in modern times) on one issue, that issue was tariff reform.

How did **tariffs** influence George Washington's controversial decision to sign **Jay's Treaty**?

The first major foreign policy challenge for President Washington occurred when France and Britain waged war against each other in the early 1790s. Fearing that involvement in the European war would hurt the fledgling United States, Washington issued a proclamation of neutrality on April 22, 1793, urging American citizens to be impartial and warning them against aiding or sending war materials to either side.

Tariffs: A Divisive Political Issue?

The nation nearly faced a secession crisis over tariffs thirty years prior to the Civil War. The crisis led to a contentious relationship between President Andrew Jackson and Vice President John C. Calhoun, who led South Carolina's fight against tariffs that included threats to secede from the Union over the issue. During a ceremonial state dinner to mark the birth date of Thomas Jefferson, Jackson rose to make a toast. Looking directly at Calhoun, Jackson said, "Our federal union! It must be preserved." Calhoun replied: "The Union, next to our liberty, most dear."

Tariff issues contributed to impeachment proceedings against President John Tyler.

The only time a president ever focused his entire Annual Address on one issue, that issue was tariff reform.

President Woodrow Wilson called a special session of Congress to pass tariff reform. When legislation stalled, he spoke directly to the people in what is considered the first modern presidential press conference, claiming that senators were caving in to special interests. The resulting popular pressure encouraged the Senate to quickly pass the treaty reform bill.

Washington sent John Jay on a treaty-making mission to London. The outcome, Jay's Treaty of 1794, outraged France; it did not uphold the French-American alliance of 1778, and the treaty benefited Britain. Despite reservations, Washington signed the treaty to keep open trade from Britain that supplied the Treasury with tariff revenues. (See The President Leads: Foreign Policy—Treaties and Trade, for more on Jay's Treaty.)

What was the "Tariff of Abominations"?

During the mid-1820s, President John Quincy Adams urged Congress to pass a higher tariff rate that would increase federal revenues and support Adams's program for internal improvements. Adams faced a hostile Congress filled with supporters of Andrew Jackson, whom Adams had defeated in the controversial election of 1824 and who was running against Adams for president in 1828. Jackson's supporters in Congress amended Adams's tariff bill to include a significantly higher tax on imported raw materials. Since the tax would be especially hard on New England manufacturers, who would have to pay higher prices for their raw materials, Congress thought Adams—a New Englander—would reject the bill. Instead, Adams signed it into law.

The bill proved very unpopular, earned the nickname the "Tariff of Abominations," and contributed to Adams's defeat in 1828. The tariff led to a sharp rise in the prices of various goods, causing hardships for manufacturers as well as consumers.

How did **tariffs** nearly lead to **South Carolina seceding** from the Union in 1832?

The tariff of 1828 inspired John C. Calhoun, a congressman from South Carolina and vice president to Andrew Jackson from 1829 to 1832, to propose what he called the Theory of Nullification, which claimed that states had the right to nullify federal laws that were against the state's interest. When South Carolina attempted to nullify the tariff of 1828, Southerners expected Jackson to side with South Carolina on the states' rights issue, but Jackson sided with the federal government.

Another tariff, passed in 1832, brought Jackson and Calhoun into deeper conflict. Calhoun had resigned as vice president near the end of Jackson's first term and was elected senator of South Carolina. He defended South Carolina's Nullification Ordinance of November 1832, which was intended to block enforcement of the tariff in that state. Jackson responded with a Nullification Proclamation and a call to Congress to authorize military suppression of any defiance of federal law. A compromise tariff, negotiated by U.S. representative Henry Clay of Kentucky, proved agreeable to both sides and helped them avoid a final confrontation.

How did a **tariff veto** lead to **impeachment proceedings against President John Tyler**?

John Tyler had a difficult relationship with Congress, even though he was in the same Whig Party as the Congressional majority. Tyler had been a states' rights Democrat until he left the party to join the Whigs in 1836 in protest over the actions of President Andrew Jackson. Tyler was selected as William Henry Harrison's running mate on the Whig ticket of 1840 because, as a Virginian and states' rights advocate, he was popular in the south. Tyler became president when Harrison died just shy of a month into his term.

Instead of following the Whig Party platform as president, Tyler stuck to his states' rights and constructionist philosophy and was soon at odds with Whig plans for expanding government programs. The Whig Party severed ties with the president in 1841.

Tyler had already outraged Whigs by twice vetoing measures to create a new Bank of the United States. When he vetoed a protective tariff in 1842, the House of Representatives adopted a resolution charging him with offenses justifying impeachment. The impeachment measure failed to pass the House, and the president succeeded in forcing Congress to pass separate bills for a more moderate tariff.

What **tariff issues confronted presidents during the mid-nineteenth century**?

Democrat James K. Polk, elected in 1844, was one of the strongest and most successful presidents of the nineteenth century. Among his accomplishments was pressuring Congress to revoke a tariff bill of 1845.

During the 1850s, the desire to expand international trade led President Franklin Pierce to negotiate a tariff reciprocity treaty with England, gaining U.S. fishing rights in the waters off Canada in return for granting Canada trade privileges with the United States. Later in the 1850s and reflecting growing divisiveness between the federal government and Southern states, James Buchanan appointed a collector to enforce federal tariff laws in Charleston, South Carolina.

Republican Chester Alan Arthur sought tariff reductions in the early 1880s, but Congress ignored him despite a large and growing budget surplus. Grover Cleveland followed Arthur as president and he, too, wanted to lower the tariff. Cleveland believed that government aid and regulation should be kept to a minimum. The protective tariff contributed not only to higher prices for consumers but also to the development of business trusts. In 1887, Cleveland devoted his entire Annual Message to Congress to an attack on the high tariff. No other president had ever given his entire message on a single topic. Cleveland's move focused nationwide attention on the tariff and emphasized his leadership. But a bill passed by the House in July 1888 contained only moderate reductions in the rates.

Cleveland staked his reelection in 1888 on the tariff issue. His opponent, Benjamin Harrison, backed the protective tariff and earned the support of business. That support helped Harrison win electoral votes of large states in the east and midwest, providing him with an electoral college victory though he registered almost one hundred thousand fewer popular votes than Cleveland.

Why were **tariffs so significant during the 1890s**?

The United States enjoyed a budget surplus during the 1880s. Supporters of tariffs wanted them to continue in the 1890s as a way of protecting American manufacturers during a period of rapid industrialization. Those against argued that tariffs contributed to higher prices for consumer goods and to the development of trusts. President Benjamin Harrison, elected in 1888, supported the McKinley Tariff Act, created by U.S. representative (and future president) William McKinley of Ohio, that set tariffs at record highs.

Harrison was defeated in the 1892 election by his predecessor, Grover Cleveland. Many of Cleveland's policies had been reversed by Harrison, so Cleveland, in turn, planned to rescind policies backed by Harrison. When a severe economic downturn hit the United States during the first year of Cleveland's term, the president cited the McKinley tariff as a major contributor to economic woes. But Cleveland failed to convince Congress to pass meaningful tariff reform. The Wilson-Gorman Tariff of 1894 did not meet his campaign promise to lower the tariff. Cleveland refused to sign the bill, but he declined to veto it as well, and the nation had a new tariff, not tariff reform.

William McKinley, elected president in 1896, wanted to further increase tariff rates. Congress obliged him with the Dingley Tariff (1897).

How did **tariff issues** help define the presidencies of **William Howard Taft and Woodrow Wilson**?

When William Howard Taft took office in 1909, tariff reform was demanded by an American public faced with continually rising costs for consumer goods. Taft called a special session of Congress early in his presidency to address tariff reform. He got what he wanted from the House of Representatives with the Payne-Aldrich Act of 1909, which called for lowering or eliminating many tariffs. But the Senate added several attachments to the bill, many of which actually increased tariffs. Taft not only signed the compromised legislation, he called it the best tariff in history and took a cross-country tour to promote the bill. The press and public quickly ridiculed the legislation. As an outcome, Taft began his administration on a negative tone from which he never really recovered. Taft finished third when he ran for reelection in 1912.

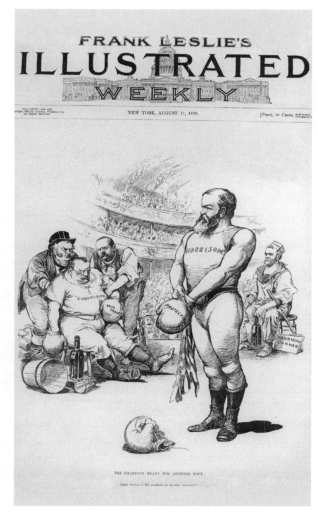

Illustrating their differences on the tariff issue in the 1888 presidential campaign, this cartoon shows Benjamin Harrison standing in a boxing ring wearing a glove labeled "protection," with a man in his corner representing labor. Grover Cleveland, in the other corner looking exhausted and beaten, wears a glove with the label, "free trade." *Library of Congress.*

Woodrow Wilson won the election of 1912 by defeating incumbent president Taft and former president Theodore Roosevelt. As Wilson's first order of business, he called a special session of Congress to pass tariff reform, as he had promised during his presidential campaign. Wilson appeared in person before a joint session of Congress and stressed his determination to lead the legislation. It was the first time in over one hundred years that a president addressed a special session of Congress. (John Adams, president from 1797 to 1801, was the last president to have done so.) A tariff reform bill, sponsored by U.S. representative Oscar W. Underwood of Alabama, lowered rates by an average of 10 percent. However, debate in the Senate threatened the legislation with significant changes or defeat. Wilson responded by going public and charging that special business and industry interests were pressuring senators to defeat the legislation. Opposition quickly faded, and the Underwood Act passed the Senate and was signed into law by Wilson. The show of strength helped make Wilson an effective leader.

POLICIES AND PROGRAMS, BOOMS AND BUSTS

What is the significance of the phrase "It's the Economy, Stupid"?

The phrase was an internal slogan for the Bill Clinton presidential campaign in 1992 pasted on the wall of the "War Room" at Clinton's campaign headquarters in Little Rock, Arkansas. The Clinton campaign promised active measures to improve the economy of the United States. Ultimately, it was the candidates' positions on the economy that decided the election in favor of Clinton.

The fortunes of many presidents have depended on the performance of the economy, whether or not booms or busts could be directly attributed to the president's policies. Among those presidents who benefited from a strong economy at the beginning of their administration are James Monroe and Herbert Hoover. Monroe survived the Panic of 1819 to win a landslide reelection in 1820, while Hoover was widely viewed as ineffective in combating what became the Great Depression and was defeated in his bid for reelection. William McKinley benefited from an upturn in the economy early in his administration and was credited for pro-business policies that sustained economic growth throughout his first term. McKinley won reelection in 1900.

Presidents Martin Van Buren and Grover Cleveland faced severe economic crises (the Panic of 1837 and the Panic of 1893, respectively) early in their terms and were blamed when conditions failed to improve. In both cases, voters went for candidates from the opposing parties in the next election. The most dramatic example of the state of the economy as a determining factor in the fate of an incumbent president occurred in the 1992 election. George Bush had enjoyed extremely high approval for his handling of the 1991 Gulf War. A sluggish economy, however, made him vulnerable in the following year's presidential election, which he lost to Clinton.

What was the Embargo Act of 1807?

Britain and France were at war, and American commerce was caught in the crossfire. President Thomas Jefferson sought to protect American life and shipping and to pressure the warring nations by suspending commerce. The Embargo Act of 1807 forbade all international trade to and from American ports. In January 1808, the embargo was

---

Hoover Hears the Heat

Perceived by many as not doing enough to combat the effects of the Great Depression, Herbert Hoover became an object of gallows humor:

- Hoover blanket: A wrap used by a homeless and jobless person to keep warm
- Hoover flag: An empty pocket turned inside out
- Hoover wagon: A broken-down automobile
- Hooverville: A makeshift village of shacks made of cardboard or found wood

---

extended to inland waters and land commerce, halting a burgeoning trade with Canada. The daring attempt to use economic pressure in a world at war was not successful. Britain and France stood firm. Enforcement was difficult, especially in New England, where merchants disliked the program. When Congress, against much opposition, passed an act to make enforcement more rigid the following year, resistance approached the point of rebellion—again especially in New England. On March 1, 1809, the embargo was superseded by the Nonintercourse Act. This allowed resumption of all commercial trade except with Britain and France.

What presidents were **considered ineffective** by voters during **times of economic crisis**?

Martin Van Buren inherited a downward spiraling economy and within weeks of his inauguration the Panic of 1837 struck, with disastrous results for the national economy and the revenues of the federal government. The Panic, the worst depression to hit the American economy to that time, was related to actions by Van Buren's predecessor, Andrew Jackson, who transferred federal funds to state banks. The state banks had been excessive in issuing loans, and when a strong economy weakened in 1837 many customers could not repay their loans and faced financial ruin. Van Buren called a special session of Congress, but he limited his recommendations to the establishment of an independent treasury system to separate the government's funds from all banks and banking activities. Van Buren was criticized by congressional Whigs for failing to recommend aid to the business community, and the public viewed him as indifferent during a time of distress.

Grover Cleveland's entire second administration was consumed by the most severe depression the country had yet experienced, the Panic of 1893. Within a year after his inauguration, four million people were unemployed out of a population of about sixty-five million. Cleveland believed the Sherman Silver Purchase Act and the

McKinley Tariff, both passed in 1890, had caused the panic of 1893 and the subsequent depression and focused his energy on having them repealed. He was successful in having the Sherman Act rescinded, but there was no noticeable effect on the depression. Like Van Buren, Cleveland was viewed as heartless in a time of need.

Herbert Hoover took office in March 1929 at a time of unprecedented prosperity. In October of that year, however, stocks began falling rapidly and the market crashed. Financial panic set in, as many investors lost their savings and many banks failed. Hoover believed that aid and job creation should come from local governments, not from the federal government. In February 1930, the stock market seemed to be balancing out, and Hoover announced that the worst was over. But unemployment continued to rise (reaching twelve million by mid-1932), banks continued to foreclose on mortgages, and a severe drought hurt farmers on the Great Plains. Hoover supported a program to provide indirect relief to the unemployed by lending money to insurance companies, banks, farm organizations, railroads, and state, county, and city governments to stimulate economic activity and employment. The result was a perception that Hoover never directly addressed those hit hardest.

Which presidents' **economic recovery efforts** were frustrated by **inflation**?

Upon taking office in 1969 and faced with inflation, Richard Nixon tried tightening the federal money policy, but it did not stop inflation. From 1971 to 1974, the Nixon administration tried various phases of wage and price controls, but the controls were frequently changed and difficult to enforce. An oil embargo by the Organization of Petroleum Exporting Countries (OPEC) during 1973 and 1974 sharply raised energy costs. The federal government was preoccupied with the Watergate hearings and did not take effective action.

When Gerald Ford became president in 1974, energy shortages contributed to a recession and increases in inflation. At first, Ford emphasized reduced spending, balanced budgets, and tight monetary policy as a means to combat inflation, but in early 1975, Ford focused on relieving the recession. Ford urged tax cuts, steps to reduce the national dependence on foreign oil imports, and substantial reductions in spending. Over a two-year period, he vetoed more than fifty pieces of legislation that, in his view, increased spending. Ford's anti-inflation program was primarily a public-relations attempt called WIN (Whip Inflation Now) that included federal spending reduction and voluntary price controls. Ford even addressed Congress with a WIN button on his suit. The program had no effect on the economy.

By mid-1976, the recession showed signs of easing. Jimmy Carter had criticized Ford's economic policies and defeated Ford in the presidential election. After four years, however, inflation and unemployment were worse, fueled in part by erosion of the value of the U.S. dollar and a large trade deficit, much of it a result of U.S. dependence on foreign oil.

> ## Deflating Inflation
>
> Inflation, rapidly rising prices of commodities and services, was traditionally viewed as the result of an increase in the quantity of money without a corresponding increase in the quantity of goods and services coming on the market. Beginning in the 1950s, inflation was also explained as the result of wages that exceed labor productivity, creating higher operating costs and forcing producers to raise their prices to consumers. During the 1980s, however, a long period of inflation was stopped in the traditional manner—by tighter control of money by the Federal Reserve. The actions taken by Fed chairman Paul Volcker, with the blessings of the administration of President Ronald Reagan, were controversial at the time but became a common strategy by the 1990s.

Which presidents benefited from a **healthy economy** without taking much action?

Following the end of the War of 1812 in 1815, the nation was expanding, political conflicts were few, and the economy was on an upward cycle. Shortly after taking office in 1817, James Monroe toured the nation. Even in New England, where opposition to the War of 1812 had been most vocal, Monroe was hailed. A Boston newspaper, the *Columbian Centinel,* exclaimed that the new president has ushered in "an era of good feelings." John Quincy Adams, who followed Monroe as president, would later write that the Monroe years would be looked back on as "the Golden Age of this Republic." Since Monroe favored a limited federal government, he did not propose major programs, even after the economy took a downward spin in 1819. Monroe remained popular in spite of the downturn: he swept the Electoral College vote in 1820 (except for one electoral voter who cast a vote for Adams to ensure that George Washington would remain the only president who captured every electoral vote).

During his first term, which began in 1885, Grover Cleveland presided over a large budget surplus and a time of business growth—the apex of the "Gilded Age." Although Cleveland pursued some business, financial, and government reforms, he served more as a "preventative president," focusing on improving and protecting programs already in place, rather than aggressively enacting new ones.

Calvin Coolidge was a low-key leader whom some commentators labeled a "do-nothing" president. But his approach was reassuring when he took office after the death of Warren G. Harding in 1923 and the subsequent revelation of numerous scandals of the Harding administration. Though he proposed little legislation, Coolidge championed tax cuts that sustained economic growth during the 1920s.

The administration of Dwight D. Eisenhower did not initiate bold economic programs, and Americans seemed to like it that way during a period of general prosperity and growth beginning in the mid-1950s.

> ### H. L. Mencken on President Coolidge
>
> The often bitingly sarcastic journalist H. L. Mencken found some praise for the low-key Calvin Coolidge: "His failings are forgotten; the country remembers only the grateful fact that he let it alone."

Which **presidents exerted the most influence on the economy**?

War presidents Abraham Lincoln, Woodrow Wilson, and Franklin D. Roosevelt exerted virtually complete management of the economy. When the Civil War began in 1861, Congress was not in session. Before asking for congressional authorization, and in violation of the Constitution, Lincoln entrusted public funds to private agents in New York to purchase arms and supplies. The Lincoln administration also made the crucial decision to finance the Union effort by borrowing money through the sale of war bonds. Salmon P. Chase, secretary of the treasury, effectively made war finance a broad, democratic, and patriotic campaign, which won support after early Union losses. Working with financier Jay Cooke, the government orchestrated a massive public-relations campaign that convinced over six hundred thousand citizens to buy over $1 billion worth of securities.

During World War I, Woodrow Wilson nationalized U.S. railroads; established the Food Administration to allocate foodstuffs to the U.S. Armed Forces, the Allies, and the general population of the United States; and created a Shipping Board to manage merchant shipping. The Council of National Defense was established in 1916 to oversee the government's economic planning and wartime supply efforts. Under this organization were the War Industries Board and the War Labor Board, which worked to convince manufacturers and unions to cooperate with each other and the government. The Wilson administration did not impose rationing or end the production of consumer goods, and the economy boomed. Millions of civilians left farms and small towns to work in industrial plants in major cities. More than sixty million Americans bought war bonds to help finance a portion of the war effort.

World War II effectively ended the Great Depression and brought prosperity: unemployment dropped from 17 percent in 1939 to one percent in 1944; personal income doubled; and because of wartime rationing and the government halting the production of nonessential goods (like refrigerators and cars), citizens accumulated savings. President Franklin D. Roosevelt created many new agencies to conduct the war:

- The War Production Board (WPB) had the power to mobilize the nation's resources.

- The Board of Economic Warfare (BEW), replaced by the Office of Economic Warfare (OEW), oversaw agencies created to administer critical materials, including the Rubber Administration, the Petroleum Administration, the Solid Fuels Administration, and the Smaller War Plants Corporation.

A cartoon satirizing the change of emphasis in Franklin D. Roosevelt's government, from concentrating on the New Deal to winning World War II. *Getty Images.*

- The Office of Price Administration (OPA) established price ceilings and rationing.
- The National Defense Mediation Board (NDMB) managed the labor force that was producing war materials with the goal of quick and amicable settlement of disputes. When this agency failed to resolve a dispute between the United Mine Workers (UMW) and steel companies, the NDMB was replaced by the National War Labor Board (NWLB), which successfully handled several major disputes.

Which presidents have **intervened in strikes**?

The effects of a severe economic downturn in 1873 continued to be felt for the rest of the decade. When railroads began to cut wages in the summer of 1877, employees of the Baltimore and Ohio line in Martinsburg, West Virginia, went on strike. The state militia was poorly equipped and many members refused to take action against the strikers. The governor and railroad owners appealed to President Rutherford B. Hayes to send in federal troops. Hayes hoped that the workers and the companies would solve their own problems, but he reluctantly sent troops in after federal court orders were issued that stated that strikers were in contempt of court.

In response, strikes spread across the country and became known collectively as the Great Strike. A few railroads restored wages and negotiated with the workers, but

221

most companies, backed by the state militias and federal troops, ended the Great Strike with force.

Grover Cleveland sent federal troops to crush the Pullman strike in 1893. The strike obstructed railroads and interfered with postal delivery. A federal injunction against the strike had been ignored. Cleveland's action was effective, but also excessive and costly. Eugene V. Debs was among several union leaders who were sent to jail for violating the injunction without a court order, a jury trial, or a conviction. Organized labor gained momentum in response to the president's actions.

In 1902, Theodore Roosevelt forced the coal industry to settle a prolonged strike by agreeing to accept the recommendations of an independent arbitration committee appointed by Roosevelt. The president was praised for his even-tempered approach, and the independent arbitration committee proved to be fair to both sides in the dispute.

During the Great Depression, militant workers used "sit-down" strikes in factories to protest wages. Franklin D. Roosevelt expressed opposition to the sit-down strikes, but his lack of action against them was blamed for encouraging growing activism of organized labor.

In 1947, President Harry S. Truman vetoed the Taft-Hartley Act because he felt it unfairly weakened the bargaining power of unions. Still, Truman intervened several times in labor-management disputes in the railroad, coal, and steel industries. Faced with a steel strike during the Korean War, Truman ordered steel mills to be seized to keep them in operation. The U.S. Supreme Court rejected the president's argument that he had inherent powers to seize firms in emergencies.

In 1962, President John F. Kennedy persuaded striking United Steel Workers members to accept a contract he hailed as "non-inflationary." A few days later, the United States Steel Corporation announced an increase of 3.5% in its prices, and most other steel companies did likewise. Infuriated, Kennedy pressured the companies to repeal the increase.

When air traffic controllers went on strike during the Ronald Reagan administration, the president called the strike illegal because it endangered public safety. He fired 11,800 workers. While Kennedy had been faulted by business for his action in 1962, Reagan was faulted by labor for his action two decades later.

Which presidents were active **against trusts and monopolies**?

The cycle of booms and busts that occurred following the Civil War to the 1890s contributed to the formation of monopolies and trusts, but no effective action was taken against unfair business practices until after the turn of the century. There is evidence that William McKinley was going to address the problems in his second term, which began in 1901, but McKinley was assassinated that year. Theodore Roosevelt succeeded to the presidency and became known as the "trust buster."

During Roosevelt's presidency, the Justice Department launched forty-three lawsuits against trusts. The most notable victory for the administration came against the Northern Securities Company, a group of several railroads run as if they were one company—an arrangement that allowed them to control rates and overwhelm competing railroads.

Roosevelt, though, was more interested in business reform than prosecution. In 1903, he signed the Elkins anti-rebate railroad bill, which ended a practice by railroads of granting special rebates on freight rates as a perk. Roosevelt effectively pressured Congress to create the Bureau of Corporations within the new Department of Commerce and Labor to investigate and report on corporations; up to that time there were few ways to monitor business practices.

Roosevelt was a master of self-publicity, unlike his successor, William Howard Taft. Roosevelt is remembered as the "trust buster," but the Taft administration initiated twice as many antitrust suits against big corporations and had more resounding success. Taft's attorney general, George Wickersham, went after the biggest trust of them all—the Standard Oil Company, led by John D. Rockefeller. Through a series of corporate mergers, the Standard Oil Company conglomerate dominated the energy industry. The anti-trust case went to the Supreme Court, which ordered the Standard Oil Company to disband.

The U.S. Steel Corporation—the first billion-dollar company in history—was next on the docket for the Taft administration. U.S. Steel had purchased several brokerage firms in 1907 that owned stock in the Tennessee Coal and Iron Company. The Tennessee Company was allegedly facing financial collapse, which would ruin the brokerage firms and precipitate a financial crisis. The Taft administration argued that the purchase was made under false pretenses and violated the Sherman Anti-Trust Act. In this case, the Taft administration failed to win conviction. In the process, the administration lost some crucial business support and angered Theodore Roosevelt, whose name was mentioned in the suit as having been informed while he was president of the plans of U.S. Steel. Roosevelt ran against Taft for the Republican nomination in the 1912. When Republicans held their support for Taft, Roosevelt ran as a third-party candidate in the general election. Roosevelt outpolled Taft and finished second in the election to Woodrow Wilson.

The administration of Woodrow Wilson helped push through Congress the Federal Trade Commission bill. The bill, which outlawed "unfair" trade practices and created a Federal Trade Commission to issue "cease and desist" orders to prevent unfair competition, was signed into law in 1914.

The Bill Clinton administration supported antitrust proceedings against the Microsoft Corporation with mixed results. Three years after Clinton left office, some portions of the case were still being argued and similar antitrust allegations against Microsoft were pursued by the European Union.

Which president **exerted the most control over a peacetime economy**?

When Franklin D. Roosevelt took office in March 1933, more than thirteen million workers were unemployed. Roosevelt gave a spirited inaugural address, declaring to Americans that "the only thing we have to fear is fear itself." Roosevelt called a special session of Congress and began acting. Congress immediately passed the Emergency Banking Act to provide aid to banks. Then, through the Economy Act, the government made cuts in payments to federal workers, freeing up some $500 million that went to local and state agencies as relief grants. People were put to work through agencies that coordinated a range of programs, from large-scale construction projects to conservation and clean-up work.

Roosevelt set up agencies that reformed banking policies, helped guide negotiations between management and labor, and established minimum wage and maximum work hours. To help speed legislation, the administration sometimes wrote bills that were quickly debated and passed by Congress and signed by the president—all in one day on several occasions. An amazing amount of legislation was passed during his first one hundred days in office, followed by more legislation in 1934 and 1935.

In spite of these actions, a full economic recovery did not happen until the United States shifted to a wartime economy. Nevertheless, many programs introduced during the Roosevelt administration provided relief and inspired confidence that the government was concerned about the welfare of its citizens. "Roosevelt understood," noted historian Garry Wills, "the importance of psychology—that people have to have the courage to keep seeking a cure." Several New Deal programs continued beyond the end of the Great Depression.

What president's economic policies were most **opposite those of the New Deal**?

It can be argued that presidents who initiated the fewest economic programs were most different than Franklin D. Roosevelt. However, Ronald Reagan took aggressive steps to dismantle the large government approach of Franklin D. Roosevelt's New Deal and Lyndon B. Johnson's Great Society.

Reflecting his philosophy that "government isn't the solution to our problems, government *is* the problem," Reagan undertook large budget reductions in domestic programs and produced substantial tax cuts for individuals and businesses. The theory of supply-side economics—generating growth by stimulating a greater supply of goods and services, thereby increasing jobs—was a mainstay of the Reagan approach and came to be known as Reaganomics. Budget cuts in 1981 of $39 billion were followed by the passage of a 25 percent tax cut for individual taxpayers and faster tax write-offs for businesses. Reagan was determined to reduce the growth of the national government, restore the power of the states in the federal system, reduce government expenditures through massive domestic budget cuts, expand the military and defense establishments, and lower taxes.

Major Acts of the New Deal

Act or Program	Acronym	Year Enacted	Significance
Agricultural Adjustment Act	AAA	1933	Protected farmers from price drops by providing crop subsidies to reduce production, and educational programs to teach methods of preventing soil erosion.
Civil Works Administration	CWA	1933	Provided public works jobs at $15/week to four million workers in 1934.
Civilian Conservation Corps	CCC	1933	Sent 250,000 young men to work camps to perform reforestation and conservation tasks. Removed surplus of workers from cities, provided healthy conditions for workers and money for families.
Federal Emergency Relief Act	FERA	1933	Distributed millions of dollars of direct aid to unemployed workers.
Glass-Steagall Act	FDIC	1933	Created federally insured bank deposits ($2,500 per investor at first) to prevent bank failures.
National Industrial Recovery Act	NIRA	1933	Created to enforce codes of fair competition, minimum wages, and to permit collective bargaining of workers.
National Youth Administration	NYA	1935	Provided part-time employment to more than two million college and high school students.
Public Works Administration	PWA	1933	Received $3.3 billion appropriation from Congress for public works projects.
Rural Electrification Administration	REA	1935	Encouraged farmers to join cooperatives to bring electricity to farms.
Securities and Exchange Commission	SEC	1934	Regulated stock market and restricted margin buying.
Social Security Act	SSA	1935	Provided pensions and unemployment insurance, as well as aid to blind, deaf, disabled, and dependent children.
Tennessee Valley Authority	TVA	1933	Federal government built a series of dams to prevent flooding and sell electricity. First public competition with private power industries.
Wagner Act	NLRB	1935	Allowed workers to join unions and outlawed union-busting tactics by management.
Works Progress Administration	WPA	1935	Employed 8.5 million workers in construction and other jobs, and provided work in arts, theater, and literary projects.

Greg D. Felmeth. "New Deal Programs." *U.S. History Resources.* http://home.earthlink.net/~gfeldmeth/chart.newdeal.html (accessed on July 3, 2004).

President Bill Clinton (right) is accompanied by former presidents (from left) Gerald Ford, Jimmy Carter, and George Bush on his way to signing the North American Free Trade Agreement, which called for the removal of tariffs and other trade barriers on most goods produced and sold in North America. The trade agreement had roots in the 1970s before being signed into law in 1993. *AP/Wide World Photos.*

What was the **outcome of Reaganomics**?

The Reagan administration's economic policies had mixed results early, then the American economy picked up momentum and growth beginning in 1983. Except for a sudden downturn in 1987, the American economy was strong for most of the 1980s. However, massive tax cuts, large increases in defense spending, and trade deficits contributed to doubling the national debt from deficit levels of the 1970s. Economists are divided in their opinions about the effects of budget deficits: in the short term, the deficits may be necessary to help stimulate a sluggish economy; in the longer term, budget deficits threaten financial stability and often lead to inflation. The steadily increasing national debt became a major campaign issue in the 1992 presidential elections and helped Democrat Bill Clinton defeat George Bush, who was Reagan's vice president and his successor as president.

With its emphasis on tighter money control, Reaganomics supported the action of the Federal Reserve to fight inflation, which had plagued the American economy for over a decade. As the country emerged from recession in 1983, a large and speedy fall of the inflation rate helped the economy become robust until the late 1980s.

What credit does **Bill Clinton** receive for the **robust economy of the 1990s**?

During the Clinton administration, the federal budget deficit that had weakened the economy in the early 1990s was cut in half, and then in 1998 the United States had a federal budget surplus of $70 billion, the first surplus since the mid-1960s. Clinton expanded earned-income credit for the working poor, significantly reduced the number of government workers, introduced targeted domestic programs on education, health, and the environment, and sponsored a welfare reform bill that established time limits for benefits. In 1997, Congress enacted a major tax cut, the first since 1981, and Clinton negotiated a deficit-reduction package.

Many private sector factors contributed to the health of the American economy during the 1990s. Additionally, the acrimonious relationship between Clinton and the Republican-led Congress was sometimes beneficial. Clinton was forced to target his spending plans and declared in a State of the Union Address that "the era of big government is over." That statement was significant, coming from a Democratic president who shared the view that government can improve social and economic problems in the tradition of Franklin D. Roosevelt, Harry S. Truman, John F. Kennedy, and Lyndon B. Johnson.

Congress kept spending in check, and passed a welfare reform bill and the 1997 tax cut. But an earlier attempt by Congress in 1995 to cut the president's expenditures in order to fund a tax break met with a stalemate. Neither side would budge on the budget. When Congress refused to pass temporary funding measures until the budget was approved, the government literally closed down. Public backlash went against Republicans in Congress, and Clinton won credit for defending such programs as Social Security and Medicare.

THE PRESIDENT LEADS: FOREIGN POLICY

PROGRAMS AND STATEMENTS

What is the **president's role in U.S. foreign policy**?

The president is the chief diplomat of the United States as well as commander in chief of the armed forces. The president negotiates and signs international treaties, agreements, and pacts with the heads of foreign nations. Treaties negotiated by the president must be approved by two-thirds majority of the U.S. Senate.

What was controversial about **George Washington's Proclamation of Neutrality (1793)**?

During Washington's presidency (1789–1797), Great Britain and France were at war. Britain had the world's best navy and continued to maintain a military presence in the North American interior around the Great Lakes. France had been a significant U.S. ally during the American Revolution (1775–1783), and two treaties of French-American alliance of 1778 were still in force.

Concerned that the young United States would be vulnerable by being involved in war, Washington issued a proclamation of neutrality on April 22, 1793. The proclamation urged American citizens to be impartial and warned them against aiding or sending war materials to either the British or the French.

Americans were divided on the war. Alexander Hamilton, Washington's secretary of the treasury, wanted to continue trade with Great Britain. He argued the treaties with France were no longer valid since they had been signed by the government of Louis XVI, which was overthrown in the French Revolution (1789). Thomas Jefferson countered that the treaties were still valid because they had been made by an enduring nation. Jefferson and his supporters were outraged that the United States would turn

229

President James Monroe (standing) and advisers discuss the Monroe Doctrine, which proved to be one of the most significant and enduring statements of American foreign policy. Painted by Clyde Deland in 1823, the illustration includes John Quincy Adams (on far left), who would succeed Monroe as president, and John C. Calhoun (next to door), who would become a controversial vice president during Andrew Jackson's first term. *Getty Images.*

away from France, whose support had been critical for the success of the American Revolution just a decade earlier.

What was the **Monroe Doctrine**?

Revolutions in Spain's South American colonies had been occurring during the first two decades of the nineteenth century. When an alliance of Russia, Austria, France, and Prussia helped restore the monarchy of Spain in the early 1820s, there was concern in Great Britain and in the United States that the alliance would also help Spain to maintain its colonies in the Americas. In 1823, England's foreign minister proposed that the United States and England issue a joint statement against European intervention in the affairs of the Americas.

President James Monroe, influenced by John Quincy Adams, his secretary of state, decided instead to assert American independence in foreign policy. In his Annual Message to Congress in December 1823, Monroe declared that the United States would regard any interference in the internal affairs of the Americans as an unfriendly act.

Greeted with enthusiasm by Americans, what became known as the Monroe Doctrine went largely unnoticed internationally. Nevertheless, the Monroe Doctrine was a

An Excerpt from the Monroe Doctrine

[The] occasion has been judged proper for asserting, as a principle in which the rights and interests of the United States are involved, that the American continents, by the free and independent condition which they have assumed and maintain, are henceforth not to be considered as subjects for future colonization by any European powers....

Our policy in regard to Europe, which was adopted at an early stage of the wars which have so long agitated that quarter of the globe, nevertheless remains the same, which is, not to interfere in the internal concerns of any of its powers; to consider the government de facto as the legitimate government for us; to cultivate friendly relations with it, and to preserve those relations by a frank, firm, and manly policy, meeting in all instances the just claims of every power, submitting to injuries from none. But in regard to those continents circumstances are eminently and conspicuously different.

It is impossible that the allied powers should extend their political system to any portion of either continent without endangering our peace and happiness; nor can anyone believe that our southern brethren, if left to themselves, would adopt it of their own accord. It is equally impossible, therefore, that we should behold such interposition in any form with indifference.

sign of the emergence of the United States as an international power and proved to be one of the most significant and enduring statements of American foreign policy. Several subsequent presidents cited the Monroe Doctrine to explain their actions to confront foreign intervention in the Americas.

Which presidents **invoked or expanded on the Monroe Doctrine**?

In 1842, John Tyler extended the Monroe Doctrine to the Hawaiian Islands when Britain became interested in the area. In 1848, James K. Polk invoked the Monroe Doctrine when France's influence in Mexico encouraged the possibility that the Yucatan Peninsula might become a French protectorate. France was again involved in Mexican affairs in the mid-1860s, helping arm factions loyal to a prince whom France wanted to become emperor of Mexico. Invoking the Monroe Doctrine, Andrew Johnson sent a warning to France that led to France withdrawing a military force.

Grover Cleveland made use of the Doctrine twice—to spur negotiations instead of war in a mid-1880s border dispute between Venezuela and British Guiana, and to support Cuba in the early 1890s in its struggle for independence from Spain. However,

231

Cleveland only exerted diplomatic pressure on Spain, which went ahead and suppressed the Cuban rebellion.

The (Theodore) Roosevelt Corollary to the Monroe Doctrine was asserted in 1904 to protect Latin American countries from military action over debts they owed to European nations. Germany had threatened action against Venezuela in 1903. The United States assumed financial management of foreign debts of the Dominican Republic under the Roosevelt Corollary.

In the twentieth century, the United States itself has intervened in the affairs of Latin American countries. Following World War II, Pan-American agreements asserted the principle that an attack on one country of the western hemisphere was to be considered an act of aggression against all the countries of the hemisphere. The Organization of American States, founded in 1948, continues the principle of the Monroe Doctrine through cooperation among nations of the Americas.

When did a **proposed canal across Panama first become a presidential concern**?

The Clayton-Bulwer Treaty of 1850, negotiated by the Zachary Taylor administration with Britain, provided for shared control over a future canal or other route across Central America.

Which other presidents addressed the **prospect of a canal in Panama during the nineteenth century**?

Preliminary plans for a canal across Panama or Nicaragua were made by Spain as early as the eighteenth century. Spain abandoned those plans when its colonies began revolting early in the nineteenth century. The Monroe Doctrine, announced in 1823, suggested that any canal-building across Central America should be controlled by the United States. That policy was explicitly stated by President Rutherford B. Hayes in 1880.

In 1881, construction of a canal on the Panama route began under a concession granted by Colombia in 1878. The attempt by the French Canal Company failed because of money and health woes, but the engineering plans were sound. The Spanish-American War (1898), fought in the Caribbean Sea and Pacific Ocean, demonstrated the need for quicker passage between the Atlantic and Pacific Oceans than sailing around South America. President William McKinley appointed the Isthmian Canal Commission in 1899, and the group submitted a report in 1901 recommending a route through Nicaragua. In 1901, the United States negotiated the Hay-Pauncefote Treaty with Great Britain, permitting U.S. control, operation, and protection of a canal. In January 1902, the Isthmian Canal Commission filed a supplementary report recommending construction of a canal on the Panama route.

What controversy surrounded **Theodore Roosevelt and the Panama Canal**?

On January 22, 1903, the Roosevelt administration and Colombia signed the Hay-Herrán Treaty, which allowed a canal to be built across Panama. However, Colombia's legislature refused to ratify the treaty.

Later that year, Panama, which was under the control of Colombia, revolted and declared its independence on November 3, 1903. The United States recognized the new government of Panama on November 6, and a week later Panama signed a treaty with the United States providing for the construction and operation of the canal in Panama. The treaty, which granted sovereignty to the United States for a ten-mile-wide strip—the Canal Zone—in which to construct the canal, was approved by the U.S. Senate on February 23, 1904.

Roosevelt is alleged to have encouraged the 1903 revolution for independence in Panama. The revolution conveniently began after the U.S. warship *Nashville* docked in Colón, Panama.

Why did **Jimmy Carter sign away rights to the Panama Canal**?

The Treaty Concerning the Permanent Neutrality and Operation of the Panama Canal and the Panama Canal Treaty, both signed by President Jimmy Carter in 1978, were the outcome of fourteen years of effort to turn over to Panama its major resource. In January 1964, two dozen Panamanians were killed and hundreds were injured when a group of students entered the Canal Zone and attempted to raise the flag of Panama. Treaties were drafted by the administrations of Lyndon B. Johnson in 1967 and Richard Nixon in 1971 for turning control of the canal over to Panama, but the tentative agreements were ultimately rejected by Panama. In March 1973, the United Nations Security Council introduced a resolution for a "just and equitable" solution to the dispute and "effective sovereignty" for Panama, but the United States vetoed the motion.

Henry Kissinger, secretary of state to Presidents Nixon and Gerald Ford, served as the principal negotiator for the United States with Panama beginning in 1973 and reached an agreement with Panamanian officials in September 1977, when Jimmy Carter was president. The treaties governed the operations and defense of the Canal through December 31, 1999, and guaranteed the permanent neutrality of the Canal. An orderly and complete transfer of jurisdiction over the Canal and the Zone from the United States to Panama occurred in 2000.

The treaties of 1978 were opposed by the more right-wing conservatives in the United States as undermining national security. The Carter administration argued in a large public relations campaign that the agreements represented "fairness, not force" in U.S. foreign relations. As with all treaties, those with Panama required two-thirds majority approval (66 votes) in the U.S. Senate. Two "reservations" were added to the 1978 treaties: one allowed for American armed intervention in Panama if the Canal closed, and the other was an agreement to station American troops in Panama after 1999. Panama agreed to the amendments and the treaties passed the U.S. Senate by a vote of 68–32.

Which president was the **first to actively seek to acquire Cuba**?

Plans to acquire Cuba, then a colony of Spain, became a focus of the Franklin Pierce administration (1853–1857). A combination of events made for good timing: Cuba had seized a U.S. merchant ship, *Black Warrior,* and Spain was facing internal turmoil. Pierce told his European ministers, led by James Buchanan, minister to England and later Pierce's successor as president, to pressure Spain to cede or sell Cuba to the United States. After a meeting of America's ministers in Europe in Ostend, Belgium, the ministers produced the Ostend Manifesto, a proposal to purchase Cuba through pressure from European bankers with hints that the United States might otherwise seize the island.

Intended as a document for viewing only within the administration, the contents of the Ostend Manifesto were leaked to the press and created a controversy. At the time, America was bitterly divided over the expansion of slavery. Interest in Cuba, already a slave colony, was viewed by abolitionists as another attempt by pro-slavery forces to extend their power. The Ostend Manifesto damaged the Pierce administration and any prospects for purchasing Cuba.

Which other presidents had **aggressive foreign policy programs toward Cuba during the nineteenth century**?

James Buchanan pursued acquisition of Cuba throughout his administration (1857–1861), but with the nation growing more divided over the issue of slavery, the acquisition had no chance of winning approval. Rebel uprisings in Cuba against Spain occurred during the administration of Ulysses S. Grant (served 1869–1877) and the second administration of Grover Cleveland (served 1893–1897), but neither president offered military support for the rebels. During Grant's time in office, Spain captured a rebel-owned steamer, the *Virginius,* which was illegally registered as an American vessel. Fifty-three crewmen and passengers aboard were executed; several were Americans. Amid cries for retribution, Grant's secretary of state, Hamilton Fish, negotiated a settlement that included reparations for families of the executed Americans.

What were presidents' **policies toward Cuba following the Spanish-American War**?

American troops left Cuba in 1903 after the United States had taken possession of the island with the defeat of Spain in the Spanish-American War (1898). The U.S. government did not interfere with Cuban affairs, even during the Cuban revolution of the 1950s when Fidel Castro took power and Cuba became a communist nation.

The Dwight D. Eisenhower administration backed a covert plan to use exiled Cuban nationals in an attempt to overthrow Castro. That military operation, known as the Bay of Pigs Invasion, occurred during the Kennedy administration (see The President Leads: Commander in Chief—Military Action).

The United States had no diplomatic or economic relations with Cuba from the late 1950s through the 1990s. The American invasion in 1983 of the Caribbean island of Grenada during the Reagan administration occurred in part over concern the island would become a base for Soviet-Cuban operations. To offset Cuban influence in Nicaragua, the Reagan administration used public and covert support for the anti-communist Contras of Nicaragua.

Responding to a wave of Cuban refugees seeking entry into the United States in 1994, Bill Clinton reversed the U.S. policy of giving asylum to those seeking to escape Cuba. The Clinton administration then worked out an agreement with the Cuban government to allow more refugees into the country. In 1999, a small group of refugees attempted to escape Cuba by boat, but the boat sank in rough weather and most of the refugees drowned. Among those saved was a six-year-old boy, Elian Gonzalez, whose mother was among those who drowned. Gonzalez was taken to the United States in preparation for return to Cuba. The boy's parents had divorced, and his father, who remained in Cuba, sought the boy's return.

Gonzalez had relatives in the United States who were part of a large Cuban exile community that left the island after the communist takeover in 1959. The Gonzalez relatives were adamant that Elian not be returned to Cuba. After weeks of dispute, an American court ordered Gonzalez to be returned to his father. When relatives refused, government agents from the Justice Department stormed the house where Gonzalez was kept, forcibly removed him, and returned the boy to his father in Cuba.

The Clinton administration sought to ease travel restrictions to Cuba. The administration of George W. Bush, which followed Clinton, tightened restrictions and reinforced economic sanctions against Cuba.

Was there much in the way of **foreign policy action during the Civil War**?

Abraham Lincoln spent little time on foreign policy during the Civil War, but he helped calm difficulties with Spain that could have led to war and succeeded in maintaining diplomatic ties with Great Britain during a tense period of British-American relations. In an 1861 incident, for example, a Union captain stopped a British boat, removed two Confederate emissaries to Britain, and took them into custody. Lincoln released the emissaries.

Why did **Ulysses S. Grant pursue annexation of Santo Domingo**?

The Grant administration envisioned an American naval base in Santo Domingo as a means for more power in the region and to protect a future canal across the isthmus of Central America. Santo Domingo had won independence from Spain, but a faction sought reunification in order to address Santo Domingo's severe economic problems and corruption. Emissaries aligned with President Bonaventura Báez of Santo Domingo approached Grant's secretary of state, Hamilton Fish, with an offer to sell the country to the United States. Fish was suspicious of the plan, but Grant was interested and pursued the matter through his secretary, Orville E. Babcock. Babcock negotiated a treaty of annexation as a first option and an agreement for a naval station as a second option.

Grant's plans for Santo Domingo had little support in his administration and in Congress. Grant attempted to sway U.S. senator Charles Sumner of Massachusetts, head of the Foreign Relations Committee, but Sumner had been among the most fierce abolitionists in Congress and was not going to compromise the black self-government of Santo Domingo. He led the Foreign Relations Committee to a 5–2 rejection of the treaty. The Grant administration pressured the Senate for a full vote, needing two-thirds majority for acceptance. The vote failed, 28–28, with nineteen members of Grant's own party rejecting the treaty. Previous to the vote, it was revealed that Babcock had offered $100,000 and weapons to assist Báez with opposition in his country. Despite the embarrassment of the revelation, Grant allowed Babcock to remain in the administration. Two years later, Babcock was implicated in other administration scandals.

Grant continued to press for annexation of Santo Domingo after the annexation treaty was rejected in 1871, despite no sign of additional support. At the very end of his second term, Grant raised the issue again in his last message to Congress.

When did **imperialism** become a presidential issue?

Imperialism was a concern for some Americans during the 1870s, when Ulysses S. Grant sought to annex Santo Domingo. The United States had never before pursued purchase or annexation of land outside the North American continent. But the issue of imperialism really heated up during the 1890s. An American-inspired revolt against the monarchy of Hawaii led to the formation in 1892 of an independent republic, which negotiated a treaty of annexation with U.S. president Benjamin Harrison. But Harrison left office before the Senate could vote on the treaty.

Grover Cleveland, elected in 1892, rescinded the treaty, pending an investigation of American involvement in the overthrow of the Hawaiian monarchy. Cleveland's stance on Hawaii and then on Cuba, where he warned Spain against quelling a rebellion in its colony but took no action, indicated his concern about the United States becoming an imperialistic nation.

William McKinley succeeded Grover Cleveland in 1897 and sent the Hawaii annexation treaty to Congress as a resolution, where it passed in both houses. The following year, by virtue of victory in the Spanish-American War (1888), the United States took

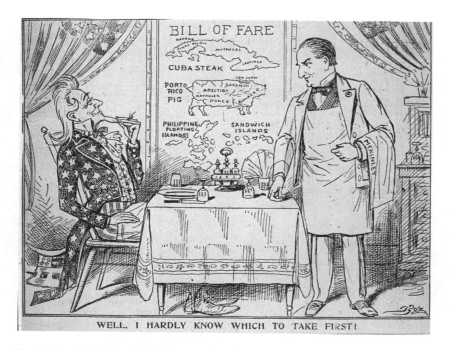

Cartoon showing President William McKinley as a waiter taking orders from Uncle Sam. On the menu is "Cuba Steak, Porto Rico Pig, Philippine Floating Islands," and the "Sandwich Islands," reflecting concern about American imperialism by some of the American public. *Getty Images.*

possession of Cuba and the Philippines. American imperialism became an issue in the 1900 presidential campaign for Democrat William Jennings Bryan in his bid to unseat McKinley. However, voters showed little interest in the issue.

Which president pursued the **"Open Door" trade policy** with China?

In 1898, the United States annexed Hawaii and took possession of the Philippines following victory in the Spanish-American War. Among other benefits, the two sets of islands served as way stations in a Pacific Ocean trade route to China. At that time, Japan, England, France, Russia, and Germany had already established presences in China and took advantage of the decentralized Chinese political organization. In September 1898, McKinley issued a foreign policy statement demanding U.S. access to China: "Asking only the open door for ourselves, we are ready to accord the open door to others." Attempting to maintain a monopoly over trade in China, the other nations did not welcome McKinley's Open Door policy.

An opportunity for gaining access to China occurred in 1900 when the Boxers, a secret Chinese martial arts society, laid siege to the entire foreign diplomatic corps in the British embassy in Peking (now Beijing), China. The Boxer Rebellion was eventually put down by an international coalition. McKinley agreed to lend troops to the coalition in return for support for the Open Door policy.

237

Richard and Pat Nixon at the Great Wall of China in 1972 as part of their historic visit. *Library of Congress.*

Which **presidents enjoyed positive developments in Chinese-American relations**?

In the early 1840s, President John Tyler asked Congress to authorize funding for a mission to China for the negotiation of a commercial treaty. Tyler was concerned about Great Britain's domination of the Chinese market. The English-Chinese Opium Wars, fought over Britain's illegal import of opium, had just ended and Britain enjoyed access to more Chinese ports than any other world power. Britain had also taken permanent possession of Hong Kong.

After debate, Congress agreed to fund the mission. The resulting Treaty of Wanghia (1844) became the first bilateral agreement between China and the United States. Trade between the United States and China later flourished.

Richard Nixon's successful effort at reconciliation and normalization of relations between the United States and China was enormously significant. Diplomatic channels had been closed since the communist takeover of China in 1949. To achieve his goal, Nixon used a strategy called "triangular diplomacy." Antagonism had developed during the 1960s between China and the Soviet Union, the world's two most powerful communist nations. Through triangular diplomacy, American negotiators offered something of value to both sides through intermediaries. Meanwhile, Nixon sent Secretary of State Henry Kissinger on a secret mission to Peking (now Beijing), China, to discuss a presidential visit with Chinese leaders.

Ping-Pong Diplomacy

The United States and China did not have official diplomatic relations from 1949 until 1972. Secret relations were established in 1969 to prepare the way for an official visit to China by President Richard Nixon in 1972. The first public sign of normalizing of relations between the two nations occurred in April 1971, when an American table-tennis team was invited to play in China. The team enjoyed a reception with Chinese premier Zhou Enlai. Later, a Chinese team was sent to the United States as part of what was dubbed "Ping-Pong diplomacy."

On July 15, 1971, Nixon made the surprise announcement that he had been invited to visit China and had accepted. In China, Nixon met with Chinese revolutionary leaders Mao Zedong and Zhou Enlai, enjoyed considerable fanfare, and traveled to historic sites, all covered by a large press entourage. Along with reestablishing relations, Nixon's visit to China led to an agreement that the United States would reduce its military presence in Taiwan and China would decrease its support for North Vietnam, which was engaged against the United States in the Vietnam War. These results were summarized in the Shanghai Communiqué. Increase trade, tourism, and cultural contacts followed Nixon's historic trip to China.

George Bush expanded trade relations with China from 1989 to 1992. During the 1992 presidential campaign, Bill Clinton argued against further expansion of trade until China showed improvement in human rights. But Clinton reversed himself after being elected president in 1992, asserting that expanding trade would encourage China to become more capitalistic and democratic. This policy, called engagement, sought to expand contact and trade between China and the world's democracies. After several years of negotiations and some tense confrontations, the Clinton administration and Chinese leaders signed an agreement in late 1999 to dramatically lower China's tariffs on U.S. goods. Another ten months elapsed as the U.S. Senate debated the agreement, but the historic China trade bill was signed into law by Clinton in October 2000.

What was **"Big Stick" diplomacy**?

"Speak softly and carry a big stick" was the way Theodore Roosevelt described his approach to foreign policy. When he assumed the presidency in 1901, several Latin American countries were behind on debt payments to European nations. Concerned that other nations might follow Germany's example of threatening action against Venezuela in 1903, Roosevelt announced what became known as the Roosevelt Corollary to the Monroe Doctrine in 1904. Roosevelt pledged to protect Latin American nations from military action, and he insisted that the United States assumed the right

THE BIG STICK IN THE CARIBBEAN SEA

New York Herald cartoon illustrating President Theodore Roosevelt's "big stick" diplomacy. *AP/Wide World Photos.*

to intervene to ensure Latin American states met their financial responsibilities to other nations.

After the U.S. Navy made an impressive showing in the Spanish-American War (1898), Roosevelt continued to expand it. In 1907, a "Great White Fleet" of American ships went on a world cruise to demonstrate the "big-stick" side of Roosevelt diplomacy.

Which president's foreign policy was dubbed **"Dollar Diplomacy"**?

William Howard Taft's administration attempted to use trade and economic opportunity as a means for offering stability to troubled nations in Central and Latin America. Taft described his policy as "substituting dollars for bullets." According to Taft, modern diplomacy was built on commercial interaction. Dollar Diplomacy, as Taft's policy was increasingly called in the press, met with modest success at best.

What were **Woodrow Wilson's policies on Latin America**?

Woodrow Wilson's administration signed treaties with thirty Latin American nations to provide a means for quickly addressing conflicts. Attempting to soothe lingering ill-feelings in Colombia over Theodore Roosevelt's encouraging the Panamanian revolution of 1903, Wilson negotiated a treaty with reparations, but it was rejected by the U.S. Senate. Under Wilson, the United States tried but was unsuccessful in bringing stability to Nicaragua, Haiti, and the Dominican Republic. The United States had to intervene and maintain military occupation in Haiti and the Dominican Republic in 1915 and 1916.

How did **U.S. foreign policy toward Central and Latin America** change under Calvin Coolidge?

The United States had mixed results at best with Latin American foreign policy from 1900 to 1925. Military skirmishes between the United States and Mexico between 1914 and 1917 and unsuccessful diplomatic efforts by the United States in Nicaragua by William Howard Taft and Woodrow Wilson were among many attempts to help bring stability to highly volatile areas. Calvin Coolidge restored diplomatic relations with Mexico and began repairing relations with Latin American nations. Preferring quiet diplomacy to large-scale programs such as the (Theodore) Roosevelt Corollary to the Monroe Doctrine or the Dollar Diplomacy of William Howard Taft (see above for more information), Coolidge administration officials avoided a conflict with Mexico on foreign oil rights and settled a disagreement over Mexican recognition of a new government in Nicaragua. Coolidge's efforts set the stage for the next big foreign policy program toward Central and South America, Franklin D. Roosevelt's Good Neighbor policy of the 1930s and 1940s that emphasized cooperation and trade to maintain stability in the western hemisphere.

What was the significance of the **Kellogg-Briand Pact (1928)**?

Woodrow Wilson had called World War I "the war to end all wars" and had faith that a league of nations working cooperatively could address international conflicts before they escalated into war. Warren G. Harding's secretary of state, Charles Evans Hughes, negotiated a pact to limit naval power among the United States, Japan, France, England, and Italy. And Calvin Coolidge, too, sought international cooperation for avoiding war and an arms race. Coolidge supported a multilateral declaration renouncing war as an instrument of national policy and agreeing to settle disputes by peaceful means and through the World Court established at the Hague, in the Netherlands. These items were incorporated into international law through the Kellogg-Briand Pact of 1928. The pact was named for Frank Kellogg, Coolidge's secretary of state, and Kellogg's French counterpart, Aristide Briand. Sixty-two nations signed the pact.

What was the **Stimson Doctrine**?

Like his immediate predecessors, Herbert Hoover hoped to avoid another major world war and an arms race. The Naval Treaty of April 22, 1930, signed at the London Naval Conference of 1930, placed limits on the number of small naval vessels nations could construct as well as on battleships and cruisers. Despite such treaties and the Kellogg-Briand Pact of 1928 (see above), aggression by one nation against another became more widespread again in the 1930s.

When Japan invaded Manchuria in September 1931, Hoover faced his first major crisis in foreign policy. In January 1932, the Hoover administration announced the "Stimson Doctrine," named after Hoover's secretary of state, Henry L. Stimson. The Doctrine declared that any territorial acquisition not in accord with existing treaties would not be recognized by the United States. However, invoking the Stimson Doctrine had no effect on Japanese aggression in China, and other nations did not provide the support needed for the doctrine to have significance.

Why did Franklin D. Roosevelt refuse U.S. participation in international currency stabilization in 1933?

The stock market crash of 1929 and the economic hard times that followed in the United States had international repercussions. Investment in European bonds contracted sharply, for example, as did the American market for imports. World trade sagged, furthering international economic hardships. The London Economic Conference was convened in 1933 to pursue international currency stabilization. However, President Franklin D. Roosevelt, shortly after assuming office in 1933, announced that the United States would not participate in international currency stabilization efforts. Roosevelt wanted to focus on problems at home.

What was Roosevelt's foreign policy prior to the United States entering World War II?

Increasing foreign trade was one way Roosevelt hoped to help stimulate the U.S. economy. He improved diplomatic relations with the Soviet Union, which was still struggling to modernize after enduring heavy damage in World War I. His "Good Neighbor" policy toward Central and South American nations was based on reciprocal trade agreements.

After World War II began in 1939, Congress proclaimed American neutrality. Congress had placed an embargo on shipping armaments to warring nations earlier in the 1930s. The embargo was lifted after the war started for nations that could pay cash and transport arms on their own ships. Despite American neutrality, Roosevelt arranged the Lend Lease Act (1940), where Great Britain received fifty American destroyers; in exchange, Britain leased military bases in the Pacific to the United States.

What was controversial about Roosevelt's strategies at the Yalta conference (1945)?

As World War II was winding down in Europe, British prime minister Winston Churchill, Soviet premier Joseph Stalin, and President Franklin D. Roosevelt met at Yalta in the Crimea region of the Soviet Union in February 1945 to discuss postwar Europe. The leaders agreed to require Germany's unconditional surrender and to set

British prime minister Winston Churchill, U.S. president Franklin D. Roosevelt, and Soviet premier Joseph Stalin meet at Yalta in 1945 to discuss postwar Europe. *Library of Congress.*

up four zones of occupation in postwar Germany to be run by the United States, U.S.S.R, Britain, and France.

Most of the agreements were kept secret until after the war. The most controversial of these concerned Eastern Europe, where the Soviet Union occupied several nations. Roosevelt did not demand Soviet evacuation of those nations after Stalin promised free elections would be held following the war. Roosevelt believed help from the Soviet Union was still needed to defeat Germany, and Stalin promised to enter the war against Japan within three months after Germany was defeated. Stalin did not keep the promise for free elections and instead installed governments dominated by the Soviet Union, moves that precipitated the Cold War.

How did **Harry S. Truman** differ from Roosevelt regarding the **Soviet Union**?

Truman succeeded to the presidency on April 12, 1945, following the death of Roosevelt. When Truman attended the Potsdam Conference in Germany with British prime ministers Winston Churchill and Clement Attlee and Soviet premier Joseph Stalin to review plans for postwar Europe and to discuss action against Japan, he already saw indications that the Soviet Union was intending to dominate Eastern Europe, in violation of the Yalta Conference agreement.

Following the end of World War II, the large American war army was demobilizing, making it difficult for Truman to aggressively protest the Soviet military presence

Yalta Conference Agreement on Poland

World War II began when Germany invaded Poland in 1939. The Cold War essentially began when the Soviet Union broke its promise to hold free elections in Eastern European nations, including Poland, and instead installed and supported governments dominated by the Soviet Union. The following excerpt from the Yalta Conference agreement is an example of the broken pledge:

VII. POLAND

The following declaration on Poland was agreed by the conference:

A new situation has been created in Poland as a result of her complete liberation by the Red Army. This calls for the establishment of a Polish Provisional Government which can be more broadly based than was possible before the recent liberation of the western part of Poland. The Provisional Government which is now functioning in Poland should therefore be reorganized on a broader democratic basis with the inclusion of democratic leaders from Poland itself and from Poles abroad. This new Government should then be called the Polish Provisional Government of National Unity....

This Polish Provisional Government of National Unity shall be pledged to the holding of free and unfettered elections as soon as possible on the basis of universal suffrage and secret ballot. In these elections all democratic and anti-Nazi parties shall have the right to take part and to put forward candidates.

and domination in Eastern Europe. Instead, Truman found opportunity to confront Soviet expansionism in Greece and Turkey. World War II had just ended, and the Cold War had begun.

What was the **Truman Doctrine**?

The Truman Doctrine was an attempt to check Soviet expansion into Turkey and Greece. The Truman Doctrine granted aid to anticommunist forces in those nations. Congress approved $250 million for Greece and $150 million for Turkey and promised assistance to other nations threatened "by armed minorities or by outside pressure."

What was the **Marshall Plan**?

The European Recovery Plan, better known as the Marshall Plan, helped rebuild European economies devastated by World War II and strengthened democratic govern-

President Ronald Reagan in Berlin, Germany, in 1987, challenging Soviet leader Mikhail Gorbachev to expand freedom in his country and in Eastern Europe and exhorting him to tear down the Berlin Wall. *Getty Images.*

ments. The architect of the plan was George C. Marshall, secretary of state to Harry S. Truman. The United States spent over $12.5 billion over a four-year period, helping rebuild Western Europe, including what was then West Germany.

What was the **Berlin Airlift**?

After ensuring that Eastern European communist governments were allied with the Soviet Union, the Soviets closed off access to Berlin—which bordered both East and West Germany—to its World War II allies, Britain, France, and the United States, which shared control of postwar Germany. Truman countered the move by ordering airlifts of essential supplies to Berlin, a policy that lasted nearly a year and helped maintain a Western presence in the city. Truman's humanitarian gesture helped solidify anti-Soviet sentiments in noncommunist nations.

What **other presidential policies are associated with Berlin**?

In 1961, the Berlin Wall was erected by the Soviet Union to separate East and West Germany and to ensure that the Soviets could better control East Germany. President John F. Kennedy asked Congress for increased military spending and called up reserve troops. Fifteen hundred armed American troops traveled a legal route that passed through East Germany and into Berlin. They were not challenged. Kennedy himself

245

made a well-publicized trip to West Berlin in 1963. Before a cheering crowd, he showed American support by declaring *"Ich bin ein Berliner"* ("I am a Berliner").

In 1987, Ronald Reagan visited West Germany at a time when the Soviet Union was undergoing reform and promising more under the leadership of General Secretary Mikhail Gorbachev. Reagan gave a memorable speech that made reference to Kennedy's Berlin speech, using German language on occasion, as Kennedy had done and uttering a challenge to Gorbachev to prove he was sincere in expanding freedom: "General Secretary Gorbachev, if you seek peace, if you seek prosperity for the Soviet Union and Eastern Europe, if you seek liberalization: Come here to this gate! Mr. Gorbachev, open this gate! Mr. Gorbachev, tear down this wall!"

What were the **roots of American involvement in Vietnam**?

In 1954, France abandoned its southeast Asian colony of Indochina after failing to quell a communist uprising. A peace agreement signed in Geneva, Switzerland, that year established a provisional military border and a nearly three-mile-wide demilitarized zone. All French military forces were to regroup south of that line (South Vietnam) and all communist military forces north of the line (North Vietnam). Small numbers of U.S. military advisers were sent to South Vietnam for antiguerrilla operations beginning in 1954.

China had assisted the communist insurgency against the French, and threat of Chinese communist domination of the area led Presidents Dwight D. Eisenhower and John F. Kennedy to send additional advisers. The number of advisers increased during the Kennedy administration from about seven hundred to more than fifteen thousand. In 1962, communist Chinese invaded the northern border of India, and Kennedy believed that additional assistance and economic aid were necessary in South Vietnam to help against communist forces.

When did the **Peace Corps** begin?

John F. Kennedy established the Peace Corps in March 1961 as one of his first presidential actions. The government-sponsored program trains volunteers for social and humanitarian service in underdeveloped areas of the world. Kennedy introduced the concept of the Peace Corps during a campaign speech in 1960 at the University of Michigan in which he challenged students to serve their country in the cause of peace by living and working in developing countries.

What was Richard Nixon's **policy of détente with the Soviet Union**?

"Détente" is defined as a relaxation of strained relations or tensions between nations. President Nixon pursued a policy of détente with the Soviet Union after taking office in 1969. Talks soon began on the limitation of strategic arms. An interim pact, negoti-

Reagan in Berlin, Germany

Ronald Reagan made a memorable speech in Berlin in 1987, at a time when the Soviet Union was undergoing reform and promising more freedom under the leadership of General Secretary Mikhail Gorbachev. As noted on the *Ronald Reagan Foundation* Web site ("Tear Down This Wall!: Remarks at the Brandenburg Gate, West Berlin, Germany, June 12, 1987"), Reagan's speech culminated with a challenge to Gorbachev to prove he was sincere in expanding freedom:

Twenty-four years ago, President John F. Kennedy visited Berlin, speaking to the people of this city and the world at the City Hall. Well, since then two other presidents have come, each in his turn, to Berlin. And today I, myself, make my second visit to your city.

We come to Berlin, we American presidents, because it's our duty to speak, in this place, of freedom. But I must confess, we're drawn here by other things as well: by the feeling of history in this city, more than 500 years older than our own nation; by the beauty of the Grunewald and the Tiergarten; most of all, by your courage and determination. Perhaps the composer Paul Lincke understood something about American presidents. You see, like so many presidents before me, I come here today because wherever I go, whatever I do: *Ich hab noch einen Koffer in Berlin.* (I still have a suitcase in Berlin.)....

We hear much from Moscow about a new policy of reform and openness. Some political prisoners have been released. Certain foreign news broadcasts are no longer being jammed. Some economic enterprises have been permitted to operate with greater freedom from state control.

Are these the beginnings of profound changes in the Soviet state? Or are they token gestures, intended to raise false hopes in the West, or to strengthen the Soviet system without changing it? We welcome change and openness; for we believe that freedom and security go together, that the advance of human liberty can only strengthen the cause of world peace. There is one sign the Soviets can make that would be unmistakable, that would advance dramatically the cause of freedom and peace.

General Secretary Gorbachev, if you seek peace, if you seek prosperity for the Soviet Union and Eastern Europe, if you seek liberalization: Come here to this gate! Mr. Gorbachev, open this gate! Mr. Gorbachev, tear down this wall!

ated in Helsinki, Finland, was taken to Moscow in May 1972 to coincide with Nixon's visit to the Soviet Union for signing by the president and his counterpart, Soviet Premier Leonid Brezhnev.

In 1973, Soviet party leader Leonid Brezhnev visited the United States. He and Nixon signed a nuclear nonaggression pact and several agreements for science, transportation, and cultural exchanges. Nixon revisited Russia in 1974, but he and Brezhnev did not achieve a final agreement on limiting the proliferation of nuclear weapons.

What was notable about the **Nixon administration's Middle East policy**?

A cease-fire in the Middle East was negotiated by Nixon's first secretary of state, William Rogers, in 1970. Henry Kissinger, who succeeded Rogers as secretary of state in 1973, effectively pressured military disengagements between Israel, Egypt, and Syria. The United States and the Soviet Union cooperated in exerting diplomatic pressure on the combatants. Nixon visited Israel and four Arab nations in mid-1974 and enjoyed a warm reception.

What was the **Ford administration's legacy in the Middle East**?

With war between Israel and its Arab neighbors a constant threat, the Gerald Ford administration managed to help maintain an uneasy peace between nations. In September of 1975, Secretary of State Henry Kissinger negotiated a pact signed by Egypt and Israel that established an unofficial demilitarized zone between the nations that was monitored by U.S. civilian technicians.

What was the significance of Ford's signing the **Helsinki Agreement** in 1975?

President Ford and leaders of thirty-six nations met in Helsinki, Finland, in July 1975. At the meeting, the Soviet Union, criticized for having censored and jailed dissidents, agreed to observe international human rights principles. Among the outstanding examples of Soviet campaigns to discredit individuals who challenged their nation's policies were Alexander Solzhenitsyn, winner of the Nobel Prize for Literature in 1970, and Andrei Sakharov, who would win the Nobel Peace Prize in 1975 a few months after the Helsinki Agreement. A physicist, Sakharov was credited as the founder of the Soviet's hydrogen bomb, but he became vilified by his government for his outspokenness for human rights and democracy.

In exchange for the Soviet Union's agreement to observe human rights principles, the United States and other Western countries agreed to recognize the boundaries created by Soviet influence in Eastern Europe after World War II. This was the first time the United States and the West showed formal acceptance of Soviet influence over Eastern bloc nations. By formally recognizing the legitimacy of the Soviet satellite nations, Ford hoped for expanded cultural and diplomatic exchanges.

Selling Out to the Soviets?

The most vocal critics of the Yalta Agreement (1945) and the Helsinki Agreement (1975) charge Franklin D. Roosevelt and Gerald Ford, respectively, for selling out to the Soviets on their domination of Eastern Europe. Roosevelt believed he needed continued Soviet support for the World War II effort and postwar peace. He did not question Soviet occupation of several Eastern European nations at the time in exchange for a promise—written into the Yalta Agreement—for free elections in those nations following the end of World War II. However, the free elections pledge was never honored by the Soviets.

Gerald Ford was willing to formally recognize the Soviet-drawn borders of postwar Eastern Europe in the Helsinki Agreement as a means for easing international tensions and promoting better relations. In exchange, the Soviet Union pledged to obey international principles for human rights. After some initial easing of restrictions on free speech and freeing some political prisoners, the Soviet Union soon returned to suppressing dissidents.

In his 1979 autobiography, *A Time to Heal,* Ford admitted that many of his advisers were uneasy about the Helsinki Agreement, but he ultimately sided with his secretary of state, Henry Kissinger, and hoped that the Agreement would ease international tensions and promote further cooperation. However, the agreement became a liability in Ford's bid for election to president in 1976. He narrowly won the Republican nomination over Ronald Reagan, who criticized the Helsinki Agreement, and lost a narrow election to Jimmy Carter. Ford had mistakenly downplayed Soviet influence over Eastern Europe during a televised debate with Carter.

Was **Jimmy Carter's emphasis on human rights** a new approach in American foreign policy?

Presidents who preceded Jimmy Carter had criticized human rights violations in other nations, but Carter was the first president to make human rights a basic tenet of American foreign policy. Carter's pleas to the Soviet Union to honor their pledge in the Helsinki Agreement (1975), to observe international human rights principles, ultimately angered the Soviet government as an intervention in its internal affairs. The spirit of détente between the United States and the Soviet Union begun by Richard Nixon in 1969 and affirmed by Gerald Ford in his acceptance of the Helsinki Agreement vanished by the end of Carter's presidency.

Even so, Carter and Soviet premier Leonid Brezhnev signed the Strategic Arms Limitation Treaty (SALT II) in Vienna, Austria, in June 1979. The treaty set limits on

Soviet and U.S. nuclear weapons. However, the treaty did not receive the necessary two-thirds majority approval in the U.S. Senate.

Why did Jimmy Carter order the United States to **boycott the 1980 Summer Olympics**?

To protest the Soviet invasion of Afghanistan in 1980, Carter ordered the U.S. Olympic Team to boycott the Summer Olympic Games that year, which were held in Moscow. The Soviet Union later responded by boycotting the 1984 Summer Olympic Games held in Los Angeles, California.

How did **American policy toward the Soviet Union change under Ronald Reagan**?

U.S. president Ronald Reagan and Soviet leader Mikhail Gorbachev meet in Switzerland on November 19, 1985. *AP/Wide World Photos.*

Reagan abandoned the détente policies of the administrations of Richard Nixon and Gerald Ford and the Nixon-supported Strategic Arms Limitation Treaty (SALT I) of 1972 as well as Jimmy Carter's SALT II agreement of 1978. Vehemently anticommunist, the Reagan administration continued Carter's criticism on human rights abuses in the Soviet Union and acted swiftly to counter the dramatic Soviet military and naval buildup of the 1970s. Reagan approved a new generation of nuclear missiles, accelerated development of a new bomber, and supported huge increases in defense spending. These were naturally viewed as aggressive actions by the Soviet Union, but tensions increased over the Soviet's continued war in Afghanistan, the downing of a South Korean airliner by a Soviet military plane in 1983, U.S. deployment of intermediate-range missiles in Western Europe, and the proposed Strategic Defense Initiative (SDI), a satellite-based defense system nicknamed "Star Wars" after the popular movie.

The Soviet Union, meanwhile, was facing leadership problems: Premier Leonid Brezhnev died in 1982; his successor, Yuri Andropov, died in 1984; and Andropov's successor, Konstantin Chernenko, died in 1985. Failure in Afghanistan, growing demands for independence within its European satellite nations, and economic hardships were plaguing the Soviet Union at the same time. When Mikhail Gorbachev became premier in 1985, the Soviet Union changed from hard-line leadership: Gor-

> ## Soviet Leadership Changes
>
> **D**uring his first term, President Ronald Reagan did not meet with his Soviet counterpart. When asked why by a member of the press, Reagan replied, "I would, but they keep dying on me." Soviet premier Leonid Brezhnev died in 1982; his successor, Yuri Andropov, died in 1984; and Andropov's successor, Konstantin Chernenko, died in 1985. The more youthful Mikhail Gorbachev took the helm following Chernenko.

bachev promoted policies of *glasnost* (openness) and *perestroika* (economic reform) along with a commitment to arms reduction.

When Reagan and Gorbachev met in Geneva, Switzerland, in late 1985, they both expressed a willingness to negotiate arms-reduction talks. Reagan believed the U.S. arms buildup had put him in a position of strength. Nearly two years later, Reagan and Gorbachev agreed on the INF Treaty (intermediate-range nuclear forces) and began discussing a strategic arms reduction treaty (START). Gorbachev visited the United States in December 1987 to sign the INF treaty and proved to be popular among Americans.

What were **Reagan's policies in Central and South America**?

The Reagan administration used public and covert means to counter communist influence in Grenada, El Salvador, and Nicaragua. Congress had prohibited military aid to the Nicaraguan Contras, a group fighting the pro-Soviet Sandinistas. Members of the Reagan administration funneled funds to the Contras.

What did George Bush mean by the phrase, the **"new world order"**?

Bush used the phrase "new world order" on several occasions. He is most frequently associated with the phrase with reference to the collapse of the Soviet Union, which began disintegrating in 1989 and dissolved into a loose confederation of independent republics and unaffiliated states in 1991. The collapse left the United States as the world's lone superpower, leading the world, in Bush's view, to a new spirit of cooperation—a new world order.

The first major speech in which Bush used the term "new world order" occurred on September 11, 1990, when he addressed Congress on the crisis in Kuwait, which had been invaded by Iraq a month earlier. Bush listed four objectives in the Persian Gulf to avoid a United Nations military response: "Iraq must withdraw from Kuwait completely, immediately and without condition. Kuwait's legitimate government must be restored. The security and stability of the Persian Gulf must be assured. American citizens abroad must be protected."

251

Bush followed with a fifth objective:

We stand today at a unique and extraordinary moment. The crisis in the Persian Gulf, as grave as it is, also offers a rare opportunity to move toward an historic period of cooperation. Out of these troubled times, our fifth objective—a new world order—can emerge: a new era, free from the threat of terror, stronger in the pursuit of justice, and more secure in the quest for peace. An era in which the nations of the world, east and west, north and south, can prosper and live in harmony.

Later, in his State of the Union speech on January 29, 1991, two weeks after air strikes began on strategic targets in Iraq, Bush again referred to the new world order: "What is at stake is more than one small country, it is a big idea—a new world order, where diverse nations are drawn together in common cause to achieve the universal aspirations of mankind: peace and security, freedom, and the rule of law. Such is a world worthy of our struggle, and worthy of our children's future."

What was **George Bush's policy on the Middle East**?

Peace talks arranged by Bush were initiated between Israel and its Arab neighbors. To help ease Palestinian tensions with Israel, Bush declined to support $10 billion in loan guarantees to Israel unless Israel stopped building settlements in territories it occupied. When Yitzhak Rabin succeeded Yitzhak Shamir in 1992, the new Israeli government suspended construction and financing of most new settlements. Soon after, Bush and Rabin came to an agreement on the loans.

What were **Bill Clinton's Middle East peace efforts**?

Israeli Prime Minister Yitzhak Rabin and Palestinian leader Yasser Arafat signed a peace accord in the White House Rose Garden in September 1993. After Rabin was assassinated by a Jewish extremist in November 1995, however, Benjamin Netanyahu won a close race and stopped the transfer of occupied lands to the Palestinians, claiming the Palestinians had not done enough to apprehend anti-Israeli terrorists. After many attempts, Clinton in 1998 persuaded Netanyahu and Arafat to sign a second treaty in Wye River, Maryland. The Wye River Accord promised an Israeli withdrawal from Palestinian lands in exchange for a Palestinian promise to arrest terrorists and to revoke a section of the Palestinian charter calling for the destruction of Israel. Netanyahu delayed action, however.

After Israelis elected Ehud Barak prime minister in May 1999, Clinton arranged for Barak and Arafat to meet at Camp David, Maryland, in 2000 to resolve the outstanding issues in the peace process. Negotiations faltered over the future of East Jerusalem and the "right of return" for Palestinian refugees. After weeks of difficult negotiations, the two parties announced they could not reach any agreement. When violence erupted between Palestinians and the Israeli army soon after, the peace process gradually faded.

How was **Bill Clinton able to authorize a $20 billion loan to Mexico without congressional approval**?

Mexico's currency dropped dramatically in value in 1994. Clinton wanted to provide aid to Mexico, which was the fastest-growing consumer of U.S. goods. At first, Clinton proposed a $40 billion loan guarantee, but after failing to win support in Congress for the loan guarantee package, he drew upon the federal Exchange Stabilization Fund. Established during the 1930s and put under control of the president and treasury secretary, the fund was created to allow presidents to quickly intervene in foreign currency markets to support the U.S. dollar. Citing concern that the devalued peso would also impact the American southwest and possibly lead to a new wave of illegal immigrants crossing the border from Mexico into the United Stares, Clinton acted on his own authority to offer Mexico $20 billion in U.S. government short-term loans and loan guarantees to stabilize the peso. The four top leaders in Congress joined with the president in a joint statement of agreement on the need for the new policy.

The initiative staved off a financial crisis in Mexico and had the effect of raising the value of the peso and Mexican stocks. Mexico maintained a strict fiscal and monetary policy, which encouraged additional private investment. Mexico paid off three-quarters of its debt, with interest, years ahead of schedule.

Did **Clinton apply his engagement policy elsewhere** in foreign relations?

In July 2000, Vietnam and the United States signed a trade agreement that opened the possibility for normalized trade relations between the two countries. Clinton became the first American president to visit the country since the Vietnam War. The policy of engagement, a new openness in relations between Hanoi and Washington, was used as a means to encourage democracy and free market economics to Vietnam.

What was **Clinton's policy toward Iraq**?

Following the Gulf War (1991), the United Nations imposed economic sanctions on Iraq and Iraq agreed to allow UN weapons-inspection teams into the country to ensure that Iraq was complying with an agreement to dismantle its program for creating weapons of mass destruction. Following frequent diplomatic showdowns and repeated uncooperativeness with weapons-inspectors, Clinton, together with British prime minister Tony Blair, authorized renewed air strikes against Iraq beginning in December 1998.

253

Which nations were linked as an **"axis of evil"** by George W. Bush?

In his State of the Union Address delivered on January 29, 2002, President George W. Bush identified three regimes that "sponsor terror" and threaten "America or our friends and allies with weapons of mass destruction."

In the president's words:

North Korea is a regime arming with missiles and weapons of mass destruction, while starving its citizens. Iran aggressively pursues these weapons and exports terror, while an unelected few repress the Iranian people's hope for freedom.

Iraq continues to flaunt its hostility toward America and to support terror. The Iraqi regime has plotted to develop anthrax, and nerve gas, and nuclear weapons for over a decade. This is a regime that has already used poison gas to murder thousands of its own citizens—leaving the bodies of mothers huddled over their dead children. This is a regime that agreed to international inspections—then kicked out the inspectors. This is a regime that has something to hide from the civilized world. States like these, and their terrorist allies, constitute an axis of evil, arming to threaten the peace of the world.

What was the **Doctrine of Preemption** of the George W. Bush administration?

Under the doctrine of "preemption," the United States could strike militarily against another sovereign nation if it considered that nation to pose an imminent threat. Cited by critics to be in abrogation of several principles of international law, the doctrine was implemented following the terrorist attacks on the United States of September 11, 2001, and can be said to have been enacted with the war in Iraq in 2003.

What was the Bush **"Roadmap for Peace" policy** on the Israeli-Palestinian conflict?

On March 14, 2003, President George W. Bush announced the Roadmap for Peace, a performance-based and goal-driven development of peace between Israeli and Palestinian states. Bush stated: "The United States has developed this plan over the last several months in close cooperation with Russia, the European Union, and the United Nations. Once this road map is delivered, we will expect and welcome contributions from Israel and the Palestinians to this document that will advance true peace. We will urge them to discuss the road map with one another. The time has come to move beyond entrenched positions and to take concrete actions to achieve peace."

The Roadmap specifies the steps for the two parties to take to reach a settlement, and a timeline for doing so, under the auspices of what is called the Quartet—the United States, the European Union, the United Nations, and Russia. The timeline specified by the Roadmap was undermined by continuing violence: Phase I: Ending Terror and Violence, Normalizing Palestinian Life, and Building Palestinian Institutions—Present to May 2003; Phase II: Transition—June 2003–December 2003; and Phase III: Permanent Status Agreement and End of the Israeli-Palestinian Conflict—2004–2005.

TREATIES AND TRADE

Which president agreed to a treaty that **paid a ransom for hostages held by pirates**?

In 1785, ten American sailors were captured by Barbary pirates, who controlled the Mediterranean Ocean from the port city of Algiers. At the time, the United States was under the Articles of Confederation and had neither the naval power nor a centralized government to negotiate freedom for the hostages.

As president and chief diplomat of the United States following ratification of the Constitution, George Washington agreed to the Treaty of Algiers (1791), which included a ransom payment of $800,000 for the prisoners and an annual tribute of $24,000 as the price of security against piracy.

On a positive note, the embarrassing situation strengthened Washington's position with Congress on the need for improving U.S. naval forces. Congress passed a resolution in 1794 authorizing construction of six frigates. By the early 1800s, the United States had sufficient naval power for President Thomas Jefferson to break the treaty and confront the pirates.

Have any other presidents been involved in **ransom negotiations**?

Thomas Jefferson paid $60,000 in ransom to Tripoli for the release of the crew of the *Philadelphia,* a frigate than ran aground in Tripoli Bay while pursuing pirates. The vessel was taken over by pirates, who took the crew hostage and used the ship to fire upon other American frigates. Americans eventually boarded the *Philadelphia* and burned it.

In modern times, insurgents hired by the CIA were captured by Cuba during the failed Bay of Pigs invasion (1961). Cuba's leader, Fidel Castro, demanded a ransom for their release, but President John F. Kennedy refused. Eventually, $53 million in food and medical supplies was raised by businesses and private donors to free the prisoners.

A congressional investigation in 1987 revealed that members of the Ronald Reagan administration illegally sold arms to Iran to try and influence a political organization there that had ties to a group in Lebanon that was holding American hostages. What became known as the Iran-Contra scandal also included an illegal funneling of

What Is a Treaty?

A treaty is a formal agreement between two or more sovereign states. Under the Constitution, treaties are negotiated through the executive branch and must be approved by two-thirds vote of the Senate.

funds from the arms sale to a group (the Contras) in Nicaragua that opposed communists in that country.

What were **Washington's reservations for signing Jay's Treaty** in 1795?

Washington's Proclamation of Neutrality in 1793 concerning war between Britain and France did not deter British forces from stopping and searching American ships at sea. Britain claimed to be seeking military deserters in their war with France, but they began seizing U.S. cargoes as well on suspicion that they were intended for Britain's enemies. These actions and Britain's suspension of trade rights between the United States and the West Indies (a British colony) in 1794 led many Americans to begin calling for war.

Washington sent John Jay on a treaty-making mission to London. Jay had negotiated the Treaty of Paris (1783) that ended the American Revolution and in 1789 he had been appointed the first chief justice of the Supreme Court by President Washington, a post he held until 1795.

Jay's Treaty, signed by the United States and Britain, did not address British aggression at sea and did not open up U.S. trade with the West Indies. Nevertheless, Washington supported the treaty because it helped avoid war with Britain and contained the agreement that Britain would abandon forts on what is now the American side of the Great Lakes by June 1, 1796.

Jay's Treaty was not popular in the United States and only passed approval in the U.S. Senate after two weeks of debate and by the slimmest possible two-thirds majority vote, 20–10. The treaty was successful in two respects: it helped the United States avoid war with Great Britain, and forts assumed by the United States on the Great Lakes proved vital for protecting westward expansion into the Ohio Valley and the Great Lakes region.

What was the **Treaty of San Lorenzo** (1796)?

Spain possessed land in the southeast from the Atlantic coast to the Mississippi River south of the Thirty-first Parallel (the present-day Georgia-Florida border). Spain used its control of New Orleans and the mouth of the Mississippi River to obstruct American exporting and to check American expansion. Kentucky had become a state in 1792, and

Tennessee in 1796. Both the United States and Spain claimed a large area, called the Yazoo Strip, between the borders of Florida and Tennessee and west of Georgia.

After some reluctance, Spain agreed to the Treaty of San Lorenzo, negotiated by George Washington's secretary of state, Thomas Jefferson. The treaty recognized the Thirty-first Parallel as the southern boundary of the United States, granted access to Americans to all of the Mississippi River, and provided a three-year privilege for Americans to warehouse goods in New Orleans for export.

In his Farewell Address (1796), Washington cited the Treaty of San Lorenzo as an example of how the American government works to help its citizens.

What was the **Adams-Onis Treaty** (1819)?

President James Monroe sought to obtain Florida from Spain. An opportunity occurred when General Andrew Jackson and his forces entered Florida in 1818 in pursuit of Seminole Indians who had made raids across the border in Georgia. In the process, Jackson captured two Spanish forts and executed two British citizens who had encouraged Seminoles to make the raids in Georgia.

While Congress called for Jackson to be reprimanded for exceeding his orders, Monroe accepted Jackson's explanation that he was responding to events as they happened. The forts were returned to Spain. Recognizing the futility of protecting its far-off possession, however, Spain agreed to negotiate the ceding of Florida. John Quincy Adams, Monroe's secretary of state, negotiated the Adams-Onis Treaty in which Spain ceded Florida to the United States.

What was the significance of the **Webster-Ashburton Treaty** (1842)?

The U.S.-Canadian border between Maine and New Brunswick had long been in dispute, nearly leading to war in the late 1830s. Major General Winfield Scott was sent to the area by President Martin Van Buren in case of war, but a temporary, diplomatic solution was worked out. The Webster-Ashburton Treaty, negotiated on President John Tyler's behalf by Secretary of State Daniel Webster, settled the Maine boundary dispute.

Which president **first actively sought trade with Japan**?

Millard Fillmore sent Commodore Matthew Perry on a mission in the Pacific Ocean that included delivering a letter to the Japanese emperor that requested a trade treaty. Perry set out with four ships from Norfolk, Virginia, in November 1852 and arrived at Edo (modern-day Tokyo) in July 1853. He was directed to Nagasaki, the only Japanese port open to foreigners. After Perry refused to leave Edo and cleared the decks of his ship as a show of military strength, he was allowed on shore in an elaborate ceremony. Perry delivered letters to two princes representing the emperor and promised to return for a reply within twelve months.

Fillmore had also dispatched Perry to protect America's growing trade with China, and Perry visited Hong Kong before returning to Japan. A treaty was concluded with Japan in March 1854 and Perry returned to the United States in January 1855. By then, Franklin Pierce had become president, and it was he who ratified the treaty after it was approved by the Senate.

Why was **trade with Japan controversial in the 1970s and 1980s**?

A trade deficit, particularly with Japan, contributed to a weak American economy during the 1970s. The American automobile industry was especially hard hit. When gasoline prices soared in the 1970s, Americans demanded smaller, more fuel-efficient cars—a trend that had been developing since the 1960s. The American automobile industry was slow to act, and when demand for fuel-efficient cars was peaking, Japanese automakers had already introduced cars that were fuel-efficient without compromising performance. By 1980, Japan passed the United States as the world's largest automaker.

Japan had trade restrictions in place to protect the Japanese auto industry. Presidents Gerald Ford and Jimmy Carter sought concessions from Japan, and within the United States there was growing consumer sentiment to "buy American." However, as early as 1969, American and Japanese auto companies had been pursuing joint ventures, a trend that continued until many Japanese car models and brands were fully assembled within the United States.

In March 1981, trade talks between Japanese foreign minister Masayoshi Ito and members of the administration of Ronald Reagan resulted in the Japanese agreeing to self-imposed, "voluntary restraints." Some members of the Reagan administration argued for tariffs on Japanese cars, but voluntary restraints, improvements by American automakers, and further cooperation between American and Japanese automakers created a fairer arrangement and helped reduce the trade deficit between the nations. The trade deficit was lessened further in the 1990s during the Bill Clinton administration when the American economy boomed and exports to Japan rose as much as 30 percent in 1996.

Which treaty addressed **British aid to the Confederacy**?

In the Treaty of Washington with Great Britain in May 1871, Ulysses S. Grant's secretary of state, Hamilton Fish, settled claims arising from British aid to the Confederacy during the Civil War. The treaty provided for international arbitration to assess financial damages to the United States against Great Britain for allowing Confederate cruisers, most notably the *Alabama,* to be built and supplied in England—a violation of British neutrality. The arbitration tribunal awarded $15.5 million in damages to the United States.

Why was the **Treaty of Versailles so controversial** in the United States?

Even though the Treaty of Versailles was more punitive towards Germany than Woodrow Wilson wanted, he accepted the final version of the treaty because it included the creation of the League of Nations, with responsibility for executing the treaty and preventing future wars. The Treaty of Versailles stripped Germany of its colonies, placed a huge liability for reparations, and severely reduced the German Army. Wilson held hope that American leadership in the League of Nations would eventually lead to reducing punishment on Germany.

Wilson was confident the Treaty of Versailles would be accepted at home. However, opposition to theLeague of Nations began even before Wilson presented the treaty for approval by the U.S. Senate. Of greatest concern to Senate Republicans led by Henry Cabot Lodge, chairman of the Foreign Relations Committee, was a collective security clause that committed U.S. military forces to League resolutions.

Wilson not only demanded speedy discussion and approval of the treaty, he insisted as well that no changes or amendments would be acceptable. When it became obvious the Senate wanted lengthy debate and some revisions to the treaty, Wilson went before the public. He traveled more than eight thousand miles and delivered forty speeches. The physical strain on Wilson was too great. He nearly collapsed following a speech at Pueblo, Colorado, on September 25, 1919, and a week later he suffered a severe stroke and paralysis of the left side of his body.

The Senate twice voted on the Versailles Treaty, on November 19, 1919, and again on March 19, 1920. Led by Lodge, a significant portion of the Senate insisted on revisions to remove commitments of American forces and leadership to the League. No changes were acceptable to Wilson, and he insisted that Democrats should vote to reject the amended treaty.

What was the **outcome of the Treaty of Versailles** in the United States?

At the very beginning of his presidency, Woodrow Wilson made a bold move by appealing directly to the public to pressure the U.S. Senate that was delaying and complicating a tariff reform bill. The gamble worked: the tariff measure passed, Wilson was able to fulfill a campaign pledge, and he was immediately established as a strong president. Seven years later, near the end of his presidency, Wilson again appealed to the public, this time to pressure the Senate to approve the Treaty of Versailles. In a public letter published on January 8, 1920, he urged the people to decide the issue in "the great and solemn referendum": the election of 1920.

Wilson lost his last big gamble. Tired of war and international issues, voters turned in landslide numbers to Republican Warren G. Harding and his "Return to Normalcy" campaign theme over Democratic candidate James M. Cox. The referendum of the election of 1920 helped Harding fulfill two key campaign pledges: he concluded a separate peace treaty with Germany and made it plain that the United States would never enter the League of Nations.

When was **NATO formed**?

The North Atlantic Treaty Organization (NATO) was established in 1949 to support the North Atlantic Treaty signed in Washington, D.C., in April of that year. The treaty was signed by twelve nations to "reaffirm their faith in the purposes and principles of the Charter of the United Nations and their desire to live in peace with all peoples and all governments. They are determined to safeguard the freedom, common heritage and civilisation of their peoples, founded on the principles of democracy, individual liberty and the rule of law. They seek to promote stability and well-being in the North Atlantic area. They are resolved to unite their efforts for collective defence and for the preservation of peace and security."

Key to the treaty was Article V: "The Parties agree that an armed attack against one or more of them in Europe or North America shall be considered an attack against them all...." President Harry S. Truman was a leading proponent for the formation of NATO as a practical way to check Soviet expansionism in Europe. The Article V provision made an attack against European allies of the United States equivalent to an attack on the United States itself. NATO provided a means for a combined military force of member nations to quickly mobilize. Dwight D. Eisenhower served as the first Supreme Allied Commander of NATO. He left the post in the spring of 1952, and in the fall of that year Eisenhower was elected president of the United States.

When were **NATO military forces first engaged**?

NATO was not involved in a military engagement until 1999. President Bill Clinton called on the alliance to help with United Nations peacekeeping efforts in the former Yugoslavia. U.S. general Wesley Clark was Supreme Allied Commander of NATO at the time. NATO waged an aerial bombing campaign for eleven weeks against Serbia and Montenegro during the Kosovo War to stop the killings of civilians in Kosovo.

What was the **Trade Expansion Act** (1962)?

To encourage cooperation with western European nations, President John F. Kennedy requested that Congress improve his bargaining position by authorizing him with greater discretion in offering tariff reductions. Congress obliged with the Trade Expansion Act. Kennedy hoped to increase cooperation with European nations to coincide with the growth of the European Common Market. However, Kennedy's plans were consistently frustrated by the actions of French president Charles de Gaulle. He vetoed Britain's entry into the Common Market and compromised prospects for more active trading among member nations of NATO.

What were the **Camp David Accords**?

In September 1978, Jimmy Carter brought Israeli prime minister Menachem Begin and Egyptian president Anwar Sadat together at Camp David, Maryland, to forge a peace agreement between their nations. Begin and Sadat announced two agreements: an Israeli-Egyptian peace treaty, and a commitment for working toward a five-year transition for Palestinians toward self-government. Begin and Sadat shared the Nobel Prize for Peace in 1978 for their historic agreement, which they officially signed on March 26, 1979.

The peace agreement ended thirty years of conflict that resulted in several wars between Israel and Egypt. The commitment for Palestinian self-government was not successful and was superseded by several subsequent attempts to forge an agreement for Palestinian statehood.

How did the **North American Free Trade Agreement (NAFTA)** develop?

The roots of NAFTA reach back to liberal trade agreements between Canada and the United States during the 1970s. A new free trade agreement between the United States and Canada began on January 1, 1989. The two nations extended negotiations to include Mexico in order to form a trilateral agreement that the respective govern-

Egyptian president Anwar Sadat, U.S. president Jimmy Carter, and Israeli prime minister Menachem Begin clasp hands on the north lawn of the White House after signing the peace treaty between Egypt and Israel on March 26, 1979. *AP/Wide World Photos.*

ments believed would improve their economies and strengthen political cooperation among the nations. Talks involving the members of the George Bush administration began in February 1991 and resulted in a draft North American Free Trade Agreement (NAFTA) in 1992. NAFTA set up a schedule for the elimination of tariffs over a fifteen-year period and restructured trade between the United States and Mexico and between Mexico and Canada. All tariffs between the United States and Canada would end by the year 1998; those between the United States and Mexico would be eliminated by 2008.

An often contentious, year-long debate over NAFTA occurred in the U.S. Senate and among candidates for president in the 1992 election. NAFTA was approved by the U.S. Congress in November 1993. NAFTA was negotiated by the Bush administration and signed into law by Bill Clinton, who defeated Bush in the 1992 election.

What were **debates about NAFTA among presidential candidates**?

The American economy was weak in 1992. Increasing trade and protecting the United States from job losses were at the top of the agenda of the three major candidates, incumbent president George Bush and challengers Bill Clinton and Ross Perot. As the Senate, business and labor, and American citizens debated the merits of NAFTA, businessman Perot became a leading public spokesman for those rejecting NAFTA. "That giant sucking sound" of employment and dollars rushing out of the country was how

Perot succinctly stated his view on NAFTA. NAFTA itself became a larger issue in 1993, when it was presented for approval to the U.S. Senate. Perot and Al Gore, Clinton's vice president, debated NAFTA on the nationally televised *Larry King Show* and Perot made NAFTA a major issue in the 1996 presidential campaign.

Job losses, lowered production, lower wages, plant closings, and massive investment of U.S. dollars in Mexico, rather than at home, are frequently cited by opponents of NAFTA as the results of the agreement. Proponents argue that NAFTA provides improved balance of trade, encourages business competition, and opens up the Mexican market for American goods. In the 2000 and 2004 presidential elections, the two major candidates supported NAFTA.

The issue of job losses from 2001 to 2004 was significant in the 2004 presidential campaign, but neither George W. Bush nor John Kerry directly blamed NAFTA. Bush supported tax cuts he began introducing in 2001 as the means to stimulate the economy; the first signs of economic recovery and growth began to show in 2004. Bush and Kerry cautioned against protectionism and extolled the value of fair competition that NAFTA represented. Kerry urged a more direct plan to address job losses through taxes and regulations that would make it less attractive for businesses to relocate or to outsource production overseas.

Why did the **George W. Bush administration rescind several treaties**?

Shortly after entering office, Bush stated that he would not sign the Kyoto Protocols on global warming. The protocols were established under the United Nations Framework Convention on Climate Change, which agreed in Kyoto, Japan, in 1997, that thirty-nine industrialized nations must cut emissions of six greenhouse gases to an average of 5.2 percent below 1990 levels by the period 2008–2012. The gases contribute to global warming.

The protocols were signed by Bush's predecessor, Bill Clinton, but he did not present it to the U.S. Senate, knowing it would be rejected because it did not restrict greenhouse emissions from third-world nations. Clinton's efforts to amend the protocols were unsuccessful, ending in November 2000 after European nations refused to accept his compromise.

Bush sought to "unsign" the treaty authorizing establishment of the International Criminal Court in The Hague. He believed the court posed a potential threat to U.S. military commanders. Bush also rescinded treaties made with the former Soviet Union that placed limits on new weapons and defense systems. In 2002, he ordered the deployment of a missile defense system with interceptors based at sea and in Alaska and California.

CRISIS AND DIPLOMACY

What was the **controversy of Citizen Genet** during George Washington's presidency?

Following the execution of France's King Louis XVI in 1793 and the establishment of a new French government, Citizen Edmond Genet was named the new French minister to the United States. He arrived in Charleston, South Carolina, and toured northward, with great fanfare, to the nation's capital, which at that time was Philadelphia, Pennsylvania. Genet insisted that the United States honor its treaty obligations (of 1778) to France and provide aid in its war with Great Britain, but Washington had already issued a proclamation of neutrality concerning the war. Certain that the United States still needed the assistance of France, Genet acted in ways that suggested he held a position of authority to direct U.S. policy.

When Genet's actions, which included leading armed expeditions in what was then Spanish-held Florida, were publicized in a newspaper, Genet admitted to them, expecting American citizens would support him. Instead, Genet's standing was compromised, yet he continued to undermine the U.S. government. In 1794, a new French minister, Jean Antoine Joseph Baron Fauchet, arrived in the United States with orders to arrest Genet and return him to France.

Washington granted Genet asylum and Genet avoided the guillotine—his likely fate had he been returned to France. Genet married a daughter of New York governor (and future U.S. vice president) George Clinton, and they settled in rural New York.

What was the **XYZ Affair**?

France and England had been at war for four years when John Adams took office in 1797. Both nations stopped American ships at sea and seized cargoes they believed were destined for their enemies. Jay's Treaty (1795) had produced a level of understanding between the United States and Great Britain. Adams sent a team of diplomats in the summer of 1797 to negotiate an agreement with France. However, French foreign minister Charles-Maurice de Talleyrand-Périgord refused to meet with the Americans. Instead, he sent three aides and several demands, including a $250,000 payment by the United States to begin the negotiations.

Adams learned of the demands by dispatch. Some member of his cabinet urged war against France and an alliance with England. Adams decided to prepare for war but to continue negotiations. Congress pressed Adams to make public the French demands. He did so, but referred to the three French envoys as X, Y, and Z. The American public was outraged at French conduct, and war fever swept the country. An unofficial conflict ensued on the seas between France and the United States called the

Quasi War (1798–1800). Meanwhile, Adams was able to use the XYZ Affair to win support from Congress for expanding the army and creating a separate naval force.

What **crises with Italy and Chile** were addressed by Benjamin Harrison?

Harrison had to address a diplomatic crisis with Italy after three Italian nationals were among nine people lynched by a New Orleans mob in 1891. The violence followed acquittal and mistrial verdicts for the Italians, who were alleged to have taken part in an organized-crime conspiracy and the ambush slaying of the city's police superintendent. The Italian government broke off diplomatic relations with the United States over the incident. Harrison managed to restore diplomatic ties, and the United States paid an indemnity to the Italian government.

Another international crisis for Harrison occurred with Chile after two American sailors were killed in that country. Reparations and an apology from the Chilean government helped settle the matter.

What **peace agreement was mediated by Theodore Roosevelt**?

The Russo-Japanese War (1904–1905) was fought over Manchuria and Korea. After diplomatic attempts failed between Russia and Japan to negotiate the areas into spheres of influence, Japan attacked and bottled up the Russian fleet and then won a series of land and sea battles. However, with Japan facing economic problems and Russia humiliated by a poor military showing, both sides wanted peace. Through the mediation of President Theodore Roosevelt, a peace treaty was negotiated in Portsmouth, New Hampshire. Roosevelt's performance earned him the Nobel Peace Prize.

During negotiations for the Treaty of Portsmouth, Roosevelt treated Japan as he would a major power, which Japan had become by defeating Russia in a series of battles in the Russo-Japanese War. He cultivated friendly relations with Japan and ensured that American interests in the Philippines would be respected by Japan, while the United States respected Japan's influence over Korea. In November 1908, the United States recognized Japan's influence over Manchuria, while Japan affirmed the Open Door policy in China that had provided access to the United States.

What was notable about **Woodrow Wilson's peace efforts during and after World War I**?

Woodrow Wilson's pursuit of peace brought him unprecedented international stature for an American president. As he worked to maintain American neutrality—World War I began in 1914 and the United States did not enter the conflict until 1917—he attempted to bring the warring factions together for peace talks by having them state their terms for peace. Once the United States entered the war, Wilson clearly spelled out the U.S. mission in his Fourteen Points Address to Congress on January 8, 1918.

An Excerpt from Woodrow Wilson's Fourteen Points

President Woodrow Wilson addressed U.S. Congress on January 8, 1918, during which he presented his Fourteen Points, which included his idea for the League of Nations. A portion of the opening statement and Point XIV, which describes the League of Nations, appears below.

> We entered this war because violations of right had occurred which touched us to the quick and made the life of our own people impossible unless they were corrected and the world secure once for all against their recurrence. What we demand in this war, therefore, is nothing peculiar to ourselves. It is that the world be made fit and safe to live in; and particularly that it be made safe for every peace-loving nation which, like our own, wishes to live its own life, determine its own institutions, be assured of justice and fair dealing by the other peoples of the world as against force and selfish aggression. All the peoples of the world are in effect partners in this interest, and for our own part we see very clearly that unless justice be done to others it will not be done to us. The programme of the world's peace, therefore, is our programme; and that programme, the only possible programme, as we see it, is this....
>
> XIV. A general association of nations must be formed under specific covenants for the purpose of affording mutual guarantees of political independence and territorial integrity to great and small states alike.

The Fourteen Points proposed the League of Nations, an international body that could address future conflicts once peace was restored.

The Fourteen Points, the United States' entry into the war, and Wilson's mediation efforts helped the warring nations reach an armistice in November 1918. The following month, Wilson and a large body of advisers sailed from New York to take part in the peace conference in Paris. It would be the first time a sitting American president had left the country for an extended period. For his efforts, Wilson was award the Nobel Peace Prize in 1919.

Which twentieth-century presidents faced **tense developments in Chinese-American relations**?

Following World War II, President Harry S. Truman attempted to persuade Chinese Nationalists and Communists to work together in one government, hoping Nationalist leader and American ally Chiang Kai-shek would remain in power. But communists made sustained military advances and drove Nationalist leaders from mainland China to the island of Taiwan in 1949.

The following year, the United States participated in the United Nations effort to assist South Korea, which had been invaded by the army of North Korea, in what became the Korean War (1950–1953). After having pushed the invading North Korean army back across the Thirty-eighth Parallel that separated the two Koreas, Truman and General Douglas MacArthur, commander in chief of the Far East and supreme commander of the UN forces, decided to pursue the North Korean army further and defeat them. Thousands of Chinese soldiers entered the conflict after UN forces crossed the Thirty-eighth Parallel and helped force UN troops into a retreat. From that point in late 1950, the Korean War was essentially a stalemate.

Dwight D. Eisenhower, like Truman, supported Chiang Kai-shek. When Chinese communist forces bombarded Nationalist outposts on Quemoy, Matsu, and the Tachen islands, Eisenhower requested and received the Formosa Resolution from Congress. With congressional backing to use military force, Eisenhower ordered the Seventh Fleet to patrol off mainland China. Unable to move on the islands, China ceased the bombardment.

U.S.-Chinese relations were volatile early in Bill Clinton's presidency. Clinton angered China when his administration allowed the Taiwanese president Lee Teng-hui to visit the United States in 1995. Then, as Taiwan's 1996 elections approached, China conducted extensive military maneuvers near the island, leading Clinton to send two aircraft carriers to the region to reemphasize U.S. defense of Taiwan. In both of these situations Clinton was influenced in his decisions by strong support for Taiwan in Congress.

In 1997, Chinese president Jiang Zemin visited the United States, and in 1998 Clinton visited China. Relations were progressing until May 1999 when a U.S. warplane on a mission over Serbia bombed the Chinese embassy in Belgrade in the former Yugoslavia. Massive demonstrations in China against the United States and Chinese government protests added to the tension. It was determined that the maps used to plan the bombing mission were inaccurate. Meanwhile, investigations in 1998 and 1999 disclosed that China had been working for decades to steal U.S. technology secrets, and may have stolen documents and computer files of nuclear secrets from U.S. government laboratories.

George W. Bush faced his first foreign policy test in early spring of 2001 when an American EP-3E surveillance plane on a routine mission over the South China Sea was clipped by a Chinese F-8 fighter. The American pilot was forced to make an emergency landing on southern Hainan Island. All 24 military personnel onboard were unharmed, but China kept them in custody. After eleven tense days of confrontation, the crew and plane were allowed to return to the United States. Chinese diplomats accepted a U.S. letter of regret about the South China Sea encounter. Bush's response to the crisis—he neither made public apologies nor threats, preferring instead to allow diplomats to negotiate a solution—was praised as an effective means of handling the situation.

What **crises in the Middle East** were faced by **President Eisenhower**?

In 1953, Mohammad Mosaddeq, prime minister of Iran, nationalized oil fields held by British companies and diverted the profits to his own treasury. He was also suspected of negotiating for Soviet aid. The Eisenhower administration authorized the Central Intelligence Agency to contribute money and expertise to supporters of Shah Mohammad Reza Pahlavi in a coup that toppled Prime Minister Mosaddeq. In response to U.S. aid, the Shah agreed to share 40 percent of Iran's oil with a development consortium that included the United States.

In 1955, the Soviet Union began to sell arms to Egypt, which was involved in an undeclared war with Israel. After the United States declined to finance a huge dam at Aswan on the Nile River in 1956, the Soviet Union agreed to supply the funds. Egypt then nationalized the Suez Canal, and a combined force from England, France, and Israel attacked Egypt. The Eisenhower administration preferred a diplomatic solution and peace was restored, but the Soviet Union continued to become a strong force in the Middle East.

A military revolution in Iraq abolished the monarchy in that country in 1958 and created instability in the nation. When a similar uprising seemed imminent in Lebanon, Eisenhower ordered a marine detachment there. The crisis ended without incident.

What **developments in the Cold War** occurred during the **Eisenhower administration**?

The arms race escalated during the 1950s. The Soviet Union became a nuclear power. After the United States successfully tested a hydrogen bomb in 1952, the Soviets were successful in 1953. Aircraft and missile delivery systems were perfected, Intercontinental Ballistic Missiles (ICBMs) became dependable, and the first nuclear-powered Polaris submarine armed with nuclear missiles was put to sea in 1960. Since a defense policy based on the threat of nuclear retaliation was less expensive than maintaining conventional armies, both the United States and the Soviet Union began a consistent escalation in nuclear weapons.

The death of Soviet premier Joseph Stalin in 1953 held some promise for a thaw in the Cold War, particularly after his successor, Nikita Khrushchev, criticized Stalin's legacy. The 1955 Geneva Summit between the United States and the Soviet Union was the first between the two nations since the 1945 Yalta and Potsdam conferences. At the summit, Eisenhower proposed an "Open Skies" policy in which the Soviet Union and the United States would each establish air bases in each others' nation. The offer was refused, as was Eisenhower's proposal for the reunification of Germany.

Also in 1955, the Soviet Union organized East Germany, Hungary, Poland, Czechoslovakia, Rumania, and Bulgaria, into a military alliance called the Warsaw Pact. When two of the nations attempted to assert independence in 1956, the Soviets responded by allowing some liberalization in Poland, but sent a military expedition

The Missile Gap?

During the 1950s, some Americans became concerned that the United States was falling behind in the arms race with the Soviet Union. Press commentators and politicians began speaking of the "missile gap" and urged more defense spending. Democrats seized on the issue during the 1960 campaign for the presidential nomination—the "missile gap" phrase was used by leading contenders John F. Kennedy and Lyndon B. Johnson. However, evidence from U-2 spyplane missions over the Soviet Union beginning in 1955 showed no evidence of an arms buildup any larger than what the Soviet Union was known to possess. Problem was, the U-2 spyplane missions were top secret, and the U.S. military could not provide the public with information that would fill the gap in perception versus the reality of the Soviet weapons cache.

into Hungary to crush rebellion. The Soviets warned that U.S. intervention would provoke a general war. The practical problem of fighting a conflict so far removed from U.S. resources in the center of the Soviet establishment of satellite nations deterred the Eisenhower administration from intervening.

The United States and Soviet Union did not resume relations until 1959, when Vice President Richard Nixon visited the Soviet Union and Khrushchev visited the United States. A planned summit in Paris in 1960, where Eisenhower hoped to win agreement on a treaty for arms limitations and a ban on atmospheric tests of nuclear weapons, was compromised two weeks prior to the meeting. A U.S. spyplane was shot down over the Soviet Union.

What was the U-2 Incident?

U-2 spyplanes, which had been flying over the Soviet Union since the mid-1950s, were capable of flying high in the atmosphere, beyond Soviet air defenses. However, the Soviets had developed an improved surface-to-air missile by 1960. Just two weeks before a U.S.-Soviet summit in Paris in 1960, President Eisenhower authorized the flight of a U-2 spyplane to make photographic runs over defense areas in the Soviet Union. Soviets shot down the plane. The United States claimed that it was a weather forecasting plane that had flown off course. Just before the Paris summit meeting, however, Soviet premier Nikita Khrushchev announced that the pilot, CIA agent Francis Gary Powers, had survived the destruction of his plane and was being held as a prisoner.

What was the Cuban Missile Crisis?

In October 1962, President John F. Kennedy was shown aerial reconnaissance photographs of missile bases under construction in Cuba with Soviet materials and super-

President John F. Kennedy confers with his brother, Attorney General Robert F. Kennedy, at the White House during the buildup of tensions between the United States and Soviet Union over the Cuban Missile Crisis. *AP/Wide World Photos.*

vision. Nuclear weapons could reach much of the United States as well as other targets in the Western Hemisphere from the bases. Kennedy revealed the finding in a radio and television address and reported that the United States was placing a naval and air quarantine on all offensive weapons bound for Cuba: U.S. warships would stop and search Soviet vessels.

The threat of war, possibly nuclear war, loomed for a week. When Soviet ships bound for Cuba, probably carrying arms, turned away and sailed back across the Atlantic, the first sense of relief could be felt. "We're eyeball to eyeball," said Kennedy's secretary of state, Dean Rusk, "and I think the other fellow just blinked." The Soviet Union dismantled and withdrew its hardware for launching missiles from Cuba.

Other than the thirteen days of the Cuban Missile Crisis, how was the **Kennedy administration's relations with the Soviet Union**?

In June 1961, President Kennedy attended a summit in Vienna, Austria, where he spoke with Soviet premier Nikita Khrushchev on the status of Berlin, Germany. Khrushchev had threatened to sign a treaty with the East German government that would give Soviets complete control of access to Berlin. After the construction of the Berlin Wall to prevent East Berliners from escaping to the West, Kennedy won congressional support to increase defense spending and ordered National Guard and

> ## Kennedy and Khrushchev
>
> During a break at a summit in Vienna, Austria, John F. Kennedy inquired about a medal Soviet premier Nikita Khrushchev was wearing. After the Soviet leader identified it as a peace medal, Kennedy replied, "I hope you get to keep it."

reserve units into active service. The treaty between the Soviet Union and East Germany was never signed.

Later, in September 1961, Kennedy responded when the Soviet Union resumed nuclear weapons tests. He ordered underground and atmospheric nuclear tests. After lengthy negotiations that began in the fall of 1961, the United States, Britain, and the Soviet Union signed a limited nuclear test-ban treaty in 1963. The treaty forbade atmospheric testing of nuclear weapons and was later signed by most other nations of the world. It was the first agreement for arms limitation since the Cold War began.

What was "Shuttle Diplomacy"?

Henry Kissinger continued as secretary of state after Richard Nixon resigned in 1974 and Vice President Gerald Ford assumed the presidency. Kissinger had negotiated a fragile military disengagement in the Middle East in 1973, which he helped sustain by shuttling back and forth between nations while preparing formal summit meetings between them. Kissinger also made several trips to the Soviet Union to lay the groundwork for summit meetings between President Ford and Soviet premier Leonid Brezhnev. Because Kissinger traveled among nations so frequently for face-to-face meetings, his method was called shuttle diplomacy.

Ford was a shuttling president, making goodwill trips to several countries. He became the first sitting president to visit Japan.

What was the Iran hostage crisis?

On November 4, 1979, a group of anti-American protestors in Tehran, Iran, stormed the American embassy, captured fifty-two American workers, and held them hostage. What became known as the Iran Hostage Crisis lasted 444 days.

The hostage-taking was led by radical Iranian students, who had helped fuel what became an Islamic Revolution in Iran that forced the nation's leader, Mohammad Reza Pahlavi, the Shah of Iran, to flee the country earlier in 1979. The Shah had been supported by the United States since the 1940s. Disparity between a small, wealthy minority of Iranians and the larger public, and continual crackdowns on dissidents by the Shah fueled revolutionary fervor and anti-American sentiments. The triumphant return of Ayatollah Ruhollah Khomeini, a supreme religious leader who had been exiled in 1963 for publicly criticizing the Shah, completed the transformation of Iran into an Islamic Republic.

The exiled Shah of Iran was granted refuge in the United States by President Jimmy Carter to receive medical treatment for cancer. Revolutionaries in Iran demanded the Shah be returned to Iran to stand trial. Demonstrations in Iran became increasingly violent, culminating with the takeover of the American embassy, an act that was praised by the Ayatollah Khomeini.

The American hostages were subjected to humiliations and endless interrogations. The crisis harmed the Carter administration, which was frustrated in attempts to secure the release of the hostages. International pressure, economic sanctions, and a rescue mission (see The President Leads: Commander in Chief—Military Action) all failed. Carter's unstinting support for the Shah and his inability to resolve the crisis contributed to his landslide defeat to Ronald Reagan in the presidential election of 1980. Iran finally released the hostages on January 20, 1981, the very day Carter was replaced as president by Reagan.

Why did George W. Bush declare a **War on Terror**?

In response to the terrorist attacks on the United States on September 11, 2001, Bush proclaimed himself a war president, leading the nation in a War on Terror. By making this official pronouncement, Bush gained leverage when asking Congress to authorize funds for military operations and made possible the enactment of emergency measures associated with the USA PATRIOT Act. Viewed by Congress and the president as a series of emergency interim regulations during a time of crisis or war, the PATRIOT Act expanded powers for search and surveillance by the Federal Bureau of Investigation (FBI).

Why was **Afghanistan the first target in the War on Terror**?

Camps used for training terrorists were based in Afghanistan and supported by the radical Islamic group, the Taliban, that governed the nation. Afghanistan was the base for the Al Qaeda organization and its leader, Osama bin Laden, who were believed responsible for organizing the attacks on the United States on September 11, 2001. The Taliban refused U.S. demands to turn bin Laden over to the United States, and instead offered to negotiate, to put bin Laden on trial in an Islamic court, and to turn him over to a third country if the United States provided evidence of his guilt. The Bush administration rejected these offers and demanded the entire Al Qaeda organization be eliminated. When the demands were not met, the war in Afghanistan (2001) began.

How was the **war in Iraq linked with the War on Terror**?

Believing that Iraq possessed weapons of mass destruction that could be used in a terrorist attack, President George W. Bush sought and received support from Congress for using force against Iraqi leader Saddam Hussein. Iraq was supposed to have destroyed its weapons of mass destruction as part of the treaty that ended the Gulf War (1991). Verification of the destruction was made impossible by Hussein, who frequently delayed and frustrated attempts by United Nations weapons inspectors to complete inspections of Iraqi sites suspected of making or housing the weapons.

Bush attempted to build an international coalition for military action against Iraq, like that which combined in 1991 to swifly expel Iraqi forces from Kuwait in the Gulf War. He sought backing from the UN Security Council, but the Council instead endorsed stricter weapons inspections without linking them to a threat of military consequences.

What **arguments were made against the war in Iraq**?

Few nations joined the international coalition led by the United States and Great Britain to oust Saddam Hussein from power. Those that declined favored continued UN inspections to ensure weapons of mass destruction existed in Iraq or had been destroyed. Americans who agreed believed that diplomatic and United Nations sponsored efforts had not been exhausted.

In addition, it was disclosed during the summer of 2003 that some intelligence information suggesting a weapons program was still alive in Iraq was erroneous. That information had been used by the Bush administration to justify the military operation in Iraq to the UN Security Council and to the American people in his State of the Union Address.

Some argued as well that Iraq did not have a record of state-sponsored international terrorism and no direct links to Al Qaeda, the terrorist organization that organized the September 11, 2001, attacks on the United States, which led to the U.S. War on Terror.

Finally, there was concern about the future of Iraq once the Saddam Hussein regime was toppled. The war against Iraq moved swiftly, but the peace—establishing an orderly government and society—proved more difficult to win.

THE PRESIDENT LEADS: COMMANDER IN CHIEF

PREPAREDNESS

What is the president's role as **commander in chief**?

As outlined by the Constitution, Article II, Section 2, "The President shall be Commander in Chief of the Army and Navy of the United States, and of the Militia of the several States, when called into the actual Service of the United States." As commander in chief, the president has the authority to place U.S. military forces on alert and to authorize military force.

How do the **executive and legislative branches cooperate on military matters**?

Though the president has the authority to order U.S. forces into battle, Congress is empowered by the Constitution to raise and support the armed forces and has the authority to declare war. The president usually requests a formal declaration of war from Congress before committing U.S. forces to military action. However, as commander in chief, the president is responsible for ensuring that the military is prepared to defend U.S. interests and to act in a timely and legal manner.

Which presidents emphasized **buildup of the navy**?

During the first three presidential administrations, American commercial ships were challenged by pirates as well as vessels from England and France, who were at war with each other. George Washington requested appropriations for warships, but Congress acted only after the Treaty of Algiers (1791), where the United States paid a ransom to pirates for the release of Americans taken hostage and agreed to pay an annual tribute—the equivalent of modern-day protection money demanded by mobsters. After the Treaty of Algiers, Congress approved money for six frigates during Washington's term. The Department of Navy was founded in 1798 during the administration of John Adams, and the U.S. Navy had forty-nine vessels to fight the Quasi-War with France (1798–1800).

Thomas Jefferson used the navy to defeat pirates in the Barbary War (1801–1805), but then he deemphasized warships in favor of smaller, lighter gunboats. The gunboats later proved ineffective during the War of 1812 against larger British warships. American warships fared well against the British. By the time of the Mexican War (1846–1848), the navy had sixty-three vessels, which were used to blockade ports and carry soldiers for amphibious operations.

The navy was expanded under Abraham Lincoln during the Civil War and was effective in blockading Confederate ports as well as stopping or destroying blockade runners. However, the Confederate navy enjoyed some success on the high seas, a factor cited in naval appropriation requests from postwar presidents Ulysses S. Grant and Chester Alan Arthur.

With the Spanish-American War (1898), where in the course of three months the navy won major victories off the shores of Cuba and the Philippines, the American navy became a supreme power. Presidents William McKinley and Theodore Roosevelt expanded the navy further. As a show of American might and "big stick" diplomacy, Roosevelt ordered a world cruise of the "great white fleet" of sixteen new battleships from 1907 to 1909.

During the twentieth century, expansion and modernization of the navy was continuous. Thirty-two battleships and almost two thousand other vessels, including Eagle Boats built in automobile plants converted to wartime shipbuilding operations, were available during World War I. The Fleet Marine Force was created in 1933 and dedicated to large-scale amphibious assault.

What was the **Quasi-War** between France and the United States?

War between France and England began in 1793 during the Washington administration and continued to the presidency of John Adams, which began in 1797. Near the end of Washington's term, the president wanted to change his ambassador to France. Washington believed that James Monroe was too sympathetic to France when the United States was committed to neutrality. The French government rejected Monroe's replacement and ordered him out of the country. Then the executive branch of the French government, a commission of five men called the Directory, authorized the seizing of American ships on suspicion they were carrying materials to the British.

Adams inherited that situation. After discussions with his cabinet members, Adams opted for diplomacy instead of war. Instead, an undeclared naval war between the United States and France—called the Quasi-War—occurred from 1798 to 1800. It was the first major conflict in which the U.S. Navy participated.

Washington Didn't Retire Here

After having fought in the 1750s in the French and Indian Wars, having led the Continental Army during the American Revolution (1775–1783), and having served as president (1789–1793), George Washington looked forward to retirement after his first term as president. Instead, he was convinced to run for reelection in 1792 because the young United States was experiencing disunity. Following the end of his second term, Washington was finally able to retire to his Virginia home in early 1797. His retirement wasn't entirely restful. Later in 1797, John Adams, Washington's successor, asked him to be on call to lead American troops in case tensions between France and the United States escalated into war.

Which five presidents asked Congress to **officially declare war**?

Five commanders in chief have followed the process for sustained military involvement as outlined in the Constitution by asking Congress to declare war: James Madison, War of 1812 (1812); James K. Polk, Mexican War (1846); William McKinley, Spanish-American War (1898); Woodrow Wilson, World War I (1917); and Franklin D. Roosevelt, World War II (1941).

When was the **first time a president asked Congress to declare war**?

James Madison asked for a formal declaration of war from Congress in 1812. The United States declared War on Great Britain on June 12, beginning the War of 1812.

What controversy surrounded the **Declaration of War with Mexico** in 1846?

Even after the U.S. annexation of Texas in 1845, a border dispute continued between the United States and Mexico: the Rio Grande was recognized as the border by the United States, while Mexico recognized the traditional border of the Neuces River, more than one hundred miles north of the Rio Grande. U.S. president James K. Polk had been hoping to convince Mexico to cede California to the United States. After being rebuffed by the Mexican government, Polk ordered an army force under General Zachary Taylor to camp along the Rio Grande. In April 1846, an American patrol suffered casualties in a border skirmish, and Polk went before Congress on May 11 to demand a declaration of war, claiming that "Mexico invaded American territory and shed American blood."

Polk's claim was disputed by some congressmen, including U.S. senator Daniel Webster of Massachusetts, who called a declaration of war unconstitutional, unnecessary, and unjust. Webster, like many northerners, viewed the war as a pretext for expanding the nation by force and inviting the expansion of slavery. First-term U.S. representative Abraham Lincoln of Illinois was another war critic. Lincoln questioned

General Zachary Taylor, nicknamed "Old Rough and Ready," was a hero in the Mexican War. Shown here with his horse, Old Whitey, Taylor became so popular that the Whig Party nominated him as its presidential candidate in 1848. He won the election. *Library of Congress.*

President Abraham Lincoln visiting soldiers at one of the bloodiest battlefields of the Civil War, Antietam, in Maryland, October 1, 1862. *Getty Images.*

the truth of the report that Americans had been fired upon and killed. He challenged Polk to show him the exact spot where American blood had been shed.

How did **President Lincoln define the Civil War** in order to carry out his constitutional duties as commander in chief?

When forces representing the Confederate States of America fired on Fort Sumter, a federal fort in South Carolina, in 1861, the U.S. Congress was not in session. Lincoln declared that the attack opposed federal laws in a manner "too powerful to be suppressed by ordinary judicial proceedings." Using his authority under the Militia Act of 1792, Lincoln called for seventy-six thousand militia volunteers. Four states—Virginia, North Carolina, Tennessee, and Arkansas—responded by joining the Confederacy.

Throughout the war, Lincoln was careful to make it clear that his main purpose as president was to preserve the union. His actions were taken to suppress a rebellion and to protect free national elections. Lincoln reaffirmed this stance in his major speeches, including his second inaugural address in 1865: "Both parties deprecated war, but one of them would make war rather than let the nation survive, and the other would accept war rather than let it perish, and the war came."

Why did **William McKinley** hesitate to go to **war with Spain**?

Spain had been confronting insurrections in its colony of Cuba for several years prior to its aggressive suppression of rebellion on the island in 1894. Many Cubans were herded

Militia Act of 1792

President Abraham Lincoln responded to the Confederacy's firing on Fort Sumter by using his authority under the Militia Act of 1792 to call for seventy-six thousand militia volunteers. By citing the Militia Act, Lincoln ensured that his actions were legal. Below is an excerpt from Section One of the Militia Act of 1792.

> Be it enacted by the Senate and House of Representatives of the United States of America in Congress assembled, That whenever the United States shall be invaded, or be in imminent danger of invasion from any foreign nation or Indian tribe, it shall be lawful for the President of the United States, to call forth such number of the militia of the state or states most convenient to the place of danger or scene of action as he may judge necessary to repel such invasion, and to issue his orders for that purpose, to such officer or officers of the militia as he shall think proper; and in case of an insurrection in any state, against the government thereof, it shall be lawful for the President of the United States, on application of the legislature of such state, or of the executive (when the legislature cannot be convened) to call forth such number of the militia of any other state or states, as may be applied for, or as he may judge sufficient to suppress such insurrection.

into internment camps, where malnutrition and disease became rampant. Like his predecessor, Grover Cleveland, McKinley took office believing he could use diplomatic pressure to convince Spain to free Cuba. Meanwhile, public sentiment for war was fueled by stories printed in major newspapers about Spanish atrocities in Cuba. The stories were often sensationalistic, reflecting a commercial "war" for customers between Joseph Pulitzer's *New York World* and William Randolph Hearst's *New York Journal*.

After first urging reform, then Cuban autonomy, McKinley provided Spain with opportunities to abandon the island. The mysterious destruction of the American battleship *Maine* in the harbor of Havana in February 1898, however, stoked sentiment for war. McKinley tried diplomacy for two more months. Finally, lack of progress in diplomacy led McKinley to address Congress and ask for a declaration of war in April 1898.

What events led **Woodrow Wilson** to ask Congress to declare **war on Germany** in 1917?

Wilson made a public appeal to Americans in August 1914 to be "impartial in thought as well as in action" after war erupted in Europe. However, Great Britain soon began using its sea power to monitor trade among neutral countries; Germany announced it would

Colonel Theodore Roosevelt and his "Rough Riders" on Kettle Hill in the battle for San Juan, Puerto Rico, 1898, during the Spanish-American War. *Library of Congress.*

use submarines against enemy ships; and Britain and France declared a blockade against all commerce to and from Germany. All of these actions challenged American interests.

When a German submarine torpedoed the British liner *Lusitania* without warning in 1915, killing more than one hundred Americans on board, Wilson warned Germany that such further actions would lead to America entering the war. After Germany agreed to cooperate, Wilson used diplomacy to pursue peace talks among the warring nations.

Wilson and Congress worked on legislation to strengthen the armed forces, and Wilson began stressing "preparedness" as an early campaign theme for his reelection in 1916. However, he switched to the more popular slogan, "He Kept Us Out of War," based on the enthusiastic response that neutrality received at the Democratic National Convention that summer.

Shortly after Wilson won reelection in November 1916, Germany announced a proclamation of unlimited submarine warfare against all sea commerce. Wilson broke diplomatic relations with Germany on February 3, 1917, and two months later, the presidential candidate who "kept us out of war" was a president asking Congress to declare war. Congress adopted the war resolution on April 6, 1917.

What were the **"undeclared wars"** preceding the official U.S. entry into World War II?

The U.S. Congress adopted and Franklin D. Roosevelt approved several neutrality acts during the mid-1930s even as regimes in Germany, Italy, and Japan were becoming

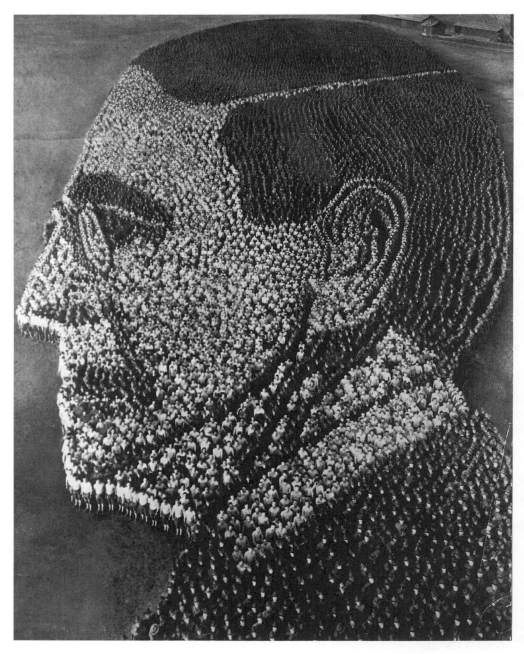

Showing great support for their president, twenty-one thousand officers and soldiers at Camp Sherman, Ohio, come together to form an unusual portrait of Woodrow Wilson. *Getty Images*.

belligerent. Early in 1939, Roosevelt lobbied Congress to lift a neutrality act that called for an embargo on armaments to all nations at war. He was unsuccessful until after Germany attacked Poland in September 1939 and World War II formally began.

Aerial photograph, taken by a Japanese pilot, during the raid on Pearl Harbor, December 7, 1941. *Library of Congress.*

In 1940, Roosevelt negotiated the Lend Lease Act: the United States leased fifty old American destroyers and, in return, Great Britain leased bases in the Pacific to the United States. After Germany attacked the Soviet Union in June 1941, the lend lease policy was applied to the Soviet Union as well.

Before entering World War II, U.S. destroyers began escorting convoys of Allied ships part way across the Atlantic. In the process, they gained and shared intelligence about the location of German submarines. When a German submarine fired a torpedo at the American destroyer *Greer* in September 1941, Roosevelt ordered U.S. warships to shoot on sight at hostile German ships. By December, the United States and Germany were engaged in an undeclared war in the Atlantic.

In the Pacific, Roosevelt countered Japanese expansionism with an embargo of vital goods, including iron and steel scrap. He demanded that Japan halt its aggression in China and Indochina, and his administration increased aid to China. Japan turned the undeclared war into full-scale war by attacking the American naval station at Pearl Harbor, Hawaii, on December 7, 1941, and by moving on the East Indies for oil and minerals.

What events led up to the **Japanese attack on Pearl Harbor**?

The attack on Pearl Harbor is generally regarded as a surprise act of aggression made without warning. The Roosevelt administration had protested Japan's expansionism in

Asia with unstinting support for China and Indochina and had placed embargoes on vital goods to Japan. Some commentators argued that these actions and others were deliberate provocations by the Roosevelt administration to heighten conflict and bring the United States into World War II.

By late November 1941, peace negotiations between the United States and Japan were stalled. U.S. intelligence information suggested the Japanese would attack the Indies. Japan did attack the Indies, but also executed a carefully planned strike to paralyze the U.S. Navy. The U.S. Fleet had been transferred to Pearl Harbor, Hawaii, in the summer of 1940, likely as a show of force against Japanese aggression. Instead, Pearl Harbor became the target through which Japan could inflict great damage on the U.S. Navy while pursuing further aggression in the Pacific.

What is the official government finding on **American preparedness for Pearl Harbor**?

After World War II ended, Congress formed the Joint Committee on the Investigation of the Pearl Harbor Attack. The Commission, which held hearings from November 1945 to May 1946, found failure in the methods used by the Army and Navy to detect an approaching hostile force.

Actions resulting from the commission's findings included the creation of the Central Intelligence Agency (CIA) in 1947 to address intelligence-sharing failures. The Department of Defense was created in 1949, putting the separate military services under one cabinet department. The commission did not fault the Roosevelt administration directly and found no evidence that the administration provoked Japan into military action against the United States as a means for bringing the America into World War II.

When did **Harry S. Truman first learn of the atomic bomb**?

Truman was sworn into office on April 12, 1945, following the death of Franklin D. Roosevelt. The new president met with Roosevelt's cabinet members and asked them to remain in their positions. Secretary of War Henry L. Stimson stayed in the room after the other cabinet officials left. Stimson informed Truman that the United States had developed an atomic bomb. It was the first time Truman had heard the weapon was available.

What **factors and advice did Truman consider** before deciding to use a nuclear weapon?

The United States had lost over four hundred thousand military personnel during World War II by July 1945; Germany had surrendered, but war still raged in the Pacific when Truman became president and learned that the United States had developed an atom bomb. The United States was planning a final assault on Japan and had won a commitment from Soviet premier Josef Stalin at the Potsdam Conference (July 17 to August 2, 1945) that the Soviet Union would enter the war against Japan. On July 26, 1945, the Allied Powers issued an ultimatum to Japan demanding its unconditional surrender. The Japanese government did not reply.

U.S. military leaders expected that as many as a half-million people would die in a final assault before Japan could be successfully invaded and overcome. Faced with those staggering losses, prepared to bring the war to an end, and certain Japan would not surrender otherwise, President Truman decided to use the atomic bomb if Japan did not surrender by August 3, 1945. Meanwhile, Secretary of War Henry L. Stimson sought input from a variety of advisers. Among them was a group of scientists who built the bomb. Physicists Arthur H. Compton, J. Robert Oppenheimer, Enrico Fermi, and Ernest O. Lawrence concluded that a technical demonstration of the bomb was not likely to persuade Japan to end the war. The physicists found no acceptable alternative to military use as a way to demonstrate the power of the bomb.

Some historians and World War II leaders, including Britain's Winston Churchill, believed that Japan's defeat was certain without use of the atom bomb.

What events led to the **Korean War**?

Korea was conquered by Japan during World War II. At the end of the war, Korea was partitioned at the Thirty-eighth Parallel into democratic South Korea and communist North Korea. The Korean War (1950–1953) was a United Nations effort to assist South Korea, which had been invaded by the army of North Korea. The administration of Harry S. Truman had pressured the UN Security Council for a resolution to use military force—UN troops and ships, led by the United States—to defend South Korea.

What president first used the term **"Domino Principle"** to explain why communist expansion needed to be challenged?

In a news conference on April 7, 1954, President Dwight D. Eisenhower was asked to explain the relevance of Indochina, the French colony in southeast Asia (see sidebar) that France was abandoning. Indochina would be partitioned into four nations—Laos, Cambodia, and North and South Vietnam. Communist North Vietnam would soon begin attempting to overthrow the democratic government of South Vietnam in what became the Vietnam War.

Explaining that communist expansion in southeast Asia would have repercussions on all nations in Asia, Eisenhower stated, "You have a row of dominoes set up, you knock over the first one, and what will happen to the last one is the certainty that it will go over very quickly. So you could have a beginning of a disintegration that would have the most profound influences."

Eisenhower on the "Domino Principle"

In a news conference on April 7, 1954, President Dwight D. Eisenhower responded to Copley Press news correspondent Q. Robert Richards's request to comment on the strategic importance of Indochina to the free world:

You have, of course, both the specific and the general when you talk about such things.

First of all, you have the specific value of a locality in its production of materials that the world needs.

Then you have the possibility that many human beings pass under a dictatorship that is inimical to the free world.

Finally, you have broader considerations that might follow what you would call the "falling domino" principle. You have a row of dominoes set up, you knock over the first one, and what will happen to the last one is the certainty that it will go over very quickly. So you could have a beginning of a disintegration that would have the most profound influences.

Now, with respect to the first one, two of the items from this particular area that the world uses are tin and tungsten. They are very important. There are others, of course, the rubber plantations and so on.

Then with respect to more people passing under this domination, Asia, after all, has already lost some 450 million of its peoples to the Communist dictatorship, and we simply can't afford greater losses.

But when we come to the possible sequence of events, the loss of Indochina, of Burma, of Thailand, of the Peninsula, and Indonesia following, now you begin to talk about areas that not only multiply the disadvantages that you would suffer through loss of materials, sources of materials, but now you are talking really about millions and millions and millions of people.

Finally, the geographical position achieved thereby does many things. It turns the so-called island defensive chain of Japan, Formosa, of the Philippines and to the southward; it moves in to threaten Australia and New Zealand....

So, the possible consequences of the loss are just incalculable to the free world.

What are the historical views on **John F. Kennedy's leadership during the Cuban Missile crisis**?

Kennedy generally receives praise for his handling of the Cuban Missile Crisis (see The President Leads: Foreign Policy—Crisis and Diplomacy) for firm and decisive action in ordering a naval blockade of Cuba and demanding the Soviet Union remove nuclear weapons and supplies from Cuba. By responding with a quarantine to prevent additional Soviet shipments to Cuba, Kennedy set up a showdown with Soviet premier Nikita Khrushchev. Khrushchev backed down before the United States used more drastic military measures, such as air strikes against the missile sites or an invasion of Cuba. The Soviets withdrew their weapons in exchange for a public pledge that the United States would not invade Cuba.

Critics of Kennedy's leadership during the Cuban Missile Crisis argue that he risked nuclear war and brought humiliation to Khrushchev that contributed to his ouster from power in 1964. Khrushchev was replaced with more hard-line leaders (a troika that was eventually dominated by Leonid Brezhnev) who escalated the Soviet weapons buildup. Adlai E. Stevenson, ambassador to the United Nations under Kennedy, had advocated a trade in which the United States removed its missiles from Turkey in return for a withdrawal of the Soviet missiles from Cuba. Critics of Kennedy's handling of the crisis argue that diplomacy may have been effective and would have avoided a potential nuclear war and later tensions in Soviet-American relations.

What events led to **American military participation in the Vietnam War**?

In 1964, North Vietnam appeared capable of overrunning South Vietnam. President Lyndon B. Johnson wanted to increase U.S. military involvement in Vietnam beyond the use of advisers. On August 4, 1964, the U.S. destroyer *Maddox* was attacked by North Vietnamese torpedo boats in the Gulf of Tonkin. Johnson claimed the U.S. ship was in international waters and the attack was unprovoked. He asked Congress for authority to defend American lives in Vietnam, and Congress granted him the power in the Tonkin Gulf Resolution.

It remained unclear whether or not the *Maddox* was engaged in helping South Vietnam commando forces conduct a raid on North Vietnam. The issue is one of many that contributed to the "credibility gap" between official government statements and the realities of the war. Following the Tonkin Gulf Resolution, Johnson began authorizing air strikes on North Vietnam to retaliate for Viet Cong raids against U.S. installations in South Vietnam. In March 1965, Johnson authorized sustained bombing raids. American marines began landing in South Vietnam soon after, and there were over 165,000 American troops in Vietnam by November of 1965. Over 460,000 American troops were stationed in Vietnam in May 1967.

The Tonkin Gulf Incident

n excerpt from President Johnson's Message to Congress, August 5, 1964:

Last night I announced to the American people that the North Vietnamese regime had conducted further deliberate attacks against U.S. naval vessels operating in international waters, and I had therefore directed air action against gunboats and supporting facilities used in these hostile operations. This air action has now been carried out with substantial damage to the boats and facilities. Two U.S. aircraft were lost in the action.

After consultation with the leaders of both parties in the Congress, I further announced a decision to ask the Congress for a resolution expressing the unity and determination of the United States in supporting freedom and in protecting peace in southeast Asia....

Two days later, Congress responded by issuing a joint resolution concerning the Tonkin Gulf Incident:

Resolved by the Senate and House of Representatives of the United States of America in Congress assembled,

That the Congress approves and supports the determination of the President, as Commander in Chief, to take all necessary measures to repel any armed attack against the forces of the United States and to prevent further aggression.

Section 2. The United States regards as vital to its national interest and to world peace the maintenance of international peace and security in southeast Asia. Consonant with the Constitution of the United States and the Charter of the United Nations and in accordance with its obligations under the Southeast Asia Collective Defense Treaty, the United States is, therefore, prepared, as the President determines, to take all necessary steps, including the use of armed force, to assist any member or protocol state of the Southeast Asia Collective Defense Treaty requesting assistance in defense of its freedom.

Section 3. This resolution shall expire when the President shall determine that the peace and security of the area is reasonably assured by international conditions created by action of the United Nations or otherwise, except that it may be terminated earlier by concurrent resolution of the Congress.

Why was the **Vietnam conflict an undeclared war**?

Neither Presidents Lyndon B. Johnson nor Richard Nixon asked Congress for a Declaration of War. The Tonkin Gulf Resolution became the legal basis for U.S. involvement in the Vietnam War.

What was the **War Powers Act** (1973)?

The War Powers Act was intended by Congress to reaffirm Article I, Section 8, of the Constitution and ensure that "the collective judgment of both the Congress and the President will apply to the introduction of United States Armed Forces into hostilities, or into situations where imminent involvement in hostilities is clearly indicated by the circumstances, and to the continued use of such forces in hostilities or in such situations."

America was still involved in the Vietnam War at the time of the act. Neither the Vietnam War nor the Korean War that preceded it was declared war, and Congress wanted to curtail the possibility of a future long-term and costly commitment of American troops. However, the War Powers Act is not considered to have been effective. Several military operations have been introduced by presidents under the clause that military action can be ordered in "a national emergency created by attack upon the United States, its territories or possessions, or its armed forces." In addition, the War Powers Act offers presidents some leeway: "The President in every possible instance shall consult with Congress before introducing United States Armed Forces into hostilities or into situations where imminent involvement in hostilities is clearly indicated by the circumstances, and after every such introduction shall consult regularly with the Congress until United States Armed Forces are no longer engaged in hostilities or have been removed from such situations."

Nevertheless, the War Powers Act requires the president to report on military engagements, and those reports can affect the level of funding and support Congress authorizes.

How has **public opinion about the Vietnam War** affected presidents?

As early as the Tonkin Gulf resolution of 1964 that preceded the involvement of American troops in the Vietnam War, some Americans doubted whether their political and military leaders were being truthful in statements about the Vietnam conflict. As casualties began to mount, the Johnson administration continued to project a positive view toward the war. Critics of the war cited a "credibility gap"—a belief that official reports on the war were questionable, misleading, or incomplete.

The credibility gap contributed to Lyndon B. Johnson's dramatic slide in approval. Johnson followed his landslide victory in the 1964 presidential election with large-scale domestic accomplishments in civil rights and government programs. By early 1968, however, Johnson had lost so much support that he quickly withdrew his bid for reelection.

The War Powers Act

The excerpt below from the War Powers Act (1973) is a description of how the president is required to inform Congress whenever United States Armed Forces are introduced into hostilities.

Sec. 4. (a) In the absence of a declaration of war, in any case in which United States Armed Forces are introduced—

(1) into hostilities or into situations where imminent involvement in hostilities is clearly indicated by the circumstances;

(2) into the territory, airspace or waters of a foreign nation, while equipped for combat, except for deployments which relate solely to supply, replacement, repair, or training of such forces; or

(3) in numbers which substantially enlarge United States Armed Forces equipped for combat already located in a foreign nation; the president shall submit within 48 hours to the Speaker of the House of Representatives and to the President pro tempore of the Senate a report, in writing, setting forth—

(A) the circumstances necessitating the introduction of United States Armed Forces;

(B) the constitutional and legislative authority under which such introduction took place; and

(C) the estimated scope and duration of the hostilities or involvement.

Sec. 4. (b) The President shall provide such other information as the Congress may request in the fulfillment of its constitutional responsibilities with respect to committing the Nation to war and to the use of United States Armed Forces abroad

Sec. 4. (c) Whenever United States Armed Forces are introduced into hostilities or into any situation described in subsection (a) of this section, the President shall, so long as such armed forces continue to be engaged in such hostilities or situation, report to the Congress periodically on the status of such hostilities or situation as well as on the scope and duration of such hostilities or situation, but in no event shall he report to the Congress less often than once every six months.

Illustrating the "credibility gap," this cartoon by Jules Feiffer shows President Lyndon B. Johnson asking several people if they believe him. The cartoon appeared in the *Village Voice,* May 13, 1967. *Library of Congress.*

The credibility gap widened during the administration of Richard Nixon, Johnson's successor. In 1971, the *New York Times* printed the Pentagon Papers, top-secret documents that revealed a history of covert operations in Vietnam (for more on the Pentagon Papers, see Presidents and the Judiciary—The Judiciary Influences the Presidency). Secret bombing raids and expansion of the war into countries that neighbored Vietnam during the Nixon administration further eroded public trust in the presidency.

Beginning in the 1980s, presidential and vice presidential candidates were routinely questioned about their activities during the Vietnam War. Vice President Dan Quayle (elected with George Bush in 1988) had avoided the wartime draft by serving briefly in the National Guard before entering law school. Bill Clinton (elected president in 1992) was accused of draft-dodging. He had indicated to recruiters that he planned to join an ROTC program at the University of Arkansas, but he did not attend that college. After drawing a lottery number with a very low chance that he would be drafted, Clinton applied for the draft.

Vietnam War service was not a significant issue during the 2000 presidential election. Vice President Dick Cheney (elected with George W. Bush in 2000) took deferments, first as a college student, and later as a married man. Democratic nominee Al Gore had served in Vietnam as a journalist. Republican nominee George Bush served in the Texas National Guard during the Vietnam War. However, in his bid for reelection in 2004, Bush faced allegations that he hadn't served his entire tour of duty with the National Guard. The issue became significant as he campaigned against Democratic nominee John Kerry, who had served with distinction in Vietnam. Kerry received a Silver Star, Bronze Star with Combat V, and three awards of the Purple Heart for his service in combat. Upon his return from Vietnam, Kerry protested continued American involvement in Vietnam. Kerry's antiwar stance then became an issue.

How did **George Bush get authority** for military engagement in the **Gulf War** (1991)?

After the army of Iraq invaded Kuwait on August 2, 1990, the United Nations passed a series of resolutions condemning the invasion. The resolutions and subsequent diplomatic efforts failed to convince Iraq to withdraw from Kuwait. The Bush administration worked closely with the UN in its attempts for a diplomatic solution. A month after the invasion, Bush spoke before Congress and a national television audience to reinforce support for the UN and demonstrate American resolve to the Iraqis. Bush won a resolution from Congress to use force to expel Iraq from Kuwait.

The UN set a date, January 15, 1991, by which Iraqi forces were to abandon Kuwait. When the date passed, several nations took part in strategic air strikes against Iraqi military targets. A month later, land forces entered Kuwait and expelled the Iraqi occupiers within one hundred hours.

What was the **9/11 commission**?

The National Commission on Terrorist Attacks Upon the United States (also called the 9/11 Commission) was an independent, bipartisan commission created by congressional legislation and approved (by signature) by President George W. Bush in late 2002. Bush initially opposed the commission. It was chartered to prepare a full and complete account of the circumstances surrounding the September 11, 2001, terrorist attacks, including preparedness for and the immediate response to the attacks. The commission was also mandated to provide recommendations designed to guard against future attacks.

Bush and Vice President Dick Cheney testified before the commission, as did their respective predecessors, Bill Clinton and Al Gore. Among others who testified was Richard Clarke, a counterterrorism adviser for the administrations of Ronald Reagan, George Bush, Bill Clinton, and George W. Bush. Clarke told the commission that the George W. Bush administration failed to heed his warnings about terrorist threats before September 11, 2001. In his testimony and in his book, *Against All Enemies,* Clarke also charged that Bush undermined the war on terror by invading Iraq instead of focusing on Al Qaeda, the terrorist network led by Osama bin Laden that was responsible for the September 11 attacks.

The commission asked Bush's national security adviser, Condoleezza Rice, to testify. Arguing Rice's testimony would be a violation of executive privilege, Bush initially refused to allow Rice to testify. The administration agreed after pressure to reverse its position.

The commission released its final report on July 22, 2004. Upon releasing the report, commission chairman Tom Kean, a former Republican governor of New Jersey, concluded the attacks "were a shock, but should not have come as a surprise." He added: "By September 2001, the executive branch of the U.S. government, the news media, and the American public had received clear warning that Islamic terrorists meant to kill Americans in high numbers."

What were reasons cited by **nations that declined to join the American-led coalition in the Iraqi War**?

France, Germany, China, Russia and several Arab states were the most notable nations that declined to participate in the Iraq War. They were among many nations that wanted to continue diplomatic efforts to make Iraq abide by United Nations sanctions regarding development and use of weapons of mass destruction (WMD). They wanted to give the Iraqi regime time to cooperate with UN inspections and comply with UNSC Resolution 1441 (passed in November 2002), which demanded that Iraq disclose and destroy any matériel related to WMD. Finally, the invasion of Iraq was viewed as undermining the rule of international law. Iraq is a sovereign nation, and interference in its internal affairs by other nations violates international law.

What **nations joined the American-led coalition in Iraq**?

Sharing the Bush administration's view that Saddam Hussein was a ruthless dictator who violated UN resolutions, carried on rearmament, was uncooperative with UN weapons inspectors, and harbored weapons of mass destruction (WMD), thirty-three nations were involved in or supported coalition efforts. They included Albania, Australia, Azerbaijan, Bulgaria, the Czech Republic, Denmark, the Dominican Republic, El Salvador, Estonia, Georgia, Honduras, Hungary, Italy, Japan, Kazakhstan, Latvia, Lithuania, Macedonia, Moldova, Mongolia, the Netherlands, New Zealand, Nicaragua, Norway, the Philippines, Poland, Portugal, Romania, Singapore, Slovakia, South Korea, Spain, Thailand, Ukraine, and the United Kingdom.

What is meant by the terms **"exit strategy"** and **"winning the peace"**?

"Exit strategy" is a business term that defines a plan used to get out of a business or project when one is ready to move on to something else, or the method a venture capitalist or business owner intends to use to get out of an investment. Exit strategy has been applied to military operations to ensure that the United States does not become bogged down in a prolonged conflict. Despite American military superiority, the United States was not able to achieve resolution in social and political conflicts of the

Korean and Vietnam Wars, for example. After enormous costs in terms of human life, hardware, and investment, the United States reached points where continued military involvement had little opportunity for political and social success.

The terms exit strategy and "winning the peace" came into use regarding military conflict following the Vietnam War. The terms were frequently applied during the Iraq War: after the United States successfully toppled the regime of Saddam Hussein, violence and social chaos continued as the United States attempted to restore order and instill democracy. A war can be won in days, weeks, or months. Winning the peace means translating military success into an enduring political success.

MILITARY ACTION

Is it true that the first offensive U.S. military action was directed against **pirates**?

The Quasi-War (1798–1800) engaged the French and U.S. navies whenever French ships attempted to stop an American commercial vessel to seize its cargo. U.S. warships were on a defensive alert. On the other hand, in what is called the Barbary War (1801–1805), President Thomas Jefferson ordered a naval squadron to the Mediterranean Sea to blockade and take aggressive action against Tripoli, a pirate haven, which had declared war on the United States.

The Barbary States that harbored pirates on the coast of North Africa demanded tribute payments from foreign powers to sail in the Mediterranean. Presidents George Washington and John Adams paid out more than $2 million in tributes during their administrations. When Tripoli declared war on the United States in 1801, believing that the other Barbary States were receiving a disproportionate share of the tributes, Jefferson decided to challenge the entire tribute practice. Without asking Congress to declare war, Jefferson dispatched four vessels to engage in spirited protection of U.S. shipping in the Mediterranean. The naval war, also known as the Tripolitan War, lasted four years before a peace treaty was signed in 1805. As a result of the war, the United States no longer paid tributes to pirates, and American sailors received practical experience in naval warfare.

What **challenges did James Madison face** as commander in chief during the **War of 1812**?

Despite having vessels victimized for years by British and French ships, the United States did not prepare for the War of 1812 by building up its navy. Public and political support for war was mixed, especially in New England where opposition was fierce. Early in the war, the United States suffered disastrous defeats, surrendering Detroit and retreating on the Niagara River frontier. The national treasury was bankrupt and the army was poorly equipped and trained. Washington, D.C., was overrun and the White House was burned in 1814.

Jefferson Sidesteps the Constitution

Ideologically, Thomas Jefferson was a constructionist, believing the Constitution is meant to be taken literally. For example, Jefferson was against large government expenditures that exceeded government revenue. He insisted a constitutional amendment was necessary to authorize such action by the federal government. However, when faced with a small window of opportunity for making the Louisiana Purchase in 1803, Jefferson abandoned his principles to seize the opportunity of making the deal. Jefferson also went against his constructionist principles when he committed U.S. naval forces to the Barbary War (1801–1805) without asking Congress for a formal declaration of war. The Constitution gives Congress, not the president, the power to declare war.

Madison's best move during the war was to expand the powers of his secretary of state, James Monroe, and place him in a dual role as secretary of war. Monroe quickly secured loans to help finance the war; lifted the spirits of soldiers and attracted new recruits by increasing the size of land parcels war veterans could claim after their military service; and combined state and federal armies, which had been fighting separately, into one force. Meanwhile, a series of victories by the United States helped even out the conflict: Commodore Oliver Perry won a key naval victory in Lake Erie in 1813 (and uttered the memorable phrase, "We have met the enemy and they are ours"); after Perry won control of Lake Erie, General (and future president) William Henry Harrison retook Detroit and pursued a British and Native American allied force into Canada, where Americans were victorious in the Battle of the Thames (river).

These successes of the U.S. Army and Navy sapped British enthusiasm for prolonging the conflict. That the United States had survived a poor early showing and achieved a standoff was a cause for pride for the young nation. A peace agreement was reached in December 1814, but the news hadn't reached New Orleans, where future president Andrew Jackson led Americans to a surprising and overwhelming victory over British forces in January 1815. News that the treaty had been signed arrived about the same time in Washington, D.C., as a report of Jackson's triumph in the Battle of New Orleans. Great celebrations and a feeling of national unity followed.

Madison has the distinction, then, of having been a poor commander in chief of an unpopular war that accomplished little but from which he and the nation emerged stronger.

Which **presidents benefited** from their association with the **War of 1812**?

James Madison was most effective during his last two years in office, after the end of the War of 1812.

James Monroe was credited as an effective war leader after taking over as Madison's secretary of war in 1814. He succeeded Madison as president and ushered in the "Era of Good Feelings," a wave of national pride following the war that Monroe extended further by visiting many regions of the country.

Andrew Jackson became a national hero for his leadership in the Battle of New Orleans. He lost the disputed election of 1824, but easily won the following two presidential elections.

William Henry Harrison added the Battle of the Thames in the War of 1812 to the impressive list of significant battles he participated in. He would be elected president in 1840, twenty-five years after the end of the war.

Zachary Taylor was elected president in 1848 after his success in the Mexican War (1846–1848), but his war glory began at Fort Harrison, Indiana, during the War of 1812. Taylor was part of a company of fifty men who withstood an assault by some four hundred Native Americans allied with the British and fighting behind Tecumseh, the famed Native American warrior who was later killed at the Battle of the Thames. Taylor was promoted after his heroism at Fort Harrison, but he was returned to the rank of captain after the war. Furious at the demotion, he resigned his military commission. President Madison intervened, restoring Taylor's rank and packing him off to Green Bay, Wisconsin, to a fort in the western frontier.

What **challenges did James K. Polk** face as commander in chief during the **Mexican War**?

The Mexican War (1846–1848), called "Mr. Polk's War" by detractors, was protested by such notable historical figures as Abraham Lincoln (a congressman at the time) and writer Henry David Thoreau. Ulysses S. Grant fought in the war, but in *The Personal Memoirs of U.S. Grant* (1885), he called the Mexican War "one of the most unjust ever waged by a stronger nation against a weaker nation."

Polk hoped to force Mexico to cede California to the United States and wanted to take advantage of Mexicans angered by the U.S. annexation of Texas, which occurred just before Polk took office. He ordered an army squadron to guard the disputed Texas-Mexico border: the United States claimed the Rio Grande as the border, while Mexico recognized the traditional border of the Neuces River, more than one hundred miles north of the Rio Grande. When Mexican and U.S. soldiers engaged in a skirmish, Polk saw an opportunity. Speaking before Congress, Polk claimed that American blood had been shed on American soil and successfully urged Congress to declare war.

Once the war began, Polk won credit for his close supervision of military campaigns, though Generals Zachary Taylor and Winfield Scott resented Polk's dispatches. Following American victory, the Treaty of Guadalupe Hidalgo (1848) gave the United States California, and Mexico surrendered claims to Texas and most of present-day

New Mexico. Polk is credited as having shown astute political and military skills in the Mexican War.

Which **presidents benefited** from their association with the **Mexican War**?

In every presidential election from 1848 to 1872, at least one presidential candidate either fought in or actively protested the Mexican War. Zachary Taylor, one of two commanding generals of the Mexican War, was elected president in 1848. The other commanding general, Winfield Scott, was defeated in his bid for president in 1852. A popular war hero, Scott won the Whig Party nomination over the sitting president, Millard Fillmore. Scott lost the 1852 election to Franklin Pierce, who had served under Scott's command during the Mexican War.

Ulysses S. Grant, winner of the 1868 and 1872 presidential elections, fought in the Mexican War and earned several distinctions for bravery. This photograph was taken in 1864 by Mathew Brady when Lt. General Grant commanded the Army of the Potomac. *AP/Wide World Photos.*

John C. Frémont, who in 1856 became the first-ever presidential candidate of the Republican Party, fought in California, then a province of Mexico, during the Mexican War. Under the orders of President James K. Polk, Frémont led the Bear Flag Revolt, an army of American settlers in California, in their successful overthrow of Mexican forces and leadership. Frémont lost the 1856 election, but the next Republican candidate, Abraham Lincoln in 1860 and 1864, won two terms as president. Lincoln had actively protested the Mexican War as a first-term congressman from Illinois in 1846. Ulysses S. Grant, winner of the 1868 and 1872 presidential elections, fought in the Mexican War and earned several distinctions for bravery.

What **challenges did Abraham Lincoln face** as commander in chief during the **Civil War**?

Congress was not in session when forces representing the Confederate States of America fired on Fort Sumter, a federal fort in South Carolina, in April 1861, a month after Lincoln took office. Using his authority under the Militia Act of 1792, Lincoln called for seventy-six thousand militia volunteers and entrusted public funds to private agents in New York to purchase arms and supplies. He made plain his main purpose for war was to preserve the Union. When Congress returned, Lincoln had to contend with a strong faction that wanted a more vigorous offensive against the Confederacy and the immediate emancipation of slaves.

Many of America's best and seasoned officers served the Confederacy. Union forces fared poorly for much of the early part of the war. Lincoln changed army commanders several times before finding in Ulysses S. Grant in 1864 a supreme commander who would fully utilize the Union advantage in manpower and resources. However, Grant's willingness to sustain high casualties received some criticism in the press.

Lincoln waited until a moment of Union strength to issue the Emancipation Proclamation, which freed slaves in states that had seceded from the Union. After the Union army fared well in September 1862 at the Battle of Antietam, Lincoln released the Emancipation Proclamation. The Battle of Antietam (Maryland) saw the bloodiest day of the American Civil War, as more than six thousand soldiers died and seventeen thousand were wounded in less than seven hours of fighting. The Union Army forced the Confederate Army back into Virginia, but Union general George McClellan did not aggressively pursue them. Lincoln removed him from command in November 1862.

Financing the war was another challenge. Secretary of the Treasury Salmon P. Chase negotiated a loan with state banks for $150 million and raised funds through the sale of government bonds. When the government ran short of funds in 1862, Chase helped pressure Congress to pass the Legal Tender Act. This law introduced "greenbacks" (for their color), the first official paper currency of the United States. Greenbacks allowed the federal government to pay creditors and soldiers. Later, in July 1862, Lincoln signed a measure raising taxes and introducing new taxes on a large variety of items.

Which presidents were **Civil War veterans**?

Ulysses S. Grant was Supreme Commander of the Union Armies during the final year of the Civil War. His popularity in the North assured his election to president in 1868, the first post–Civil War presidential election. Grant was reelected in 1872.

Rutherford B. Hayes (elected in 1876) fought with valor in the war for the entire four years. Reports of his heroism on the battlefield were widely known back in Cincinnati, Ohio, where he had settled in 1849. Hayes was nominated for a seat in Congress in 1864 while he was still fighting in Virginia. Replying to a letter requesting that he return home to campaign, Hayes wrote "I have other business just now. Any man who would leave the army at this time to electioneer for Congress ought to be scalped." Still, he won the election as a Republican in a district that usually voted Democratic.

Like Hayes, James A. Garfield (elected president in 1880) was also elected to Congress while serving in the Union army. Reportedly, President Abraham Lincoln encouraged Garfield to accept the position because he needed further support in Congress. Garfield remained in uniform and fought heroically at the Battle of Chickamauga in September 1863.

Chester Alan Arthur, who succeeded to the presidency when Garfield was assassinated in 1881, was named to the honorary post of engineer in chief of the state militia

Remember the *Maine*?

William McKinley showed restraint despite growing support in the United States for war against Spain, which had brutally repressed a rebellion in its colony of Cuba. When an explosion destroyed the American battleship U.S.S. *Maine,* anchored in Havana Harbor in February 1898, the clamor for war grew considerably. McKinley continued to urge caution until results of an official investigation into the explosion were completed, but growing public settlement and Spain's refusal to commit to reform or grant autonomy to Cuba led him to ask Congress to declare war in April 1898.

The investigation into the explosion of the *Maine* in 1898 pointed to sabotage. In 1912, a government commission examined damage to the hull of the ship and agreed with the original finding that an underwater mine had destroyed the *Maine.* In 1974, however, a team led by Admiral Hyman Rickover concluded that a fire had started on board, ignited the ammunition magazine, and led to explosions that sunk the *Maine.*

in New York in 1860. When the Civil War began in 1861, he was in charge of recruiting and equipping soldiers from the state.

Benjamin Harrison fought in the war from 1862 to 1865. Short and stocky, he was nicknamed "Little Ben" by the men he led as colonel. His group fought under General William Tecumseh Sherman at the end of the war, at which time Harrison attained the rank of brigadier general.

William McKinley (elected president in 1896 and 1900) volunteered to fight when the war began and served in a regiment led by Hayes. He became an officer on Hayes's staff and fought with distinction in several battles.

Which president **ducked Civil War service**?

After being pressed into service, Grover Cleveland hired a man to replace him—a legal maneuver at the time under the Federal Conscription Act. Cleveland was from a family of nine children who fell on hard times when their father died in 1853. Sixteen at the time, Cleveland abandoned plans for college to support his family. He had a thriving law practice at the outbreak of the Civil War in 1861 and was still helping support his family at the time.

What **challenges did William McKinley face** as commander in chief during the **Spanish-American War**?

McKinley is praised for showing restraint during a period when newspapers like Joseph Pulitzer's *New York World* and William Randolph Hearst's *New York Journal*   299 were printing sensational stories about Spain's conduct in Cuba and agitating for war. McKinley used diplomacy to challenge Spain's ongoing efforts to suppress insurrection in Cuba, urging reform and then Cuban autonomy, and providing Spain with opportunities to abandon the island. The mysterious destruction of the American battleship *Maine* fueled the sentiment for war, but McKinley waited two more months before lack of progress led him to address Congress and ask for a declaration of war.

The Spanish-American War lasted little more than four months. By the time the armistice was signed in August 1898, the United States occupied Cuba and Puerto Rico and had defeated the Spanish fleet defending the Philippine Islands. The United States helped prepare Cuba to become an independent republic, retained Puerto Rico as a territory, and acquired the Philippine archipelago. McKinley named future president William Howard Taft as governor of the Philippines, charging him with the duty of guiding it toward self-government.

Which president responded to the **Boxer Rebellion**?

"Boxers" was a term used by Westerners for a group of Chinese rebels who called themselves Righteous and Harmonious Fists. The rebels were intent on ridding their country of foreign influences and began a campaign of violence against foreigners in 1900. Japan, England, France, Russia, and Germany had established strong commercial presences in China, taking advantage of the decentralized Chinese political organization. President William McKinley dispatched five thousand U.S. troops to an international expedition to rescue Western residents in China, hoping the U.S. participation would lead to better access to the Chinese market that was dominated by the other nations. The Righteous and Harmonious Fists, or Boxers, were overcome in August 1900, and the U.S. military assistance opened the door for larger American trade in China.

Which president sent troops to quell **rebellion in the Philippines**?

Among the results of U.S. victory in the Spanish-American War was acquisition of the Philippines, which sparked heated debate over whether the United States should administer faraway lands. The United States could not return the islands to Spain, and the Philippines had been so dominated by Spain that there was fear of anarchy if the island was not provided with a transitional government. According to Alan Brinkley in his book *The Unfinished Nation: A Concise History of the American People*, President McKinley believed the Filipinos were "unfit for self-government" and it was the responsibility of the United States "to take them all and to educate [them], and uplift and Christianize them, and by God's grace do the very best we could by them."

Spain agreed to an offer of $20 million for the islands as part of the Treaty of Paris that ended the Spanish-American War. After lengthy debate, Congress approved the treaty on February 6, 1899, by a single vote more than the required two-thirds majority. That same day, there was a Filipino insurrection against U.S. occupation, as there

Theodore Roosevelt Goes to War

Theodore Roosevelt became recognized as a military leader during the Spanish-American War. Appointed assistant secretary of the Navy in 1897 by William McKinley, Roosevelt began helping prepare the navy for a possible war with Spain. When the battleship *Maine* mysteriously exploded and sank off the coast of Cuba, a colony of Spain, Secretary of the Navy Joseph D. Long was out of the country. As next in command, Roosevelt used his authority to instruct George Dewey, the commander of the Navy's Asian fleet, to sail for Hong Kong and prepare for action in the Philippines, a colony of Spain. When war was declared in April 1898, Dewey attacked and quickly defeated the Spanish fleet at Manila Bay in the Philippines.

Roosevelt wanted to see action after war was declared, even though he was already thirty-nine and had served for three years in the National Guard, where he attained the rank of captain. He resigned from his government position after war against Spain was declared to serve as lieutenant colonel in the First U.S. Volunteer Cavalry. Organizing his own unit of "Rough Riders," Roosevelt was quickly popular in Cuba and Puerto Rico with a U.S. press contingent. Promoted to colonel, he led a wild, perhaps reckless, but quickly successful charge on Kettle Hill in the battle for San Juan, Puerto Rico, and became a national hero through press reports. After Spain surrendered in the three-month Spanish-American War, Roosevelt received additional publicity for his efforts on behalf of bringing troops home as quickly as possible.

had been previously against Spanish occupation. The United States responded with military force and a prolonged occupation, engaging over two hundred thousand troops and suffering over forty-three hundred casualties. At least fifty thousand Filipinos were reportedly killed in the war that lasted over two-and-a-half years.

Which president was frustrated by **Pancho Villa**?

A series of revolutions in Mexico early in the twentieth century left the country unstable and ruled by the military dictatorship of Victoriano Huerta. President Woodrow Wilson supported Huerta's rivals. When American sailors were arrested at Tampico, Mexico, Wilson ordered the navy to occupy Veracruz, Mexico. A battle ensued and war seemed imminent. Wilson accepted the mediation offered by Argentina, Brazil, and Chile.

When the opposition party in Mexico, the Constitutionalists, occupied Mexico City in August 1914, Wilson officially recognized one of its factions. The head of the other faction, Pancho Villa, responded by leading a bandit foray across the border and sack-

Congress Declares War in 1917

Following Woodrow Wilson's War Message to Congress on April 2, 1917, Congress voted to declare war. Reprinted below is the "Joint Resolution Passed by the United States Senate and House of Representatives, Effective April 6, 1917, at 1:18 P.M."

> WHEREAS, The Imperial German Government has committed repeated acts of war against the Government and the people of the United States of America; therefore, be it
>
> Resolved, by the Senate and House of Representatives of the United States of America in Congress assembled, That the state of war between the United States and the Imperial German Government, which has thus been thrust upon the United States, is hereby formally declared; and
>
> That the President be, and he is hereby, authorized and directed to employ the entire naval and military forces of the United States and the resources of the Government to carry on war against the Imperial German Government; and to bring the conflict to a successful termination all the resources of the country are hereby pledged by the Congress of the United States.

ing the town of Columbus, New Mexico, on March 9, 1916. Wilson sent an expedition under General John J. Pershing into Mexico to pursue and apprehend Villa and his forces. After Villa drew Pershing deep into Mexico and battled from an advantageous position at Carrizal, Wilson was faced with either asking Congress to declare war or accepting mediation. The United States was already attempting to remain out of World War I. Wilson withdrew the expedition in January 1917.

What **challenges did Woodrow Wilson face** as commander in chief during World War I?

World War I began in 1914, but the United States did not enter until 1917. A massive mobilization effort was needed to expand the American military. By the time of the armistice in November 1918, over four million had served in the U.S. military.

The Wilson administration introduced the first draft since the Civil War. Considered a controversial move when announced, the draft proved successful, as more than 24 million men registered and 2.7 million more were drafted.

Wilson assumed enormous power as a wartime president as the government took control over vital industries and railroads. The Food Administration was established to

A Different Kind of War Hero

Herbert Hoover was in London, England, with his family when World War I broke out in 1914. Trained as a geologist, Hoover had been a top executive with a British mining firm for ten years before starting an international consulting firm staffed with engineers. At the onset of the war, thousands of Americans living or traveling in Europe found their travel restricted and their money devalued. Working with the U.S. ambassador to England, Hoover formed the Committee of American Residents in London for assistance to American travelers and backed the organization with his personal assets of over $10 million. The Committee organized lodging and assistance for stranded Americans and arranged travel home within six weeks.

Hoover's efforts led to his appointment as head of the Committee for Relief to Belgium. Overrun by Germany early in World War I, Belgium was facing a severe food shortage. Hoover arranged to distribute food and supplies to the Belgium people in need.

The administration of Woodrow Wilson then named Hoover America's "food czar." As head of the U.S. Food Administration, established when the United States entered World War I, Hoover instituted a volunteer food conservation program to reduce consumption at home and ensure food supplies were available for American soldiers. When the war ended, Hoover headed several programs that distributed food and clothing to war refuges in Europe. He founded the American Relief Administration to fight famine in Europe, and won a $100 million appropriation from Congress to help finance the effort.

Hoover became a popular international figure for his relief efforts. He was voted among the top ten greatest living Americans in a *New York Times* poll conducted shortly after the war.

allocate food among the U.S. Armed Forces, the Allies, and the general population of the United States. Financing the war effort was a concern, but production of war supplies as well as consumer goods fueled a booming economy, and more than sixty million Americans ultimately bought war bonds.

Civil rights suffered during the Wilson administration in an effort to curtail war dissent. The Espionage Act of 1917 and Sedition and Alien Acts of 1918, initiated by the administration, cracked down on antiwar activity. More than three thousand people were prosecuted under the laws. Socialist Party leader Eugene V. Debs was sentenced to ten years in prison for claiming the United States was not a democracy (see Presidents and the Judiciary—The Judiciary Influences the Presidency). In 1919, the Wilson administration began cracking down on labor activists. The "Palmer Raids," named after Attorney General Alexander M. Palmer, brought more than four thousand arrests of alleged labor agitators.

What were **Franklin D. Roosevelt**'s major actions during **World War II**?

Before the United States entered World War II in December 1941, President Franklin D. Roosevelt signed the Selective Training and Service Act of 1940, which created the country's first peacetime draft. The act formally established the Selective Service System as an independent federal agency. As the United States entered a state of preparedness, the defense industry flourished, creating jobs, stimulating the economy and effectively ending the Great Depression. Roosevelt maintained close ties with Allied Nations and negotiated the Lend Lease Act in 1940: the United States leased fifty old American destroyers and, in return, Great Britain leased bases in the Pacific to the United States. The U.S. fleet was transferred to Pearl Harbor, Hawaii, in the summer of 1940, likely as a show of force against Japanese aggression in the Pacific.

After Japan attacked Pearl Harbor in December 1941, Roosevelt made a speech to the American people to rally them for war. More than fifteen million Americans would serve in the military forces during World War II, and millions of others worked in industries that supported the war effort. Several new government agencies were created to monitor industries. Rationing was instituted to ensure materials, supplies, and food would be in ready supply for combat needs.

Among Roosevelt's most controversial decisions was the internment of Japanese Americans. Executive Order 9066 established ten internment camps to house all Japanese—citizens and non-citizens—residing on the west coast of the United States. None of the inmates had committed any criminal acts, nor were they ever tried in a court of law. Within weeks, the U.S. government forced over 120,000 people of Japanese ancestry—70 percent of whom were American-born citizens—to leave their homes and move to the camps. On a more positive note, Roosevelt also issued an Executive Order establishing a special army combat team consisting of Japanese American volunteers. The group fought heroically and with distinction in France and Italy.

Roosevelt was elected to a fourth term in office in 1944, as a majority of Americans (and historians) approved of his overall handling of the war. He died on April 12, 1945, a month before the surrender of Germany.

What **challenges did Harry S. Truman face** as commander in chief during the **Korean War**?

Determined to address communist aggression following World War II, the administration of Harry S. Truman pressured the UN Security Council for a resolution to use military force—UN troops and ships, led by the United States—to defend South Korea after it was invaded by communist North Korea in 1950. By the time troops arrived, North

Roosevelt's War Message to the American People

President Franklin D. Roosevelt addressed the American people following the Japanese attack on Pearl Harbor, Hawaii, on December 7, 1941:

Yesterday, December 7, 1941—a date which will live in infamy—the United States of America was suddenly and deliberately attacked by naval and air forces of the Empire of Japan.

The United States was at peace with that nation and, at the solicitation of Japan, was still in conversation with its Government and its Emperor looking toward the maintenance of peace in the Pacific. Indeed, one hour after Japanese air squadrons had commenced bombing in Oahu, the Japanese Ambassador to the United States and his colleague delivered to the Secretary of State a formal reply to a recent American message. While this reply stated that it seemed useless to continue the existing diplomatic negotiations, it contained no threat or hint of war or armed attack.

It will be recorded that the distance of Hawaii from Japan makes it obvious that the attack was deliberately planned many days or even weeks ago. During the intervening time the Japanese Government has deliberately sought to deceive the United States by false statements and expressions of hope for continued peace....

Always will we remember the character of the onslaught against us. No matter how long it may take us to overcome this premeditated invasion, the American people in their righteous might will win through to absolute victory.

I believe I interpret the will of the Congress and of the people when I assert that we will not only defend ourselves to the uttermost but will make very certain that this form of treachery shall never endanger us again.

Hostilities exist. There is no blinking at the fact that our people, our territory and our interests are in grave danger.

With confidence in our armed forces—with the unbounded determination of our people—we will gain the inevitable triumph—so help us God.

I ask that the Congress declare that since the unprovoked and dastardly attack by Japan on Sunday, December seventh, a state of war has existed between the United States and the Japanese Empire.

After U.S. general Douglas MacArthur (left) publicly disagreed with President Harry S. Truman's decision to negotiate with North Korea during the Korean War, he was fired. They are pictured here at the Wake Conference in 1950. *Getty Images.*

Korean forces besieged the Pusan Peninsula and had taken Seoul, the capital city of South Korea. General Douglas MacArthur, the U.S. commander in the Pacific, used air attacks to stabilize Pusan and then followed with a daring, amphibious counterattack at Inchon. North Koreans were forced to retreat with heavy losses, and Seoul was liberated.

MacArthur ordered troops to continue pursuing the North Korean army beyond the Thirty-eighth Parallel, hoping for a complete defeat of the communist army. However, after the UN forces entered North Korea, China joined North Korea in a counterattack that drove the United States and UN troops back into South Korea. From that point, the winter of 1950–1951, the war became a virtual stalemate.

Why did **Truman fire General Douglas MacArthur**?

After U.S. forces recovered Seoul, the capital of South Korea, in spring of 1951 for the second time, President Truman proposed negotiations with North Korea, hoping for a truce and wanting to avoid having the war spread further in Asia and possibly involving the Soviet Union.

MacArthur disagreed publicly. Declaring "there is no substitute for victory," MacArthur advocated another advance into North Korea that would be coordinated with an attack on China by Chiang Kai-shek, the Chinese leader who had been defeated by communists and had created a stronghold on the island of Taiwan. MacArthur found supporters in Congress. Truman fired MacArthur for challenging his authority as commander in chief.

Firing Yankee Leaders: A Lincoln Tradition

Harry S. Truman's dismissal of General Douglas MacArthur was not without precedent. Abraham Lincoln replaced several Union generals during the Civil War before finally settling on Ulysses S. Grant. Lincoln expressed displeasure at not winning by frequently changing his field commander.

George McClellan led the Union army from spring 1861 to November 1862. After a series of Union defeats, Lincoln replaced McClellan with Ambrose Burnside until January 1863, when Burnside was replaced by Joseph Hooker, who lasted until June. George Meade was head of Union forces during the pivotal month of July 1863, when the Union army stopped a Confederate advance led by General Robert E. Lee at Gettysburg, Pennsylvania. Lincoln ordered Meade to pursue Lee's forces, which had retreated from Gettysburg but were halted by flooding of the Potomac River. Meade responded slowly, and Lee's forces escaped.

Meanwhile, Union forces under the leadership of General Ulysses S. Grant took Vicksburg, Mississippi, in July 1863 after several attempts. Grant was then sent to Chattanooga, Tennessee, where the Union army had bogged down. Grant led Union forces in three significant battles to take control of Chattanooga, a key east-west railroad junction. In March 1864, Lincoln commissioned Grant as supreme commander of the Union armies.

Just two years earlier, Grant's preparedness was questioned when his forces were overrun in the Battle of Shiloh before regrouping and holding their line. Several military leaders at the time suggested Lincoln should remove Grant from a leadership role. "I can't spare this man," replied Lincoln. "He fights."

MacArthur returned to the United States for a rousing, hero's welcome before crowds in New York City and Washington, D.C. He addressed a joint session of Congress, where he justified his conduct in Korea and his bold plan for fighting communism. Many congressmen applauded MacArthur's plans. However, a subsequent congressional investigation concluded that MacArthur had violated his orders from the commander in chief. Omar Bradley, chairman of the Joint Chiefs of Staff, emphasized that MacArthur risked involving the United States in a large-scale Asian land war against China, and possibly the Soviet Union, as well. It would be "the wrong war, at the wrong place, at the wrong time, and with the wrong enemy," concluded Bradley.

Which president **ended the Korean War**?

During his campaign for the presidency in 1952, Dwight D. Eisenhower pledged to roll back communism by escalating American involvement in the Korean War. Eisenhower's threats included sending tactical nuclear weapons to U.S. Air Force bases in Okinawa off the coast of Japan. That action, perhaps, and certainly the staggering cost of the war on both sides, led to a truce negotiated between North Korea and UN forces in July 1953.

What was the **Bay of Pigs invasion** (1961)?

A revolution in Cuba resulted in the rise to power of communist Fidel Castro in 1959. As Castro nationalized property, U.S. companies were shut down and thousands of anti-Castro Cubans, or Cuban nationalists, entered the United States. A team of nearly a thousand Cuban nationalists was trained in military operations by the Central Intelligence Agency (CIA). The nationalists were to be transported back to Cuba, landed on a beach in the Bay of Pigs, and move inland, joining with an anti-Castro uprising within Cuba. The United States planned to back the insurgents with air support.

Upon taking office in 1961, John F. Kennedy approved the plan that had begun during the administration of his predecessor, Dwight D. Eisenhower. What is called the Bay of Pigs Invasion was a disaster. The nationalist uprising within Cuba never materialized, and Kennedy therefore refused to provide air support because such use would be considered an invasion and an act of aggression. The CIA-trained insurgents were quickly defeated and taken prisoner by Cuban forces.

Kennedy took full responsibility for the fiasco. His forthrightness helped ease the controversy for most Americans, except for a strong and vocal anti-Kennedy faction.

How did **American involvement in the Vietnam War escalate** during the Johnson administration?

The United States sent military advisors to assist South Vietnam in stemming aggression by communist North Vietnam beginning in 1954 during the Eisenhower administration. The number of advisers grew consistently until numbering over fifteen thousand during the administration of John F. Kennedy, who succeeded Eisenhower. Lyndon B. Johnson became president in 1963 after Kennedy was assassinated. He continued the policy, but in 1964 he became concerned that South Vietnam was going to be overrun. Congress passed the Tonkin Gulf Resolution in 1964 that authorized the president to defend American lives in Vietnam.

In early 1965, Johnson began authorizing air strikes on North Vietnam to retaliate for Viet Cong raids against U.S. installations in South Vietnam. In March 1965, the bombing raids became more regular. American marines began landing in South Vietnam, followed by additional military personnel: there were over 165,000 American troops in Vietnam by November 1965. Some 460,000 American troops were stationed in Vietnam in May 1967.

The United States soon became bogged down in defending South Vietnam. Johnson had hoped that escalating American military involvement would disrupt and slow the infiltration of insurgents and supplies from the north and bring the North Vietnamese into peace negotiations. Johnson had hoped to prevent the reunification of Vietnam under communist leadership.

As casualties mounted, Americans began protesting the war. Johnson's popularity plummeted. Early in his reelection bid in 1968, he announced he was dropping from the race after a poor showing in the New Hampshire primary.

Were **American troops sent to places other than Vietnam during Johnson's administration**?

Juan Bosch, a socialist, was elected president of the Dominican Republic in 1962, but he was overthrown the following year. In April 1965, his supporters rebelled. Concerned that communists would seize control of the revolution, Johnson ordered more than twenty thousand troops to restore order. American intervention led to a cease-fire.

What changes did **Richard Nixon** make in **Vietnam War policy**?

Upon taking office in 1969, Nixon began a plan for withdrawing American troops: twenty-five thousand troops came home by August, and eighty thousand by the end of 1969. Nixon instituted a policy of Vietnamization, where Vietnamese soldiers were better trained and equipped to defend their nation.

Although troop numbers and casualties declined, American war activities escalated as air and ground forces entered Cambodia in 1970 in pursuit of Viet Cong soldiers and supply lines. The United States began bombing supply lines in Laos in 1971. In March 1972, American bombing raids began in North Vietnam for the first time in three years.

Peace talks, which had progressed sporadically for years, finally yielded a breakthrough in December 1972. On January 23, 1973, President Nixon spoke to the nation: "A cease-fire, internationally supervised, will begin at 7:00 P.M. this Saturday, January 27, Washington time. Within 60 days from this Saturday, all Americans held prisoners of war throughout Indochina will be released. There will be the fullest possible accounting for all of those who are missing in action. During the same 60-day period, all American forces will be withdrawn from South Vietnam. The people of South Vietnam have been guaranteed the right to determine their own future."

The 1973 Nobel Peace Prize was shared by Henry Kissinger, Nixon's secretary of state, and Le Duc Tho of North Vietnam for their success at ending the conflict. However, Le Duc Tho declined to accept the award, declaring that a true peace did not yet exist in Vietnam.

U.S. military involvement in Cambodia continued until August 15, 1973, when bombing in support of the anticommunist regime was halted by agreement between Nixon and Congress. The Senate Armed Services Committee held hearings on the bombing of Cambodia: the Nixon administration allegedly allowed bombing raids to be carried out during a time when Cambodia's neutrality was officially recognized. Meanwhile, true peace did not exist in Vietnam: in 1974, North Vietnam announced it was renewing hostilities.

How did the **Vietnam War end**?

In 1975, a sustained North Vietnamese offensive forced South Vietnamese troops to begin withdrawing from northern provinces; the withdrawal quickly became a disorganized retreat. When communists began moving on Saigon, President Gerald Ford, who succeeded to the presidency in August 1974 after the resignation of Richard Nixon, announced that the Vietnam War was "finished." As Saigon fell, Ford ordered an evacuation of American citizens and Vietnamese sympathizers. More than one hundred thousand Vietnamese refugees entered the United States.

What was the *Mayaguez* incident?

Cambodian gunboats seized an American merchant ship, the *Mayaguez,* in May 1975, claiming the ship had entered their territorial waters. The U.S. government countered by insisting the *Mayaguez* had been safely off the Cambodian coast. The United States and Cambodia had poor relations at the time. Cambodia had fallen to the Khmer Rouge on April 16, 1975.

President Gerald Ford authorized military force to prevent the ship and crew of 39 to be taken to the Cambodian mainland. U.S. planes patrolled and bombed the mainland to prevent Cambodian interference with the American rescue operation. Two U.S. destroyers and an aircraft carrier entered the scene and engaged in action with Cambodian gunboats. Marines landed on an island where the crew was believed to be held. Meanwhile, the *Mayaguez* was recovered and the boat's crew was delivered to an American ship by a small Cambodian boat. Forty-one American lives were lost in the incident.

What was **Operation Eagle Claw** during the Iran hostage crisis?

Operation Eagle Claw was an April 1980 attempt to rescue American hostages who had been held in Iran since November 4, 1979. The operation failed when helicopters malfunctioned during a desert sandstorm. The mission was abandoned, but a helicopter collided with a plane during the retreat and eight Americans were killed.

What **military actions against communism and terrorism were taken by Ronald Reagan**?

In October 1983, Reagan ordered the invasion of Grenada, a Caribbean island where communist insurgents were amassing power. Reagan claimed Americans on the island were in jeopardy and that the country could become the site of a Cuban-Soviet military base.

A terrorist attack on a U.S. peacekeeping contingent in Beirut, Lebanon, killed 241 marine servicemen just two days before the Granada invasion. Combined with an airline hijacking in June 1985, in which 39 passengers were released after 17 days but a member of the U.S. Navy was murdered, the Reagan administration began aggressive targeting of terrorism. Libyan leader Muammar al-Qaddafi was a prime target for having sponsored terrorist training. Tension between the two nations dated from early in Reagan's presidency, when two Libyan jets were downed by U.S. planes in the Gulf of Sidra during military exercises. In October 1985, terrorists hijacked the Italian ocean liner *Achille Lauro* and murdered an elderly American passenger. U.S. planes intercepted a plane carrying the hijackers and forced it to land in Italy. Later that year, Libya was involved in helping sponsor bombings of the Rome and Vienna airports. After Libyan involvement was proven, American planes attacked several sites in and around Tripoli, Libya's capital, during the spring of 1986.

How did **George Bush help forge an international coalition to fight Iraq** in the Gulf War (1991)?

George Bush helped forge a broad international coalition against Iraq that included support of virtually all United Nations members, including Arab nations often reluctant to challenge their neighbors. With UN endorsement, Bush ordered the largest deployment of American forces (over four hundred thousand soldiers) since the Vietnam War. Bush asked for and received from Congress the authority to use all necessary means to expel Iraqi forces from Kuwait.

Bush achieved his goals of minimizing U.S. casualties, returning control of Kuwait to its government, and formulating a broad international coalition. Operation Desert Storm, as the mission was called, was well-defined and legally sanctioned. The Gulf War was over in less than two months.

Why didn't **George Bush order the invasion of Iraq and the overthrow of Saddam Hussein?**

Invasion of Iraq to oust its leader, Saddam Hussein, was neither legal nor part of the war planning. The United Nations issued an endorsement for the Gulf War and the U.S. Congress prepared a resolution that granted Bush authority to expel Iraqi forces from Kuwait. Following the war, Hussein quickly crushed internal postwar revolts by Kurds and Muslims. Bush sent relief aid to refugees fleeing Hussein's forces. Then, in 1992, as Hussein's troops continued to attack Shi'i Muslims, Bush enlisted France and Britain to support a "no-fly zone," enforced largely by U.S. aircraft, barring Iraq from sending planes into the disputed territory. The Gulf War was pursued with patience, international cooperation, a well-defined plan, and commitment of necessary resources.

Where did **Bill Clinton order air strikes** and send American troops in peacekeeping efforts?

When Clinton took office in 1993, the United States was involved in a United Nations peacekeeping effort, Operation Restore Hope, in Somalia. A crisis of starvation was eased by the operation, but the political situation in Somalia was still in turmoil. After the relief effort, U.S. force levels were reduced and command of relief, disarmament, and reconstruction work was assumed by the UN. By June, however, fighting between two factions resumed in Somalia. In early October 1993, eighteen U.S. Army Rangers were killed and seventy-five were wounded in a firefight. American public opinion and most member of Congress pressured Clinton to withdraw U.S. troops. After the United States pulled out, almost twenty thousand UN troops remained to try to maintain order.

Working with the United Nations, the United States threatened an invasion of Haiti when a military junta refused to yield power to Jean-Bertrand Aristide, a democratically elected president. After the junta relinquished power, American troops entered Haiti to keep the peace.

In 1994, Clinton deployed troops in Kuwait after Iraq, in protest of UN sanctions and the enforcement of a no-fly zone following its defeat in the Gulf War (1991), began to threaten Kuwait again. Two years later, Clinton ordered air strikes against Iraq for again violating the terms of peace.

By planning limited air strikes against Bosnian Serbs, the Clinton administration helped convince the Serbs, Muslim, and Croats of Bosnia to negotiate, leading to the November 1995 Dayton Peace Accords. The country was partitioned under a multiethnic leadership, with NATO peacekeeping troops to enforce the cease-fire.

In the summer of 1998, the Kosovo Liberation Army began a campaign for independence from Serbia, the most powerful republic in the Yugoslav federation. Serbian president Slobodan Milosevic responded by launching an attack against ethnic Albanians who populated the region. Clinton called on the international community to take action. The UN demanded a cease-fire, and North Atlantic Treaty Organization (NATO) threatened Serbia with military action if it did not stop the attacks in Kosovo. Milosevic signed a cease-fire agreement in October 1998.

What were reasons for the U.S. war in **Afghanistan**?

Following the terrorist attacks of September 11, 2001, President George W. Bush demanded that Afghanistan's ruling Taliban regime turn over Osama bin Laden, mastermind of the Al Qaeda terrorist organization, to the United States. Addressing a joint meeting of Congress on September 20, Bush vowed to direct "every means of diplomacy, every tool of intelligence, every instrument of law enforcement, every financial influence, and every necessary weapon of war" to defeat the "global terror network." Congress granted Bush the authority to use military force.

Grading the War in Afghanistan

One year after the war in Afghanistan, *Time* magazine "graded" the effort in an October 14, 2002, article titled "Grading the Other War: Does Our Fighting in Afghanistan Hold Any Lessons for a Battle with Iraq? A Report Card on the Afghan War's Uneven First Year." The grades follow:

Subject	Grade	Comments
Regime change	A	Destroyed the Taliban at minimal cost in U.S. lives. Liberated Afghan people; established new government. Job well done.
The manhunt (for Al Qaeda operatives and Osama Bin Laden)	B-	Has shown steady improvement but failed to accomplish main goals. Needs to make more progress before moving on.
Civilian casualties	C+	Did well during the fall but slipped back this summer. Needs to ease up on the bombing and get aid moving to locals.
Nation	Incomplete	U.S. showing more enthusiasm for least favorite building subject, but could still need years to complete the course.

After Taliban leaders delayed presenting information to the United States and its allies regarding the whereabouts of bin Laden, the U.S. military launched air strikes against Taliban targets in Afghanistan beginning on October 7, 2001. The action was endorsed by the UN Security Council. Targets included military aircraft, airfields, and antiaircraft installations followed by attacks on terrorist camps and the Taliban military. A ground force followed. In just over two months, the Taliban had been overthrown and the country was in the hands of coalition forces. Osama bin Laden remained elusive, and U.S. troops were still in Afghanistan a year later.

What is **Operation Iraqi Freedom**?

Operation Iraqi Freedom was intended to end the regime of Saddam Hussein and to identify and eliminate Iraq's weapons of mass destruction (WMD). During the summer of 2002, President George W. Bush encouraged the United Nations to hold Iraq accountable for having frustrated the attempts of UN weapons inspectors to ensure that Iraq had destroyed its WMD, as mandated by the treaty that ended the Gulf War (1991). On October 16, 2002, Congress authorized and Bush signed a resolution authorizing him to use force if necessary against Iraq.

The United Nations Security Council debated whether or not to include authorization of the use of force in Resolution 1441, which ordered Iraq to disarm and to provide UN inspectors unrestricted access. Eventually, the resolution demanded Iraq

President George W. Bush announcing the end of major combat operations in Iraq aboard the aircraft carrier USS *Abraham Lincoln. AP/Wide World Photos.*

comply with weapons inspectors or face "serious consequences." Formal inspections began in Iraq in November 2002. In his State of the Union Address in late January 2003, Bush stated that if Saddam Hussein would not disarm, the United States would lead a coalition to forcibly disarm Iraq.

After a final deadline passed, the invasion of Iraq began on March 19, 2003. Baghdad, the capital of Iraq, fell to coalition forces on April 9, 2003. On May 1, 2003, Bush announced an end to major combat operations.

The war in Iraq was supported by a majority of Americans. Those who opposed the war sided with those nations that wanted more time for weapons inspectors to complete their investigations. A year after the end of major combat operations, no evidence was found that Iraq had continued developing WMD, which had been the main pretext the Bush administration argued for military action against Iraq. The cost of the war and the potential of a long-term commitment were also cited by opponents, who argued that the cost on the United States was far greater for having moved early on Iraq and without broad international participation.

The peace in Iraq proved more difficult than the war. Sustained insurgent attacks left more Americans dead after the end of major combat operations than during the war. Controversy over contracts awarded to firms for rebuilding Iraq and reports of mistreatment of Iraqi prisoners contributed to opposition of American policy. A majority of Americans disapproved of U.S. policy in Iraq a year after the war had ended. Another pretext for war—Iraq as a sponsor of terrorism, with connections to Al Qaeda—was dismissed by the 9/11 Commission.

Proponents of the war point to the removal of Iraq's brutal dictator as a humanitarian action and ending a rogue regime that was a threat to the Middle East and, through terrorism, a global threat. The often messy and sometimes violent aspects of rebuilding Iraq were viewed as a necessary prelude to establishing democracy and returning sovereignty to the nation by June 30, 2004. Sovereignty was officially returned to Iraq on June 28.

ILLNESS AND DEATH, ASSASSINATION AND SCANDAL

ILLNESSES OF THE PRESIDENTS

Which **presidential and vice presidential candidates hid illnesses** during their campaigns?

Many sitting presidents and new hopefuls hid illnesses at election time. Franklin D. Roosevelt kept his deteriorating heart condition quiet during his 1944 reelection campaign. In fact, President Roosevelt's personal physician asserted that there was "nothing wrong organically with him at all…. He's perfectly okay." Roosevelt suffered from hypertension and died the following year from a cerebral hemorrhage after serving just three months of his fourth term. During the 1960 presidential campaign, John F. Kennedy successfully hid his long-rumored and publicly denied struggle with Addison's disease, a failure of the adrenal glands, for which the Massachusetts senator received cortisone injections and other medications. George McGovern's 1972 running mate, U.S. senator Thomas Eagleton of Missouri, was forced to quit the ticket within a month of the Democratic National Convention after the media revealed allegations of electroshock therapy treatment for his clinical depression. McGovern at first defended Eagleton, then asked him to step down.

While in times past, the media often cooperated by not publicizing candidates' health conditions, today the press makes much of presidential hopefuls' health status. Recent tabloid coverage includes Bill Bradley's irregular heartbeat, John McCain's recurring skin cancer (both were candidates for nomination in 2000), and John Kerry's prostate-cancer surgery. Following a precedent set by late-twentieth-century candidates, including McCain, Kerry authorized the release of his medical records in 2003, proving he was fit to run the executive office.

Which **presidents hid illnesses during their tenure in office**?

During the nineteenth and much of the twentieth century, presidents frequently hid illnesses in order to perpetuate an image of a strong, virile leader. Beginning in the nineteenth century, presidents such as Chester Alan Arthur, who suffered from a kidney condition called Bright's disease, worked with trusted insiders to keep their deteriorating health under wraps. (Arthur, in fact, died the year following the end of his term in 1885.) The most prominent example is Franklin D. Roosevelt, who concealed his inability to walk without support from the public eye by almost never being photographed or depicted in a wheelchair. However, Roosevelt also hid the hypertension and heart failure he developed during his third term. Warren G. Harding, who hid his heart disease, died of heart failure a little over two-and-a-half years into his term. John F. Kennedy suffered from many conditions, including Addison's disease, a condition his personal physician kept from the public. Many presidents chose not to disclose their medical problems for fear of political consequences; however, this has often been at odds with the public's concern for presidential accountability and disclosure to the populace.

Other presidents, especially later in the twentieth century, have been forthcoming about their medical conditions. President Dwight D. Eisenhower was one later president who was especially candid with his health. President Lyndon B. Johnson chose at first not to reveal information about his infected gall bladder, but later changed his mind, even showing reporters the scar from his successful surgery. Today, a president's health is almost a matter of public record, although presidents often cite their right to privacy as a reason for not disclosing health issues. George W. Bush had four non-cancerous skin lesions removed in December 2001, and Vice President Dick Cheney has been straightforward regarding his heart disease.

Was **Andrew Jackson sick** when he assumed the presidency?

Jackson biographer Robert Remini called Andrew Jackson "one of the most colossal, legendary figures to stride across American history." Nevertheless, when Jackson assumed the presidency in 1829, he was sixty-two years old, sickly, thin, and, according to one observer, a "tottering scarecrow in deadly agony." At the time, Jackson was suffering from rotting teeth, chronic headaches, poor eyesight, and constant pain and internal bleeding from two bullets lodged in his body—which were the result of two separate duels. The new president was also in emotional pain, having just lost his wife, Rachel, to a heart attack in December 1828 after an especially bitter presidential campaign that assaulted her character.

The hot-tempered Jackson was shot in 1806 and 1813. The earlier duel with lawyer Charles Dickinson, over comments made about a horse-race bet and possibly slurs against Rachel, resulted in two broken ribs and a bullet being lodged near one of Jackson's lungs. Since the bullet landed two inches from Jackson's heart, it was never

In 1991, over 140 years after Zachary Taylor's death, his remains were exhumed to determine if the president had been poisoned. Tests revealed no evidence of foul play. *AP/Wide World Photos.*

removed by surgery, but instead caused repeated attacks of internal infection and bleeding. In the 1813 duel with Jesse Benton, Jackson took a bullet in his left shoulder, causing him much pain until he had it removed in 1832. According to Remini's *The Life of Andrew Jackson* (1990), "No anesthesia was available, of course, so Jackson simply bared his arm, gritted his jaws, … and said 'Go ahead.'" As a result of the remaining bullet wound, Jackson's health became progressively worse during his second term in office, and he experienced constant abdominal pain and frequent headaches. He died in 1845, likely from heart failure.

What were the circumstances surrounding **Zachary Taylor's ill health**?

Although the former soldier was nicknamed "Old Rough and Ready" by his army colleagues, Zachary Taylor assumed the presidency in 1849 in questionable health. Later that year, the president was bedridden with an attack of diarrhea and high fever that was almost fatal. Almost a year later, during a Fourth of July celebration in 1850, the president became sick and was diagnosed with the gastrointestinal disorder *cholera morbus*. Although his doctors tried all forms of popular remedies, including opium, bloodletting, and purging, President Taylor died on July 8, after just sixteen months in office. His wife, Peggy Taylor, refused to let his body be embalmed. Historian Clara Rising advocated the theory that President Taylor was poisoned and did not die of natural causes. This theory led to the 1991 exhumation of Taylor's body, which did not reveal evidence of foul play.

Conspiracy: Rest in Peace

A conspiracy theory developed around the death of Zachary Taylor. Taylor was opposed to the Compromise of 1850 and his death literally cleared the way for passage of the bills that made up the Compromise. The president died a little more than a year into his term, diagnosed as having a gastrointestinal disorder, *cholera morbus*. Taylor's stomach ailment, according to those who suspected foul play, was similar to the effects of arsenic poisoning. According to the conspiracy theory, Taylor was slipped some arsenic in the cold water or cherries in iced milk he consumed that day while listening to patriotic speeches on a hot fourth of July at a ceremony marking the beginning of construction of the Washington monument. The theory lived on until 1991, when Taylor's relatives agreed to have his corpse disinterred so tissue samples could be tested for traces of arsenic. No significant traces were found, and the conspiracy theory (and Taylor) were finally laid to rest.

Is it true that **Chester Alan Arthur had Bright's disease**?

Yes. Although Arthur did not know that he was ill when he became president in 1881, many of the president's inner circle noticed that he was becoming increasingly depressed, irritable, and apathetic. In 1882, the *Chicago Tribune* reported that the president's temperament was "sluggish," and that it required "a great deal for him to get to his desk and begin the dispatch of business." At some point during his first year in office, the president was diagnosed with Bright's disease, a fatal kidney disorder. Arthur's staff kept his illness a secret, calling it "pure fiction" when news leaked from the *New York Herald.* Few of Arthur's friends were aware of his condition, which was not made public until after his death in 1886. At the time of his death, Arthur was suffering from an enlarged heart, high blood pressure, and a malarial infection.

What were the circumstances around **President Cleveland's secret illness**?

In July 1893, after developing a cancerous tumor on his left jaw, President Grover Cleveland had a secret operation to remove the lesion. In order to keep it from his cabinet and White House staff, his doctors removed it while the president was "sailing" on a private yacht off the Massachusetts coast. So as not to attract attention, the surgeons performed the operation inside the president's mouth without making an external incision. Two weeks later, the doctors performed a second surgery, again while on the yacht, to remove additional tissue. The doctors made the president a vulcanized rubber plate, which restored his speaking voice so well that when he reappeared in public no one could detect that anything abnormal had taken place during the president's brief respite. Despite Cleveland's carefully guarded attempts at secrecy, news leaked to the press. However, rather than admit he had a cancerous lesion, the president told the press that he had his wisdom teeth pulled.

Cleveland's cancer is typically associated with heavy tobacco use and alcohol consumption. The president often drank beer and smoked both cigars and pipes. In September 1917, Cleveland's operation was revealed to the public in a *Saturday Evening Post* article written by one of his surgeons, William Keen, who later expanded his story into the book, *The Surgical Operations on President Cleveland in 1893.*

What happened after President **Woodrow Wilson suffered a stroke while in office**?

Woodrow Wilson, who hid his chronic circulatory disease and high blood pressure, suffered a major stroke during his second term in office in October 1919. The stroke occurred after the president embarked on a rigorous cross-country speaking tour to gain support for his recent League of Nations plan, which would establish an international peacekeeping organization in the aftermath of World War I. Both his wife, first lady Edith Wilson, and his attending physician kept the president's stroke hidden from the public for seventeen months. The cabinet and the press were told that the president had suffered a nervous breakdown. Key staff members, including Vice President Thomas Marshall, were not informed of the severity of the president's condition.

During this time, the work of the president essentially came to a halt. Neither the U.S. Constitution nor previous situations in the White House provided any guidelines for dealing with the incapacity of a president, and Wilson chose not to relinquish any of his duties—even though he was unable to carry them out—and no one challenged his decision. Instead, the first lady, at her sole discretion, briefed the president on what she felt was important, and in effect, served as his chief of staff during this time. In her memoirs written in 1938, Edith Wilson said of her role, "I studied every paper sent from the different Secretaries or Senators, and tried to digest and present in tabloid form the things that, despite my vigilance, had to go to the President. I, myself, never made a single decision regarding the disposition of public affairs." Wilson died in February 1924, in deteriorating health.

What were the circumstances surrounding **President Harding's poor health**?

When Warren G. Harding was elected to the presidency in 1920, he was suffering from high blood pressure and heart disease. The president may also have suffered a series of nervous breakdowns earlier in his life, which he had treated at the J. P. Kellogg sanitarium in Battle Creek, Michigan, between 1889 and 1901.

In June 1923, President Harding embarked on a tiring cross-country public-relations tour dubbed the Voyage of Understanding, during which he planned to convey his administration's policies to average Americans. At the end of the trip in Alaska, the president became ill and returned to San Francisco, California, where his health became worse. Reportedly at this time he received news about the looming Teapot Dome scandal, which would not come to light until after his death. Although the official word to the press was that the president had suffered from food poisoning, other doctors, including an eminent cardiologist, found that President Harding had an enlarged heart and was suffering from heart disease. In addition, the president was under severe stress, as he was trying to cope with the problems of his administration. The American public was never notified of the president's condition, and when Harding died in a San Francisco hotel room just days after checking in, the official cause of death was stroke. Although a sensational book appeared in 1930 titled *The Strange Death of President Harding*—which suggested that the first lady poisoned her husband out of revenge for his extramarital affairs or to spare his impeachment from office—historians generally discount the story. The book made headlines because Florence Harding never permitted an autopsy, a procedure not mandated at the time by the state of California.

What were some of the **health problems that President Eisenhower experienced in office**?

President Dwight D. Eisenhower suffered three medical crises during his two terms in office. In September 1955, he suffered a heart attack; in June 1956, he underwent surgery for Crohn's disease, a disorder that can cause obstruction in the intestines; and in November the following year, he had a mild stroke. When President Eisenhower had his heart attack, he told his press secretary, James Hagerty, to tell the press "everything" about his condition. Although he broke with tradition by releasing detailed information about his health to the public, much of what the public learned was carefully managed by Eisenhower's inner circle. Although he reportedly believed it was not in the president's best interest to run for reelection, lead cardiologist Paul White told a press conference that the president "should be able to carry on an active life for another five to ten years." Less than a year later, the president's operation for a bowel obstruction did not stop him from running for reelection, undertaking an active campaign schedule to squelch rumors that he was not fit to hold another term as president.

In late 1957, after Eisenhower had suffered a stroke and displayed a mild speech impediment, Eisenhower's advisers became concerned about the president's ability to carry out his duties. However, prior to the stroke, Eisenhower and Vice President Richard Nixon had exchanged letters documenting the transfer of presidential authority in the event that Eisenhower became incapacitated. Because there was not yet a constitutional amendment in place to discuss the transfer of authority in the event of an incapacitated president (the Twenty-fifth Amendment was ratified in 1967), both presidents John F. Kennedy and Lyndon B. Johnson followed the same written format during their terms as president.

Did **John F. Kennedy have a range of health problems**?

Yes. Although President John F. Kennedy projected an image of youth and vigor, he had a long-standing history of health problems. Kennedy never publicly confessed that he had Addison's disease—an incurable disorder of the adrenal glands with which he was diagnosed in 1947—and even went to great lengths to hide it. Entering the election campaign of 1960 in the wake of President Dwight D. Eisenhower's health problems, Kennedy most likely realized America would not elect a sick president. When rumors surfaced about his disease, Kennedy's personal physician boldly claimed, "John F. Kennedy has not, nor has he ever, had ... Addison's disease."

Kennedy biographer Robert Dallek said in a 2002 *Atlantic Monthly* article, "When Kennedy ran for and won the presidency, he was essentially gambling that his health problems would not prevent him from handling the job." These included back problems, for which the president underwent major surgery while a U.S. senator, took steroid treatments, and wore a back brace. Medical historians have also speculated that Kennedy had celiac disease, which is often linked to Addison's disease, and may have been the cause of Kennedy's gastrointestinal upsets. In addition, President Kennedy suffered from allergies and an overly sensitive stomach, and took a whole host of medications, including cortisone shots for his Addison's disease and lomotil for his diarrhea. Kennedy was hospitalized more than three dozen times in his life, and accounts of his childhood mention bouts of scarlet fever, measles, and whooping cough.

Which president planned to keep his **gall bladder operation a secret**?

During Labor Day weekend in 1965, President Lyndon B. Johnson experienced a gall bladder attack. When Johnson's doctors informed him that he had to have his gall bladder removed, initially Johnson was reluctant to inform the press. However, after consulting with former president Dwight D. Eisenhower, Johnson felt it was in his—and the public's—best interest to disclose the details of the surgery, which included the removal of a kidney stone. In accordance with his Type A personality, Johnson projected an image of being in control. He showed the press his surgical scan and signed a major antipoverty bill from his hospital room. In November 1966, President Johnson returned to the hospital to have a nonmalignant growth removed from his throat, and a small hernia repaired. Once again, the administration was straightforward about the president's health condition.

Did **Richard Nixon keep certain health facts hidden**?

Yes. Richard Nixon had viral pneumonia and advanced phlebitis (vein inflammation) in one leg during his presidency. Soon after Nixon resigned in 1974, he had emergency surgery to remove a blood clot that developed from the phlebitis.

What is the **Twenty-fifth Amendment** and how does it relate to **presidential illness**?

The Twenty-fifth Amendment, ratified in 1967, discusses the procedures to be followed if the office of the president or vice president is vacant, or if the president is disabled. Section 3 deals with the president's disability, and allows the president of his volition to turn over the power of his office to the vice president. It states that the vice president shall serve as acting president whenever the president sends the presiding officers of the House and Senate a letter stating that he is unable to execute the duties of his office. The president will reassume his duties upon notifying these congressional leaders of his recovery by letter.

Section 4 of the Twenty-fifth Amendment makes provisions for the vice president to serve as acting president when the vice president and a majority of cabinet members, or any other group that Congress chooses by law, sends Congress a letter stating that the president is disabled. When the president has recovered, he sends a letter notifying the congressional leaders of his recovery. If the vice president and other department heads disagree, Section 4 outlines the steps they must take in order to determine whether the vice president should continue as acting president or whether the president can carry out his duties.

Who was the **first president to invoke the Twenty-fifth Amendment**?

Ronald Reagan. Although he was the oldest president in America's history (almost seventy-eight when he left office), Ronald Reagan was athletic and physically fit. In July 1985, President Reagan declared that he would be incapacitated while undergoing surgery to remove cancerous polyps from his colon. In anticipation of the surgery, he sent a letter to the Speaker of the House of Representatives and the president pro tem of the Senate notifying them that he was temporarily turning over the powers of the presidency to Vice President George Bush. "I have determined that it is my intention and direction that Vice President George Bush shall discharge powers and duties in my stead, commencing with the administration of the anesthesia to me," the letter stated in part.

The surgery was successful, although about two feet of Reagan's colon was removed. Under the terms of the Twenty-fifth Amendment, Vice President Bush assumed presidential duties until Reagan was able to resume them, about eight hours later. Reagan became the first president to formally invoke the transfer of power terms as outlined the amendment.

Which presidents since Ronald Reagan have invoked the **disability clause of the Twenty-fifth Amendment**?

Since Reagan, only one president has felt it necessary to invoke the disability clause of the Twenty-fifth Amendment. George W. Bush followed Reagan's example in June 2002,

Sections 3 and 4 of the Twenty-fifth Amendment

Section 3. Whenever the President transmits to the President pro tempore of the Senate and the Speaker of the House of Representatives his written declaration that he is unable to discharge the powers and duties of his office, and until he transmits to them a written declaration to the contrary, such powers and duties shall be discharged by the Vice President as Acting President.

Section 4. Whenever the Vice President and a majority of either the principal officers of the executive departments or of such other body as Congress may by law provide, transmit to the President pro tempore of the Senate and the Speaker of the House of Representatives their written declaration that the President is unable to discharge the powers and duties of his office, the Vice President shall immediately assume the powers and duties of the office as Acting President.

Thereafter, when the President transmits to the President pro tempore of the Senate and the Speaker of the House of Representatives his written declaration that no inability exists, he shall resume the powers and duties of his office unless the Vice President and a majority of either the principle officers of the executive department or of such other body as Congress may by law provide, transmit within four days to the President pro tempore of the Senate and the Speaker of the House of Representatives their written declaration that the President is unable to discharge the powers and duties of his office. Thereupon Congress shall decide the issue, assembling within forty-eight hours for that purpose if not in session. If the Congress within twenty-one days after receipt of the latter written declaration, or, if Congress is not in session within twenty-one days after Congress is required to assemble, determines by two-thirds vote of both Houses that the President is unable to discharge the powers and duties of his office, the Vice President shall continue to discharge the same as Acting President; otherwise, the President shall resume the power and duties of his office.

when he declared himself incapacitated while undergoing a colonoscopy. At that time, he temporarily transferred presidential authority to Vice President Richard Cheney.

The elder President George Bush faced two serious health issues during his presidency: an irregular heartbeat and Grave's disease. Although he did not invoke the Twenty-fifth Amendment in either case, in 1991 he announced that he would do so if he needed to receive electric shock therapy for his irregular heartbeat. In that case, he would have temporarily transferred power to his vice president, Dan Quayle. President Bill Clinton was never seriously ill during his presidency, although he privately made a contingency plan with his vice president, Al Gore, should he become incapacitated.

ASSASSINATIONS AND NEAR-DEATH

What is the **"twenty-year curse"**?

The twenty-year presidential curse has also been called "Tecumseh's curse" after Tecumseh, the Shawnee Indian chief who supposedly cast it. Tecumseh's brother, Tenskwatawa, and his men where defeated during the Battle of Tippecanoe in 1811. According to the curse, presidents elected in a year ending in "0" would die in office. Indeed, every president elected from 1840 through 1960 in the years ending in "0" died in office.

The first president to succumb to the "curse" was William Henry Harrison, who, after being elected in 1840, caught a cold during his inauguration ceremony and died just a month later of pneumonia. Interestingly, it was Harrison, then governor of the Indiana Territory, who defeated Tenskwatawa and his men at the battle. Twenty years later, in 1860, Abraham Lincoln was elected president, then died from an assassin's bullet in 1865. The curse continued with the following election-year winners: 1880, with the assassination of James A. Garfield in 1881; 1900, with the assassination of William McKinley in 1901; 1920, with the death of Warren G. Harding from heart failure in 1923; 1940, with the death of Franklin D. Roosevelt from a stroke in 1945; and 1960, with the assassination of John F. Kennedy in 1963. Elected in 1980, Ronald Reagan was the first president to survive—some say break—the curse, having lived through an assassination attempt at the hands of John Hinckley Jr. in 1981.

The Twenty-Year Curse

Year elected	President	Death in office
1840	William Henry Harrison	Died of pneumonia shortly after inauguration
1860	Abraham Lincoln	Assassinated in 1865
1880	James A. Garfield	Assassinated in 1881
1900	William McKinley	Assassinated in 1901
1920	Warren G. Harding	Died in 1923
1940	Franklin D. Roosevelt	Died in 1945
1960	John F. Kennedy	Assassinated in 1963

Which **presidents were assassinated**?

Threats against the presidency have been commonplace since the creation of the executive office. Four presidents—Abraham Lincoln, James A. Garfield, William McKinley, and John F. Kennedy—were killed while in office. On April 14, 1865, John Wilkes Booth, a disillusioned actor who thought he was saving the South, shot President Lincoln, who died the next morning. President Garfield was shot on July 2, 1881, by a disgruntled job-seeker who had been hoping for a position in the government. The presi-

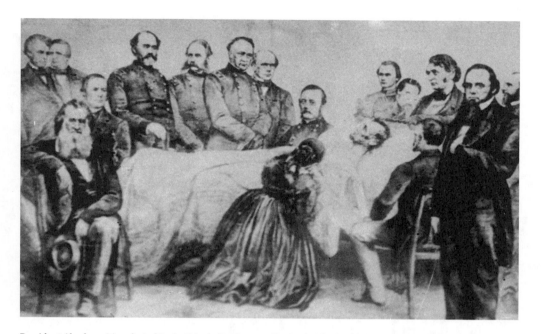

President Abraham Lincoln in his deathbed after he was shot on April 14, 1865. First lady Mary Todd Lincoln kneels beside her husband, and members of the cabinet surround them. The photograph was apparently given by Mrs. Lincoln to a friend and held by that family for several generations. *AP/Wide World Photos*.

dent died of complications from gunshot wounds on September 19. On September 6, 1901, extremist Leon F. Czolgosz shot President McKinley while he was standing in a reception line at the Buffalo Pan-American Exposition; the president died eight days later. On November 22, 1963, Lee Harvey Oswald allegedly shot President Kennedy while he was riding through Dallas, Texas, in a motorcade. At age forty-six, Kennedy was the youngest president to die in office.

What were the **circumstances around Abraham Lincoln's assassination**?

After serving one month of his second term, Abraham Lincoln was shot the night of April 14, 1865, and died the following morning. John Wilkes Booth, an actor, shot Lincoln at close range in the back of the head in the presidential box at Ford's Theatre in Washington, D.C., while the president, the first lady, and friends were attending an evening performance of *Our American Cousin*. Booth struggled with and stabbed Lincoln's theater companion, Henry Rathbone, before leaping onto the stage and escaping out a back door. The assassination occurred just six days after the end of the Civil War (1861–1865).

On April 26, federal authorities shot and killed Booth when they found him hiding in a barn a few miles outside of Washington. Booth was a Southern sympathizer during the Civil War and held President Lincoln responsible for the South's struggle during the

327

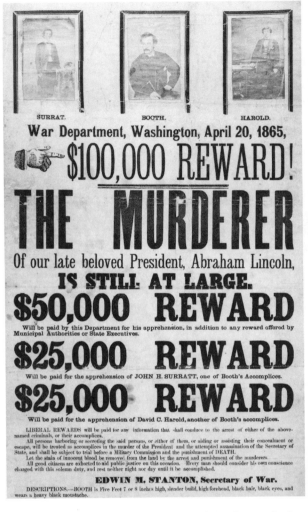

Poster advertising a reward for the capture of Lincoln assassination conspirators, with photographs of John H. Surratt, John Wilkes Booth, and David E. Herold. *Library of Congress.*

war. Although Booth originally planned to kidnap Lincoln and hold him in exchange for Confederate soldiers being held in Union prison camps, his plans turned to assassination shortly after General Robert E. Lee surrendered the South at Appomattox on April 9. Two days later, Lincoln had spoken to a White House crowd and suggested that some voting rights would be granted to African Americans—a speech that Booth witnessed firsthand. Although some historians argue that Lincoln's assassination was part of a larger conspiracy theory, they are certain that Booth did not operate alone. Booth and his small band of associates agreed that men of Lincoln's cabinet—including Vice President Andrew Johnson and Secretary of State William Seward—would also be killed. Booth hoped that the resulting chaos and instability in the executive branch would trigger a comeback for the South.

Is it true that **Lincoln's secretary of state was stabbed** and that **other men were involved in Lincoln's assassination**?

Yes. By January 1865, Lincoln's assassin, John Wilkes Booth, had organized a small group of co-conspirators to help him carry out his plan to derail Lincoln's administration. This group of approximately eight individuals included men that were originally going to kidnap Lincoln. George A. Atzerodt was assigned to kill Vice President Andrew Johnson at the Kirkwood House where Johnson lived, and Lewis Powell was scheduled to kill Secretary of State William Seward, with the assistance of David E.

Booth's Little Red Book

When John Wilkes Booth was captured and shot on April 26, 1865, a little red book, which Booth used as his diary, was recovered from his body. Historians have used Booth's entries, such as the following excerpt, to gain entry into the assassin's psyche:

> Until today nothing was ever thought of sacrificing to our country's wrongs. For six months we had worked to capture, but our cause being almost lost, something decisive and great must be done. But its failure was owing to others, who did not strike for their country with a heart. I struck boldly, and not as the papers say. I walked with a firm step through a thousand of his friends, was stopped, but pushed on. A colonel was at his side. I shouted Sic semper before I fired. In jumping broke my leg. I passed all his pickets, rode sixty miles that night with the bone of my leg tearing the flesh at every jump. I can never repent it, though we hated to kill. Our country owed all her troubles to him, and God simply made me the instrument of his punishment. The country is not what it was. This forced Union is not what I have loved. I care not what becomes of me. I have no desire to outlive my country.

Historians have used the diary to discuss various conspiracy theories. Indeed, the diary itself has been surrounded in mystery. Although it was given to Secretary of War Edwin Stanton, the diary was not used as evidence in the 1865 Conspiracy Trial. In 1867, the diary reappeared in a forgotten War Department file with eighteen pages missing, although the number of pages missing varies, depending on the source consulted. Today, Booth's diary is on display at Ford's Theatre.

Herold. Although all the attacks were scheduled to take place the night Lincoln was shot, only one other attack took place. Powell stabbed Seward, who received knife wounds to his face and neck but recovered. Within days, the government had arrested Booth's co-conspirators, who were tried by a military tribunal and found guilty. Atzerodt, Powell, Herold, and Mary E. Surratt were hanged in July 1865, while others received prison sentences. Seward continued on as secretary of state, serving in Johnson's administration until 1869.

What were the **circumstances surrounding James A. Garfield's death**?

Medical historians acknowledge that if President Garfield were shot today, he would have lived. However, in 1881, medical technology was unable to save the president after he was shot, and instead contributed to the president's death.

Illustration of the assassination of President James A. Garfield by Charles Guiteau in 1881. *AP/Wide World Photos.*

On July 2, 1881, the new president—only four months into his term—was shot at the Baltimore and Potomac Railway Station, in Washington, D.C., while in route to his twenty-fifth class reunion. His thirty-nine-year-old assassin, Charles Guiteau, shot him once in the arm, and a second time in the back, as the president was walking across the train station with Secretary of State James Blaine. Doctors probed with their fingers and non-sterile instruments for weeks attempting to discover the location of the second shell. Alexander Graham Bell, who had invented a metal-detecting device, was called in to try to locate the bullet. Probing the president's body repeatedly had caused a number of serious infections and blood poisoning that finally led to the president's death on September 19, 1881. After the president's autopsy, doctors realized they had been probing the wrong side of the president's body. Although the bullet had entered to the right of Garfield's spine, it had migrated downward and to the left. In fact, a cyst had formed around the bullet, making it harmless. Had Garfield been allowed to recover naturally, he probably would have been back at his desk in a few weeks.

Was **Charles Guiteau insane**?

Unlike President Lincoln's assassin before him, Charles Guiteau acted alone. He was obsessed with President Garfield. Before the assassination, he demanded, almost on a daily basis, to meet the president. He was convinced that Garfield should have appointed him to a diplomatic post, and when he was finally banned from the White House, he decided to kill the president. "I was thinking over the political situation," Guiteau wrote, disgruntled, "and the idea flashed through my brain that, if the president was out of the way, everything would go better." After stalking the president for weeks, Guiteau was waiting at the train depot when President Garfield arrived, and fired his revolver at close range. Guiteau had a long history of mental instability, violence, and erratic behavior. Although his lawyer pleaded innocence by reason of insanity, Guiteau was convicted of President Garfield's murder and hanged on June 30, 1882.

What **happened to President McKinley**?

William McKinley was shot twice on September 6, 1901, by Leon Czolgosz, while attending the Pan-American Exposition in Buffalo, New York. During a public reception, Czolgosz stood in line to greet the president, then suddenly fired two shots at the president's abdomen. The assassin's gun was disguised beneath his handkerchief-wrapped hand, and none of the guards noticed anything strange about him as he patiently waited his turn to pay his respects to the president. One of the bullets penetrated McKinley's stomach, as he fell backward into the arms of a guard. Although he was rushed to a nearby hospital, doctors could not locate the wanton bullet, so instead cleaned the abdominal cavity and stitched the president up.

President McKinley survived eight days and died September 14, 1901. The cause of death was gangrene poisoning. After a long search during McKinley's autopsy, practitioners still could not locate the fatal bullet. A popular president, McKinley was six months into his second term when he was killed. For more than thirteen hours, Americans were without a president, since Vice President Theodore Roosevelt was hiking in the Adirondack Mountains when the president died and could not be sworn in immediately.

Czolgosz, a twenty-eight-year-old unemployed mill worker and anarchist, was convicted of murder and electrocuted in December after stating he was proud to have accomplished his goal of killing a president so hostile to the "good working people." Many Americans labored long hours in poorly paid jobs as big businesses controlled commerce and squelched labor unions. "I don't believe," Czolgosz said, "one man should have so much and another should have none." Interestingly, historians later learned Czolgosz used the alias Fred Nieman, a name whose origin means "no man" or "nobody."

How was **John F. Kennedy assassinated**?

John Kennedy was shot November 22, 1963, while riding in an open motorcade through downtown Dallas, Texas, in front of a large crowd that had gathered that day. Kennedy went to Dallas to gain Texan support for his reelection the following year. Witness accounts vary as to the number of shots that rang out as Kennedy's car passed the Texas School Book Depository building. At least two, possibly three or four, bullets hit the president and a fellow passenger, Texas governor John Connally, who survived. A bullet struck the back of President Kennedy's neck and tore through his windpipe, a second bullet shot through the president's head, blowing away a portion of his skull. Although the president was rushed to a local hospital, he was pronounced dead almost immediately.

The Dallas political climate was one of the most heated in America. At the height of the civil rights movement, ultraconservative groups violently opposed President Kennedy's liberal policies. Many specifically opposed the president's handling of the communist threat. Although both Connally and U.S. senator J. William Fulbright of Arkansas had asked the president to reconsider his Dallas trip, the president retorted, "If anyone wanted to kill you, you wouldn't be around."

The accused gunman, Lee Harvey Oswald, a communist sympathizer and worker at the book depository, was arrested later that day. While being transported from a Texas jail two days later, Oswald was gunned down by Jack Ruby, a Dallas nightclub owner. In 1964, Ruby was convicted of murder and sentenced to death. Oswald never confessed to the crime, but his death caused many to believe a larger conspiracy involving organized crime, a group of right-wing anticommunist zealots, or perhaps others were responsible for the assassination of President Kennedy.

Members of the Kennedy family at the funeral for the assassinated John F. Kennedy in November 1963. In the front row stands the late president's daughter Caroline (left), wife Jackie, and son John Jr. Behind them are brothers Edward and Robert.

What was the **Warren Commission**?

With Lee Harvey Oswald's death and many questions about President Kennedy's assassination left unanswered, President Lyndon B. Johnson, on November 29, 1963, appointed a commission to investigate the assassination under the leadership of Supreme Court Chief Justice Earl Warren. Although it was formally called the President's Commission on the Assassination of President Kennedy, colloquially it has been referred to as the Warren Commission. After ten months of investigation, the Warren Commission concluded, "The shots which killed President Kennedy and wounded Governor Connally were fired by Lee Harvey Oswald." However, vast disagreement about the number of shots fired, the direction from which they came, and other details existed between Governor Connally and key eyewitnesses. Many refused to believe that Oswald was the only assassin. In 1977, the U.S. House of Representatives reopened the investigation, and in 1979 the House Select Committee on Assassins ruled that Kennedy was "probably" killed as the result of a conspiracy, but was "unable to identify the other gunman or the extent of the conspiracy."

Although in 1994 Congress appointed a federal Assassination Review Board to gather records about Kennedy's assassination and make them public, no single assassination theory predominates. Over the years, both the FBI and CIA have been implicated, as well as the Dallas Police Department and organized crime groups. The assassination occurred after the failed Bay of Pigs invasion to topple the communist Cuban government of Fidel Castro and America's increased military presence in South Vietnam. As a result, anti-Castro Cuban exiles, pro-Castro Cubans, and Vietnamese groups all became suspect over the years.

Which presidents survived assassination attempts?

In 1835, President Andrew Jackson came face to face with a deranged man carrying two pistols. After both guns misfired, causing Jackson no physical harm, he whacked the attacker with his cane. The attacker, Richard Lawrence—who believed himself to be King Richard III of Great Britain—spent the next few decades in a mental hospital after a jury released a verdict of not guilty by reason of insanity. Former president Theodore Roosevelt was stalked during his 1912 election campaign as a candidate of the Bull Moose Party. Although he took a bullet in his chest, he continued on with his business that evening. In February 1933, President-elect Franklin D. Roosevelt escaped the bullet of an assassin, who ended up harming a handful of onlookers, including Mayor Anton Cermak of Chicago, who had gathered to hear Roosevelt speak at Miami's Bay Front Park. Roosevelt wasn't hit at all, but Cermak was rushed to a nearby hospital, and died two and a half weeks later. Likewise, Presidents Harry S. Truman and Gerald Ford were not touched in the instances where people attempted to take their lives. The last president to be injured at the hands of a gunman was President Ronald Reagan, whose left lung was punctured after John Hinckley Jr. attempted to kill him in March 1981.

Did George Washington narrowly escape kidnappers?

Yes. During the American Revolution, while George Washington was commander-in-chief of the army, several men attempted to kidnap or kill him. The 1776 conspiracy involved William Tyron, the Tory governor of New York; David Matthews, the Tory mayor of New York City; and a host of other men, including General Washington's bodyguard, eighteen-year-old Private Thomas Hickey, a deserter from the British Army. In April 1776, just after Washington arrived in New York, the conspirators—who were all Loyalist sympathizers—plotted to help the British take control of the state. An unsigned letter sent to the *Pennsylvania Journal* indicated that upon the arrival of British troops into the region, the American Loyalists were instructed to "murder all the staff officers, blow up the [ammunition] magazines, and secure the passes of the town." However, before the plan could take effect, Hickey, who was sitting in jail for attempting to pass counterfeit notes, revealed the plot to his cellmate who exposed the conspiracy.

Matthews was jailed, and other co-conspirators were implicated. However, Hickey was the only man to be executed, marking the first military execution in the Continental Army. A court martial tried Hickey, found him guilty, and sentenced him to hanging, which occurred in a field near Bowery Lane on June 28, 1776. That day, Washington wrote the following comment in his orderly book: "The unhappy fate of Thomas Hickey, executed this day for mutiny, sedition, and treachery; the General hopes will be a warning to every soldier, in the Army, to avoid those crimes and all others, so disgraceful to the character of a solider and pernicious to his country, whose pay he receives and bread he eats."

How did **Theodore Roosevelt's eyeglass case save his life**?

On the evening of October 14, 1912, as Bull Moose candidate Theodore Roosevelt was preparing to deliver a campaign speech in Milwaukee, Wisconsin, he was shot by thirty-six-year-old John Schrank. According to Schrank, on September 15 of that year, a deceased William McKinley, whose assassination in 1901 made Vice President Roosevelt the new president, appeared to Schrank in a dream, instructing him to kill Roosevelt. As Roosevelt exited his hotel, Shrank approached the former president and shot a bullet into his chest. Before the assassin could fire again, he was tackled to the ground. Roosevelt coughed into his hand, and when he didn't see blood he knew that the bullet hadn't pierced his lungs. In fact, the bullet had hit his breast pocket, which was filled with a thick, folded copy of the speech Roosevelt was about to deliver and a metal eyeglass case—two items that took the full force of the bullet and undoubtedly saved his life. While bleeding, Roosevelt delivered his fifty-minute speech with the added line, "It takes more than one bullet to kill a Bull Moose." He was rushed to a Chicago hospital for treatment, where he recovered, although he ultimately lost the election that year to Democrat Woodrow Wilson. Shrank spent the rest of his life in mental hospitals.

Did **Franklin D. Roosevelt have his life threatened** before his inauguration as president?

Yes. After he was elected president in November 1932, but before his inauguration in March 1933, President-elect Franklin D. Roosevelt faced an assassination attempt. On February 15, 1933, after Roosevelt had finished delivering a speech at Miami's Bay Front Park, thirty-two-year-old anarchist Giuseppe Zangara fired five rounds from a revolver into the crowd. At the time, Roosevelt was chatting with Chicago mayor Anton Cermak, who was hit by one of the bullets in his right lung. Four other bystanders were injured. Roosevelt fled the scene with Secret Service agents and Mayor Cermak in tow, whom they rushed to the hospital. Although President Roosevelt was not hit, Cermak died from complications of gunshot wounds nineteen days later. Zangara was tried on assault, attempted assassination of the president, and the murder of Cermak. He was sentenced to death and died in the electric chair on March 20, 1933, just weeks after President Roosevelt was inaugurated.

What were the circumstances surrounding the **assassination attempt on Harry S. Truman**?

On November 1, 1950, two Puerto Rican nationalists, Griselio Torresola and Oscar Collazo, shot at presidential guards while attempting to enter Blair House—the Washington, D.C., residence where the Trumans lived during White House renovations—while President Truman was taking a nap in an upstairs bedroom. As fanatical members of the Puerto Rican Nationalist Party, Torresola and Collazo planned to assassinate Truman in an effort to draw attention to their cause of gaining independence for Puerto Rico, a U.S. possession since the Spanish-American War.

In a flurry of gunfire, one of the guards shot and killed Torresola, and others wounded Collazo as he attempted to make his way up the house's front steps. Two guards were seriously injured, and one was shot dead. The president was unharmed, and left out the back door to continue on with the day's pressing appointments—dedicating a statue in Arlington National Cemetery less than an hour after the assassination attempt. Unshaken, President Truman commented, "A president has to expect these things." Although Collazo was tried and sentenced to death, Truman, who did not believe in capital punishment, converted Collazo's death sentence to life imprisonment. In 1979, President Jimmy Carter granted Collazo clemency.

Was **Gerald Ford** injured during his **assassination attempts**?

Amazingly, no. In September 1975, two separate attempts to assassinate President Gerald Ford were made. On September 5, while President Ford was in Sacramento, California, to discuss the national epidemic of violent crime, Lynette "Squeaky" Fromme, a follower of imprisoned cult leader Charles Manson, pointed a gun at Ford. Secret Service agents rushed to the president's defense and captured Fromme. No one was injured. Seventeen days later, in San Francisco, California, forty-five-year-old Sara Jane Moore fired a gun at the president as he greeted onlookers outside the St. Francis Hotel. An ex-Marine jostled Moore and the bullet instead wounded a cabdriver. Both women received life sentences.

When Fromme attempted to assassinate Ford, it marked the first time a female tried to kill the president of the United States. Both women admitted trying to gain attention for their causes. Fromme hoped that her trial would draw attention to Manson, eventually granting him a new trial. Moore, a left-wing sympathizer and former FBI informant, hoped her act of assassination would help her gain entrance into her former radical Leftist circles.

What were the details surrounding **Ronald Reagan's assassination attempt**?

On March 31, 1981, John Hinckley Jr. fired a gun at Ronald Reagan as the president left the Hilton Hotel in Washington, D.C. Hinckley was obsessed with actress Jodie Foster and was hoping that the assassination attempt would get her attention and gain her affection. Hinckley fired six shots within nine seconds, one of which ricocheted off the presidential limousine and entered Reagan's body under his left arm. It then hit a rib and traveled into his lung, which was bleeding profusely as Reagan was rushed to

"I Am in Charge." Not!

When Ronald Reagan was shot by John Hinckley in March 1981, Vice President George Bush was away from Washington, D.C. Reporters first reached Reagan's secretary of state, Alexander Haig, for a statement. While trying to reassure the American people that the government was operating smoothly, Haig declared: "I am in charge." The press and public quickly seized on the blunder by Haig, who was actually fourth in line of succession. Haig's credibility was never the same. He resigned from the Reagan administration in 1982 and later faced frequent reminders of his remark when challenging George Bush for the 1988 Republican presidential nomination.

The actual sequence of succession in case of illness or death of the president has changed several times after the Constitution originally stated that the office of president "shall devolve" upon the vice president. Since 1967, the line of succession has comprised elements of the Twentieth Amendment (1933), the Presidential Succession Law of 1947, and the Twenty-fifth Amendment (1967). The successor must meet the same requirements as those outlined in the Constitution for the president. The line of succession:

1. Vice President
2. Speaker of the House
3. President pro tempore of the Senate (The president pro tempore presides over the Senate when the vice president is absent. By tradition, the position is held by the senior member of the majority party.)
4. Secretary of State
5. Secretary of the Treasury
6. Secretary of Defense
7. Attorney General
8. Secretary of the Interior
9. Secretary of Agriculture
10. Secretary of Commerce
11. Secretary of Labor
12. Secretary of Health and Human Services
13. Secretary of Housing and Urban Development
14. Secretary of Transportation
15. Secretary of Energy
16. Secretary of Education
17. Secretary of Veterans Affairs
18. Secretary of Homeland Security

George Washington University Hospital. In surgery, doctors located the bullet, an inch from the president's heart, and removed it.

Although no one was killed, the president's press secretary, James Brady, was seriously injured and permanently disabled when one of Hinckley's bullets entered his skull. Secret Service agent Timothy McCarthy suffered wounds from shielding the president with his body and taking a shot in the chest, and Metropolitan Police officer Tom Delahanty was shot in the neck.

After the shooting, the president did not invoke the Twenty-fifth Amendment, although his aides intensely debated whether the president should have taken that step. Back at the White House, Secretary of State Alexander Haig mistakenly declared that he was "in charge," pending the return of Vice President George Bush, who was out of the country at the time. Hinckley, who was captured at the scene, was tried and found not guilty by reason of insanity. He was committed to St. Elizabeth's psychiatric hospital, the same institution where Andrew Jackson's would-be assassin, Richard Lawrence, lived out his existence more than one hundred years earlier.

Did **anyone ever try to kill Bill Clinton** while he was president?

Yes. During Bill Clinton's presidency, two events occurred within months of one another. In September 1994, Frank Eugene Corder killed himself when he crashed a stolen Cessna airplane into the lawn of the White House. The Clintons were not in the building at the time, and no one was injured. Most have concluded that Corder's act was a suicide by an individual wishing to make a particular statement by crashing into the White House, rather than an assassination attempt. In October, Francisco Martin Duran fired between twenty-five and thirty rounds from an assault rifle at the White House from the sidewalk on Pennsylvania Avenue. While attempting to reload his rifle, he was tackled by a tourist. The president, who had just returned from a trip to the Middle East, was in the family quarters of the White House and was not injured. Duran was convicted of attempting to assassinate the president and sentenced to forty years in prison.

What is the **role of the Secret Service**?

In 1865, President Abraham Lincoln signed into law a bill that created the Secret Service within the U.S. Treasury Department. Although it was originally put in place to reduce the counterfeiting of U.S. currency, it gradually took on a larger role. Secret Servicemen guarded President William McKinley on an informal, part-time basis; however, public sentiment after McKinley's assassination in 1901 demanded better protection of the nation's chief executive. In 1902, the secretary of the treasury charged the Secret Service with officially guarding the president on a full-time basis. In 1922, at the request of President Warren G. Harding, the White House Police was created to guard the White House buildings and grounds, and in 1930 that group came under the supervision of the Secret Service. Today, the Secret Service protects the president, the vice president, their families, former presidents and their wives and children, and visiting dignitaries and heads of state.

Despite its dedicated mission and well-qualified personnel, the Secret Service is not foolproof. John F. Kennedy was assassinated despite sophisticated security measures and a full Secret Service team that was put in place. Suggestions that came from the 1963–1964 Warren Commission included the creation of a committee of cabinet members to oversee presidential security. The commission also advised that the Secret Service be granted more money and manpower, and that various government departments work together on security measures. By 1973, the Secret Service had more than tripled its work force. In 2003, the Secret Service, whose budget was $1.3 billion, became part of the Department of Homeland Security.

Were there any **protective measures in place before the Secret Service**?

John Tyler, who witnessed the assassination attempt on President Andrew Jackson, became the first president to hire an official bodyguard. In fact, Congress assigned four plain-clothed armed guards to the White House. They were called "doormen" at the time, and soon became Washington's Metropolitan Police. Abraham Lincoln and his family were usually protected by the Metropolitan Police; however, on the night President Lincoln was shot, his bodyguard, John Parker, had left his post. President James A. Garfield was left wide open for attack, since he did not have a bodyguard on hand when he was shot. President William McKinley's public event had stepped-up security measures, including extra Exposition police and soldiers outside the meeting area, and Buffalo, New York, detectives and Secret Service agents posted near the president and at the receiving line. The Secret Service was new at this time, having recently expanded its authority to protect the president. Although a full-time Secret Serviceman, George Foster, was assigned to President McKinley, he and others were poorly positioned and unable to defend the president from attackers.

DEATH AND GRIEVING IN THE WHITE HOUSE

Which **presidents lost children during their presidency**?

Six men—John Adams, Thomas Jefferson, Franklin Pierce, Abraham Lincoln, Calvin Coolidge, and John F. Kennedy—lost children while serving as (or about to serve as) chief executive. Adams's grown son Charles died in 1800, shortly after the president lost his reelection bid. Jefferson's grown daughter Mary died in 1804. Pierce lost all three of his sons at an early age. Eleven-year-old Benny, his only surviving child, was killed in a train accident in January 1853, two months before Pierce's inauguration.

Abraham Lincoln lost his son William ("Willie") in 1862 in the middle of the Civil War. His death devastated first lady Mary Lincoln's psyche and furthered the president's empathy toward the nation's tremendous suffering. Calvin Coolidge Jr. died after contracting blood poisoning from an infected blister in 1924. John F. Kennedy lost his son Patrick two days after he was born on August 7, 1963.

How did **Franklin Pierce's son's death** affect the president and first lady?

President-elect Franklin Pierce and his family were preparing to move to Washington, D.C., in late January 1853. After losing two children earlier in life (three-day-old Franklin in 1836 and four-year-old Frank in 1839) his only surviving child, Benjamin ("Benny") died. The family was traveling to Boston via train, when the train jumped the tracks and rolled down an embankment, killing Benny almost instantly.

Benny had been the main focus of his slightly emotionally unbalanced mother, Jane Pierce. With each successive death of her children, Jane became increasingly intolerant of her husband's political career, and believed that God had taken her youngest son so that her husband could pursue the duties of the presidency without the distraction of children. After Benny's death, Mrs. Pierce became an emotional recluse. She moved into the White House, shrouded herself in black, and rarely emerged from the upstairs living quarters. She frequently wrote letters to her dead son. In the first lady's absence, the second wife of Mrs. Pierce's uncle, Abby Kent Means, fulfilled the role of White House hostess. Franklin Pierce barely endured the stress caused by his wife's grief-induced mental illness, and was a weak leader. Many historians mention his bouts of drinking.

How did the **death of Abraham Lincoln's son** affect the president?

When Abraham Lincoln assumed the presidency in 1861, he had already lost one son, Edward ("Eddie") to tuberculosis in 1850. During the dark days of the Civil War, President Lincoln found great joy in playing with his sons William ("Willie") and Thomas ("Tad"), whose childish antics livened up the White House and kept the staff engaged in the Lincolns' life. Many, such as White House secretary Noah Brooks, noted that Lincoln's open expression of love toward his sons helped him cope with the pressures of the presidency and his own bouts of depression. On February 20, 1862, eleven-year-old Willie died of typhoid fever with the president at his bedside. A devastated Lincoln broke down and cried. After spending some time alone with Willie, the president went back to his desk and continued working. Although Lincoln continued on with his presidential duties, he found it difficult to accept his son's loss. Eventually his grief transformed into a personal resolution to preserve the Union and halt the loss of life soldiers and their families were experiencing. Willie was the only child of a president to die inside the White House.

339

Is it true that **President and Mrs. Lincoln conducted séances** in the White House?

Yes. Mary Todd Lincoln was an emotionally unstable first lady. By most accounts, it was the death of her son Willie in 1862 that sent her over the emotional edge. She did not attend her son's funeral and found it difficult to care for her older son, Tad, and soon President Lincoln hired a personal nurse to care for her. Layered in black mourning clothes, Mrs. Lincoln was obsessed with communicating with her dead son. She frequently sought out spiritualists who promised to put her in touch with Willie, and on more than half a dozen occasions séances were held in the White House. Historians believe that President Lincoln attended at least one of these gatherings, primarily out of curiosity and a desire to discern what was contributing to his wife's increasing emotional instability. Although she emerged from mourning a year after Willie's death, Mrs. Lincoln continued to have bouts with mental illness.

How did **Calvin Coolidge's son die**?

On July 7, 1924, Calvin Coolidge's son, Calvin Coolidge Jr., died from blood poisoning after he developed a blister on his foot from playing tennis. "Cal" had been away at school and returned to the White House to spend summer vacation with his parents and his older brother John. Just a few days after the tennis match, Cal's blister had become infected and poisoned his blood; by July 6, the doctors said his condition was terminal, although a final attempt to surgically remove the poison was made at Walter Reed Hospital, where Cal died. Cal was popular with the press for his forthrightness, having once said to a friend, "I think you are mistaken in calling me the first boy of the land since I have done nothing. It is my father who is President. Rather, the first boy of the land would be some boy who has distinguished himself through his actions." America earnestly mourned the death of President's Coolidge son, and the first family was flooded with phone calls, telegrams, and notes of condolences.

Although President Coolidge was reelected later that year, he said in his autobiography that when his son died, "the power and the glory of the Presidency went with him." First lady Grace Coolidge said that the president "lost his zest for living." Biographers, including Dr. Robert Gilbert in *The Tormented President* (2003), have suggested that Coolidge's son's death caused the president to experience a deep depression that lasted until the end of his second term. Gilbert maintains that the depression led Coolidge to lose interest in working with Congress, despite the fact that the Republican Party controlled both houses, and his relationship with the legislature became more tense. In addition, the president's leadership style changed: He noticeably withdrew from his daily responsibilities, and increasingly Coolidge delegated more responsibilities to his cabinet.

Which **first ladies died during their time at the White House**?

Three first ladies—Letitia Tyler, Caroline Harrison, and Ellen Wilson—died during their residency in the White House. Mrs. Tyler arrived at the White House paralyzed from a stroke, and thus was never healthy enough to serve a public role. She stayed in the upstairs living quarters of the White House, and only came downstairs on one occasion: when her daughter Elizabeth was married in January 1842. Nevertheless, when she died later that year from a second stroke, she was mourned in the building's East Room, where public officials and dignitaries whom she had never met paid their last respects.

During Benjamin Harrison's campaign for reelection, Mrs. Harrison contracted tuberculosis. She died in October 1892, a few weeks before Election Day. She didn't live to see her husband defeated that November by Democrat Grover Cleveland. Ellen Wilson, Woodrow Wilson's first wife, died on August 6, 1914, just several days after President Wilson announced U.S. neutrality in World War I. She died in the White House of Bright's disease, a kidney condition.

Five wives of presidents died before their husbands took office: Martha Jefferson (died in 1782, nineteen years before Thomas Jefferson became president); Rachel Jackson (died in 1828, three months before Andrew Jackson became president); Hannah Van Buren (died in 1819, eighteen years before Martin Van Buren became president); Ellen Arthur (died in 1880, a year before Chester Alan Arthur became president); and Alice Roosevelt (Theodore Roosevelt's first wife, who died in 1884, seventeen years before her husband became president). In addition, Abigail Fillmore died a few weeks after Millard Fillmore left office in 1853.

Is it true that **President McKinley's wife was an invalid**?

First lady Ida McKinley was a lifelong invalid dependent upon her husband. High-strung after the death of her two young daughters, five-month-old Ida in 1873 and four-year-old Katherine in 1875, she battled epileptic seizures and phlebitis. As first lady, she also suffered from depression, hysteria, and headaches. Ever the devoted husband, William McKinley constantly attended to his wife's physical and emotional needs. He sat next to his wife during White House dinners, politely covering her face with a napkin when she had a seizure. Many nights he rocked her to sleep. After the president died in September 1901, Ida McKinley did not attend the funeral. She lived the rest of her life in Canton, Ohio, where she died in May 1907.

SCANDALS, RUMORS, AND AFFAIRS

What was the nature of **George Washington's relationship with Sally Fairfax**?

Sarah "Sally" Fairfax was the wife of George Washington's friend and neighbor, George William Fairfax. Although Washington had strong feelings for Mrs. Fairfax, it appears that the infatuation did not proceed further. In September 1758, at the time he was engaged to Martha Dandridge Custis, his soon-to-be wife, Washington penned a letter to Sally expressing his love. George and Martha were married the following January, and the newlyweds spent much time visiting the Fairfaxes at their Virginia estate, Belvoir. Just how much Mrs. Washington and Mr. Fairfax knew of the infatuation is uncertain. However, the Fairfaxes did not share General Washington's vision for an independent America, and they sailed for England in 1773, where they lived permanently thereafter. The 1758 letter became a matter of public scrutiny when it was published some years later, in 1877, by the *New York Herald*. Its publication opened rumors of an extramarital affair, although history does not bear out that the relationship was consummated sexually.

Who was **Sally Hemings**?

After Thomas Jefferson's wife Martha died in 1782, it was widely speculated that Jefferson engaged in a number of romances. His relationship with Sally Hemings, one of his slaves, with whom it is rumored he fathered several illegitimate children, was reported in the press when he ran for president in 1800. Sally was the daughter of a slave mother, Elizabeth Hemings, and a white owner, John Wayles, Jefferson's father-in-law. When Jefferson's younger daughter Polly traveled to France (where Jefferson was U.S. ambassador) in 1787, Sally accompanied her. According to some historians, shortly thereafter the affair most likely began. Jefferson returned to the United States in early 1789 and Sally later followed, but only after Jefferson promised that he would free her children when each reached the age of twenty-one. She was visibly pregnant when she returned to Jefferson's estate, Monticello, and gave birth to her first child in late 1789 or early 1790. Sally herself admitted to the affair with Jefferson, asserting that he had fathered all seven of her children, five of whom lived to maturity and were all freed at twenty-one.

Jefferson's biographers are divided over whether the president did indeed father Hemings's children. Some have suggested that Peter Carr, Jefferson's nephew, was the father. A DNA study conducted by Dr. Eugene Foster on descendents of Hemings and Carr, as well as a descendent of Jefferson's paternal uncle Field Jefferson, concluded that Eston Hemings (Sally Hemings's son) was Thomas Jefferson's son. Results published in the British science journal *Nature* in 1998 discounted Carr as the father. The results, however, could not effectively rule out another potential father, Thomas Jefferson's younger brother, Randolph, since he and Jefferson both shared the same Y chromosome pattern. After the study was published, the Thomas Jefferson Memorial Foundation issued a statement in January 2000 that maintained there is a strong likelihood that Thomas Jefferson was the father of at least one and perhaps all of Sally Hemings's children, although controversy continues to exist.

Why was **Thomas Jefferson's relationship with Aaron Burr contentious**?

Throughout his term as Thomas Jefferson's vice president from 1801 to 1805, Aaron Burr was a controversial figure. He was not a political ally of Jefferson's—having vied for the presidency himself during the contentious election of 1800. In July 1804, Aaron Burr shot and killed his political rival, Alexander Hamilton, in a duel. Although the action, for which Burr was never tried, is frequently mentioned in history books as a testimony to Burr's bitter nature, Burr's main source of contention with Jefferson stems from an event known as the "Burr conspiracy."

While vice president, Burr developed a treasonous plan to form a new country (with himself as leader) out of lands acquired under the Louisiana Purchase. He tried to persuade Britain and then Spain to assist in financing the operation, which would begin with a coup d'état in Washington. James Wilkinson, commanding officer of the army and governor of the Louisiana Territory, who was originally involved in the scheme, ended up exposing Burr's plan to President Jefferson in late 1806.

Burr was arrested in 1807 and tried with a small group of co-conspirators for treason (see Presidents and the Judiciary—The Judiciary Influences the Presidency). His actions thoroughly discredited Burr as a public official, and he spent several years in exile in England. Wilkinson, though no longer governor of the Louisiana Territory, was an incompetent military leader who continued to be a thorn in the side of Jefferson, and after him, President James Madison. George Clinton picked up the post of Jefferson's vice president from 1805 until 1809 (and also continued on as Madison's first-term vice president until Clinton died in 1812).

What was the **controversy surrounding Andrew Jackson's wife, Rachel**?

When Andrew Jackson married Rachel Donelson Robards in August 1791, neither party knew that she was still married to her first husband. Rachel's divorce from her first husband, Lewis Robards, had not yet gone into effect. (Although the Kentucky legislature passed a resolution granting Robards permission to sue for divorce, he had not done so.) Although Jackson and Rachel remarried legally in 1794, their 1791 "marriage" had made Rachel a bigamist and Jackson an adulterer—slurs Jackson's detractors railed at him during the presidential election of 1828 and charges he would continually defend. The gossip and campaign backstabbing contributed to Rachel's ill health, and she died of a heart attack in December 1828, just months before Jackson's inauguration as president.

What was the **Petticoat War**?

The Petticoat War refers to one of the first major political scandals to strike the American presidency. It was dubbed a war for the infighting that took place in Andrew Jackson's cabinet over a woman named Peggy Eaton, the wife of Jackson's secretary of war, John Eaton. Eaton had met Peggy while she was still married and while he was a senator from Tennessee. As the daughter of a Washington, D.C., tavern keeper, Peggy had a reputation for being promiscuous: she was banned from White House social functions and society dinners beginning with James Monroe's administration. In 1829, when

Jackson assumed the presidency, many Washington wives shunned Peggy, despite the fact that she was now married to a prominent member of the president's cabinet. Jackson was sensitive to Peggy's social ostracism (having endured verbal attacks against his wife Rachel), and empathetic toward her. Jackson refused to remove Eaton from his cabinet, as a group of congressman had suggested, and he purposely invited Peggy to his cabinet dinners.

By the second year of Jackson's administration, the so-called "Petticoat War" had divided Jackson's cabinet and alienated Jackson from his vice president, John C. Calhoun, who refused to socialize with the Eatons. In early 1831, Secretary of State Martin Van Buren and Eaton resigned from the cabinet and, at Van Buren's suggestion, Jackson asked for the resignations of his remaining cabinet members. He was then free to rebuild his cabinet, which he promptly did, although one holdover from the original cabinet remained: Postmaster General William Barry. Calhoun resigned in December 1832, the only vice president besides Spiro Agnew in 1973 to formally resign. Jackson was so grateful to Van Buren's loyalty that he made him his running mate in the election of 1834. As for Eaton, he enjoyed a healthy post as governor of Florida and U.S. minister to Spain before he died in 1856. Peggy remained a figure of controversy: At age sixty, she married a nineteen-year-old dancing instructor who stole all her money and ran away with her granddaughter to Italy. Eaton died in poverty in 1879, at the age of ninety-three.

Was **James Buchanan a closet homosexual**?

James Buchanan was the only president to never marry, causing many to speculate about his sexuality. Some scholars, including sociologist James Loewen, believe that Buchanan had a longstanding homosexual relationship with William Rufus King, who served nearly three decades in the Senate. Before the presidency, Buchanan and King were roommates in Washington for twenty-three years. King went on to serve as Franklin Pierce's vice president, although he died from tuberculosis a month after being sworn in. Rumors of the men's affair circulated throughout Washington. About town they were often called "the Siamese twins." Andrew Jackson nicknamed King "Miss Nancy," and James K. Polk's law partner referred to King as "Buchanan's better half." When Aaron Brown, a representative from Tennessee, wrote to Sarah Polk, he called King "Mrs. B." Any remaining evidence of the affair—including letters exchanged between King and Buchanan—is circumstantial.

Was **Mary Todd Lincoln a Confederate spy**?

Mary Todd Lincoln, the wife of President Abraham Lincoln, was a controversial first lady subject to intense scrutiny. Throughout her husband's administration, Mrs. Lincoln was the target of slanderous comments, which led to a brief investigation by a joint committee of Congress. Mrs. Lincoln came from a prominent slave-holding family in Kentucky with firm roots in the South, and when the Civil War broke out her brother and three half brothers fought on the side of the Confederacy. Amidst rumors that Mrs. Lincoln was a Confederate spy, secretly aiding the Confederate Army, a congressional committee met to investigate. President Lincoln boldly defended his wife, claiming, "I, of my own knowledge, know that it is untrue that any of my family hold treasonable communication with the enemy." The committee dropped its investigation, although murmurings still persisted. Historians generally agree that there is little evidence to support the fact that Mrs. Lincoln's allegiance to the North was divided. However, the destruction of the South and the death of several of her family members in the war took a toll on her fragile psyche.

What were some of the **scandals that plagued the Grant administration**?

Ulysses S. Grant was never found to be personally involved in the scandals that rocked his office, but many members of his administration were implicated. The first scandal, 1869's "Black Friday" on the New York gold exchange, involved Wall Street conspirators who attempted to corner the available gold supply and prevent the government from selling gold by enlisting Grant's brother-in-law, Abel Corbin, as co-conspirator. In the Crédit Mobilier scandal of 1872, Vice President Schuyler Colfax, vice presidential candidate Henry Wilson, and other prominent politicians were involved in the operations of the Crédit Mobilier Co., a corporation established by the promoters of the Union Pacific to siphon off the profits of railroad construction. When Congress discovered that Crédit Mobilier officials were padding construction budgets and illegally taking in funds for themselves, U.S. representative Oakes Ames of Massachusetts, who managed much of Crédit Mobilier's affairs, sold select stockholders (including Colfax and Wilson's wife) $33 million worth of Crédit Mobilier stock at below market value. The scandal erupted during Grant's reelection campaign.

In 1875, Secretary of the Treasury Benjamin Bristow exposed the Whiskey Ring scandal, in which a group of corrupt officials and businessmen were accused of pocketing millions of dollars in liquor taxes. Since the end of the Civil War, liquor taxes were raised up to eight times the price of the liquor. Large distillers—mainly in St. Louis, Milwaukee, and Chicago—bribed Internal Revenue Service (IRS) agents and other government officials in order to retain the tax proceeds. When the operation was exposed, it compromised key leaders, including IRS supervisor John McDonald and Grant's private secretary, Col. Orville E. Babcock. Accusations were also made against President Grant's oldest son, Frederick Dent Grant, and the president's brother, Orvil. After Bristow broke the conspiracy by rallying secret investigators to gather evidence, more than $3 million in taxes was recovered and 110 conspirators were convicted.

The 1876 impeachment charges against Secretary of War William W. Belknap, on suspicion of accepting bribes from Indian agents, made Belknap the first U.S. cabinet official ever to have impeachment charges drawn up against him. Ultimately, Belknap was acquitted because he resigned prior to the opening of the Senate trial. During his

State of the Union address, held in December 1876, President Grant acknowledged his administration's failures: "It is but reasonable to suppose that errors of judgment must have occurred.... It is not necessarily evidence of blunder on the part of the executive because there are these differences of views. Mistakes have been made, as all can see and I admit."

What **scandalous story broke while Grover Cleveland was campaigning for president**?

During the presidential campaign of 1884, the *Evening Telegraph,* a Buffalo, New York, newspaper, published a story claiming that Democratic candidate Grover Cleveland was the father of a child out of wedlock. With Republicans milking the story for all it was worth, Cleveland decided to come forward with the truth: In 1874, Cleveland had an affair with Maria Halpin, who gave birth to a son in September of that year and, claiming Cleveland as the father, named him Oscar Folsom Cleveland. Although he was uncertain of the child's paternity and opted not to marry Halpin, Cleveland decided to pay child support. This included paying the child's expenses once he was admitted to an orphanage because of Halpin's heavy drinking and parental neglect. Cleveland's candidness helped end the scandal. He won the 1884 election with 49 percent of the popular vote. Oscar was eventually adopted by a financially stable New York family and grew up to be a doctor.

What was the **Teapot Dome scandal**?

The Teapot Dome scandal involved officials who illegally leased government-owned oil reserves in Teapot Dome, Wyoming. At the heart of the scandal was Secretary of the Interior Albert B. Fall, who upon his appointment to the Department of the Interior in 1921, coerced Secretary of the Navy Edwin Denby into turning control of the oil fields over to his department. Fall then secretly leased the Teapot Dome reserves to various oil companies in exchange for personal "gifts" totaling almost $400,000. The excessive development of public lands led conservationists to urge U.S. senator Robert LaFollette of Wisconsin to investigate the matter more closely. In 1923, a U.S. Senate committee, the Public Lands Committee, was charged with investigating the government's private drilling program. Led by U.S. senator Thomas J. Walsh of Montana, the committee uncovered numerous cabinet documents that implicated both Fall and drilling contractors Harry Sinclair of Mammoth Oil and Edward Doheny of Pan-American Oil.

President Warren G. Harding died just before news broke of his administration's Teapot Dome scandal. In 1924, President Calvin Coolidge ordered the Justice Department to begin investigations; however, because Attorney General Harry Daugherty was friends with Fall, the president appointed a special counsel to investigate. Congress also began to pressure Coolidge to dismiss Denby because of his role in delivering the oil reserve and, under pressure, Denby resigned. In the end, both the Public

Lands Committee and the courts determined that a conspiracy existed between the Interior Department and the drilling companies. In 1929, Fall was convicted of bribery, served a year of prison time, and assessed a steep fine, which he never paid (see also Presidents and the Judiciary—The Judiciary Influences the Presidency).

Did **Warren G. Harding have more than one extramarital affair**?

Historians recognize that Warren Harding engaged in two long-term extramarital affairs, one of which produced a daughter. In 1905, as lieutenant governor of Ohio, Harding began an extramarital affair with Carrie Phillips, the wife of a

Cartoon showing the juggernaut of scandal rolling toward the White House after members of President Warren G. Harding's government were implicated in the Teapot Dome scandal. *Getty Images*.

longtime friend. Harding and Phillips saw each other regularly, even vacationing together with their spouses, until 1914, when Florence Harding discovered the affair. Although Harding promised to break the relationship, he did not, and he faced public scandal during his campaign for the presidency in 1920. Campaign manager Albert Lasker offered Phillips and her husband $20,000, a European vacation, and a monthly allowance if the Phillipses remained out of the United States until after the election. The couple complied, and Harding was elected president on the Republican ticket that year. In 1963, many of Harding's letters to Carrie Phillips were uncovered, confirming the affair. After reading the letters, Harding biographer Francis Russell stated that "she was the one great love of his life."

During this time, Harding also conducted an affair with Nan Britton, a woman he met first met in 1910, began writing letters to in 1914 (when she was almost eighteen years old), and with whom he began sexual relations in 1917. Britton gave birth to a daughter in 1919, whom Harding supported financially. Britton visited the White House occasionally, where, according to Britton, the two shared many intimate moments. After Harding died in 1923, Britton published *The President's Daughter* (1927), in which she chronicled her relationship with the president.

How did **Franklin D. Roosevelt's mistress affect his marriage with Eleanor**?

Franklin D. Roosevelt's almost thirty-year affair with Lucy Page Mercer, his wife Eleanor's social secretary for a time, probably began in the summer of 1916. Several years later, in 1918, Eleanor discovered some of the love letters Mercer had written to Roosevelt, and confronted her husband about the affair. Although Eleanor offered her husband a divorce

347

and Roosevelt promised to stop seeing Mercer, he continued the affair, intermittently, until his death in 1945. While not the only affair that Roosevelt engaged in (he also had a long-term relationship with his personal secretary, Missy LeHand, for many years), it is the one that seems to have had the most profound effect on their marriage.

Most accounts mention that after Eleanor first learned of her husband's affair with Mercer, she began to create a life for herself outside of her role as "Mrs. Roosevelt." She grew more independent and became a pioneering first lady by becoming active in significant social causes, carving out a niche for herself in the White House. Rather than a traditional marriage relationship, Eleanor and Franklin developed more of a partnership, and Eleanor drew emotional support from other women. Her relationship with Associated Press reporter and lesbian Lorena Hickok, who moved into the White House in 1941 and shared a working relationship with the first lady, has been the source of some gossip.

Is it true that **John F. Kennedy had several extramarital affairs**?

John F. Kennedy is known to have engaged in numerous extramarital affairs, several of which took place during his tenure as president, from 1961 to 1963. The affairs became public at various times after his death in 1963. Most prominent was Judith ("Judy") Campbell, reputed girlfriend of Mafia boss Sam "Momo" Giancana. Although she wrote about her affair with JFK in her 1977 book *My Story,* Campbell's recounting of the relationship changed over time. Other women include artist Mary Pinchot Meyer; Pamela Turnure, Jackie Kennedy's press secretary; and actress Marilyn Monroe, with whom Kennedy reportedly carried on a relationship well into his presidency.

Why didn't **JFK's affairs come to light during his presidency**?

John F. Kennedy's presidency took place in an era when the media was more apt to take a hands-off approach to covering a president's personal life, especially in the areas of health and sexual relations. Although the media was vaguely aware of JFK's sexual exploits, they agreed not to publicize them. This is almost unimaginable to a twenty-first century citizenry, whose public officials are barraged by the media spotlight and exposed to the press's tell-all philosophy. In the 1970s, journalists began linking Kennedy to various women, portraying him as a less-than-perfect husband with a penchant for extramarital affairs. Reports about Kennedy's well-disguised Addison's disease also began to surface at that time, forcing reporters to examine their responsibility to scrutinize the physical conditions and private lives of their public officials.

What was Richard Nixon's **Checkers speech**?

In 1952, the *New York Post* reported that vice presidential candidate Richard Nixon had set up a secret fund of $18,000 through which he processed contributions from wealthy donors to help underwrite his political expenses. In September of that year, Nixon, a U.S. senator from California at the time, appeared on television to defend himself and deny the charges. During what has popularly been called the "Checkers Speech," Nixon said that the only gift he received as a senator was his cocker spaniel Checkers, who was given to him by a man in Texas after hearing Nixon's wife, Pat, say in a radio interview that her children would like to have a dog. In his remarks, Nixon commented that his children loved the dog, and "regardless of what they say about it, we're gonna keep it." In what the public perceived to be a humanistic moment of candor, they voiced their support for the vice presidential candidate, who was swept into office in 1952 alongside Republican presidential candidate Dwight D. Eisenhower.

What were the circumstances of Vice President **Spiro Agnew's resignation**?

Although the Watergate scandal would forever tarnish the administration of Richard Nixon, Vice President Spiro Agnew (who was not involved in Watergate) did not escape his own set of federal accusations and charges. In August 1973, federal prosecutors alleged that Agnew received illegal payment, or kickbacks, from contractors who wished to do business with the state of Maryland during his tenure as Baltimore County executive from 1963 to 1967 and as governor of the state from 1967 to 1969. Prosecutors also charged that he continued to accept bribes as vice president. In order to avoid criminal persecution, in October 1973 Agnew resigned from the office of vice president, becoming the second vice president in America's history to do so. Pleading "no contest" to charges of tax fraud (Agnew did not report income he received in 1967, whether it was in the form of legitimate political contributions or not), Agnew was fined and placed on probation. In his 1980 book, *Go Quietly ... Or Else,* Agnew continued to plead his innocence, claiming he resigned in order to avoid confrontation with White House chief of staff Alexander Haig.

What was the **Watergate scandal**?

Watergate was the most far-reaching presidential scandal to take place since the Harding administration's Teapot Dome scandal. The Watergate scandal generally refers to the events that occurred in the administration of Richard Nixon between 1972 and 1974. It began with the connection of five members of Nixon's Committee to Reelect the President (CREEP) with a burglary at the Democratic National Committee headquarters at the Watergate Complex in Washington, D.C., and ended with the resignation of President Nixon. In between, Nixon and key staff repeatedly denied knowledge of the burglary plan and attempted to cover up their involvement.

In October 1972, the *Washington Post* reported that FBI agents established that the Watergate break-in stemmed from a massive campaign of political spying and sabotage conducted on behalf of the Nixon reelection campaign. Although initial allegations came through the publication of *Washington Post* articles written by reporters

Bob Woodward and Carl Bernstein, government investigations started in February 1973 when the Senate established a committee (called the Select Committee on Presidential Campaign Activities) to investigate. During the investigation, it was revealed to the committee in testimony that Nixon had an audio taping system installed in the White House to record his daily conversations for posterity. Seeking to discover whether the tapes implicated the president in an attempt to cover up the scandal, the committee and a special prosecutor demanded access to the tapes. Claiming executive privilege, Nixon withheld these tapes until October 1973, at which time he turned over a few of the tapes. In May 1974, the House Judiciary Committee began impeachment hearings, and the Supreme Court ordered Nixon to release more tapes, one of which (referred to as the "Smoking Gun" conversation) clearly implicated Nixon in the cover-up. After the release of these tapes, it became clear that President Nixon would be impeached by the House and convicted in the Senate trials.

After becoming the first president to resign, Richard Nixon bids farewell to his staff members outside the White House before boarding a helicopter on August 9, 1974. *AP/Wide World Photos.*

Although President Nixon resigned in August 1974 under the threat of impeachment and didn't serve any jail time, twenty-five of Nixon's aides served prison sentences as a result of their participation in the Watergate cover-up. Key aides found guilty in the Watergate scandal included White House counsel John Dean; Charles ("Chuck") Colson, special presidential counsel; chief domestic affairs adviser John Ehrlichman; H. R. "Bob" Haldeman, Nixon's chief of staff; White House assistant and CREEP counsel G. Gordon Liddy; and Attorney General and CREEP director John Mitchell.

What was the **"Saturday Night Massacre"**?

On October 20, 1973, at the height of the Watergate scandal, an event called the "Saturday Night Massacre" took place at the hands of sitting president Richard Nixon. He ordered Attorney General Elliot Richardson to fire Watergate special prosecutor Archibald Cox. Cox had denied President Nixon's request that instead of turning over recorded conversations he accept summarizations of the Watergate tapes. Rather than execute this order, Richardson resigned his position from the Justice Department in protest. When Assistant Attorney General William Ruckelshaus refused to comply with President Nixon's request, Nixon fired him, although Ruckelshaus had already written a letter of resignation. The order to fire Cox was ultimately carried out by Solicitor General Robert Bork, but much damage had been done. In the immediate aftermath of the event, Richardson and Ruckelshaus held a live, televised press conference in which Richardson declared, "At stake, in the final analysis, is the very integrity of the governmental processes I came to the Department of Justice to help restore."

Congress perceived the act of firing Cox as a blatant abuse of presidential power. In the weeks that followed the Saturday Night Massacre, even as the president agreed to turn over the tapes, members of Congress increasingly indicated they would support impeachment against President Nixon. Although Nixon defended his actions in a November press conference—during which he insisted, "I have never obstructed justice" and "I'm not a crook!"—there were cries for his resignation. As a result of the Watergate scandal, the Ethics in Government Act was passed in 1978. The act established the Office of Independent Counsel, an independent, special prosecutor who has the authority to investigate alleged crimes and impeachable conduct committed by select government officials.

What was the **backlash of Watergate toward the office of the president**?

After the Watergate scandal and President Nixon's resignation, many people simply did not trust the presidency. Every component of the executive office was turned inside out, from the abuse of national security and executive privilege to the misuse of large campaign donations. The willingness of a president and his aides to use respected government agencies like the Federal Bureau of Investigation, the Internal Revenue Service, and the Central Intelligence Agency in unlawful and unethical ways against their "enemies" was an exploitation many Americans could not accept. As a result, the public cited great disillusionment with the national government in general, and the presidential office in particular.

What was **"Billygate"**?

President Jimmy Carter's brother, Billy, was widely viewed by the press and the public as a fun-loving, average American. However, by 1979, Billy's antics, like beer-drinking and carrying on in public, were highlighted by the press, who took every opportunity to expose the shenanigans of President Carter's kid brother. National headlines claimed that Billy violated a federal statute by accepting a $220,000 loan from the Libyan government—considered terrorists by the U.S. government. Billy had accepted the funds as a portion of a fee owed to him for helping broker the sale of Libyan crude oil to the Charter Oil Company of Florida. However, Billy had not registered as an agent of a foreign power, which a 1933 federal law required of someone serving as a liaison for a foreign firm. Congress investigated the matter and their suspicion that Billy was acting as an agent of the Libyan government, a scandal dubbed "Billygate" by the press. Although no evidence surfaced that the Carter administration had done anything illegal, the investigation exposed the federal government's recent ties to the Libyan government, including their discussions to possibly secure Libyan assistance with the freeing of American hostages held in Iran. Further, President Carter came under fire himself, as the press questioned whether the president had shown a lack of judgment in not restraining his brother's relationship with the Libyans.

What was the **Iran-Contra Affair**?

In October and November 1986, two related secret U.S. government operations were publicly exposed, which ended up implicating Reagan administration officials in illegal activities.

One involved U.S. assistance of military activities of Nicaraguan Contra rebels from 1985 to 1986; the other involved the sale of U.S. arms to Iran (which was at war with its neighbor Iraq) in violation of U.S. policy and United Nations sanctions. Reagan administration officials admitted that some of the proceeds from the sale of U.S. arms to Iran had been diverted to the Contras. The sale of the arms to Iran was intended to help secure the release of American hostages held in Lebanon by a group with ties to Iran. Proceeds from the arms sales were diverted to support the anticommunist guerrilla war of the Contra rebels fighting to overthrow their government.

The scandal broke when the Lebanese magazine *Ash-Shiraa* reported that the United States had been secretly selling weapons to Iran in exchange for the release of seven American hostages held by pro-Iranian groups in Lebanon. President Ronald Reagan, denying any involvement in the scandal, set up a presidential commission known as the Tower Commission (after its chair, former U.S. senator John Tower of Texas) to investigate. Key in the resulting investigation was Lt. Col. Oliver North, aide to U.S. national security adviser John Poindexter, whose testimony implicated himself, Poindexter, Secretary of Defense Casper Weinberger, and Robert McFarlane, the assistant to the president for national security affairs. Although the Tower Commission found no direct evidence implicating President Reagan, the U.S. Congress issued a report in November 1987 that claimed Reagan carried the "ultimate responsibility" for his aides' actions, and that his administration exhibited "secrecy, deception, and disdain for the law." Although North and Poindexter were convicted, they both avoided serving jail time.

What was the **Whitewater scandal**?

Whitewater is the name of an early scandal that broke during the Clinton administration. Members of the Republican Party accused President Bill Clinton of covering up financial misdealings with regard to his investments dating back to 1978. The accusation centered around a failed savings and loan company operated by Clinton business

President Bill Clinton on January 26, 1998, emphatically denying having an affair with former White House intern Monica Lewinsky. First lady Hillary Clinton stands by his side. *Getty Images.*

associates, James and Susan McDougal, who had questionable business dealings in real estate on the Whitewater River in Arkansas. James McDougal was accused of wrongly using money from his failing savings and loan in the 1980s to benefit the Whitewater venture he had created with the Clintons. The scandal soon centered around the mysterious missing and resurfacing of billing records from Hillary Clinton's Rose Law Firm, which could have revealed Hillary Clinton's legal work for McDougal and implicated her in the business transactions.

Once the charges of a possible cover-up were made, a special prosecutor was assigned, which after a series of events ultimately became Kenneth Starr, a conservative attorney and former federal judge who headed the Whitewater investigation as well as the resulting Paula Jones and Monica Lewinsky sex-scandal investigations. By the end of 1999, no indictment or specific charges of criminal activity by the president or Hillary Clinton had resulted from Whitewater. Fourteen of the Clintons' Arkansas associates were ultimately convicted and imprisoned for their Whitewater associations, including the McDougals and Jim Guy Tucker, Clinton's successor as governor of Arkansas when Clinton resigned after being elected president.

In March 2002, the saga came to an end when the third prosecutor, independent counsel Robert Ray, issued his final report, concluding that investigators lacked insufficient evidence to prove either Bill or Hillary Clinton "knowingly participated in the criminal financial transactions used by McDougal to benefit Whitewater." According to the Associated Press, "the Clintons' lawyer called the five-volume report—the product of a $70 million, six-year investigation—the most expensive exoneration in history." Many political analysts understand that while the case against the Clintons may have ultimately been dismissed, the Whitewater investigation created irreparable damages to the Clinton legacy, including prompting a presidential impeachment and creating bitter divisions between Republicans and Democrats.

How did the **Clinton administration's atmosphere of scandal** reach beyond the office of the president?

Several of Bill Clinton's aides were implicated by the media and questioned before the grand jury in Clinton's Whitewater investigation, and several members of Clinton's cabinet, including Agriculture secretary Mike Espy, Interior secretary Bruce Babbitt, and Energy secretary Hazel O'Leary, were the subjects of their own investigations. In addition, although Clinton and his staff were found guiltless, an investigation into the Democratic Party's 1996 fundraising methods resulted in jail terms for some Democratic Party donors. Even the behavior of Clinton's accusers did not escape the media's watchful eye, as seen in the number of Republican congressmen who found their extramarital affairs the subject of news headlines, including Robert Livingston, who was slated to become Speaker of the House before his scandal erupted. The most talked-about effect of Clinton's follies was the abrupt resignation of Republican Speaker of the House Newt Gingrich. Gingrich resigned after the House lost five Republican seats, and the Senate remained almost unchanged, in the midterm elections of 1998, despite the Clinton administration scandals.

What **scandal broke during the George W. Bush administration**?

In April 2004, as the U.S. military continued to occupy Iraq, an Iraqi prison abuse scandal broke. Discriminating photographs of physical, mental, and sexual abuse at the hands of U.S. soldiers at the Iraqi Abu Ghraib detention facility were aired on *60 Minutes II,* igniting international outcry. Most of the abuses reportedly took place between October and December 2003. As the scandal broke, the Bush administration fought accusations that Secretary of Defense Donald Rumsfeld had authorized the expansion of a secret program that encouraged physical and sexual abuse of prisoners to acquire intelligence information. The Central Intelligence Agency responded to the allegations of prisoner abuse by investigating in early May, as President George W. Bush appeared on an Arab television show to address the scandals. May also saw the first court-martial of a U.S. soldier in connection with Iraqi prisoner mistreatment, as the U.S. federal government scrambled to hold the military accountable. Many people called for Rumsfeld's resignation, and admonished Bush for not doing more to either prevent the abuse or reprimand Rumsfeld. The public and news media also began seriously discussing its desire to see the United States pull out of Iraq, and commented that President Bush's handling of the scandal and the overall war would be key to his reelection in November 2004.

PRESIDENTS AND CONGRESS

NORMAL RELATIONS

What is the relationship between the **executive and legislative branches**?

The framers of the Constitution wanted strong executive and legislative branches. Several key functions are shared: many presidential appointments are subject to the approval of Congress; Congress passes legislation, but the president signs it into law; the presidential administration negotiates treaties, but the treaties are subject to approval by Congress; and Congress declares war, but the president can initiate military action. The president has the power to veto legislation. Congress, in turn, may override a presidential veto with a vote by two-thirds majority of both houses. Congress must approve the executive budget, and Congress has the power to impeach all nonmilitary members of the executive branch, including the president.

What **precedents were established by George Washington** in the relationship between the president and Congress?

Washington took great care to respect the separation of powers between the executive and legislative branches. He did not campaign for or against candidates and did not comment on legislation being debated. Wanting advisors to consult with and to help him, Washington established the cabinet and instituted the power to select executive advisors and remove them if necessary.

Washington believed a presidential veto should be used only if the constitutionality of legislation was in question. Washington vetoed two bills during his two terms in office. The first veto was on apportionment—the number of representatives in Congress for each state. The Constitution called for a common number to apply to all states. Congress passed a measure that took the entire U.S. population of citizens into

BORN TO COMMAND.

OF VETO MEMORY.

HAD I BEEN CONSULTED.

KING ANDREW THE FIRST.

Cartoon depicting President Jackson as King Andrew I. Jackson's veto of the bill passed by Congress to renew the charter of the National Bank brought one of the most bitter political issues of the period. *AP/Wide World Photos.*

account, then apportioned representatives among the states, but also provided an additional member to eight states. After receiving the first veto in U.S. history, Congress dropped its bill in favor of apportioning representatives at "the ratio of one for every thirty-three thousand persons in the respective States."

Washington's other veto concerned a military organization bill that, he argued, would have put light dragoons (infantry that rode horseback) out of service.

What is a **veto** and a **pocket veto**?

When presented with legislation passed by both houses of Congress, the president may sign it into law within the ten-day period prescribed in the Constitution (Article I, Section 7), let it become law without his signature, or veto the bill. All bills and joint resolutions, except those proposing amendments to the Constitution, require the president's approval before they become law. Amendments to the Constitution, which require a two-thirds vote of approval in each chamber, are sent directly to the states for ratification.

If Congress adjourns after sending a bill to the president, the president may withhold his signature. The bill neither becomes law nor is returned to Congress for further action. This practice is known as a "pocket veto." Congress does not have the opportunity or the constitutional authority to override a pocket veto.

President George Bush attempted to use the pocket veto while Congress was on recess but had not adjourned. Instead, since Bush hadn't returned the bills to Congress and the ten-day period for the president to act had elapsed, Congress considered the bills enacted.

Who was the **first president to significantly wield veto power** over Congress?

The first six presidents vetoed a total of ten bills over a span of forty years. Andrew Jackson, the seventh president, vetoed twelve bills during his eight years in office.

Presidential Vetoes

President	Vetoes	Pocket Vetoes	Total	Vetoes Overridden
George Washington	2	0	2	0
John Adams	0	0	0	0
Thomas Jefferson	0	0	0	0
James Madison	5	2	7	0
James Monroe	1	0	1	0
John Quincy Adams	0	0	0	0
Andrew Jackson	5	7	12	0
Martin Van Buren	0	1	1	0
William Henry Harrison	0	0	0	0
John Tyler	6	4	10	1
James K. Polk	2	1	3	0
Zachary Taylor	0	0	0	0
Millard Fillmore	0	0	0	0
Franklin Pierce	9	0	9	5
James Buchanan	4	3	7	0
Abraham Lincoln	2	5	7	0
Andrew Johnson	21	8	29	15
Ulysses S. Grant	45	48	93	4
Rutherford B. Hayes	12	1	13	1
James A. Garfield	0	0	0	0
Chester Alan Arthur	4	8	12	1
Grover Cleveland	304	110	414	2
Benjamin Harrison	19	25	44	1
Grover Cleveland	42	128	170	5
William McKinley	6	36	42	0
Theodore Roosevelt	42	40	82	1
William Howard Taft	30	9	39	1
Woodrow Wilson	33	11	44	6
Warren G. Harding	5	1	6	0
Calvin Coolidge	20	30	50	4
Herbert Hoover	21	16	37	3
Franklin D. Roosevelt	372	263	635	9
Harry S. Truman	180	70	250	12
Dwight D. Eisenhower	73	108	181	2
John F. Kennedy	12	9	21	0
Lyndon B. Johnson	16	14	30	0
Richard Nixon	26	17	43	7
Gerald Ford	48	18	66	12
Jimmy Carter	13	18	31	2
Ronald Reagan	39	39	78	9
George Bush	29	15	44	1
Bill Clinton	36	0	36	2
George W. Bush	0	0	0	0

President John Tyler's vetoes of the tariff bill and another on reestablishing a national bank were considered by Congress to be excessive use of executive power. *Library of Congress.*

Two of Jackson's vetoes were especially noteworthy. His 1830 veto of the Maysville Road bill sent a discouraging message to those in Congress who wanted to use tax money on internal improvement programs. Jackson's bank veto of 1832 left the United States without a national bank. Both of these vetoes reflected Jackson's insistence on limiting the authority and power of the federal government.

When was the **first time Congress overrode a presidential veto**?

In 1842, President John Tyler vetoed a bill to raise tariffs. Congress overrode the veto and began considering impeachment hearings against the president. Tyler's vetoes of the tariff bill and another on reestablishing a national bank were considered by Congress excessive uses of executive power.

Were there presidents who **never used their veto power**?

Yes, seven presidents never vetoed legislation: John Adams, Thomas Jefferson, John Quincy Adams, William Henry Harrison, Zachary Taylor, Millard Fillmore, and James A. Garfield. In addition, George W. Bush did not use his veto power heading into the final months of his 2001–2005 term in office.

Harrison and Garfield served for less than a year, and Taylor served little more than a year. Fillmore served less than three years, while each of the Adamses served only one term. Jefferson is the only two-term president never to have vetoed legislation.

THE PRESIDENT INFLUENCES CONGRESS

Why do **presidents deny congressional requests for information** on the basis of **executive privilege**?

The Constitution makes no mention of executive privilege. Under the constitutional principle of separation of powers, however, presidents have claimed a privilege to resist certain requests for information by Congress and the judiciary branch. In 1796, President George Washington refused a request by the House of Representatives for documents relating to the negotiation of Jay's Treaty (for more information on the treaty, see The President Leads: Foreign Policy—Treaties and Trade). Washington argued that since the Senate alone is responsible for approving treaties, the House had no right to request the material. Washington provided some documents to the Senate.

Executive privilege is recognized by the courts as a practice that ensures presidents can get candid advice in private without fear of it becoming public.

What are some **examples of presidents using executive privilege**?

Andrew Jackson defied the Senate when it demanded to see documents in which the president stated his reasons for withdrawing government assets from the national bank and placing them in state banks. The president informed the Senate that it had no constitutional authority to make such a request.

Grover Cleveland utilized executive privilege to withhold information from Congress. Cleveland's use of executive privilege was most noteworthy because it helped restore power to the presidency in the mid-1880s that had been waning since the mid-1860s, when Congress overrode President Andrew Johnson's veto to pass the Tenure of Office Act. Under the Act, all federal officials whose appointment required Senate confirmation could not be removed by the president without the consent of the Senate.

In 1885, the Republican-dominated Senate wanted to check the power of Cleveland to appoint and remove officials. Cleveland was the first Democrat to be elected president in nearly thirty years. Cleveland refused to supply information on those he removed from federal positions as he trimmed the federal government and weeded out employees whose jobs had been secured as political favors. Cleveland defended the right of the president to withhold from Congress all information of a private or confidential nature and to determine what material was to be classified. When the Senate threatened to block all his appointments, Cleveland rallied public support for his position. In March 1887, the Tenure of Office Act was repealed.

Theodore Roosevelt declined to give to the Senate papers relating to the antitrust case the administration was developing against U.S. Steel. The Senate targeted an administration official in the Justice Department and threatened him with a contempt charge and jail if he refused to turn over documents. Roosevelt had the documents transferred to the White House, assumed responsibility for them and stated, "The only way the Senate or the committee can get those papers now is through my impeachment."

During the 1950s, President Dwight D. Eisenhower resisted demands by U.S. senator Joseph McCarthy of Wisconsin and others for testimony and personnel records of federal officials. Eisenhower insisted, according to Stephen E. Ambrose (in *Eisenhower: Soldier and President,* 1991) that "it is not in the public interest that *any* ... conversations or communications, or *any* documents or reproductions" relating to advice from "any executive branch official whatsoever be disclosed." The administration denied over forty Congressional requests.

Richard Nixon used executive privilege as a stonewalling technique as the Senate Watergate Committee investigation deepened. He claimed executive privilege to prevent aides from testifying and to withhold tapes he made of his White House conversations. When Watergate special prosecutor Leon Jaworski attempted to follow up on a federal subpoena for specific tapes, Nixon again refused, and the legal challenge was ultimately decided by the Supreme Court (see Presidents and the Judiciary—The Judiciary Influences the Presidency). Bill Clinton also invoked executive privilege in a case that was decided by the Supreme Court (see the question on *Clinton v. Jones* in Presidents and the Judiciary—The Judiciary Influences the Presidency).

During the George W. Bush administration, the question of executive privilege arose when Comptroller General David Walker, head of the nonpartisan Government Accounting Office, announced he would sue Vice President Dick Cheney to obtain information about the National Energy Policy Development Group Cheney had chaired. Since the GAO is an arm of Congress, the administration contended that its efforts to obtain information about discussions within the executive branch violated the constitutional principle of separation of powers.

Bush claimed executive privilege to avoid having his national security adviser, Condoleezza Rice, testify before the National Commission on Terrorist Attacks Upon the United States (also known as the 9/11 Commission), citing separation of the executive and legislative branches of government. After public and political pressure, Bush relented.

The first time Bush used executive privilege was to keep Congress from seeing documents of prosecutors' decision-making in federal cases ranging from a decades-old Boston murder to a Clinton-era fund-raising probe.

Which presidents faced **little congressional opposition**?

Thomas Jefferson was the leader of the Democratic-Republicans, which became the dominant party in the 1800 election, winning the presidency and both houses of Congress. The opposing Federalist Party never recuperated and faded shortly after the War of 1812. James Monroe, the first president elected after the War of 1812, enjoyed a period when the Democratic-Republicans were the only powerful national party.

Jefferson was the first president to make recommendations to Congress on legislation. He interacted with congressmen on a regular basis by inviting selected members to dinner parties, sometimes holding as many as three dinners per week while Congress was in session. Discussion of politics was forbidden, but good food and camaraderie was helpful in shoring up support.

Monroe faced little opposition during his first term. He invited congressmen to call on him at the Executive Mansion (White House) and Congress was dependent on the executive branch for information and data, having little in staff and services in those days. The growing power of such congressmen as Henry Clay of Kentucky during Monroe's administration helped extend the influence of Congress. Monroe vetoed a bill on internal improvements that was championed by Clay, believing a Constitutional Amendment was necessary to authorize Congress to use public funds for internal improvements. But it was Clay who engineered the Missouri Compromise (1820), a major federal decision made by Congress and dutifully signed into law by the President because he found no constitutionally questionable grounds on which to object.

How did **Andrew Jackson create congressional coattails** in the election of 1832?

Democrat Jackson and congressional members of the Whig Party clashed in 1832 after Jackson vetoed a bill that would have rechartered the National Bank for another twenty years. Whigs viewed Jackson as having taken on the power of a monarch and took their case to the people in the 1832 election. Jackson welcomed the challenge. His popular appeal helped Democrats maintain control of Congress, as Jackson brushed away his Whig opponent Henry Clay, 219 electoral votes to 49.

Why was **James K. Polk** so successful in his early **relations with Congress**?

As the first dark-horse candidate to become president, Polk rode into the White House on a wave of popular support for annexation of Texas and limited federal influence, in the tradition of Andrew Jackson. Polk had been a force of congressional opposition to John Quincy Adams beginning in 1825 and a close congressional ally for Andrew Jackson when he took office in 1829. During the 1830s, Polk was Speaker of the House. As president, Polk approached his dealings with Congress with a combination of forcefulness and savvy, and he had a Democratic majority behind him. Finally, Polk had a clear and determined agenda: 1) reestablish an independent treasury system; 2) lower tariffs; 3) settle the Oregon Territory dispute with Great Britain; and 4) acquire California from Mexico.

The first two agenda items were quickly enacted, and there was strong popular support for assuming control over the Oregon territory. The slogan "54°40' or Fight!," which referred to the northernmost boundary of Oregon territory, had been a campaign slogan for Polk and the expansionist-minded Democratic Party, and Polk reasserted the sentiment in his inaugural address by insisting that the United States was entitled to the whole of Oregon Country. Great Britain, which shared control of the region with the United States, insisted on sovereignty over present-day British Columbia and south to the Columbia River in present-day Washington (south of 49° latitude) to the Pacific Ocean. Polk offered to use the 49° line, which already served as the boundary between the United States and Canada east of the Rockies, to continue from the Rockies west to the Pacific. After a year, the two nations officially agreed on June 6, 1846, to a treaty with the boundary set at 49°. The Senate approved the treaty on June 12, 1846.

During the final two years of his administration, Polk faced a more difficult time with Congress, especially as he took steps for war with Mexico. While he lost some support over the Mexican War (1846–1848), Polk did achieve the fourth goal of his presidential agenda—obtaining California from Mexico—by pursuing and winning the war.

How did **Millard Fillmore's support for Congress contribute to his failure to be elected president**?

Fillmore had been a powerful, four-term congressman from New York before becoming Zachary Taylor's vice president. In his role as president of the Senate, Fillmore attended Congress and listened to debate over the Compromise of 1850. Taylor intended to veto any legislation that permitted the expansion of slavery, but Fillmore informed him that if he was to cast the tie-breaking vote in the Senate, he would vote in favor of the Compromise.

Taylor died while in office in 1850, and Fillmore assumed the presidency. Upon becoming president, Fillmore asked for and received the resignations of Taylor's cabinet and selected his own. Fillmore and his cabinet announced their support for the Compromise and helped to ensure passage of its various components, including the Fugitive Slave Law.

Fillmore hoped the legislation would be a final statement on slavery as an issue for the states, not the federal government. He was wrong. The nation, and Fillmore's Whig Party, grew more divisive over slavery. Fillmore was passed over as the Whig Party's nominee for president in 1852.

Why did **Abraham Lincoln face few congressional challenges** to his actions as commander in chief?

The Civil War began in April 1861 and the new session of Congress did not begin until July. Lincoln was able to take unprecedented powers in the meantime, some of which are considered unconstitutional. When Congress opened its session, it had few options other than to support the president in a war already underway. Under his "war power," Lincoln had expanded the armed forces, drew funds from the Treasury that had not been appropriated by Congress, and suspended the writ of *habeas corpus* (a judicial mandate to a prison official to bring an inmate to the court to determine whether or not the inmate is imprisoned lawfully and should remain or be released from custody). According to Article I, Section 9, Clause 2, of the U.S. Constitution, "The Privilege of the Writ of Habeas Corpus shall not be suspended, unless when in Cases of Rebellion or Invasion the public Safety may require it." This power is given to Congress by the Constitution, not the president.

The Republican-dominated Congress passed several nonmilitary legislative measures that Lincoln supported and that had been blocked for years by congressmen from states that seceded from the Union. Together, the president and Congress passed the Homestead Act (opening up Western lands free for settlement), the Land-Grant College Act, and the Pacific Railroad Act, among others.

What **battles did Rutherford B. Hayes win over Congress**?

Hayes pressed for much needed civil service reform upon taking office. Many administrations since the late 1820s had filled government positions with men based primarily on their political loyalty. Following the many scandals of the Ulysses S. Grant administration that preceded Hayes's, civil service reform was a popular cause. However, Hayes's own Republican Party was dominated by two political machines, the Stalwarts, based in New York, and the Half-Breeds, a more New England–based faction. Knowing he had little chance to have reform passed by Congress, Hayes issued an executive order in June 1877 forbidding federal civil servants to take an active part in politics.

Hayes went after the biggest political machine, the Stalwarts, who used the New York Customhouse as a base of operations. The Customhouse collected huge amounts of tax money. An investigation revealed the Customhouse was overstaffed, and many of the employees did little work. Hayes was successful in removing Customhouse officials, including Chester Alan Arthur, who would later become president.

After Democrats won control of the House of Representatives in the mid-term election of 1878, they attempted to attach riders (unrelated measures attached to legislation) to fund projects in their district Hayes would otherwise veto. Hayes vetoed the measures. Congress was eventually forced to drop riders attached to army appropriation bills.

How did **Chester Alan Arthur** use public sentiment to **force Congress to act on stalled legislation**?

When James A. Garfield succeeded Rutherford B. Hayes as president, he immediately introduced reforms to curtail the power of political machines. After Garfield was assassinated in the summer of 1881, his first year in office, Vice President Arthur became president. Arthur, who himself had benefitted from a political machine, continued Garfield's initiative, but Congress ignored him. To pressure Congress, Arthur turned to the public, which had demanded reforms, and aligned himself with a grassroots agency called the National Civil Service Reform League. Arthur drafted legislation that was sponsored by U.S. senator George Pendleton of Ohio. The momentous Pendleton Civil Service Reform Act was passed by Congress and signed into law by Arthur in 1883. The act established the Civil Service Commission to oversee federal appointments, administer competency tests, and ensure that civil service employees do not actively participate in partisan efforts.

Why did **Benjamin Harrison lose a reelection bid** despite having an **excellent record with Congress**?

Harrison was an effective but uninspiring leader whose relatively quiet presidency was facing increasing labor unrest and an economic downturn in an election year. He had been outpolled in the 1888 election, but he achieved an electoral college victory by taking most of the large states.

During his administration, Harrison worked effectively with Congress to pass the Sherman Antitrust Act, which outlawed trusts and monopolies that hindered trade. The Sherman Silver Purchase Act increased the money supply, a policy favored by small farmers and urban laborers. The McKinley Tariff Act set tariffs at record highs to protect American manufacturers during a period of rapid industrialization. The Dependent Pension Act benefitted Civil War veterans, even though the system was abused by some and nearly doubled the cost of the pensions for the government.

Voters in 1892 who preferred a tighter monetary policy turned to Grover Cleveland (who had lost to Harrison four years earlier), while Harrison competed with Populist Party candidate James B. Weaver for the farm and labor vote.

How did **Woodrow Wilson and Congress work together effectively**?

During the campaign of 1912, Wilson had promised tariff reform as one of the first acts he would pursue if elected president. Shortly after he was inaugurated, Wilson called a special session of Congress to pass tariff reform. A reform bill stalled in the Senate and it was threatened with significant changes or defeat. Wilson responded by going public and charging that special business and industry interests were pressuring senators to defeat the legislation. Opposition quickly faded, and the Underwood Act passed the Senate and was signed into law by Wilson.

Wilson continued to press Congress, especially the Democratic majority, with his agenda, called the New Freedom. In short order, Congress passed a bill creating the Federal Reserve Board, the Clayton Antitrust Act, the Federal Trade Commission (FTC) Act, and the first peacetime income tax in the nation's history.

The early success Wilson enjoyed was not long lasting. Foreign policy issues with Mexico and the outbreak of World War I took attention away from domestic policies, and the Democratic majority Wilson worked with during his first two years gradually faded.

How did the **Hoover administration fare with Congress** before and after the stock market crash of 1929?

Herbert Hoover took office at a time of sustained prosperity and enjoyed large Republican majorities in Congress. Hoover did not believe in large government programs, but he worked effectively with Congress to pass the Agricultural Marketing Act that

"Give 'em Hell, Harry!"

Harry S. Truman borrowed a campaign theme from a remark shouted by a supporter at a campaign rally, where Truman was railing against the "Do-nothing Eightieth Congress." The supporter yelled out, "Give 'em hell, Harry!" Truman would say later, "Well, I never gave anybody hell—I just told the truth on those fellows and they thought it was hell."

established the Federal Farm Board to ensure crop prices remained at stable rates and to provide loans for agricultural cooperatives. Hoover also supported the Hawley-Smoot Tariff, the highest peacetime tariff in the nation's history. The midterm election of 1930 occurred after the stock market crash of 1929 and the onset of the Great Depression. Voters responded by turning a Democratic minority in the House of Representatives into a majority, and the Republican majority in the Senate was reduced to a margin of one. Hoover worked sparingly with Congress. Rather than support federal relief and work programs, Hoover urged state and local governments to expand public works projects.

How was **Franklin D. Roosevelt able to win congressional support** during his **first hundred days** in office?

Roosevelt was elected on his promise of an aggressive federal approach to combat the economic crisis of the Great Depression. Beginning with a rousing inaugural address in which he assured Americans that "the only thing we have to fear is fear itself—nameless, unreasoning, unjustified terror," Roosevelt called a special session of Congress and began working with them. He showed flexibility, used his executive powers to secure congressional cooperation, and rallied support from the people through press conferences, speeches, and fireside chats over the radio.

How did **Harry S. Truman** make his case to the public about what he called a **"do-nothing Congress?"**

During 1948, an election year, Truman made what he called the "Do-nothing Eightieth Congress" an issue in the campaign. He called Congress into an emergency summer session to address such domestic issues as inflation and foreign crises related to the Cold War. Congress was not able to accomplish much. Truman cited the lack of action by Congress in his "Give 'em hell" speeches and in informal chats with voters who attended his rallies. Truman successfully fought off a challenge from within his own party and defeated the favored Republican candidate, New York governor Thomas Dewey, in a surprising election upset.

How did **Lyndon B. Johnson energize Congress** to act on sweeping and historic legislation?

Congress had been slow to act on programs sponsored by the John F. Kennedy administration. Following Kennedy's assassination in 1963, Lyndon B. Johnson, Kennedy's successor, pushed through Congress and signed into law the Tax Reduction Act and the Civil Rights Act in 1964. Preparatory work by the Kennedy administration and the national mood to honor him following his death helped make Congress more receptive to the programs. The civil rights movement, following the 1963 March on Washington, had become a more vocal presence and helped pressure passage of the Civil Rights Act. Johnson's excellent political skills, honed over twenty years as a powerful congressman, were a decisive factor as he personally and publicly lobbied Congress to pass the measures.

Johnson won the presidency in a landslide in 1964, and Democrats won firm majorities in both houses of Congress (67–33 in the Senate, 295–140 in the House). Johnson had plenty of programs for Congress to act upon, having introduced his vision of the Great Society during the 1964 campaign. Johnson asked for and received legislation to improve the nation's cities, environment, educational system, and quality of life (a full list of Great Society programs appears in The President Leads: Domestic Issues—Social Programs and Civil Rights). The amount of social and economic legislation passed in 1965 and 1966 rivaled that of the New Deal of Franklin D. Roosevelt during the Great Depression.

Why was **Ronald Reagan more successful with Congress than his immediate predecessors**?

Reagan won election in 1980 in a landslide against an incumbent president, Jimmy Carter, and on his coattails came the first Republican majority in the Senate since 1954. Republicans made gains in the House of Representatives as well. Reagan's conservative policies had enough support from Southern Democrats to help push through legislation he wanted. Reducing the growth of the national government, moving federal programs to the states, making massive budget cuts to trim expenditures, and expanding defense spending proved to be popular causes for many in Congress. Reagan effectively pressured Congress for budget cuts of $39 billion and for passage of a 25 percent tax cut. None of the three presidents who preceded Reagan—Richard Nixon, Gerald Ford, and Jimmy Carter—enjoyed an effective relationship with Congress. Only Carter enjoyed a majority in Congress from his own party, but Carter's relationship with Congress started slowly and never really developed momentum. Reagan, on the other hand, counted on immediate support from his party, and Republicans were ready to back the popular president.

What was **George W. Bush's relationship with Congress**?

Republican George W. Bush began his presidency with a majority of his party in the House and an evenly split Senate. After the 2002 midterm elections, he would enjoy a

Republican majority in the Senate as well. Congress supported a massive tax cut proposed by Bush and generally showed little opposition to his policies. Following the terrorist attacks on September 11, 2001, Congress gave Bush sweeping war powers. Bush did not veto legislation during the first three-and-a-half years of his presidency.

What **historical success occurred in the midterm elections of 2002**?

In November 2002, Republicans regained control of the Senate, fifty-one to forty-eight, with one independent. It was the first time the party holding the White House took control of the Senate in a midterm popular election since voters began directly electing senators in 1914. Before then, senators were elected by state legislatures.

CONGRESS V. PRESIDENT

Why did **James Madison face difficulties with a Congress** dominated by his own party?

Democratic-Republicans dominated the American political scene during the first two-and-a-half decades of the nineteenth century. The party initially attracted a variety of people from the different regions of the country united in their belief in limited power for the federal government. They contrasted with Federalists, who supported a strong federal government. However, by 1810, the debate over the role and powers of the federal government was increasing waged within the Democratic-Republican party.

Madison's presidency began in 1809 after the failed embargo against trade with England and France imposed by Thomas Jefferson as an effort to pressure those nations to stop interfering with American ships at sea. The midterm election of 1810 brought to Congress "war hawks" Henry Clay of Kentucky and John C. Calhoun of South Carolina who wanted a more aggressive policy against Great Britain. When Britain continued to violate American neutrality at sea and was accused of helping incite Native American uprisings in what was then the Northwest (Ohio, Indiana, Illinois, and Michigan), Madison began siding with the war hawks and asked Congress to declare war in 1812.

The war was opposed by some Democratic-Republicans in Congress as well as in New England. Congress failed to fund the war effort with taxes and did not increase the navy. A group of antiwar Democratic-Republicans senators called themselves the Invincibles and found an ally with Madison's secretary of state, Robert Smith. Madison fired Smith and replaced him with James Monroe, who quickly helped to rally the American war effort (for more information on the War of 1812, see The President Leads: Commander in Chief—Military Action).

Congress challenged Madison with legislation he disliked. Madison had planned to use the veto sparingly, like his predecessors: George Washington used the veto only twice, and John Adams and Thomas Jefferson did not use the veto at all. In contrast, Madison would end up vetoing seven bills during his presidency. Congress passed bills that provided land to the Salem Meeting House Baptists in the Mississippi Territory and the incorporation of an Episcopal church in Alexandria, Virginia. In his veto messages, Madison cited the First Amendment, which prohibits the government establishment of religion, in the Mississippi case, and argued the Episcopal church case not only violated the First Amendment but actually provided a government sanction for the church to take a leading role in education and caring for the poor. These functions were a "public and civic duty," according to Madison.

When the War of 1812 ended in early 1815, Madison's relations with Congress improved considerably. His last two years in office were the best of his two terms.

Which other presidents had **difficulties with congressional majorities of their own party**?

John Tyler succeeded to the presidency following the death of William Henry Harrison and challenged the agenda of his own Whig Party. Tyler believed in limited government and states' rights, while the Whig Party pursued policies that expanded the role of the federal government. Tyler was kicked out of the Whig Party during his presidency.

Abraham Lincoln and a Republican Congress disagreed about plans for readmitting seceded states and dealing with members of the Confederacy as the Union began dominating the Civil War. Following Lincoln's assassination shortly after the Confederate surrender, Congress assumed control of Reconstruction.

Theodore Roosevelt's progressive views on social and economic reform alarmed many of his fellow Republicans in Congress. Roosevelt took great pains to explain to the public that his economic reforms and trust-busting activities were not antibusiness. Harry S. Truman faced opposition from congressional Democrats of the South over his pursuit of civil rights legislation and uses of executive orders, including one that desegregated the military.

Dwight D. Eisenhower successfully battled congressional Republicans over the "Bricker Amendment," a proposal by U.S. senator John Bricker of Ohio to place limits on the ability of presidents to negotiate treaties. Eisenhower also faced challenges as he attempted to implement foreign policy measures to combat communism. U.S. Senate majority leader Robert Taft of Ohio advocated more isolationist policies. John F. Kennedy achieved little in his domestic policy plans, especially in civil rights legislation and tax reduction. A coalition of Southern Democratic congressmen regularly joined Republicans to oppose Kennedy's domestic initiatives.

Jimmy Carter was more moderate than the Democratic majority in Congress during his presidency and vetoed several bills he considered wasteful spending. The Democratic Congress overrode two of Carter's vetoes. George Bush exerted influence over Congress by vetoing 44 pieces of legislation. However, he began losing support from his own party when he agreed to end a budget showdown with Congress in 1990 by accepting a deal that included new taxes. He had campaigned in 1988 with the famous pledge, "Read my lips; no new taxes."

Why was **John Quincy Adams** the first president to face a **hostile Congress**?

Adams won the disputed election of 1824, which splintered the Democratic-Republican Party into two factions: those who believed in enlarging the federal government to direct internal improvement projects backed Adams and his secretary of state, Henry Clay; and those who believed in limiting the federal government and in states' rights backed Andrew Jackson, who would become head of the new Democratic Party in 1828. When Adams took office in 1825, Jackson supporters formed the majority in the Senate and united to thwart virtually all legislation supported by Adams. Regarded as an abolitionist, Adams was viewed with suspicion by congressmen from slave states. After the midterm election of 1826, Adams became the first president to face opposition majorities in both houses of Congress.

Cartoon by John R. Fischetti in 1953 showing President Dwight D. Eisenhower and the GOP elephant playing golf, the President's favorite sport. "This hole's easy—wait'll y'see the rest of the course" refers to the difficulties Eisenhower was having with Congress in the early days of his presidency. *Library of Congress.*

Why did **Congress consider impeaching John Tyler**?

John Tyler left the Democratic Party for the Whig Party in 1836 to protest the immense power wielded by President Andrew Jackson, but he continued to have more in common with the states' rights and limited government approach of Jacksonian Democrats than the more national-minded Whigs. Still, he was added to the Whig ticket as a vice presidential candidate because of his appeal to Southern voters as a Virginian. Tyler became vice president when William Henry Harrison was inaugurated in 1841, then succeeded to the presidency when Harrison died less than a month later. Whigs believed Tyler would follow the party's congressional leadership and platform.

Tyler proved to be more independent. He vetoed two bills to create a new national bank. Following the second veto, his cabinet resigned with the exception of Secretary of State Daniel Webster. When Tyler quickly appointed a new cabinet, Whigs kicked him out of the party. In 1842, Tyler vetoed a tariff bill. Whigs in Congress were outraged. They began exploring grounds for impeaching the president, and they overrode Tyler's veto—the first time Congress had ever overridden a presidential veto. The House adopted a resolution charging him with offenses justifying impeachment. However, the resolution to begin impeachment hearings failed 127 to 83.

Which presidents faced **significant sectional opposition from Congress**?

Sectional differences were common beginning with the birth of the nation, but they did not interfere significantly with presidential policies until the 1820s when John Quincy Adams was consistently thwarted by supporters of Andrew Jackson, who was a favorite in states outside the northeast. But sectional opposition was most significant during the 1850s with divisiveness over slavery. Franklin Pierce and James Buchanan, presidents from Northern states, supported states' rights and sincerely believed that the Compromise of 1850 offered a final statement on slavery. "I fervently hope," said Pierce in his inaugural address, "that the question [of slavery] is at rest, and that no sectional or ambitious or fanatical excitement may again threaten the durability of our institutions or obscure the light of our prosperity."

When Pierce took office in 1853, there was already fierce reaction in the North against the Compromise of 1850. The Kansas-Nebraska Bill of 1854, which proposed to create the new territories of Kansas and Nebraska and allow their settlers to decide for themselves whether to permit slavery, was furiously debated in Congress. Pierce experienced delays in winning approval for several appointments and for approval of the Gadsden Treaty, a land purchase of over seventy-five thousand square miles that filled out much of the southernmost portion of present-day New Mexico and Arizona that had not been part of the treaty that ended the Mexican War.

James Buchanan, who succeeded Pierce, declared in his inaugural address that "the great object of my administration will be to arrest … the agitation of the slavery question at the North and to destroy sectional parties." But Buchanan was immediately confronted with the problem of the territory of Kansas, where two governments existed, the proslavery Lecompton organization and an antislavery Topeka faction. Buchanan asked Congress to approve the Lecompton constitution, allow Kansas to enter as a slave state, and then allow citizens to make a new constitution if they desired. The measure was rejected by Congress, and statehood for Kansas did not occur until the very end of Buchanan's presidency. The midterm elections of 1858 further eroded Buchanan's power, as antislavery Republicans came to power in Congress.

Following Republican Abraham Lincoln's election to president in 1860, South Carolina seceded from the Union on December 20, 1860. Buchanan hoped to save the union by calling for a constitutional convention, but Congress refused to act on that proposal and others by the lame duck Buchanan.

Following the Civil War, President Andrew Johnson was essentially overwhelmed by northern Republicans in Congress (see below). During the twentieth-century, Presidents Franklin D. Roosevelt and Harry S. Truman contended with a Southern wing in their Democratic party that was opposed to civil rights legislation. Roosevelt took little action in civil rights during his first two terms out of concern he might lose key support from Southern congressmen for his New Deal program. Truman's pursuit of civil rights improvements through executive order and legislation angered the Southern wing of his party, leading to the creation of a faction called Dixiecrats. The Dixiecrats ran their own candidate, South Carolina governor Strom Thurmond, against Truman in the 1948 presidential election.

How did **Congress differ with Abraham Lincoln over Reconstruction**?

In December 1863, President Lincoln proposed a comprehensive plan for reconstructing the union by bringing back states that had seceded. Called the Ten Percent Plan, the policy included pardon and amnesty to Confederates who would swear loyalty to the Union and proposed to return control of local governments to the civil authorities when 10 percent of the 1860 voting population participated in elections. Emancipation of slaves and guarantees of civil rights and voting rights for African Americans were proposed in the program. Governments operating under the Ten Percent Plan were soon established in Louisiana and Arkansas and petitioned Congress for readmission.

Congress objected to the plan, in part because many Republicans wanted more stringent rules for readmission and believed Congress should set the terms for Reconstruction. Congress passed the Wade-Davis bill (sponsored by U.S. senators Benjamin F. Wade of Ohio and U.S. representative Henry W. Davis of Maryland), which provided for the appointment of provisional military governors in the seceded states. When a majority of a state's white citizens swore allegiance to the Union, a constitutional convention could be called. Each state's constitution was to be required to abolish slavery and disqualify Confederate officials from voting or holding office.

Disagreeing especially with the final two items, President Lincoln pocket-vetoed the bill. He believed states should voluntarily abolish slavery and viewed the disqualification of Confederate officials as too harsh. When Congress reassembled in December 1864, just after Lincoln was reelected, it pressured Lincoln to drop his support to

JOHNSON AS KING SUPPORTED BY SEWARD AND WELLES. IN THE DISTANCE
HENRY WARD BEECHER, WENDELL PHILLIPS, CHARLES SUMNER, AND OTHER
ABOLITIONISTS ARE FORMED IN LINE FOR EXECUTION
(From a cartoon by Thomas Nast; published in *Harper's Weekly*, November 3, 1866)

Cartoon by Thomas Nast published in *Harper's Weekly* (November 3, 1866) shows President Andrew Johnson as a king supported by his secretary of state, William Seward. Lined up in the background are former congressional abolitionists awaiting execution. The cartoon satirizes Johnson's version of Reconstruction, which did not include civil rights protection for ex-slaves. *Getty Images.*

readmit Louisiana. Reconstruction policy was still being debated when the Civil War ended in April 1865 and Lincoln was assassinated.

How did **Congress differ with Andrew Johnson over Reconstruction**?

Johnson believed in limited federal government and wanted to reestablish state governments in the South as quickly as possible. After assuming the presidency in April 1865 when Lincoln was assassinated, Johnson modified Lincoln's Ten Percent Plan (see above) to speed up development of new state constitutions. He required that states ratify the Thirteenth Amendment (which includes the abolishment of slavery), repudiate Confederate debts, and nullify secession ordinances. When states met those conditions, Johnson, as the temporary wartime authority, would recognize their restoration to the Union. Congress was not in session when Johnson proposed his plan and states began meeting the obligation.

When Congress returned in December 1865, the battle between the executive and legislative branches over Reconstruction was renewed.

Northerners were concerned about protecting the basic rights of citizenship of freedmen. Republican majorities refused to agree that the Southern states were ready to assume their rights and did not seat the Southern congressional representatives from states that met the obligations of Johnson's program. Johnson believed that Congress was overstepping its bounds. He vetoed civil rights legislation and refused to

> ## In the Office, 24/7
>
> Edwin Stanton won distinction as secretary of war under Abraham Lincoln for helping administer the Union war effort. He had a less than distinguished history under Andrew Johnson, Lincoln's successor. Johnson tried to remove Stanton from his position, but Stanton refused. He barricaded himself in his office in the War Department building. A guard was posted to protect him and to ensure department records were not seized. Stanton remained there for several weeks, until the outcome of Johnson's impeachment trial in the Senate.

endorse a new constitutional amendment granting African Americans rights of citizenship. The remainder of Johnson's term was acrimonious. Congress succeeded in controlling Reconstruction and passing laws that limited presidential authority, including the Tenure of Office Act.

What was the **Tenure of Office Act**?

The Tenure of Office Act was one of several examples of Congress assuming power over the presidency during the administration of Andrew Johnson. Passed in 1867 by Congress over Johnson's veto, the Tenure of Office Act concerned federal officials appointed by the President that required confirmation by the Senate. Under the Tenure of Office Act, such officials could not be removed from their position by the president without the consent of the Senate. If the Senate was not in session, the president could suspend an official, but once the Senate reconvened it had to approve the removal or the official would have to be reinstated by the president.

The Tenure of Office Act was tested by Johnson during the summer of 1867, when Congress was not in session. Johnson's secretary of war, Edwin Stanton, was a confidante to Republicans in Congress who wanted a harsher Reconstruction program toward the South following the Civil War than what Johnson was pursuing. The congressional group is known historically as the Radical Republicans. Johnson wanted to remove Stanton, and he found a potential loophole in the Tenure of Office Act: Stanton was an appointee of Abraham Lincoln's and had remained in the cabinet following Lincoln's death and Johnson's succession to the presidency.

In August 1867, Johnson sent Stanton a letter that stated, "Public considerations of high character constrain me to say that your resignation as Secretary of War will be accepted." When Stanton refused to resign (replying to Johnson that "public considerations of a high character ... constrain me not to resign"), Johnson was forced to send Stanton a second letter announcing he had been suspended from office, ordering him to cease all exercise of authority, and transferring his power to Ulysses S. Grant as

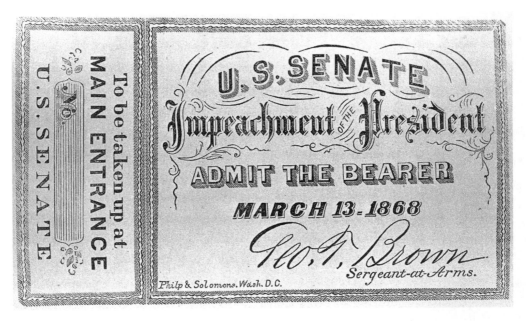

Ticket for admission into the impeachment trial of President Andrew Johnson, 1868. *AP/Wide World Photos.*

Johnson's new secretary of war. Five months later, in January 3, 1868, the new Congress convened and refused to approve Stanton's removal by a vote of thirty-five to sixteen. Johnson, in turn, refused to accept the Senate's decision and called the Tenure of Office Act an unconstitutional infringement on the power of the executive.

Impeachment hearings against Johnson began in a few days. Meanwhile, Stanton remained in his office and had a guard posted to protect him and to ensure department records were not seized. Stanton remained in the War Department building for several weeks, until the outcome of Johnson's impeachment trial in the Senate.

The Tenure of Office Act was repealed by Congress in 1887 under pressure by President Grover Cleveland.

What was the **prosecution's case in Andrew Johnson's impeachment trial** (1868)?

The House of Representatives approved eleven articles of impeachment against Johnson for actions related to his attempt to remove Secretary of War Edwin Stanton from office (see answer above) and for remarks he made in speeches in Cleveland and St. Louis where he defamed Congress. Article X of the Articles of Impeachment describes Johnson's public speeches against Congress: "utterances, declarations, threats and harangues, highly censurable in any, are peculiarly indecent and unbecoming in the Chief Magistrate of the United States, by means whereof the said Andrew Johnson has

Words of Impeachment?

Reprinted below is an excerpt from Article X of the eleven Articles of Impeachment against Andrew Johnson. The first two paragraphs of the excerpt (reprinted in their original form) are quotes from a Johnson speech about Congress to an audience in St. Louis, Missouri. The final paragraph is commentary on the speech by those congressmen who drafted the Articles of Impeachment against Johnson.

"Well, let me say to you, if you will stand by me in this action, if you will stand by me in trying to give the people a fair chance? Soldiers and citizens? … God be willing, I will kick them [Congress] out. I will kick them out just as fast as I can.

"Let me say to you, in concluding, that what I have said is what I intended to say; I was not provoked into this, and care not for their menaces, the taunts and the jeers. I care not for threats, I do not intend to be bullied by enemies, nor overawed by my friends. But, God willing, with your help, I will veto their measures whenever any of them come to me."

Which said utterances, declarations, threats and harangues, highly censurable in any, are peculiarly indecent and unbecoming in the Chief Magistrate of the United States, by means whereof the said Andrew Johnson has brought the high office of the President of the United States into contempt, ridicule and disgrace, to the great scandal of all good citizens, whereby said Andrew Johnson, President of the United States, did commit, and was then and there guilty of a high misdemeanor in office.

brought the high office of the President of the United States into contempt, ridicule and disgrace, to the great scandal of all good citizens, whereby said Andrew Johnson, President of the United States, did commit, and was then and there guilty of a high misdemeanor in office."

During Johnson's impeachment trial in the Senate, the president's lawyers argued that Johnson's attempt to remove Stanton was a test of the constitutionality of the Tenure of Office Act. They contended as well that since Stanton had been appointed by Abraham Lincoln, the Tenure of Office Act did not apply to Stanton's position.

When arguments were completed in Johnson's impeachment trial, the Senate voted first to determine whether each of the eleven articles were grounds for impeachment. The Senate voted against all but three of the articles. Concerned that they might not have the two-thirds majority to find Johnson guilty (needing thirty-six of fifty-four votes), Republican Senate leaders delayed the impeachment vote to woo twelve Republicans considered swing voters. When the Senate voted on the first of the articles, six of the twelve swing votes were for acquittal, as expected, but a seventh not-guilty vote, by U.S. senator Edmund Gibson Ross of Kansas, saved Johnson. Thirty-five senators had voted guilty, one short of the majority needed to remove Johnson from office. After ten days, the final two votes were taken, and they also ended 35–19, one short of the necessary two-thirds majority.

"I almost literally looked down into my open grave," said Ross, recounting his feelings when he rose to give his vote on Johnson's impeachment. His Senate career was over because of the vote. He was shunned by fellow Republicans and failed to win reelection. Ross's vote "may well have preserved for ourselves and posterity constitutional government in the United States," wrote John F. Kennedy in *Profiles in Courage,* his 1955 Pulitzer Prize–winning collection of essays on courageous Americans.

Why do historians claim that **Congress was more powerful than the president** from 1865 to 1885?

Congress assumed control over the post–Civil War Reconstruction policy during the presidency of Andrew Johnson. Through the Tenure of Office Act (see above) in 1867, Congress assumed greater power concerning presidential appointments that it had previously. Congress nearly succeeded in removing Johnson from office. Johnson's successor, Ulysses S. Grant, did not plan to exert influence over Congress, and he succeeded. When Grant did show initiative, he was thwarted, as in his failed effort to annex Santo Domingo. Several congressmen were involved in scandals during the Grant presidency, and even in poor economic times that began in 1873, Congress voted itself a retroactive pay raise in 1876. Rutherford B. Hayes and Chester Alan Arthur had little success with Congress as well.

Why did **Congress reject the Treaty of Versailles and the League of Nations**?

U.S. Senate majority leader and Foreign Relations Committee chairman Henry Cabot Lodge led the fight against approval of the Treaty of Versailles that ended World War I. He represented those Americans who believed the treaty would undermine U.S. sovereignty and force the nation into unwanted obligations. Article 10 of the League of Nations covenant was of special concern to Lodge for suggesting the United States would go to war in support of the territorial integrity of any member state of the League of Nations.

President Woodrow Wilson lobbied for support but refused to attach any reservations or amendments to the treaty. He went on a nationwide speaking tour to rally public support, but was unsuccessful and suffered a stroke during the journey that left him largely incapacitated during the final year of his presidency.

When did **Congress** begin to more actively **challenge Franklin D. Roosevelt's policies**?

Roosevelt worked effectively with Congress to pass significant legislation from 1933 to 1935 to combat the Great Depression. The president had encountered some challenges from the left to increase taxes against the wealthy and from the right against the growing power of union labor, but an enormous amount of legislation passed through Congress and was signed into law by the president. After the economic recovery suffered a setback in 1937, Congress made cuts in relief spending and public works. Republican gains in the midterm elections of 1938 further eroded Roosevent's power, but as the nation shifted to a wartime economy at the end of the 1930s with the outbreak of World War II, the economy picked up significantly and New Deal programs began fading. Roosevelt then assumed enormous powers as a wartime president when America entered World War II in 1941.

OVERWEIGHTED.

Cartoon from *Punch* magazine (March 25, 1919) in which Woodrow Wilson offers the dove of peace an olive branch too heavy to carry. *Getty Images.*

How did Harry S. Truman and Dwight D. Eisenhower respond to **McCarthyism**?

On February 9, 1950, U.S. senator Joseph McCarthy of Wisconsin made a speech in which he claimed he had a list of fifty-seven people in the State Department that were known to be members of the American Communist Party. As McCarthy began receiving publicity and making larger accusations, Truman was facing erosion of public support over the Korean War (1950–1953) and an economy beset by inflation. Truman attempted to rally public support against McCarthy, but his efforts were not effective. Many congressmen refused to challenge McCarthy for fear of political fallout.

After Republicans made gains in Congress in 1952, the party leadership appointed McCarthy chairman of the Senate Permanent Subcommittee on Investigations. President Dwight D. Eisenhower, elected in 1952, resisted demands by McCarthy and others for testimony and personnel records of federal officials. McCarthy's excessively mean-spirited and hollow accusations were eventually exposed on national television in 1954. The Senate, by a vote of 65–22 in early December 1954, condemned McCarthy for "conduct that tends to bring the Senate into dishonor and disrepute."

Why did **Lyndon B. Johnson begin losing the support of Congress**?

Following his landslide election victory in 1964, Johnson worked with Congress to pass sweeping social legislation as part of his Great Society and War on Poverty programs in 1965 and 1966. However, his continuing escalation of American involvement in the Vietnam War beginning in 1965 gradually resulted in decreasing support for the president. Republicans made congressional gains in the midterm election of 1966 and Johnson began facing challenges he hadn't experienced previously from Congress, especially as he attempted to maintain funding for his social programs while sharply increasing military spending.

Why were **Richard Nixon's relations with Congress strained** even before the Watergate scandal?

Republican Richard Nixon narrowly won election in 1968 and entered office facing Democratic majorities in both Houses of Congress. He failed to rally Congress to support his welfare reform plan and generally dealt with Congress indirectly, attempting to press his programs through speeches and other public forums. The Senate rejected two of his nominees to the Supreme Court because of their civil rights views and issues relating to their ethics.

Nixon also faced increasing congressional restraints on his military authority during the Vietnam War. Early in 1971, news reports of a failed, U.S.-supported invasion of Laos contradicted the president's statements. In 1973, it was revealed that Nixon preserved secrecy over U.S. bombing in Cambodia by sending false reports to the Senate. Congress prohibited the president from further use of American ground combat troops in Cambodia and Laos.

Nixon won a landslide reelection in 1972, but Republicans were not able to ride his coattails for congressional gains.

What **congressional actions contributed to Nixon resigning** from office?

After news stories linked the Watergate break-in and other illegal activities to the Committee to Reelect the President (CREEP), Nixon's political organization, the U.S.

> ## Memorable Phrases and Statements from the Watergate Scandal
>
> "What did the president know and when did he know it?" —Howard Baker, Tennessee Republican and co-chair of the Senate Watergate Committee
>
> "I am not a crook." —Richard Nixon, denying his involvement in the Watergate scandal to a group of newspaper editors
>
> "Expletive deleted" —a frequent editorial insertion in transcripts of tapes recorded in the Oval Office to replace coarse language
>
> "Deep Throat" —the name (from the title of a pornographic movie) given to the secret source that informed *Washington Post* reporter Bob Woodward of the depth of executive branch involvement in Watergate and other illegal activities

Senate voted (70-0) in February 1974 to form the Senate Select Committee to Investigate Campaign Practices (commonly called the Watergate Committee or the Ervin Committee, after its chairman, U.S. senator Sam Ervin of North Carolina). Hearings of the committee were broadcast daily to a national audience and often provided dramatic testimony: White House special counsel John Dean implicated Nixon in the Watergate cover-up, contradicting Nixon's emphatic assertions that he had no knowledge of the events; and White House aide Alexander Butterfield revealed the existence of a secret recording system that Nixon had installed in the White House.

Watergate special prosecutor Archibald Cox obtained a subpoena for the tapes from U.S. Circuit Court judge John Sirica, who had presided over the arraignment of the Watergate burglars. Nixon refused to turn over the tapes, then later ordered Attorney General Elliot J. Richardson to fire Cox. After Richardson refused and resigned, it was left up to Solicitor General Robert Bork to complete what was dubbed the "Saturday Night Massacre."

An ongoing court battle ensued over the tapes until the Supreme Court ruled against the president in *United States v. Nixon* on July 24, 1974 (see Presidents and the Judiciary—The Judiciary Influences the Presidency). Meanwhile, the Senate Watergate Committee continued its investigation and turned in a summary of its findings to the House of Representatives. The House Judiciary Committee recommended impeachment around the same time tapes were released by the White House that clearly showed Nixon involved in the Watergate conspiracy. Nixon resigned from office two weeks later, on August 9, 1974.

Why did **Gerald Ford veto over fifty pieces of legislation** in less than two years?

When Ford took office in August 1974 following Richard Nixon's resignation, the country was in an economic recession compounded by high inflation. Ford called for

President Gerald Ford testifying on his "full, free and absolute pardon" of former president Richard Nixon before the U.S. House Committee on the Judiciary in 1974. *AP/Wide World Photos.*

substantial reductions in spending, but Democratic majorities in Congress wanted to continue funding broad social programs and offering assistance to the poor and the unemployed. Ford vetoed more than fifty pieces of legislation that he believed increased government spending.

Why was **Gerald Ford questioned by the U.S. House Committee on the Judiciary**?

Ford was called to appear before the U.S. House Committee on the Judiciary to explain his reasons for granting a "full, free and absolute pardon" to former president Richard Nixon "for all offenses against the United States which he … has committed or may have committed or taken part in." In general, public, media, and congressional response to the pardon was negative. The pardon precluded possible indictments that might have provided answers to some of the remaining issues related to Watergate. Some critics charged that Ford had made a secret deal with Nixon that led to Ford's appointment to vice president.

Ford replied to the Committee that there were no deals connected with the pardon and that his actions were intended to end the domination of Watergate on American affairs and help the former president regain his health.

Which other **presidents have testified before congressional committees**?

According to the U.S. Senate Historical Office, two presidents and one vice president testified before congressional committees prior to Gerald Ford. President Abraham Lincoln appeared before the House Judiciary Committee on February 13, 1862, to testify on the premature publication in the *New York Herald* newspaper of a portion of his Annual Message to Congress on the same morning that it was sent to Capitol Hill. A correspondent for the newspaper was a close friend of Mary Todd Lincoln, and many assumed that the first lady was the source of the leak. Lincoln assured committee members that no member of his family was involved.

Ulysses S. Grant's vice president, Schuyler Colfax, testified before the House Select Committee to Investigate the Crédit Mobilier scandal in January 1873. President Woodrow Wilson testified at the White House before members of the Senate Foreign Relations Committee on August 19, 1919, concerning the treaty of peace with Germany and establishment of a League of Nations. The president opened by reading a statement and then answered questions for three-and-a-half hours, after which he invited committee members to stay for lunch. Despite Wilson's efforts, the Senate twice rejected the Treaty of Versailles, and the United States never joined the League.

In 2004, President George W. Bush and Vice President Dick Cheney testified in the White House before the National Commission on Terrorist Attacks Upon the United States (the 9/11 Commission). Former President Bill Clinton and his vice president, Al Gore, also testified before the commission.

Why was **Ronald Reagan less successful with Congress during his second term**?

In the midterm elections of 1986, Democrats gained five seats in the House and took control of the Senate, 55–45. Even before Democrats were emboldened to challenge Reagan's programs, the administration admitted late in 1986 that some members had been secretly selling arms to Iran, with some of the profits possibly going to guerrilla fighters in Nicaragua—actions that were illegal. The final two years of the Reagan administration were dominated by congressional investigations, including the Iran-Contra hearings and Senate deliberations over Reagan's appointments to fill a Supreme Court vacancy. The Senate voted 58–42 to rejected Reagan's nomination of Robert Bork on grounds that his strong conservative views and constructionist philosophy would make him disinclined to protect individual rights and liberties that had been upheld by the Supreme Court since the 1950s. Douglas Ginsburg, Reagan's second appointment, withdrew from consideration after it was revealed that he had smoked marijuana while teaching at Harvard University. Reagan's third choice for the vacancy, Judge Anthony M. Kennedy, was approved.

What was the result of the **Iran-Contra hearings**?

After news stories broke in 1986 about illegal sales of arms by the Reagan administration to Iran and a connection linking the sales to illegal financial support for an anticommunist group called the Contras in El Salvador, Ronald Reagan appointed a bipartisan Presidential Commission to investigate what became known as the Iran-Contra scandal. The Tower Commission, named after its head, former U.S. senator John Tower of Texas, implicated several administration officials in illegal activities. Though the commission could not determine Reagan's role, if any, in the scandal, it criticized the president for loose supervision of his national security staff.

Meanwhile, a congressional investigation turned up evidence that Reagan had authorized the arms sales. Even if he hadn't, the commission concluded, he had either been misinformed or was unaware of actions undertaken by officials in his own administration. The congressional committee concluded that Reagan had "clearly failed to take care that the laws be faithfully executed" and that the president bore "ultimate responsibility" for wrongdoing by his aides.

What was **Bill Clinton's relationship with the Republican-controlled Congress**?

Bill Clinton's presidency began slowly: many of his appointments were delayed or not approved by Congress; he moved quickly on a controversial topic—homosexuals in the military—before Congress, the military, and the general public had opportunities for debate; and his pursuit of a national health-care policy faced challenges from the beginning. Clinton was successful in helping win Senate approval for the North American Free Trade Agreement (NAFTA) and passage of the Family and Medical Leave Act of 1993.

In 1994 midterm elections, Republicans made substantial gains and had rallied around a "Contract with America," promising to move quickly on a wide variety of federal legislation within one hundred days. A sweeping welfare reform bill passed Congress and was signed into law by Clinton, and both sides claimed credit for the legislation. Republican resistance to Clinton programs became heated and led to a stalemate over the president's 1995 budget. Congress wanted spending cuts to fund a tax cut, but Clinton refused. Without an approved budget, and rejection by Congress of temporary funding measures, the government literally shut down in late 1995. National parks, museums, and many government agencies were closed. Congress took the brunt of the blame for the shutdown. A booming economy and Clinton's defense of the Social Security and Medicare programs contributed to his reelection in 1996.

During Clinton's second term, his relationship with Congress became more acrimonious. Congress continued to pursue what became a five-year investigation of Clinton's involvement in a real estate deal dating back to 1978. The president was not charged with wrongdoing in the Whitewater investigation. However, Kenneth Starr, the special prosecutor investigating the Whitewater scandal was given evidence that Clinton had engaged in an extramarital affair during the winter of 1995–1996 with a White House intern. Denials of the affair by the president and the intern, Monica Lewinsky, were grounds for perjury. Both had denied the relationship in testimony in another case, a lawsuit by Paula Jones, a former government worker in Arkansas, claiming sexual harassment by Clinton when he was governor of Arkansas. The affair and the charge of perjury led Congress to vote to impeach Clinton. Congress failed to convict Clinton in the president's impeachment trial in the U.S. Senate.

How did Congress come to **impeach Clinton**?

On September 21, 1998, Whitewater special prosecutor Kenneth Starr released a report detailing evidence that President Clinton committed perjury in a civil suit brought against him by Paula Corbin Jones and coached and influenced aides who testified before a Grand Jury convened by Starr. The Starr Report also included all of the testimony of Monica Lewinsky concerning her affair with Clinton during the winter of

High Crimes and Misdemeanors

According to Article II, Section 4, of the Constitution, "The President, Vice President and all civil officers of the United States, shall be removed from office on impeachment for, and conviction of, treason, bribery, or other high crimes and misdemeanors."

Still, impeachment boils down to a matter of political judgment. Framers of the Constitution wanted to address actions that warranted removal of a federal official from office. Those actions fall under the category of treason, bribery, and "high crimes and misdemeanors." Treason and bribery were used in a draft of the Constitution, but George Mason and James Madison wanted to include other "great and dangerous offenses." Mason proposed adding "high crimes and misde-meanors" to cover other offenses that would warrant impeachment. Many of those who opposed the impeachment of Bill Clinton argued that his actions did not jeopardize the nation as "great and dangerous offenses."

1995–1996 and which she denied in a signed affidavit related to the Jones case (for more on *Clinton v. Jones,* see Presidents and the Judiciary—The Judiciary Influences the Presidency).

On October 8, 1998, a little over two weeks after the Starr Report was released, the House of Representatives voted in favor of conducting an inquiry into Starr's allegations. The results were presented to the House Judiciary Committee, which voted strictly along partisan lines on four articles of impeachment against the president. On December 19, 1998, the House voted to impeach Clinton on two of the articles.

The impeachment trial began in the Senate on January 7, 1999, and ended on February 12. A two-thirds majority vote of guilty (sixty-six of ninety-nine) was needed to remove Clinton from office. Article I (perjury) had forty-five guilty votes, and Article II (obstruction of justice) had fifty guilty votes.

What was the **aftermath of the Clinton impeachment**?

Democrats made gains in Congress in the midterm elections of 1998, held while Congress was conducting an inquiry on grounds for impeaching the Democratic president. Polls routinely showed 65 percent of the electorate did not support impeachment. The Whitewater Investigation concluded in 2000 with no official charges brought against President or Mrs. Clinton. In 2000, the Independent Prosecutor Act was allowed to expire, and Hillary Rodham Clinton was elected to the U.S. Senate. After sitting out the election of 2000, when it was feared that Clinton's presence on the campaign trail would hurt the presidential bid of Al Gore, Clinton gradually

383

Former president Bill Clinton shakes hands with a fan at his book signing for his autobiography titled *My Life* in 2004. *AP/Wide World Photos.*

returned to the public eye. In 2004, he wrote an instantly bestselling memoir and went on a long book-publicity tour.

How did **George W. Bush bypass Congress to make judicial appointments**?

Bush seated two of his nominees for federal appeals courts in 2004 without the required Senate approval by appointing them while Congress was in recess. An approval vote on both judges had been filibustered by Democrats for months. Both appointments were temporary: the judges would face confirmation hearings in January of the year following their appointment.

Bush's actions were based on a loose interpretation of Article II, Section 2, Clause 3, of the Constitution: "The President shall have Power to fill up all Vacancies that may happen during the Recess of the Senate, by granting Commissions which shall expire at the End of their next Session."

PRESIDENTS AND THE JUDICIARY

THE PRESIDENT INFLUENCES THE JUDICIARY

How did **Washington influence the development of the federal judiciary**?

The U.S. Constitution provided for an independent judiciary to consist of a Supreme Court and lower courts, but did not offer specifications. Article III of the Constitution established the judicial branch as one of the three separate and distinct branches of the federal government. The Constitution stated that federal judges are appointed for life and can be removed from office only through impeachment and conviction by Congress of "Treason, Bribery, or other high Crimes and Misdemeanors."

George Washington supported the Judiciary Act of 1789 that created the Supreme Court, three circuit courts, and thirteen district courts. The cabinet-level office of attorney general was also created by this act. The president is the chief enforcer of federal laws, and the attorney general is the agent of the president in prosecuting cases before the federal courts.

Washington appointed members of the first Supreme Court, which included John Jay as chief justice. Jay had been elected to the Continental Congress in 1774 and 1775, drafted the first constitution of New York State, and was one of the commissioners (with Benjamin Franklin and John Adams) who negotiated the Treaty of Paris with Great Britain, ending the American Revolution. Jay did much to establish the credibility of the Supreme Court.

What were the **"midnight appointments" of John Adams**?

Early in 1801, Adams's "midnight appointments" set the stage for the first conflict between the executive and judicial branches. Adams had proposed legislation in 1799   385 to reorganize the judiciary and increase the number of federal courts and judges, but Congress did not pass the measure. Adams was defeated in the election of 1800 and his political party, the Federalists, lost control of both houses of Congress. The lame duck president and the lame duck Federalist Congress passed the Judiciary Act of 1801 that Adams had proposed earlier. Adams used his authority under the Act to pack the courts with Federalist judicial appointments during the final two months and up to the last days of his administration. He believed a Federalist judiciary was necessary to offset an incoming president (Thomas Jefferson) and Congress dominated by one party, the Democratic-Republicans.

Adams had another major impact on the federal judiciary: he appointed John Marshall as chief justice of the U.S. Supreme Court in 1800. Marshall, who would serve as chief justice for thirty-four years, established the court's power as equal to the executive and legislative branches and authored the court's first major decision, the *Marbury v. Madison* case.

When was a **Supreme Court justice impeached for political reasons**?

Upon taking office, Thomas Jefferson reacted to the "midnight appointments" (see above) of John Adams by seeking to repeal the congressional action that created numerous judgeships for Adams to fill before leaving office. He also sought to impeach judges who expressed strong political views against Jefferson's Democratic-Republican Party. Jefferson was successful in having John Pickering, a New Hampshire federal district court judge and violent alcoholic, removed from office. Pickering was removed through the standard process: an impeachment vote in the House of Representatives, a trial in the Senate, and a vote on removal from office, requiring two-thirds majority, by the Senate. Pickering was removed in 1803.

Jefferson took his next aim at U.S. Supreme Court Associate Justice Samuel Chase. Chase was targeted by the Democratic-Republican president for impeachment on grounds of partisanship. Among many examples of partisanship, Chase once ordered a federal marshal to remove from a jury panel "any of those creatures or persons called democrats."

The impeachment proceedings occurred in January and February of 1805. Chase argued that his non-criminal behavior did not meet the definition of "high Crimes and Misdemeanors" the Constitution lists as grounds for impeachment. That view held ground and the impeachment failed. The attempt to removed Chase was the last time a presidential administration actively pursued the impeachment of a federal judge because he was a political enemy.

How did **James Madison reinforce the balance between the presidency and the judiciary**?

President Madison was asked by Pennsylvania governor Simon Snyder to intervene against a Supreme Court decision. The case began in 1803—before either Madison or

Snyder were in office—when a U.S. prisoner on a British ship seized control of the vessel and, according to laws of the time, claimed the ship as a "sea prize"—a ship or cargo captured during wartime. A passing U.S. boat then seized the ship and claimed it as a sea prize for the state of Pennsylvania. After the boat arrived in Pennsylvania, the original claimant sued the state of Pennsylvania, and a federal court ruled in his favor. After a decade passed without return of the ship to the plaintiff, the U.S. Supreme Court ordered a federal marshal to arrest the defendants. Governor Snyder ordered the state militia to protect the defendants while he appealed for intervention from President Madison, a fellow Democratic-Republican.

Madison refused to intervene, arguing that the president is required to carry out rulings of the court. Madison's action was a significant and lasting precedent for upholding the balance of powers between the executive and judicial branches.

Which **president refused to carry out an order of the Supreme Court**?

Andrew Jackson did not believe the Supreme Court should act as the final arbiter of constitutional issues. This view may have been a response to his antagonistic relationship with Chief Justice John Marshall, but he had an opportunity to refuse to follow the court in its ruling on the Cherokee Nation in Georgia. Under a treaty with the United States, the Cherokees were entitled to remain in their native Georgia homeland. In the 1820s, however, Georgia was expanding and settlers encroached on valuable Cherokee land. After the state legislature enacted laws to confiscate the land, the Cherokee Nation appealed to the Supreme Court, but the Court ruled in *Cherokee Nation v. Georgia* (1831) that it had no authority to hear the dispute.

The following year, however, the Court ruled in *Worcester v. Georgia* that Cherokees were entitled to federal protection from the actions of the state governments. After the ruling, Jackson expressed his opinion: "John Marshall has made his decree. Now let him enforce it." Jackson failed to intervene when the state of Georgia defied a Supreme Court order and conducted an execution of a Cherokee prisoner.

Cherokees were eventually forced to move by the federal government. A group of Cherokees represented by a minor chief signed the Treaty of New Echota (1835), a legal document that allowed Jackson to remove all Cherokees from the southeast. The treaty was approved by two-thirds of the Senate (by one vote), and in 1838 the United States began the removal of Cherokees to Oklahoma.

Which presidential administrations have had **controversial ties to Supreme Court justices**?

While the Supreme Court deliberated before issuing the *Dred Scott* decision in 1857, incoming president James Buchanan wrote a letter to a justice from the North urging him to side with Southerners on the court against Dred Scott, the appellant. Scott was an African American slave whose owner was an officer in the U.S. Army. The officer took Scott with him from Missouri, a slave state, for a long period while he was stationed in Illinois and Wisconsin, both free states. Scott returned with his owner to Missouri, where the owner died in 1846. With the assistance of abolitionist lawyers, Scott sued for his freedom in court. The case went to the U.S. Supreme Court.

Two days before Buchanan's inauguration in March 1857, a majority decision (seven of nine justices) agreed that no slave or a descendant of a slave was a U.S. citizen, or ever had been a U.S. citizen. As a non-citizen, the court stated, Scott had no rights and could not sue in a Federal Court and must remain a slave.

Buchanan had pressured the northern judge because he believed the ruling would reinforce states' rights and help end the growing national divisiveness over slavery. Instead, the *Dred Scott* decision further inflamed abolitionists.

In 2004, attorneys for two public interest groups, the Sierra Club and Judicial Watch, argued before the Supreme Court for the release of records related to a task force on energy head by Dick Cheney, vice president under George W. Bush. They contended the vice president's contacts with industry leaders were improper while he was developing government policy that benefited their businesses. Lawyers for the administration argued that forcing Cheney to disclose his task force's 2001 contacts with industry executives and lobbyists would hurt the administration's ability to receive candid advice. The case was complicated because Supreme Court Justice Antonin Scalia had taken a hunting trip earlier in the year with Cheney.

What was significant about **Abraham Lincoln's appointments to the Supreme Court**?

Lincoln had battled with Chief Justice Roger B. Taney, a states' right supporter of slavery, from the beginning of his presidency in 1861. Taney had authored the *Dred Scott* decision of 1857 (see above) and challenged Lincoln's assumption of far-ranging war powers as commander in chief during the Civil War. When Taney died in 1864, Lincoln replaced him as chief justice with Salmon P. Chase, a longtime opponent of slavery. In all, Lincoln made five appointments to the Supreme Court, all of them against slavery and supportive of the great powers he assumed as a war president. Among the appointments was Samuel Freeman Miller, who supported Lincoln's war measures as well as civil rights measures that followed the war.

What were some **significant presidential appointments of minorities to the Supreme Court**?

Woodrow Wilson's nomination of Louis D. Brandeis as the first Jewish Supreme Court justice was extremely controversial. Some opposition was based on Brandeis's earlier rulings against big business concerns, but much more was rooted in anti-Semitism.

Cartoon satirizing the "court packing" controversy involving Franklin D. Roosevelt. Roosevelt, the "ingeniuous quarterback," is telling the referee (Congress) that he immediately wants six substitutes for his team (the Supreme Court). Drawn by C. K. Berryman, the cartoon published in the *Washington Star,* February 6, 1937. *Library of Congress.*

Nevertheless, Brandeis was confirmed by a Senate vote of forty-seven to twenty-two. He had a distinguished career on the court and was known as a champion of civil liberties.

Thurgood Marshall, the first African American to serve on the Supreme Court, was appointed by Lyndon B. Johnson. Marshall had argued the *Brown v. Board of Education* case in 1954 (see below) and was nominated by John F. Kennedy to serve on the Second Court of Appeals in 1961. Marshall served nearly twenty-five years on the court and was known as a champion of civil rights.

Sandra Day O'Connor, the first female Supreme Court justice, was appointed by Ronald Reagan in 1981. O'Connor proved to be an important swing vote on the court during her more than two decades of service, a period when justices were often accused of partisanship.

What was the **"court packing" controversy** involving Franklin D. Roosevelt?

Many of the programs passed as part of the New Deal of Roosevelt's administration were challenged in the courts. Constitutional issues arose over the extensive powers and controls the government was taking to address economic woes of the Great Depression. The Supreme Court struck down numerous New Deal measures in 1935 and 1936 (see below). Roosevelt was furious at the Court, believing it was behind the times in its "horse and buggy" decisions.

389

Roosevelt Takes His Case to the People

Franklin D. Roosevelt went public to defend his proposal for reorganizing the federal judiciary and appointing a new Supreme Court justice for every justice who had reached the age of seventy. He made public speeches and addressed the issue in his weekly "Fireside Chat" radio address. Below is an excerpt from his "Fireside Chat on Reorganization of the Judiciary," broadcast March 9, 1937.

> Last Thursday I described the American form of government as a three-horse team provided by the Constitution to the American people so that their field might be plowed. The three horses are, of course, the three branches of government—the Congress, the executive, and the courts. Two of the horses, the Congress and the executive, are pulling in unison today; the third is not.
>
> Those who have intimated that the president of the United States is trying to drive that team, overlook the simple fact that the president, as chief executive, is himself one of the three horses. It is the American people themselves who are in the driver's seat. It is the American people themselves who want the furrow plowed. It is the American people themselves who expect the third horse to fall in unison with the other two.

Following his reelection in 1936, Roosevelt began pursuing an idea first developed in 1913 by James C. McReynolds, attorney general under President Woodrow Wilson. Under the proposal, a president would be able to appoint a new judge for every federal magistrate who reached the age of seventy and had not retired. Since there was nothing in the Constitution specifying the number of Supreme Court justices, Roosevelt adapted the idea to the Supreme Court, where six justices were over seventy, including four conservatives who routinely ruled against New Deal policies.

Presented to Congress as the Judicial Reform Act of 1937, the bill caused an immediate uproar. Opponents, including many Democrats, contended Roosevelt was trying to subvert the Constitution. Roosevelt attempted to win support for his plan by speaking to the American people during a radio address and on a speaking tour, but he could not rally enough support and soon abandoned the plan.

About the same time, the Court suddenly began to uphold New Deal legislation. In quick succession in March and April 1937, for example, the Court sustained the National Labor Relations Act and the Social Security Act. Charles Evans Hughes became a key swing vote on the Court, having moved from opposing New Deal measures to upholding them. "A switch in time saves nine" became a humorous way for explaining how the Supreme Court suddenly swung in Roosevelt's favor after he had proposed revising it.

Why were **so many court federal appointments** made by Presidents **Kennedy and Carter**?

In May 1961, a judiciary act passed by Congress enacted administrative reform of the judiciary and created more than 70 new federal judgeships. During his nearly three years in office, John F. Kennedy appointed 126 federal judges, while his predecessor, Dwight D. Eisenhower, appointed 175 over eight years. However, Kennedy was forced to negotiate on appointments with U.S. senator James Eastland of Mississippi, chairman of the Senate Judiciary Committee and opponent of racial integration. Kennedy's appointment to the Second U.S. Circuit Court of Appeals of Thurgood Marshall, a distinguished African American later appointed to the Supreme Court by Lyndon B. Johnson, was held up by Eastland, who insisted on Kennedy providing a federal judgeship to Harold Cox, a segregationist and a former college roommate of Eastland's, as a return favor.

Faced with a huge backlog of cases in the federal courts, Congress in 1978 passed legislation creating 152 new federal judgeships—the greatest expansion of the federal judiciary in the nation's history. Jimmy Carter filled new and existing seats with more minorities than any other previous president.

What was **Ronald Reagan's policy of judicial restraint**?

Reagan believed that the Supreme Court, beginning in the 1950s, was involved more in actively interpreting the constitution rather than following the "original intent" of the founding fathers. Decisions such as those against school prayer and for abortion rights were viewed by Reagan as examples of government interference. Reagan had the opportunity to appoint three Supreme Court justices. In 1981, he selected Sandra Day O'Connor, a conservative-leaning Arizona judge and former state senator as the first woman to serve on the Supreme Court. In 1986, he promoted William Rehnquist, the most conservative of the justices at the time, to Chief Justice of the Supreme Court, and nominated conservative Antonin Scalia to an empty seat. Reagan's final nominee, Robert Bork, an outspoken political conservative, did not win approval by the U.S. Senate (see Presidents and Congress—Congress v. President). Another conservative judge, Anthony M. Kennedy, was appointed by Reagan instead and was approved by the Senate.

Reagan's selections showed judicial restraint in their subsequent decisions. However, the restraint meant that Reagan's hopes for reversing decisions on abortion and school prayer were not likely to occur. Rather than changing rulings, judges who practice restraint usually uphold precedents—even those they would not have approved in the first place.

What was the **"litmus test"** applied by Presidents Reagan, George Bush, and George W. Bush in their federal judicial appointments?

The "litmus test" for appointing federal judges is a policy of carefully screening nominations to the federal bench to ensure a conservative influence on the interpretation of the law. Appointees by the three presidents tended to side with conservatives who sought to restrict abortion, affirmative action, and the rights of criminal defendants, and to increase the influence of religion in public life.

THE JUDICIARY INFLUENCES THE PRESIDENCY

What is the **role of the Supreme Court in presidential impeachment trials**?

The Chief Justice of the Supreme Court presides over the impeachment trial of the president. The trial is conducted in the U.S. Senate and prosecuted by members of the House of Representatives following a House vote on articles of impeachment. Salmon P. Chase carried out this constitutional duty during Andrew Johnson's impeachment in 1868 and William H. Rehnquist during Bill Clinton's impeachment in 1998.

Upon entering the office of the presidency, Thomas Jefferson was set on reducing the federal judiciary. Through his efforts came the case of *Marbury v. Madison,* and with the result was the principle of judicial review. *Library of Congress.*

What was the lasting significance of *Marbury v. Madison* in 1803?

Believing that the federal government should have limited powers, Thomas Jefferson entered office in 1801 with plans to reduce the federal judiciary, especially since it was dominated by members of the opposing party, the Federalists. He asked Congress to repeal the Judiciary Act of 1801 (see above) and to eliminate many judgeships. Since the Constitution mandates that federal judges have lifetime tenures, however, his plans contradicted the Constitution.

A repeal bill reached the Senate in January 1802 and the vote ended in a tie. In such cases, the president of the Senate—the vice president, in this case Aaron Burr—casts the deciding vote. Burr surprised Jefferson by advising the Senate to reconsider the legislation. The bill eventually passed, and Jefferson signed it into law.

These actions coincided with a dispute over one of John Adams's "midnight

Presidents v. Marshall

John Marshall helped establish the role of the Supreme Court by establishing the principle of judicial review, to declare laws unenforceable if they violate the Constitution. Marshall ended the practice whereby each justice wrote his own opinion in every case, and instead encouraged one majority opinion. In *Marbury v. Madison,* he wrote that it is "emphatically the province and duty of the judicial department to say what the law is."

The Marshall court made several rulings that angered Presidents Thomas Jefferson and Andrew Jackson. Most significantly, he established the Court's ability to interpret the Constitution, rather than taking a strictly literal, constructionist approach. In *McCulloch v. Maryland* (1819), for example, Marshall addressed the implied powers of Congress that extended the scope of the legislative branch. Since Congress had the power to collect taxes, regulate commerce, raise armies, and declare war, Marshall argued, it also should have the power to create a national bank, even though the power is not explicitly stated in the Constitution. Ex-presidents Jefferson and James Madison severely criticized that stand.

appointments" to the federal judiciary (see above). Jefferson's secretary of state, James Madison, refused to process Adams's appointment of William Marbury as justice of the peace in the District of Columbia. Marbury responded by petitioning the Supreme Court a writ of mandamus, an order forcing Madison to deliver the commission.

Led by Chief Justice John Marshall, the Supreme Court used the case to establish its power to rule on the constitutionality of acts of Congress. The Court ruled that Marbury was entitled to his appointed position, but the Supreme Court could not force Madison to process the appointment.

Though Madison and the Jefferson administration won the case, Marshall established the principle of judicial review. He ruled that part of the Judiciary Act of 1789 (see above) that gave the Supreme Court the power to issue writs of mandamus was unconstitutional because the Constitution did not explicitly impute this power to the Supreme Court. So, the Supreme Court was stripped of this right while earning the more powerful role of judicial review—that federal courts have the power to declare laws unenforceable if they violate the Constitution. Marshall wrote that it is "emphatically the province and duty of the judicial department to say what the law is."

What is the background of the **Aaron Burr trial** of 1807 and why did the executive and judicial branches clash?

Aaron Burr was a significant and colorful figure in the early days of the republic. He fought with distinction in the American Revolution, became a leading lawyer in New

Chief Justice John Marshall helped establish the role of the Supreme Court by establishing the principle of judicial review, to declare laws unenforceable if they violate the Constitution. *AP/Wide World Photos.*

York, and served one term as vice president as a result of the controversial election of 1800. (For more on the controversy, see Presidential Elections—The Electoral College.) Thomas Jefferson arranged to have Burr dropped from the Democratic-Republican ticket in 1804, and Burr ran for governor of New York. During the gubernatorial campaign, New Yorker Alexander Hamilton, a bitter enemy of Vice President Burr's, called him unfit for office, and Burr responded to Hamilton's frequent derogatory statements about him by challenging Hamilton to a duel. Burr shot Hamilton in the chest during the duel, and Hamilton died soon after.

In 1805, Burr moved on to the frontier the United States had acquired two years earlier in the Louisiana Purchase. He conspired with several pro-British forces and other allies, including James Wilkinson, General-in-Chief of the Army, to rebel against the United States and establish a new nation on the frontier. As the conspirators delayed in executing their plan, Wilkinson became agitated and finally informed President Jefferson about the planned rebellion. Jefferson authorized a local Ohio militia to raid an estate in Ohio that served as the conspirators' base of operations. The rebellion was crushed. Burr was not present, but he was arrested a few months later. After lengthy pretrial and grand jury hearings, Burr's trial for treason began on August 3, 1807.

The trial was held in Richmond, Virginia. John Marshall, Chief Justice of the Supreme Court, happened to be in Richmond and decided he would hear the case. Marshall proceeded to rule much of the evidence presented against Burr as inadmissible. The prosecution had to prove treason as required by Article III, Section 3, of the Constitution:

> Clause 1: Treason against the United States, shall consist only in levying War against them, or in adhering to their Enemies, giving them Aid and Comfort. No Person shall be convicted of Treason unless on the Testimony of two Witnesses to the same overt Act, or on Confession in open Court.

The defense argued that since the planned rebellion had been crushed before "levying war" and Burr was not present when the base of operations was captured, witnesses against Burr could not testify that Burr was engaged in an "overt Act" of rebellion. Marshall ruled that the prosecution failed to show how Burr assembled men and materials for revolt, and with little evidence remaining the jury had no choice but to return a not-guilty verdict against Burr.

Jefferson had declared Burr guilty before the trial began and was furious at the proceedings of the trial. Essentially, by ordering the militia to crush a rebellion before it could take place, Jefferson had removed the possibility of convicting Burr for treason as it is defined by the Constitution.

What **challenges did Abraham Lincoln face over his war powers**?

When forces representing the Confederate States of America fired on Fort Sumter, a federal fort in South Carolina, in 1861, the U.S. Congress was not in session. President Lincoln responded by using his authority under the Militia Act of 1792 to call for volunteers and to begin military action. On April 19, 1861, Lincoln declared a naval blockade of the South. Congress passed a resolution authorizing the blockade in July 1861.

In 1863, owners of some of the ships seized between the time of the president's blockade proclamation and authorization of it by Congress challenged the legality and constitutionality of the blockade. After lower federal courts rejected the challenges, the owners combined their actions into one case, the *Prize Cases,* and appealed to the Supreme Court. The Court ruled five-to-four to uphold Lincoln's action as valid under the emergency powers inherent in the president's war powers.

Chief Justice Roger B. Taney dissented. He argued the Constitution did not explicitly provide for such emergency powers and the Constitution's grant to the president to wage war did not extend to suppressing an internal rebellion. All three of the justices Lincoln had appointed by that time voted with the majority opinion.

What presidents had stakes in the 1895 and 1917 **trials of Eugene Debs**?

Eugene Debs was a labor and political activist who formed the American Railroad Union (ARU) in 1892 to organize all railroad workers into one union, regardless of craft or skill. A severe economic downturn occurred in 1893, and the following year workers at the Pullman Sleeping Car Company went on strike to protest wage cuts. Debs led the ARU in a sympathy strike. When national railroad traffic was affected, President Grover Cleveland called in federal troops to break the strike. Violence ensued and more than two dozen people were killed in confrontations. A federal judge issued an injunction ordering the ARU to stop the strike and then sentenced Debs to six months in jail for violating the injunction.

The government tried Debs for conspiracy in 1895, since the strike interfered with the federal mail. The case was adjourned and then the trial was never reconvened. Lawyers for Debs, including famed attorney Clarence Darrow, had succeeded in making the government's desire to crush the union an issue in the trial and had subpoenaed George Pullman, owner of the Pullman company. His reluctance to testify in open court probably influenced the sudden adjournment, and the case against Debs folded. Meanwhile, the imprisonment of Debs by a court order, without jury trial or

Theodore Roosevelt on Big Business

In Theodore Roosevelt's *An Autobiography* (1913), he issued an opinion on big business:

> Where a company is found seeking its profits through serving the community by stimulating production, lowering prices or improving service, while scrupulously respecting the rights of others (including its rivals, its employees, its customers, and the general public), and strictly obeying the law, then no matter how large its capital, or how great the volume of its business it would be encouraged to still more abundant protection, or better service by the fullest protection that the Government could afford it.

conviction, and the use of a blanket injunction in the strike was widely criticized and contributed to the decline in Cleveland's popularity.

Debs became a socialist after the 1896 election and a perennial presidential candidate. Between 1914 and 1917, Debs made several speeches arguing against U.S. involvement in World War I. After the United States entered the war in 1917, Congress passed and President Woodrow Wilson signed into law the Espionage Act. The act made it a felony to interfere with the recruiting of troops, to disclose information on national defense, and to refuse to perform military duty. After making a speech in Canton, Ohio, where he criticized the Espionage Act, Debs was arrested and sentenced to ten years in the Atlanta Penitentiary. While in jail in 1920, he was the presidential candidate of the Socialist Party and received over nine hundred thousand votes. Debs was pardoned by President Warren G. Harding in December 1921.

How did the U.S. Supreme Court react to "trust-busting" efforts of Theodore Roosevelt and William Howard Taft?

When Theodore Roosevelt took office in 1901 following the assassination of William McKinley, he began addressing the concern about monopolies that had been a growing national problem during the 1890s. He is remembered as a progressive president (progressivism was an early twentieth century political term for those favoring business and social reform).

The major antitrust victory for the Roosevelt administration came when the U.S. Supreme Court upheld the government's dissolution of the Northern Securities Company in 1904. Northern Securities was founded by railroad builder James J. Hill to protect his railroad company from the booms and busts of business. Roosevelt directed his attorney general, Philander C. Knox, to challenge the holding company. In March 1904, the Supreme Court, by a five-to-four decision, declared that Northern Securities was a trust—an unfair business operation that overwhelmed competition. Hill spent another year appealing the ruling, but it was upheld unanimously by the Supreme Court on March 6, 1905. The victory solidified Roosevelt's reputation as a "trust buster."

More than forty antitrust suits were initiated during the years Roosevelt was president. However, Roosevelt was not against large corporations and preferred to use legislation to regulate them. He pushed through Congress legislation that created a new department of commerce and labor with a bureau of corporations charged with investigating the operations and conduct of interstate corporations. During an economic downturn in 1907, Roosevelt allowed the merger of the U.S. Steel Corporation with the Tennessee Coal, Iron, and Railroad Company. That merger would be challenged by the administration of William Howard Taft, who had served in Roosevelt's cabinet as secretary of war and who succeeded him as president.

Taft proved to be the bigger trust-buster—initiating twice as many antitrust cases and winning major cases against the U.S. Steel Corporation (the first billion-dollar corporation in history and headed by J. P. Morgan), the American Tobacco Company, and the Standard Oil Company (headed by John D. Rockefeller).

What was momentous about **Supreme Court decisions on freedom of speech during Woodrow Wilson's presidency**?

In addition to Eugene Debs being arrested after making a speech during which he criticized the Espionage Act of 1917 (see question above), the government prosecuted Americans for criticizing the Conscription Act (1918) that introduced the military draft for service in World War I. When the act passed, the Socialist Party, headquartered in Philadelphia, Pennsylvania, began distributing leaflets that urged men who were drafted to "not submit to intimidation."

Charles T. Schenck, general secretary of the Socialist Party, was arrested for sedition for authorizing publication of the pamphlets. After Schenck was found guilty, the case made its way to the Supreme Court (*Schenck v. U.S. Appeal*). The Supreme Court unanimously affirmed guilt on Schenck's part, with Chief Justice Oliver Wendell Holmes writing a memorable opinion: "The question in every case [of free speech] is whether the words are used in such circumstances and are of such a nature as to create a clear and present danger that they will bring about the substantive evils that Congress has a right to prevent."

What was the result of **trials in the Teapot Dome scandal** of Warren G. Harding's administration?

After years of litigation on the Teapot Dome scandal (see Illness and Death, Assassination and Scandal—Scandals, Rumors, and Affairs), Albert Fall, Harding's secretary of

Harding's Ghostly Presence

The defense lawyer in the Teapot Dome trial of former secretary of the interior Albert Fall played on the sympathy of the jury by invoking the ghost of President Warren G. Harding "from his sacred tomb in Marion [Ohio]" to vouch for Fall's innocence.

the interior, was found guilty and sentenced to prison. It was the first time a cabinet member was convicted of a felony and served a prison sentence.

A Senate investigation disclosed that Fall had received kickbacks for leasing federal oil reserves at Teapot Dome, Wyoming, and Elk Hills, California, without competitive bidding. The investigation began shortly after the death of Harding, who was replaced by Vice President Calvin Coolidge. Coolidge assigned a special counsel made up of one Democrat and one Republican to prosecute cases connected with the scandal. Over a half-dozen trials ensued. Fall was tried in 1926 and acquitted for criminal conspiracy to defraud the government on the Teapot Dome contracts.

Fall was tried again in 1927, this time for criminal conspiracy to defraud the government on the Teapot Dome lease. A mistrial was called when it was revealed that Fall's codefendant Harry L. Sinclair, head of the Sinclair Consolidated Oil Company, had hired detectives to shadow the jurors. At the next trial, in 1928, Fall was excused when his doctors reported that he was dying. In 1929, Fall was put on trial for having accepted a bribe to execute the contract and lease of Teapot Dome development. Fall appeared frail and in a wheelchair, and his lawyer demanded Fall should be vindicated "before he passes into the Great Beyond." Nevertheless, Fall was found guilty. The jury recommended mercy, and Fall was sentenced to one year and a $100,000 fine. Fall appealed, but the conviction was upheld.

Fall entered prison via an ambulance, but emerged walking a year later. He never paid the $100,000 fine and lived for twelve more years.

Why were several **New Deal programs** of Franklin D. Roosevelt **struck down by the judicial branch**?

Some of the early New Deal measures were written, debated, passed, and signed into law in one day. Many of them were challenged on constitutional grounds. (For a full list of New Deal programs, see The President Leads: The Economy—Policies and Programs, Booms and Busts.)

The Supreme Court struck down a portion of the National Industrial Recovery Act in January 1935, and in May of that year the National Recovery Act (NRA) was completely invalidated as an improper regulation of intrastate business. In striking down the Agricultural Adjustment Administration (AAA) in 1936, the Supreme Court ruled that the general welfare clause of the Constitution (Section 8, Clause 1) did not support the AAA's processing tax for regulating agricultural production. According to Section 8, Clause 1, "The Congress shall have Power To lay and collect Taxes, Duties, Imposts and Excises, to pay the Debts and provide for the common Defence and general Welfare of the United States; but all Duties, Imposts and Excises shall be uniform throughout the United States."

What was significant about the Supreme Court's 1952 ruling on **Harry S. Truman's seizure of steel mills**?

Faced with a strike by steelworkers during the Korean War, Truman seized steel mills to keep them operating. Steelworkers were demanding higher wages. Mill owners wanted to raise steel prices despite the fact that Congress had passed price-control legislation to battle post–World War II inflation. Truman sided with workers, but after nearly three months of negotiation between workers and owners failed to result in an agreement, he authorized government seizure of the steel factories, claiming his right to use emergency war powers to protect national security.

The mill owners sought and received a legal injunction against the government. The Supreme Court upheld the injunction in a six-to-three decision. Truman's action, according to the ruling, violated the principle of the "Separation of Powers": the emergency powers granted to a president during wartime, the Court argued, do not extend to seizure of private property to settle a domestic dispute. A strike ensued for nearly two months after the ruling before a settlement was reached.

What was the significance of *Brown v. Board of Education of Topeka, Kansas* (1954)?

The Supreme Court voted unanimously in *Brown v. Board of Education of Topeka, Kansas* that the policy of "separate but equal" facilities for African Americans and whites was inherently discriminatory against African Americans. In the words of Chief Justice Earl Warren, "We conclude that the doctrine of 'separate but equal' has no place. Separate educational facilities are inherently unequal." The significance of the ruling was reflected in conferences and celebrations on its fiftieth anniversary in 2004. On October 26, 1992, Congress passed Public Law 102-525 establishing the Brown v. Board of Education National Historic Site to commemorate the landmark Supreme Court decision aimed at ending segregation in public schools.

The Supreme Court ruling did not set a time schedule for desegregating school systems, instead calling for a "prompt and reasonable start toward full compliance" and "with all deliberate speed." While several states and the District of Columbia moved quickly to desegregate their school systems, others delayed or defiantly opposed the ruling. Some Southern members of Congress voiced determination to have the decision reversed and urged their states to resist. President Dwight D. Eisen-

Warren Court vs. Conservative Ideology

When Dwight D. Eisenhower appointed Earl Warren to the Supreme Court in 1953, he expected Warren would support a conservative philosophy. As attorney general of California during World War II, Warren authorized the mass deportation of Japanese American citizens to internment camps after the Japanese attack on Pearl Harbor in Hawaii. Popular among Republicans, Warren had been a three-term governor of California (1942–1953), was Thomas E. Dewey's running mate in the 1948 election, and had been a serious contender for the 1952 Republican presidential nomination.

According to *Earl Warren: The Judge Who Changed America*, Vice President Richard Nixon convinced Eisenhower to promise Warren the next seat available on the U.S. Supreme Court because Nixon viewed Warren as a rival—the court position would remove the popular Warren as a future opponent of Nixon, according to this view. Even in 1955, a Gallup Poll revealed that if Eisenhower did not seek a second term, Warren was the number one choice among Republican and Independent voters to succeed him, leading Nixon three to one.

Under Chief Justice Warren, the Supreme Court ruled against segregation in public education, liberalized obscenity standards, curbed Congress's ability to terminate citizenship, and challenged police misconduct. The Warren Court admitted sociological as well as legal evidence in reviewing cases. Warren was an unlikely figure to become a hero as an upholder of civil liberties. Nixon would later write in his memoirs, "Like many political moderate conservatives, I felt that some Supreme Court justices were too often using their own interpretations of the law to remake American society according to their own social, political and ideological precepts."

hower was concerned about losing support from congressional Democrats from the South who favored many of his policies. Eisenhower did not take action until 1957, when he sent federal troops to Little Rock, Arkansas, to stop a white crowd from preventing nine black students from entering Central High School.

What was the case of the **"Pentagon Papers"**?

The *New York Times v. United States* (1971) case involved papers stolen from the Pentagon and given to the press by Daniel Ellsberg, a former Defense Department staff member. Classified documents relating to the Vietnam War, the Pentagon Papers, as they were called by the *New York Times,* revealed that the United States had been much more deeply involved in Vietnam than the government had reported. The documents showed that the United States had supported much of the failed French stand in Indochina in 1954, then began covert action against North Vietnam that same year, after France had abandoned Indochina and the former colony was partitioned into North and South Vietnam, Laos, and Cambodia. The documents also gave evidence that the United States ensured that a South Vietnamese leader loyal to the United States took power, even without elections that were mandated by the 1954 treaty between France and North Vietnam. Among other revelations, the documents indicated the Lyndon B. Johnson administration overstated to Congress and the public what happened in the Gulf of Tonkin in August 1964. An incident there led to the Tonkin Gulf resolution that authorized Johnson to take military action against North Vietnam (see The President Leads: Commander in Chief—Preparedness).

When these documents began to appear in the *New York Times,* Richard Nixon's attorney general, John Mitchell, secured a temporary restraining order to stop publication. The *Washington Post,* which also had a copy of the papers, began printing them as well until a restraining order stopped them. The Nixon administration prepared a case against the *New York Times.* On June 18, 1971, five days after the first story appeared in the *Times,* the government presented five authorities in a district court to testify that publication of the Pentagon Papers threatened national security. The court refused to file an injunction against the *Times.* An appeals court agreed with the decision the following day. The administration appealed to the Supreme Court, which upheld the ruling by a 6–3 vote on June 30, 1971. The Court ruled the government must meet a heavy burden of justification to restrain the press from its First Amendment rights to publish.

What was the effect of the *Roe v. Wade* (1973) decision on presidents?

Presidential candidates beginning in 1976 routinely stated their position on *Roe v. Wade.* Originally a case in Texas arising from a state law prohibiting abortion, the U.S. Supreme Court ruled that such a law was a violation of the right of personal privacy guaranteed by the due process clause of the Fourteenth Amendment, as well as a violation of rights set forth in the First, Third, Fourth, Fifth, and Ninth Amendments. The ruling, in effect, made abortion a legal procedure.

Presidents Richard Nixon, Ronald Reagan, George Bush, and George W. Bush expressed their opposition to *Roe v. Wade.* They viewed the decision as representing judicial flexibility and broad constructionist philosophy. Presidents Jimmy Carter and Bill Clinton supported the ruling.

What was the significance of *United States v. Nixon* (1974)?

The *United States v. Nixon* case (1974) centered on a subpoena ordering President Richard Nixon to produce tapes and writings related to the Watergate investigation. After the Nixon administration released to the public edited transcripts of forty-three conversations, Nixon's lawyer wanted the subpoena revoked. The judge who issued the

Cartoon satirizing the controversy surrounding President Richard Nixon's refusal to turn over the White House tapes to the House Judiciary Committee, which was responsible for investigating the Watergate cover-up. *Library of Congress.*

subpoena, John Sirica, ruled the release did not meet the specifications of the subpoena. An appeal was heard by the U.S. Supreme Court in July 1974.

Nixon claimed executive privilege (the right to keep private forms of communication like taped conversations and memos that allow an administration to function) and also claimed that the principle of separation of powers gave him, as president, judicial immunity. The Court ruled against Nixon on both claims. On executive privilege, the Court agreed that a high level of confidentiality extended to matters of national security, but not if it involves withholding evidence.

Nixon was ordered to turn over specified tapes and other documents to the Watergate Special Prosecutor, Leon Jaworski. There was concern whether Nixon would comply. Nixon did, and the tapes and documents showed that the president, despite his repeated denials, had indeed been involved in the cover-up of the Watergate break in.

The Supreme Court decision was rendered on July 24, 1974. Nixon announced he would comply the following day. A little over two weeks later, on August 8, 1974, Nixon announced his resignation from the presidency, effective the following day.

What was the significance of the *Clinton v. Jones* (1997) Supreme Court ruling?

In *Clinton v. Jones,* the Supreme Court ruled for the first time that a sitting president could stand trial in civil cases. Paula Corbin Jones had sued President Bill Clinton, alleging that she suffered several "abhorrent" sexual advances by him while she was an Arkansas state employee and Clinton was the state's governor during the 1980s. Jones claimed her continued rejection of Clinton's advances led to punitive action by her state supervisors. Clinton sought to invoke his presidential immunity to completely dismiss the Jones suit against him. A District Court judge denied Clinton's immunity request, but ordered a stay of any trial in the matter until after Clinton's presidency.

After several appeals, the case went before the Supreme Court in 1997. After the Supreme Court ruling, an Arkansas federal judge dismissed Jones's lawsuit on April 1, 1998, on grounds that Jones could not prove key instances of sexual harassment. An

Break-ins and Wiretaps

Daniel Ellsberg and Anthony Russo Jr. collaborated to steal the top-secret, forty-seven-volume *History of U.S. Decision-Making Process on Vietnam Policy* that became known as the Pentagon Papers. The government began preparing a case against Ellsberg and Russo shortly after the *New York Times* began publishing the Pentagon Papers on June 13, 1971. On that day, the Pentagon Papers shared front-page news in the *Times* with a report on the White House wedding of Tricia Nixon, the president's daughter.

Preliminary indictments against Ellsberg and Russo were issued on June 28, 1971, and more formal indictments occurred on December 30, 1971. In the meantime, on September 3, 1971, Nixon administration associates G. Gordon Liddy and E. Howard Hunt Jr. burglarized the office of Ellsberg's psychiatrist, looking for evidence of other conspirators but finding nothing of substance. The trial of Ellsberg and Russo encountered numerous delays and was stopped after a month in July 1972 when it was revealed the government had been secretly taping communication between the defendants.

When the trial resumed in January, the Watergate scandal was in full swing. On April 26, 1973, Watergate special prosecutors learned of the break-in on Ellsberg's psychiatrist's office, and soon after it was learned that Nixon administration officials had conducted more illegal wiretaps of the defendants' conversation than previously admitted. The entire case against Ellsberg and Russo was dismissed.

appeals court dismissed the case in December, citing an $850,000 settlement the parties reached in November 1998.

What was the significance of *Bush v. Gore* (2000)?

The 2000 presidential election was the closest in history. Either candidate would have won the election if they gained the twenty-five electoral votes of Florida. Exit polls indicated that the Democratic candidate, Vice President Al Gore, would win Florida and news agencies began predicting after the polls closed that Gore would get Florida's electoral votes and seemed headed for an electoral college victory. Around 10:00 P.M. Eastern Standard Time, however, actual vote tallies indicated a narrower margin than exit polls, and many agencies took back their projection, citing the Florida vote as too close to call. Meanwhile, accusations of voting irregularities, defective voting machines, confusing ballots, and unfair vote-counting methods surfaced.

Because the Republican candidate, Texas governor George W. Bush, led by only 525 votes after all the ballots were counted, the Gore campaign pressed for a manual recount in counties where most of the irregularities had been reported. A legal battle

An Excerpt from the Supreme Court's Decision in *Bush v. Gore*

Given the Court's assessment that the recount process underway was probably being conducted in an unconstitutional manner, the Court stayed the order directing the recount so it could hear this case and render an expedited decision. The contest provision, as it was mandated by the State Supreme Court, is not well calculated to sustain the confidence that all citizens must have in the outcome of elections. The State has not shown that its procedures include the necessary safeguards. The problem, for instance, of the estimated 110,000 overvotes has not been addressed, although [Florida Supreme Court] Chief Justice [Charles] Wells called attention to the concern in his dissenting opinion.

> Upon due consideration of the difficulties identified to this point, it is obvious that the recount cannot be conducted in compliance with the requirements of equal protection and due process without substantial additional work. It would require not only the adoption (after opportunity for argument) of adequate statewide standards for determining what is a legal vote, and practicable procedures to implement them, but also orderly judicial review of any disputed matters that might arise.

ensued within Florida, with the Florida Supreme Court calling for a manual recount of ballots that voting machines reported as having no vote for president, to find any votes those machines might have missed. The Bush campaign appealed this Florida ruling to the U.S. Supreme Court.

On December 12, 2000, shortly before the deadline for the state of Florida to certify its vote, the U.S. Supreme Court ordered that the recounts be halted. The 5–4 opinion, written by Chief Justice William Rehnquist, found that the recounts were being conducted in a manner that violated the Equal Protection Clause of the U.S. Constitution, and therefore had to stop. The recounts were being done without a well-defined, uniform standard for evaluating the ballots. Since the ongoing recount was unconstitutional, and there was little time left before the deadline to certify the vote, the Supreme Court ruled that no recount could take place. This decision effectively decided the election in favor of Bush.

The Supreme Court decision fell strictly along ideological lines: the court's five most conservative justices voted in favor of Bush and the four more liberal justices issued dissents in which they accused the majority of endangering the Supreme Court's legitimacy by the partisan appearance of its ruling. Justices Stephen G. Breyer and David Souter, who was nominated by George Bush and took his seat in 1990, argued in their official dissents that the Court should have allowed Florida to start a new recount, using constitutionally valid standards, even though time was short.

What was significant about the **Supreme Court's rulings on affirmative action** in 2003?

The U.S. Supreme Court decided the constitutionality of affirmative action by upholding in a 5–4 vote for the use of race as a factor to achieve "diversity" in college admissions. At issue was the University of Michigan Law School's practice of considering the race of applicants to ensure a "critical mass" of minority students attended the university. In the majority opinion, Justice Sandra Day O'Connor wrote, "The Equal Protection Clause does not prohibit the Law School's narrowly tailored use of race in admissions decisions to further a compelling interest in obtaining the educational benefits that flow from a diverse student body."

In a companion case, the Supreme Court ruled 6–3 against a University of Michigan undergraduate admissions policy, arguing that the policy violated the Equal Protection Clause of the Fourteenth Amendment or Title VI of the Civil Rights Act of 1964. The admissions process automatically granted a preference to applicants from certain minority groups. The court struck it down, claiming the specific method employed was too broad and mechanical and consequently violated the equal protection clause of the U.S. Constitution.

President George W. Bush had directed his attorney general to file a brief against the affirmative action policies. On January 15, 2003, he remarked on the Michigan affirmative action cases:

> The Supreme Court will soon hear arguments in a case about admission policies and student diversity in public universities. I strongly support diversity of all kinds, including racial diversity in higher education. But the method used by the University of Michigan to achieve this important goal is fundamentally flawed.

> At their core, the Michigan policies amount to a quota system that unfairly rewards or penalizes prospective students, based solely on their race. So, tomorrow my administration will file a brief with the court arguing that the University of Michigan's admissions policies, which award students a significant number of extra points based solely on their race, and establishes numerical targets for incoming minority students, are unconstitutional.

What was the controversy over rights of U.S. citizens designated as **"enemy combatants" during the George W. Bush administration**?

At the end of June and in early July 2004, the U.S. Supreme Court ruled in three cases against the Bush administration's argument that judges should play no role in supervising the war on terror. The court ruled that an American citizen seized in Afghanistan could not be detained indefinitely as an enemy combatant without providing the accused access to lawyers and courts.

The two other cases involved foreign nationals held at the U.S. naval base in Guantanamo Bay, Cuba. "The court affirmed adherence to due process at a time of grave and truly legitimate concerns about national security," stated Walter E. Dellinger, a professor at Duke Law School, in an article by Jeffrey Rosen, law professor at George Washington University, in the July 4, 2004, issue of the *New York Times*.

LEGACIES OF THE PRESIDENTS

REMEMBERING THE PRESIDENTS

What is a president's **legacy**?

A legacy, or what a person leaves behind for others, is open to many interpretations. Historians and political scholars have attempted to assess the president's effectiveness as a leader, his accomplishments in office, and his contributions to society. As political scholar James McGregor Burns noted, "We want everything: a strong leader, a consensus builder, a good manager, a policy expert, a great communicator, an ethical model, a visionary, a negotiator." Although opinions differ, George Washington, Abraham Lincoln, and Franklin D. Roosevelt consistently rank as strong leaders and great presidents. By most accounts, these men defined or redefined the presidency, and strengthened the position as a national office. Theodore Roosevelt, Andrew Jackson, and Harry S. Truman generally receive strong appraisals and often rank just below the top presidents. At the other end of the spectrum, weak leaders whose administrations were riddled with scandal, such as Ulysses S. Grant and Warren G. Harding, or who proved ineffective, including James Buchanan and Andrew Johnson, are seen as far less successful. However, ratings change from decade to decade, as historians and biographers gain deeper perspective on the man and the times during which he governed.

What is **George Washington's legacy**?

"First in war, first in peace, first in the hearts of his countrymen." That's how Richard Henry Lee, a Virginia congressman and Revolutionary War veteran, eulogized George Washington. Indeed, Washington is a legend in American history. As a revolutionary war hero, Washington was a stellar leader in the fight for an independent America. He was the only president to be elected unanimously by the electoral college, since at the time of the presidential elections, no one could conceive of anyone better than the dignified Washington to run the country. Indeed, Washington went a long way toward establishing the office of the president. During his first term as president, Washington joined the states together and helped lay the groundwork for the workings of the federal government. Washington appointed the first cabinet, which had four members, and appointed the first ten justices of the U.S. Supreme Court. As the nation's chief executive, he did not interfere with the policy-making powers that he felt the Constitution gave Congress, and he established a strong separation of powers among the executive and legislative branches. He was the first president to exercise use of the veto, a powerful tool in the presidency today that he used judiciously.

Washington also set the climate for a self-determined foreign policy. When the French Revolution led to war with France and England, Washington insisted that the fledgling United States remain neutral. By refusing to seek a third presidential term, Washington set the precedent for informal term limits on the executive office.

C-SPAN Ranks the Presidents

For its twentieth anniversary, the cable network C-Span conducted a survey of historians to rate presidents in each of ten categories ("qualities of presidential leadership") as part of the network's *American Presidents: Life Portraits* series broadcast from March to December 1999.

The ten categories were: 1) public persuasion; 2) crisis leadership; 3) economic management; 4) moral authority; 5) international relations; 6) administrative skills; 7) relations with Congress; 8) vision/setting agenda; 9) pursued equal justice for all; and 10) performance within context of times.

Listed below are the overall results of the survey of 58 historians, combining the ratings of each president across ten categories. Complete results and information are available at http://www.americanpresidents.org/survey/.

Ranking	President	Ranking	President
1	Abraham Lincoln	22	Jimmy Carter
2	Franklin Delano Roosevelt	23	Gerald Ford
3	George Washington	24	William Howard Taft
4	Theodore Roosevelt	25	Richard Nixon
5	Harry S. Truman	26	Rutherford B. Hayes
6	Woodrow Wilson	27	Calvin Coolidge
7	Thomas Jefferson	28	Zachary Taylor
8	John F. Kennedy	29	James Garfield
9	Dwight D. Eisenhower	30	Martin Van Buren
10	Lyndon Baines Johnson	31	Benjamin Harrison
11	Ronald Reagan	32	Chester Arthur
12	James K. Polk	33	Ulysses S. Grant
13	Andrew Jackson	34	Herbert Hoover
14	James Monroe	35	Millard Fillmore
15	William McKinley	36	John Tyler
16	John Adams	37	William Henry Harrison
17	Grover Cleveland	38	Warren G. Harding
18	James Madison	39	Franklin Pierce
19	John Quincy Adams	40	Andrew Johnson
20	George Bush	41	James Buchanan
21	Bill Clinton		

How was **George Washington "promoted" many years after leaving office**?

George Washington was the first man in American history to become a lieutenant general. General Washington commanded the Continental Army as a four-star general from 1775 to 1781. Many years after his death, Washington was promoted to the position of six-star "General of the Armies of Congress" by the order of President Jimmy Carter, who felt America's first president should also be America's highest military official.

What were **Thomas Jefferson's contributions to the presidency**?

A true "Renaissance man," America's third president was a lawyer, architect, scientist, musician, writer, educator, and horticulturist. After signing the Declaration of Independence, Jefferson served as governor of Virginia, ambassador to France, the nation's first secretary of state under George Washington, and vice president under John Adams. In fact, Jefferson is the only vice president in America's history to be elected to two terms as president. As president from 1801 to 1809, his greatest achievement was the Louisiana Purchase, which involved the purchase of the vast Louisiana Territory from France for $15 million (or three cents an acre). The purchase of the region, which consisted of the land between the Mississippi River and the Rockies, nearly doubled the size of the United States. Although the U.S. Constitution does not specifically grant the president the power to buy territory, Jefferson argued it was an assumed power under the president's treaty-making power. He is also known for signing into law the 1807 bill that banned the importation of slaves into the United States. To his credit or perhaps detriment, Jefferson helped found one of America's first political parties, the Democratic-Republicans.

Why didn't **Jefferson's gravestone** mention his tenure as president of the United States?

In some ways, Jefferson's final years were spent defending his legacy. During this time, Jefferson wrote his autobiography and political tracts, became increasingly concerned about the preservation of historical documents, and defended his role as an opposer of slavery and as the author of the Declaration of Independence. At key points in his life, Jefferson had written up lists of his accomplishments, and on the verge of his death in 1826, he composed his own epitaph, which read: "Author of the Declaration of American Independence, of the Statute of Virginia for religious freedom, and Father of the University of Virginia." Although no one knows for sure why, Jefferson's gravestone does not mention that he was president of the United States. Scholars speculate that he ranked his work as president below his other accomplishments.

Which early American leaders had **presidencies that were inferior to their other accomplishments**?

While much good can be found in the early-nineteenth-century presidents, historians have noted that several had presidencies that did not seem to live up to their other

Father of the Declaration of Independence

As the Declaration of Independence's primary author, Thomas Jefferson of Virginia holds the title "Father of the Declaration of Independence."Formally adopted on July 4, 1776, by the Continental Congress, the Declaration of Independence announced the birth of America as a new nation and set forth a philosophy of human freedom that would become a dynamic force throughout the entire world. Interestingly, Jefferson was not supposed to write the document. Despite his reputation as a writer, he expected John Adams of Massachusetts, the foremost public leader for independence, to draw up the document. But Adams, who was busy on the committees for foreign treaties and the Board of War, turned down Jefferson's request to draft the declaration. (Historians say Adams regretted his decision for the rest of his life.)

Meanwhile, the Second Continental Congress had formed a committee composed of Jefferson, Adams, Benjamin Franklin of Pennsylvania, Robert R. Livingston of New York, and Roger Sherman of Connecticut to prepare a statement concerning independence. The now-famous document was drafted by Jefferson as its principal author, with some assistance from Adams and Franklin. A total of forty-seven alterations, including the insertion of three complete paragraphs, was made to the text before it was presented to Congress on June 28, 1776.

accomplishments. These include Thomas Jefferson, James Madison, and John Quincy Adams. Jefferson, an ideological leader in the American Revolution, helped frame the reasons for the colonies to break free from Great Britain. His strong beliefs in human rights, a government derived from the people, and the separation of church and state helped lay the groundwork for the Declaration of Independence. As one of America's Founding Fathers, he did much to set the United States on its own independent footing, accomplishments that tend to overshadow his other achievements in political office. James Madison, too, did much for the fledgling United States. Madison is called the "Father of the Constitution" for his contributions as a political theorist and practical politician as he looked to replace the Articles of Confederation with an enduring national republic. Madison advocated a strong but limited national government and did his best to lead the country through two terms, although he was criticized for his handling of the War of 1812 against Great Britain.

John Quincy Adams enjoyed a robust political career before and after his presidency, first as minister to Prussia (served 1797–1801) under his father's administration, then as a Federalist U.S. senator from Massachusetts (served 1803–1808), and then as James Monroe's secretary of state (served 1817–1825). In 1814, Adams was also the chief negotiator of the Treaty of Ghent, a peace agreement with Great Britain that ended the War of 1812. Historians count Adams as one of the most accomplished secretaries of state, being the chief architect of the Monroe Doctrine of foreign policy for a unilateralist United States. Although his presidential administration was filled with such bold moves as creating federally funded roads and canals and calling for the creation of a national observatory, Adams was an unpopular president. After his tenure as America's chief executive, Adams served with distinction in the U.S. House of Representatives from 1831 to 1848, where he was a strong advocate of nationalism and denounced the doctrine of states' rights to protect the institution of slavery.

What was the **Age of Jackson**?

The "Age of Jackson" is the term used to frame Jackson's administration from 1829 to 1837, and to a lesser extent from 1837 to 1849, during which the Jacksonian Democrats held power. During these years, democracy began to expand, as states rewrote their constitutions and extended the right to vote to all free white males. Although inequalities existed, by the late 1830s, the United States had become a full democracy for adult white males. Jackson was a symbol of the new age of democracy, the "age of the common man." Jackson, who enjoyed wide support among Americans, was the first leader of the modern Democratic Party. The rival Whig Party was to a large extent anti-Jacksonian before dissolving in the 1850s and giving way to the Republican Party and the basic two-party system that functions to this day.

How did **Andrew Jackson strengthen the presidency**?

When Andrew Jackson took office in 1829, he brought a new strength to the presidency. His detractors called him "King Andrew" for his authoritative rule and liberal use of the presidential veto to squelch bills introduced by Whigs in Congress. However, many historians argue that he did not act as a supreme ruler who felt he was above politics but, to the contrary, as a political infighter who saw his role as protecting the people from the excesses of Congress. His presidency was one part of a long struggle to define the nature of governmental power and authority, and to determine where the real power of government lies: in Congress or in the White House. Jackson saw the office of president as a protection against the power usurpers of the other branches of government.

Two achievements dominate Jackson's administration. The first is Jackson's vetoing of the Second Bank of the United States, and the second is his handling of South Carolina's Ordinance of Nullification—which cut to the heart of states' rights versus the preservation of the federal Union. Jackson ordered troops to Charleston, South Carolina, when officials voted to nullify, or cancel, federal tariff laws. Although South Carolina threatened to secede from the union if the president tried to collect the taxes, Congress supported the president by authorizing him to use force to collect them. Ultimately, the federal government and South Carolina reached a compromise, the tariff was lowered, and South Carolina abandoned its nullification legislation. The

The Jackson Spirit

Lawyer and educator Washington McCartney spoke of the impact Andrew Jackson had on his countrymen:

> The spirit of an age sometimes descends to future generations in the form of a man ... in proportion as an individual concentrates within himself, the spirit which works through masses of men, and which moves, and should move them through the greatest cycles of time, in that proportion, he becomes entitled to their admiration and praise.... Because his countrymen saw their image and spirit in Andrew Jackson, they bestowed their honor and admiration upon him.

compromise, written by U.S. senator Henry Clay of Kentucky, reaffirmed a constitutional law that said while an individual state has a right to create legislation, it cannot overrule the federal government or the other states.

What were **James K. Polk**'s contributions to the presidency?

James K. Polk, the first "dark horse" candidate, won the presidency in 1844 by a narrow margin. He campaigned on a platform that advocated westward expansion, including the annexation of Texas, a hotly debated issue in political circles. The addition of Texas, which occurred after Polk's election but before his inauguration, extended the boundaries of the United States to the Rio Grande. The reestablishment of an independent treasury system, and the acquisition of territory from Mexico, which eventually became the states of California, New Mexico, Arizona, Utah, and parts of Colorado and Wyoming, also occurred during his presidency. During the county's war with Mexico, Polk drew on the spirit of expansionism. He was single-minded and determined in his goals as president and is credited with being the most effective president in the twenty-four-year period between the time Andrew Jackson left office in 1837 and Abraham Lincoln entered office in 1861. According to Harry S. Truman, who ranked Polk as one of America's most successful presidents, he knew "exactly what he wanted to do in a specified period of time and did it, and when he got through with it he went home."

What kind of president was **Abraham Lincoln**?

Consistently ranked as one of the top presidents, Abraham Lincoln is easily among the most notable leaders in America's history. Lincoln is remembered for his humility, courage, and fairness in light of the controversies he faced as America's chief executive from 1861 to 1865. Lincoln was a shrewd lawyer and accomplished politician who had

Abraham Lincoln giving his famous Gettysburg Address at the dedication of the Gettysburg National Cemetery during the Civil War in 1863. The painting, by Fletcher C. Ransom, was completed in 1863. *Getty Images.*

served in the Illinois state legislature and as a member of the U.S. House of Representatives before his presidential nomination. As one of America's wartime presidents, and the only one to govern during a civil war, Lincoln did much to strengthen the president's role as commander in chief of the armed forces.

Lincoln set a precedent for using emergency powers in times of crisis, although his decisions don't escape controversy. In 1861, he restricted civil liberties by suspending the writ of habeas corpus in several states before extending the suspension to all states in 1863. Although he insisted that the action was necessary to put down the insurrection of the Confederacy that threatened the Union, it allowed for the indefinite detainment of those suspected of sympathizing with the Confederate cause. Habeas corpus, guaranteed by the Constitution, dictates that someone accused of a crime will be brought before a court to decide the legality of the charges brought against him or her.

Although Lincoln despised war and was empathetic toward the lost lives, he never strayed from his commitment to preserve the Union. He issued the historic Emancipation Proclamation in 1863, and delivered his Gettysburg Address in Pennsylvania later that year. The Emancipation Proclamation set in motion emancipation of all slaves and abolition of slavery. When the Civil War came to a close, Lincoln urged for humane treatment of the South, insisting, "Let them have their horses to plow with" and "I want no one punished." Although Lincoln's second term ended abruptly by assassination, he was able to see an end to America's Civil War.

Why is **William McKinley** considered the first modern president?

Certain biographers and presidential scholars describe William McKinley as an important figure in American politics because of the significant contributions he made to strengthening and broadening the powers of the presidency. During the Spanish-American War of 1898, during which the United States went to war with Spain over Cuba's independence, McKinley did much to direct the military effort. During this brief war, the United States destroyed the Spanish fleet outside Santiago Harbor in Cuba, captured the Philippines, and occupied Puerto Rico. At the end of the war, McKinley's acquisition of land—Puerto Rico, Guam, and the seventy-two hundred islands of the Philippines—and his securing the ratification of the Treaty of Paris in the Senate underscored his expansive view of presidential power. He acted as chief diplomat in the negotiation of the treaty and, as moral leader, embarked on a tour of the West and South to rally popular opinion for his postwar policies. Presidential commissions governed these new territories with little interference from Congress.

After the Spanish-American War, McKinley pursued an aggressive (and to some, imperialistic) foreign policy. He is credited with expanding American trade to China through his Open-Door policy. McKinley sent troops to China to join an international force during the Boxer Rebellion without congressional authorization. Although his second term as president was cut short by an assassin, McKinley is remembered as ushering in the era of the modern president. Congress had exerted authority over the presidency following Lincoln's assassination; Grover Cleveland had some success in reestablishing the power of the presidency during his terms (he was elected to nonconsecutive terms in 1884 and 1892), but McKinley was the most powerful president after Lincoln. He made tough foreign-policy decisions that contributed to the United States' rise as a world power, and by most accounts laid the groundwork for future presidents' boldness in foreign-policy matters. In 1976, President Ronald Reagan said, "There have been people who suggest my ideas would take us back to the days of McKinley. Well, what's wrong with that? Under McKinley, we freed Cuba."

In what ways was **Theodore Roosevelt** a maverick?

Historians consider Theodore Roosevelt, the twenty-sixth president of the United States, a strong leader for both his domestic- and foreign-policy achievements. In 1901, Vice President Roosevelt assumed the office of president when William McKinley was assassinated, making Roosevelt, at age 42, the youngest man to become president. Roosevelt was then elected to a full term in 1904 with a landslide victory. As president, Roosevelt followed in McKinley's footsteps, excelling at international policy and steering the United States more actively into world politics. He was the first president to travel outside the United States while still in office, and is credited with single-handedly ensuring the construction of the Panama Canal, which opened trade routes between the Atlantic and the Pacific. His enforcement of the Monroe Doctrine prevented foreign bases from being built in the Caribbean and maintained that the United

States had had a responsibility to intervene in Latin America whenever necessary. In 1906, he received the Nobel Peace Prize for his work in the negotiations that led to the Treaty of Portsmouth, ending the Russo-Japanese War in 1905. This accolade made him the first American to win a Nobel Prize.

Roosevelt effectively used the press to promote himself and his causes. With the public's support, Roosevelt began assuming presidential powers not specifically listed in the Constitution and believed it was his right to do so as a "steward of the people." Unless the law forbade it, Roosevelt wrote that he "did and caused to be done many things not previously done by the president." For example, in an effort to foster conservationism, Roosevelt used the executive order, which was traditionally a wartime power, to set aside lands for preservation and for public use. Roosevelt became known as the "Father of Conservation" and signed legislation that established 5 national park units and 18 national monuments. He empowered the U.S. Forestry Service in 1905, increasing forest reserves from 43 million acres to 194 million acres while he was president.

Roosevelt used his diplomatic skills at home, settling a 1902 coal strike by negotiating with workers and mine owners. Roosevelt became known as a "trust buster," forcing the railroad monopoly in the Northwest to break apart. These actions gained Roosevelt the support of middle-class America, who hailed him as a workingman's hero. As the symbol of progressivism, Roosevelt secured the passage of the Elkins Act (1903) and the Hepburn Act (1906) for regulation of the railroads, the Pure Food and Drug Act and the Meat Inspection Act (both 1906) for consumer protection, and the Employers' Liability Act (1908) for labor.

What is **Woodrow Wilson**'s legacy?

Woodrow Wilson, who served as America's twenty-eighth president from 1913 to 1921, began his first term as an active president who initiated and directed policy, appearing before a joint session of Congress to ask the legislative branch to act on his tariff reform package. His larger reform package, called the New Freedom and consisting of tariff, banking, labor, and tax-related reforms, passed Congress by the end of his first year in office. This package expanded the executive branch substantially by creating the Department of Labor, the Federal Reserve, the Federal Trade Commission, and the Internal Revenue Service. During Wilson's two terms, he supported four constitutional amendments, the largest number since the passage of the Bill of Rights in 1791: the Sixteenth Amendment gave Congress the power to impose income taxes based on individual income, not population; the Seventeenth Amendment provided for the direct election of senators; the Eighteenth Amendment instituted prohibition; and the Nineteenth Amendment granted women the right to vote. He is also credited with putting together one of the most effective cabinets in presidential history.

Along with these and other domestic accomplishments, Wilson is also generally known for his successes in foreign affairs. As a twentieth-century wartime president,

The Progressive Presidents

The Progressive era of presidential leadership, which took place in the United States between 1895 and 1920, was characterized by a campaign for economic, social, and political reform. Ignited by rapidly increasing industrialism and business trusts on the one hand, spreading city slums and sweatshops on the other, those aligning themselves with the Progressive movement attempted to relieve these social ills by creating laws that would provide more power to the common people and slow the excesses of capitalism.

Under the leadership of William Jennings Bryan, the Democratic Party led a movement of agrarian reformers and supported women's suffrage. The party established a graduated income tax rather than the previous property tax, giving less power to those who had hidden property in stocks and bonds. A strong progressive president, Theodore Roosevelt helped establish increased government regulation of business in an effort to curtail illegal business practices and government monopolies that limited competition. Under President Woodrow Wilson, progressivism continued with tariffs, banking, labor, and tax reforms.

Wilson saw the United States through World War I. As an idealist and ardent believer in world peace and democracy, he generated public support for World War I (the "war to end all wars"), issued his Fourteen Points for Peace in January 1918, and led the vision to establish the peace-keeping League of Nations. When he returned from the Paris Peace Conference in 1919, he was heralded in the United States and abroad as an effective leader who took direct control of American foreign police. For his efforts, he won the Nobel Peace Prize in 1920. Although Wilson's vision for a League of Nations would be cut short by his lack of support in the U.S. Senate and his dehabilitating stroke, he became an inspiration to future wartime presidents.

Who was the first president since the Civil War to make a **public statement for civil rights**?

President Warren G. Harding was the first president since the Civil War (1861–1865) to make a public statement for civil rights. And despite mixed reviews of his effectiveness as a president, historians consistently cite him as an early-twentieth-century proponent for civil rights. On October 26, 1921, in a speech in Birmingham, Alabama, President Harding advocated civil rights for all Americans. Earlier, he reversed President Woodrow Wilson's policy of excluding African Americans from federal positions, supported an anti-lynching bill, and advocated the establishment of an interracial commission to find ways to improve race relations. While both Republicans and Democrats played a role in derailing these presidential initiatives,

417

Harding remained true to his underlying philosophy of civil rights and equal treatment for all.

Why is **Franklin Roosevelt** considered one of the **greatest presidents**?

Franklin D. Roosevelt assumed the presidency in March 1933 when the country was in the midst of the Great Depression. During this time of severe economic crisis, between thirteen and fifteen million people were unemployed. Roosevelt's response was to take charge. With enormous determination and the full support of Congress, Roosevelt enacted his "New Deal," a series of economic measures designed to reinvigorate the economy and restore the confidence of the American people in their political and financial institutions. Roosevelt's New Deal was the largest set of relief policies and federal domestic legislation to be enacted in U.S. history. These policies led to the establishment of a range of administrative agencies between 1933 and 1935, all of which were meant to provide relief for those in need, recovery for the nation at large, and long-range reform of the nation's economic institutions. (A list of New Deal programs appears in The President Leads: The Economy—Policies and Programs, Booms and Busts.)

Among the most significant pieces of New Deal legislation achieved by Roosevelt and Congress was the Banking Act of 1933, which brought an end to the panic that choked the nation's banking system. Other significant New Deal measures included the establishment of the Works Progress Administration (WPA), the Civilian Conservation Corps (CCC), and the Agricultural Adjustment Administration (AAA). The most enduring measure of the New Deal was the 1935 Social Security Act, which led to the establishment of the Social Security Administration and the creation of a national system of old-age pensions and unemployment compensation. In addition, the New Deal created a number of significant regulatory (or "alphabet") agencies, including the Securities and Exchange Commission (SEC), the Federal Housing Administration (FHA), the National Labor Relations Board (NLRB), the Civil Aeronautics Authority (CAA), and the Federal Communications Commission (FCC).

The first two terms of Roosevelt's presidency helped stave off the worst effects of the Great Depression, but it was the switch to a wartime economy during World War II that ended the Great Depression.

How did the **New Deal expand the power of the presidency**?

The New Deal era of the 1930s marked a major turning point in both the power of the presidency and U.S. economic history. This period, more than any other, defined the federal government as an active and extensive participant in regulating the nation's private economy. President Roosevelt's New Deal program, meant to get the country back to work after the Great Depression, marked the first time that the federal government regulated businesses to such a large extent, and became the provider of social security for the people. With its "alphabet" agencies and numerous work and social programs, the New Deal instituted a number of reforms in almost every area of the economy: finance, agriculture, labor, industry, and consumer protection. Although conservatives argue that the New Deal brought *too much* government intervention in the economy, most historians agree that the New Deal's greatest achievements transcended economic statistics—that in an uncertain world climate, the New Deal maintained and even restored the faith of the American people in their government.

What are the key accomplishments of **Harry S. Truman**'s presidency?

Harry S. Truman abruptly assumed the presidency after President Franklin D. Roosevelt died from a cerebral hemorrhage in 1945. As vice president under Roosevelt, Truman was not kept abreast of such vital policy matters as the development of the atomic bomb, and when he assumed the presidency he described the incredible shock and weight the position placed on him. With World War II drawing to a close, Truman authorized the use of atomic bombs against Japan. In many respects, he picked up where Roosevelt left off, leading the United States in helping form the United Nations (UN) and instituting the 1947 Marshall Plan (or European Recovery Program) to help rebuild a wartorn Europe. However, Truman was never able to garner the same kind of loyalty from the American people that FDR enjoyed.

His Truman Doctrine—in which he stated, "It must be the policy of the U.S. to support free peoples who are resisting attempted subjugation by armed minorities or by outside pressures"—initiated a foreign policy of "containment" to prevent the spread of communism. Through the UN, President Truman supported the creation of the state of Israel in 1948 and continued to fight for peace and freedom with his 1949 Four Point Program. This innovative program marked the beginning of U.S. commitment to aid underdeveloped nations in Latin America, Asia, and Africa. At a time when the Cold War gripped the world, Truman outlined his plans for the North Atlantic Treaty Organization (NATO). He took aggressive and controversial action when communist forces invaded South Korea in 1950, ultimately preserving South Korean independence, though at the cost of many lives as well as the support of the American people and the press.

On the domestic front, Truman is known for promoting his Fair Deal, which instituted a number of improvements at home, such as the allocation of federal funds for new housing, an increase in the minimum wage, extension of Social Security benefits, and desegregation of the armed forces. Portions of the president's Fair Deal legislation failed to pass in Congress, and historians generally discuss the program with mixed reviews. Truman promoted civil rights legislation but met resistance from Congress.

How is **Dwight D. Eisenhower** remembered?

Although his standing as an effective president has improved over the years, Eisenhower is remembered mainly for ensuring peace after the end of the Korean War. Elected in 1952, Eisenhower brought a new prestige into the executive office, having

President John F. Kennedy delivering his inaugural address after taking the oath of office on January 20, 1961. Incoming vice president Lyndon B. Johnson and outgoing vice president Richard Nixon are seated behind Kennedy. *AP/Wide World Photos.*

served as the commanding general of the Allied forces in Europe during World War II. Upon returning from a victorious D-Day, Eisenhower was hailed a hero by the American people, and entered the presidency with immense public support. As president, he was able to bring closure to the Korean War and focused his administration on easing the tensions of the Cold War. However, his administration is also remembered for its duplicity, having stockpiled nuclear weapons while discussing disarmament plans with the Soviet Union. Although Eisenhower was the first twentieth-century Republican president to be elected to two terms, his failed Paris Peace Summit of 1960 ended his presidency on a weak note. His "Farewell Address," in which he warned of a growing relationship in the military-industrial complex, is frequently cited as a notable criticism of defense spending.

Did **John F. Kennedy** have any successes as president?

John F. Kennedy enjoyed several successes in his brief time as the country's thirty-fifth president, from 1961 to 1963. Kennedy is credited with establishing the Peace Corps and proposing civil rights legislation to Congress. He is largely praised for his handling of the Cuban Missile Crisis. Unlike the failed Bay of Pigs invasion that haunted the opening of his administration, Kennedy met the Cuban Missile Crisis with determination and resolve. He carried out tough negotiations that resulted in the withdrawal of Soviet missiles from communist Cuba. Though Cold War tensions were high, Kennedy would not live to see his administration play a role in the world's tumultuous times.

Americans mourned the assassination of JFK in 1963, not because of his long list of presidential accomplishments, but because Kennedy had come to represent a robust idealism. His administration had been dubbed "Camelot," as Americans recall the president's leadership style, confidence, and personality, as well as first lady Jacqueline's style and grace under pressure. JFK's optimism and eloquence fill his public speeches, many of which are still liberally quoted.

What was **Lyndon B. Johnson's downfall** as president?

When John F. Kennedy's death elevated Lyndon B. Johnson to the presidency in 1963, Johnson effectively pressured Congress to pass the civil rights legislation Kennedy had introduced and Congress had delayed acting on. Elected president in 1964, Johnson established his plan for a "Great Society," declared a federally funded "war on poverty," and enacted a series of landmark pieces of legislation that included the most far-reaching civil rights laws since the Reconstruction legislation following the Civil War. After his success with the 1964 Civil Rights Act outlawing discrimination in employment, Johnson used his considerable political skills to win passage of the 1965 Voting Rights Act and the 1968 Civil Rights Act barring discrimination in housing. (A full list of Great Society programs appears in The President Leads: Domestic Issues—Social Programs and Civil Rights.)

The Johnson administration's war against communism in Vietnam overshadowed his legislative successes at home. Johnson's escalation of American military involvement in the Vietnam War from 1965 to 1968 turned him from a popular successor of Kennedy to a beleaguered leader who withdrew early from his bid for reelection in 1968. By the end of his presidency, anger over the war and the loss of thousands of American soldiers had triggered ongoing protests across the country. Most historians assess Johnson as a great social reformer who became overwhelmed by the Vietnam War.

What was **Ronald Reagan's greatest achievement** as president?

Reagan was a strong chief executive whose program of deregulation and cutbacks in government contrasted with Johnson's expansion of federal programs. Reagan's economic program of tax cuts and deregulation helped stimulate and reinvigorate the American economy, although budget deficits sapped economic strength at the end of the decade. However, historians cite Reagan's "finest hour" as his accomplishments during his second term. With the rise of Soviet leader Mikhail Gorbachev in 1985, Reagan began nuclear disarmament talks began between the United States and the Soviet Union. In 1987, the two leaders signed the Intermediate-Range Nuclear Forces (INF) Treaty, in which both countries agreed to destroy hundreds of nuclear missiles and permit on-site inspections to ensure treaty compliance. Many considered the treaty a break-

President George W. Bush escorts former first lady Nancy Reagan at a funeral service for former president Ronald Reagan. In the middle row (left to right) are former presidents and first ladies George and Barbara Bush, Jimmy and Rosalynn Carter, and Gerald and Betty Ford. In the front row are first lady Laura Bush, Vice President Dick Cheney and his wife Lynne, and former president Bill Clinton. *AP/Wide World Photos.*

through agreement that put the end of the Cold War into tangible reach. In a 1988 visit to the United States, Gorbachev announced an unprecedented reduction in Soviet armed forces and agreed to withdraw troops from Eastern Europe and Afghanistan.

In 1994, Ronald Reagan announced that he had Alzheimer's disease. On June 5, 2004, he died from the neurological disorder. As CNN announced his death and discussed his legacy, they confirmed that Reagan will be remembered as the man "who launched the modern-day conservative political movement with the 'Reagan Revolution,'" quickened the end of the Cold War, and reinvigorated the Republican Party.

What was **George Bush's greatest strength**?

George Bush's diplomatic and military actions are an enduring mark of his legacy. In late 1989, President Bush sent U.S. troops into Panama to capture General Manuel Noriega, the country's dictator. Although he acted boldly without congressional approval, Bush asserted he was moving in the spirit of the Monroe Doctrine and acting well within his powers as America's commander in chief. Less than a year later, following Iraq's invasion of Kuwait in mid-1990, Bush helped forge a coalition of thirty nations to restore Kuwaiti sovereignty. With the success of Operation Desert Storm, Bush led the world in his vision for collective security known as the "New World Order."

Meanwhile, a series of world events, including the dismantling of a communist Soviet Union under Soviet president and Bush ally Mikhail Gorbachev, eventually brought about the end of the Cold War. The reunification of Germany and democratization of much of the rest of Eastern Europe followed during Bush's presidency. Bush and Gorbachev signed the Strategic Arms Reduction Treaty (START), which guaranteed deep cuts in both U.S. and Soviet nuclear arsenals over a period of seven years. As President Bush left office, only three countries—China, Cuba, and North Korea—had retained their communist regimes.

Despite these enormous changes and Bush's deft handling of the Gulf War, Bush did not win a second term. The American public criticized the president for a weak economy and budget deficits, and instead elected Democrat Bill Clinton into the White House.

How will **Bill Clinton** be remembered?

Presidential scholars have not yet decided how to rate the forty-second president. In a December 2000 *New York Times* article, President Clinton is described as having

Future president Bill Clinton shakes hands with President John F. Kennedy on an American Legion Boys Nation trip to the White House in 1963. *Getty Images.*

"striking strengths, glaring shortcomings." Clinton ran his administration intent on making his mark as a Democratic social reformer, yet many remember his failed attempts at overhauling America's health-care system. Although his years in the White House from 1993 to 2001 were rife with scandal—especially the Monica Lewinski affair, which ultimately led to Clinton's impeachment in 1998—Clinton completed his tenure as president with high public-approval ratings. He presided over the longest sustained growth of the American economy and projected a visionary yet limited domestic program despite the divided government that characterized his presidency (in 1994, for the first time in 40 years, Republicans controlled both houses of Congress). Whether or not his administration was successful, scholars credit Clinton with sidestepping numerous political minefields that could have brought about his demise.

Clinton became the first Democratic since Franklin D. Roosevelt to be elected to a second term, the first to lead America in a post–Cold War world, and the first elected president to be impeached. His post-presidential years have been spent as an independent ambassador, effective fundraiser for the Democratic Party, and a writer. His autobiography, *My Life,* released in June 2004, quickly became a hot seller.

Which presidents delivered **notable farewell addresses**?

When it comes to notable farewell addresses, historians are quick to cite George Washington's 1796 farewell address to the presidency. Washington spoke of the political climate around him. He warned his fellow Americans of the fractious nature of political parties and their ability to upset domestic tranquility. Washington called for leaders to lay aside party leanings and unite for the common good, exercising an "American character" totally free of foreign attachments and alliances with countries that threatened America's development. For decades, Washington's farewell address was read annually in Congress.

Other farewell speeches, such as Harry S. Truman's 1953 farewell speech, speak to broader issues that are typically found in other presidential addresses. In Truman's case, he briefly imparted the vision of the end of the Cold War. Dwight D. Eisenhower, when he left office in 1961, warned against the establishment of a "military-industrial complex" and spoke of the necessary evils of an arms race: "A vital element in keeping the peace is our military establishment. Our arms must be mighty, ready for instant action, so that no potential aggressor may be tempted to risk his own destruction." Richard Nixon's resignation speech, delivered in August 1974, expressed his great sadness in leaving office, acknowledged that mistakes had been made, and expressed the need to start "that process of healing which is so desperately needed in America." Ronald Reagan's farewell speech in January 1989 spoke of his achievements in boosting both the economy and the nation's morale. Echoing the vision of early Puritan leader John Winthrop, Reagan encouraged Americans to remember their country as a "shining city upon a hill."

Who was responsible for establishing the **presidential library system**?

Presidential libraries—the repository for the papers, records, and other historical materials of U.S. presidents—are a legacy of almost every president. For much of the nineteenth and early twentieth century, presidents dispersed their papers randomly among libraries, historical societies, and private collections. Many of the collections prior to the presidency of Herbert Hoover, reside in the Library of Congress. In 1939, President Franklin D. Roosevelt established the presidential library system when he donated his personal and presidential papers to the National Archives and Records Administration (NARA) of the federal government. In an effort to keep his papers public, he also established a library at his estate in Hyde Park, New York. At the dedication of his library in 1941, Roosevelt summarized his philosophy for leaving a legacy of his presidential paperwork: "To bring together the records of the past and to house them in buildings where they will be preserved for the use of men and women in the future, a nation must believe in three things: It must believe in the past. It must believe in the future. It must, above all, believe in the capacity of its own people so to learn from the past that they can gain in judgment in creating their own future."

In 1955, Congress passed the Presidential Libraries Act, which established a system of privately constructed and federally maintained libraries. The act encouraged other presidents to donate their historical materials to the government, ensuring the preservation of presidential papers and their availability to the public. However, the Presidential Records Act of 1978 changed the long-held belief that a president's papers were his own. According to NARA, this law established that the presidential records that document the "constitutional, statutory, and ceremonial duties of the President" are the property of the U.S. government, and must be turned over to the archivist of the United States after the president leaves office.

Which president is known for keeping an **extensive diary**?

James K. Polk governed America for only four years, from 1845 to 1849, but he left behind a unique legacy: a thorough, written account of his administration. Except for the journals of John Quincy Adams, Polk kept the most extensive personal notes of any American president. On August 26, 1845—about five-and-a-half months after he took office—Polk made his first entry, which had been prompted by a conversation he had with his secretary of state, James Buchanan, the details of which he wanted to note for future reference. Polk went on to produce a total of 25 volumes, each containing 100 to 250 handwritten pages. Recognized today as one of the most valuable documents for studying the American presidency, the diary provides a rare behind-the-scenes glimpse of decision-making in the White House, and has helped historians more objectively assess the contributions of America's eleventh president. The diary was first published in book form in 1910.

LIFE AFTER THE PRESIDENCY

What do presidents *do* after **leaving office**?

There is no designated role for presidents after they leave office. For the most part, their activities depend on their standing in the eyes of the American people, their stature within their political party, and their ambition to continue in the public arena. Some are happy to "retire" to their hometowns, others settle in to pen their memoirs, others actively pursue careers in the private sector, and still others continue to serve their country. For some individuals, what they do after the presidency contributes significantly to their legacy, being respected as humanitarians, peace-makers, diplomats, even presidential advisers to their successors. History reveals varied attempts at finding a fulfilling work life after having held the most powerful job in the nation.

Which **presidents remained active in politics** after their presidencies?

The phrase "politics after the presidency" brings to mind a handful of notable men, not the least of whom was John Quincy Adams, the only president to be elected to the U.S. House of Representatives after serving as president. Adams served for seventeen

425

years in the House (1831–1848), gaining a reputation as a persuasive speaker. He is known for fighting against the long-standing House "gag rule" that prohibited members from submitting antislavery positions on the floor; he finally saw its repeal in 1844. Of his position in the House, he later wrote, "No election or appointment ever gave me so much pleasure." Similarly, Andrew Johnson, although he left his presidency disgraced, managed to serve briefly in the Senate, from March to July 1875, before his death by stroke that summer. It was his second stint as a U.S. senator, having served from 1857 to 1862. In his only floor speech as a post-presidential senator, Johnson criticized the Grant administration and its Reconstruction policy.

America's second president and John Quincy Adams's father, John Adams, emerged from retirement briefly in 1820 to become a presidential elector, casting his vote for James Monroe during his reelection campaign. The following year, he was chosen as a delegate to revise the Massachusetts Constitution of 1779, a document he had had profound influence over years earlier. In 1829, former presidents James Madison and James Monroe both served on the Virginia Constitutional Convention. Former president Martin Van Buren twice served as an elector: In 1852, he voted for fellow Democrat Franklin Pierce, and in 1856 he voted for James Buchanan.

Which **former presidents decided to run for the presidency again**?

In 1848, eight years after his presidency ended, Martin Van Buren ran on the Free Soil Party ticket for president. Although Van Buren did not win, the Free Soil platform drew enough votes from Democratic opponent Lewis Cass to ensure a Whig victory for Zachary Taylor. In 1856, Millard Fillmore ran for the presidency again on the American, or Know-Nothing, Party ticket, polling more than eight hundred thousand ballots in that November's election, but ultimately coming in third to the winner, Democrat James Buchanan. Grover Cleveland also attempted a comeback in 1892, although unlike Van Buren and Fillmore, Cleveland won the presidential election that year with the Democratic Party's support, becoming the only president in American history to serve non-consecutive terms. He defeated incumbent president Benjamin Harrison four years after Harrison had defeated incumbent president Cleveland. After two terms as a successful Republican president, Theodore Roosevelt ran for the presidency on the Progressive ticket in 1912. He came in second place ahead of his successor, Republican incumbent William Howard Taft, but behind Democratic opponent Woodrow Wilson.

Which presidents **served in some military capacity after they left office**?

Three former presidents served the United States in largely symbolic military positions after their terms as president: George Washington, Ulysses S. Grant, and Dwight D. Eisenhower. Washington reluctantly accepted the position of commander in chief of the American military in 1798 when war with France was looming, and for a few months went about raising an army. As the threat of war subsided, Washington entered retirement without participating in active duty. Nevertheless, Washington remains the only former president to have commanded the American military after his term as president. A financially depleted Grant served as an honorary, paid general in the army during the last months of his life. Eisenhower served as a restored five-star general of the U.S. Army, although he never saw active duty.

Which presidents **achieved significant accomplishments in education or law** after leaving office?

After completing his second term as president, Thomas Jefferson stewarded the establishment of the University of Virginia, acting as the chairman of its development commission. Jefferson and his commission chose Charlottesville as the approved site for the campus, after which Jefferson designed the campus, led fundraising efforts, hired a building staff, developed curriculum, and recruited a fledgling faculty. The university opened its doors in March 1825 to high acclaim, and to Jefferson's credit.

Rutherford B. Hayes found time after the presidency to serve as a trustee of Ohio State University and other midwestern colleges. After winning the Republican nomination for a second term of office in 1892, Benjamin Harrison lost the election to Democrat Grover Cleveland. At this time, he also experienced the loss of his wife, Caroline. A dejected Harrison returned to his hometown of Indianapolis, where he set up a law practice and wrote actively on politics. He became a law instructor at Stanford University, and published both a political treatise, *This Country of Ours* (1897), and a memoir, *Views of an Ex-President* (1901).

After Grover Cleveland left the presidency, he and his wife Frances moved into their new estate in Princeton, New Jersey. In 1899, Cleveland became a professor of public affairs at Princeton. In 1901, he became a trustee of the university, and a few short years later president of the Board of Trustees. After the presidency, William Howard Taft and his wife settled in New Haven, Connecticut, where Taft became a Kent Professor of Law at Yale University. While teaching at Yale from 1913 to 1921, Taft also became president of the American Bar Association and delivered speeches around the nation. Taft achieved his ultimate career goal when he was named Chief Justice of the Supreme Court in 1921 by President Warren G. Harding.

Which presidents were **happy to "retire" at home**?

In contrast to ongoing achievers, some presidents felt they had accomplished a full lifetime of work by the time they left the executive office. George Washington retired to his estate in Mount Vernon before dying there in December 1799. Similarly, James Madison, Andrew Jackson, and, ultimately, Thomas Jefferson, all retired to their plantations, where, for the most part, they attended to the duties of running their large estates. They frequently entertained guests and caught up with correspondence. Jefferson and Madison often enjoyed long hours of conversation, Madison's estate, Montpelier, being just a short distance from Jefferson's home. John Adams settled into retirement in his Braintree (now Quincy), Massachusetts, estate, called Old House, where he focused on the "labors of agriculture and amusements of letters."

When he left the presidency, Rutherford B. Hayes said, "Nobody ever left the Presidency with less regret, less disappointment, fewer heartburnings ... than I do." Returning home to his estate in Fremont, Ohio, to lead a quiet life, Hayes oversaw the farms he owned in Ohio, Minnesota, North Dakota, and West Virginia. However, Hayes also became active in social reform. Lyndon B. Johnson retired to his Texas ranch, where he wrote his 1971 memoir, *The Vantage Point,* and became a very private figure.

Is it true that **George Washington only lived a few years after leaving the presidency**?

Yes. When George Washington retired to his Mount Vernon estate to resume his intermittent "career" as an independent farmer, he had no intention of leaving his well-loved home. He quickly adapted to the normal routine of plantation living, making a daily inspection by horseback of his farms. Although Washington had had bouts of smallpox, malaria, respiratory infections, and pneumonia during his lifetime, the ex-president was in fairly good health until late 1799. At that time, after riding for hours in a snowstorm, Washington developed a severe throat infection that led to his death on December 14—just a few years after leaving office. By contrast, America's second president, John Adams, lived more than twenty-five years beyond the last year of his term as president.

What did **Thomas Jefferson do after leaving office**?

Jefferson's Virginian estate, Monticello, was a working plantation, though it rarely produced enough wheat and tobacco to keep Jefferson and his large staff afloat. Like fellow Virginia residents James Madison and James Monroe, Jefferson experienced financial precariousness and debt. The consummate horticulturalist, Jefferson performed scientific and agricultural experiments at his plantation. He served as president of the American Philosophical Society from 1797 to 1815. Continuing in the spirit of his "Renaissance man" personality, Jefferson studied the classics, worked as an architect, and spent almost a decade energized around founding the University of Virginia. By the time the university opened in March 1825, Jefferson was in failing health. He died at Monticello on July 4, 1826, just several hours before the death of another great founding father, John Adams. The two founding fathers did not speak to each other for over a decade after Jefferson's inaugural in 1801, which Adams—the outgoing president—did not attend. They renewed their friendship a decade before they both died. Among Adams's last words were, "Jefferson still survives," not knowing Jefferson had died earlier that day.

Life After the Presidency

President	Jobs After the Presidency
George Washington	Planter, lieutenant-general of all the U.S. armies
John Adams	Writer
Thomas Jefferson	Writer, gentleman farmer, rector at the University of Virginia
James Madison	Rector at the University of Virginia
James Monroe	Writer, regent at the University of Virginia
John Quincy Adams	U.S. representative from Massachusetts
Andrew Jackson	Gentleman farmer
Martin Van Buren	Activist for Free Soil Party
William Henry Harrison	Died in office
John Tyler	Lawyer, chancellor of the College of William and Mary, member of the Confederate House of Representatives
James K. Polk	Died 103 days after leaving office
Zachary Taylor	Died in office
Millard Fillmore	Rogue political activist, chancellor of the University of Buffalo
Franklin Pierce	Gentleman farmer
James Buchanan	Writer
Abraham Lincoln	Died in office
Andrew Johnson	U.S. senator from Tennessee
Ulysses S. Grant	Political activist, writer
Rutherford B. Hayes	Education activist, president of the National Prison Reform Association
James A. Garfield	Died in office
Chester Alan Arthur	Lawyer
Grover Cleveland	Reelected president
Benjamin Harrison	Lawyer, lecturer
William McKinley	Died in office
Theodore Roosevelt	Hunter, writer
William Howard Taft	Professor, chief justice of the U.S. Supreme Court
Woodrow Wilson	Retired in poor health
Warren G. Harding	Died in office
Calvin Coolidge	Writer, president of the American Antiquarian Society
Herbert Hoover	Chair of the Hoover Commission on administrative reform
Franklin D. Roosevelt	Died in office
Harry S. Truman	Writer
Dwight D. Eisenhower	Writer
John F. Kennedy	Died in office
Lyndon Johnson	Rancher, writer
Richard Nixon	Writer
Gerald Ford	Writer
Jimmy Carter	Writer, humanitarian, Nobel-prize winning statesman
Ronald Reagan	Writer
George Bush	Private citizen
Bill Clinton	Writer, independent ambassador

Source: Infoplease.com, http://www.infoplease.com/ipa/A0768854.html (accessed on July 5, 2004).

What **major contribution did Thomas Jefferson make** to preserving the government?

After the presidency, Thomas Jefferson was the driving force behind the second Library of Congress. During the War of 1812, the British burned down the original Library when they destroyed many of Washington, D.C.'s buildings and landmarks. In 1815, Jefferson sold his entire sixty-five-hundred-volume personal library to the government, for almost $24,000, which greatly helped the president with his personal debts. However, the sale of his works was not solely a financial endeavor. Jefferson believed that an active mind was tied to a healthy government; indeed, that self-government depended on the unrestrained study of truth by an informed and active citizenry. Unfortunately, much of Jefferson's collection was destroyed in another fire in 1851. Today, the complete Thomas Jefferson Papers from the Manuscript Division make up the core of the Library of Congress. His papers consist of approximately twenty-seven thousand documents, dating from 1606 to 1827. These papers, which include correspondence, commonplace books, financial account books, and manuscript volumes, make up the largest collection of original Jefferson documents in the world.

What was **James Madison's notable contribution to political science**?

Historians credit James Madison with principal authorship of the U.S. Constitution at the 1787 Constitutional Convention in Philadelphia. Although he actively participated in the debates and in the drafting of the document, he also took the most complete set of notes at that convention, capturing the essence and, in some cases, the exact words of the framers. In 1821, four years after leaving the presidency, Madison began formulating his notes on the Constitutional Convention, and they became a part of the 1840 edition of his papers. Why Madison did not publish them before his death in 1836 is unclear. He might have wanted to keep the account of the proceedings confidential, as the framers originally agreed, until the death of the delegates. Scholars concur that Madison's notes are invaluable in providing Americans with a definitive insight into the intent of the Constitution, and stand as a unique component of the president's legacy.

How did **John Tyler spend his years after the presidency**?

John Tyler left the presidency with few political allies, having alienated both political parties during his term from 1841 to 1845. He left for his home, Sherwood Forest, in Virginia, to retire with his second wife Julia, though it wouldn't be long before he became active in politics again. Although he was originally a Whig when he ran as William Henry Harrison's vice presidential running mate in 1840, after the presidency Tyler returned to the Democratic Party and supported the Compromise of 1850 and the Kansas-Nebraska Act of 1854, both of which made possible the expansion of slavery. In both 1852 and 1856, Tyler set his eyes on the presidency, hoping that the Democratic conventions would choose him as a compromise candidate. When that didn't happen, Tyler sponsored and presided over the "Richmond Convention," a peace convention that looked toward finding a compromise between the Northern and Southern states in order to avoid Civil War. When the convention failed, he encouraged Virginia to secede from the Union. Tyler then became a member of the Provisional Congress of the Southern Confederacy. He subsequently won election to the Confederate House of Representatives, but died in early 1862 before he could take his seat. Tyler was the only former president to lobby for the rebel South. He also spent his post-presidential years on another legacy: "His Accidency" fathered seven children after he turned fifty-five. Tyler was the grand-uncle of Harry S. Truman.

What did **Rutherford B. Hayes do for social causes**?

Rutherford B. Hayes kept his pledge to serve only one term and left the White House in 1881. While tending to his midwestern farms, the former president spent much time as a humanitarian and social reformer. Hayes biographer Ari Hoogenboom confirmed this as part of Hayes's legacy, noting, "With the exception of Jimmy Carter, no retired president has been more involved in social causes than Hayes." Throughout his life, Hayes was an advocate of public education for all races. He served as director of the George Peabody Educational Fund and the John F. Slater Fund, both of which were dedicated to the cause of African American education, including improving schools in the rural South. As president of the Slater Fund, Hayes gave a scholarship to W. E. B. Du Bois, a future educator and civil rights leader, who would help found the National Association for the Advancement of Colored People (NAACP) in 1909. The Slater Fund also embraced the education of African American females, a liberal concept at that time in history. In the early 1890s, Hayes actively participated at the Lake Mohonk Conferences, which sought to find ways to integrate the full participation of African Americans and Native Americans into mainstream American life.

Hayes also actively supported prison reform, serving as president of the National Prison Reform Association from 1883 until his death in 1893. As a leader in that organization, Hayes fought for the more humane treatment of prisoners.

Which president served as **chief justice of the Supreme Court** after his presidential term?

In June 1921, President Warren G. Harding appointed William Howard Taft to the position of chief justice of the U.S. Supreme Court. Taft served on the Court for eight-and-a-half years and wrote more than 250 opinions before retiring in February 1930. He is the only individual who served as both president and as a member of the Supreme Court. He helped pass the 1925 Judges Act, which enabled the Supreme Court to give priority to cases of national importance. Interestingly, Associate Justice Charles Evans Hughes resigned from the court in 1916 to become a Republican presidential candidate in the race with Woodrow Wilson. Hughes lost to incumbent Wilson by a small electoral-vote margin. In 1930, Hughes returned to the high court when President Herbert Hoover appointed him Hughes chief justice, after Taft resigned due to poor health.

Which president was involved in **humanitarian relief efforts**?

Herbert Hoover received much blame for the nation's economy during the Great Depression and left office in 1933 an unpopular leader. Hoover had been a hero during World War I for his leadership in food distribution and relief efforts. His post-presidential reputation began to thrive beginning with a tour of Europe in 1938. There, he met German dictator Adolf Hitler. Shortly afterward, he became one of the first Americans to denounce Nazi persecution of the Jewish people. After World War II, Hoover returned to his roots in relief work when in 1946 President Harry S. Truman appointed him coordinator of food relief for all of wartorn Europe. From 1947 to 1949, as chairman of the Hoover Commission, he embarked on a two-year-long study of the bureaucracy of the executive branch, and his suggestions for streamlining government were incorporated into the Reorganization Act of 1949 with the blessing of President Truman. Under President Dwight D. Eisenhower, from 1953 to 1955, Hoover chaired the Commission on Government Operations, which recommended the establishment of the Department of Health, Education, and Welfare.

What did **Gerald Ford do after the presidency**?

After losing to Georgia governor Jimmy Carter in the 1976 presidential campaign, Gerald Ford soon began a rather active post-presidential career. He served as an adjunct professor of government at the University of Michigan, wrote his memoirs, and was a founding member of the Washington, D.C.–based American Enterprise Institute, a public-policy think tank. He also accepted many prestigious corporate board memberships, participated in civic activities, and lectured widely on such issues as congressional/White House relations, federal budget policies, and domestic and foreign policy issues. In 1982, Ford established the AEI World Forum, an international gathering of former and current world leaders and business executives to discuss political and business policies impacting current issues. In 1999, President Bill Clinton awarded Ford the Presidential Medal of Freedom, America's highest civilian honor.

How did **Jimmy Carter excel after he left the presidency**?

After leaving the presidency in 1981, Jimmy Carter pursued an active humanitarian career in which he continued to pursue human rights, a major concern of his presidency. In 1982, he founded the Carter Center, an Atlanta-based organization "committed to advancing human rights and alleviating unnecessary human suffering." According to its mission statement, the center's goal is to secure peace settlements in third-world military conflicts, protect human rights, and fight disease. As a nonprofit, nongovernmental organization, the center has strengthened democracies in Asia, Latin America, and Africa, and has sent 47 election-monitoring delegations to these areas in order to ensure fair elections; helped farmers double or triple grain production in fifteen African countries; mediated or worked to prevent civil and international conflicts in areas such as Ethiopia, North Korea, Bosnia, Sudan, and Venezuela; intervened to organize medical support to prevent unnecessary diseases in Latin America and Africa, including the near eradication of Guinea worm disease; and strived to diminish the stigma against mental illness.

Carter is also known for his work as a volunteer for Habitat for Humanity, an organization that builds low-cost residential housing in the United States and abroad. An accomplished author of eighteen books, Carter also lectures widely. In 2002, Carter won the Nobel Peace Prize for his efforts "to find peaceful solutions to international conflicts, to advance democracy and human rights, and to promote economic and social development."

Has **former President Bush** begun a second career as an **elder statesman**?

When George Bush lost the 1992 presidential election to Bill Clinton, he returned with his wife Barbara to their home in Houston, Texas, and retired from public life. Unlike many mid- to late-twentieth-century presidents before him who continued on as elder statesmen or presidential advisers—such as Harry S. Truman, Dwight D. Eisenhower, or Richard Nixon—Bush was content to stay out of the public spotlight. When his son, George W. Bush, assumed the presidency in 2001, the press reported the new administration's conscious effort to avoid any appearance of influence from the elder Bush, primarily to assert the younger Bush's independence as a leader. However, the *New York Times* reported that the former president advised his son on how to gently reopen negotiations with North Korea. In the aftermath of the September 11, 2001, terrorist attacks, George W. Bush dispatched his father to London as his personal representative to a memorial service for British subjects who were killed in the World Trade Center attacks. Drawing on his own experiences before and after the 1991 Gulf War, in late 2003 the senior Bush cautioned his son against acting unilaterally in the U.S. war in Iraq.

FIRST LADIES

PRESIDENTRESSES: MARTHA TO SARAH

How did **Martha Washington** help establish the office of first lady?

As the original first lady, Martha Dandridge Custis Washington used her charm and grace to lend prestige to the position of first lady. At her Mount Vernon estate, Martha had acquired great administrative skills, at one time overseeing all tasks from the planting schedule to the meal planning to the operation of sixteen spinning wheels. When the Revolutionary War took her general husband George to the battlefields, Martha accompanied him, nursing the sick and knitting socks for soldiers, even during the dreadful winter of 1776 at Valley Forge, Pennsylvania. Of this time on the battlefield, she wrote: "I am still determined to be cheerful and happy, in whatever situation I may be; for I have also learned from experience that the greater part of our happiness or misery depends upon our dispositions, and not upon our circumstances."

Her graciousness on the front lines—described as "sweeten[ing] the cares of a hero and smooth[ing] the rugged pains of war"—followed her to the White House, where she set a precedent of dignified humility. The first lady fulfilled social obligations with grace, presiding over Friday evening "drawing rooms," where men and women of the day mingled with the president and his wife. During these events, "Lady Washington," as she was known, remained seated, and then promptly rose to announce her departure at bedtime. The Washingtons entertained in a formal style, sending the message that the new republic's government was on equal standing with the more established European governments. Despite this formality, Martha's hospitality made her guests feel welcome.

What was the **office of the first lady** like in the **1800s**?

In the late 1700s and throughout the 1800s, and especially before the Civil War, first ladies were primarily social figures who were rarely seen outside of Washington, D.C.

Confines of the "Office" of First Lady

Martha Washington was a graceful first lady. But she acknowledged the limits she faced as the nation's most high-profiled woman:

> I lead a very dull life and know nothing of what passes in the town. I never go to any public place, indeed I think I am more like a state prisoner than anything else. There [are] certain bounds set for me which I must not depart from and as I cannot say and do as I like I am obstinate [and] stay at home a great deal.

During the campaign process, candidates avoided discussing their wives and families even when they were a potential asset. Once in office, the first lady was responsible for serving as White House hostess, transforming the president's house into a livable home environment for her family, raising her children, and caring for sick family members. Presidents often relied on their behind-the-scenes wives for support and advice, who—despite little public power—could express their ideas to America's chief executives.

In the late 1800s, first ladies became more visible as they helped with their husbands' campaigning and as popular magazines started to cover the first lady and her family in the White House. As noted in the Smithsonian National Museum of American History's "First Ladies" exhibition, "Notions of proper conduct for women made the role a contradiction, and forced first ladies to walk a fine line between publicly supporting their husbands and avoiding the appearance of interfering in politics." Notwithstanding social mores and limitations for women during this time, the nineteenth century did see a few politically active wives, such as Abigail Adams, Dolley Madison, and Sarah Polk. Others contributed to the office in unique ways, putting their stamp on cultural and historic preservation or speaking out for social causes. Many accomplished groundbreaking feats as women and did much to eventually elevate the office of first lady—something that their twentieth-century successors would build upon and forever be indebted to.

How did **Abigail Adams** differ from Martha Washington?

Abigail Smith Adams, wife to second president John Adams, came from a rich heritage of Congregational ministers. Her intelligence, integrity, and strength—the result of her grooming in a New England Puritan family—helped prepare her for the years ahead. During the Revolutionary War, when her husband was away from home serving in the Continental Congress, Abigail ran the family farm and raised four children alone. Her ongoing time alone, and the self-reliance she developed during this period, influenced her thoughts about the status of women. She is remembered in history books for a letter she wrote to her husband while he was developing a code of laws for

Abigail Adams: A Prolific Letter Writer

From the beginning of their courtship in 1761 and continuing through the years of politics, Abigail and John Adams exchanged more than eleven hundred letters. While her husband was serving in the American Revolution, and Abigail was at home tending the family farm, the two engaged in a series of letters that reveal much about their relationship and Abigail's personality. An ardent Federalist, Abigail was not afraid to express her political views or advise her husband. Once, when a neighbor complained because Abigail had sent one of her servants to school, she wrote to John, "Merely because his face is black, is he to be denied instruction?" In March 1776, when her husband was serving in the Continental Congress, she wrote, "I long for independence.... In the new code of laws which I suppose it will be necessary for you to make, I desire you would remember the ladies. ... If particular care and attention is not paid to the ladies, we are determined to foment a rebellion, and will not hold ourselves bound by any laws in which we have no voice or representation."

The Adams's correspondence is part of the Adams Family Papers collection of the Massachusetts Historical Society. Many of their key letters are included in the six-volume *Adams Papers: The Adams Family Correspondence,* edited by Lyman H. Butterfield, et al. Several other volumes of letters have been published, including *Letters of Mrs. Adams, Wife of John Adams,* which was edited by Charles Francis Adams, Abigail's grandson; and *New Letters of Abigail Adams, 1788–1801,* edited by Stewart Mitchell.

the fledgling country, in which she said, "Remember the ladies, and be more generous and favorable to them than your ancestors. Do not put such unlimited power into the hands of husbands. Remember all men would be tyrants if they could." Her forward-thinking ideas established Abigail Adams as a forerunner of the women's rights movement that would come about in the next century. Besides speaking up for women, Abigail also spoke out against slavery.

When John Adams became vice president to George Washington, Abigail was often seated next to Mrs. Washington during the first administration's formal dinners and receptions. Abigail learned a lot as the quiet observer of Martha Washington's social graces, and continued the tradition of formal entertaining when her husband became president in 1797. Although the couple moved into the White House while it was still under construction, Abigail dutifully hosted receptions and dinners on her husband's behalf. As first lady, her tact and articulation offset her husband's gruff disposition. She was known to quietly advise him on political matters and appointments, and the president lamented when he chose Vans Murray as his minister to France without consulting her. As the mother to John Quincy Adams, America's sixth president, Abigail was the first of two women in history to be the wife of one president and the mother of another (Barbara Bush was the other), although she didn't live long enough to see her son inaugurated. Despite this and other firsts, she is remembered as a first lady of character, and as the first intimate presidential adviser.

Why is there **no discussion of Mrs. Jefferson** in the chronicles of first ladies?

Thomas Jefferson, who took office in 1801, is the first of several presidents to govern in the White House without a first lady at his side. Thomas Jefferson was widowed in 1782, when his wife Martha Wayles Skelton Jefferson died, after many years of being weakened by complications from childbirth. Jefferson had become adept at handling social affairs, however he occasionally called on the assistance of Dolley Madison, wife to Jefferson's secretary of state, James Madison. Jefferson's daughter Patsy, who was now grown up and married to Thomas Mann Randolph Jr., also served for a brief time as White House hostess.

Three other men—Andrew Jackson, Martin Van Buren, and Chester Alan Arthur—were also widowers during their entire White House tenures. Two presidents—John Tyler and Woodrow Wilson—lost wives during their tenures as president, but remarried before they left office. Three other presidents had different circumstances: William Henry Harrison died after a month in the White House and his wife, Anna Symmes Harrison, never made it to Washington, D.C.; James Buchanan was a bachelor, never marrying during his life; and Grover Cleveland began his presidency as a bachelor but married at the White House during his first term in office.

Out of all early first ladies, who holds the title as the **"nation's hostess"**?

James Madison's wife, Dolley Payne Todd Madison, was the first first lady to embrace entertaining at the White House. An outgoing, widowed Quaker, the personable Dolley married Madison, who was seventeen years her senior, and quickly shed her traditional Quaker dress for fine fashions. Dolley and "Little Jemmy," as she called the five-foot, four-inch Madison, were introduced by Aaron Burr, then (in 1794) a New York senator. As first lady, Dolley was described in social circles as dressing like a queen, and Washington socialite Margaret Bayard Smith said, "It would be absolutely impossible for any one to behave with more perfect propriety than she did." She was fond of wearing a turban, and started a fashion trend called the Dolley turban. Beginning with the first inaugural ball she hosted when Madison became president in 1809, Dolley quickly rose in social circumstances as the consummate hostess. Conscious of the fact that her predecessor, Abigail Adams, was known for favoring her husband's supporters at social events, Dolley treated everyone with equal respect, and quickly earned the reputation of being unbiased, graceful, and charming. She also broke ground by visiting legislators' families in their own homes, thus bridging the gap between the executive and legislative branches. Later, it would become clear that Mrs. Madison was politically astute.

In keeping with her hostess role, Dolley is also known to have introduced social dancing to the White House—notably the waltz. She was the first president's wife to renovate the interior of the White House, which she did with the assistance of two appropriations from Congress: one for $12,000 for general repairs, and another for $14,000 for new furnishings. During the War of 1812, the British attacked and burned down the White House. Dolley fled under British pursuit, but not before removing artist Gilbert Stuart's priceless portrait of George Washington and an original copy of the Declaration of Independence. While the White House was being rebuilt, Dolley entertained in the Madison's temporary residence, the Octagon House, without a break in style or tone.

Beginning with the first inaugural ball she hosted when her husband became president in 1809, Dolley Madison embraced entertaining at the White House and quickly rose in social circumstances as the consummate hostess. *Library of Congress.*

What **White House tradition** did **Dolley Madison** reportedly establish?

Some historians believe that Dolley Madison started the tradition of the annual Easter egg roll. Dolley became enamored with an ancient Egyptian tradition her son, John Payne Todd, told her about, which involved rolling colorful hard-boiled eggs against the bases of the pyramids. Dolley dyed hundreds of eggs and invited local children to an egg-rolling celebration on the Monday after Easter. At that time, the roll was held at the nearby Capitol. When the children created a commotion one year, Congress responded in 1878 by passing the Turf Protection Law, which prohibited children from using the grounds for future egg-rolling events. President Rutherford B. Hayes, alerted to the plight of the children by his wife Lucy Hayes, vetoed the law and opened the gates of the White House to children. The first official White House Easter Egg Roll was held that year, and it has been a White House tradition ever since.

When did the **term "first lady" come into popular usage**?

Although Martha Washington was referred to as "Lady Washington," in the early nineteenth century this title of nobility gave way to more informal titles for the president's wife. Terms such as "Mrs. President" and "Presidentress" were used until 1849, when, at the funeral of Dolley Madison, the term "first lady" was applied to describe the recently departed president's wife. The term "first lady" became consistently used in the early twentieth century when Charles Nirdlinger's play about Dolley, *Dolly Madi-*

son, or the First Lady of the Land was performed in New York in 1911 to wide acclaim. Although certain first ladies preferred other titles (Jackie Kennedy, for example, was partial to "Mrs. Kennedy"), the term "first lady" has been applied to all presidents' wives beginning in the twentieth century.

How did a *belle Americaine* change history before she set foot in the White House?

Elizabeth Kortright Monroe, wife of James Monroe, accompanied her husband to France in 1794 when he was U.S. minister to France under George Washington. They arrived in Paris during a time of turmoil, and Elizabeth played a dramatic role in saving the life of the wife of imprisoned French statesman Marquis de Lafayette, who was also imprisoned and expecting death by guillotine. As a commissioned major general in the U.S. Continental Army in 1777, Monsieur Lafayette had become a close associate of George Washington, and in France he advanced the American cause. With only her servants in her carriage, Mrs. Monroe visited the prison and asked to see Madame Lafayette. Soon after this gesture of American interest was exposed, the French government released Madame Lafayette, rather than risk losing their ally. The Monroes became very popular in France, and Elizabeth was called *la belle Americaine*.

What was **Elizabeth Monroe's time in the White House** like?

Upon returning home to the White House, Elizabeth Monroe led a reserved life as first lady from 1817 to 1825. She suffered from epileptic seizures, which she carefully hid, and had an aloof and "haughty" personality—two traits that made her stand out from her predecessor, the much-loved, jovial Dolley Madison. When it came to social calls and entertaining in general, Elizabeth insisted on formality and a less democratic manner than Dolley had established. She rarely returned social calls. Washington society denounced the first lady's cold and reserved manner and formally chided the behavior of the Monroes' oldest daughter, Eliza, who, as social hostess for her mother on several occasions, had offended many socialites. Eventually, Elizabeth Monroe sought a compromise by hosting very formal and elegant European-style dinners balanced by American style "drawing room" receptions. By developing a new style of entertaining, Elizabeth Monroe contributed to ridding the first ladyship of outdated social obligations.

Which early **president's wife hit the campaign trail** on behalf of her husband?

During the contentious election of 1824, when none of the four candidates received a majority of the votes, Democratic-Republican contender John Quincy Adams asked his wife to hit the campaign trail on his behalf. Because she was more endearing and sociable than her husband, and probably the better of the two to undertake the job, Louisa Catherine Johnson Adams agreed to defy tradition and campaign for her husband.

Adams gave her the names of congressmen's wives to visit. She also acted as her husband's hostess, entertaining those callers who had come to meet her husband. She hosted dinners for members of Congress and was probably the first to hold an "open house" in the White House. She traveled to Philadelphia and Maryland, where she met with journalists. A political aficionado, she kept up with current events and attended congressional debates when she was in Washington. Although future first ladies—such as Eleanor Roosevelt, Lady Bird Johnson, and Hillary Clinton—would go on to actively campaign for their husbands, Louisa Adams was a woman well ahead of her time.

Which **nineteenth-century first ladies relinquished their duties as social hostess**?

An ailing Elizabeth Monroe is the first of several wives who found little joy in their responsibilities as first ladies. Letitia Christian Tyler, who served as first lady for a little more than a year, was confined to her bedroom after a major stroke. Her daughter-in-law, Priscilla Cooper, served as the White House hostess with elegance and flair. Letitia died in the White House in September 1842, after suffering a second stroke. A frail Peggy Taylor also served for a little more than a year, due to her husband Zachary's death in 1850. As a recluse, the only time the public saw her was when she went to church. All of the duties of the first lady went to her third daughter, Mary Elizabeth Taylor. Abigail Powers Fillmore was bookish and a bit reserved, and preferred for her outgoing and beautiful daughter, Mary Abigail Fillmore, to perform most White House social duties.

Although she served as first lady for her husband's entire term from 1865 to 1869, Eliza McCardle Johnson was suffering from tuberculosis when her husband entered the presidency after Abraham Lincoln's assassination. Uninterested in politics, she spent her time in her upstairs bedroom, often with family. Unlike many other first ladies before her who had embraced the office, Eliza denounced it, saying, "It's all very well for those who like it—but I do not like this public life at all. I often wish the time would come when we could return to where I feel we best belong." Except for two public appearances, she remained entirely out of the public eye for most of her husband's term, and left all first lady duties to her daughter, Martha Johnson Patterson. Eliza's hesitancy toward her social obligations was due in part to ill health and in part to the public's criticism of her predecessor, Mary Todd Lincoln.

What was **Julia's Tyler's personality** like?

The second wife of President John Tyler, young debutante Julia Gardiner Tyler loved the privileges that accompanied the role of first lady. She was constantly attended to by twelve personal maids and reveled in riding through town in her white-horse-drawn carriage. Because she required it, she was treated like royalty, and as such is known for introducing the song "Hail to the Chief" as the president's "announcement"

First lady Sarah Polk defied the traditions of the day by setting aside domestic duties to serve as her husband's confidante and political assistant. She oversaw President James K. Polk's appointments, assisted him with his correspondence, helped him write speeches, and highlighted newspaper articles for his review. *Getty Images.*

song. Julia married the president in office (he was the first president to do so) in 1844, with only eight months left until the end of his term. After the death of her husband in 1862, Julia solicited Congress for a pension for herself but was denied. When Congress agreed to a pension for Mary Lincoln in 1870, they voted to grant Mrs. Tyler an annual pension of $1,200. After James A. Garfield's assassination in 1881, Congress voted to grant a uniform amount of $5,000 annually to Julia and several other presidential widows, including Lucretia Garfield, Mary Lincoln, and Sarah Polk. In 1958, federal law would provide automatic pensions for presidential widows.

How did **Sarah Polk** defy the traditions of the day as both woman and first lady?

Sarah Childress Polk, wife of James K. Polk, was more partial to matters of politics than to those of homemaking. During the presidential election of 1844, when a man said he would not vote for James K. Polk because his opponent's wife made better butter, Sarah responded by saying, "If I get to the White House, I expect to live on $25,000 a year [the president's salary] and I will neither keep house nor make butter." Although women were largely valued at that time in history for their domestic skills and social graces, Sarah Polk lived up to her word and instead served the president as his confidante and political assistant. In the White House, Sarah oversaw his appointments, assisted him with his correspondence, helped him write his speeches, and highlighted newspaper articles for his review. A devout Presbyterian, she banned hard liquor, dancing, and card playing in the White House, but nevertheless held many White House receptions and parties. Because she didn't have children, Sarah was able to involve herself in all aspects of her husband's career, and men such as Henry Clay, Andrew Jackson, and Franklin Pierce all testified to her expansive knowledge of history and politics.

After her husband's death in 1849, Sarah left the White House to run the Polks' cotton plantation in Mississippi, which she did with a great business sense, until the Civil War forced her to sell it. She retired to her home in Nashville, Tennessee, called Polk Place, where during the Civil War she was known for her neutrality, welcoming both Union and Confederate officers.

HOSTESSES: HARRIET TO CAROLINE

Who was **Harriet Lane**?

Not a first lady in the traditional sense of the word, Harriet Lane fulfilled the role of White House hostess for America's only bachelor president, James Buchanan. President Buchanan was Harriet's uncle and legal guardian. Besides enthusiastically living up to her role as efficient and lively socialite, Lane had attained a large art collection of European works. When she donated this to the government, the Smithsonian Institution called her the "First Lady of the National Collection of Fine Arts." After leaving the White House, marrying, and losing her two young sons to rheumatic fever, Lane donated a large sum of money to the Johns Hopkins Hospital in Baltimore for the purpose of creating a home for invalid children. In 1912, the Harriet Lane Home for Invalid Children opened its doors as the first children's hospital in the United States affiliated with an academic medical center. In its day, the five-story facility was considered innovative, with isolation wings to prevent the spread of contagious diseases as well as housing chemistry and bacteriology labs. Over the years, it became an acclaimed pediatric facility, and in the 2000s the Harriet Lane Primary Care Center for Children serves thousands of children each year.

How did **Mary Todd Lincoln** unsettle the position of first lady?

Rather than rise to the occasion, Mary Todd Lincoln had a difficult time in the position of first lady. Her emotional instability after the loss of her children, criticism and suspicion over her Southern background, and her lavish spending and shopping sprees made her the target of scandal and vicious attacks. When her son Willie died in the White House in 1862, it sent the first lady over the edge, and she turned to spiritualism and séances to govern her relationship with her deceased son. Her uncontrollable habit of shopping and spending placed the family in enormous debt: At one time, her unpaid clothing debt totaled $27,000—$2,000 more than President Lincoln's annual salary. Mary was never her husband's political confidante, and their relationship became strained during the White House years. In terms of her official functions, she reviewed troops and made inspections of ships, and acted as hostess to a number of state dinners and White House social events. But her duties were cut short by her instability, and when Lincoln was assassinated Mary slipped into further despair. While she spent many years trying to obtain a government pension, she suffered the death of her son Tad before her oldest son, Robert, finally committed her to a mental institution. She died tormented and on the brink of poverty, the most tragic of all the first ladies.

How did **Julia Grant** turn the office of first lady around?

Julia Dent Grant was the first first lady to serve two complete terms in her role since Elizabeth Monroe. She loved the position of first lady, and quickly went about cleaning

First lady Lucy Hayes was nicknamed "Lemonade Lucy" for her habit of serving lemonade and fruit juices at White House functions. She is seen here with two of her children, son Scott and daughter Fannie (standing), and one of their friends in the White House conservatory, which she expanded during her time as first lady. *AP/Wide World Photos.*

and refurbishing the White House, readying it to become the center of Washington social life. Although Julia Grant hosted many state dinners and threw elaborate parties, she was not criticized for it as Mary Lincoln had been. She was a refreshing breath of fresh air to Washington society after the volatile and unpredictable Mary Lincoln and the reclusive Eliza Johnson. Julia became known for her Tuesday-afternoon receptions given for "any and all." When asked whether "colored visitors" would be permitted, Julia replied, "Admit all." However, unbeknownst to the first lady, her staff denied entrance to African Americans. Although she attempted to persuade her husband, Ulysses S. Grant, in political matters, Julia had little or no effect on the president's policies. After the presidency, Julia continued to make a name for herself. Although her husband died in 1885 from throat cancer, she returned to Washington social circles, and as a "Grand Dame" befriended Frances Cleveland and Caroline Harrison. There she penned her memoirs—the first president's wife to do so—although they wouldn't be published until 1975.

Who was **Lemonade Lucy**?

"Lemonade Lucy" was the nickname the press teasingly gave first lady Lucy Ware Webb Hayes for her habit of excluding alcoholic beverages from White House functions, choosing instead to serve lemonade and fruit juices. Although the custom at the time was to serve alcohol at state functions, Hayes's custom was supported by her husband, President Rutherford B. Hayes, an ex–poker-playing, cigar-smoking, drinker, who gave up his vices to join the Sons of Temperance and traveled to make speeches on their behalf. Although the Women's Christian Temperance Union supported Lucy's ban, she never actually belonged to that organization. In response to her detractors, Lucy said, "It is true that I shall violate a precedent; but I shall not violate the Constitution which is all that, through my husband, I have taken an oath to obey.

How did **Lucy Hayes expand the role of first lady**?

Lucy Hayes was considered a "new" woman of the late nineteenth century. She was one of America's first presidential wives to be college educated, and the first to graduate from college (Cincinnati's Wesleyan Female College, in 1852). Her interest in social causes began on the battlefield, as she nursed her husband, Rutherford B. Hayes, during the Civil War and worked in camps and hospitals throughout the North. During her husband's three postwar terms as governor of Ohio, she accompanied him on visits to state reform schools, prisons, and asylums, and fought to improve their conditions. During the temperance movement that characterized her time in the White House from 1877 to 1881, Lucy became an advocate of the cause. For a brief time, she supported woman's suffrage, but her long-term interests involved education and alleviating homelessness.

As first lady, Lucy took an interest in refurbishing the White House to reflect its history, and was responsible for expanding the collection of portraits of former presidents and first ladies. She began the first significant art collection at the executive mansion, improved the landscaping of its grounds, and expanded the White House conservatory. She balanced her time as first lady with her time with her children. Although she supported her husband's career, she pursued her own interests and often influenced those around her; for example, as a strong believer in the value of education, she allowed the staff to take time off to pursue their studies. As a charitable personality, she consistently gave money to alleviate homelessness, and fed and clothed the impoverished who arrived at the White House steps. She was the first of the presidents' wives to travel across America, and when she did so in 1880 the press called her the "First Lady of the Land."

Which first lady drew up an **inventory of the White House's contents**?

Lucretia Randolph Garfield was first lady for less than a year, but her time in the White House is not without its accomplishments. She was intensely interested in the history of the executive mansion and, with the aid of the Library of Congress, drew up a list of all the building's contents. Although her project was cut short in May 1881, a few months before her husband James Garfield was shot by an assassin, the beginnings of her list were later referenced by Grace Coolidge and Lou Hoover.

What role did **Lucretia Garfield** play in making presidential wives more visible in the late 1800s?

Lucretia Garfield, fondly nicknamed "Crete," was active in her husband's political career from the start. In 1880, when her husband James A. Garfield ran for the presidency, she and James created the front-porch campaign, a presidential campaign in which the candidate makes speeches, literally from his front porch, instead of traveling to secure votes. Although previously women worked behind the scenes during presidential campaigns (for example, making banners or cooking for events), Crete was one of the first to step out in front of the public. She was also the first candidate's wife to have her photograph appear on a campaign poster. After James Garfield won the presidential election, Lucretia traveled from their home in Ohio to New York under the assumed name of "Mrs. Greenfield." Once there, she served as a liaison between her husband and Stalwart faction head Roscoe Conkling to discuss cabinet appointments. She quietly passed her recommendations along to Garfield, becoming his well-trusted confidante during his brief time in office. Had the Garfield administration not been cut short by the president's assassination in 1881, it is likely that Lucretia would have gone on to become a politically active first lady.

What were **Frances Cleveland**'s strengths as first lady?

When twenty-one-year-old Frances Folsom married President Grover Cleveland in the White House in June 1886, she became the youngest first lady in history and the first to marry a president in the White House. Neither her inexperience nor her youth hindered her in her role as first lady, and she quickly started other precedents. While it was customary to host public receptions, Frances added a Saturday reception so that working women could attend her events. Furthering the causes of working women, Frances posted the accepted hourly rate for a seamstress's services so that ladies of society could not cheat them out of their going rate. Her support of working women was acknowledged in these subtle ways; as first lady she never aggressively spoke out for any issue. She became a popular hostess in Washington circles and soon won the admiration of the nation—advertisers capitalized on her beauty and popularity by using her image to sell everything from toothpaste to sewing machines. After Grover Cleveland's first term as president ended in 1889, the couple retired to private life. But they quickly returned to the White House in 1893, after Cleveland won the presidential election of 1892. There, Frances gave birth to her daughter Esther, the only president's child to be born in the White House. Although she spent her second term concerned with the press's obsession with her children and her husband's health, she nevertheless exited the White House in 1897 as a much-loved and highly regarded first lady.

How did **Caroline Harrison** use her influence to help women?

Caroline Lavina Scott Harrison, wife of president Benjamin Harrison, presided over official White House functions, but went beyond her predecessors when she arranged painting classes for the wives of government officials. As a student at Oxford Female Institute, Caroline developed her love for drama, music, art, and painting, and she carried these loves into the White House. In 1890, she used her position as first lady to get women admitted to Johns Hopkins Medical School: she agreed to raise funds for the school only if women were admitted. Also that year, she became the first president-general of the newly formed Daughters of the American Revolution (DAR). In February 1892, Caroline gave the first recorded speech by a first lady at the first congress of the DAR. At that gathering, she urged Americans to support their country by "buying American." She was responsible for putting up the first Christmas tree in the White House and establishing the historical collection of White House china.

A political poster widely used during the presidential campaign of 1888, when Grover Cleveland and running mate Allen G. Thurman were the Democratic candidates. The image of popular first lady Frances Cleveland is prominently placed. *AP/Wide World Photos.*

Which early first ladies were known for **championing social causes**?

Although much of the work of the nineteenth-century first lady was tied up in social functions and diplomacy, a few mavericks reached beyond the conventions of the office and became involved with social causes. Perhaps the first to do this was Dolley Madison. Dolley took a special interest in children, and in 1815 established the first federally funded child welfare program, a home for orphans of the War of 1812. She personally made clothes for the children of the Washington City Orphans Asylum. Mary Lincoln pioneered an unpopular cause when she worked with the Contraband Relief Association to feed and house thousands of escaped slaves who had fled to Washington, D.C. Lucy Hayes, as the embodiment of the ideal late-nineteenth-century woman, supported the temperance movement, education, and the alleviation of homelessness.

EXPANDED ROLE: IDA TO LOU

How did **Ida McKinley** hide her epilepsy?

Ida McKinley suffered from emotional frailty and epilepsy, yet she still appeared in public to give the impression of being an active wife. Her image appeared on cam-

447

paign buttons and posters before she became first lady, and Ida supported her husband with his 1896 front-porch campaign. Although she did not appear frequently in public, America was familiar with the future first lady's face. When he took office, President William McKinley chose to include his wife in social functions—even breaking tradition by seating her next to him at state dinners—and came to her assistance whenever she had a seizure. The president refused to seclude his wife in an upstairs bedroom, and as such paved the way for future first ladies, including Nellie Taft, who suffered from a major stroke in 1909, and then recuperated; Florence Harding, whose time in the White House was spent fighting a kidney disorder; and Mamie Eisenhower, who, along with her husband, would encounter heart problems during her time as first lady.

Which first lady began the practice of **hiring a social secretary**?

While Julia Tyler was the first presidential wife to have a White House social secretary, Edith Carow Roosevelt, wife of Theodore Roosevelt, initiated the policy of hiring a social secretary at the government's expense. The job of Mrs. Roosevelt's social secretary was to prepare the hundreds of invitations for White House functions and keep lists of attending guests. Edith also broke ground by hiring caterers to prepare meals for state banquets, and put the chief usher in charge of running the White House's daily duties and managing domestic personnel. She did these things to free up time for her six rambunctious, animal-loving children—the most to ever live at the White House. Out of a need for privacy, Edith was successful in convincing Congress to expand the president's house by creating the West Wing for executive offices, thus turning the second floor into private quarters for the first family. Among other firsts, she began to seriously catalog the contents of the White House; started the practice of hanging first lady portraits in the East Corridor of the White House; and started a collection of china samples used by previous presidential administrations.

How was **Nellie Taft** active in her husband's political career?

Helen "Nellie" Taft was strong-willed, ambitious, and extremely interested in politics. She visited the White House to attend the christening of the daughter of President and Mrs. Hayes thirty years before she became first lady. As her husband William Howard Taft climbed the political ladder—beginning with his post under President William McKinley as commissioner to the Philippines—Nellie encouraged him to pursue the nation's executive office. Nellie campaigned so vigorously for her husband during the presidential election of 1908 that incumbent president Theodore Roosevelt rebuked her for her aggressive behavior. Of her role in her husband's campaign, she said, "The ups and downs of such a campaign, the prophecies, the hopes, the fears aroused by favorable and opposing newspapers were all new and trying to me, and in a way I think I was under as great a nervous strain as my husband was."

First lady Helen "Nellie" Taft set a precedent for future first ladies when she rode with her husband to the White House after his inauguration. The Tafts are seen here in the first official presidential automobile in 1909. *AP/Wide World Photos.*

Taft won the election, and Nellie set a precedent for future first ladies when she rode with her husband to the White House after his inauguration. Nellie actively involved herself in her husband's role as president: he was the first presidential wife to attend all her husband's cabinet meetings. After suffering a severe stroke in May 1909, she recovered in 1911 and continued to oversee both the daily White House functions and extravagant social events. After the presidency, she stood by her husband as he achieved his dream of becoming chief justice of the U.S. Supreme Court in 1921.

How did **Ellen Wilson** fold social causes into the first lady's job description?

Woodrow Wilson's first wife, Ellen Louise Wilson, entered the White House in 1913 at the height of the reform-oriented Progressive era. As a believer in actively promoting social causes, she chose slum clearance in Washington as her personal project. Indeed, Ellen was no stranger to helping those less fortunate than she, having earlier established a scholarship at the Berry School near her hometown of Rome, Georgia. The scholarship was for the education of underprivileged and rural mountain children, given in honor of Ellen's brother, who drowned in 1905 in the Etowah River with his wife and young son.

During her seventeen months as first lady, before she died from kidney disease, Ellen fought to change conditions for impoverished African Americans living in slums and alleys. In 1913, she partnered with Charlotte Hopkins of the National Civic Feder-

President Woodrow Wilson and first lady Edith Bolling Wilson. *AP/Wide World Photos.*

ation to further her cause, becoming the organization's honorary chair, and she bought shares in a housing company that built model homes for the poor. She led the drafting of a congressional bill that proposed to clear Washington's slums, but the legislation stalled in Congress. As she lay dying, Congress passed Ellen Wilson's Alley Bill of 1914, and she became the first president's wife to see legislation she had inspired pass through Congress. Ironically, while Ellen worked hard to eradicate the conditions that poor blacks lived in, she did not believe in their equality and advocated separate facilities for blacks and whites in government buildings. The Alley Bill was eventually ruled unconstitutional, and the slum cause would have to wait until another first lady—Eleanor Roosevelt—revived an interest in Washington's downtrodden.

Why is **Edith Wilson** referred to as "Mrs. President"?

Woodrow Wilson's second wife, Edith Bolling Wilson, has received both respect and criticism from scholars for the role she played during her husband's debilitating stroke while he was president of the United States. When President Wilson was stricken in October 1919, Edith began screening visitors, reviewing the president's mail, and deciding when to present him with executive matters. However, some historians claim that her role went beyond that, and that she was, in effect, acting president for a time. Although Edith consulted with her husband's advisers, evidence supports the fact that she was at least in the decision-making process, possibly at the prompting of Wilson's doctors, during the months her husband was incapacitated. In *My Memoir* (1939),

Edith denied claims that she took over a role that should naturally have fallen to the vice president. Maintaining that she "never made a single decision regarding the disposition of public affairs" and that all decisions were Wilson's, she defended her role as first lady: "The burning question was how best to serve the country— and yet protect the president."

How did **Florence Harding** carefully court the press?

Florence Kling Harding was a strong-willed woman who was dedicated to advancing her husband's career. As Warren G. Harding rose through Ohio politics and became a U.S. senator, Florence directed all her energies into ensuring

First lady Grace Coolidge, holding Rebecca, the family's pet raccoon. When she became first lady, Grace chose what came naturally as her social cause: education and child welfare. *AP/Wide World Photos.*

his success. When he became the Republican nominee for president in 1920, "the Duchess," as Warren fondly called her, worked hard to guarantee his election. That is why her words when he assumed the presidency—"Well, Warren, I have got you the Presidency; what are you going to do with it?"—surprised few.

During his campaign, she courted the press to receive a favorable public image, a habit she continued as first lady. She carefully shielded her emotional precariousness and hot temper, both of which were flared by President Harding's extramarital affairs. To perpetuate her and her husband's image as "just plain folks," she often personally greeted tourists at the White House. She countered criticisms of his administration by starting such traditions as afternoon teas on the South Lawn for servicemen who had been wounded in the line of duty. And in an effort to preserve the president's declining public image, the couple embarked on a widely publicized cross-country "Voyage of Understanding" tour in June 1923. Shortly after her husband died on that tour and his administration was implicated in the Teapot Dome scandal, Florence Harding burned almost all of Harding's presidential papers.

What social cause did **Grace Coolidge** choose to stand for?

Grace Goodhue Coolidge once said that the White House was "a great opportunity for service." When she became first lady, Grace chose what came naturally as her social cause: education and child welfare. Before she married future president Calvin Coolidge in 1905, Grace had taught deaf children at the Clarke School for the Deaf in Northampton, Massachusetts. As first lady, she often invited children from the school to the White House and spoke of their plight to the press. After she left the White House, Coolidge was honored by the National Institute of Social Sciences for "fine personal influence exerted as First Lady of the Land." She supported a variety of children's organizations, including the Association for the Aid of Crippled Children, the Girl Scouts, the Campfire Girls, and several children's hospitals. During World War II, Grace was active in the Red Cross and other relief agencies.

By the time of the Coolidge administration, how many **first ladies had graduated from college**?

By 1923, when Calvin Coolidge assumed the presidency, Grace Coolidge was one of the first college-educated first ladies. She graduated from the University of Vermont in 1902. The accolade of the first presidential spouse to hold a college degree goes to Lucy Hayes, who was an 1852 graduate of Wesleyan Female College (later Ohio Wesleyan University). Frances Cleveland graduated in 1885 from Wells College. Three other first ladies before 1923 attended college, but did not graduate: Lucretia Garfield, Helen Taft, and Ellen Wilson.

How did **Lou Hoover** set off a controversy when she hosted a tea to honor congressional wives?

In 1930, Lou Henry Hoover, wife of President Herbert Hoover and an outspoken feminist, hosted a series of teas to honor the wives of members of Congress. While this event was in keeping with established first lady protocol, Lou's way of handling the event was unique. In assembling the list of attendees, she discovered that one of the congressmen, Oscar De Priest of Illinois, was an African American. The Republican politician was the first black man to be elected to Congress since Reconstruction. Since Washington, D.C., was racially segregated, Lou was cautioned against inviting his wife, Jessie. She compromised by later hosting a special tea party for Mrs. De Priest, and only those congressional wives who would be comfortable around a black woman were invited. Jessie De Priest became the first African American White House guest since Teddy Roosevelt invited educator Booker T. Washington and his wife there for lunch nearly thirty years previously.

The press's coverage of the event set off a controversy. Much of the southern segregationist press denounced her decision, calling it an "arrogant insult to the South and to the nation." Although northern newspapers celebrated the first lady's effort to "put into practice the brotherhood of man," talk arose of the Republican Party's defeat in the presidential election of 1932. Lou embarked on a tour of Southern states to squelch fears, but she became ever-increasingly leery of the press from then on.

Which president's wife ran the **Girl Scouts**?

Lou Hoover was the first president's wife to serve as both national president (1922–1925) and honorary president (1929–1933) of the Girl Scouts. As an independently

The Fascination with the First Lady

In *The White House: The First Two Hundred Years,* Betty Boyd Caroli comments on the public's interest with first ladies:

> No topic in American politics offers a more interesting contradiction than the role of the presidential spouse. This is not a job in the sense that it is paid, yet it is full-time work. It results from a private relationship yet becomes the subject of considerable public attention. Political scientists frequently ignore it, but individual first ladies—even candidates for the job—become the focus of innumerable magazine articles, television interviews, and books that quickly climb to the top of the best-seller list. The same newspapers that choose not to review books on the subject of first ladies, even those from the oldest, most scholarly presses, will run front-page articles on an individual first lady whenever she makes a speech, takes a trip, or catches the flu. It is not surprising that historian Louis Gould concluded: "The First Lady is an institution in American government that is as important as it is ill-defined."

wealthy first lady, she helped finance some of their programs, and drew support for their organization. Lou also became the first presidential wife to speak on radio, when she tried to promote awareness of the Great Depression's effect on women and children. In keeping with her husband's domestic policy, she encouraged self-reliance and was careful not to promote government intervention of society's ills. Lou's activism for women and children while in the White House was an extension of the time she spent with her husband Herbert as a relief worker in London. During World War I, she mobilized the Society of American Women to provide clothing, shelter, and food for stranded Americans in London. When Hoover was appointed official chairman of the Commission for Belgian Relief, Lou organized a California branch of the Commission and raised funds for one of the first food ships to be sent to Belgium from California.

How did twentieth-century women speak up for **women's rights**?

Ardent feminist and America's second first lady Abigail Adams insisted, "I will never consent to have our Sex considered in an inferior point of light." Clearly she was a first lady ahead of her time. For the most part, women in the twentieth century—president's wives included—became more vocal in their support for feminism as the women's movement began to gain momentum. Nellie Taft was an early advocate of women's suffrage, but it wasn't until 1920, when women gained the right to vote, that first ladies showed more public support for women's rights. Florence Harding became an honorary member of the National Women's Party, which sponsored the first proposed Equal Rights Amendment in 1923. Lou Hoover encouraged women to vote. Eleanor Roosevelt was in many ways the embodiment of feminism, insisting, "It is essential for a woman to develop her own interests."

When the new Equal Rights Amendment was proposed in 1972, Pat Nixon became the first president's wife to publicly support it. After Betty Ford assumed the post of first lady in 1974 she wholeheartedly embraced the ERA and made it her personal cause. However, it was Lady Bird Johnson who fully articulated the twentieth-century woman's dilemma, when she said, "American women are undergoing a quiet revolution in our lifetime. We have learned to master dishwashers, typewriters, and voting machines with reasonable aplomb. We must now try to make our laws catch up with what has happened to us as we bounce in and out of the labor market and raise a family."

THE MODERN FIRST LADY: ELEANOR TO LAURA

What is the **modern first lady's job description**?

The role of the first lady has progressed over time from a largely ceremonial one to one of great influence. According to historian Betty Boyd Caroli, the twentieth-century first lady fulfills multiple roles as campaigner; communicator for the president; a complement to, or extension of, the president's domestic and foreign-policy programs; and a designer/curator of the White House. Since the 1960s, every first lady had chosen a special cause to call her own and has spoken on behalf of an issue she felt strongly about. Several, such as Eleanor Roosevelt, Betty Ford, and Hillary Clinton, have championed more than one humanitarian, social, or cultural cause.

In order to accomplish these and other public tasks, the first lady has her own office, budget, and staff. The staff of the Office of First Lady is comprised of aides who handle correspondence, maintain scheduling, and undertake the speech writing necessary to support an active speaking schedule. After leaving office, all first ladies since 1963 have published their own autobiographies, with the exception of Pat Nixon, whose daughter penned her story.

Does the first lady **receive a salary** for her efforts?

No. Even though the first lady works hard, she is not on the government payroll. Her position as the president's wife is not mentioned in the U.S. Constitution. The presidents' wives are unpaid government workers who, for the most part, sculpt their job descriptions to their individual personalities and interests.

A Living Legacy

Lady Bird Johnson: "My image will emerge in deeds, not in words."

Betty Ford: "Any woman who feels confident in herself and happy in what she is doing is a liberated woman."

Rosalynn Carter: "I was determined to be taken seriously."

Nancy Reagan: "I have opinions, he has opinions. We don't always agree. But neither marriage nor politics denies a spouse the right to hold an opinion and the right to express it."

Barbara Bush: "You really only have two choices: You can like what you do, or you can dislike it. I choose to like it, and what fun I've had."

Hillary Clinton: "Our lives are a mixture of different roles. Most of us are doing the best we can to find whatever the right balance is for our lives. For me the elements of that balance are family, work, and service."

Laura Bush: "The role of the First Lady is whatever the First Lady wants it to be."

Why was **Eleanor Roosevelt considered one of the most powerful first ladies** of the twentieth century?

For the twelve years she served as first lady, Eleanor Roosevelt pursued an almost independent career from her husband, President Franklin D. Roosevelt. One journalist described her as a "Cabinet minister without portfolio—the most influential woman of our times." Eleanor wrote a daily newspaper column, "My Day," hosted a weekly radio program, toured the country as a professional speaker, and wrote for national periodicals, in addition to fulfilling her role as first lady. In 1938, her speaking and writing engagements had earned her more than $100,000—more than the president's salary. She actively traveled the globe pursuing various social causes to write about and act on, becoming in 1934 the first presidential wife to fly to a foreign country.

A champion of the underprivileged, Eleanor is known for her extensive social work. As the "eyes and ears" of her husband's administration, she entered mine shafts, walked slum neighborhoods, and worked in war zones. In 1933, she supported public-housing projects and sponsored the creation of Arthurdale, a model community for poverty-stricken West Virginia miners. Designed to promote self-sufficiency by providing a factory and schools, Arthurdale embraced the first lady's philosophy: "One must not do too much for people, but one must help them to do for themselves." She later worked with the housing division of the Public Works Administration and the Washington Housing Authority to devise planned communities. In alignment with FDR's philoso-

phy and New Deal programs, in 1935 she helped found the National Youth Administration, a government agency that helped young people find jobs. A strong supporter of workers' rights, she lobbied for the National Labor Relations Act, supported the concept of a living wage, and urged the passage of the Fair Labor Standards Act.

As a civil-rights leader, she befriended members of the black activist community, including Mary McLeod Bethune, lobbied against the poll tax, backed the Southern Tenant Farmer's Union, and argued for the inclusion of African Americans in government posts and programs. Her support of civil rights came to a head when she resigned from the Daughters of the American Revolution because the group refused to let African American opera signer Marian Anderson appear at Constitutional Hall. Despite racial segregation in Washington, D.C., Eleanor arranged for the singer to perform on the steps of the Lincoln

First lady Eleanor Roosevelt with a group of U.S. soldiers during her special White House party to honor servicemen. During World War II, Mrs. Roosevelt visited England and the South Pacific to foster good will among the Allies and boost the morale of the troops. *Getty Images.*

Memorial to an audience of seventy-five thousand. An equally controversial move was her support of the Anti-Lynching Bill, designed to end the murder of blacks at the hands of white antagonists.

How did **Eleanor Roosevelt** support FDR during **World War II**?

During World War II, Eleanor became the first presidential wife to be appointed to an official government post when she became deputy director of the Office of Civilian

Defense. Although she resigned from the post, she worked in an unofficial capacity for the government throughout the war. She served on behalf of refugees, lobbying Congress for passage of the Child Refugee Bill, which, had it passed, would have allowed ten thousand Jewish children a year to enter the United States above the standard quota for German immigrants. On the home front, she supported women working outside the home and called for their employment in defense industries. Eleanor played a pivotal role in convincing FDR to establish the Fair Employment Practices Commission, which outlawed racial discrimination in industries that received federal contracts, called for equal treatment of African Americans in the military, and helped ensure that black units had the same opportunities as their white counterparts. She became the personal pen-pals of several soldiers and used her popular "My Day" newspaper column to present soldiers' concerns to Congress and the public.

After President Roosevelt died in 1945, Eleanor became the U.S. delegate to the United Nations, where she served as chair of the commission that drafted the Universal Declaration of Human Rights. When she died in 1962, both historians and average Americans agreed that Eleanor was a trailblazing first lady.

Which first lady broke new ground by **holding regular meetings with women journalists**?

Eleanor Roosevelt set a precedent—that has not been followed since—when she held weekly news conferences solely for women reporters. Before that, she broke new ground in 1933 as the first presidential wife to hold a press conference. Roosevelt's press conferences were a vehicle to discuss current events, her husband's New Deal programs, and any one of Eleanor's humanitarian projects—as well as to promote jobs for women in the media. Although some first ladies since Roosevelt have had dedicated meetings with the press when an occasion called for it, none cultivated a dedicated following of female journalists like Eleanor had.

How did **Bess Truman** stand in stark contrast to Eleanor Roosevelt?

Unlike Eleanor Roosevelt, a powerful figure who almost single-handedly redefined the role of the first lady in the twentieth century, Bess Truman was a more reluctant public figure. She is known for limiting her official appearances and for often visiting her hometown of Independence, Missouri, to get away from Washington, D.C., and protect her privacy. As a more reclusive first lady, she said, according to biographer Marian Means, "I am not the one who is elected. I have nothing to say to the public."

Bess Truman became known as her husband's silent partner. Uninvolved in social causes, she stated: "A woman's place in public is to sit beside her husband, be silent, and be sure her hat is on straight." Despite this statement, some historians suggest that Bess Truman was very much a part of President Truman's political decisions, functioning as a behind-the-scenes confidante as he formulated his foreign policy.

What was **Mamie Eisenhower**'s concept of **feminism**?

Ike and Mamie Eisenhower, shortly after their wedding on July 1, 1916. *AP/Wide World Photos.*

Marie "Mamie" Eisenhower once said, "Ike runs the country, and I turn the lamb chops." In her two terms as first lady, she and husband Dwight D. "Ike" Eisenhower lived in the White House for most of the 1950s. In an article for *Today's Woman* magazine, Mamie expressed her ideas about feminism and women's professions: "Let's face it. Our lives revolve around our men, and that is the way it should be. What real satisfaction is there without them? Being a wife is the best career that life has to offer a woman."

Interestingly, Mamie delved into volunteer work at servicemen's canteens in Washington and for the Red Cross during her years as General Eisenhower's army wife. After Eisenhower returned from World War II and began to actively campaign for the U.S. presidency in 1952, Mamie appeared on the Gallup Poll's list of Top 10 Most Admired Women in America. As president and first lady, they entertained heads of state and Mamie embraced her role as social hostess.

How did **Jackie Kennedy** take **White House restoration** to a new level?

Jacqueline Bouvier Kennedy's legacy as first lady includes her restoration of the White House, her success in stimulating interest in the arts and culture, and the style, grace, and poise she brought to the role of first lady. Educated in fine art and literature, "Jackie" established in 1961 the White House Historical Association. She set up a White House Fine Arts Committee to oversee and authenticate her work, hired a White House curator, and redecorated the mansion with early nineteenth-century furnishings and museum-quality paintings. Not satisfied to only replace curtains and carpets, Jackie was determined to restore the White House as a historical and cultural icon. She built on earlier, smaller-scale attempts to do so, notably by Grace Coolidge, Lou Hoover, and Mamie Eisenhower.

In February 1962, Mrs. Kennedy gave a guided tour of her efforts to millions of
Americans via television broadcast. By asking for donations, courting the press, and

actively involving the public in the process, Jacqueline Kennedy helped make Americans feel that they had played a part in recreating history. She soon published a guidebook for visitors, *The White House: A Historic Guide,* and promoted legislation to have the White House raised to museum status. Through her efforts, Jackie fueled a nationwide interest in architectural preservation. Hugh Sidey, White House correspondent for *Time* magazine during the Kennedy administration, noted, "She really was the one who made over the White House into a living stage—not a museum—but a stage where American history and art were displayed." Jackie influenced husband John F. Kennedy's appreciation of art and history, and the president folded those values into his administration by supporting preservation of Lafayette Square and redevelopment of Pennsylvania Avenue, as well as appointing the first presidential arts adviser.

How was **Jackie Kennedy** one of the most **private first ladies**?

After John F. Kennedy's assassination, Jackie Kennedy carefully guarded her privacy. However, a closer look at her role of first lady reveals a very private mother and wife, intent on giving her children, Caroline and John, the most "normal" upbringing life in the White House could offer. Her personal philosophy was, "If you bungle raising your children, I don't think whatever else you do well matters very much."

Jackie restricted the number of photographs the press took of her children, read and played with her children constantly, and opened a nursery school inside the executive mansion for her children. She conveyed her desire for privacy in a memo to her press secretary shortly after moving into the White House: "I feel strongly that publicity in this era has gotten completely out of hand—and you really must protect the privacy of me and my children—but not offend [the media]. My press relations will be minimum information given with maximum politeness." True to her word, during her time in the White House, Jackie was select in granting interviews and posing with her family for photographs.

How did **Lady Bird Johnson secure a successful presidential campaign for her husband**?

Claudia "Lady Bird" Taylor Johnson was the first presidential wife to run her husband's campaign for president and campaign for him while he stayed in Washington, D.C. In 1964, when Lyndon B. Johnson was running for his first elected term, Lady Bird embarked on a whistle-stop tour throughout the South aboard a train dubbed the "Lady Bird Special." In forty-seven stops in four days, Lady Bird traveled to eight southern states to challenge opposition to the passage of the Civil Rights Act and to demonstrate the South's importance to the president and first lady. Some southern Democrats threatened to leave the Democratic Party, potentially costing President Johnson the election. As a southerner herself, Lady Bird was concerned with the region's support for her husband. "I knew the Civil Rights Act was right and I didn't mind saying so," Lady Bird said, "but I also loved the South and didn't want it used as the whipping boy of the

Democratic Party." Her southern roots and empathy of the region's social history allowed Lady Bird to voice her husband's politics without alienating voters.

Despite opposition in some states, such as South Carolina, Lady Bird's efforts were praised by the press. An *Atlanta Constitution* editorial noted that Lady Bird's tour reminded southerners that the president was "the son of a southern tenant farmer and that he asks for the vote of this state not as a distant theorist but as a native southerner who understands his kin." Lyndon B. Johnson won the presidency that year, as Lady Bird won the respect of many Americans for actively participating in her husband's political career.

What was **Lady Bird Johnson's beautification program**?

Lady Bird Johnson played an active role in her husband's administration. During her tenure as first lady, she made 164 speeches, participated in 718 scheduled activities, and took 47 official trips. She promoted many of Lyndon B. Johnson's Great Society and War on Poverty programs, including Head Start, VISTA, and Job Corps. However, her signature cause involved promoting environmental protection and beautifying the nation's landscapes and highways. She created a First Lady's Committee for a More Beautiful Capital, which included tree and flower plantings in Washington, D.C., then expanded her program to include the entire United States. She lobbied for the passage of the Highway Beautification Act of 1965, which included restrictions on billboards along the nation's highways. Of these accomplishments, Lady Bird reflected, "We walked the problem of the environment on to center stage and put it on the national agenda—clean water, clean air, the amenities in all parks, in urban areas, all of that became a part of the national thinking."

How is **Pat Nixon** linked to the concept of volunteerism?

First lady Patricia "Pat" Nixon did not support one particular cause, but rather encouraged volunteerism from all Americans. She traveled around the nation, recognizing and encouraging those who spent their time in volunteer service, a concept she called "the spirit of people helping people." She applauded those who donated their time and money to day-care centers, hospitals, and shelters, and invited many Americans who embraced this ideal to the White House. In keeping with this spirit, she traveled to more than eighty countries, many times alone and on humanitarian missions. She often visited orphanages and hospitals, and once visited a leper colony in Panama. In June 1970, Pat flew supplies gathered by volunteers to earthquake-devastated Peru. For this, the Peruvian government awarded her the country's highest honor, the Grand Cross of the Order of the Sun.

Which first lady was known for fighting for the **Equal Rights Amendment**?

First lady Elizabeth "Betty" Ford stepped into the office of first lady as an ardent feminist who spoke her mind on often controversial issues. In 1972, when the Equal

Rights Amendment (ERA) passed in the Senate, many women worked to try to get the required thirty-eight states to pass the amendment within the allotted seven years. After supporting ERA as the wife of a congressman, Betty Ford moved to the forefront of this movement when she became first lady in 1974. She gave speeches, contacted state legislators, and influenced her husband, President Gerald Ford, to proclaim "Woman's Equality Day" in support of the ERA. She was known for "working the phones"—calling state legislators from the White House to encourage them to vote for the amendment. She once said, "Being ladylike does not require silence." Although her husband did not share all her views, she voiced her opinion on a range of issues, from premarital sex to abortion. In November 1981, when the National Organization for Women (NOW) organized a series of rallies in support of the ERA, former first lady Betty Ford was among the notable speakers. Time ran out in 1982, and the ERA failed to become law.

How did **Betty Ford's battle with breast cancer** affect her legacy as first lady?

When Betty Ford contracted breast cancer and underwent subsequent treatment, including a mastectomy, in 1974, she became the first presidential wife to be candid about the details of her health. In her autobiography, *The Times of My Life* (1978), Betty revealed her thoughts after her mastectomy: "Thinking of all those women going for cancer checkups because of me, I'd come to recognize more clearly the power of the woman in the White House. Not my power, but the power of the position, a power which could be used to help." By speaking out about her breast cancer, Betty Ford became a very respected first lady. In an era when breast cancer was rarely discussed, she greatly expanded the public's awareness of the disease, inspired thousands of women to have routine mammograms, pushed researchers to work toward prevention and cure, and encouraged others to establish breast cancer support groups.

After her husband left office in 1977, Betty revealed her dependency on alcohol and prescription drugs. In 1982, she founded a rehabilitation clinic, the Betty Ford Center, in Rancho Mirage, California, which has treated thousands of people for alcoholism and drug dependency. Betty Ford's legacy as a first lady reaches beyond her achievements in office, and includes her candor in discussing her personal struggles. In 1999, Gerald and Betty Ford were awarded with the Congressional Gold Medal for their humanitarian and charitable achievements.

Which first lady supported **mental health programs**?

Rosalynn Smith Carter once said, "A first lady is in a position to know the needs of the country and do something about them." Her husband, President Jimmy Carter, publicly acknowledged her role as "political partner," admitting, "There's seldom a decision I make that I don't first discuss with her. She's got superb political judgment." During her husband's tenure as governor of Georgia from 1971 to 1975, Rosalynn took a serious interest in mental health. She was appointed to the Governor's Commission to Improve Services for the Mentally and Emotionally Handicapped, and served as honorary chairperson for the Georgia Special Olympics for Retarded Children. During the presidential campaign season of 1976, Rosalynn was elected to the board of directors of the National Association of Mental Health.

As first lady of the United States from 1977 to 1981, Rosalynn continued to speak out on behalf of the mentally ill. She broke tradition by opening her own East Wing office, became active honorary chair of the President's Commission on Mental Health, sat in on cabinet meetings, and met with cabinet members individually to discuss specific mental-health issues. Her efforts resulted in the passage of the Mental Health Systems Act of 1980, which helped increase the number of America's community mental health centers. In an effort to obtain increased funding for mental healthcare, she testified before a congressional committee, becoming the second presidential wife to do so (the first was Eleanor Roosevelt).

Rosalynn co-authored two books related to mental illness, *Helping Yourself Help Others: A Book For Caregivers* (1994) and the award-winning *Helping Someone with Mental Illness: A Compassionate Guide for Family, Friends, and Caregivers* (1998). She continued to be an advocate for mental health programs, human rights, and conflict resolution through her work at the Carter Center in Atlanta, founded by Rosalynn and Jimmy Carter in 1982. She created and chairs the Carter Center's Mental Health Task Force. Each year, she hosts the Rosalynn Carter Symposium on Mental Health Policy, bringing together leaders of the nation's mental health organizations to address critical issues. Besides her volunteer work for Habitat for Humanity, a network of volunteers who build homes for the underprivileged, Rosalynn donates her time to Project Interconnections, an organization that provides housing for homeless people who are mentally ill.

Which first lady captured the media's attention when she ordered over $200,000 worth of china for the White House?

Nancy Reagan attempted to make the White House elegant with the purchase of $209,000 worth of new china—a decision that was not well received by the public once it made headline news. Indeed, Nancy Reagan's penchant for $20,000 designer dresses and other flamboyancies were often the subject of press reports. When the bad press started to elicit criticism of the first lady, President Ronald Reagan's staff began to work on Nancy's image, which included donating her gowns to museums and embracing social causes. Despite a rather active campaign against drug abuse and an ever-increasing role in President Reagan's administration after his surgery for cancer in 1985, reporters did not hesitate to list the "gifts" Nancy acquired and left the White House with: after just two terms in office, more than $1 million worth of dresses, jewelry, shoes, and accessories.

Which first lady sponsored the **"Just Say No" anti-drug campaign**?

Nancy Reagan's "Just Say No" anti-drug campaign was the one major policy program the first lady heralded during her tenure as first lady to Ronald Reagan from 1981 to 1989. Based on the response Nancy felt a youth should give when confronted with drugs and alcohol ("Just say no!"), this pioneer campaign involved a bevy of public service announcements, speeches, and "Just Say No to Drugs" clubs among children around the nation.

In response to her efforts, Congress funded a "National Crusade for a Drug-Free America" and the first lady traveled to sixty-five cities in thirty-three states, the Vatican, and eight foreign countries in the course of eight years. Her mission was to "bring public awareness, particularly parental awareness, to the problems of drug abuse." Nancy also held two international drug conferences in an effort to alert the international community to how drugs and alcohol damage the youth population.

Which first lady took a special interest in **adult literacy**?

As first lady from 1989 to 1993, Barbara Bush established an adult literacy campaign in response to the twenty-three million Americans who were functionally illiterate. Believing that "reading to children early and often is the single most important thing parents can do to prepare them to start school ready to learn," she established the Barbara Bush Foundation for Family Literacy in 1989 to support family literacy programs, break the intergenerational cycle of illiteracy, and establish literacy as a value in every American family. The foundation has funded more than three hundred family literacy programs in more than forty states. In support of her campaign, Bush regularly appeared on "Mrs. Bush's Story Time," a national radio program that stressed the importance of reading aloud to children, and authored two books, *C. Fred's Story* and the best-selling *Millie's Book,* the profits of which benefited her literacy cause.

How did **Hillary Clinton** introduce the concept of a **political partner** during her husband's campaign for the presidency?

Hillary Rodham Clinton was not shy about vocalizing her assets when her husband, Bill Clinton, was running for president in 1992. "If you vote for my husband, you get me, it's a two-for-one blue-plate special." Her words marked a political climate where presidential wives had risen to the status of "political partner" or "associate president." Hillary was one of the few presidential wives who had an accomplished decades-long career (as a prominent Arkansas attorney) before she entered the White House, and she joined the list of those twentieth-century women before her, such as Eleanor Roosevelt, Lady Bird Johnson, Betty Ford, and Rosalynn Carter, who made major contributions to their husbands' administrations.

From her office in the West Wing, Hillary played a pivotal role, advising President Clinton in his appointment selection and chairing the presidential task force on

U.S. senator and former first lady Hillary Clinton greets her fans at a book signing for her autobiography, *Living History,* in 2003. *AP/Wide World Photos.*

health care. By becoming the first presidential wife to set up an office just steps from the president's Oval Office, she sent a message that she was key to the administration. In taking charge of reforming America's health care system, Hillary was responsible for creating a detailed set of policy proposals and lobbying those ideas before congressional committees. Although her nationwide health care plan failed to pass Congress, her efforts marked the first time a first lady orchestrated a major legislative initiative.

How is **Hillary Clinton a first**?

Hillary Rodham Clinton has achieved many firsts: she was the first presidential wife to graduate from Yale Law School, the first presidential wife to have an office in the West Wing, and the first presidential wife to run for office under a "co-presidency" banner, with the slogan, "Two for the Price of One." She is perhaps most celebrated as the only presidential wife to have won a seat in the U.S. Senate. She assumed her seat in Congress just a couple weeks before the end of President Clinton's tenure in 2001, making her a senator while also the wife of a sitting president.

How did **Laura Bush** carve out a niche for herself as a first lady?

Laura Bush, a former public-school teacher and librarian, has said, "I have a lifelong passion for introducing children to books." As first lady to President George W. Bush, Laura is dedicated to advancing education in America and supports President Bush's

Former President George Bush with his wife Barbara, their son, President George W. Bush, and first lady Laura Bush on January 27, 2002. *AP/Wide World Photos.*

initiative to ensure that no child is left behind in school or in life. She has stated, "Our challenge is to reach all children early so that every child starts school with the skills needed to learn." To that end, she created the "Ready to Read, Ready to Learn" program, which educates parents and policy makers about early childhood education and the importance of reading aloud to and with children. She helped develop a public-service magazine series called *Healthy Start, Grow Smart* to provide parents with information about their infant's cognitive development and health. Other educational programs she has heralded include "Reach Out and Read," which encourages early literacy as a standard component of pediatric primary care, and "Teach for America," which recruits recent college graduates to short-term teaching careers in needy communities.

Presidents and Vice Presidents of the United States

Number	President	Political Party	Vice President	Term
1	George Washington	Federalist	John Adams	1789–1797
2	John Adams	Federalist	Thomas Jefferson	1797–1801
3	Thomas Jefferson	Democratic-Republican	Aaron Burr	1801–1805
			George Clinton	1805–1809
4	James Madison	Democratic-Republican	George Clinton	1809–1812
			None	1812–1813
			Elbridge Gerry	1813–1814
			None	1814–1817
5	James Monroe	Democratic-Republican	Daniel D. Tompkins	1817–1825
6	John Quincy Adams	Democratic-Republican	John C. Calhoun	1825–1829
7	Andrew Jackson	Democratic	John C. Calhoun	1829–1832
			None	1832–1833
			Martin Van Buren	1833–1837
8	Martin Van Buren	Democratic	Richard M. Johnson	1837–1841
9	William Henry Harrison	Whig	John Tyler	1841
10	John Tyler	Whig	None	1841–1845
11	James K. Polk	Democratic	George M. Dallas	1845–1849
12	Zachary Taylor	Whig	Millard Fillmore	1849–1850
13	Millard Fillmore	Whig	None	1850–1853
14	Franklin Pierce	Democratic	William Rufus King	1853
			None	1853–1857
15	James Buchanan	Democratic	John C. Breckinridge	1857–1861
16	Abraham Lincoln	Republican	Hannibal Hamlin	1861–1865
		National Union	Andrew Johnson	1865
17	Andrew Johnson	National Union	None	1865–1869
18	Ulysses S. Grant	Republican	Schuyler Colfax	1869–1873
			Henry Wilson	1873–1875
			None	1875–1877
19	Rutherford B. Hayes	Republican	William A. Wheeler	1877–1881
20	James A. Garfield	Republican	Chester Alan Arthur	1881

Number	President	Political Party	Vice President	Term
21	Chester Alan Arthur	Republican	None	1881–1885
22	Grover Cleveland	Democratic	Thomas Hendricks	1885
			None	1885–1889
23	Benjamin Harrison	Republican	Levi P. Morton	1889–1893
24	Grover Cleveland	Democratic	Adlai E Stevenson	1893–1897
25	William McKinley	Republican	Garret A. Hobart	1897–1899
			None	1899–1901
			Theodore Roosevelt	1901
26	Theodore Roosevelt	Republican	None	1901–1905
			Charles W. Fairbanks	1905–1909
27	William Howard Taft	Republican	James S. Sherman	1909–1912
			None	1912–1913
28	Woodrow Wilson	Democratic	Thomas R. Marshall	1913–1921
29	Warren G. Harding	Republican	Calvin Coolidge	1921–1923
30	Calvin Coolidge	Republican	None	1923–1925
			Charles G. Dawes	1925–1929
31	Herbert Hoover	Republican	Charles Curtis	1929–1933
32	Franklin D. Roosevelt	Democratic	John Nance Garner	1933–1941
			Henry A. Wallace	1941–1945
			Harry S. Truman	1945
33	Harry S. Truman	Democratic	None	1945–1949
		Democratic	Alben W. Barkley	1949–1953
34	Dwight D. Eisenhower	Republican	Richard Nixon	1953–1961
35	John F. Kennedy	Democratic	Lyndon B. Johnson	1961–1963
36	Lyndon B. Johnson	Democratic	None	1963–1965
			Hubert Humphrey	1965–1969
37	Richard Nixon	Republican	Spiro Agnew	1969–1973
			None	1973
			Gerald Ford	1973–1974
38	Gerald Ford	Republican	None	1974
			Nelson Rockefeller	1974–1977
39	Jimmy Carter	Democratic	Walter Mondale	1977–1981
40	Ronald Reagan	Republican	George Bush	1981–1989
41	George Bush	Republican	Dan Quayle	1989–1993
42	Bill Clinton	Democratic	Al Gore	1993–2001
43	George W. Bush	Republican	Dick Cheney	2001–

Presidential Trivia

Items of national interest that may have escaped the previous pages ...

George Washington

- He proclaimed the first national Thanksgiving Day in 1789.
- He caught smallpox while in the Caribbean when he was nineteen. He was left with scars on his face, but the early exposure helped build up his immunity to a disease that killed many during the Revolutionary War.
- Cream of peanut was his favorite soup.

John Adams

- He was the first of six presidents to graduate from Harvard. The others are John Quincy Adams, Theodore Roosevelt, Franklin D. Roosevelt, John F. Kennedy, and George W. Bush (business school).
- Died on July 4, 1826, 50 years to the day of the signing of the Declaration of Independence and on the same day as Thomas Jefferson. They were the only two presidents to have signed the Declaration of Independence.
- His great-great grandparents, John and Priscilla Alden, were Pilgrims who landed at Plymouth Rock in 1620.

Thomas Jefferson

- He often wore slippers around the White House.
- He played the violin.
- An inventor, he constructed an early copying machine (two pens connected by a mechanical arm: when one pen was used the other moved simultaneously) as well as a swivel chair, a dumb waiter (for retrieving wine without having to leave the dining room), and other inventions. Introduced a specie of the olive tree to North America.

James Madison

- At 5'4" tall and weighing less than 100 pounds, he was the smallest president.
- His last words were, "I always talk better lying down."
- He was the first president to wear long pants, rather than knee-length breeches.

James Monroe

- He was the first president to travel on a steamship.
- He was the first president to have been a U.S. senator.
- After more than 40 years of public service, he had little money after leaving the presidency and was forced to move in with his daughter. He died in her home on July 4, 1831, making him the third of the first five presidents to die on Independence Day.

John Quincy Adams

- He was the first president to be interviewed by a female journalist. Adams had rebuffed Anne Royall, but knowing the president swam in the buff on early mornings in the Potomac River, Royall went to the river, gathered the president's clothes, and sat on them until she had her interview.
- He traveled to Berlin, Germany, in 1797 to serve as a diplomat but was prevented from passing through the Berlin gates because the guard had never heard of the country, the United States, that Adams was representing.
- Like his father, Adams served as a minister to England. His own son, Charles Francis Adams, served in that capacity in the administration of Abraham Lincoln.

Andrew Jackson

- As a boy in North Carolina during the Revolutionary War, he was beaten by a British soldier when he refused to shine the soldier's boots.
- As president, he used government money to buy 20 spittoons for the East Room—a shrewd investment that protected the White House carpets.
- He was the first president to ride in a train.

Martin Van Buren

- He was the first president born after the American Revolution and so the first to be born as an American, not as a British citizen.
- He was called the "Little Magician" and the "Red Fox of Kinderhook" (his hometown) because of his slyness and cunning as a politician.
- He and his wife (who died 18 years before Van Buren became president) spoke Dutch at home.

William Henry Harrison

- He was the only president who studied to become a doctor.
- Tippecanoe and Tyler Too: both were born in Charles City County, Virginia, marking the only time a president (Harrison) and vice-president (Tyler) were from the same county.
- His father, Benjamin Harrison, served three terms as governor of Virginia and signed the Declaration of Independence.

John Tyler

- While vice president, he was playing marbles when word came that President Harrison had died.
- He was elected to the Confederate House of Representatives.
- Tyler was the grand uncle of Harry S. Truman.

James K. Polk

- He was the first president to have his photo taken while in office.
- He banned dancing in the White House and didn't like music, except for hymns.
- The first gaslight in the White House was installed during his administration.

Zachary Taylor

- He refused all mail that had postage due. The letter notifying him of his nomination for president was returned, then several days later the nomination letter arrived, prepaid.
- Souvenir horsehairs from Whitey, Taylor's army horse that he kept on the White House lawn, were a popular item.
- He was due to be sworn in as president on March 4, 1849, but refused on religious reasons because it was a Sunday. Since the terms of the previous president (Polk) and vice president (George M. Dallas) had ended, David Rice Atchison, president pro tempore of the Senate, was the legal president until Taylor was sworn into office on March 5.

Millard Fillmore

- He was a member of the Anti-Masonic Party in the late 1820s and early 1830s, which opposed secret fraternal orders, including those whose members included Presidents Washington, Monroe, and Jackson.
- He was the first chancellor of University of Buffalo, now SUNY Buffalo.
- He refused an honorary degree from Oxford University, contending he had done nothing to deserve the honor.

Franklin Pierce

- At forty-nine, he was the youngest elected president (1852) until Theodore Roosevelt (1904), who was forty-six when he was elected.
- He was the first president to have a Christmas tree in the White House.
- His campaign biography was written by the eminent author Nathaniel Hawthorne.

James Buchanan

- He served in the administrations of Pierce, Polk, and Jackson. When he was appointed minister to Russia in Jackson's first term, the president stated, "It was as far as I could send him out of my sight, and where he could do the least harm. I would have sent him to the North Pole if we had kept a minister there!"
- He put a bounty of $250 for the capture of abolitionist John Brown. Brown responded with a $2.50 bounty on Buchanan.
- He liked to give parties that featured sauerkraut and mashed potatoes.

Abraham Lincoln

- He was the first president to receive a patent (for a floating drydock, May 22, 1849, patent #6469).
- He was the tallest president (6'4") and the first one born outside the original thirteen states.
- He was not the featured speaker at the dedication of the Gettysburg Battlefield as a national cemetery. Edward Everett, a noted orator and congressman from Massachusetts, spoke for two hours and his speech was widely reported in the press. Lincoln spoke for less than two minutes, but his Gettysburg Address is recognized as among the finest American speeches.

Andrew Johnson

- He escaped removal from office by one impeachment vote. Among those who voted against conviction was Republican senator Benjamin Wade, who would have become president if Johnson had been found guilty (the vice presidency was vacant).
- He never attended school. He was taught to read by his wife and by a minister.
- Johnson married at the youngest age of all the presidents: he married a 16-year-old girl when he was 18.

Ulysses S. Grant

- His given name was Hiram Ulysses Grant, but he had been called Ulysses as a youth. The congressman who recommended him to West Point thought his name was Ulysses and his middle name Simpson, his mother's maiden name. Grant kept the name. While at West Point, he set a high-jump record that lasted more than 25 years.

- His favorite breakfast was a cucumber soaked in vinegar.

- He preceded the modern tradition among presidents of inviting championship sports teams to the White House. After baseball's first all-professional team, the Cincinnati Red Stockings, completed a cross-country, undefeated season in 1869, they were rewarded with a private audience with President Grant. The president complimented what he called "the western Cinderella club" for its skills and winning ways.

Rutherford B. Hayes

- He had the first telephone installed in the White House, then spoke with Alexander Graham Bell, who was 13 miles away. He also had the first typewriter in the White House.

- The first president to travel to the West Coast, he and the first lady went by rail, stagecoach, horse, steamer, yacht, ferry, and ambulance wagon. In San Francisco, he attended a reunion of his Civil War regiment.

- He was wounded four times during the Civil War.

James Garfield

- He was the only man to be a congressman, senator-elect, and a president-elect at the same time (1880).

- He was the first left-handed president.

- A great debater, he made a speech before Congress in 1879 in which he contended the legislative body was attempting to usurp the authority of the president.

Chester Alan Arthur

- He was nicknamed Elegant Arthur.

- He was an excellent fly fisherman.

- Calling the White House a barracks, he had furniture carted out and hired Louis Tiffany to redecorate.

Grover Cleveland

- The Baby Ruth candy bar was named for his daughter. Ruth was born between terms of the only president to serve nonconsecutive terms.

- The Clevelands retired to Princeton, New Jersey, where the ex-president died in 1908. Frances Cleveland would live until 1947. She was invited to a reception attended by President Truman. During small talk, the president learned she had once lived in Washington, D.C., and asked where she had resided in the city. "In the White House," she replied.

- Cleveland was nicknamed His Obstinacy and the Preventative President for frequently blocking new legislation, but he lived up to his motto, "Public office is a public trust."

Benjamin Harrison

- He was not an inspiring leader, as indicated by his collection of nicknames: "Kid Glove" Harrison, for his refusal to spar during debates when he first sought office in Ohio (he lost his first two elections); "Little Ben," as a Civil War commander (a reference to his small stature, not his fighting ability); and "the Centennial President," because he was inaugurated 100 years after George Washington.

- He was the first president to attend a baseball game.

- His father was the only man to be a son of one president (William Henry Harrison) and father of another.

William McKinley

- He liked to wear a white vest and a lucky red carnation in his buttonhole.

- He was the first president to ride in an automobile—a Stanley Steamer—and his inauguration in 1896 was the first to be filmed and audio taped. Thomas Edison's new motion picture camera and gramophone captured the moment.

- He once said, "I have never been in doubt since I was old enough to think intelligently that I would sometime be made President."

Theodore Roosevelt

- He owned a guinea pig named Father O'Grady and a snake named Emily Spinach.

- He was the first president to ride in an airplane. He rode in a Wright biplane on October 11, 1910, in St. Louis, Missouri.

- The Teddy Bear originated from a hunting trip where Roosevelt refused to shoot a young bear. A book, *The Adventures of the Roosevelt Bears,* soon followed, and then came the toy. Roosevelt himself did not like being called Teddy, preferring TR or Teedy, which he was called when he was a boy.

William Howard Taft

- Nicknamed "Big Bill" and "Big Lub," he was the largest president, denting the scales at over 300 pounds and standing 6'2". A special 7-foot-long, 41-inch-wide bathtub was installed in the White House for him. The tub could accommodate four normal-sized people.

- Taft was the first president to have a car at the White House (he had the White House stables converted into a four-car garage), to throw out the first ball to begin the professional baseball season, and the first president to be buried in the National Cemetery in Arlington, Virginia.

- His father, Alphonso Taft, was secretary of war under President Grant. Taft's son, Robert, served in the U.S. Senate from 1938 to 1953, was nicknamed Mr. Republican, and was expected to be the party's presidential nominee in 1952, but then Dwight D. Eisenhower announced that he was a Republican. Taft's grandson was elected to the U.S. Senate in 1979, and his great-grandson was elected governor of Ohio in 1996.

Woodrow Wilson

- He wrote a book called *Congressional Government* (1885) that criticized the power Congress had assumed over the presidency beginning in 1866, after the Civil War. After being elected president in 1912, Wilson quickly assumed influence over Congress, but at the end of his second term, Congress held the power—rejecting the Wilson-negotiated Treaty of Versailles and his proposal for the League of Nations.
- Taught at Bryn Mawr and Wesleyan University (where he also coached football) before becoming president of Princeton University.
- His vice president, Thomas Riley Marshall, coined the phrase, "What this country needs is a good five-cent cigar."

Warren G. Harding

- His dog, Laddie Boy, delivered the president his newspaper each day. Laddie Boy enjoyed a birthday party and a cake made of dog biscuits, and he had his own chair for cabinet meetings.
- He hosted weekly poker games at the White House while he was president. Attorney General Harry Daugherty attended and brought along Jess Smith, an official in the Justice Department who often brought the booze. Prohibition was in effect at the time.
- He was the first president to visit Alaska.

Calvin Coolidge

- A man of few words, he was called "Silent Cal." A reporter approached the president and said, "I bet someone that I could get more than two words out of you." Coolidge replied, "You lose." When Coolidge died, columnist Dorothy Parker asked, "How can they tell?"
- He was not camera-shy. He was photographed wearing a full headdress of feathers given to him by Native American leaders on one occasion, and on another he wore a cowboy outfit. Off-hours shots of Coolidge showed him plowing his Vermont farm and fishing—wearing hat, suit, tie, and waders.
- He was the first president to make a radio broadcast, the only one born on the Fourth of July, and probably the only one who liked having his head rubbed with Vaseline while he ate breakfast in bed.

Herbert Hoover

- He was the first president to have a telephone on his desk.
- Charles Curtis, Hoover's vice president, was the only nonwhite person to be elected vice president of the United States. He was a Native American of the Kaw tribe.
- An avid fisherman, he once said "that comprehensive list of human rights, the Declaration of Independence, is firm that all men (and boys) are endowed with certain inalienable rights, including life, liberty, and the pursuit of happiness, which obviously includes the pursuit of fish."

Franklin D. Roosevelt

- Genealogists have determined that Roosevelt was related to George Washington, John Adams, James Madison, John Quincy Adams, Martin Van Buren, William Henry Harrison, Zachary Taylor, Ulysses S. Grant, Benjamin Harrison, Theodore Roosevelt, and William Howard Taft.

- He was the first president to appear on television, April 30, 1939, at the opening of the World's Fair in New York; to have his own airplane; to travel through the Panama Canal; to visit a foreign country during wartime; and to name a woman to his cabinet. Superstitious, he never traveled on a Friday and would not sit at a table if there were twelve others seated.

- He served hot dogs to the king and queen of England, and his dog, Major, once bit the British prime minister, Ramsey McDonald.

Harry S. Truman

- His middle name is actually "S." Both of his grandfathers had names beginning with an "S," and his parents made a shrewd political move to give their boy a middle initial that paid tribute to both and did not offend either grandfather.

- He noticed that on one rug in the White House, the head of the eagle on the presidential seal was turned the wrong way. Instead of facing the olive branch, the eagle's head pointed toward the arrows (see the presidential seal on the cover of this book). Truman ordered the rug restitched.

- Bess Truman may have been the most athletic first lady, having run track and played baseball and tennis.

Dwight D. Eisenhower

- He played college football for Army and was injured trying to tackle Jim Thorpe.

- He was the first nominee to travel by airplane while campaigning, and he initiated the use of *Air Force One.* A man of the 1950s, he liked to eat TV dinners while watching westerns.

- A putting green was installed on the White House lawn for Eisenhower to practice his golf shots. He was the first president to have a hole-in-one, scoring his ace on February 2, 1968, at the Seven Lakes Country Club in Palm Springs, California.

John F. Kennedy

- He was the youngest man to be elected president as well as the first Roman Catholic and the first Pulitzer Prize winner (for *Profiles in Courage,* 1956, a collection of eight essays on U.S. senators who risked their political careers fighting for their causes).

- Kennedy's secretary was named Lincoln, and Lincoln's was named Kennedy. Both presidents were assassinated, and they were succeeded by vice presidents named Johnson. Kennedy's assassin shot from a warehouse and was later captured in a theater. Lincoln's assassin shot him in a theater and fled to a warehouse. Lincoln and Kennedy were first elected to Congress (1846 and 1946, respectively) and to the presidency (1860 and 1960) 100 years apart. The vice presidents who succeeded them were born 100 years apart. Both of the assassins commonly used their first, middle, and last names, and they, too, were born 100 years apart (1839 and 1939). Lincoln was killed at Ford's Theatre, and Kennedy was killed in a Ford automobile.

- Jack (as he was often called) and Jackie (as the first lady was often called) both worked as reporters: Jack for the Hearst International News Service in 1946, and Jackie as the "inquiring camera girl" for the *Washington Times-Herald* in the early 1950s.

Lyndon B. Johnson

- He signed the Voting Rights Act of 1965 with the same pen Abraham Lincoln used to sign the Emancipation Proclamation (1863).

- He was the first president to deliver his State of the Union Address in prime time.

- He kept three televisions in the Oval Office to keep track of the three broadcast networks at the time.

Richard Nixon

- He once worked at a game booth at the Slippery Gulch Rodeo.

- He was the first U.S. president to attend a regular season National Football League game while in office. He attended practices of the Washington Redskins while in office, and head coach George Allen allowed him to call a play. Nixon called a reverse. The play worked in practice, but when Allen used it in a 1971 playoff game, the play lost 13 yards.

- He was the first president to visit all 50 states and the first to talk to people on the moon—the *Apollo 11* astronauts in 1969 via radio-telephone.

Gerald Ford

- His resume includes flipping burgers and working as a fashion model.

- He started as center on the University of Michigan Wolverines' national championship football teams of 1932 and 1933, and he was the Most Valuable Player of the 1933 team. He played in the 1934 East-West College All-Star Game and was offered contracts by the Green Bay Packers and Detroit Lions. Ford instead went to law school.

- Although a good athlete, Ford could never quite master golf. He remarked that he knew his game was improving when he was hitting fewer spectators with errant golf shots.

Jimmy Carter

- He was the only president who had commanded a submarine and the first to have been born in a hospital.

- He was the only president known to have been attacked by a rabbit. According to the Associated Press, the beast breached Secret Service security and swam toward a canoe from which Carter was fishing in a pond. "It was hissing menacingly, its teeth flashing and nostrils flared, and making straight for the president, forcing the chief executive to beat back the beast with a canoe paddle." Carter believed the rabbit was fleeing in panic from some predator. A White House staff photographer was on hand and captured the attack as well as the president's successful self-defense.

- The only president to be awarded the Nobel Peace Prize after leaving office, Carter was cited by the Nobel committee for his "untiring effort to find peaceful solutions to international conflicts, to advance democracy and human rights, and to promote economic and social development."

Ronald Reagan

- He kept a jar of jelly beans on his desk.
- He was the first U.S. president to address Japan's legislature.
- In 1926, while still in high school, he became a lifeguard and, according to his presidential library's Web site, saved seventy-seven lives over seven summers.

George Bush

- He liked to play horseshoes.
- "Poppy" Bush played first base and was captain of the 1948 Yale University baseball team. The scouting report: good fielder but a relatively weak hitter; batted .251 with 2 home runs and 23 RBIs in 51 games during his two seasons. The Yale team won eastern regional titles and played in the first College World Series. Bush met Babe Ruth shortly before Ruth's death in 1948 during a Yale-Princeton pregame ceremony.
- First dog Millie had her own room in the White House.

Bill Clinton

- He was the first president born after World War II.
- He was named William Jefferson Blythe IV at birth. After his father's death (two months before the future president was born), his mother married Roger Clinton. He began using his stepfather's last name while in grade school and formally changed his name to William Jefferson Clinton when he was 15.
- He was the second president to card a hole-in-one when he aced the par-3, 125-yard sixth hole at Harborside International Golf Course in Chicago, 2001.

George W. Bush

- He was the first president to run a marathon: in 1993, at age 46, he ran and finished the Houston Marathon in 3:44:52.

- He assembled a group of partners that purchased the Texas Rangers baseball franchise in 1989. He served as managing general partner of the team until he was elected governor of Texas in 1994.
- He was the head cheerleader at his Massachusetts prep school.

Presidential Landmarks

George Washington

Birthplace:

George Washington Birthplace
  National Monument
1732 Popes Creek Rd.
Washington's Birthplace, VA 22443-5115
(804) 224-1732
http://www.nps.gov/gewa/

Home and burial:

Mount Vernon
Historic Mount Vernon
P.O. Box 110, 3200 Mount Vernon
  Memorial Highway
Mount Vernon, VA 22121
(703) 780-2000
http://www.mountvernon.org/

John Adams

Birthplace and home:

Adams National Historical Park
135 Adams St.
Quincy, MA 02169-1749
(617) 773-1177
http://www.nps.gov/adam/

Burial:

United First Parish Church
1306 Hancock St. (Quincy Center)
Quincy, MA 02169

(617) 773-1290
http://www.ufpc.org/

Thomas Jefferson

Home, burial, and museum:

Monticello
P.O. Box 316
Charlottesville, VA 22902
(434) 984-9800
http://www.monticello.org/

James Madison

Home and burial:

James Madison's Montpelier
P.O. Box 911
Orange, VA 22957
(540) 672-2728
http://www.montpelier.org/

Museum:

James Madison Museum
129 Caroline St.
Orange, VA 22960-1532
(540) 672-1776
http://www.jamesmadisonmus.org/

James Monroe

Home:

Ash Lawn–Highland
1000 James Monroe Pkwy.

Charlottesville, VA 22902-8722
(434) 293-9539
http://www.ashlawnhighland.org/

Burial:

Hollywood Cemetery
412 South Cherry St.
Richmond, VA 23220
(804) 648-8501
http://www.hollywoodcemetery.org/

Museum and library:

**James Monroe Museum and
  Memorial Library**
908 Charles St.
Fredericksburg, VA 22401
(540) 654-1043
http://www.artcom.com/museums/vs/gl/
  22401-58.htm

John Quincy Adams

Birthplace:

Adams National Historical Park
135 Adams St.
Quincy, MA 02169-1749
(617) 773-1177
http://www.nps.gov/adam/

Burial:

United First Parish Church
1306 Hancock St. (Quincy Center)
Quincy, MA 02169
(617) 773-1290
http://www.ufpc.org/

Andrew Jackson

Home, burial, and museum:

The Hermitage
4580 Rachel's Lane
Hermitage, TN 37076
(615) 889-2941
http://hermitage.org/

Martin Van Buren

Home:

Martin Van Buren National Historic Site
1013 Old Post Rd.
Kinderhook, NY 12106
(518) 758-9689
http://www.nps.gov/mava/home.htm

Burial:

Kinderhook Reformed Cemetery
Albany Ave.
Kinderhook, NY 12106
(518) 758-6401

William Henry Harrison

Birthplace:

Berkeley Plantation
12602 Harrison Landing Rd.
Charles City, VA 23030
(804) 829-6018

Home and museum:

**Grouseland: William Henry
  Harrison Mansion**
3 West Scott St.
Vincennes, IN 47591
(812) 882-2096
http://www.grouselandfoundation.org/

Burial:

Harrison Tomb State Memorial
Cliff Rd.
North Bend, OH 45052
(800) 686-1535
http://www.ohiohistory.org/places/
  harrison/

Historic site and museum:

Tippecanoe Battlefield
200 Battle Ground Ave.
Battle Ground, IN 47920
(765) 567-2147
http://www.tcha.mus.in.us/battlefield.htm

John Tyler

Home:

Sherwood Forest Plantation
State Rte. 5
14501 John Tyler Memorial Highway
Charles City, VA 23030-3544
(804) 829-5377
http://www.sherwoodforest.org/

Burial:

Hollywood Cemetery
412 South Cherry St.
Richmond, VA 23220
(804) 648-8501
http://www.hollywoodcemetery.org/

James K. Polk

Birthplace and museum:

James K. Polk Memorial State
  Historic Site
P.O. Box 475
Pineville, NC 28134
(704) 889-7145
http://www.ah.dcr.state.nc.us/sections/hs/
  polk/polk.htm

Home:

James K. Polk Ancestral Home
301 West Seventh St.
Columbia, TN 38401
(931) 388-2354
http://www.jameskpolk.com/

Burial:

Tennessee State Capitol
600 Charlotte Ave.
Nashville, TN 37243
(615) 741-1621
http://tnmuseum.org/exhibitions/special
  collections/capitol.html

Zachary Taylor

Burial:

Zachary Taylor National Cemetery
4701 Brownboro Rd.
Louisville, KY 40207
(502) 893-3852
http://www.cem.va.gov/nchp/zacharytaylor.
  htm#nb

Millard Fillmore

Home and museum:

Millard Fillmore House (Museum)
24 Shearer Ave.
East Aurora, NY 14052
(716) 652-8875
http://rin.buffalo.edu/c_erie/comm/cult/
  muse/agen/mfh.html

Burial:

Forest Lawn Cemetery
1411 Delaware Ave.
Buffalo, NY 14209
(716) 885-1600
http://www.forest-lawn.com/fillmore.htm

Franklin Pierce

Burial:

Old North Cemetery
North State St.
Concord, NH

Home:

Pierce Homestead
Routes 9 and 31
Hillsborough, NH 03244
(603) 478-3165
http://www.franklinpierce.ws/homestead/
  contents.html

Home:

Pierce Manse
14 Penacook St.

Concord, NH 00302-0425
(603) 224-5954
http://www.newww.com/free/pierce/pierce.
  html

James Buchanan

Home:

Wheatland
1120 Marietta Ave.
Lancaster, PA 17603
(717) 392-8721
http://www.wheatland.org/

Burial:

Woodward Hill Cemetery
538 East Strawberry St.
Lancaster, PA 17602

Abraham Lincoln

Birthplace:

Abraham Lincoln Birthplace National
  Historic Site
Sinking Spring Farm,
  2995 Lincoln Farm Rd.
Hodgenville, KY 42748
(270) 358-3137
http://www.nps.gov/abli/

Home:

Lincoln Boyhood National Memorial
P.O. Box 1816, Highway 162
Lincoln City, IN 47552-1816
(812) 937-4541
http://www.nps.gov/libo/index.htm

Home and historic site:

Lincoln's New Salem State Historic Site
R.R. 1, Box 244A
Petersburg, IL 62675
(217) 632-4000
http://www.lincolnsnewsalem.com/

Home and museum:

Lincoln Home National Historic Site
413 S. Eighth St.
Springfield, IL 62701-1905
(217) 492-4241
http://www.nps.gov/liho/index.htm

Assassination site and museum:

Ford's Theatre National Historic Site /
  The House Where Lincoln Died (across
  the street)
511 Tenth St. N.W.
Washington, DC 20004
(202) 426-6924
http://www.nps.gov/foth /index.htm

Burial:

Lincoln Tomb
Oak Ridge Cemetery
Springfield, IL 62702
(217) 782-2717
http://www.state.il.us/HPA/hs/Tomb.htm

Library and museum:

Abraham Lincoln Presidential Library
  and Museum
112 North Sixth St.
Springfield, IL 62701
(217) 785-0348
Library is due to open in 2004; museum
  is due to open in early 2005

Museum:

Lincoln Museum
200 E. Berry St.
Fort Wayne, IN 46802
(260) 455-3864
http://www.thelincolnmuseum.org/

Museum:

Abraham Lincoln Library and Museum
U.S. Highway 25E
Harrogate, TN 37752
(423) 869-6235

http://www.lmunet.edu/museum/

Andrew Johnson

Birthplace:

Andrew Johnson Birthplace
Mordecai Historic Park
1 Mimosa St.
Raleigh, NC 27604
(919) 834-4844
http://www.itpi.dpi.state.nc.us/vvisits/
  mordecai.html

Homes and burial:

Andrew Johnson National Historic Site
P.O. Box 1088
College and Depot Streets
Greeneville, TN 37744
(423) 638-3551
http://www.nps.gov/anjo/

Museum and library:

President Andrew Johnson Museum
  and Library
Tusculum College
P.O. Box 5026
Greeneville, TN 37743
(423) 636-7348
http://ajmuseum.tusculum.edu/

Ulysses S. Grant

Birthplace and museum:

Grant's Birthplace
Routes 52E and 322
Point Pleasant, OH 45143
(513) 553-4911
http://www.ohiohistory.org/places/grantbir/

Home and historic district:

Grant's Boyhood Home
219 E. Grant Ave.
Georgetown, OH 45121
(937) 378-4222

http://www.ohiohistory.org/places/grant
  boy/index.html

Home:

Ulysses S. Grant National Historic Site:
  White Haven
7400 Grant Rd.
St. Louis, MO 63123
(314) 842–3298
http://www.nps.gov/ulsg/

Home:

Grant Home State Historic Site
500 Bouthillier St.
Galena, IL 61036
(815) 777-3310
http://www.granthome.com/grant_home.
  htm

Cottage and death site:

Grant Cottage State Historic Site
Mount McGregor
P.O. Box 990
Saratoga Springs, NY 12866-0897
(518) 587-8277
http://www.artcom.com/museums/vs/gl/
  12866-82.htm

Burial:

General Grant National Memorial:
  Grant's Tomb
Riverside Dr. and 122nd St.
New York, NY 10027
(212) 666-1640
http://www.nps.gov/gegr/

Civil War surrender site:

Appomattox Court House National
  Historical Park
Highway 24, P.O. Box 218
Appomattox, VA 24552
(434) 352-8987
http://www.nps.gov/apco/

Rutherford B. Hayes

Home, burial, museum, and library:

Rutherford B. Hayes Presidential Center
Spiegel Grove
Fremont, OH 43420
(800) 998-7737
http://www.rbhayes.org/

James A. Garfield

Birthplace:

James A. Garfield Birthplace
4350 S.O.M. Center Rd.
Moreland Hills, OH 44022
(440) 248-1188
http://www.morelandhills.com/historical.
  html

Home and museum:

James A. Garfield National Historic Site
8095 Mentor Ave.
Mentor, OH 44060
(440) 255-8722
See http://www.nps.gov/jaga/

Burial:

James A. Garfield Monument
Lake View Cemetery
12316 Euclid Ave.
Cleveland, OH 44106-4393
(216) 421-2665
http://www.lakeviewcemetery.com/

Chester Alan Arthur

Birthplace:

Chester A. Arthur State Historic Site
Route 36
Fairfield, VT 05455
(802) 828-3051
http://www.dhca.state.vt.us/HistoricSites/
  html/arthur.html

Burial:

Albany Rural Cemetery
Cemetery Ave.
Menands, NY 12204
(518) 463-7017

Grover Cleveland

Birthplace and museum:

Grover Cleveland Birthplace State
  Historic Site
207 Bloomfield Ave.
Caldwell, NJ 07006
(973) 226-0001
http://www.westessexguide.com/gcb/
  index.htm

Burial:

Princeton Cemetery
29 Greenview Ave.
Princeton, NJ 08540
(609) 924-1369
http://www.princetonol.com/patron/
  cemetery.html

Benjamin Harrison

Home, museum, and library:

President Benjamin Harrison Home
1230 North Delaware St.
Indianapolis, IN 46202
(317) 631-1888
http://www.presidentbenjaminharrison.
  org/

Burial:

Crown Hill Cemetery
700 West 38th St.
Indianapolis, IN 46208
(317) 925-8231
http://www.crownhill.org/cemetery/index.
  html

William McKinley

Birthplace:

McKinley Birthplace Home and Research
  Center
40 S. Main St.
Niles, OH 44446
(330) 652-1774
http://www.mckinley.lib.oh.us/museum/
  reconstruction.htm

Burial, library, and museum:

William McKinley Presidential Library
  and Museum
800 McKinley Monument Dr., NW
Canton, OH 44708
(330) 455-7043
http://www.mckinleymuseum.org/

Museum:

National McKinley Birthplace Memorial
40 N. Main St.
Niles, OH 44446
(330) 652-1704
http://www.mckinley.lib.oh.us/memorial.
  htm

Theodore Roosevelt

Birthplace and museum:

Theodore Roosevelt Birthplace National
  Historic Site
28 E. 20th St.
New York, NY 10003
(212) 260-1616
http://www.nps.gov/thrb/

Home and museum:

Sagamore Hill National Historic Site
20 Sagamore Hill Rd.
Oyster Bay, NY 11771-1807
(516) 922-4447
http://www.nps.gov/sahi/home.htm

Historic site and museum:

Theodore Roosevelt Inaugural National
  Historic Site
641 Delaware Ave.
Buffalo, NY 14202
(716) 884-0095
http://www.nps.gov/thri/

Burial:

Youngs Cemetery
Cove Neck Rd. and Cove Rd.
Oyster Bay, NY 11771
http://www.nps.gov/sahi/youngs.htm

William Howard Taft

Birthplace and museum:

William Howard Taft National
  Historic Site
2038 Auburn Ave.
Cincinnati, OH 45219
(513) 684-3262
http://www.nps.gov/wiho/

Burial:

Arlington National Cemetery
Arlington, VA 22211
http://www.arlingtoncemetery.org/histori
  cal_information/william_taft.html

Woodrow Wilson

Birthplace and museum:

Woodrow Wilson Birthplace
18-24 N. Coalter St.
Staunton, VA 24402-0024
(540) 885-0897
http://www.woodrowwilson.org/

Home:

Boyhood Home of President
  Woodrow Wilson
419 Seventh St.
Augusta, GA 30901

(706) 722-9828
http://www.wilsonboyhoodhome.org/

Home:

Woodrow Wilson Boyhood Home
1705 Hampton St.
Columbia, SC 29201-3419
(803) 252-1770
http://www.historiccolumbia.org/houses/
  woodrow.htm

Home:

Woodrow Wilson House
2340 S St. N.W.
Washington, DC 20008
(202) 387-4062
http://www.woodrowwilsonhouse.org/

Burial:

Washington National Cathedral
Massachusetts and Wisconsin Avenues,
  N.W.
Washington, DC 20016-5098
http://www.cathedral.org/cathedral/

Warren G. Harding

Home and museum:

Harding Home
380 Mount Vernon Ave.
Marion, OH 43302
(740) 387-9630
http://www.ohiohistory.org/places/
  harding/

Burial:

Harding Tomb
Vernon Heights Blvd.
Marion, OH 43302
(740) 387-9630
http://www.ohiohistory.org/places/hard
  tomb/

Calvin Coolidge

Museum:

Black River Academy Museum
14 High St.
Ludlow, VT 05149
(802) 228-5050
http://www.okemovalleyvt.org/frame.
  html?target=107

Library and museum:

**Calvin Coolidge Presidential Library
  and Museum**
Forbes Library
20 West St.
Northampton, MA 01060
(413) 587-1014
http://www.forbeslibrary.org/coolidge/
  coolidge.shtml

*Historic site, birthplace, home, museum,
and burial:*

**President Calvin Coolidge State
  Historic Site**
Vermont Route 100A, Box 79
Plymouth, VT 05056
(802) 672-3773
http://www.dhca.state.vt.us/HistoricSites/
  html/CoolidgeTour.html

Herbert Hoover

*Historic site, birthplace, home, museum,
library, and burial:*

**Herbert Hoover Presidential
  Library-Museum**
210 Parkside Dr.
West Branch, IA 52358
(319) 643-5301
http://hoover.nara.gov/index.html

Home:

Hoover-Minthorn House
115 S. River St.

Newberg, OR 97132
(503) 538-6629

Franklin D. Roosevelt

Birthplace and burial:

Home of Franklin D. Roosevelt National
  Historic Site
4079 Albany Post Rd.
Hyde Park, NY 12538
(845) 229-9115
http://www.nps.gov/hofr/hofrhome.html

Vacation home:

Roosevelt Campobello
  International Park
459 Route 774
Welshpool, New Brunswick, E5E 1A4
  Canada
(506) 752-2922

Also, P.O. Box 97
Lubec, ME 04652
http://www.nps.gov/roca/ and
  http://www.fdr.net/

Historic site and death site:

FDR's Little White House State
  Historic Site
401 Little White House Rd.
Georgia Highway 85 Alternate
Warm Springs, GA 31830
(706) 655-5870
http://www.fdr-littlewhitehouse.org/

Library and museum:

Franklin D. Roosevelt Presidential
  Library and Museum
4079 Albany Post Rd.
Hyde Park, NY 12538
(800) FDR-VISIT
http://www.fdrlibrary.marist.edu/

Harry S. Truman

Birthplace:

Harry S. Truman Birthplace State
  Historic Site
1009 Truman Ave.
Lamar, MO 64759
(417) 682-2279
http://www.mostateparks.com/trumansite
  .htm

Home:

Truman Farm Home
12301 Blue Ridge Blvd.
Grandview, MO 64030-1159
(816) 254-2720
http://www.nps.gov/hstr/learning_place/
  farm/farm_page_1.htm

Home and museum:

Harry S. Truman National Historic Site
223 N. Main St.
Independence, MO 64050-2804
(816) 254-9929
http://www.nps.gov/hstr/

Museum:

Harry S. Truman Little White House
111 Front St.
Key West, FL 33040
(305) 294-9911
http://www.trumanlittlewhitehouse.com/

Library, museum, and burial:

Harry S. Truman Library and Museum
500 W. U.S. Highway 24
Independence, MO 64050
(800) 833-1225
http://www.trumanlibrary.org/

Dwight D. Eisenhower

Birthplace:

Eisenhower Birthplace State
  Historic Site

609 S. Lamar Ave.
Denison, TX 75020
(903) 465-8908
http://www.eisenhowerbirthplace.org/

Home:

Eisenhower National Historic Site
97 Taneytown Rd.
Gettysburg, PA 17325
(717) 338-9114
http://www.nps.gov/eise/home.htm

Home, burial, library, and museum:

**Dwight D. Eisenhower Library
 & Museum**
200 Southeast Fourth St.
Abilene, KS 67410
(785) 263-6700
http://www.eisenhower.utexas.edu/

John F. Kennedy

Birthplace:

John F. Kennedy National Historic Site
83 Beals St.
Brookline, MA 02446
(617) 566-7937
http://www.nps.gov/jofi/

Assassination site:

The Sixth Floor Museum at Dealey Plaza
411 Elm St., Suite 120
Dallas, TX 75202
(214) 747-6660
http://www.jfk.org/

Burial:

Arlington National Cemetery
Arlington, VA 22211
http://www.arlingtoncemetery.org/
 historical_information/JFK.html

Library and museum:

**John Fitzgerald Kennedy Library
 and Museum**

Columbia Point
Boston, MA 02125
(866) JFK-1960
www.jfklibrary.org

Museum:

John F. Kennedy Hyannis Museum
397 Main St.
Hyannis, MA 02601
508-790-3077
http://www.hyannischamber.com/JFK
 Museum.asp

Lyndon B. Johnson

Birthplace and burial:

**Lyndon B. Johnson National
 Historical Park**
P.O. Box 329
Johnson City, TX 78636
(830) 868-7128
http://www.nps.gov/lyjo/

Home:

**Lyndon B. Johnson State Park and
 Historic Site**
P.O. Box 238
Stonewall, TX 78671
(830) 644-2252
http://www.tpwd.state.tx.us/park/lbj/lbj.
 htm

Library and museum:

**Lyndon Baines Johnson Library
 and Museum**
2313 Red River St.
Austin, TX 78705
(512) 721-0200
http://www.lbjlib.utexas.edu/

Richard Nixon

Birthplace, library, museum, and burial:

Richard Nixon Library and Birthplace
18001 Yorba Linda Blvd.

Yorba Linda, CA 92886
(714) 993-5075
http://www.nixonfoundation.org/

Gerald Ford

Library:

Gerald R. Ford Library
1000 Beal Ave.
Ann Arbor, MI 48109
(734) 205-0555
http://www.fordlibrarymuseum.gov

Museum:

Gerald R. Ford Museum
303 Pearl St. NW
Grand Rapids, MI 49504-5353
(616) 254-0400
http://www.ford.utexas.edu/

Jimmy Carter

Historic site and museum:

Jimmy Carter National Historic Site
300 N. Bond St.
Plains, GA 31780
(229) 824-4104
http://www.nps.gov/jica/

Library and museum:

Jimmy Carter Library and Museum
441 Freedom Parkway
Atlanta, GA 30307–1498
(404) 865-7100
http://www.jimmycarterlibrary.org/

Ronald Reagan

Birthplace and museum:

Ronald Reagan Birthplace
119 S. Main St.
Tampico, IL 61283
(815) 438–2130

Home and museum:

Ronald Reagan Boyhood Home
816 S. Hennepin Ave.
Dixon, IL 61021
(815) 288-3404

Library, museum, and burial:

Ronald Reagan Presidential Library
and Museum
40 Presidential Drive
Simi Valley, CA 93065
(805) 522-2977
http://www.ronaldreaganmemorial.com/

George Bush

Library and museum:

George Bush Presidential Library
and Museum
1000 George Bush Drive West
College Station, TX 77845
(979) 691-4000
http://bushlibrary.tamu.edu/

Bill Clinton

Birthplace:

President Clinton's Birthplace Home
117 S. Hervey St.
Hope, AR 71802
870-777-4455
http://clintonbirthplace.org/

Hope, Arkansas, Sites
Hempstead County Economic
  Development Corporation
P.O. Box 971, Hope, AR 71802-0971
(870) HOPE-USA
http://www.hopeusa.com/clinton/believe.
  html

Hot Springs, Arkansas, Sites
Hot Springs Convention and Visitors
  Bureau
134 Convention Blvd., Box K

Hot Springs National Park, AR 71902
(800) 543-2284
http://www.hotspringsar.com/info/clinton/

Library:

William J. Clinton Presidential Center
1200 President Clinton Ave.
Little Rock, AR 72201
Scheduled to open in November 2004
http://www.clintonpresidentialcenter.org/
  library.htm

George W. Bush

No public landmarks at this time.

General

Presidents museum:

Museum of the American Presidents
130 North Massanutten St.
Strasburg, VA 22657
(540) 465-5999
http://www.waysideofva.com/presidents/

Vice presidents museum:

United States Vice Presidential Museum
Dan Quayle Center
815 Warren St.
Huntington, IN 46750
(260) 356-6356
http://www.quaylemuseum.org/

First ladies library and museum:

**Saxton McKinley House / National First
  Ladies' Library**
331 S. Market Ave.
Canton, OH 44702
(330) 452-0876
http://www.firstladies.org/

Pets museum:

Presidential Pet Museum
1102 Wrighton Rd.
Lothian, MD 20711
(410) 741-0899
http://www.presidentialpetmuseum.com/

The Constitution of the United States

We the People of the United States, in Order to form a more perfect Union, establish Justice, insure domestic Tranquility, provide for the common defence, promote the general Welfare, and secure the Blessings of Liberty to ourselves and our Posterity, do ordain and establish this Constitution for the United States of America.

ARTICLE I.

SECTION 1. All legislative Powers herein granted shall be vested in a Congress of the United States, which shall consist of a Senate and House of Representatives.

SECTION 2. The House of Representatives shall be composed of Members chosen every second Year by the People of the several States, and the Electors in each State shall have the Qualifications requisite for Electors of the most numerous Branch of the State Legislature.

No Person shall be a Representative who shall not have attained to the Age of twenty five Years, and been seven Years a Citizen of the United States, and who shall not, when elected, be an Inhabitant of that State in which he shall be chosen.

Representatives and direct Taxes shall be apportioned among the several States which may be included within this Union, according to their respective Numbers, which shall be determined by adding to the whole Number of free Persons, including those bound to Service for a Term of Years, and excluding Indians not taxed, three fifths of all other Persons.

The actual Enumeration shall be made within three Years after the first Meeting of the Congress of the United States, and within every subsequent Term of ten Years, in such Manner as they shall by Law direct. The Number of Representatives shall not exceed one for every thirty Thousand, but each State shall have at Least one Representative; and until such enumeration shall be made, the State of New Hampshire shall be entitled to chuse three, Massachusetts eight, Rhode Island and Providence Plantations one, Connecticut five, New York six, New Jersey four, Pennsylvania eight,

Delaware one, Maryland six, Virginia ten, North Carolina five, South Carolina five and Georgia three.

When vacancies happen in the Representation from any State, the Executive Authority thereof shall issue Writs of Election to fill such Vacancies.

The House of Representatives shall chuse their Speaker and other Officers; and shall have the sole Power of Impeachment.

SECTION 3. The Senate of the United States shall be composed of two Senators from each State, chosen by the Legislature thereof, for six Years; and each Senator shall have one Vote.

Immediately after they shall be assembled in Consequence of the first Election, they shall be divided as equally as may be into three Classes. The Seats of the Senators of the first Class shall be vacated at the Expiration of the second Year, of the second Class at the Expiration of the fourth Year, and of the third Class at the Expiration of the sixth Year, so that one third may be chosen every second Year; and if Vacancies happen by Resignation, or otherwise, during the Recess of the Legislature of any State, the Executive thereof may make temporary Appointments until the next Meeting of the Legislature, which shall then fill such Vacancies.

No person shall be a Senator who shall not have attained to the Age of thirty Years, and been nine Years a Citizen of the United States, and who shall not, when elected, be an Inhabitant of that State for which he shall be chosen.

The Vice President of the United States shall be President of the Senate, but shall have no Vote, unless they be equally divided.

The Senate shall chuse their other Officers, and also a President pro tempore, in the absence of the Vice President, or when he shall exercise the Office of President of the United States.

The Senate shall have the sole Power to try all Impeachments. When sitting for that Purpose, they shall be on Oath or Affirmation. When the President of the United States is tried, the Chief Justice shall preside: And no Person shall be convicted without the Concurrence of two thirds of the Members present.

Judgment in Cases of Impeachment shall not extend further than to removal from Office, and disqualification to hold and enjoy any Office of honor, Trust or Profit under the United States: but the Party convicted shall nevertheless be liable and subject to Indictment, Trial, Judgment and Punishment, according to Law.

SECTION 4. The Times, Places and Manner of holding Elections for Senators and Representatives, shall be prescribed in each State by the Legislature thereof; but the Congress may at any time by Law make or alter such Regulations, except as to the Place of Chusing Senators.

The Congress shall assemble at least once in every Year, and such Meeting shall be on the first Monday in December, unless they shall by Law appoint a different Day.

SECTION 5. Each House shall be the Judge of the Elections, Returns and Qualifications of its own Members, and a Majority of each shall constitute a Quorum to do Business; but a smaller number may adjourn from day to day, and may be authorized to compel the Attendance of absent Members, in such Manner, and under such Penalties as each House may provide.

Each House may determine the Rules of its Proceedings, punish its Members for disorderly Behavior, and, with the Concurrence of two-thirds, expel a Member.

Each House shall keep a Journal of its Proceedings, and from time to time publish the same, excepting such Parts as may in their Judgment require Secrecy; and the Yeas and Nays of the Members of either House on any question shall, at the Desire of one fifth of those Present, be entered on the Journal.

Neither House, during the Session of Congress, shall, without the Consent of the other, adjourn for more than three days, nor to any other Place than that in which the two Houses shall be sitting.

SECTION 6. The Senators and Representatives shall receive a Compensation for their Services, to be ascertained by Law, and paid out of the Treasury of the United States. They shall in all Cases, except Treason, Felony and Breach of the Peace, be privileged from Arrest during their Attendance at the Session of their respective Houses, and in going to and returning from the same; and for any Speech or Debate in either House, they shall not be questioned in any other Place.

No Senator or Representative shall, during the Time for which he was elected, be appointed to any civil Office under the Authority of the United States which shall have been created, or the Emoluments whereof shall have been increased during such time; and no Person holding any Office under the United States, shall be a Member of either House during his Continuance in Office.

SECTION 7. All bills for raising Revenue shall originate in the House of Representatives; but the Senate may propose or concur with Amendments as on other bills.

Every Bill which shall have passed the House of Representatives and the Senate, shall, before it become a Law, be presented to the President of the United States; If he approve he shall sign it, but if not he shall return it, with his Objections to that House in which it shall have originated, who shall enter the Objections at large on their Journal, and proceed to reconsider it. If after such Reconsideration two thirds of that House shall agree to pass the Bill, it shall be sent, together with the Objections, to the other House, by which it shall likewise be reconsidered, and if approved by two thirds of that House, it shall become a Law. But in all such Cases the Votes of both Houses shall be determined by Yeas and Nays, and the Names of the Persons voting for and against the Bill shall be entered on the Journal of each House respectively. If any Bill shall not be returned by the President within ten Days (Sundays excepted) after it shall have been presented to him, the Same shall be a Law, in like Manner as if he had signed it, unless the Congress by their Adjournment prevent its Return, in which Case it shall not be a Law.

Every Order, Resolution, or Vote to which the Concurrence of the Senate and House of Representatives may be necessary (except on a question of Adjournment) shall be presented to the President of the United States; and before the Same shall take Effect, shall be approved by him, or being disapproved by him, shall be repassed by two thirds of the Senate and House of Representatives, according to the Rules and Limitations prescribed in the Case of a Bill.

SECTION 8. The Congress shall have Power To lay and collect Taxes, Duties, Imposts and Excises, to pay the Debts and provide for the common Defence and general Welfare of the United States; but all Duties, Imposts and Excises shall be uniform throughout the United States;

To borrow money on the credit of the United States;

To regulate Commerce with foreign Nations, and among the several States, and with the Indian Tribes;

To establish an uniform Rule of Naturalization, and uniform Laws on the subject of Bankruptcies throughout the United States;

To coin Money, regulate the Value thereof, and of foreign Coin, and fix the Standard of Weights and Measures;

To provide for the Punishment of counterfeiting the Securities and current Coin of the United States;

To establish Post Offices and Post Roads;

To promote the Progress of Science and useful Arts, by securing for limited Times to Authors and Inventors the exclusive Right to their respective Writings and Discoveries;

To constitute Tribunals inferior to the supreme Court;

To define and punish Piracies and Felonies committed on the high Seas, and Offenses against the Law of Nations;

To declare War, grant Letters of Marque and Reprisal, and make Rules concerning Captures on Land and Water;

To raise and support Armies, but no Appropriation of Money to that Use shall be for a longer Term than two Years;

To provide and maintain a Navy;

To make Rules for the Government and Regulation of the land and naval Forces;

To provide for calling forth the Militia to execute the Laws of the Union, suppress Insurrections and repel Invasions;

To provide for organizing, arming, and disciplining the Militia, and for governing such Part of them as may be employed in the Service of the United States, reserving to the States respectively, the Appointment of the Officers, and the Authority of training the Militia according to the discipline prescribed by Congress;

To exercise exclusive Legislation in all Cases whatsoever, over such District (not exceeding ten Miles square) as may, by Cession of particular States, and the acceptance of Congress, become the Seat of the Government of the United States, and to exercise like Authority over all Places purchased by the Consent of the Legislature of the State in which the same shall be, for the Erection of Forts, Magazines, Arsenals, dock-Yards, and other needful Buildings; And

To make all Laws which shall be necessary and proper for carrying into Execution the foregoing Powers, and all other Powers vested by this Constitution in the Government of the United States, or in any Department or Officer thereof.

SECTION 9. The Migration or Importation of such Persons as any of the States now existing shall think proper to admit, shall not be prohibited by the Congress prior to the Year one thousand eight hundred and eight, but a tax or duty may be imposed on such Importation, not exceeding ten dollars for each Person.

The privilege of the Writ of Habeas Corpus shall not be suspended, unless when in Cases of Rebellion or Invasion the public Safety may require it.

No Bill of Attainder or ex post facto Law shall be passed. No capitation, or other direct, Tax shall be laid, unless in Proportion to the Census or Enumeration herein before directed to be taken.

No Tax or Duty shall be laid on Articles exported from any State.

No Preference shall be given by any Regulation of Commerce or Revenue to the Ports of one State over those of another: nor shall Vessels bound to, or from, one State, be obliged to enter, clear, or pay Duties in another.

No Money shall be drawn from the Treasury, but in Consequence of Appropriations made by Law; and a regular Statement and Account of the Receipts and Expenditures of all public Money shall be published from time to time.

No Title of Nobility shall be granted by the United States: And no Person holding any Office of Profit or Trust under them, shall, without the Consent of the Congress, accept of any present, Emolument, Office, or Title, of any kind whatever, from any King, Prince or foreign State.

SECTION 10. No State shall enter into any Treaty, Alliance, or Confederation; grant Letters of Marque and Reprisal; coin Money; emit Bills of Credit; make any Thing but gold and silver Coin a Tender in Payment of Debts; pass any Bill of Attainder, ex post facto Law, or Law impairing the Obligation of Contracts, or grant any Title of Nobility.

No State shall, without the Consent of the Congress, lay any Imposts or Duties on Imports or Exports, except what may be absolutely necessary for executing its inspection Laws: and the net Produce of all Duties and Imposts, laid by any State on Imports or Exports, shall be for the Use of the Treasury of the United States; and all such Laws shall be subject to the Revision and Controul of the Congress.

No State shall, without the Consent of Congress, lay any duty of Tonnage, keep Troops, or Ships of War in time of Peace, enter into any Agreement or Compact with another State, or with a foreign Power, or engage in War, unless actually invaded, or in such imminent Danger as will not admit of delay.

ARTICLE II.

SECTION 1. The executive Power shall be vested in a President of the United States of America. He shall hold his Office during the Term of four Years, and, together with the Vice-President chosen for the same Term, be elected, as follows:

Each State shall appoint, in such Manner as the Legislature thereof may direct, a Number of Electors, equal to the whole Number of Senators and Representatives to which the State may be entitled in the Congress: but no Senator or Representative, or Person holding an Office of Trust or Profit under the United States, shall be appointed an Elector.

The Electors shall meet in their respective States, and vote by Ballot for two persons, of whom one at least shall not lie an Inhabitant of the same State with themselves. And they shall make a List of all the Persons voted for, and of the Number of Votes for each; which List they shall sign and certify, and transmit sealed to the Seat of the Government of the United States, directed to the President of the Senate. The President of the Senate shall, in the Presence of the Senate and House of Representatives, open all the Certificates, and the Votes shall then be counted. The Person having the greatest Number of Votes shall be the President, if such Number be a Majority of the whole Number of Electors appointed; and if there be more than one who have such Majority, and have an equal Number of Votes, then the House of Representatives shall immediately chuse by Ballot one of them for President; and if no Person have a Majority, then from the five highest on the List the said House shall in like Manner chuse the President. But in chusing the President, the Votes shall be taken by States, the Representation from each State having one Vote; a quorum for this Purpose shall consist of a Member or Members from two-thirds of the States, and a Majority of all the States shall be necessary to a Choice. In every Case, after the Choice of the President, the Person having the greatest Number of Votes of the Electors shall be the Vice President. But if there should remain two or more who have equal Votes, the Senate shall chuse from them by Ballot the Vice President.

The Congress may determine the Time of chusing the Electors, and the Day on which they shall give their Votes; which Day shall be the same throughout the United States.

No person except a natural born Citizen, or a Citizen of the United States, at the time of the Adoption of this Constitution, shall be eligible to the Office of President; neither shall any Person be eligible to that Office who shall not have attained to the Age of thirty-five Years, and been fourteen Years a Resident within the United States.

In Case of the Removal of the President from Office, or of his Death, Resignation, or Inability to discharge the Powers and Duties of the said Office, the same shall devolve on the Vice President, and the Congress may by Law provide for the Case of Removal, Death, Resignation or Inability, both of the President and Vice President, declaring what Officer shall then act as President, and such Officer shall act accordingly, until the Disability be removed, or a President shall be elected.

The President shall, at stated Times, receive for his Services, a Compensation, which shall neither be increased nor diminished during the Period for which he shall have been elected, and he shall not receive within that Period any other Emolument from the United States, or any of them.

Before he enter on the Execution of his Office, he shall take the following Oath or Affirmation: "I do solemnly swear (or affirm) that I will faithfully execute the Office of President of the United States, and will to the best of my Ability, preserve, protect and defend the Constitution of the United States."

SECTION 2. The President shall be Commander in Chief of the Army and Navy of the United States, and of the Militia of the several States, when called into the actual Service of the United States; he may require the Opinion, in writing, of the principal Officer in each of the executive Departments, upon any subject relating to the Duties of their respective Offices, and he shall have Power to Grant Reprieves and Pardons for Offenses against the United States, except in Cases of Impeachment.

He shall have Power, by and with the Advice and Consent of the Senate, to make Treaties, provided two thirds of the Senators present concur; and he shall nominate, and by and with the Advice and Consent of the Senate, shall appoint Ambassadors, other public Ministers and Consuls, Judges of the supreme Court, and all other Officers of the United States, whose Appointments are not herein otherwise provided for, and which shall be established by Law: but the Congress may by Law vest the Appointment of such inferior Officers, as they think proper, in the President alone, in the Courts of Law, or in the Heads of Departments.

The President shall have Power to fill up all Vacancies that may happen during the Recess of the Senate, by granting Commissions which shall expire at the End of their next Session.

SECTION 3. He shall from time to time give to the Congress Information of the State of the Union, and recommend to their Consideration such Measures as he shall judge necessary and expedient; he may, on extraordinary Occasions, convene both Houses, or either of them, and in Case of Disagreement between them, with Respect to the Time of Adjournment, he may adjourn them to such Time as he shall think proper; he shall receive Ambassadors and other public Ministers; he shall take Care that the Laws be faithfully executed, and shall Commission all the Officers of the United States.

SECTION 4. The President, Vice President and all civil Officers of the United States, shall be removed from Office on Impeachment for, and Conviction of, Treason, Bribery, or other high Crimes and Misdemeanors.

ARTICLE III.

SECTION 1. The judicial Power of the United States, shall be vested in one supreme Court, and in such inferior Courts as the Congress may from time to time ordain and establish. The Judges, both of the supreme and inferior Courts, shall hold their Offices during good Behavior, and shall, at stated Times, receive for their Services a Compensation which shall not be diminished during their Continuance in Office.

SECTION 2. The judicial Power shall extend to all Cases, in Law and Equity, arising under this Constitution, the Laws of the United States, and Treaties made, or which shall be made, under their Authority; to all Cases affecting Ambassadors, other public Ministers and Consuls; to all Cases of admiralty and maritime Jurisdiction; to Controversies to which the United States shall be a Party; to Controversies between two or more States; between a State and Citizens of another State; between Citizens of different States; between Citizens of the same State claiming Lands under Grants of different States, and between a State, or the Citizens thereof, and foreign States, Citizens or Subjects.

In all Cases affecting Ambassadors, other public Ministers and Consuls, and those in which a State shall be Party, the supreme Court shall have original Jurisdiction. In all the other Cases before mentioned, the supreme Court shall have appellate Jurisdiction, both as to Law and Fact, with such Exceptions, and under such Regulations as the Congress shall make.

Trial of all Crimes, except in Cases of Impeachment, shall be by Jury; and such Trial shall be held in the State where the said Crimes shall have been committed; but when not committed within any State, the Trial shall be at such Place or Places as the Congress may by Law have directed.

SECTION 3. Treason against the United States, shall consist only in levying War against them, or in adhering to their Enemies, giving them Aid and Comfort. No Person shall be convicted of Treason unless on the Testimony of two Witnesses to the same overt Act, or on Confession in open Court.

The Congress shall have power to declare the Punishment of Treason, but no Attainder of Treason shall work Corruption of Blood, or Forfeiture except during the Life of the Person attainted.

ARTICLE IV.

SECTION 1. Full Faith and Credit shall be given in each State to the public Acts, Records, and judicial Proceedings of every other State. And the Congress may by general Laws prescribe the Manner in which such Acts, Records and Proceedings shall be proved, and the Effect thereof.

SECTION 2. The Citizens of each State shall be entitled to all Privileges and Immunities of Citizens in the several States.

A Person charged in any State with Treason, Felony, or other Crime, who shall flee from Justice, and be found in another State, shall on demand of the executive Authority of the State from which he fled, be delivered up, to be removed to the State having Jurisdiction of the Crime.

No Person held to Service or Labour in one State, under the Laws thereof, escaping into another, shall, in Consequence of any Law or Regulation therein, be discharged from such Service or Labour, But shall be delivered up on Claim of the Party to whom such Service or Labour may be due.

SECTION 3. New States may be admitted by the Congress into this Union; but no new States shall be formed or erected within the Jurisdiction of any other State; nor any State be formed by the Junction of two or more States, or parts of States, without the Consent of the Legislatures of the States concerned as well as of the Congress.

The Congress shall have Power to dispose of and make all needful Rules and Regulations respecting the Territory or other Property belonging to the United States; and nothing in this Constitution shall be so construed as to Prejudice any Claims of the United States, or of any particular State.

SECTION 4. The United States shall guarantee to every State in this Union a Republican Form of Government, and shall protect each of them against Invasion; and on Application of the Legislature, or of the Executive (when the Legislature cannot be convened) against domestic Violence.

ARTICLE V.

The Congress, whenever two thirds of both Houses shall deem it necessary, shall propose Amendments to this Constitution, or, on the Application of the Legislatures of two thirds of the several States, shall call a Convention for proposing Amendments, which, in either Case, shall be valid to all Intents and Purposes, as part of this Constitution, when ratified by the Legislatures of three fourths of the several States, or by Conventions in three fourths thereof, as the one or the other Mode of Ratification may be proposed by the Congress; Provided that no Amendment which may be made prior to the Year One thousand eight hundred and eight shall in any Manner affect the first and fourth Clauses in the Ninth Section of the first Article; and that no State, without its Consent, shall be deprived of its equal Suffrage in the Senate.

ARTICLE VI.

All Debts contracted and Engagements entered into, before the Adoption of this Constitution, shall be as valid against the United States under this Constitution, as under the Confederation.

This Constitution, and the Laws of the United States which shall be made in Pursuance thereof; and all Treaties made, or which shall be made, under the Authority of the United States, shall be the supreme Law of the Land; and the Judges in every State shall be bound thereby, any Thing in the Constitution or Laws of any State to the Contrary notwithstanding.

The Senators and Representatives before mentioned, and the Members of the several State Legislatures, and all executive and judicial Officers, both of the United States and of the several States, shall be bound by Oath or Affirmation, to support this Constitution; but no religious Test shall ever be required as a Qualification to any Office or public Trust under the United States.

ARTICLE VII.

The Ratification of the Conventions of nine States, shall be sufficient for the Establishment of this Constitution between the States so ratifying the Same.

DONE in Convention by the Unanimous Consent of the States present the Seventeenth Day of September in the Year of our Lord one thousand seven hundred and Eighty seven and of the Independence of the United States of America the Twelfth. In Witness whereof We have hereunto subscribed our Names.

Go. Washington
President and deputy from Virginia

New Hampshire
John Langdon
Nicholas Gilman

Massachusetts
Nathaniel Gorham
Rufus King

Connecticut
Wm Saml Johnson
Roger Sherman

New York
Alexander Hamilton

New Jersey
Wil Livingston
David Brearley
Wm Paterson
Jona. Dayton

Pennsylvania
B Franklin
Thomas Mifflin
Robt Morris
Geo. Clymer
Thos FitzSimons
Jared Ingersoll
James Wilson
Gouv Morris

Delaware
Geo. Read
Gunning Bedford jun
John Dickinson
Richard Bassett
Jaco. Broom

Maryland
James McHenry
Dan of St Tho Jenifer
Danl Carroll

Virginia
John Blair
James Madison Jr.

North Carolina
Wm Blount
Richd Dobbs Spaight
Hu Williamson

South Carolina
J. Rutledge

Charles Cotesworth Pinckney
Charles Pinckney
Pierce Butler

Georgia
William Few
Abr Baldwin

Attest: William Jackson, Secretary

AMENDMENT I.

Congress shall make no law respecting an establishment of religion, or prohibiting the free exercise thereof; or abridging the freedom of speech, or of the press; or the right of the people peaceably to assemble, and to petition the Government for a redress of grievances.

AMENDMENT II.

A well regulated Militia, being necessary to the security of a free State, the right of the people to keep and bear Arms, shall not be infringed.

AMENDMENT III.

No Soldier shall, in time of peace be quartered in any house, without the consent of the Owner, nor in time of war, but in a manner to be prescribed by law.

AMENDMENT IV.

The right of the people to be secure in their persons, houses, papers, and effects, against unreasonable searches and seizures, shall not be violated, and no Warrants shall issue, but upon probable cause, supported by Oath or affirmation, and particularly describing the place to be searched, and the persons or things to be seized.

AMENDMENT V.

No person shall be held to answer for a capital, or otherwise infamous crime, unless on a presentment or indictment of a Grand Jury, except in cases arising in the land or naval forces, or in the Militia, when in actual service in time of War or public danger; nor shall any person be subject for the same offense to be twice put in jeopardy of life or limb; nor shall be compelled in any criminal case to be a witness against himself, nor be deprived of life, liberty, or property, without due process of law; nor shall private property be taken for public use, without just compensation.

AMENDMENT VI.

In all criminal prosecutions, the accused shall enjoy the right to a speedy and public trial, by an impartial jury of the State and district wherein the crime shall have been committed, which district shall have been previously ascertained by law, and to be informed of the nature and cause of the accusation; to be confronted with the witnesses against him; to have compulsory process for obtaining witnesses in his favor, and to have the Assistance of Counsel for his defence.

AMENDMENT VII.

In Suits at common law, where the value in controversy shall exceed twenty dollars, the right of trial by jury shall be preserved, and no fact tried by a jury, shall be otherwise re-examined in any Court of the United States, than according to the rules of the common law.

AMENDMENT VIII.

Excessive bail shall not be required, nor excessive fines imposed, nor cruel and unusual punishments inflicted.

AMENDMENT IX.

The enumeration in the Constitution, of certain rights, shall not be construed to deny or disparage others retained by the people.

AMENDMENT X.

The powers not delegated to the United States by the Constitution, nor prohibited by it to the States, are reserved to the States espectively, or to the people.

AMENDMENT XI.

The Judicial power of the United States shall not be construed to extend to any suit in law or equity, commenced or prosecuted against one of the United States by Citizens of another State, or by Citizens or Subjects of any Foreign State.

AMENDMENT XII.

The Electors shall meet in their respective states, and vote by ballot for President and Vice-President, one of whom, at least, shall not be an inhabitant of the same state with themselves; they shall name in their ballots the person voted for as President, and in distinct ballots the person voted for as Vice-President, and they shall make distinct lists of all persons voted for as President, and of all persons voted for as Vice-President and of the number of votes for each, which lists they shall sign and certify, and transmit sealed to the seat of the government of the United States, directed to the President of the Senate;

The President of the Senate shall, in the presence of the Senate and House of Representatives, open all the certificates and the votes shall then be counted;

The person having the greatest Number of votes for President, shall be the President, if such number be a majority of the whole number of Electors appointed; and if no person have such majority, then from the persons having the highest numbers not exceeding three on the list of those voted for as President, the House of Representatives shall choose immediately, by ballot, the President. But in choosing the President, the votes shall be taken by states, the representation from each state having one vote; a quorum for this purpose shall consist of a member or members from two-thirds of the states, and a majority of all the states shall be necessary to a choice. And if the House of Representatives shall not choose a President whenever the right of choice shall devolve upon them, before the fourth day of March next following, then the Vice-President shall act as President, as in the case of the death or other constitutional disability of the President.

The person having the greatest number of votes as Vice-President, shall be the Vice-President, if such number be a majority of the whole number of Electors appointed, and if no person have a majority, then from the two highest numbers on the list, the Senate shall choose the Vice-President; a quorum for the purpose shall consist of two-thirds of the whole number of Senators, and a majority of the whole number shall be necessary to a choice. But no person constitutionally ineligible to the office of President shall be eligible to that of Vice-President of the United States.

AMENDMENT XIII.

1. Neither slavery nor involuntary servitude, except as a punishment for crime whereof the party shall have been duly convicted, shall exist within the United States, or any place subject to their jurisdiction.

2. Congress shall have power to enforce this article by appropriate legislation.

AMENDMENT XIV.

1. All persons born or naturalized in the United States, and subject to the jurisdiction thereof, are citizens of the United States and of the State wherein they reside. No State shall make or enforce any law which shall abridge the privileges or immunities of citizens of the United States; nor shall any State deprive any person of life, liberty, or property, without due process of law; nor deny to any person within its jurisdiction the equal protection of the laws.

2. Representatives shall be apportioned among the several States according to their respective numbers, counting the whole number of persons in each State, excluding Indians not taxed. But when the right to vote at any election for the choice of electors for President and Vice-President of the United States, Representatives in Congress, the Executive and Judicial officers of a State, or the members of the Legislature thereof, is

denied to any of the male inhabitants of such State, being twenty-one years of age, and citizens of the United States, or in any way abridged, except for participation in rebellion, or other crime, the basis of representation therein shall be reduced in the proportion which the number of such male citizens shall bear to the whole number of male citizens twenty-one years of age in such State.

3. No person shall be a Senator or Representative in Congress, or elector of President and Vice-President, or hold any office, civil or military, under the United States, or under any State, who, having previously taken an oath, as a member of Congress, or as an officer of the United States, or as a member of any State legislature, or as an executive or judicial officer of any State, to support the Constitution of the United States, shall have engaged in insurrection or rebellion against the same, or given aid or comfort to the enemies thereof. But Congress may by a vote of two-thirds of each House, remove such disability.

4. The validity of the public debt of the United States, authorized by law, including debts incurred for payment of pensions and bounties for services in suppressing insurrection or rebellion, shall not be questioned. But neither the United States nor any State shall assume or pay any debt or obligation incurred in aid of insurrection or rebellion against the United States, or any claim for the loss or emancipation of any slave; but all such debts, obligations and claims shall be held illegal and void.

5. The Congress shall have power to enforce, by appropriate legislation, the provisions of this article.

AMENDMENT XV.

1. The right of citizens of the United States to vote shall not be denied or abridged by the United States or by any State on account of race, color, or previous condition of servitude.

2. The Congress shall have power to enforce this article by appropriate legislation.

AMENDMENT XVI.

The Congress shall have power to lay and collect taxes on incomes, from whatever source derived, without apportionment among the several States, and without regard to any census or enumeration.

AMENDMENT XVII.

The Senate of the United States shall be composed of two Senators from each State, elected by the people thereof, for six years; and each Senator shall have one vote. The electors in each State shall have the qualifications requisite for electors of the most numerous branch of the State legislatures.

When vacancies happen in the representation of any State in the Senate, the executive authority of such State shall issue writs of election to fill such vacancies: Provided, That the legislature of any State may empower the executive thereof to make temporary appointments until the people fill the vacancies by election as the legislature may direct.

This Amendment shall not be so construed as to affect the election or term of any Senator chosen before it becomes valid as part of the Constitution.

AMENDMENT XVIII.

1. After one year from the ratification of this article the manufacture, sale, or transportation of intoxicating liquors within, the importation thereof into, or the exportation thereof from the United States and all territory subject to the jurisdiction thereof for beverage purposes is hereby prohibited.

2. The Congress and the several States shall have concurrent power to enforce this article by appropriate legislation.

3. This article shall be inoperative unless it shall have been ratified as an Amendment to the Constitution by the legislatures of the several States, as provided in the Constitution, within seven years from the date of the submission hereof to the States by the Congress.

AMENDMENT XIX.

The right of citizens of the United States to vote shall not be denied or abridged by the United States or by any State on account of sex.

Congress shall have power to enforce this article by appropriate legislation.

AMENDMENT XX.

1. The terms of the President and Vice President shall end at noon on the 20th day of January, and the terms of Senators and Representatives at noon on the 3d day of January, of the years in which such terms would have ended if this article had not been ratified; and the terms of their successors shall then begin.

2. The Congress shall assemble at least once in every year, and such meeting shall begin at noon on the 3d day of January, unless they shall by law appoint a different day.

3. If, at the time fixed for the beginning of the term of the President, the President elect shall have died, the Vice President elect shall become President. If a President shall not have been chosen before the time fixed for the beginning of his term, or if the President elect shall have failed to qualify, then the Vice President elect shall act as President until a President shall have qualified; and the Congress may by law provide

for the case wherein neither a President elect nor a Vice President elect shall have qualified, declaring who shall then act as President, or the manner in which one who is to act shall be selected, and such person shall act accordingly until a President or Vice President shall have qualified.

4. The Congress may by law provide for the case of the death of any of the persons from whom the House of Representatives may choose a President whenever the right of choice shall have devolved upon them, and for the case of the death of any of the persons from whom the Senate may choose a Vice President whenever the right of choice shall have devolved upon them.

5. Sections 1 and 2 shall take effect on the 15th day of October following the ratification of this article.

6. This article shall be inoperative unless it shall have been ratified as an Amendment to the Constitution by the legislatures of three-fourths of the several States within seven years from the date of its submission.

AMENDMENT XXI.

1. The eighteenth article of Amendment to the Constitution of the United States is hereby repealed.

2. The transportation or importation into any State, Territory, or possession of the United States for delivery or use therein of intoxicating liquors, in violation of the laws thereof, is hereby prohibited.

3. The article shall be inoperative unless it shall have been ratified as an Amendment to the Constitution by conventions in the several States, as provided in the Constitution, within seven years from the date of the submission hereof to the States by the Congress.

AMENDMENT XXII.

1. No person shall be elected to the office of the President more than twice, and no person who has held the office of President, or acted as President, for more than two years of a term to which some other person was elected President shall be elected to the office of the President more than once. But this Article shall not apply to any person holding the office of President, when this Article was proposed by the Congress, and shall not prevent any person who may be holding the office of President, or acting as President, during the term within which this Article becomes operative from holding the office of President or acting as President during the remainder of such term.

2. This article shall be inoperative unless it shall have been ratified as an Amendment to the Constitution by the legislatures of three-fourths of the several States within seven years from the date of its submission to the States by the Congress.

AMENDMENT XXIII.

1. The District constituting the seat of Government of the United States shall appoint in such manner as the Congress may direct: A number of electors of President and Vice President equal to the whole number of Senators and Representatives in Congress to which the District would be entitled if it were a State, but in no event more than the least populous State; they shall be in addition to those appointed by the States, but they shall be considered, for the purposes of the election of President and Vice President, to be electors

appointed by a State; and they shall meet in the District and perform such duties as provided by the twelfth article of Amendment.

2. The Congress shall have power to enforce this article by appropriate legislation.

AMENDMENT XXIV.

1. The right of citizens of the United States to vote in any primary or other election for President or Vice President, for electors for President or Vice President, or for Senator or Representative in Congress, shall not be denied or abridged by the United States or any State by reason of failure to pay any poll tax or other tax.

2. The Congress shall have power to enforce this article by appropriate legislation.

AMENDMENT XXV.

1. In case of the removal of the President from office or of his death or resignation, the Vice President shall become President.

2. Whenever there is a vacancy in the office of the Vice President, the President shall nominate a Vice President who shall take office upon confirmation by a majority vote of both Houses of Congress.

3. Whenever the President transmits to the President pro tempore of the Senate and the Speaker of the House of Representatives his written declaration that he is unable to discharge the powers and duties of his office, and until he transmits to them a written declaration to the contrary, such powers and duties shall be discharged by the Vice President as Acting President.

4. Whenever the Vice President and a majority of either the principal officers of the executive departments or of such other body as Congress may by law provide, transmit to the President pro tempore of the Senate and the Speaker of the House of Representatives their written declaration that the President is unable to discharge the powers and duties of his office, the Vice President shall immediately assume the powers and duties of the office as Acting President.

Thereafter, when the President transmits to the President pro tempore of the Senate and the Speaker of the House of Representatives his written declaration that no inability exists, he shall resume the powers and duties of his office unless the Vice President and a majority of either the principal officers of the executive department or of such other body as Congress may by law provide, transmit within four days to the President pro tempore of the Senate and the Speaker of the House of Representatives their written declaration that the President is unable to discharge the powers and duties of his office. Thereupon Congress shall decide the issue, assembling within forty eight hours for that purpose if not in session. If the Congress, within twenty one days after receipt of the latter written declaration, or, if Congress is not in session, within twenty one days after Congress is required to assemble, determines by two thirds vote of both Houses that the President is unable to discharge the powers and duties of his office, the Vice President shall continue to discharge the same as Acting President; otherwise, the President shall resume the powers and duties of his office.

AMENDMENT XXVI.

1. The right of citizens of the United States, who are eighteen years of age or older, to vote shall not be denied or abridged by the United States or by any State on account of age.

2. The Congress shall have power to enforce this article by appropriate legislation.

AMENDMENT XXVII.

No law, varying the compensation for the services of the Senators and Representatives, shall take effect, until an election of Representatives shall have intervened.

Resources

Anthony, Carl Sferrazza. *America's First Families: An Inside View of 200 Years of Private Life in the White House.* New York: Touchstone, 2000.

Barber, James David. *The Presidential Character: Predicting Performance in the White House.* 4th ed. Englewood Cliffs, NJ: Prentice-Hall, 1992.

Boller, Paul F., Jr. *Presidential Anecdotes.* Rev. ed. New York: Oxford University Press, 1996.

Boller, Paul F., Jr. *Presidential Campaigns.* Rev. ed. New York: Oxford University Press, 1996.

Boller, Paul F., Jr. *Presidential Wives: An Anecdotal History.* New York: Oxford University Press, 1988.

Buchanan, Bruce. *Presidential Campaign Quality: Incentives and Reform.* Upper Saddle River, NJ: Pearson/Prentice Hall, 2004.

Burke, John P., and Fred I. Greenstein. *How Presidents Test Reality.* New York: Russell Sage Foundation, 1989.

Busch, Andrew. *Horses in Midstream: U.S. Midterm Elections and Their Consequences, 1894–1998.* Pittsburgh: University of Pittsburgh Press, 1999.

Campbell, James E. *The American Campaign: U.S. Presidential Campaigns and the National Vote.* College Station: Texas A&M University Press, 2000.

Caroli, Betty Boyd. *First Ladies.* New York: Oxford University Press, 1995.

Chase, James S. *Emergence of the Presidential Nominating Convention, 1789–1832.* Urbana: University of Illinois Press, 1973.

Clarke, James W. *American Assassins: The Darker Side of Politics.* Princeton, NJ: Princeton University Press, 1982.

Congressional Quarterly. *Cabinets and Counselors: The President and the Executive Branch.* Washington, DC: Congressional Quarterly, 1989.

Cronin, Thomas E., ed. *Inventing the American Presidency.* Lawrence: University of Kansas Press, 1989.

CQ Press. *Presidential Elections 1789–2000.* Washington, DC: CQ Press, 2002.

Cunliffe, Marcus. *American Presidents and the Presidency.* 2nd ed. New York: American Heritage Press, 1972.

DeGregorio, William A. *The Complete Book of U.S. Presidents.* 5th ed. Fort Lee, NJ: Barricade Books, 2001.

DiClerico, Robert E. *The American President.* 5th ed. Upper Saddle River, NJ: Prentice-Hall, 2000.

Fields, Alonzo. *My Twenty-One Years in the White House.* New York: Coward-McCann, 1960.

Freidel, Frank, and William Pencak, eds. *The White House: The First Two Hundred Years.* Boston: Northeastern University Press, 1994.

Greenstein, Fred I. *The Presidential Difference: Leadership Style from FDR to Clinton.* New York: The Free Press, 2000.

Hart, Roderick P. *Campaign Talk: Why Elections Are Good for Us.* Princeton, NJ: Princeton University Press, 2000.

Hellweg, Susan A., Michael Pfau, and Steven R Brydon. *Televised Presidential Debates: Advocacy in Contemporary America.* New York: Praeger, 1992.

Hoover, Irwin H. *Forty-Two Years in the White House.* Boston and New York: Houghton Mifflin Co., 1934.

Kunhardt, Philip B. Jr., et al. *The American President.* New York: Riverhead Books, 1999.

Mayer, Kenneth. *With the Stroke of a Pen: Executive Orders and Presidential Power.* Princeton, NJ: Princeton University Press, 2002.

Mitchell, Jack. *Executive Privilege: Two Centuries of White House Scandals.* New York: Hippocrene Books, 1992.

Neustadt, Richard E. *Presidential Power and the Modern Presidents: The Politics of Leadership from Roosevelt to Reagan.* New York: The Free Press, 1990.

Parks, Lilian Rogers, and Frances Spatz Leighton. *My Thirty Years Backstairs at the White House.* New York: Fleet Publishing, 1961.

Plissner, Martin. *The Control Room: How Television Calls the Shots in Presidential Elections.* New York: The Free Press, 1999.

Rogers, Donald W., and Christine B. Scriabine. *Voting and the Spirit of American Democracy: Essays on the History of Voting and Voting Rights in America.* Urbana: University of Illinois Press, 1992.

Sifakis, Carl. *Encyclopedia of Assassinations.* New York: Facts on File, 1991.

Thayer, George. *Who Shakes the Money Tree? American Campaign Practices from 1789 to the Present.* New York: Simon & Schuster, 1974.

Utter, Glenn H., and Ruth Ann Strickland. *Campaign and Election Reform.* Santa Barbara, CA: ABC-CLIO, 1997.

Wayne, Stephen J. *The Road to the White House, 2000: The Politics of Presidential Elections—Postelection Edition.* New York: St. Martin's Press, 2001.

Wead, Doug. *All the Presidents' Children: Triumph and Tragedy in the Lives of America's First Families.* New York: Atria Books, 2003.

West, J. B., with Mary Lynn Kotz. *Upstairs at the White House: My Life with the First Ladies.* New York: Coward, McGann & Geoghegan, 1973.

Index

Note: (ill.) indicates photos and illustrations.

518

M

S

T

X

Y

Z